Praise for Norman L. Macht's
Connie Mack and the Early Years of Baseball

"[Macht] tells Mack's story with incredible detail with liberal helpings of personal anecdotes and descriptions. . . . To know Mack's life story is to know much of the personalities and politics behind the birth of the American League. *Connie Mack and the Early Years of Baseball* is an excellent story of an amazing American."
—*Dubuque (IA) Telegraph-Herald*

"Masterful. . . . A must read for all historians of the national pastime."
—*Pennsylvania Magazine of History and Biography*

"A biography of Mack cannot help but be a history of baseball in the first half of the twentieth century, and this biography is a feast of interesting facts and judgments."
—**George F. Will**, syndicated columnist and author of *Men at Work: The Craft of Baseball*

"[Includes] many fascinating details of baseball from the 1880s to 1914."
—*Boston Globe*

"A mother lode of data, stories, perceptions about one of the legendary figures in the history of the national pastime."
—**Harvey Frommer** on Sports

"Macht has turned out a book which provides a true insight into baseball and its beginning as the National Pastime."
—**Ernie Harwell**, Hall of Fame broadcaster for fifty-four years, the last forty-two for the Detroit Tigers

"As a catcher and manager, Connie Mack deserves much of the credit for writing 'The Book' on baseball strategy and the managing of men. How he did it all is told here for the first time."
—**Roland Hemond**, three-time winner of Major League Baseball's Executive of the Year award

"Comprehensive and interesting portrait of one of baseball's most successful managers. . . . A compelling look at a legend and an era."
—*Kirkus Reviews*

CONNIE MACK

THE TURBULENT AND
TRIUMPHANT YEARS
1915—1931

NORMAN L. MACHT

CONNIE MACK

THE TURBULENT AND TRIUMPHANT YEARS

1915–1931

UNIVERSITY OF NEBRASKA PRESS | LINCOLN AND LONDON

Library of Congress
Cataloging-in-Publication Data

Macht, Norman L. (Norman Lee), 1929–
Connie Mack: the turbulent and triumphant
years, 1915–1931 / Norman L. Macht.
p. cm.   Includes index.
ISBN 978-0-8032-2039-3 (cloth: alk. paper)
1. Mack, Connie, 1862–1956. 2. Baseball man-
agers—Pennsylvania—Philadelphia—Biogra-
phy. 3. Baseball team owners—Pennsylvania—
Philadelphia—Biography. 4. Philadelphia
Athletics (Baseball team)—History. I. Title.
GV865.M215M333 2012   796.357092—dc23
[B]   2011035517

Set in Minion by Bob Reitz.
Designed by A. Shahan.

To departed friends
Ernie Harwell
Joe Hauser
Jim Smith
Bill Werber

CONTENTS

ILLUSTRATIONS   *following page* 298

The Mack family house at 604 West Cliveden

The Mack family in 1926

Jack Nabors, Michael Mack, and Doc Ebling

Bench made of bats

Branch Rickey

Kenesaw Mountain Landis and Jack Hendricks

Earle Mack

Connie Mack, 1921

Stanley "Bucky" Harris and Connie Mack, 1926

Al Simmons

Connie Mack during the Roaring Twenties

The A's 1924 Christmas card

Joe Hauser

Dick Richards and Connie Mack

Mack and the A's in Fort Myers

The A's in the Royal Palm Pharmacy in Fort Myers

The A's in front of Thomas Edison's Fort Myers home, 1926

Thomas Edison and Connie Mack, 1927

Connie Mack watching batting practice

Light-heavyweight champion Tommy Loughran

Connie Mack, c. 1925–30

Eddie Collins, Ty Cobb, and Connie Mack, 1927

Illustrations (continued)
following page 298

ACKNOWLEDGMENTS I am indebted to the following players or their families for sharing their memories with me for this part of the Connie Mack story: Walter Anderson, Roger Cramer, Joe Hauser, Ted Lyons, Rudel Miller, Tommy Thomas, Shag Thompson, Dib Williams, Whitey Witt; the families of Mickey Cochrane, Eddie Collins, Jimmie Dykes, Jim Moore, Ed Rommel, and Ira Thomas; and, above all, the children and grandchildren and cousins and friends of Connie Mack.

Without Jim "Snuffy" Smith's zealous pursuit of truth and accuracy in all matters, I would have fallen farther short of the holy grail of getting it all right. I will miss him.

The letters to Sr. Florence from Connie Mack are quoted with the permission of the Sisters of Charity, Leavenworth, Kansas.

My MVP and clean-up hitter in the lineup was copy editor Bojana Ristich.

This ancient typewriter tapper is indebted to David Smith and Tom Ruane and the other creators and maintainers of Retrosheet.org, whose efforts have shortened the writing time and lengthened the lives of baseball researchers seeking an accurate record of the past. A tip of the fedora also to baseball-reference.com, especially for its minor league records, and to Frank Vaccaro and all his contributors for compacting more than a hundred years of baseball-season sports pages from Chicago, Boston, New York, and Washington newspapers onto a stack of discs as thin as a quarter-pounder.

The Society for American Baseball Research (SABR) remains a rare source of accurate information among the fields of fallible websites.

Had all these magic wands been available at my desk thirty years ago, these first two volumes of the life of Connie Mack would have been completed by a younger man.

Print sources include primarily several Philadelphia newspapers and papers from other AL cities, *The Sporting News, Baseball Magazine,* and the *Saturday Evening Post.* Useful were *Connie Mack,* by Fred Lieb (New York:

G. P. Putnam's Sons, 1945), and *Baseball, The Golden Age*, by Harold Seymour (New York: Oxford University Press, 1971).

I cited sources for direct attribution wherever possible. Recognizing that some sportswriters of the time were more creative than others in inventing or paraphrasing quotes, I have tried to identify and rely on those who had the highest reputations for accuracy.

Many people have contributed to this work in a variety of ways. They include Lisa A. Ancelet, Texas State University; Karen Abramson, Archivist, Brandeis University; Craig and Dawn Budner; Bob Buege; Liz Cook, Archivist, Guilford College; Anne Crews; Forrest Cuch; Charles "Smiley" Denver; Joe Duff; Rob Edelman; Jim Elfers; Tom Erickson; John Evans; Ruth Feldman; Dick Fitzgerald; Sr. Helen Forge, Sisters of Charity, Leavenworth, Kansas; Betsy Foster; Nancy S. Garner; Judge Jim Getty; Larry Gieschen; Willie Gravitte; Bill Grier; Garrett Grier; Rock Hoffman; Bill Jenkinson; H. E. "Gene" Johnson; Francine Keyes, Rotary International; April M. Krause, Person County Museum of History, Roxboro, North Carolina; Gerry Lynam; Stanley Macht; Karen Mahony, Canisius (NY) High School; Gwendolyn Marquez; William J. McClain; Murray McComas; Glenn Miller, *Ft. Myers News-Press*; Jim Moore; Frank Phelps; Frank Richards; Hugh Richards; Rob Rodriguez; Dick Rosen; Charlie Ruedebusch; Gabriel Schechter; Fred Schuld; Ron Selter; Riley Seymore; Terry Sloope; Jon Sparks; Lyle Spatz; Mark Stang; Steve Steinberg; Judge Ralph G. Thompson; Bob Timmerman; Joe Tumelty; Lenny Wagner; Bob Warrington; Frank Weedon; and Bill Weis.

INTRODUCTION The following appeared in the January 1915 issue of the prestigious one-hundred-year-old literary magazine the *North American Review*:

The world-wide reputation which [Senator] Henry Cabot Lodge acquired some years ago as the Editor of this *Review* he is now regaining as the father-in-law of the Honorable [Congressman] Augustus Peabody Gardner, M. C. It is interesting, therefore, to note the following conversation as reported by [editor] Dr. St. Clair McKelway in the *Brooklyn Eagle*:

"You read the newspapers, don't you?" asked Mr. Gardner.

"Certainly," replied Senator Lodge.

"Do you read them thoroughly?"

"I believe I do."

"Did you ever hear of Connie Mack?" inquired Mr. Gardner.

"Connie Mack?" repeated Mr. Lodge.

"Yes, Connie Mack."

"You mean Norman Mack [onetime political power in New York], don't you?"

"I do not. I mean Connie Mack."

"I do not think I ever heard of him," replied Mr. Lodge, after a period of thought.

"And still you assert that you read the newspapers thoroughly," remarked Mr. Gardner.

"But who is Connie Mack?" inquired the Senator.

"He is a person," declared Mr. Gardner, impressively, "who is probably better known to several millions of American citizens than Henry Cabot Lodge."

Although characteristically disrespectful, if not indeed, positively unfilial on the part of August Peabody, we may not deny the approximate accuracy of his assertion. As a strategist, Mr. Connie Mack is the Admiral Mahan† of the diamond, and is, moreover, undoubtedly more widely known though hardly "better" known to millions than the distinguished Senator. . . .‡

† Rear Admiral Alfred Thayer Mahan, considered the world's foremost theorist of military sea power, who had died December 1, 1914.
‡ Lodge had been a senator for twenty-one years.

CONNIE MACK

THE TURBULENT AND
TRIUMPHANT YEARS
1915–1931

1 | THE FEDERAL LEAGUE
GOES TO COURT

Following the same formula that Ban Johnson, Connie Mack, and their allies had used to break the National League's monopoly on major league baseball in 1901, the well-heeled Federal League had launched an independent league that claimed major league status in 1914. Waving rolls of cash and the banner of the rights of free Americans to sell their services to the highest bidder, the Feds sowed dissension and distraction among big league players, forcing club owners to induce stars to sign long-term contracts at sharply increased salaries.

The minor leagues had been hit the hardest by the Feds' inroads. Very few clubs showed a profit. The higher leagues lost scores of players and attendance plummeted. The National Commission was flooded with complaints from minor league players who had not been paid their full salaries. Roster and salary cuts were deep and widespread. Ban Johnson suggested that a half dozen minor leagues shut down to avoid inevitable losses in 1915. (Nine of the forty-one that operated in 1914, including the Tri-State League, a fertile source of players for Mack, did shut down.) Mack's closest friend among minor league owners, Jack Dunn in Baltimore, faced Federal League competition across the street from his Oriole Park. Unable to obtain a nickel's worth of aid from the major leagues, he surrendered the city to the Terrapins and moved to Richmond, Virginia.

Despite poor attendance and heavy losses, the Federal Leaguers showed no signs of letting up in their efforts to join or disorganize organized baseball. Congressman Thomas Gallagher, Democrat from Cook County, Illinois, had introduced resolutions in 1912 and 1913 for the House of Representatives to investigate "the baseball trust." Both were referred to the Committee on Rules, where they died because, according to Gallagher, "the players refused to testify concerning conditions." It's more likely the Rules Committee had more important matters to address.

Connie Mack was not alone in refusing to be drawn into any further bidding wars against the Federal League. Charles Ebbets said his players could go ahead and jump. "I shall not enter into further competition with the Feds to see which of us shall be held up. My players can take it or leave it."

Nor would Mack compete with the Feds to sign semipros or college boys. He knew how much of a gamble they were and how few amounted to anything. When he was interested in a recruit, he said, "the first thing I asked him was whether any other club had made a proposition or communicated with him." If he said no, Mack would offer him a tryout.

A war-weary Mack said, "If there should be another baseball war, I would get out of the game. I have been through three of these disastrous wars and I've had enough."

The Feds enlisted oil tycoon Harry Sinclair to back a club in Newark in 1915 as a stepping stone into Manhattan, giving them a lineup of twelve millionaire backers. They talked of launching their own minor league system. In the fall of 1914 they had signed baseball's greatest pitcher, Walter Johnson, who later bullfrogged out of their net and bounced back to Washington. When the Feds sought a peace treaty that would accept them as an equal major league, they were rebuffed.

So the Feds charged the National and American Leagues with being a monopoly in restraint of trade, in violation of the amended Sherman antitrust law. On January 5, 1915, they filed a ninety-two-page bill of complaint, attacking the ten-day clause in the player contracts, which allowed a club to release a player with ten days' notice, and the reserve clause, which supposedly bound a player to a club for life. They sued for damages and the dissolution of the National Agreement in federal court in Chicago, Judge Kenesaw M. Landis presiding.

The suit listed eleven "prayers" for injunctive relief which, if granted, would effectively invalidate the National Agreement under which organized baseball was organized and nullify every major and minor league contract.

It didn't help their cause that the Feds came into court with hands as dirty as a coal miner's face at quitting time. At least three of their club owners—Robert B. Ward, Charles Weeghman, and Phil Ball—had tried to buy into the allegedly tyrannical trust they now prayed be abolished. And their own contracts contained the same kind of clauses they were denouncing.

It's difficult to find any writers or club owners who took the suit seriously.

Publicly, major league magnates were unanimous in considering it nothing more than a gnat-sized nuisance. National Commission chairman August A. "Garry" Herrmann called it "the dying squeal of a beaten crowd."

While the rest of the world was absorbed by headlines of an earthquake in Italy that killed twelve thousand people and a German zeppelin that crossed the English Channel and dropped bombs on six British towns, the baseball world was focused on Chicago for two weeks in January. Connie Mack was spared the trip; only the club and league presidents were subpoenaed. His affidavit, describing the Feds' overtures to Eddie Collins during the 1914 season and the subsequent signing of Collins to a new three-year contract, was among twenty-three filed by owners and managers on January 16. Publicly Mack said:

> The Federals having failed to win support in the field are trying to force themselves on a public that had shown it does not want them. I think the public reached its decision last season that the Feds are not wanted. I draw this conclusion from the poor manner in which the fans turned out to see the Feds. Surely this is an indication they are not wanted. [National and American League attendance wasn't so great either: down 30 percent.] Without the present organization, which is fair to all, baseball can't thrive as it has.

The players' affidavits had a different slant on how "fair to all" the system was, but they garnered no sympathy from the public when their lawyers tried to depict them as exploited victims, little more than slaves. More diamond stickpins were sported by the four hundred big league players than could be found in the collar boxes of a million fans.

Dave Fultz, president of the Players' Association, supported the reserve or, as it was now called, the option clause, forecasting disaster for all if every player became a free agent:

"The dissolution of the National Commission would leave the players free to dispose of their services in the open market and to the highest bidder. Professional baseball without proper organization and control would result in complete disruption of playing and business standards. Such conditions would be the forerunner of baseball chaos."

Yet at one point in the four-day hearing, National League counsel George Wharton Pepper startled Judge Landis and the six hundred spectators jammed into the two-hundred-seat courtroom by stating that the contract form adopted by the leagues a year earlier had no reserve clause and his clients were taking a chance on holding their players after the one-year option clause had expired. In effect, a player could play out his option season without signing a new contract and become a free agent (just as arbitrator Peter Seitz would interpret the reserve clause sixty years later, opening the gates to the free agency world).

The surprised Landis, wondering if he'd heard correctly, said, "Hold it," and asked Pepper to repeat what he had just said.

His eyes locked on the judge's, Pepper assured him that the reserve clause the Feds were attacking didn't exist anymore. Banging his fist on the table in front of him, Pepper emphasized what the new style of contract meant: every player who signed a 1914 contract for one year was a free agent after two years if he didn't sign a new contract, "and at the end of that second year the player is free to sign with any league in the world. That's why many clubs are signing their stars to long-term contracts with no reserve or ten-day clauses, like Eddie Collins's five-year White Sox contract."

When lawyers on both sides got into a heated discussion over just what the option clause meant, Landis rapped his gavel. "If there is confusion in your minds regarding the new contract, there is none in the mind of the court. Please proceed."

Why didn't any players test Pepper's statement by playing out their options and becoming free agents? Why didn't Dave Fultz or player/lawyer John Montgomery Ward persuade Ty Cobb or Walter Johnson or *somebody* to challenge it? The Feds called it a subterfuge, and they may have been right. The National Commission maintained a reserve list for each club, and a player could be suspended for not signing with his reserving club, effectively prohibiting him from signing with anybody else. Or such players could be labeled as contract jumpers and no other club would sign them. Collusion is an ancient concept. It's no wonder that the magnates took vows to stay out of the courts in settling disputes.

If the Feds had done any judge shopping, they picked the wrong man. That became clear on the third day of the hearing, when lawyers George Wharton Pepper and George W. Miller spent the day shredding the Feds' case. Late in the day Pepper asked the judge's indulgence for a personal remark. "I love baseball," he said to Landis.

Wagging a long index finger at the packed courtroom, Landis replied, "We'll have to keep our love and affection out of this case, I think. But I want to warn both sides that he who strikes a blow at baseball strikes a blow at a national institution."

Pepper found it prudent to shut up and sit down at that point.

Landis thoroughly enjoyed the proceedings. When Pepper made the point that labor was not considered a commodity of commerce subject to antitrust laws, the bow-tied jurist expressed surprise that playing ball was considered work:

"As a result of thirty years of observation I am shocked because you call it labor."

That prompted this poesy from humorist J. P. McEvoy of the *Chicago Herald*:

THE BASEBALL SLAVE

He romps a pair of hours per day
And draws per romp enormous pay

And romping o'er, he goes his way
To swell hotels to lurk,
Where lurking costs a gang of dough.
That night he sees a four-plunk show—
No wonder Landis lawfed: "Ho Ho!"
When lawyers called it work.

Oh, if I toted such a job,
With all that dough—a juicy gob—
I'll lay a shiner to a bob
I'd never rant and rave;
I'd never holler "I'm oppressed
Please take your foot from off my chest."
I'd wear my gyves with festive zest—
I'd love to be a slave.

More than anything, the case helped a coven of high-priced lawyers claim a lot of billable hours. Sam Weller of the *Tribune* quipped, "You can't tell the lawyers without a scorecard." And it enabled desperate baseball writers to fill acres of newsprint during the dormant interlude between the World Series and spring training.

The four days of legal arguments concluded with an extraordinary Saturday session called by Landis. At six thirty on January 30, with the snow falling outside in the 15-degree air, the judge said to Feds' lawyer Edward E.

Gates, "I have gone just about far enough in this case. The time has come when I should ask you gentlemen just what you want me to do in issuing this injunction. Do you want me to stop the teams from going on their spring training trips? Do you want me to break up the clubs, or what do you want me to do?"

No, no, no, Gates assured the court, nothing like that. Baseball's organization was imperfect, but it was stable, and the Feds had no interest in overturning the entire structure of the business. Having spent the past two hours trying to wash the Feds' unclean hands, Gates said, "We only wanted to purify the game by joining organized baseball."

In the end all it amounted to was that the Feds were merely seeking to restrain organized baseball from pursuing any further legal actions against them and the dozen or so players they had signed since the end of the 1914 season. The Feds had been forced to pay some of their captured stars who had been idled by injunctions during the 1914 season while their cases tortoised through the courts. They had $50,000 invested in new advances paid to jumpers and didn't want to see the same thing happen with them.

The magnates, the lawyers, and the winter-bound fans all went home, and the six-day bike races took over the headlines in the Chicago sporting sections.

As the weeks passed and the National Commission put off any business pending Judge Landis's decision, Cincinnati writer W. A. Phelon shrewdly observed, "I'm beginning to think we will all have long white beards before we see or hear the text of that tremendous verdict."

He was right. Landis the fan had slid the case under the posterior of Landis the judge like a wafer-thin horsehair ballpark cushion.

2 | BATTLE OF THE BULLHEADS

From 1905 through 1914, Connie Mack's Philadelphia Athletics had won 909 games and lost 593, resulting in five pennants and three World Series victories. Their ten-year .605 percentage remains second in American League annals only to the 1934–1943 New York Yankees' 982-547 .642 record. They had been profitable years, too; on November 9, 1914, the club declared a $12,000 dividend. A month later, the $50,000 from the sale of Eddie Collins was also distributed among the Shibes and McGillicuddys.

Now, in a turn of the tide of biblically epic proportions, the A's were about to embark on the worst decade ever suffered by an AL team, a .334 famine in which they would average 96 losses and finish last seven years in a row. The reversal was as unexpected as it was both precipitate and precipitous. It would force Connie Mack to adapt to changing conditions—social, economic, and baseball—in order to survive, at an age when most men were retired or deceased.

Connie Mack had built a baseball machine so perfect it had won the 1914 pennant—its fourth in five years—without hardly trying, so perfect that fans in Philadelphia and every other city in the league lost interest in turning out to watch what seemed to them a team of colorless automatons who were twice as likely to win as lose. Four other teams, including the seventh-place Yankees, drew better at home than the Athletics.

The Athletics had been favored to win the 1914 World Series over the Boston Braves, but not in Connie Mack's book. Clashes of personalities and the intrusive overtures of agents of the newly formed independent Federal League had turned his once-harmonious clubhouse family into a glum, spiritless crew by season's end. They were outplayed but not routed, swept by an inferior Braves team riding a three-month hot streak, losing two games by one run and the last by two after a 7–1 Game 1 licking.

7

James Isaminger of the *Philadelphia North American* accurately summed up the World Series outcome: "Mack's machine did not crack, it was merely out of order. The infield made only one error, and that should have been scored a hit. The A's infield was stanch, the Boston infield was dazzling."

Other writers called it the defeat of very good pitching by exceptional pitching.

In studying a man's life and times, his thinking and decisions and actions, a historian cannot look back smugly with the luxury of knowing how it all turned out. It is necessary to go back to the beginning and move forward in step with the subject, sharing his ignorance of the outcomes that would follow in the wake of his actions.

Long before the World Series loss, Connie Mack knew that two of his veteran pitchers, Chief Bender and Eddie Plank, who between them had won 476 games for him in fourteen years, were headed for the Feds. That was all right with him; he had made up his mind that he was through with them. If any other American League club wanted them and was willing to match the Feds' salary offers—which Mack was not willing to do—Mack was ready to sell them. There were no takers. The pair took the Feds' money.

After winning 80 games in three years, sturdy right-hander Jack Coombs had been sidelined by illness for two years. According to Philadelphia writer Billy Weart, Coombs had peeved Mack with some comments as far back as 1913. Mack was not so thin-skinned that he would part with a strong, healthy Coombs over some remark made by the gruff pitcher two years earlier, after carrying the ailing pitcher on the payroll at full salary all of 1913 and 1914. At thirty-two, Coombs was past his prime. Mack had waited until Coombs demonstrated that he was able to pitch again before releasing him, enabling Coombs to sign wherever he wished to go. They maintained a close friendship and working relationship throughout the many years Coombs would coach at Duke.

Star second baseman Eddie Collins was not only Mack's highest-paid player, but he had also been at the center of controversies that shattered the equanimity of the Athletics' clubhouse like a tornado ripping through the Texas panhandle. And Connie Mack truly prized harmony on his club far more than he supposedly prized money. He found a buyer for Collins at $50,000 in Charles Comiskey. Still, Mack was prepared to keep Collins despite the squalls, even if he couldn't afford him, if the player didn't want to go elsewhere. And Collins didn't, until Comiskey offered him such a fat contract to captain the White Sox that Collins said he'd be crazy to turn it down.

Throughout the winter and spring of 1914–1915, there was no howling about Connie Mack's wrecking his defending champions—because he hadn't. The myth persists that because of the loss of the 1914 World Series, Connie Mack immediately took an axe and gave his roster forty whacks, selling practically a player a day. But when the 1915 season opened, Eddie Collins was still the only player Mack had sold—"only" as in lone, not a pejorative "only." Hardly a wrecking ball.

After the December sale of Collins, Mack headed for Atlantic City for a much-needed rest before beginning the 1915 winter round of meetings, speeches, and banquets. He ignored the rumors that always seemed to surround him. Reports of a feud between him and club secretary John Shibe, which was supposed to lead to Mack's moving to the Yankees as part owner and manager, quickly fizzled out. The taciturn Shibe was no favorite of the writers; he gave them little time and less information. But nobody who knew him believed for a minute that any friction existed within the club's management family. Mack and the Shibes—Ben and his sons Tom and John—worked together with the harmony of a first-class barbershop quartet.

When Mack returned to his desk in January the outlook for his team was as bright as that of any other club in the league. He had three-fourths of his nonpareil infield—Frank "Home Run" Baker, Jack Barry, and Stuffy McInnis; his starting outfield of Eddie Murphy, Amos Strunk, and Rube Oldring; his catchers, Wally Schang and Jack Lapp; and a stable of strong-armed young pitchers who had proven themselves under fire. While picking the Red Sox as the strongest team in the league, Mack said, "The fans must not make the mistake of counting us out of the race."

But Connie Mack was never complacent. "Staying a pennant winner is as hard as keeping a rowboat on the brink of Niagara," he had been quoted as saying back in 1912. "You may do it for the moment, but soon you land in the whirlpool. Then you must start all over again."

Mack wasted no time filling that big second-base hole. In Cleveland, club owner Charles Somers's financial affairs and Napoleon "Larry" Lajoie's relations with manager Joe Birmingham had both frayed. A widespread business depression, bad real estate investments, and the closing of coal mines he owned forced Somers to relinquish to a committee of bankers control of everything except his interests in the New Orleans, Waterbury, Portland, Toledo, and Cleveland ball clubs. Claiming that nobody could play for Birmingham, Lajoie had hit a career-low .258 for the last-place Naps in his nineteenth season. To the cost-conscious bankers, who wanted the

Naps sold, the forty-year-old Lajoie, with his $9,000 salary for two more years, was an overpriced, over-the-hill liability. Charles Somers agreed. When Cleveland asked waivers on him, Branch Rickey claimed him for the Browns. But Lajoie said he wouldn't play in St. Louis.

Connie Mack hopped a train to Cleveland and conferred with Somers, the man who had put up the original stake to help launch the Athletics (and Boston and Cleveland) in 1901. On January 5 Mack telegraphed the Philadelphia papers: "Athletics have purchased release of Lajoie of the Cleveland club." Philadelphia fans whooped and hollered at the welcome news. There was probably no money involved, just the assuming of Lajoie's contract. No purchase is recorded in A's secretary Bob Schroeder's meticulous books.

(With Napoleon gone, a committee of Cleveland sports editors and club officials changed the team's name from Naps to Indians.)

Eager to welcome the King back to town, the baseball writers immediately invited Lajoie to be a guest of honor at their annual February fete. Lajoie, Connie Mack's biggest prize from his 1901 raids on the Phillies, who had then been stolen from the Athletics by a state supreme court decision after one spectacular season, was coming home. Napoleon's return subdued the travail over the sale of Eddie Collins. The King wasn't expected to fill Collins's shoes, but even an aging Lajoie was better than most any other second baseman around. Arriving a few days early, Lajoie was the guest of coach Harry Davis, and he enjoyed red carpet treatment wherever he went in the city. He was not only happy to be home again. Joining a perennial pennant winner also offered him his last opportunity to play in a World Series.

Nobody at the time considered another Athletics pennant a pipe dream. Stanley T. Milliken of the *Washington Post* was not alone when he wrote, "Those who know anything about baseball would not for a minute consider Mack's team through as a pennant possibility. The nucleus for a pennant winner still remains. The Athletics are evidently weaker than they were in 1914, but they still have an excellent chance of copping the bunting, and they will make every other team in the American League hustle to beat them out for first place."

Old-time Baltimore Orioles star Joe Kelley told Damon Runyon of the *New York American*, "Most baseball people seem to think that by [selling Collins] Connie has disposed of his chances for the pennant next season. But I doubt if Connie has any such thought. I am inclined to the belief that he has mapped out a definite scheme of action . . . and I am further inclined to the belief that Connie by no means feels he has hopelessly weakened himself."

Kelley speculated that Mack would move McInnis to second base and put Lajoie on first and that Lajoie had lost none of his old slugging ability. "Therefore Mack's plan may carry through, and if it does—well, you'll have to dip the bonnet to the old fox of Shibe Park."

Cutting costs was uppermost in the minds of major league moguls when they met at the Belmont Hotel in New York on a snowy February 3. Fielding a winning team had proven to be no guarantee of profits. The National League voted to cut rosters from twenty-five to twenty-two. Ironically, in the American meetings, the two owners habitually labeled as penny-pinchers, Clark Griffith and Connie Mack, led the opposition to cutting rosters, arguing that such a cut would weaken their clubs and aid the Feds' recruiting. They prevailed.

The Great War in Europe, precipitated by an assassin's bullets on June 28, 1914, had dragged inconclusively past the cheery three-months predictions of the jingoists. The public was distracted by the war news. Even the sports fans were reading the front page before the sports page, at the same time the competition for their hard-earned quarters was growing. In the fall of 1914 college football commanded three or four pages in the sports sections of the Philadelphia dailies. Connie Mack enjoyed a variety of sports. He often rode the train ninety miles to New York for a big football game on a Saturday afternoon.

Sporting Life began featuring coverage of football, soccer, tennis, and golf. In the final weeks of the pennant race, a full-page photo of golfers actually dominated the front page. By 1916 it would feature coverage of more than two dozen sports and recreational activities from motorcycling to "kennel." By midseason there would be no more room for box scores.

In 1913 the Associated Press had put a wire into every major league ballpark, flashing across the country the starting batteries, umpires, scores by half-inning, run-scoring plays, and other details of the action. The next year it cut back; the service consisted only of the batteries, scores by inning, pitching changes, and a few other details. Now it announced that for 1915 it was eliminating the entire service. There were too many other demands on its facilities.

Club owners began to realize they had to work for the space and publicity they had taken for granted. By 1916 the Indians would begin the practice of sending advance press releases about their stars to papers in cities where the team was scheduled. The Cubs hired an advance man to drop in at sports desks with photos and stories.

The afternoon papers complained that managers waited until game time to give out the lineups—too late to print them in the early editions for customers going to the park. Editors reminded club owners how much free promotion they were giving baseball, but at the same time circulation managers knew that at least 25 percent of their readers bought the papers for the sports news. The more space they devoted to the local teams, the more circulation. During a World Series, the evening papers' several editions each day were good for a 50 percent boost in sales.

The nascent golf craze reached the fifty-two-year-old Connie Mack, who took up the game that winter under the tutelage of a friend, Dr. Simon Carr. For the first time since his arrival in Philadelphia in 1901, there were days when Mr. Mack could be found at Pine Valley Country Club across the Delaware River in New Jersey and not in his office during the off-season. Mack was among the first to hit the links; the number of golf addicts in the country was estimated at 250,000 out of a population of 100 million. But no golf togs for the tall, lean son of East Brookfield, Massachusetts. A sweater instead of a suit jacket and an ascot instead of his usual necktie were the extent of his lowered sartorial standard. Mack picked up the game quickly. George Alvas, the pro at Cleveland's Shaker Heights Country Club, said in 1916, "Of the scores of baseball men I have played with, Connie Mack has the best form. While Connie doesn't get as low scores as some others, he makes the plays more nearly correctly. I would say his style is excellent." Whatever his score, Mack enjoyed relaxing on the links. While baseball men frowned on players touring eighteen holes in the morning before a game, Mack and his road secretary, Rudolph "Rudy" Ohl, took their clubs on the road.

On the evening of Tuesday, February 16, the ovation for Nap Lajoie was still echoing around the banquet room of the Majestic Hotel when Connie Mack cast a pall over the Philadelphia baseball writers' dinner. Cigar smoke clouding the room, the four hundred guests, sated with food, drink, and entertainment from an orchestra and vocal trio, sat back and awaited Mack's usual brief remarks exuding optimism and goodwill toward all. Mack's words, which were reported differently in various papers, stunned them. The gist of them was:

"I can't say that I've had as good a time tonight as I've had in years gone by at this banquet. I have given you a lot of surprises lately, but tonight I have a real surprise for you. Frank Baker wrote me a letter that he would not play for the Athletics the coming year. I got the letter just as I sat down to this banquet table. Frank has decided to quit the game for good. He is not going to play for the Feds or any other team."

According to the *Inquirer*, Mack went on: "Last spring I went down to see Baker about signing a contract. For years I had made this trip and I determined to sign Baker to a three-year contract, and I suggested this plan to him. After some difficulty he signed, but only with the proviso that if he wanted to, he could retire after the 1914 season."

Asked later by the *Inquirer* why he had waited for the big dinner to make the announcement, Mack reportedly said he had just received Baker's final answer that afternoon. In fact, there had been no "final" answer. Mack had received a letter, not that day, but a week earlier. He had said nothing about it, hoping that Baker might change his mind.

Baker's letter was characteristically blunt, brief, and to the point. He hated the eight months of travel involved in playing major league baseball. He was content to farm his two hundred acres in Trappe, Maryland, and would not play this season. He reminded Mack that he had reserved the right to quit after one year of the three-year contract he had reluctantly signed before the 1914 season.

That wasn't in writing, but Mack had readily acknowledged Baker's right to do so at the time and had shrugged it off. Baker talked that way every year and not just at the end of the season. A March 1914 *Sporting Life* feature, "Some Standard Headlines," had included, "J. Franklin Baker Says This is His Last Year in Baseball."

Baker's letter, written on February 8, made no mention of money or offers from the Federal League. The next day (postal service was considerably faster in those days) Connie Mack sat at a typewriter and pecked out his reply:

Mr. J. Franklin Baker
Trappe, Maryland

Dear Frank:

Yours of the 8th, inst. received, and am naturally a little surprised to find that you intend not to play ball the coming season. I remember quite well of your saying that you might not play after this season, but did not take it seriously as I supposed it was like the majority of players who make this announcement annually but still continue to play the old game of baseball. I myself would not want anyone neither would I force upon any of my players to do something that they hadn't ought to do or that they don't feel like doing. I see no reason why you should not continue to play baseball, but I realize I am not supposed to know your business, and of course it is wholly up to you as to whether you play the coming season or not. I feel that you must have been perfectly satisfied with your contract. Otherwise you would not have signed it, as it was not forced upon you. If I am wrong in this matter and you feel that you should get more money for playing baseball, then I am willing to make some concessions. Not as far as our club is concerned in paying a larger salary, for we are not in a position to do that, as we are now paying more than we can possibly take in at the gate. So it is out of the question with us as far as paying any higher salary than we are paying at the present time. If the salary is what is keeping you from playing, you might let me know what amount of salary you want and the clubs that you would prefer to play with in the American League. As you probably are aware, I disposed of Collins for the reason that we could not handle his salary. As you have always been satisfied, I sort of feel that it is not more money that you are looking for, that you are sincere about not playing baseball.

I would like a reply from you before giving out any news relating to your not playing. It is always a bad thing to give out a statement about a player not playing unless it is absolutely right that the player does not intend to play any longer. For the public begins to think that there must be some difference in the salary question. They can't see the player giving up what they term easy money. So I wish you would get right down to business with me and express yourself as to just how you feel in this matter. If you are to retire and that is your wish, you can rest assured that I will not make any further attempt to attain your services for the coming season.

With very best wishes to Mrs. Baker and yourself, I remain

Sincerely yours,
/s/ Connie Mack

Mack waited a week, received no reply from Baker, then made his startling announcement. The likelihood of the A's repeating as champions immediately dropped to remote. The Athletics needed Baker. Lajoie might approach replacing Collins. But nobody in sight could come close to taking Baker's place. There might be slicker fielders available, but Baker had driven in more runs—471—in the past four years than anybody in the major leagues. His 52-ounce bat would be missed. And Mack knew it.

Those who knew Baker well called him the squarest of men, a straight shooter whose word was good as gold. They refused to believe he would try to hold up the Athletics for more money and considered his desire to retire sincere, though his love for the game—and the money—might ultimately prevail. Maybe so. But Frank Baker covered more ground in the things he said and wrote during the next three months than he had ever covered around third base.

It wasn't about money, he told F. C. Lane, *Baseball Magazine* editor, during Lane's visit at his home in Trappe. But of course it was. Numerous statements made by Baker over the next few months would make it clear that money was the issue. At one point during the Lane interview, Baker said, "Every man has his price at which he is willing to work. I have mine. I am not stating what it is, but I will take it if it is offered. I will work for Connie Mack cheaper than I will work for anyone else. But I will not work for Connie Mack or anyone else under the conditions as they are at present."

Baker was being coy. He told Lane, "If they meet my terms, well and good. If they don't meet my terms, well and good. Either course suits me." But he wouldn't tell Mack what his terms were. By letting Mack know it was about money without naming a figure, he hoped he wouldn't be seen as asking to renegotiate a contract he had signed. That would be tantamount to breaking his word, and that was not going to happen. He would wait for Connie Mack to volunteer to tear it up and resign him at a hefty raise. And that was not going to happen either.

Baker's reference to "conditions as they are at present" concerned the departure of Bender, Plank, and Collins, making another World Series check less likely, and the apparent viability of the Federal League. Although Baker's long-term contract with the Athletics made him off limits to the Feds, he saw large raises bestowed on players like Walter Johnson to keep them in the American League. He read about Eddie Collins earning $15,000 and Nap Lajoie $9,000, while he was stuck—or had stuck himself—at $6,666.66 for another two years.

"I wish them all the luck in the world," he said of Collins and Johnson. "But I have to look out for my own interests also. If I'm not satisfied I have the right to drop out and make a living in some other way. It's clear enough, I guess. There's no mystery about that."

What angered Baker the most was the quote attributed to Mack in his remarks at the writers' dinner, alluding to his having made trips to Trappe "for years" to sign Baker and his reason for pressuring the reluctant Baker to sign a three-year contract: "I don't want to run down to Trappe every year." Neither the annual trips nor the implicit reason for the three-year contract was accurate. Mack had visited Baker in the past but only once on business, when he had pressured Baker into signing the three-year pact that the taciturn farmer now regretted.

When Connie Mack read Baker's *Baseball Magazine* interview, he fired off a hot letter to him, accusing him of putting the Athletics' management in a bad light. "You know the Athletics ball club cannot give you any more money than you are getting. If you want more, send me your terms and the name of the club you want to play with and I will get you what you want just like I did with Collins."

Baker backed off, reversing himself as if he had been caught in a pickle between third and home. He claimed he was not holding out for more money; when he was asked if he would play if offered enough money, he had meant that if he was offered some enormous sum, he would be foolish to refuse it. He denied that he was threatening to retire just to pry more out of the Athletics. F. C. Lane had twisted his words to make him look like he was quitting because he wasn't getting paid enough. Baker assured Mack that he didn't want to play anywhere but Philadelphia, and if the A's couldn't pay him a bigger salary, he wasn't going to ask for more. He'd just stay home and be a farmer.

Connie Mack was supported by most of the baseball writers, whose words swayed the public to the club's side. For all his scrabbling like a Chesapeake blue crab, Baker was seen as a contract breaker, his retirement talk a bluff. Connie Mack said he would not be held up by any player, and the working man applauded him for it.

Baker had a tough row to hoe if he was looking for public support. A general business depression was smothering the nation. Iron and steel and coal production were down. Among major league cities, unemployment ranged from 10 percent in Philadelphia to 16 percent in New York. Ninety percent of male workers in factories and mines earned less than twenty dollars a week, one-third of them less than half that amount. So a man balking at playing ball for seven months for a salary that would support a dozen ordinary families reaped little sympathy.

Nor was Mack alone in his attitude concerning the uncertainties of the times. The *New York Times* named the wealthy new owners of the Yankees, Jacob Ruppert and Cap Huston, and Jim Gaffney, owner of the world champion Boston Braves, as among those who "will not be held up by ball players because of the present conditions of the game." Bill James, who had picked up two World Series wins, had signed a three-year contract the previous July for $4,000 a year. Now he wanted the Braves to tear it up and raise it to $6,000. They turned him down. When Cap Huston was told that Baker wanted $10,000 a year and a $10,000 bonus to sign and that it would take $40,000 to buy him from the A's, he said, "Baker would cost us more than some franchises sold for not long ago."

This kind of verbal shadowboxing over money in the public arena always irritated Connie Mack. A man's salary was a private matter between employer and employee, whatever the business. On a ball club, salary publicity—especially the inflated guesses emanating from the press—was poison, causing resentment, jealousy, dissension. What's more, he knew the fans wanted to read about the players and what happened on the field, not about club owners or players whining about money and spouting pompous nonsense.

Mack was especially fed up with Baker's bobbing and weaving around his motives, his reluctance to come out with an asking price, and his hints about retiring and being content to watch his asparagus grow, while at the same time lauding Mack as the greatest manager in the business and insisting he would play for Mack at a lower salary than for anyone else.

Mack turned his attention to culling his recruits in search of a replacement for the irreplaceable slugger.

Before leaving for Jacksonville and spring training, Mack sprang another, milder surprise. He realized that he had made a mistake in appointing Ira Thomas his team captain a year ago. A catcher when he joined the Athletics in 1909, Thomas had become Mack's most trusted coach, scout, and confidant. A non-smoker or -drinker, Thomas never hung out with any of the players off the field. As the captain, he had been a major source of friction on the 1914 team; half the players thought Eddie Collins should have been their leader. Mack wasn't too stubborn to change course. He reinstated the popular Harry Davis to the position, which carried more responsibility in those days than it does now. Davis had been a loyal player and coach since the Athletics' first year in business, except for a brief, unhappy stint as manager of the Cleveland Naps in 1912. Mack's explanation for the change? He wanted Thomas to be a full-time pitching coach: "'The work of the pitchers will make or break us this year. I consider that Ira Thomas is the best man in the country for the development of young pitching talent. He has proved this to me in the past and I look for him to again show excellent results."

The A's also had a new trainer, Edward E. "Doc" Ebling. A barber who had gone to school to become a physiotherapist, Ebling had been working in a clinic with the A's team doctor, Frank Macfarland. Macfarland, who married one of Ben Shibe's daughters, had recommended Ebling to Mack as far back as 1910. But Ebling preferred private practice. In the ensuing years he had often treated some of Mack's players, who praised his work. Mack kept after him and finally persuaded him to join the A's with a contract Ebling called "too good to pass up."

Doc Ebling became another member of the Athletics family to work for Connie Mack until death did them part.

The journey to spring training was different in those days. On the morning of Friday, February 25, contingents of the Phillies and Athletics—mostly rookies and prospects—left by train for Jersey City. From there they took a ferry to New York and walked a few blocks to the Clyde Line steamship piers, where they boarded the *Apache* for the three-day trip to Jacksonville. The Brooklyn Robins were also on the ship. Despite reports of German U-boats in the Atlantic, the voyage was uneventful. The next day Mr. and Mrs. Mack, leaving their three children, ages one to three, at home in the care of Katherine's spinster sister Nan, and Tom and Ida Shibe boarded a train to Jacksonville, followed a few days later by Harry Davis and most of the veteran players.

The Athletics gathered at Sunset Park in Jacksonville on Tuesday, March 1, included the wealthy playboy C. Emory Titman, who weighed over four hundred, sometimes over five hundred, pounds. Titman rarely missed a spring training with the A's. Clad in a tent-like uniform, he worked out in the outfield. In the last exhibition game against the local club, Harry Davis let him pinch-hit for Lajoie. Titman hit a long triple but made it only as far as first base. He made an unforgettable sight for local golfers when he showed up with Mack and Ohl at the Florida Country Club decked out in golf togs.

Mack expressed his usual optimism, and nobody laughed. As always, Mack based his outlook on his pitchers, and he had an ample squad of bright, young, strong-armed, experienced hurlers working under Ira Thomas and Jack Lapp. Joe Bush, with 30 wins and two complete-game World Series appearances in two years, and Bob Shawkey, who had worked more innings than any of the veterans in 1914, looked ready to replace Bender and Plank.

Herb Pennock had grown three inches since joining the A's as an eighteen-year-old and had gained ten pounds over the winter to fill out his slender frame. John Wyckoff, twenty-four, showed signs of better control of his fastballs and curves. Twenty-year-old Rube Bressler, coming off a 10-4 debut year, was touted as this year's "next Rube Waddell."

"The making or breaking of the staff depends on the work of Wyckoff, Pennock, and Bressler," Chandler Richter predicted in *Sporting Life*.

Larry Lajoie showed up carrying ten pounds over his playing weight instead of his usual thirty. Never the speediest afoot, he had lost a few steps on the bases and some range, which he made up for by wearing a bigger glove. Skipping about with renewed enthusiasm, he looked to camp visitors years younger than he had in recent seasons, though at forty, "years younger" did not a sprightly youth connote.

Jack Barry and Stuffy McInnis were capable of shading toward second to protect the areas that now lay beyond the ever-graceful Nap's reach.

For a change, Mack split the group into two teams, each a mix of veterans and rookies. They had two workouts a day, with a lunch break either back at the Burbridge Hotel or at the ballpark, the hotel sending ham or roast beef sandwiches (egg salad on Fridays for the Catholics). It was a calm, easygoing routine. During one session on base running, Mack commented that learning to dance would help a player's work on the bases. The humor magazine *Puck* picked it up and suggested, "Somebody should invent a dance with the hook-slide in it." Mack restrained the pitchers from cutting loose for the first week. On Sunday the players golfed or toured the local ostrich and alligator farms and other sights. When it rained, they went to billiard parlors or played basketball and swam at the YMCA. When rain washed out all practice on March 13, Mack put on a raincoat and went out to a golf course with Ohl to watch an exhibition by National Open champion Walter Hagen. "I learned something about how the champion played some of those drives and approaches," he said.

The Athletics and Connie Mack lost some friends that spring. While they were in Jacksonville, their mascot, Louis van Zelst, died at his home on March 15. The bright, witty little hunchback had been the club's good luck charm since 1910. He had made every World Series trip. Death was charged to heart trouble complicated by Bright's disease, but the players believed the sad spectacle of their loss to the Braves in the 1914 World Series had broken little Louie's heart.

Philadelphia papers extolled the mascot's virtues: "In that misshapen little body, there was one of the greatest souls that ever existed. Players and fans alike loved Little Louie and of all the mascots that have appealed to the baseball world from time to time in its history, he probably was the most famous and the most appealing."

Sam Erwin, who had missed his first spring training in fifteen years, died on May 10. One of Connie Mack's close friends and volunteer assistants, Erwin had coached and managed Mack's Yannigans every spring. A powerful political ward leader, Erwin had worked for railroads above and under ground. In his youth he had helped slaves escape to the north and Canada. He had been in charge of the train that carried President Lincoln's body to lie in state in Philadelphia in 1865. Erwin operated a popular hotel on Juniper Street that was home to some of the players during the season.

On June 17 Mack's friend and chronicler Henry Beech Needham was killed in France. Needham had been a frequent traveler with the A's, guest on the bench during games, and visitor to Mack's home. Now a war correspondent, he had talked his way onto a military airplane that was shot down. His book, *The Double Squeeze*, based on his travels with the Athletics, had just been published by Doubleday, Page & Co.

The McGillicuddy family tree would bear two new names before the year ended. On August 4 Connie Mack became a grandfather for the first time when his daughter, Marguerite, gave birth to a boy, Robert McCambridge, in Chicago. On September 28 Mack's son Earle married Miss Mary Caine of Morgantown, West Virginia, in Asheville.

Connie Mack gave utility man Larry Kopf the first shot at third base in practice games. His glove was good, but his bat was full of holes. Rube Oldring was tried there, with Shag Thompson, a late-season call-up, replacing him in the outfield. Mack then gave catcher Wally Schang and outfielder Eddie Murphy a look at third.

Meanwhile, they all kept looking for Frank Baker to get off the train. Some of the players wrote to him; nobody received a reply. They hoped he would change his mind when the box scores from Florida began to bloom in the northern sports pages. Back home the fans looked for headlines announcing Baker's return. Reports that Baker had enlisted Trappe high school lads to pitch batting practice for him buoyed their hopes. Why would a man keep his batting eye sharp if he didn't expect to use it? When the players returned to the Hotel Burbridge after working out each day, they expected—hoped—to see Bake in the lobby.

A week after they arrived in Jacksonville, Mack was waiting outside the hotel one morning for Titman's limousine to take him to Sunset Park. A reporter asked if he had heard from Baker.

No, I haven't heard a line from him. I am off Bake and he should know it by this time. Certainly I would like to see him back in the lineup, but I have done all in my power to bring him around.

You see a lot in print these days about it being a money question with him; why, the latest yarn I heard was to the effect that he would play ball again if some club would give him a $10,000 a year salary. If he is waiting for this, then I don't think he will play in the big leagues. Bake never brought up the money question with me. I won't believe he is trying a hold-up game until he tells me personally that it is a question of money with him, and if this should be the case, Bake will get the greatest call he has ever had in baseball.

I am not counting on him. He is not so wonderful that he cannot be replaced. Anyone, no matter how good he is, can be replaced in business or baseball. The fellow who thinks he is so good [that] they can't get along without him is mistaken. It may take a little time, but the right fellow comes along sooner or later. . . . Bake would look good with us, but we will be out there at Shibe Park just the same if he should stick to his retirement.

Despite Mack's letter to Baker in which he had expressed his willingness to sell or trade Baker to anyone who would meet his still unspecified salary demands, when Jacob Ruppert, the new co-owner of the Yankees, said he would give Baker $10,000 if Mack would take $25,000 for him, Mack was quoted as saying he had not received any such proposition and, even if he had, Baker was not for sale or trade under any conditions.

"It is indeed a tempting offer," Chandler Richter wrote of Ruppert's bid, "but Mack's answer greatly pleased all lovers of the game, as it proved conclusively that there are many things Connie prizes more than money."

The *Los Angeles Times* commented, "Mack must be trying to play a joke on somebody, inasmuch as Col. Ruppert has a letter from him stating that he will dispose of Baker for $50,000."

The letter, if it existed, was not made public.

A Philadelphia writer contacted by the *Times* filed the following "special dispatch" on March 3:

Frank Baker will play with the New York Yankees if Connie Mack agrees to accept Col. Ruppert's offer of $25,000 for the services of the former hard-hitting Athletics third-sacker.

An interview over the long-distance phone with J. Franklin at his home in Trappe, Md., made this clear.

"I will play with the New York Yankees if they offer a liberal enough salary," said Baker, "but, of course, I would prefer to stay with the Athletics. If the report is true that Mack has been dickering with Col. Ruppert for my sale to that club I would certainly play with them. I want to play with the Athletics, and would do my best to again bring the pennant to Philadelphia, for a much smaller salary than that for which I would play with the Yankees."

Newspapers in St. Louis and New York beat the drums to get Ban Johnson involved in seeing that Baker was sold to the Browns or Yankees. The Browns, basing their appeal on the competition they faced from a Federal League club, were willing to match New York's offers of $25,000 and a $10,000 salary.

Ban Johnson was never hesitant about helping to strengthen the weaker teams in his league, but he assured one and all that Connie Mack had told him he would not part with Baker at any price.

To Mack, putting an end to the Baker talk was like trying to tag Ty Cobb. In reply to an inquiry from a St. Louis paper, Mack wired, "Baker will not be traded to any club in base ball nor sold for any sum that may be named, and that is my final statement in the case of Baker."

The word "obstinate" appeared frequently, applied to both Mack and Baker, in comments of major league magnates about the standoff. Stubbornness, not stinginess, was in Connie Mack's soul. He was digging in for this tug-o'-war with his star RBI man, at the same time silently sharing the hopes of the players and public that Baker would catch spring fever and a train south—or maybe show up dramatically at Shibe Park on opening day ready to play, and when the umpire barked out the full lineups to the crowd and he came to "Baker, third base," the cheers would rock Billy Penn atop City Hall. It made for a pleasant, exciting reverie. But it would have to be on Connie Mack's terms—that is, the terms of the contract Baker had signed—or not at all.

The early April weather was so cold that attendance was sparse on the way north. Even in good weather, barnstormers going north to open the season didn't draw as they had in earlier times. Mack said that spring training was probably two weeks longer than necessary. The young players showed up in good condition. It shouldn't take more than a few days to see if a prospect had what it took to stick. Ban Johnson agreed. Johnny Evers went further, claiming that players who took care of themselves could get into playing shape just as well in their home ballparks.

Home Run Baker did show up at Shibe Park wearing a derby and topcoat on a cool, breezy opening-day April 14 and asked Connie Mack to let him play. But not for the Athletics.

The Upland club in the Delaware County League, a member of the Interstate Association of semipro clubs, had invited Baker to play on Saturdays for $100 a game. Upland was a tiny borough less than twenty miles southwest of Shibe Park. Baker sought Mack's permission to play "a little independent baseball." He didn't say where. According to one report, Baker visited with the players on the bench before the game, but when he approached Mack, the manager looked the other way and ignored him. The *Inquirer* had him huddled in a pregame "interview" with Mack, who told another reporter he and Baker exchanged brief greetings and little else and did not talk about baseball. Asked by a reporter if he was going to return, Baker said, "I don't know. You can never tell. Baseball is an uncertain game." Harry Davis urged Baker not to lose a season's salary for the sake of his pride.

During the game, Baker told Richter he would be willing to return to the A's if someone asked him. But that someone wasn't about to ask him. As far as Connie Mack was concerned, Baker was bound to a contract that obligated him to report without a special invitation.

Richter accurately summed up the situation: "Though Mack is right in his stand, both are too bull-headed to give in."

It was reminiscent of Mack's rigidly principled stance in dealing with a pitcher, Pete Husting, in Milwaukee fifteen years earlier. A difference of opinion over an agreement on an additional twenty-five dollars a month in salary had cost him the services of a pitcher he needed, who had a law practice he could retreat to.

One way or another, on opening day or soon afterward, Baker put his request to Mack and received permission to play independent ball anywhere "outside of Philadelphia."

3 | STARTING OVER

There were vast stretches of empty seats in the upper deck when Harry Davis and Boston manager Bill Carrigan raised the 1914 pennant at Shibe Park on opening day. Why Carrigan was invited to participate was not explained. Decked out in new uniforms with blue stripes down the legs and black on the stockings (Mack had finally given in to the criticism of the team's ugly uniform of the past few years), the Athletics peaked on opening day. They took an early 2–0 lead over the Red Sox on a walk, two bunts, a fielder's choice, and a scratch single. This set the pattern for the entire season's offense: two runs constituted a big inning.

Meanwhile, Herb Pennock was sailing through 8 innings without giving up a hit. Later Joe Bush recalled in *The Glory of Their Times* that as Pennock started out to the mound for the ninth, a rookie called out, "Well, Herb, only three more men and you've got a no-hit game."

Pennock got two quick outs, then Harry Hooper hit a feeble bouncer past the mound toward Lajoie, who started slowly then lunged for it, tried to pick it up with his bare hand, but was unable to hold it.

"The players thought it was an error," Bush said, "but the scorer called it a hit. In the clubhouse the rookie got a going over" for jinxing the no-hitter by mentioning it.

Pennock's masterpiece did not set the pattern for the season's pitching. The next day Bush was knocked out in the fifth in a 5–3 loss, and from there it was all downhill.

The Home Run Baker soap opera continued when Connie Mack learned that Baker had agreed to play for Upland. To Mack, Upland was part of the Athletics' metropolitan drawing area, not far enough "outside of Philadelphia" to suit him. Infuriated, he blasted Baker for contract jumping, breaking his word, breach of good faith, and general all-around villainy. He vowed that he wouldn't have Baker back under any conditions. What's more, he wouldn't sell Baker to anybody for any price, not even "one million dollars in cash." If Baker wanted to be a farmer in Trappe, that was okay with Mack.

At this point, the public was still squarely behind Connie Mack. But that wasn't the end of the battle of the bullheads. Baker was uncomfortable with his portrayal as a contract breaker. When some of the other clubs in the Delaware County League objected to "the contract jumper" playing for Upland, John H. Crozen, an Upland millionaire who backed the local team, hired him to manage Crozen's stock farm for $10,000 a year while playing third base for the local nine "just for the fun of it." The whole situation was unseemly to Baker.

A broken rib suffered in a fall down a flight of stairs at his home kept Baker out of the Upland opener on Saturday, May 1. Sitting at home, he may have had second or third or twentieth thoughts about his predicament. His enforced idleness may have given his wife a chance to remind him, as she had done whenever he talked about quitting, that those regular checks coming from the Athletics were mighty useful compared to the sporadic income that was the farmer's lot.

Mack remained obdurate. In Boston on April 26 he said that Baker could return if he chose to, but "it will be a long while before he is put into a game. I don't care if he returns or not but he won't be sold."

After stumbling to a 4-11 record, the A's were idled by rain in New York on May 4. Mack called a meeting in a conference room at the Ansonia Hotel and lit into them. They would have to wake up and play better if they hoped to be contenders. The pitchers would have to start throwing strikes. They won three of the next four, but the loss was ugly, 11–2 to Washington; Pennock lasted 2 innings and Barry made 4 of their 7 errors.

The A's were tied for seventh, 7 games behind the Tigers, on the evening of Saturday, May 8. Having won their second straight against Washington that afternoon, they were feeling pretty good about themselves as they waited at North Philadelphia station for the train to Cleveland, where they would play a Sunday game. They were startled to see Frank Baker coming down the platform toward them, accompanied by J. Worton Weeks, a young attorney who was president of the Delaware County League, and the Upland manager, Frank Miller.

The trio approached Connie Mack. Baker began by reiterating that he really didn't want to play big league ball. He preferred to stay home. But if the Athletics needed him badly enough, he was ready to play and would report immediately or any time Mack called him. Baker had not given in. There was a big "but": Mack would have to tear up the three-year contract, releasing Baker from the 1916 part of it, to dry up the brush that was painting him a contract breaker. He was not asking for any more money.

Connie Mack did not say yes or no. Instead, he berated Baker for breaking his word by playing for Upland. "When I said you could play outside of Philadelphia, that did not mean you could play in the Delaware County League." Mack added that he might seek an injunction against his playing for Upland. But that was just steam escaping. The lawyer, Weeks, said he'd never get it.

Again Baker declared that he was ready to play right now, if—. That was as far as he would go. The rest of the players watched transfixed, hoping for a reconciliation. But Connie Mack made only noncommittal sounds. There was no way he would back down, tear up the contract, tell Baker, "Yes, we need you, please come back." He couldn't do it.

The train pulled into the station. Baker, as if begging for the impasse to be resolved—but on his terms—once more tried to melt Connie Mack's resolve by stating that he was ready to step into the batter's box with his big bat. Mack had only to say the word. Mack said nothing. He boarded the train, leaving Baker and his companions on the platform.

Before Baker returned to Trappe, a reporter for the *Philadelphia Record*, looking for a way to make the manager look bad, offered the stranded player a chance to tell the public his side of the dispute. Baker refused to take the bait. He wouldn't criticize Connie Mack. He wanted to oil the hinges on the door to the lineup, not throw sand in them. Baker said:

> I hope the A's win the pennant by 25 games. I like every man on the club and I don't wish Mack any hard luck. The Federal League doesn't enter into it. [There had been reports that Baker was ready to jump if not for the legal hurdles.] If I was a free agent today and wanted to play in the big leagues I would go to Mack and ask him for a job with the Athletics. I'd rather play in Philadelphia than anywhere. I'd like the fans to know my position in the matter. I've done what I think's right. I don't want to play ball any more than I did a month ago, but if they need me as bad as they say, I'm willing to jump in and help them out. That's what I told Connie tonight. Now it's up to him.

When the fans learned about the encounter at the railroad station, they began to shift the blame for the standoff onto Connie Mack. They got on him to let Baker play now and worry about 1916 later.

But Baker also wanted that contract-breaking stigma erased from the public mind. He claimed that Mack had misstated his position, but he had changed his position so many times, it was difficult to avoid misstating it. Baker could have simply reported and played out the 1915 season at the same salary, then quit if he wanted to, without asking for the contract to be revised. If money wasn't really the issue.

The following Monday morning, an enterprising reporter, M. A. Kelly, rode the train from Philadelphia to Trappe. When he arrived at the station, he was surprised to find that he was still three miles from the tiny village. After a long, hot hike, he finally caught up with Baker, and the twenty-nine-year-old third baseman made it clear that money was indeed the issue.

"If he does return to the game," Kelly wrote, "it will be at a decided increase in salary. The club that gets his services, he told me, 'will have to want me a whole lot.'"

"You mean you want more salary?" Kelly asked.

"That's it," Baker said.

Kelly asked if a $2,000 increase would do.

"I'll want a whole lot more than that," Baker said. "It would take more than that to get me back into it."

The season was barely a month old, and already the revolving door was spinning at third base. Kopf flopped; he was followed by Oldring, Schang, Lajoie, and at least a half dozen others who left scant footprints in the infield dirt. By the end of the season fourteen players would take a turn at third.

Mack's stable of strong young pitchers rapidly fell apart. Joe Bush was ill. Rube Bressler had a sore arm. Wyckoff was the only dependable starter. When pitchers started out well, they invariably blew up in the late innings. Mack was quoted: "No game is a cinch for us until it is over."

After one such game, umpire Billy Evans said to Mack, "Those young pitchers seem to have a habit of getting wild just when it will help the opposition the most."

To which Mack replied, "Habit? That wildness is no longer a habit with those boys. It's a disease." Make that an epidemic. It would be July 31 before an Athletics pitcher could get through a game without walking a batter.

A lack of control is not indicated solely by walking batters. The failure to deliver a pitch where it was intended to go—high or low, inside or out—led to barrages of base hits. The poor pitching was also making a mess out of Mack's scorecard. For years he had charted every pitch, but there may have been days when he gave up in disgust. Eventually he abandoned the details but never the scorekeeping.

On June 18 Joe Bush and Wilbur Davis walked the White Sox pitcher Red Faber four times in an 11–4 loss. For a while they were averaging 10 walks a game. One writer quipped, "The Allies are thinking of signing Connie Mack's pitchers. By aiming at the Azores they might be able to hit Berlin."

Reporting on a 13–5 loss in New York, the *Times* commented, "Connie watched two of his pitchers give 14 bases on balls without even uncrossing his legs."

In 153 games the A's pitchers would issue 827 free passes. Mack told a *St. Louis Post-Dispatch* writer, "If you consult the records, you'll find, I believe, my pitchers this year have established a record for wildness that probably will live for all time. [It is still the record.] My young pitchers of promise are wilder than any I have ever seen."

Whatever this said about Ira Thomas as a pitching coach went unsaid.

"My team is somewhat demoralized by this," Mack continued, "but I resent the accusation that my team is the worst club on earth. We may be playing bad ball in spots, but I have a pretty good team, with several good players. Quite naturally I am disappointed this season. I'm not sore because my club is last."

After his opening day 1-hitter, Herb Pennock won only 2 of 7 starts. Connie Mack's celebrated patience was running out. Now in his fourth year with the A's, Pennock had not progressed enough to satisfy Mack. The twenty-one-year-old lefty seemed indifferent about his future as a pitcher. The intensity, the desire to learn and improve, were missing. Regardless of ability, Connie Mack looked for men who clearly, openly enjoyed working at their job, loved to play the game each day and showed it, whatever the score or the standings. Call it competitive spirit or "zest"—the word his more loquacious friend Branch Rickey used to describe it. Collins and Barry and McInnis and Danny Murphy and Wally Schang showed it. He didn't see it in Pennock. No life in the coal mines awaited him if he didn't succeed in baseball. Coming from a wealthy family, he lacked the hunger that drove the farm boys and miners' sons, who wanted no part of milking cows or digging coal for the rest of their lives.

At least, that's the way the manager read him.

The ongoing hassle with that farmer in Trappe may have grated on Connie Mack's temper and drained his patience tank, which was not bottomless.

It ran dry in the west.

On May 17 in Chicago, Pennock lasted only 3 innings, giving up 5 runs in a 6–2 loss. Two days later the A's had a 7–4 lead over the White Sox when Pennock relieved Wyckoff in the eighth and was battered for 5 runs while Mack's collar tightened. Mack gave him another start on May 23 in Detroit. Before the game the manager imparted careful instructions on how to pitch to the Tigers' powerful lineup. The young lefty either forgot, ignored, or was unable to follow Mack's directions. The Tigers scored 3 in the first inning on 3 hits and 3 walks.

The peppery temper of Connie Mack's younger days began to percolate. When Pennock reached the dugout, Mack blew up. "Young man," he snapped, "as far as I'm concerned, you can sit on that bench all season and never pitch another ball."

Pennock coolly replied, "If you don't care for my pitching, why not trade or sell me?"

The May 24 American League Bulletin No. 54, mailed to all clubs, read: "Clubs will kindly wire this office immediately if they desire to claim the following: Philadelphia: Herbert Pennock."

Every team waived on him except the Red Sox, against whom Pennock was especially effective. Boston claimed him for $2,500. He was the first player Connie Mack had sold since Eddie Collins five months earlier.

Mack then made a curious statement to F. C. Richter. "Had I wanted to put Pennock on the market, I could have easily gotten several thousand dollars for him, but I did not. . . . I had been offered a few players, but none of them seemed to be worth the contracts they were carrying so I turned them down." Presumably Mack was suggesting that he could have gotten more from a National League club if Pennock had cleared AL waivers. Boston manager Bill Carrigan refused to play the game of gentleman's wink-and-wave that often enabled a club owner to slip a desirable player out of the league.

Mack told the *Philadelphia Press* he didn't think Pennock would ever be a winning pitcher for the Athletics. Based on what he had seen so far that year, Pennock wouldn't be missed. Mack had been scouting college games since April and had plenty of better-looking arms in the pipeline. "I have several men reporting to me in the middle of June who will more than make up for his departure. Two of the pitchers joining us will be better right now than Pennock has been."

Looking back long after Herb Pennock wound up his Hall of Fame career at forty, Connie Mack called his impetuous dismissal of Pennock "the biggest blunder of my managerial career. I was too impatient with the boy." But Mack's appraisal of the Pennock of 1915 was accurate. The young southpaw appeared in only five games for Boston the rest of that year, did not become a winning pitcher until four years later, and did not become a great pitcher until he was traded to the Yankees in 1923 at the age of twenty-nine.

It's a lot easier to look back a hundred years than to look ahead eight.

Another young left-hander, Rube Bressler, gave Connie Mack even more fits than Herb Pennock. Rube had the spirit and the nerve, but he was wild and erratic. Ira Thomas and Bressler didn't get along. Eddie Collins, a prolific and outspoken commentator throughout his playing career, had written in 1914, "You have always read how Thomas developed [Bressler]. Every time the Athletics saw that statement in print, they laughed. Why? Because Bressler hated to have Thomas warm him up. If there ever was a chance to spoil Bressler, Thomas would have done so. Rube Bressler is a pitcher because Eddie Plank took an interest in him."

Now Plank was gone and Thomas had his chance to spoil Bressler.

Rube could be a marvel one day and a poor excuse for a pitcher the next. He might throw a 1-hitter or walk 5 batters in the first inning. Unfortunately the poor-excuse-for-a-pitcher showed up most of the time. He didn't win a game until June 8 and finished the year with 4 wins and 17 losses, carrying the highest earned run average in the league: 5.20. Once the season became a lost cause, Bressler found the after-hours action more enjoyable than the daylight toil of pitching for a last-place team.

It didn't help that the defense behind the pitchers was terrible. The infield was a shambles, not just third base. It was literally a case of "Who's on first?" after Stuffy McInnis fielded a practice grounder with his nose one day. Amos Strunk, Jack Lapp, Nap Lajoie, even forty-one-year-old Harry Davis filled in for him. At one point, Lajoie, McInnis, Strunk, Oldring, and Schang—Mack's five best players—were all sidelined with injuries.

Mack took it all calmly. Injuries were the only part of the game where luck was a factor. All the rest—good bounces and bad, umpires' mistakes, the weather—evened out over time. "Fifteen years we've been mighty lucky," he said, forgetting untimely injuries to Jack Barry that he once claimed had cost him pennants. "Now I am getting my share. Good thing it is all coming at once."

He played catchers in center field and at first and third. And he went prospecting. When Nap Lajoie went down with a foot injury in late May that looked like it would sideline him for some weeks, Mack tapped a fertile source of baseball talent, Mount St. Joseph's Academy in Baltimore. Lew Malone was their eighteen-year-old star infielder, in the same bright, heads-up style of Eddie Collins. Mack wanted him to fill in immediately.

"I want to be able to finish out our season on June 2," Malone said.

"I need you now," Mack said. "Play under a different name until your school year is over."

So Lewis Ryan showed up at Shibe Park early on the morning of May 31 and played both games of the split doubleheader against Boston, drawing raves from Tim Murnane of the *Boston Globe* for his sensational play. When asked where Ryan came from, Connie Mack "absolutely refused to say where he secured [him]."

The next day he played against Washington and a Nationals' beat writer recognized him and blew his cover, but it didn't matter. The A's were rained out the next two days, and Malone had graduated when he appeared in the lineup on June 4 under his own name. Malone was a whiz in the field, but big league pitching baffled him. He began to lose his confidence at the plate, and it affected his fielding. Mack sat him down, at the same time trying to boost his failing confidence by building him up to the press. "Malone," he claimed, "is just at the stage where Collins was when he came to me and looks every bit as good. At present he is not hitting, but he will be a great hitter and a great infielder."

As it turned out, Malone wasn't and never would be. But as fallacious as Mack's ballyhoo appears in retrospect, this was typical of his management style, speaking more for the player's consumption than the public's, to give a struggling rookie's chin a lift when he needed it.

By mid-June the Athletics were 11 games out of first place. When Mack asked waivers on a long list of players, other clubs caught the whiff of prey. Comiskey was interested in Barry and Eddie Murphy. In Detroit Hughie Jennings asked him to name the price for Wally Schang. Mack withdrew all the waivers. Whether from conviction or habit or just to keep the fans interested, he proclaimed, "We will be in the race by the middle of August."

And the British were proclaiming, "The war will be over by Christmas."

Two of the pitchers who were supposed to make the fans forget Herb Pennock made their debuts against the Yankees on June 23. In the first game

Minot Crowell, late of Brown University, pitched well while losing, 3–2, in 10 innings. The second game starter was Bruno Haas, a hefty twenty-four-year-old left-hander who had been recommended by his classmate at Worcester Academy, Connie Mack's son Roy.

"Connie was so pleased with Crowell's showing," the *New York Times* said, "that between games he whispered to Bruno Haas . . . to go and do likewise. Bruno went out on the hill with a glove and uniform, just like Crowell. Thereafter his imitation of Minot was painful."

At what point does "lack of control" become "out of control"? Haas walked 16 in 9 innings, threw 3 wild pitches, and located enough pitches over the plate for the Yankees to rap out 11 hits. The A's made 6 errors, which didn't help. Mack watched the performance calmly and let Haas endure the 15–7 loss, which took a merciful two hours and five minutes. Afterward, Mack was unusually relaxed and eloquent. He reminisced about a game he had seen where a pitcher walked 18 and explained that Haas was not used to pitching off a fifteen-inch elevation.

"I signed Haas because of his wonderful control. That sounds queer, doesn't it, in view of his wildness. But I'll tell you the secret of his failure. . . . The pitching mound fooled him. Twirling on scholastic diamonds, where he stood on a level with the plate, was what he had been accustomed to. When he was lifted into the air a foot or more by the big league mound, it threw off his delivery. We are coaching him out of his trouble rapidly and I believe he will make a valuable player."

Later Mack gave the *Evening Ledger* a different spin on Haas's outing. His approach with youngsters, he said, was to let them make mistakes and learn from them, so they would be better prepared the next time he called on them. At least that was the theory.

"Had I pulled [Haas] out of the game, I might have hurt his confidence. As it was, he learned something every inning he pitched, which will come in handy on his next appearance. . . . The next time I use him I will pull him out if he gets a bad start, as he has seen most of his glaring faults, and it would hurt him to leave him in too long on his second start. I knew he was not right in the second inning, and was really anxious to see how he would act."

Haas didn't fare any better in his second chance, and Mack quickly pulled him and suggested he try playing the outfield. Haas took the suggestion and played twenty-one years in the minor leagues, nine of them as a Class C and D manager, where he made his last appearance as a pitcher at the age of fifty-five. (Haas also played one year of pro football in 1921.)

After a brief glimpse of seventh place in June, the Athletics ducked back into the basement to stay. Connie Mack no longer spoke about being back in the race by August. The pitchers he had counted on had all gone back on him. At this point, the Federal League was still feisty. It may have been a bluff, but the Feds talked openly about finding grounds in New York for 1916 and continued to woo stars to boost their credibility as a major league.

Mack's grapevine yielded the tip that Bob Shawkey was committed—if not already signed—to jump to Buffalo at the end of the season. How he could do that wasn't reported; like most of the A's, Shawkey had signed a revised contract in August 1914 to fend off the Feds, giving him a raise to $3,250 a year through 1916. More to the point, Shawkey wasn't living up to his 1914 promise. He was 6-6 and an active carrier of the base on balls virus.

When Mack let it be known that Shawkey was for sale, Charles Comiskey was interested. After a sixth-place finish in 1914, Comiskey had sworn off buying high-priced minor league stars who quickly faded. He went on a spending spree to rebuild the White Sox with established major leaguers, beginning with Eddie Collins. He offered a bundle of cash and players for Cleveland shortstop Ray Chapman and was turned down but later won the bidding for Cleveland star Joe Jackson, paying a reported $31,500 plus three players who had cost him $34,000. Contemporary reports have Ban Johnson intervening to steer Shawkey to the Yankees. Johnson was getting some heat from Jake Ruppert, who had been promised help in strengthening the Yankees when he bought the club in January. So far Ruppert had seen very little help. Shawkey wound up going to New York on June 28.

A big deal has been made of this sale by the look-back experts and critics of Connie Mack. But at the time it was considered a very small deal that made no big headlines. The *New York Tribune*, whose baseball coverage featured the stellar talents of Grantland Rice, W. O. McGeehan, and Heywood Broun, gave it no more than this at the bottom of a page:

"The Yankees purchased Bob Shawkey from the Athletics yesterday. Shawkey is a young but well-seasoned right-handed pitcher."

End of story. No price was mentioned. Other papers gave it only a one-line mention or ignored it altogether.

The $18,000 price mentioned in later accounts is way off. Such a price for a third-year pitcher would have been extraordinary for the time and made a bigger splash than it did. The Athletics' ledgers show it as $3,000.

Public reports of prices paid for players in those days are seldom reliable. Buyers and sellers rarely made official announcements. Exaggeration was as common as evasion. Sometimes a buyer would float inflated hints to impress his customers with how much he was spending to bring them a winner. Sellers generally made deflationary comments or said nothing at all. Charles Comiskey took pride in his lavish spending. Connie Mack was the silent type. To him, a club's monetary affairs, including players' salaries, were none of the public's business.

It is in the nature of the press: what they do not know they guess. It was worse when there were six or eight papers in town competing for readers. Staring at a blank sheet of copy paper with a deadline approaching and no story, sportswriters would invent a colorful exploit, start a trade rumor, spawn a myth, or add to one started by some scribe from the past facing the same dilemma. Ordinary men were turned into legends. Future writers would pick it up, embellish it, perpetuate it. Later the distinction between the tales the writers made up and the truth became blurred. In their memoirs, retired players often ended up believing it all. Connie Mack would have agreed with William Pinkerton of the detective agency, who complained, "You cannot get a thing right for a newspaperman. . . . If you write the facts down for him, he will change them about to suit himself."

Thus is history made.

After fifteen years in Philadelphia, the fifty-two-year-old Connie Mack was not yet the grand old man of baseball he would become. He had gained a sphinx-like reputation because of his reluctance to divulge his thinking in advance of completing player moves. As an earlier writer, Harry Weldon, had said, "Mack doesn't hunt quail with a brass band."

Most writers and fans didn't understand the effects on a team of premature talk of a deal that might never be consummated, nor the common practice of withholding statements until both sides could announce it simultaneously. An obviously peeved Mack told J. C. Linck of the *St. Louis Globe-Democrat*, "I never like to say what I'm going to do. That is, I don't mind telling in a general way, but as far as going into details about the players I have and what I expect to do with them—I'd rather not. I can't afford to pay any attention to my critics. They certainly didn't come out to see the team last year or the year before. They were not interested in a great team which was always winning. What do they want? I have started to build up a new team. Their objections are no worse than they were when I had a pennant winner."

At the same time Mack understood the writers' position. Over the years he would tell his beat writers, "If you have an idea that a deal may be in the works, don't come to me and ask me, for I'll deny it. Then you'll have no story. Go ahead and write what you want, then I'll deny it, and that way you'll have two stories instead of none." He was a gracious interview, expounding at length on his philosophies of baseball, the managing of players, and life in general. He enjoyed reminiscing about his own playing days and past pennant races.

But some out-of-town writers didn't know him.

The sales of Pennock and Shawkey raised speculation of more moves to come by the Athletics' leader. After the June 28 game in Washington, a *Post* writer told Mack he had heard that Jack Barry was on the market.

"You will hear a whole lot of yarns about my ball club," Mack said, "about this or that player being sold or traded, but you will find but little truth in any of them. Barry, at the present time, is suffering from an injury."

The writer persisted. "But it is reported that a deal is already pending involving Barry. How about it?"

"I would rather not discuss Barry at the present time," Mack snapped.

Connie Mack wouldn't talk about Jack Barry, but he was thinking about him. In Boston, the A's next stop, the heaviest downpour in twenty years washed out their doubleheader on Friday, July 2. Mack spent the afternoon noodling over his plans for the future of his team. His machine had broken down. Rube Oldring and Eddie Murphy were near the end of the line. Every day he was being reminded—not that he needed reminding—how uncertain a commodity pitching was. They weren't going anywhere this year. Who knew what conditions—the war in Europe, the Federal League, Frank Baker's state of mind—would exist next year?

As he watched the rain batter his hotel window, he considered the status of his shortstop, Jack Barry. Perhaps Mack's favorite among his veterans, Barry was smart, sober, dependable, creative, the best bunter and hit-and-run stroker in the league, and the most dangerous hitter in the lineup with the game on the line. In February 1914, the *Boston Post* had asked eleven experts in major league cities to pick an all-American team. Seven chose Barry at shortstop.

And yet if it was time to rebuild, where did Jack Barry fit in? He had another year left on a contract at $4,000. He was only twenty-eight, but frequent injuries had left him with prematurely old legs. He had slowed perceptibly in the field and had recently been out for two weeks with a hand injury. The departure of Eddie Collins had made a difference too. Though Collins remained a great player, the quick-thinking-in-unison combination of Barry and Collins had lifted both of them to defensive heights that neither attained thereafter without the other. Lajoie couldn't cover the ground that Collins did. That forced McInnis to play farther off first base and Barry closer to second, leaving a bigger gap between short and third.

Mack believed that Barry might have four or five years of baseball left in him as a part-time player, but he would certainly be finished when the A's would need a shortstop of the future. Why wait to begin testing fuzzy-cheeked recruits to see how they developed? The Athletics would not be as good a team without Barry, but they were 22-42 with him. They were only 2 games out of sixth place, but if they couldn't be in the thick of a pennant race, it mattered little to Connie Mack whether they finished fifth, sixth, seventh, or last while he was rebuilding.

Deep-pockets Charles Comiskey and Jake Ruppert had been after Mack to name his price for Barry, but Mack knew that Barry would prefer to finish his career closer to his home in Worcester. And that mattered to the manager.

Mack telephoned Red Sox president Joe Lannin and offered him Barry. Lannin conferred with his manager, Bill Carrigan. They didn't need a shortstop; they had a dandy in young Everett Scott. They needed a second baseman; Charles "Heinie" Wagner had a bad arm and was no longer an everyday player. They were battling Detroit and Chicago for the pennant, and Carrigan said he could use a man with Barry's abilities and leadership qualities, wherever he played.

So Lannin told Mack they had a deal. Neither disclosed the price tag, which Lannin said was "rather stiff," while Mack said, "I sold Barry for a song." The price was $10,000.

That evening Mack told the writers, "I had made up my mind to cling to Barry and it was only today that I changed my mind in regard to this matter. . . . It is simply a question of being at the bottom or at the top, and as I aim to be at the top again, I may as well start to build up all around."

Mack also used the occasion to knock down the recurrent rumors of his bailing out of Philadelphia and to eliminate the need to respond to speculation about more sales to come.

He wired the *North American*: "Prior to yesterday I had not planned to dispose of Barry. Changed my mind in order to put him with a good club where he wanted to play. This deal in no way affects my relation to the club. I am out to build a new team that will be a winner. My stock has never been for sale, and will not be unless President Shibe should disapprove of the way

I am running the club. Further deals regarding players will be made public only when completed. Will not deny any rumors relating to players."

When the Red Sox won the 1915 pennant, Mack sent Barry a telegram: "Heartiest congratulations over your great work for Boston and hope your playing will do as much in the World Series for your club."

Jack Barry found playing second base much less demanding on his arm and scarred legs. The first time he saw Eddie Collins after he went to Boston, he joked, "Listen, Collins, I just found out what an easy job you've had all this time. Playing second base, you ought to stay in baseball till the whiskers come down to your toes."

Barry later recalled, "Eddie was so mad he couldn't speak, just walked away."

Barry helped the Red Sox win two pennants and managed the team in 1917. All together he played on six pennant winners and four world champions in nine full seasons (he did not play in the 1916 Series, won by Boston). He played his last game at thirty-two before beginning a forty-year coaching career at Holy Cross.

Mack used the broom on outfielder Eddie Murphy when the A's were in Chicago on July 16. The White Sox were looking for a lead-off man.

"Mr. Mack came to me on the field before the game," Murphy told baseball historian Lee Allen, "and said, 'I'd like you to meet Clarence Rowland.' We went under the stands and when I shook hands with Rowland, who was manager of the White Sox, he said, 'You ought to know I just bought you.' So I just changed suits."

Murphy was batting .231 at the time. He had hit just .188 in the 1914 Series. But he was only twenty-three, so Mack got $11,500 for him. Murphy was never again an everyday player. Used by the White Sox primarily as a pinch hitter for the next five years, he batted .300 in that role.

(Syndicated columnist Hugh Fullerton subscribed to papers from every major league city and kept track of how many times game accounts charged players with failing to run out grounders they might have beaten out for hits. As of July 1, the National League total was fifty-three, the Federal League sixty-nine, and the American League forty-three. Cleveland led the AL with eleven; the A's were in the middle with seven; the lowest were Detroit and St. Louis with one each. Four of the Athletics' seven involved one man, "and you need but one guess to tell who he is," wrote Fullerton. My guess is Murphy.)

The popular Collins, Barry, and Murphy were all honored by the A's and fan groups on their first visits to Shibe Park in foreign uniforms. Double-barrel shotguns and silver tea sets were the usual gifts on such occasions.

But Mack was not unloading all his stars. In July he reportedly turned down $50,000 from the Browns for Baker, McInnis, and Oldring. He had no intention of letting McInnis and Oldring go.

For Connie Mack the gloom he saw among his older players who had been with him through the glory years was more painful than the daily losses. Their morale was shot. They were accustomed to the tension and excitement and challenge of a pennant race. The cellar was a strange environment. They expected to win every year, and there was something bewildering about being out of the fight. Smiles were scarcer than victories and more sorely missed by the harried manager. The quick thinking he prized and encouraged was absent. Sometimes Amos Strunk would be on first and start for second, change his mind, and turn back, invariably picked off. Finally Mack told him, "Amos, next time you get a thought, have it while you're standing on a base, not when you're between 'em."

Some of them fell into a last-place attitude and played accordingly. It's a contagious virus, the lethargy and despair that seeps through a team that started the season with great expectations and a month later was looking up at the rest of the league. The season seemed to drag on endlessly; it felt like September and it was still July. A team may lose 100 or more games a year, but each day the players were expected to go out on the field believing they would win that game. Now there were few believers.

Mack told W. J. "Billy" O'Connor of the *St. Louis Post-Dispatch:*

The hardest part of my work during the present season has been keeping the players I need in my plans in the proper frame of mind. It's only natural for a few of the boys to be disappointed at the breaking up of the old machine.

I'm not sore because my club is last. I don't mind losing if we're beaten by a better team. I can stand that, but I'm sorely disappointed this year in the fact that some of my highest-priced men have not shown the spirit of hustle and stick-to-itiveness that men of their salary and experience should.

It matters not whether I have torn down a pennant team. Conditions of unusual character now prevailing dictated that move. It is hard to maintain a winning spirit on a ball club these days. When my last good team was at its best, we were as a happy family. We were one for all and all for one.

I regret to say the same condition hardly exists today. Players of whom the club should expect most, measuring our demands from the scale of wages paid, have done least. In them I am disappointed.

Some players have not kept themselves in a winning condition. You need not drink or carouse to be out of condition, either. You can get out of what I choose to call "winning condition" by eating too much, failing to enthuse over each ball game or, worse yet, by becoming lazy. Losing your "pep," I might say. Laziness is the worst sin in baseball.

It's a problem that still challenges managers of hopeless also-rans.

"Playing for a last-place team is a test of character more than of ability," said twenty-first-century manager Jerry Narron. "Can a man reach down inside himself and bring out what's in him? A manager can try to motivate by appealing to pride or economic self-interest. But there is only so much a manager can do to motivate a team that's dead last."

A few of the A's—Jack Lapp, Wally Schang, Stuffy McInnis—never let up. Mack wanted Schang's bat and speed—and Lapp's bat—in the lineup every day, so Schang split his time between third and the outfield. "I put [him] on third base this spring," Mack said, "and he went great for thirty games. However I was obliged to switch him to the outfield and when he came back to third he wasn't so good. But I want to see more of him there before I give up." Schang had a rifle arm—threw faster than Walter Johnson, said Mack—but erratic aim and played with enthusiasm, but he never really mastered either position.

McInnis played all-out every day. His hitting never fell off. He was making spectacular plays on high, wide, and low throws, especially when Schang was playing third. In a game on June 12 he took a wide throw while almost flat on the ground, reaching out with his hand-sized glove for the throw, his bare hand on the base, as Ty Cobb raced down the line toward him. There has never been a better-fielding first baseman, nor a more deserving Hall of Famer who isn't there.

To some players stuck on a losing team, the only incentive was the hope of escape. Some took the route of trying to pump up their stats, thus making themselves more attractive to a contending club that might be willing to pay an inflated price for them. One common tactic for maintaining or improving a batting average was to bunt with a man on base, even if a sacrifice was not called for. A successful bunt might result in a hit at best or no time at bat if the runner advanced. Playing for next year—boosting the stats for next year's salary negotiations—is still practiced. Others reacted by soldiering the manager—going through the motions, hoping to exasperate the skipper into putting them on the market to be rid of them. Either way, their thinking was not about the team.

John McGraw had the same problem with the Giants. Two years after facing each other in the World Series, both Mack and McGraw had last-place teams. (For McGraw 1915 was the only year he would finish last; the Giants' 69-83 record is the best ever for a pre-expansion last-place team.) A mid-season story in the *New Orleans States* quoted McGraw: "The old spirit is gone. The players don't enthuse over victories as they used to do. . . . There's a different spirit on my club since things were upset by the Federal League." The effects of the Feds' overtures had also contributed to the Giants' decline that had cost them the 1914 pennant. Both managers knew who was "mailing it in" to collect a paycheck. Connie Mack gets all the notoriety for dismantling his 1914 Athletics, but the fact is that John McGraw did just as much housecleaning. By 1916 eight of his 1914 starters were gone, including Fred Snodgrass, Bob Bescher, Chief Meyers, Red Murray, Rube Marquard, and Al Demaree.

The multiyear contracts used by club owners to protect them from Federal League raiders had sapped the motivation of a lot of players. Ralph Davis of the *Pittsburgh Press* noted, "It is true that ballplayers are taking advantage of conditions and that many of them are not playing the game of which they are capable. They feel that they are protected; the clubs must pay them whether they play or not, and there is no incentive for them to overexert themselves."

I. E. (Irving) Sanborn of the *Chicago Tribune* lamented the effects of long-term contracts on players' ambition and aggressiveness, compared to the time when next year's salary depended on this year's performance.

Sid Keener of the *St. Louis Times* believed the long-term and guaranteed contract "makes the player safe whether he earns his pay or not . . . whether they bat .300 or .100."

The Cincinnati Reds were reported considering releasing some players without further payment on the grounds of their having failed to render ample services in exchange for their big salaries. The Cardinals took the opposite approach, promising bonuses based on the club's finish in the standings. When they finished third, every man received an extra 20 percent of his salary.

A *New York Times* account of a Yankees doubleheader loss at Philadelphia in June accused the New Yorkers of becoming "displeased at each other when the Athletics took the lead, and did not appear to be trying. In the last two innings of the first game, Keating simply floated the ball up to the plate. All told, twelve errors of commission were recorded during the afternoon, and there were many errors of omission."

The Federal League was not immune to the wave of nonchalance brought on by multiyear contracts. Club owners threatened to suspend jakers without pay. Cynics accused club owners of fining high-priced stars for poor performances as a way to cut their losses. The biggest flop was Chief Bender, who won 5 and lost 16 at Baltimore. The Terrapins cut him loose before the season ended, despite his long-term contract. (Eddie Collins wasn't surprised; Mack probably wasn't either. Both of them knew Bender well. Pitching for a last-place team in a quasi-major league, Bender had lost interest and, as Collins diplomatically put it, "When Bender loses interest he finds it hard to drive himself.")

For all the talk about harmony and players dogging it, and the playing down of the economic factors behind his actions, there is no doubt that cutting overhead was a priority for Connie Mack. He had always operated on the premise that baseball was a business. Like any business, you had to take in more than you spent to survive. "When the fans lose interest in the team and nobody comes in through the gate, you have to make changes," he maintained.

Mack remembered the effects of the Spanish-American War on the public's interest in baseball in 1898. Now the war in Europe was getting bloodier as the months passed. The Athletics had lost attendance with a winner. They were headed for a deep dip in the red ink sea this year, and there was nothing to indicate better times ahead, for baseball or the world. The Feds were still hanging in there. Mack considered it essential to bring the payroll down from the $93,000 of 1914.

He was not alone in cutting payroll. The Reds were down to nineteen players and talked of cutting down to seventeen. By mid-June only the Giants were carrying a full roster.

Connie Mack was not criticized for viewing skyrocketing salaries as a threat to the stability of baseball. On the contrary, he was hailed as a model of foresight and business acumen.

On June 22, an unidentified western club owner was quoted in a special report out of Philadelphia to the *Los Angeles Times*:

In retrenching all along the line, Connie Mack is doing this year what every club in the major leagues will be doing next season. The wise Mack is, as usual, a year ahead of everybody else. It took a lot of grit for him to do what he has done, but, like all men who do big things and accomplish great results, Connie has lots of courage.

Mack saw the handwriting on the wall and went ahead and governed himself accordingly. Philadelphia fans will profit by his foresight, for in reorganization plans Mack has had a year's start on everybody else.

Anyway, you can't keep a wonder like Mack down, for there is nobody in his class in digging up young players. No temperamental star can hold any club over his head, for he is too resourceful in getting successors. That's where he has it on the average tactician.

Two weeks later Henry P. Edwards of the *Cleveland Plain Dealer* noted that the Cleveland Naps had the highest payroll in the league in 1908, and by 1915 the Red Sox and White Sox payrolls were double what the Naps' had been, Boston topping the league at $120,000. Edwards wrote:

Now the salaries have become so abnormal . . . that first division clubs merely hope to break even, while the second division teams feel certain they will incur big losses. The inflation of salaries was due primarily to the magnates themselves. Even before the Federal League invaded the field the salaries started to jump. . . . Today finds the payrolls close to double what they were a few years ago.

Connie Mack was the first to read the handwriting upon the wall. He saw the financial abyss that was ahead of the national pastime because of the tremendous overhead expenses and it was last winter that he started to separate himself from some of his high salaried men. . . .

As it looks now, Mack is but a pioneer in a move that may be adopted by the other big league managers and the Federal Leaguers also.

The Philadelphia writers were, in the main, understanding and supportive of Mack's actions. He stood high with the local scribes. He was always available for one-on-one interviews in his office. Some writers he liked more than others, but he played no favorites when he had an announcement to make or a background briefing on some player move to explain.

So they were surprised and angered when, after refusing for six months to expound on his "real" reasons for letting Plank, Bender, Coombs, and

Collins go the preceding year, Mack inexplicably chose to break his silence with an exclusive statement dictated to the *Evening Ledger*. It ran in early July under his own byline and was picked up by *Sporting Life* and newspapers all over the United States and Canada.

Mack said he had been "caught napping." Twice before he had seen his championship teams slipping in time to begin rebuilding before they slid out of contention. Not this time. He had expected his machine to be good for another five years. Once it began deteriorating, he saw it crumbling like a sat-on cookie.

At the same time he was being lauded for his foresight in taking steps to cut back on overhead, Mack insisted the breakup of his team was not "for the sake of economy." And it wasn't—not entirely. Sure it had to do with money, but not his own or his club's money.

> The Federal League completely wrecked my club by completely chang-
> ing the spirit of the players. After that change came, there was nothing
> for me to do but protect myself and the club. Before last season the boys
> thought only of victories, but when the Federal League agents started
> offering salaries all out of proportion, they forgot there was something
> else besides money in the world. . . .
>
> Money had nothing to do with the breaking up of my team, except
> that I saw the time had come when some of the players thought of
> nothing but money, and sooner or later the team must go to pieces.
>
> I thought it all over, and decided that the break had better come right
> away. I want to say there was no chance for me to hold any of the play-
> ers I let go. They were responsible for the breaking up of the fabulous
> machine, and not the club or its policies.

Mack saw himself as taking the lead, setting the example for other clubs. The way to survive the war was not to outbid the Feds; that path led to baseball's being shipwrecked. "Somebody was forced to lead the way in preventing the ruin of baseball, and I think in a few years the fans will look back and say that I was not such a bad fellow and will agree with me in my conclusions."

The fans didn't agree at the time, and the revisionists of today still don't. Mack continues to be pilloried as a penny-pincher for doing what has today become common, as winning and losing teams alike look for ways to slash payrolls and remain competitive—or not care about remaining competitive.

Putting together a winner that is economically feasible is the challenge still facing almost every major league club. And for the most part the clubs do it without criticism.

The most explosive display of fireworks over the interview came from the *Record*'s sports editor, A. M. Gillam, who had knocked Mack continuously since the day he had banned their beat writer, William Brandt, from Shibe Park in a spat over the paper's use of a display board to recreate home games in 1914.

Gillam's attack ran twenty-four column inches; raked over some old, cold coals; and was sometimes careless with the facts:

So finally Connie Mack feels called upon to make some explanations as to the why and wherefore of his policy in breaking up the most powerful baseball machine of modern times. . . . With the drop-off in attendance, he realizes it's time now for any excuse. Connie is pretty good at making excuses, as is shown by his article explaining why it was good baseball to send up Plank, his weakest batsman, in place of Schang, his best hitter, when any sort of an outfield fly was all that was needed to win the deciding game of the worlds championship series of 1913 [it was Game 2]. He was so convincing that a great many actually believed that he meant everything he said. So very likely many will believe that Mack really had to get rid of all his best players for him to continue business at the old stand.

Mack's getting rid of practically all his high-priced players was designed not only to save money but to make sure the team could not win. This has made the games played by the Athletics this year a mere farce, a travesty on baseball. . . . A team that begins the season so hopelessly weak it is useless to look for anything better than a tail-end position will never be much of a financial success. [Nobody had picked the A's to finish last.]

On it went, Gillam criticizing Mack for resting his players before the 1914 World Series and for talking about the financial aspects of the business, which the fans didn't give a rap about.

The Gillam harangue continued for the rest of the season. A few weeks later Gillam floated an alternative conspiracy theory behind Mack's disposing of his stars:

The belief is growing that [Mack] is following orders rather than fol-lowing the dictates of his own judgment, that the breaking up of the strongest baseball machine ever put together is being done for what is considered the best interest of organized baseball. In other words, Philadelphia is now being made to suffer humiliation for too many successes. Mack has proven himself too good a manager for the other fellows, so someone higher up took a hand with the idea of equalizing things, all for the good of the game.

So now the Connie Mack who had mismanaged the 1913 World Series and the preparation for the 1914 Series was "too good a manager" for the others to match him. Gillam continued: "The American League pennant race this season is being manipulated inasmuch as Philadelphia has been officially shut out of the possibility while Chicago and New York have been strengthened for the good of the game."

Others on the *Record* took a more evenhanded view. George W. Mason wrote, "Mack will yet bring order out of chaos, and they will emerge even-tually as one worthy of battling with the leaders. When they come into their own, the present nightmare will have been forgotten, and supporters will rally to the new Athletics as they did when they were making baseball history."

In August Gillam wondered if Mack sat on the bench pining for all the players he had sent away: "But even the best of them make mistakes, and this time Mack seems to have made a bonehead that will outlive Merkle's by a century or two. He must by this time begin to realize that it's easier to tear down than build up."

Gillam was skeptical of reports that the Athletics had lost money in the past two years: "A club that is known to have profited by a half million dol-lars from World Series games alone cannot be counted out because of one rather poor season."

How Gillam came up with that half million figure is unknown. The Gi-ants had reported a profit of $75,507 from the six-game 1911 Series; the A's could not have netted more. Their net from the 1913 five-game Series was $53,315; the Series in 1905 and 1910, played in smaller parks, had gone only five games, and last year's sweep had netted them under $26,000.

By September Gillam had forgotten his claim that other clubs had forced Mack to "break up the Athletics" so somebody else could win. Now he had the rest of the league complaining about Mack's lousy team: "Something will have to be done soon to brace up the club, as the other club owners are not going to stand idly by and witness the wrecking of one of the best-paying cities in the American League circuit because of the whims of one of their number. As long as some of the other clubs were profiting by the dismemberment of the champions, there was nothing said. But the meager returns at the gate this season are likely to stir the magnates into unwonted activity when the meeting of the American League is held next winter."

The Athletics' swan dive turned off the fans completely. Attendance withered. Mack took it in stride. He didn't expect anything different and wasn't discouraged about it. He would never complain about low attendance when he had a losing team, nor wave the phony banner of "civic duty" to appeal for patronage. On June 7, discussing baseball's general slump and the world's unsettled conditions, he found no cause for alarm. He had seen enough of the roller coaster of both baseball and world history not to forfeit his optimism that things would ultimately right themselves. As for his team, he told the *Baltimore Sun:*

> The smallness of our own attendance has been commented on, but the Athletic club has no complaint to register on its treatment from this city. As a matter of fact, after 14 years here, we have only feelings of gratitude. . . .
>
> If in the interval before we get another team in the race the attendance falls off, we have no kick. We have every faith in Philadelphia as a great baseball city. Fourteen years of goodwill from press and public in Philadelphia gives us every reason to believe that as soon as our team gets going we will have the old crowds. We have had our share of the varying fortunes that go with every amusement enterprise, but in the final estimate our support from the fans has been liberal when the team deserved it. We are willing to take our medicine till the time comes.

For Connie Mack, the sudden fall from the top was not a cause for melancholy. Where other men might feel despair in disaster, he saw opportunity. For him, building a winning combination out of unknown, untried youngsters was the source of eternal youth. It had been that way when he had first become a manager more than twenty years ago. Then he had been thwarted by bosses who preferred veterans familiar to the fans. Now he was the boss and could do it his way.

"This is really the happiest period of my life," he said. "I am broke financially but full of ambition. It is like starting all over again for me, and I love base ball and love to build up teams. I have done it once and will do it again. It is a new experience for me, after the terrific strain I have been under for seven years. It is the ambition of my life to turn out this new combination—and I will do it."

In two years, he predicted, he would have a team "greater than the one I broke up."

The optimism Mack exuded was genuinely felt by him at the time. He was not blowing smoke. He never doubted that he would succeed in building another young winning combination. Baseball men didn't doubt it either. Mack's reputation as the premier Pied Piper of big league wannabes was still intact after twenty years, inspiring good-natured kidding as well as admiration.

The *Washington Post* ran this yarn:

Jack Doyle, who scouted for the White Sox last year, tells a good story how Connie Mack got [Lloyd] Davies, now one of the Athletics' young pitcher-outfielders.

"I got a tip about Davies last year," says Doyle, "and I watched him in several games up in New England. Then I followed him to his home in New Hampshire and decided to sign him for Comiskey.

"As Davies was under age, I had to call in his relatives to witness and approve the contract. His father, mother, sisters, brothers, cousins and aunts were all there when I fished out the document.

"Then, to my astonishment, I learned that Connie Mack had signed Davies when he was 7 years old and that the boy was only 17. Connie gets them when they are infants."

The *Atlanta Constitution* joined in with this item: "Connie Mack, nefarious leader of the once, etc. Athletics, continues to lure kids into baseball captivity. It is rumored that Connie goes about with a bag of stick candy in his hip pocket for this very purpose."

An unsigned column in the *Record*, probably by Mason or Brandt, lent some support to Mack's assessment of his team. "The Athletics are not as bad as their record would lead one to believe, but weighted down with a lot of second-class pitchers who have only the remotest idea of the location of the home plate, there is little wonder at the buffeting the team is getting with such consistent regularity."

But the rest of the item—"There does not seem to be a disposition toward building up a team for next year, but the owners appear to be content to allow the present aggregation to drift along for the remainder of this season, irrespective of what the club's former staunch supporters may think"—was not an accurate portrayal of what was happening.

Spring training 1916 began in June 1915. Like an audition call for a Broadway musical, a steady parade of collegians and semipros paraded from North Philadelphia station and sandlots throughout the area to Shibe Park. Still more arrived as lower minor league seasons ended, sent by the scouting of Harry Davis, Pat Flaherty, Ira Thomas, and Earle Mack, managing in Raleigh. During a four-week home stand in June, more than sixty hopefuls from all over the east and south reported to Connie Mack's Baseball Academy. For the first time in years, Mack was on hand directing the morning drills. They played intrasquad games, with Davis and Lajoie as field captains, Mack and Thomas the managers. The action stopped while mistakes were pointed out. There was constant instruction on the field and on the benches. Jack Lapp worked with the pitching prospects. He taught them control by having them throw at spots—his left shoulder, his belt buckle—for thirty minutes at a time. Jack Coombs had won 80 games in three brilliant years throwing at Lapp's left shoulder.

One enterprising reporter counted seventy-nine pitchers who came, worked out, and—mostly—went. Gradually the class was cut to twenty-five, who continued to practice while the A's went on the road for a month. Mack arranged games for them against local independent teams.

Enough of the prospects made it into the Athletics' lineup so that by season's end fifty-six players had appeared in at least one game, a record for a 154-game schedule. Thirty-five were making their big league debuts; for nineteen of those it was also their last major league appearance. Mack used twenty-seven pitchers, a record tied by the Kansas City Athletics in 1955. Twenty-four of them started at least one game, a major league record. The twenty-seven pitchers won 43 games, an average of 1.7 per man.

The few customers who came to see them didn't recognize any of them, but at least they saw youngsters hustling, and the losses were swift. On August 29 in Chicago a 5–0 defeat by the White Sox took one hour and eight minutes, then the big league record.

Mack's cheerleaders in the press, led by Chandler Richter, hailed every newcomer who showed an early flash of talent as a sure fixture in the imminent resurrection of the Athletics.

Typical of the gushers: "Young Healy, the U. Of Pittsburgh lad . . . looks like the goods. . . . One of the prettiest hitters seen here in a long time. . . . If Sheehan and Knowlson . . . improve as fast as youngsters generally do under Mack the 1916 Athletics' pitching staff will be the surprise of the race; it is safe to predict that Connie Mack is going to hand the base ball world a great shock when the Mackmen take the field next season."

Richter was certain that Mack would pull another Collins, Barry, Baker, and Bender out of his net. "Don't count the Athletics out," he wrote over and over.

Connie Mack added to the bubbling ballyhoo by hinting at "another young man who will come to me later who is the only infielder I know of who will positively be a regular next season."

This unnamed rookie failed to materialize, as none of the new infielders Mack tried would win a regular berth in 1916. But he might have been talking about Sam Crane.

Crane was a twenty-one-year-old infielder up from Harrisburg. Mack had signed him in 1914 and farmed him out. Called up in September, he had a seven-game look at second base and shortstop. Another brief look in 1916 would convince Mack that Crane would never hit enough. Mack sold him to Washington in 1917. He drifted to the minors, then played two years in Cincinnati, where he proved Mack's assessment accurate.

One day in 1929 Crane came upon a former girlfriend in a café with a man. In a rage Crane pulled out a gun and shot them both dead. He was sentenced to 18–36 years in prison. In the years that followed, Connie Mack wrote to Crane and visited him in prison. Beginning in 1935 Mack appeared on behalf of Crane at several parole board hearings. His assurances that Crane would have a job at Shibe Park did not sway the board until August 14, 1944. Crane worked for the Athletics until they left Philadelphia in 1955 and died that same year.

Years later Connie Mack Jr. would recall, "Dad always thought there was some good in every human being. If he thought a convict got a bad deal, he would try to get him paroled. This used to worry us, but you couldn't discourage him. He never forgot how to excuse human weakness."

Mack's tyros tried hard but managed to lose almost every day. They were handy targets for ridicule, especially with the Phillies heading for their first World Series using a steady lineup that included only twenty-three players all season. Despite an occasional effective pitching performance, none of

Mack's newcomers looked like anything resembling big league caliber. A column by "Right Cross" in the August 17 *New York Evening Journal* took this shot: "The rumor that Mack selects his pitchers on the morning before the games, wandering down to the docks and grabbing the most foolish-looking longshoreman he can find, may or may not be true. There seems to be something in it, judging from effects."

And the next day, in reply to a correspondent, "Right Cross" wrote: "If you are absolutely sure that your son, Amos, has not sense enough to come in out of the wet, perhaps it might be just as well to send him to Connie Mack and he will get a job on the Athletics' pitching staff. But before doing so it would be advisable to let the young man try for a position as dogcatcher in some small Jersey town. Before subjecting the young man to the humiliation of being connected with the Philadelphia Americans it is only humane to give him every chance to save himself from that fate."

Mack was well aware of how his recruits looked. This was his way of sifting: throw them into games, and if they didn't show him enough of what he was looking for, weed them out and send another bunch onto the field. During September he turned the entire team over more than once. The A's literally had the proverbial three teams: one coming, one playing, one going.

Mack reminded his critics that they had laughed when he trotted out his last kiddie corps on opening day 1908, which grew up quickly to dominate the league.

When they got on him for not keeping more veterans and working in the newcomers gradually, he replied that the mistake he'd made was not cleaning out all those whose play had been indifferent at best.

One prospect who stood out was catcher Ralph "Cy" Perkins, bought for $500 from Raleigh, where he had been tutored by Earle Mack. The nineteen-year-old Gloucester, Massachusetts, native weighed only 130 pounds, but Mack liked what he saw. Perkins made his debut as a pinch hitter on September 25 and caught most of the rest of the games.

For his 1916 pitching staff, Mack said he was counting on two veterans (probably Bush and Wyckoff, who had managed a six-game winning streak in his 10-22 record) and two recruits "who are going to become one of the powerful staffs next season. Wait and see before you scoff at the idea."

One recruit was Jack Nabors, who had made national news by pitching a 13-inning no-hitter for Newnan against Talladega in the Georgia-Alabama League on June 15. Only two Talladega batters reached base on errors. Nabors had earlier pitched a 15-inning 4-hit 1–0 win against Anniston. His record stood at 6-1.

Nabors's record-breaking no-hitter touched off a flurry of bidding for him. Scouts scrambled to Newnan to look him over. His manager, Harry Matthews, was a respected baseball man. When Matthews claimed that Nabors had the best curve he had ever seen in the minors, Connie Mack listened. Nabors's record went to 12-1. Mack outbid everybody else and paid what was reported to be the highest price ever for a Class D player, which turned out to be $500. (Another Newnan pitcher, Bill Terry, pitched a no-hitter two weeks later, but nobody bought the future Hall of Fame first baseman.)

Nabors made his debut on August 9 at home against the White Sox before a surprising Monday crowd of 2,500. It wasn't pretty. After Emory Titman waddled out to home plate to present Eddie Murphy a traveling satchel from his Philadelphia fans, Nabors hit the Sox's new lead-off man with a pitch. He walked Buck Weaver. Eddie Collins beat out a bunt. Jack Fournier hit a fly ball that Davies dropped. Happy Felsch walked. Larry Kopf let a ground ball go under his glove into left field, where Bankston booted it. Nabors forgot to cover first on a bunt. Four runs scored on one bunt hit. Once they saw how clumsy the "tall young Georgian" was, the Sox bunted him silly. Thirty-one Sox had batted and they had a 6–0 lead before a ball was hit safely to the outfield.

Chicago Tribune writer I. E. Sanborn said of Nabors, "Aside from lack of control, inability to field bunts, and slowness in covering first base, he looked like some pitcher."

The *Record*'s correspondent was gentler. "Nabors's wildness might have been due to the excitement of his first tryout and the way the heartless Sox kept kidding him."

Nabors must have remained excited the rest of the year. He had difficulty throwing his nifty curve for strikes and was 0-5 in 7 starts, despite what demon statistician Ernest J. Lanigan described as "a half balk motion that would cause Ed Walsh envy."

The *New York Times*, in its brief item on the Newnan no-hitter, gave Nabors's age as twenty. (According to the *Times*, Nabors's age declined the following year; he became "Nabors, a thin, lanky youth who will be able to vote in a few years.") The *Atlanta Constitution* in a caption under his photo pegged Nabors as twenty-four. (Two years later Indianapolis papers would call him twenty-one or twenty-two *at that time*.) The *Boston Globe* called him a very promising "raw recruit" who "appears to have everything, only lacking confidence." Philadelphia papers referred to him as the "young pitcher" and "a big country boy" as green as they come.

But all of Nabors's birth and death and census records testify that he was more "medium well" than "raw"; he was twenty-seven at the time Mack bought him. That would make the 6-foot-3 Alabaman pretty old for Class D competition. His ability to baffle that level of batters with his hook becomes less impressive.

Did Connie Mack know that Nabors was twenty-seven? If he did, this purchase was strangely contrary to all of Mack's practices at the time. He was harvesting seventeen-to-twenty-year-old high school, semipro, and college boys by the dozen at little or no cost. Even his draft picks were mostly from the lower minors. He was not about to pay record prices for twenty-seven-year-old Class D pitchers. If Mack believed that Nabors was really twenty or younger, he never spoke of it.

Tom Sheehan was another big right-hander Mack was counting on for next year. Sheehan was a legitimate twenty-one and had a 6-5 record when Mack bought him for $1,000 from the Peoria Distillers in July on the advice of Izzy Hoffman, manager of Ridgeway in the Interstate League. Sheehan won his first three starts after joining the A's, but he caught the wild bug and finished the year with 4 wins and 9 losses.

There were occasional highlights. Jack Nabors once fanned Joe Jackson with the bases loaded. On September 8 in Boston Tom Sheehan finished a 1-0 win by striking out an over-eager pinch-hitting Babe Ruth swinging at "three very bad balls" with the bases loaded in the ninth.(It was quickly followed by a lowlight in the second game; Minot Crowell walked 12 and was touched for 21 hits in a complete game 13–2 loss.)

Another walk-on pitcher, who never won a game, became a valuable member of the baseball friends and allies of Connie Mack for many years thereafter.

Tom Turner, a local high school sports star, had knocked around the minor leagues out west for about six years. Connie Mack had once given him a brief springtime look. At twenty-five, he was still pitching for Class D shoestring operations in New York, finishing the season on September 6 at Hornell of the Interstate League, not in a blaze nor even a candle of glory, but with a 3-3 record. About two weeks later he walked into Shibe Park and asked Connie Mack to take another look at him. With nothing to lose but another ball game, Mack gave him the ball to start the second game of a doubleheader against the White Sox on September 24. Like a chameleon, Turner took on the hue of the rest of Mack's pitchers. In the first inning he walked 2 batters. Fournier doubled. Joe Jackson hit a home run. In the second, 3 singles, another walk, and some errant play by Jack Lapp produced 2 more runs. That was all for Turner.

Years later Turner related this story: "I decided my pitching days were over and told Connie Mack. He told me in his droll way that he was looking for a scout who knew when a ball player was no good. I had convinced him I knew that [by] the way I had decided I was no good. Anybody could get excited about bush league stars, he told me, but it took a bird like me to tell when they wouldn't by any manner of means do. So by declaring myself unfit for big league company as a player, I became a picker of others who might be."

Turner bounced around the minor leagues for two more years, amassing a collection of pink slips, before enlisting in the army in 1917, where his thirty-year scouting and minor league executive career began, eventually leading to his ownership of the Portland Beavers.

In September the crowds dwindled down to a precious few, usually a thousand or less. On Monday, September 27, about 150, including park employees, were more interested in watching firemen battle a blazing grocery storehouse across Somerset Street behind the left-field fence while the A's were rallying for 4 runs in the ninth, falling short in a 6–5 loss to Chicago. But Cleveland and St. Louis—and occasionally the fifth-place Yankees—also drew only a few hundred spectators at home as the season wound down.

It was the Phillies' turn to capture the city's enthusiasm and headlines with pitching star Grover Alexander and slugger Gavvy Cravath. The entire baseball experience in Philadelphia was encapsulated on September 29. Alexander pitched a 1-hitter and the Phillies clinched their first pennant while the Athletics were losing in Washington by scores of 10–2 and 20–5. Perhaps more interested in seeing what stuff they were made of, not what stuff they had, Mack left Lloyd Davies in to pitch the entire first game and Tom Sheehan the second.

Mack juggled his schedule to milk the most out of it, creating doubleheaders to open up dates for more lucrative exhibition games elsewhere. With a Grand Army of the Republic reunion encampment taking place in Washington September 29–30, he switched his home games against the Nationals to the capital. (In a promotion Bill Veeck would have appreciated, the September 30 game featured the GAR's annual ten-mile race pitting the undefeated champion, seventy-year-old Col. J. L. Smith, against a ten-man relay team of fellow veterans. The race started at one thirty, with the game to follow. Fittingly, Mack started one of his prospects, Joe Sherman, who was immediately nicknamed "General"; he won his only major league start.)

The season ended on a faintly optimistic note. Rookie pitchers won two from Washington, 6–4 and 4–0, the nightcap a 2-hit debut by Elmer Myers, who immediately won a place in Connie Mack's heart to start the 1916 season. The two games took a total of two hours and forty-five minutes.

Thanks to the Phillies, total attendance in the city rose. The Athletics' count fell by 200,000—almost 60 percent—while the Phillies' more than tripled, a rise of over 300,000. The A's total of 146,223 would remain the lowest in Connie Mack's fifty years at the helm.

Connie Mack didn't care if anybody was coming through the Shibe Park turnstiles. He didn't expect them to turn out to watch what amounted to spring training games.

"It doesn't pay to argue with the press," was one of the maxims he lived by. "They'll always have the last word anyhow."

He stuck to it—most of the time. But when A. M. Gillam roasted him for "the monumental folly of Mack's tearing his team apart" while "begging the fans to come out to watch his "collection of pitiful jokes," Mack had had enough. He told Chandler Richter:

> I have not made any plea for patronage as the critic has declared, nor do I admit that the season is a monument to Connie Mack's folly. We have landed in last place and [are] drawing but a handful of fans a day, but I am more than ever convinced we did right in breaking up our team. Critics point out the fact that my recruits have failed to make good, using our present standing and our losing as a basis for the argument. That is a joke, because I have used only one player barring pitchers who is being counted on as a part of the new combination. . . . I don't expect or deserve patronage under the conditions. We will be better off and not under a handicap if fans do not turn out until I have convinced them I will make good my statement that I will have another championship team in two years. By the middle of next season I expect the machine to get its bearings and from then on it will come just as the old one did. I have wasted a year, according to my critics, but it has been a year well spent, one that I have thoroughly enjoyed. . . . Naturally I expected criticism when I tore the old team apart. I don't mind it when it comes from a source that I know is impartial. But I do object to the constant roasting.

Frank Baker didn't play a game in the American League all season, but he led the league in phony reports. One day he was seen at Shibe Park, supposedly for a peace parley with Connie Mack. In the August 22 *Record*, A. M. Gillam quoted a lengthy declaration purportedly delivered by Baker to a *Chicago Daily News* writer in Baltimore. Baker allegedly said he wanted to play ball but never for Mack. . . . Mack couldn't keep him out of baseball. . . . He wanted to play for Joe Tinker and the Chicago Feds even if he had to wait until 1917 (when his A's contract ended). . . . He was ready to go to court and force Mack's hand, etc., etc.

None of which happened.

On September 2 the *New York Times* reported Baker's sale to the Yankees was a done deal. Not so, said Cap Huston. (Relying on "authentic sources," the *Times* the next day declared that a peace treaty had been signed at the Hotel Biltmore in New York, accepting the Federal League as a third major league provided the Feds moved their Chicago club to Detroit and their St. Louis club to Washington. That "news" wasn't fit to print either.)

By then some disgruntled fans were complaining that Mack should have kept his machine together even if he had to go to the poorhouse to pay the players. It's always easy to spend someone else's money. Fans are passionate about baseball because it offers an escape from everyday life and its problems—and realities. To the man who is in the business of baseball, his passion for the game may be equal to, and may even surpass, that of the fan, but it offers no escape. It *is* his everyday life and problems.

Connie Mack didn't see the Baker standoff as a matter of money so much as a labor-management principle.

"Certain writers have been trying to force me to give in in my stand in the Baker case," he said. "But I want to ask one question. How long is any business going to last when the employees are bigger than the boss? That is my stand."

The nettlesome Baker business continued to harass Connie Mack all winter. Baker's name appeared in the papers as often as President Woodrow Wilson's:

Baker says he won't go to New York. . . . There's only one club he would play for and he won't say which one. . . . Baker buys more farmland. . . . Baker buys a seven-passenger roadster. . . . Baker meets with Huston and Donovan of the Yankees in Wilmington. . . . Baker signs with White Sox, according to "close associates of Charles Comiskey". . . . Baker denies it, says if he plays anywhere, it will be in New York. (The *New York Sun* believed the White Sox story and blasted Ban Johnson for allowing Comiskey to grab every available star.)

Mack was fed up being asked to comment on every one of these rumors. He didn't want to talk about Frank Baker. He just wanted to be rid of Baker and the whole subject. He believed that after a year-long layoff, the thirty-year-old Baker would never be the player he had been. The muscles would have lost some of their memory, the reflexes some of their snap. Apparently other club owners thought the same. Interest in acquiring Baker had cooled. Mack gave the Yankees permission to negotiate with the Trappe farmer. If they could agree on contract terms, he was now ready to sell his star-turned-thorn.

Whether it was Baker's hesitation about leaving the farm or that he and the Yankees couldn't agree on the money, it took until February 15, 1916, to close the deal. Baker credited Vernon S. Bradley of nearby Cambridge, a friend of both Mack and Baker, with persuading him that he owed it to himself, Mr. Mack, and baseball to return to the game. The Yankees paid $37,500 for him; Baker received $5,000 from the A's, either as part of the sale price or for agreeing to sign with New York.

Whatever peevishness Connie Mack may have felt toward Baker during their season-long standoff quickly dissipated. A week after the sale was concluded, Mack told a group of fifty Penn students at their Alpha Tau Omega fraternity house that he and Baker remained the best of friends. "No matter what attitude Baker took toward me and the reunion of the club, he did it with the idea of bettering his own position and I can't blame him for it. I do think however that he was badly advised." Despite everything, he said, "I hold Frank in the highest esteem."

And then the Federal League war ended. The sudden death of Brooklyn baking magnate Robert Ward, who had reportedly poured $675,000 into shoring up several clubs and paying most of the legal expenses, and the large losses in the league's second year of operation—Brooklyn, with the highest payroll, lost $60,000, and Kansas City reported a loss of $35,332.18 in its stockholders' report—motivated the Feds to meet with National League owners in New York on December 13. Both sides were ready to compromise. Two days later league president John Tener and Pirates owner Barney Dreyfuss brought the terms to the American League meeting in Chicago. According to the meeting minutes, Harry Sinclair was to buy the Cubs, with the National League putting up $50,000 of the price. (A group headed by Charles Weeghman but bankrolled primarily by chewing gum magnate William Wrigley and other business leaders wound up buying the Chicago franchise at a cost of $641,152.17.) Each league agreed to pay the Ward estate $10,000 a year for twenty years for the lease and equipment of Washington Park in Brooklyn and $25,000 each to buy out the Pittsburgh Feds. Phil Ball was later admitted into the monopolists' tent, buying the Browns. Connie Mack pronounced the proposition a very fair one, good for baseball. He was not part of the five-man AL negotiating committee and was not interested in acquiring any of the players in the Feds' going-out-of-business sale.

In other league business, a motion to expand the World Series to nine games lost on a 4–4 vote. On the pretext that players might incur injuries in an independent pursuit of extra income, the two leagues unanimously voted to ban players from barnstorming in games other than those with their own clubs.

To the relief of Judge Landis, the Feds dropped the lawsuit that Landis had sat on for a year.

The Baltimore Terrapins got nothing out of the settlement and called their lawyers.

Some estimates put everybody's operating losses for two years, including subsidies to the minor leagues to keep them afloat, plus the legal and settlement costs, at more than $10 million.

An unsigned story in the *New York Times* on December 3 supported these dreary reports. "There was a time when baseball was a good paying proposition, and that time may come again, but the last four years have been lean ones, and there will be more lean ones before there will be any fat ones. There are more clubs losing money than declaring dividends."

The article went on to describe the financial results for each club in both leagues. Of the Athletics, it reported they "dropped about $50,000 last year with a winner. They dropped the same amount this year with an eighth place club. Losing $100,000 in two years is no joke."

Fred Lieb figured the A's, Browns, and Indians had each lost between $50,000 and $100,000 for 1915 alone, "despite the fact that the clubs were run on a reduced expense basis. And with these clubs it looks as though the worst is yet to come."

(The Athletics' records show that, except for player sales, the club lost about $50,000 in 1915 but had made an equal amount in 1914.)

Businesses that are losing money can cut expenses by laying off employees or closing down factories. A baseball club can't do those things. It has to field a team and provide a place to play. Today's players rarely take salary cuts; they get raises regardless of how poor a year they had. Trading or releasing players for budget reasons is prevalent in today's free-agent world. That hasn't changed. It's what the Athletics and Indians and Browns were doing in 1915. And the rich, profitable clubs—the Giants, Yankees, White Sox, Red Sox—were buyers. Yet Connie Mack continues to be singled out—by tradition? habit? ignorance?—for avariciously wrecking his team.

Did Mack have everybody fooled in his day when he claimed the baseball war and the financial losses forced him to sell off some of his stars? If so, Grantland Rice was among the duped: "No man in baseball has done more for the game and has gotten less in the way of financial reward," Rice wrote in the *New York Tribune*. "The fact that he was paid for Collins, Baker and Barry has no significance when it is known that he had made less than two percent on his investment, with six pennant years behind him. If he could make no money with a pennant winner, where is his fortune to come from a tail-ender?"

Over the years, the question was sometimes put to Mack: If baseball was such a poor investment, why not get out of the business? Mack never directly answered it. But despite his occasional threats to quit the game if this or that happened, there simply was no other business, no other life, for him. (He had some business interests; he was a director, along with John Shibe and realtor Ted Gorsuch, of a savings and loan started in 1913 by Ira Thomas.)

Like the stage's claim on actors, the paintbrush's hold on the starving artist, the pen's grip on the struggling unpublished poet, baseball had seized Connie Mack and would never let go. Blessing or curse, win or lose, profit or loss, he was doing the only thing he ever wanted to do with his life. Nor could he go back to being just a manager, subject to the second-guessing and impatience of a club owner whose eye was always on the bottom line of the ledger. He had to do things his way, however peculiar or hopeless his way might seem to others in the game.

Connie Mack didn't want to stay in business by selling players. After the Baker sale, he said, "Now I have sold my last player. I don't believe in dealing in ballplayers. I'm not in the business of developing players in order to sell them. When I sold Eddie Collins, I did not intend to part with any of my other men. But conditions were such I soon found it would be impossible for me to hope for a winning team with the men I had left. Therefore I parted with several others. I would like to say that if ever again conditions are such that I cannot get along with my players, have them work for me and be happy and loyal about it, I will retire from the game."

Mack had almost everything he owned invested in the Athletics. He expected more red ink in 1916 and was determined to defend and protect the business he had built in the past fifteen years. But more important than the financial losses, which could be made up in better times, he was distraught by the discord that had soured the last two years. He called it disloyalty and took it personally. It's easy to say he shouldn't have, and in later years he softened his views, no longer blaming the players for looking out for their own interests. But players who considered themselves bigger than the team or the manager, on top of discontent sowed by the lure of the Feds' money—ironic in that Mack had done the same kind of sowing and luring to launch his own club—exhausted him. His beautiful baseball machine, like a totaled car, had been sold for parts.

He began to put the bitterness behind him. He looked forward with joy and optimism to the prospect of finding and developing his next crop of stars. It was the part of this business of baseball he loved the most.

"The critics say . . . that the material is no longer available in the independent and collegiate fields," he said. "Time will tell that story."

Connie Mack was the first manager to win six pennants; he did it in fourteen years in Philadelphia. Except for the first two, in 1902 and 1905, he had done it by sweeping sandlots, college campuses, and lower minor leagues for nuggets of gold. Many of his greatest players had had no professional experience when he had signed them. When he did spend money in the open market, his most expensive minor league purchase, Lefty Russell, had been an $11,000 lemon.

He was confident that his methods would work again. He told George M. Young of the *Philadelphia Public Ledger* that he intended to "fight this thing to a finish, and win." He knew what he had to do and, as always, would do it his way. And no one doubted him.

"If there are any Collinses or Bakers or Barrys out there," Heywood Broun wrote in the *New York Tribune*, "Connie Mack will find them. Into classroom, mine or ploughed field, his scouts will carry the search."

"No manager ever in the history of baseball attempted a more ambitious program," wrote James Isaminger. "Those who know the wonderful capacity of the winner of six pennants believe that, given time, he can succeed in his program. What will happen in the interval is the only matter for concern."

In 1906 Charles Somers's love affair with baseball had been cited as the direct cause of the demise of his marriage. Now, after another year of heavy losses for his Indians, the bankers who had taken control of the club demanded that it be sold, along with his minor league clubs (except New Orleans, which he pleaded to hold onto).

The official announcement on February 16, 1916, had the club being transferred to Ban Johnson on behalf of four investors for $500,000.

Taylor Spink in 1942 wrote a possibly fanciful tale of how Johnson and Charles Comiskey felt obligated to help Somers realize a good price out of gratitude for his having bankrolled the American League's launching in 1901. They persuaded one of their cronies, railroad builder James Dunn, his partner, and an old third-string Cubs catcher, Tom Walsh, to buy the club. Various accounts have Johnson and Comiskey each putting up $50,000 or $100,000 to enable Somers to net the half million. (In 1919 Johnson testified under oath that they had each loaned Dunn $100,000 and that most of it had been paid off.) Johnson's supposed "piece" of the Cleveland club would become a thorny issue later.

As soon as peace with the Federal League had been declared in Cincinnati on December 22, 1915, wartime salaries began to tumble—as much as they could. There were still enough long-term contracts in effect to push total payrolls of the two leagues close to $2 million, according to some reports. Barney Dreyfuss reckoned that no team could carry a $100,000 payroll and expect to break even.

The players who groused and held out didn't garner any sympathy from the public; the average working family was living on less than $1,000 a year and not complaining. Railroad workers were thrilled when Congress voted them a forty-eight-hour work week. To them, a ballplayer's life was easy street, whatever he was paid.

When the Red Sox tried to slash outfielder Tris Speaker's $18,000 salary in half for the 1916 season, Speaker refused to sign. To his surprise the Red Sox decided they could win without him. The Indians' new owners did something the bankers would never have approved. They paid a bundle of cash and a brace of players for the star holdout, an investment that turned around the fortunes of the downtrodden franchise by the lake.

Speaker demanded part of the sale price from the Red Sox and wouldn't sign until he got it, which was not until after he had played his first game for Cleveland. Connie Mack had had problems—and would have more in the future—with the purchase of minor league players who were promised part of their sale price from the selling club and refused to report when they didn't get it. To eliminate future bickering, he suggested a rule that would automatically give players part of their sale price, but it never went anywhere.

Some of the A's—Stuffy McInnis among them—still had a year to go on long-term contracts. Now that the Feds were dead, it was the club owners' turn to try to renegotiate salaries downward. Connie Mack had signed about a dozen of his prospects to multiyear contracts to enable him to look them over without the threat of their jumping. Now he was stuck with them.

Shag Thompson was one of them. "When the Feds were gone," he recalled, "Mack tried to cut the salaries in half of eleven of us. I had a guaranteed contract for $500 a month. He had to honor it."

Thompson started the season in an 0-for-17 drought. "One day Mack said to me, 'When are you going to start hitting?'

"I said, 'Mr. Mack, I don't care if I never get another hit for you. I'm through with you. You can farm me out. I'm not going to play another game for you.' I was mad as a goose."

Mack sent him to Omaha. The following year his contract expired. "Mack said all he could pay me was $200 a month. I told him I could make two and a half times that in the minor leagues. 'I'll buy my own release,' I said. 'How much do you want for it?' So I gave him $500 for my release and went back to Omaha.

"I liked Connie Mack. We all liked him," added Thompson, the last survivor of the 1914 A's when he died at ninety-six. "It was just he didn't pay enough."

For all the complaints about salaries—which for ballplayers was as endemic as soldiers' gripes about chow, even those who never had it so good—it's all but impossible to find anyone who knew Connie Mack and didn't like him, respect him, even love him. You could apply the Sara Lee commercial jingle to him: "Nobody doesn't like Connie Mack." Despite their year-long contentious dispute, there was never any personal animosity between Frank Baker and Mack. Three years later umpire Billy Evans reported a 1916 conversation he had had with Baker while riding on the train from New York to Washington. Evans mentioned Connie Mack: "I was under the impression there was ill feeling between them," he wrote. "I was interested to know how Baker would express himself. I expected Baker to say unkind things. . . . Imagine my surprise when Baker said, 'Connie is a great fellow to work for. I'm sorry to leave him. I spent the happiest years of my career in Philadelphia."

Through the years, even when harsh words were exchanged and partings were unpleasant, invariably players made a point of adding, "I liked the man." Allusions to his kindness and generosity, and how much they had learned from him, are common. Those who became college coaches or big league managers spoke of trying to emulate his style of leadership. The list of players who returned to the Athletics as coaches—and could have gone elsewhere—is long and impressive.

With the Feds disbanded, Jack Dunn moved his Orioles back to Baltimore. He was offered the Terrapins' almost-new ballpark for $40,000, but he didn't have the money. Connie Mack loaned him part of it and put up more for his son, Roy, to buy a piece of the club, where Roy worked as secretary and business manager until he went into the navy in 1918. Eddie Collins and Yankees third baseman Fritz Maisel, a Baltimore native, also invested in the club and became directors.

The Athletics family suffered a loss on January 27 when Joe Schroeder died at his home two blocks from Shibe Park. Schroeder, fifty-six, had been ill since the previous summer. Mack's groundskeeper since 1902, he was responsible for the design of the drainage system at Shibe Park, where the rain drained into eight separate sewer outlets in all directions from the level field. His son, Robert, had begun as a peanut vendor and was now the A's business manager.

Connie Mack continued his housecleaning in January. He sent Larry Kopf to Baltimore, surprising many fans and writers, including *Sporting Life* editor Chandler Richter, who had been touting Kopf as the shortstop of the future. But Kopf and Rube Bressler had done too much running together in the late-night league to suit Mack. Bressler, though erratic, had too much potential for Mack to give up on him. Kopf, Mack decided, did not. Kopf was one of those who had signed what he called "a cheap contract" for three years in 1914. Bought by the Reds in 1916, he was still complaining when they sent him a $2,400 contract for 1917.

Mack then asked for waivers on catcher Jack Lapp. Lapp had never stopped hustling throughout the dismal 1915 season, catching a career-high 89 games, and had his best year with the bat. But he was thirty-one, and that was too old for a Mack rebuilding program. Writing to every club asking for waivers, Mack said that building up a young team and getting rid of veterans was his only reason for disposing of Lapp. "Anyone needing an experienced catcher will get a first-class man in Lapp. If the waivers are secured, you can have him by assuming his [$3,000] contract. First club wanting his services will secure him." Comiskey immediately claimed him. Lapp caught only 34 games in 1916, his last major league season.

Two days after the sale of Baker to the Yankees, Mack bought Charlie Pick, officially from the Brooklyn Feds, though Pick had played for Jack Dunn in Richmond and never appeared in a Fed game. Mack hoped the twenty-eight-year-old veteran would fill "Grand Canyon," as James Isaminger dubbed the hole at third base. Pick disappeared into it instead.

Connie Mack could be evasive, noncommital about his plans and his business. He didn't announce contract signings because any names he didn't mention were then labeled holdouts by the writers. He would deny a report that was true rather than confirm it prematurely or break an agreement not to announce it at the time. As a player he had been tricky, tipping bats and faking foul tips when he could get away with it. As a manager he was not above the common practice of aiding and abetting minor league clubs in protecting players from the draft. During his own minor league days in Milwaukee, he had sought such cooperation. But assaults on his financial probity in dealing with other clubs infuriated him. His word, his reputation were crucial to him in his dealings with major and minor league club owners and managers. Occasionally players were "borrowed" from other clubs when a team was shorthanded, with the understanding that they would be returned. Mack was a lender more than a borrower, but the entire arrangement depended on trust between club owners. He and other managers had strings on dozens of players who were not—on paper—their property. Whenever a minor league manager or owner inadvertently or deliberately cut a string and sold a player, Mack would have nothing more to do with that individual. And when he promised to send players to a minor league club (either farmed out or outright) as a delayed payment for a player, his word had to be reliable.

It happened that a young third baseman, Jim Ritter, was drafted by Jack Dunn from Lewiston of the Class B New England League in the fall of 1915. Mack bought him from Dunn on a spring trial basis. A Lewiston official (possibly manager Arthur Irwin, whose sometimes contentious dealings with Mack went back to 1901) publicly accused Mack of using Dunn to draft Ritter, instead of drafting the player himself, in order to save a few hundred dollars. The draft price for a AA club was less than for a major league team.

The charge that he had cheated a minor league club so incensed Mack, he promptly returned Ritter to Baltimore without giving him a look.

"It is an outrage to accuse me of underhand practices in the Ritter case," Billy Weart of the *Philadelphia Telegraph* quoted Mack. "I asked Dunn to let me have Ritter for a trial and in case he failed to make good I would turn him back to Dunn. Such a thing as a frame-up is absurd. While it is no fault of Ritter that a misguided individual spread such reports, I am through with him. I would not now have Ritter if he was the best young player in the country. [He wasn't.] The young man can blame his failure to get a chance with me on the knocker connected with the Lewiston club."

Mack also had little patience with minor league managers whose word was unreliable. In January 1914 he had offered a young infielder, Harry Fritz, for sale for $500. H. D. Ramsey, manager of the Troy club, said, "I'll take him." Mack said okay; send the check. No check came. Three times Mack wrote or wired Ramsey, telling him to either send the check or cancel the deal if he wanted to so that Mack could offer the player to other clubs. Ramsey did neither.

On February 6 Mack informed Ramsey that the player was reportedly negotiating with the Federal League. His letter ended: "We will wait for reply if it reaches me by Monday morning. Just want you to send check or say you would like to call the deal off. That ought to be easy. There's only one way to play and that is the square way. Do get busy."

Ramsey didn't get busy. Fritz signed with the Chicago Feds. Mack petitioned the National Association for the $500 from Troy, and it ruled in his favor.

American League attendance had fallen 30 percent in the past two years to the lowest level since 1903. Squeezed by carryover contracts and their share of the Federal settlement costs, the AL owners argued over how to boost revenues. One faction sought to reduce the number of cheap bleacher seats. Another view contended that raising prices would further depress attendance; prices should be cut to draw more customers.

St. Louis writer John B. Sheridan, using the Browns as an average, cited a club's overhead at $280,000, including $90,000 for players' and managers' salaries. Except for maybe $15,000 from park rentals, concessions, and advertising sales, it all had to come from ticket sales.

Shibe Park seated twenty-three thousand; four parks were bigger. None had more bleacher seats, and Connie Mack was not about to shrink his bleacher capacity. With a price scale of twenty-five cents and up and attendance under two hundred thousand, even with a payroll of half the league average, there was no way the Athletics could break even. The Athletics' 1915 overhead had been about $180,000, including a $69,000 player payroll.

These were the financial facts of life the Shibes and Mack faced. Until the team started winning and attendance came back, they had to keep a lid on the payroll. But for that to happen, Mack had to corral and develop another class of low-cost, high-potential youngsters.

He had no doubt that he could do it. "I have everything I own tied up in this ball club," he said, "and I am perfectly satisfied with conditions. I'm staking my reputation on my ability to come back. I am coming back with a greater team than I ever had before."

He didn't care how long it took, how low the team finished in the meantime, or how few patrons came out to see them. To keep the audience entertained in case his team didn't, Mack spent $3,000 to have a Moller organ with eight ranks of pipes installed at Shibe Park. He put no pressure on himself to stay in the pennant race while rebuilding. He had tried that once before, after winning the 1905 pennant, and it didn't work. So he had cleaned house and started over developing young players. It had taken three years to pay off.

Despite the Athletics' disappointing 1915 season, Connie Mack's personal popularity remained high. Among his many friends was a prosperous coal transporter in Philadelphia, Edward F. Glennon. A Glennon family story that could not be verified claims that Edward Glennon once gave Mack a loan to help the A's stay in business. Whether true or not, when Glennon's son Tom was born on February 16, 1916, Connie Mack was the infant's godfather. Mack showed up at the baptism at the Church of the Nativity, and a huge crowd filled Allegheny Street outside the church just to get a glimpse of him. Nobody heckled or threw anything at him because of his last-place team.

At the winter meetings in New York, they—managers, owners, and writers—laughed when Mack, declining to bid on a couple of veteran pitchers the Feds were trying to peddle, said he had all the pitching he needed. It was a hollow-sounding boast, considering that he appeared to be going into the new season relying on the same "Connie Mack's Marching Club" that had produced the debacle of 1915.

But Mack believed he had a bunch of strong young arms. The trouble was that except for Bush, Wyckoff, and Bressler, they were just green as grass. And Mack really wasn't all that sanguine about the three veterans. Wyckoff had been wild and ended 1915 with a sore arm. Despite Richter's prediction that Wyckoff was "destined to be one of the sensations of the year," his sore arm never healed and he proved to be of little use.

Among the rookies, Mack reserved his highest praise for twenty-two-year-old Elmer Myers—"another Bender"—who had shut out Washington on two hits in his year-end debut. Signed off the Philadelphia sandlots in the fall of 1912, Myers had been entrusted to Earle Mack at Raleigh for three years of tutoring. After two break-even seasons, he had won 29 games—almost half the team's 63 wins—and lost 10, striking out 266. He had grown into what Mack considered a perfect build for a pitcher: 6-foot-2, 180 pounds. He was cool under fire. His fastball, curve, and change-up were all effective when he threw them for strikes.

Mack was less hopeful about another highly touted prospect, Bill Morrisette, a spitball artist and the slowest worker on the mound since Eddie Plank. Mack disliked the spitter. There were no more than a half dozen pitchers who could throw it consistently for strikes. He didn't like pitchers who depended on the shine ball, emery ball, or any other doctored ball to succeed and had consistently advocated banning all such pitches. But he gave Morrisette a trial because Jack Dunn called him the best prospect he had turned out in years "if Mack can keep [Bill's] mind on the game." Apparently Mack couldn't; Morrisette would make one relief appearance: 4 innings, 5 walks, 6 hits. The spitballer sailed into the sunset.

One collegian who eluded Mack's net pitched for the University of Florida against the A's that spring. Spessard Holland impressed Mack enough to be offered a contract. The future Florida governor and senator turned it down.

For all his pumping up of prospects, Mack often acknowledged that every young pitcher was a gamble. Many hard-hitting clubs fare poorly against a young pitcher they've never seen before. Mack might praise him publicly, but privately he'd withhold judgment until the youngster had faced a team more than once.

Visitors to Barrs Field in Jacksonville commented on the change in the atmosphere of the A's camp. In the past Mack had allowed his veterans to train at their own pace. Now, with so few older players, he was driving everybody hard. Writers making the rounds of the camps compared him to John McGraw as a martinet, taking charge of everything. Everybody was up at eight, on the field at nine, worked till noon, back on the field after lunch for more drills, then an intra-squad game. Overweight players jogged in the outfield. Golf was out, banned all season. Mack believed it had affected the batting eye of some of his players the previous year.

Mack and Ira Thomas worked with the pitchers, changing deliveries and moves to hold base runners close. Too many pitchers were oafs when it came to fielding bunts. Mack had them taking grounders in the infield to improve their footwork.

The catching corps that had looked strong was suddenly depleted. Cy Perkins had come down with typhoid fever on the steamer *Comanche* on the way to camp. On the second day rookie Bill Meyer split his hand. That left only Wally Schang and some greenies. When Perkins recovered, he did most of the catching on the way north and thought he'd made the team. But the day before the opener Mack called him up to the tower office and told him he was going to Atlanta to learn under Charlie Frank, whom Mack trusted more than most minor league managers. Frank had been an outfielder in the Western League when Mack was managing Milwaukee. He had managed at New Orleans for ten years, forming a solid and dependable personal working relationship with Mack. Charlie Frank never cut a string. After two years in Atlanta, Perkins would become Mack's first-string catcher and remain with the A's for eleven years.

Mack was satisfied with his outfield of Strunk, Oldring, and Jimmy Walsh. Amos Strunk had been with the A's since 1908, but he was still only twenty-six. Rube Oldring was a veteran who had given Mack ten years of outstanding service, but cellar-dwelling had sapped his motivation. When the 1915 season ended, Oldring announced he was retiring to his new farm in Shiloh, New Jersey. But when the spring training call came, he was back. He would hang up his spikes for good in June, or so he thought. When the Yankees found themselves shorthanded, they persuaded him to finish the season with them.

Except for McInnis at first base, the infield was iffy.

The brightest-looking recruit was shortstop Ladislaw Wittkowski, better known as Lawton "Whitey" Witt. Harry Davis had discovered the 5-foot-7 towhead playing in the White Mountain League in the summer of 1915. Witt was attending Bowdoin College in the fall when Mack invited him to a meeting on December 2 at the Copley Square Hotel in Boston, where Witt signed a two-year contract for $1,800 a year and a $300 bonus.

Witt was a chatterbox and a speedy left-handed batter. He was an ideal lead-off man: an expert bunter, a punch-and-judy hitter who didn't strike out often after his rookie year. He stood so far up in the batter's box that his right foot was outside the line by the time he swung. But he knew nothing about getting a jump on a pitcher, never picked it up, and was a minimal base-stealing threat.

Connie Mack assigned the nineteen-year-old Witt to room with Nap Lajoie, who took Whitey in hand and showed him how to work tobacco juice into his bats and other rites of big league life. In turn Whitey's infectious enthusiasm at shortstop rejuvenated Lajoie—as much as his forty-one-year-old legs could be rejuvenated. Lajoie led the league in longevity; this was his twenty-first season. Spring spryness would stiffen by July.

Mack intended to give Whitey Witt a year of schooling by his side on the bench. That idea lasted only until opening day, when Sam Crane once again showed he would never be the next Jack Barry. Witt went into the lineup to stay.

And, as perennial as the crocus and the daffodil, came the prophesies that after college graduations, there would appear new men who would "make a difference" in the A's lineup. Harry Davis spoke of a college infielder better than Eddie Collins who would show up in June. You'd have thought Chandler Richter was on the Athletics' payroll as a publicist, the way he continually promised his readers "great surprises" in store for A's fans, with hints of a mysterious new collegiate star who would appear out of the east—or maybe it was the west—in July, like Elijah showing up at a Passover seder, and make A's fans forget Jack Barry.

The chorus began to sound like Dickens's Mr. Micawber: something good was always bound to turn up.

Relations with the Phillies had cooled. William F. Baker, a former New York police commissioner, now headed the Phils' ownership. He had no ties to the city, no interest in getting along with Connie Mack. For the first time, the Phillies were looking down on their last-place neighbors from a pennant perch. The two teams had earlier arranged 9 spring games, some in Florida and some on the way home. There would be no city series, which was fine with Mack. They were usually played in cold, wet weather to meager gatherings. Phillies manager Pat Moran didn't like barnstorming home from Florida and proposed that those games be canceled. Mack responded by calling off the Florida games too. This teed off Baker, which didn't bother Mack. "Let the Phillies have their day," he sniffed. "Ours is coming, and sooner than most people think."

Mack then contacted Braves president James Gaffney and scheduled 5 games in Florida. The spring series with the Braves was even more painful than the 1914 World Series sweep had been. George Stallings probably enjoyed it immensely. The A's were soundly trounced and roundly ridiculed in every game. The pitchers walked everybody except the groundskeeper's dog. Only Joe Bush seemed to be making good on his vow to bear down and do the job he had failed to do in 1915.

The lousy pitching stifled whatever pepper the A's had started out with. The veterans Mack had kept—Strunk, McInnis, Oldring—believing they were still young enough to contribute to his next winning machine, were as disappointed as their leader in the poor showing of the hurlers. There's nothing more palling on a fielder's pep than to be forced to stand idly fidgeting while pitchers walk a parade of batters.

Another long season loomed.

When they split up into two squads to head north, leaving Wyckoff and Bressler behind to work the aches out of their wings, it was hard to tell which team was the Yannigans.

"They're all Yannigans," Mack was heard to mutter.

Wherever they stopped, Mack had some local semipros and college boys lined up for a look. If he put them in the lineup, he usually did so using an alias, a frequent practice for college players at the time. A third baseman whose real name may or may not have been Ralph Baker showed up one day and quickly demonstrated that he would never be known as Home Run.

Ever the optimist, Connie Mack repeated his state of the A's message of a year earlier. "By August I expect my club to have found itself. The boys will have had considerable experience by that time and I will know just what they can do."

It didn't take him that long to find out what they could do.

Jack Nabors started the opener against Babe Ruth on a cold day in Boston. Despite 8 walks in 4 innings he escaped without a run scored. Joe Bush relieved him and took the 2–1 loss on his own error and one by Charlie Pick. Catcher Wally Schang stuck his right hand in the path of a fastball and for the second straight year was put on the shelf immediately and indefinitely.

The catching load fell on the rookie Bill Meyer. They lost the next game and the next and went to New York, where it rained, keeping Connie Mack warming the cushions in the Ansonia lobby while the players went to the circus, the movies, and the bowling alleys. Then Frank Baker beat them, but not with the bat. Trailing 4–2 in the eighth, the A's loaded the bases with no outs. Baker made two outstanding defensive plays that kept them from scoring off Bob Shawkey.

So they were 0-5 when they came home and lost the home opener, 7–1, to the Red Sox. Bush faced 8 batters in a 4-run first. Errors by Pick, Lajoie, and 2 by Oldring didn't help. Half their early losses were due to leaky defense and bases on balls.

And that's the way it was going to be. Pick went on to lead all third basemen in errors despite playing only 108 games. Witt's 78 bobbles were the most by a shortstop. Lajoie's grace was no longer amazing.

They finally picked up a win when Elmer Myers outpitched Herb Pennock, 2–1, and Jack Nabors beat Boston, 6–2, before enthusiastic crowds eager to see Connie Mack's new collection of future champs.

A few weeks later, in a 4-game series against Detroit, the world saw what havoc scatter-armed pitchers could sow. On May 9 three A's hurlers handed out 18 bases on balls in a 16–2 loss. Detroit pitchers walked 12; the total of 30 is still a 9-inning record. The next day Sheehan and Nabors walked 11 and Tigers pitchers walked 7 in Detroit's 9–3 win. The 2-game total of 48 walks is still the standard for wildness.

It wasn't over. On May 11 Elmer Myers issued 10 free passes but only 3 hits and managed to edge Harry Coveleski, 3–2. The Tigers won the finale in 11 innings, 8–6, benefitting by 10 walks and 17 hits, despite punching 15 free passes themselves. In this game the two teams left 36 base runners stranded, 20 by the A's, a record once tied by the Yankees.

Final casualty count for the four games: 167 base runners on 86 walks, 68 hits, 11 errors, and 2 hit batters, with 90 left on base.

An exasperated Connie Mack allowed as how it was the dumbest exhibition of baseball he had ever witnessed by a team under his management.

For all that, the Athletics surprised the experts and the fans by playing tough. Most days they were no pushovers, at least when Bush and Myers did the pitching. They were Mack's only consistent starters, and he used them often. On May 13 Myers won his third complete game in six days, beating the Browns to move the Mackmen a half-game over St. Louis into seventh place. They enjoyed this lofty site for almost three weeks, even bobbing up to fifth for a day. The first time they faced Eddie Plank since his departure after the 1914 season, they staged a 4-run rally in the seventh to beat him.

When Myers shut out the Yankees, 1–0, on May 30, Mack hit the hyperbole button: "Myers is the best young pitcher I ever developed in my sixteen-year career with the Athletics. Today he is better than Plank, Bender, and Coombs were in their prime."

Then the A's went west, where they lost every game. They played just well enough to stave off complete discouragement. The lack of a timely hit, a surfeit of untimely errors, and oh, those bases on balls did them in. They might have won one—or lost four more—if it hadn't rained every day in Chicago. The city was packed for the Republican convention; some of the players made their way from the Chicago Beach Hotel downtown to Convention Hall to watch the GOP wrangle its way toward nominating Charles Evans Hughes to run against Woodrow Wilson. Mack held court in the hotel lobby, where he told the writers, "My youngsters have come up to my expectations"—which must have been pretty low to begin with—"but some of my veterans have fallen down this year."

McInnis was struggling well below the .200 level. Rube Oldring was talking about retiring to his farm in New Jersey and did so on July 1. Rube Bressler didn't have his head, heart, or arm in his job. After he gave up 14 walks and 16 hits in 15 innings of work, Mack had seen enough and optioned him to Newark. Newark threw him back. Mack used him to pitch batting practice before casting him off for good. Bressler went on to a long career in the National League as a .300-hitting outfielder.

Wyckoff's arm never stopped hurting. He showed nothing in his few outings. Mack tried to send him to Cleveland, but he didn't want to go. So Mack released him, and the Red Sox picked him up. He didn't help them either and never won another game for anybody.

But Mack's biggest disappointments were Tom Sheehan and Jack Nabors. No sport celebrates the forlorn along with the superstar with as much fondness as baseball. These 1916 roommates are as legendary for their losing record as Cy Young or Smoky Joe Wood for a winning year.

(Warning: The record books on Nabors are still being rewritten by the retro stats revisers, and they don't agree—yet—with what follows here. One reason for the confusion is that prior to 1950 official scoring rules for determining winning and losing pitchers were not codified. Such decisions were left to the scorers' judgment. Occasionally Ban Johnson would overrule a scorer. And in 1916 no official pitching records were published by the American League. Another reason is that the revisionists have been inconsistent in retroactively applying modern rules to ancient games.)

After his impressive April 22 win over the world champion Red Sox in his third start, the alleged "tall, slim youth" Jack Nabors started 27 more games and never won another. He finished the year with a 1-21 line according to some record books, 20 of the losses in a row, and a 1-20 line in others.

Tom Sheehan started 17 games and won none of them. His lone win came in relief on June 26; his year ended with a 1-16 line.

(In 1963 a committee of the Baseball Writers Association, chaired by Cliff Kachline, applied current scoring rules and switched Nabors's September 19 loss to Sheehan in relief, ratifying their records at 1-20 and 1-16 respectively. But the committee failed to do the same for the A's April 28 7–6 loss to Washington, a game that Nabors left in the ninth with a 6–3 lead and the tying runs on base and which *Sporting Life* at the time correctly pinned on reliever Minot Crowell, while most record books still pin it on Nabors, whose tally should be 1-19, with a record 18 losses in a row, tied by Roger Craig in 1963.)

No pair of teammates has ever matched the elegiac 2-35 combined record of Nabors and Sheehan in 1916. But they weren't really all that bad. Sure, Nabors's earned run average of 3.47 and Sheehan's 3.69 were among the highest in the league, but they were no worse than Elmer Myers's 3.66 or Stan Coveleski's 3.41, winners of 14 and 15 games. Nabors and Myers allowed almost identical base runners per nine innings. They all had their wild streaks. Myers, who was 7-2 at the start of the first western trip, won 7 and lost 21 the rest of the year. He led the league in walks—168 in 315 innings.

As often as not, this is the way the year went for Nabors and Sheehan:

On June 23 in Boston, Sheehan pitched a 2-hitter and lost, 1–0. Nabors started the next day. Harry Hooper beat out an infield hit to lead off for Boston. He reached third and stole home. From then until the ninth, Nabors held the Red Sox hitless and the A's led, 2–1. For years thereafter, Tom Sheehan enjoyed telling the story, often reprinted in anthologies, of what happened next.

Rookie catcher Mike Murphy was behind the plate. Hooper started the ninth by dragging a bunt that got by Lajoie for a single. Hal Janvrin put down a bunt that Nabors threw past first base. Runners on second and third, no outs. Witt threw out Duffy Lewis, both runners holding. Dick Hoblitzel lifted a fly ball to left. Schang caught it and threw a bullet home that beat Hooper. But the runner crashed into the catcher and Murphy dropped the ball. The score was tied.

At this point, Sheehan's yarn went, "Nabors winds up and throws the next pitch twenty feet over the hitter's head into the grandstand, the man on third scores and we lose another.

"Later I asked Nabors why he threw that one away.

"'Look,' he said, 'I knew those guys wouldn't get me another run and if you think I'm going to throw nine more innings on a hot day like this, you're crazy.'"

Great story—just not true.

What really happened, according to contemporary accounts, was that the game ended when Nabors threw a waist-high inside fastball to right-handed batter Tilly Walker that sailed right past Murphy's mitt, hit either the umpire's or Murphy's chest protector, and bounded toward the first base dugout, while Janvrin scored the winning run. The official scorer and the *Philadelphia Inquirer* called it a wild pitch, but both the *Boston Globe* and the *Herald* called it a passed ball. Everybody called it Murphy's fault and a crying shame that Nabors had to lose a pitching gem that way.

If Sheehan's account had been accurate, it would have been understandable. The A's couldn't buy a run when the pitchers did their job. In 25 games in which Nabors worked the A's scored no more than 2 runs a game. Over a 14-game stretch they scored as many as 4 runs only once. For the year the A's averaged 2.92 runs (even Chicago's 1906 Hitless Wonders had averaged almost 3.8). Their opponents scored 5.17. The A's had almost as many errors per game—2.05.—as runs.

But it wasn't just the lack of scoring or defense that contributed to the pitchers' sorry records. John McGraw considered catchers one-third responsible for good pitching; Connie Mack put it at 40 percent. With the A's, the pitchers never knew who their catcher would be from one day to the next. When Wally Schang broke his jaw crashing into a concrete wall chasing a fly ball, the catching crew consisted of rookies Bill Meyer and Ralph "Doc" Carroll, who had just joined the team from Tufts University. Carroll may not have lasted long enough to sign a contract. On the train to St. Louis on July 10 Meyer was hit with appendicitis while Mack was on a scouting trip in Kentucky. On their arrival in St. Louis Carroll informed Mack that he wasn't feeling well, didn't really much care for professional baseball, and was going home. A greenie just out of Princeton, Val Picinich, showed up and immediately became the regular catcher. Mack prevailed upon Boston president Jim Lannin to lend him catcher Ray Haley from Buffalo, which Lannin controlled, on a thirty-day trial. Mack decided to keep Haley and sent outfielder Jimmy Walsh to Boston in payment. All together the Athletics used six catchers; except for Schang they were all rookies, though a few had been in a handful of major league games in the past. Some days the pitcher and catcher had never met until they took their positions on the field. Of the five rookies, only Val Picinich went on to a long big league career, but not in Philadelphia.

The Athletics had been without a mascot since the death of Louis Van Zelst in the spring of 1915. One morning in July, a thirteen-year-old hunchback, Hughie McLoon, showed up at Shibe Park. A frequent spectator at the games, Hughie knew the players. He called to Larry Lajoie and asked what his chances were to be the A's mascot. Lajoie told him to go up to Mr. Mack's office and ask.

"I went up the steps to Connie's office and couldn't open the door," McLoon told an interviewer a few years later. "A big fellow saw me tryin' and pulled it wide for me. 'Hey, Connie,' he shouted, 'here's a big pitcher for you from the west.' I felt queer, and they all began to laugh and kid me, but I stood there and told Mr. Mack what I wanted, anyhow.

"He told me the team has been losing a bunch of games . . . and that if they won the first day I was on the job he would keep me. I tol' him I'd bring 'em luck, an' I did. The A's won 'at day and I stayed."

Neither the luck nor Hughie McLoon lasted long. Unlike the popular, sunny Van Zelst, McLoon was a sassy, hard-boiled kid who had been mascoting for various athletic teams and prize fighters around Philadelphia. He heckled umpires and opposing players, once drawing a published rebuke from player-turned-umpire and poet George Moriarty that began:

> Hey, Hughie McLoon, now you'd better watch out.
> I'm three times as mad as a guy with the gout.
> It didn't take Silk and me long to get wise
> That you were no friend of us umpiring guys.
> The first thing you know, one of these summer days,
> There'll be a new mascot at work for the A's.

McLoon would be gone after the 1918 season. During the years of Prohibition, he became an undercover informant for Smedley Butler, head of the Philadelphia police force. In 1928 his cover was exposed and he was gunned down by bootleggers.

By July 4 even Chandler Richter had given up, declaring, "There's no reason to believe the A's will get out of last place this season." It was a safe prediction; they had won 17 games and lost 47, and were 10 games out of seventh place. Stuffy McInnis had a charley horse and anemic batting average and was sent home to rest. Lajoie was hobbling from a spike wound.

It got worse. From June 27 through August 8, the Athletics won 2 games and lost 41, tying Boston's 1906 AL record of 20 consecutive losses. Joe Bush had to throw shutouts to win those two. On August 6 in Cleveland Mack jury-rigged his rotation, using Nabors, Myers, and Bush for 3 innings each. They lost again. By then their record was 19-80. They had yet to win a game in the west. Joe Bush, the "stopper," ended that losing streak on August 9 with a 7–1 win over the Tigers. Then they got hot and swept a doubleheader at New York. That was the last time the A's won two in a row.

For the entire year they would win only 13 games away from Shibe Park, a showing they would repeat in 1945.

The reformed Bush, possibly bearing down to attract interest from contending clubs, pitched his league-leading eighth shutout on August 26 at home against Cleveland, a near-perfect no-hitter marred only by a lead-off walk to Jack Graney. It was an amazing game, not because it was thrown at a heavy-hitting team, but because he had an infield behind him that couldn't stoppeth even one of three. An incident in this game probably told Nap Lajoie it was time to retire. His first time up he hit a ball over Tris Speaker's head in center field. The ball rolled to the scoreboard while Lajoie puffed into third. In April he would have scored easily. When Pick followed with an apparent single back of second, Lajoie held up before starting for home and was thrown out. After flying out to right field in his next at-bat, he never batted in the big leagues again.

Connie Mack was undaunted. It took patience to sit through the losses day after day, but that was one thing he had plenty of. He was learning how his kindergarten boys handled themselves, handled losing, making mistakes, walking batters. In addition to talent, he was always looking for heart. Heart alone wouldn't win, but he believed that talent alone wouldn't either. He was also looking for alertness and ability to learn. He didn't like what he saw.

Eighty-five years later, the June 19, 2001, *Investor's Business Daily* put Connie Mack in some very fast company for a sixth-grade dropout. In a feature, "Wisdom to Live By," Mack was quoted along with the likes of Theodore Herzl, Henry Ford, Norman Vincent Peale, Victor Hugo, Johan Wolfgang von Goethe, and Conrad Hilton.

Mack's aphorism: "More players defeat themselves than are ever defeated by an opposition team. You can't win any game unless you are ready to win."

In December he would tell Billy O'Connor of the *St. Louis Post-Dispatch*, "Ball players have not been taking their work seriously. They have been distracted and are not giving their employers full value. No team can win, you know, unless everybody on that team concentrates on the business at hand. The men on the bench must help those in the field. You've got to keep your head up every inning. If you don't, you'll lose. I find it hard to make the young players appreciate that fact."

American Association president A. J. Hickey blamed the lackadaisical attitude on the Players Fraternity. "Old-fashioned rivalry is forgotten. Players throw their arms around each other's necks instead of watching for a chance to put one over. I want to see teams go after each other with hammer and tongs to win, see blood in their eyes when they come on the field, see them at daggers' point from first to last instead of taking it out on the umpires. This frat business has made players too roommatey."

John McGraw was rebuilding by spending whatever it took to buy established players. Charles Comiskey was castigated by some writers for trying to buy a pennant. The Yankees now had the deepest pockets of all, and Jake Ruppert was digging into them freely to acquire a winner. They had the money. Connie Mack didn't. Nor had he lost confidence that he could succeed doing things the way that had worked for him in the past, the way he enjoyed building a championship team.

Not yet.

In the spring Connie Mack had told reporters:

I have never built teams as other managers do, by recruiting almost exclusively from the minor leagues. Therefore I care nothing about the charges made by my critics. I have been managing ball clubs for twenty years and have tried out every method. I managed in minor leagues and learned my lesson there. That was where I learned that minor league players after they had been sent up to the majors had to be started all over again. Big leagues is a different style. I therefore made up my mind to build from the ground up. And that is why I have so many raw recruits this year. They look unpromising at first, but from them I will build a club that will play any kind of baseball and will not have to alter the style of my players.

A Philadelphia columnist with the improbable moniker Rodman Random lauded Connie Mack for his unwavering approach to rebuilding his team: "Mack gets more national attention and publicity by sticking to his task in his own way and never swerving in the slightest degree. Fans throughout the country are more than ever convinced that Mack followed the only possible and logical method of rebuilding. That he has the courage of his convictions and carried through his plan is so greatly admired."

Connie Mack never passed up a chance to look at a prospect, as long as someone brought the player to his attention (he never acted on letters from unknown boys seeking a trial). Somewhere out there was the next budding star. He followed up every tip, usually typing his own letters of invitation to a tryout. Typical of his style is a letter to a semipro and college umpire, dated August 26, 1916, exactly as typed by him:

Mr. Jack McGowan.
Wilmington, Del.

Dear Jack:

Yours of the 16th., inst., received and please excuse delay in my replying to same. Have been very busy and my correspondence is a way behind. Am sorry you did not drop in to see me when you were in the City. When ever you are up this way, be sure and drop in will always be glad to see you.

In regards to this young player Doherty, would like to have you bring him up some Morning. Will be home all of next week except on Monday, and any day that you can come up with him, will be glad to have you do so. Let me know a few days in advance if possible, though I am pretty sure to be here all of next week.

Yours truly,
/s/ Connie Mack

(Jack McGowan's younger brother, Bill, was just breaking in as a minor league umpire prior to a thirty-year career in the American League.)

If Doherty showed up, he didn't show enough to make the Big Show.

On the road Mack frequently left the team and visited minor league towns. His first base coach, Ira Thomas, and third base coach, Harry Davis, were often absent scouring the country. Mack even scouted other teams' prospects. In St. Louis in late July he watched a tall, sturdily built lad working out at first base with the Browns. Before leaving town, Mack talked to the youngster, a gas meter reader who sold peanuts during the games. When the A's headed for Chicago, nineteen-year-old Charlie Grimm signed a contract for $125 a month and went with them. Mack put him in the outfield, where he was hitless in his debut against Eddie Cicotte.

In 1950 Grimm told a writer, with some fallibility of memory: "Connie had a poor team and a lot of youngsters around, so many he didn't have enough uniforms. So the rest of us would sit in the stands and when he needed a pinch hitter, he'd wigwag us and we would rush down, climb into the suit of the departing player, and go into the game. I got into only one game [he was in twelve] and I played very well. I was put in the outfield and I didn't have a thing to do except alternately hope and fear a ball would come my way. None did." (He made 7 putouts and 1 error.)

Mack sent Grimm to Durham in 1917, but the strings were cut when the North Carolina State League folded in May and Grimm became a free agent.

Since the end of June the trains into North Philadelphia station had brought enough students to Mack's baseball academy for him to start his own college. Some of them had never seen a grass infield. At one point, Mack's entire infield consisted of McInnis and three rookies, all New Englanders. Their average age was 20.5. Otis Lawry, a small, smart infielder who had been coached by one of Mack's former players, Monte Cross, at the University of Maine, was probably the one Harry Davis had predicted would make the fans forget Jack Barry. Or was he the one tabbed to be the next Eddie Collins? Whatever. He remained the one and only Otis Lawry.

For the rest of the season, the days began at Shibe Park with two-hour workouts, a lunch break, then another hour session until it was time for pregame practice. The veterans often showed up in the morning to get in some extra batting practice and help with the tutoring. The field was in such constant use there was no time to cut the grass. It grew so high that visiting managers complained to Ban Johnson.

The lineup Mack put on the field at game time seemed to change daily. By the end of the year fifty-one players would appear in an Athletics uniform—twenty-one of them pitchers, nineteen of them college boys. Of the fifty-one, twenty-one made their last major league appearance; for twelve of those it was also their first. As fast as recruits showed up, Mack threw them into action. It didn't take him long to decide if they had enough to stick around. The Hesselbachers, Mitterlings, and Stellbauers stayed just long enough to pick up their cups of coffee to go.

For all the ballyhoo over this phenom or that, the one-day wonders and sure things, nobody stood out. They were all so green, so raw, so lacking in the fire and dedication Mack was looking for. Grit, heart, moxie, ginger—this was the language of hustle. None of them spoke it.

Nor was Connie Mack the only baseball man to notice the decline in determination. Up in Boston the old crab Johnny Evers grouched, "Young ballplayers of today do not take their profession seriously enough. They are unwilling to take the infinite pains necessary to overcome their faults and increase what natural ability they possess."

Wild Bill Donovan of the Yankees lamented, "There are mighty few recruits who take pains to discover their own batting weakness and set out to correct it. They would rather have a pitcher in practice throw the ball they like best to hit instead of one they find hardest to hit."

Nobody, it seemed, wanted to do what it took to be the next anybody.

Perhaps that was why Connie Mack's eyes lit up when he saw a nineteen-year-old infielder sent to him by scout Mike Drennan. Jimmie Dykes was a local lad from Bryn Mawr who played second base for an amateur team managed by his father. He caught for his high school team because he had the strongest arm among the kids his age. He also had what was called a "taxicab build"—a broad, bulky rear end like the trunk of a cab.

Dykes was playing for a semipro team in Seaford, Delaware, when Mike Drennan and Cardinals' scout Joe Sugden saw him. Drennan liked his strong arm and peppery style. Sugden didn't like his big butt. Drennan invited Dykes to a morning workout at Shibe Park, where Ira Thomas hit ground balls to him for what seemed like hours to the youngster, who finally complained, "Haven't you seen enough yet?"

The rookies were not allowed in the clubhouse and had to change in the umpires' room. They were also pushed away from the batting cage by the regulars. When they chased Dykes, he fumed and started to walk away from the whole setup. Connie Mack stopped him, picked up a bat, and escorted Dykes to the plate. He wanted to get a look at the kid's swing. When Mack left the field, the others pushed Dykes out of the batting cage.

Disgusted by the way he'd been treated, the hotheaded Dykes had left the park and gone home when Mack went looking for him later.

Connie Mack had seen something he liked. Maybe it was the spirit, the hot temper that spoke to him of enthusiasm, energy, a love for the game. He had watched Jimmie flagging down the grounders Thomas drove at him, heard him complain that he'd done enough to show them he could catch the ball, and seen him stay with it until Thomas quit.

Mack wrote Jimmie a letter inviting him to his home. Dykes later recalled Mack telling him, "You have good tools, Jimmie, but you need instruction in hitting. Keep at it, plug away, and you'll make it one of these days."

Mack then offered him a contract with Gettysburg in the Blue Ridge League, one of those invisible-strings arrangements. The A's would pay thirty dollars of his hundred-a-month salary. Dykes leaped at the chance.

Until the A's hit the skids in July, attendance at Shibe Park had actually been pretty good. Maybe the organist was playing well. A growing indifference to the prolonged bloody stalemate of the Great War "over there" and general economic prosperity boosted the gate in both leagues. Attendance doubled in St. Louis, tripled in Cleveland. Visions of profit had danced in Connie Mack's head.

But not for long. As the losses and rainouts piled up, the turnstile numbers went down. Trouble in Mexico broke out when Pancho Villa raided Texas border towns. Local news in Philadelphia was dominated by the mobilizing of the National Guard for a "punitive expedition" to guard the border. The A's chaplain, Rev. Davis, went with the troops. Though the final turnstile count of 184,471 was 37,000 higher than the count in 1915, it wasn't enough to break even, no matter how low the payroll.

Other club owners had complained about Mack's unbeatable teams driving customers away. Now they were upset because he was presenting a collection of no-names that couldn't win and nobody was coming out to see them. They forgot or weren't around in the early years when Philadelphia, Boston, and Chicago teams had supported the weaker clubs at home and on the road for the first dozen years of the league.

The new Yankee magnates, Ruppert and Huston, non-baseball men that Clark Griffith regarded as "bushwhackers," were the loudest complainers. It was a common practice for clubs to reschedule Monday games to create weekend doubleheaders and open the way for more lucrative Monday exhibition games in other cities and towns. Along with sending them players, Connie Mack often did this to provide a big payday for minor league clubs in the area. They in turn sometimes gave him first call on their young prospects.

So Mack moved a game with the Yankees from Monday, September 11, to create a Saturday doubleheader and arranged to play in Ridgeway, New Jersey, on Monday and Tuesday. The Yankees then scheduled an exhibition game of their own on Monday.

Mack had another policy: whenever a contending team was in town and it was raining or storm clouds hovered, he gave the visiting manager the choice of playing or postponing the game. The situation had arisen during the last visits of Boston and Detroit, and that's the way it was when the fourth-place Yankees woke up in Philadelphia on Friday morning, September 8, and it was raining, pouring, cloudbursting. It was still pouring at game time.

Players were required to report to the ballpark regardless of the weather, so they were all at Shibe Park. If they called the game, it would have to be played on Monday. Neither Yankees manager Bill Donovan nor Mack wanted to cancel their exhibition games. So they waited. It was Donovan's call, but afterward Connie Mack took the heat. Eventually it stopped raining, and at 4:15 the managers announced the game would start. Only one reporter, George M. Young of the *Public Ledger*, and one telegrapher had shown up. They counted twenty-five people in the grandstand.

In the first inning Wally Schang hit a grand slam batting left-handed. In the second he batted from the right side and hit another home run, becoming the first to hit home runs from both sides of the plate in a game. The Athletics won, 8–2.

A few years later Jake Ruppert would refer to this game while railing against Mack and his last-place teams as a drag on the rest of the league. Ruppert overlooked the scant turnout at the Polo Grounds on October 2 of that year, when the Yankees and Nationals were battling for fourth place. According to W. O. McGeehan, "There wasn't a Cossack corporal's guard to witness the inspiring spectacle. Harry Stevens said all he sold was three beers and one highball, one ham sandwich and three hot dogs, putting them one hot dog behind the worst house of last year."

It takes courage to follow a different drummer, as Mack was doing. Buying and trading for established stars and highly touted minor leaguers may or may not win pennants, but if not, well, everybody could say a club owner was trying. Failure to win by doing what other clubs do draws no criticism. But taking a different path and failing left Mack open to ridicule.

By August the A's were 30 games behind seventh-place St. Louis; every other team was over .500. The losing streaks and tryout-camp lineups of August and September made the Athletics a fertile source of comedy material. Ring W. Lardner worked them over in the *Chicago Tribune* on September 21: "While the odds are slightly against Philadelphia winning the American League pennant by a great stretch run, there is yet a possibility of their making up the fifty and a half games which at this writing separate them from the leaders. With this possibility in mind, I visited Comiskey Park Tuesday afternoon."

After extolling the catcher [Ray Haley] as a great standing high jumper—"So effective was his work in the latter line that Nabors and Sheehan were able to accumulate but one wild pitch between them"—Lardner skewered the rest of the lineup with one-liners, then concluded, "As a whole, the club looks fairly well balanced, there being only two or three strong spots. Mr. Mack would, I believe, do well to sell McInnis, Strunk, and Schang, so his pitchers might lose with less effort."

Five days later Lardner proposed that, "as it looks kind of improbable for them to win the pennant now unless the season is extended a couple of years," a postseason series be arranged between the Athletics and Milwaukee of the American Association, losers of 106 games so far, or Oakland, which had already lost 116 games. Writing to "Friend Harvey" in his inimitable style, Lardner added, "Another reason why the Philadelphias should ought to get in a series of this kind is so they could make a hole lot more money which they certainly deserve for the help they have gave other teams to say nothing of the amusement they have gave to the fans who have been lucky enough to witness them."

There were other digs:

Connie Mack still talks about what is going on in the American League, as if he were still in it.

If the Athletics don't play better ball next year, Connie Mack might boost his receipts a bit by charging the players an admission fee.

The main difference between the Athletics and the new German submarine is that the Deutschland occasionally came up for air.

In spite of the advancing cost of white paper, most newspapers continue to include the A's in their daily "standings of the clubs."

Whitey Witt said some of the players were not above poking fun at themselves. "One day we're arriving on the train in Chicago about seven a.m. and I'm walking with Strunk and he says, 'Connie Mack's clowns coming to town.'"

Undeterred, Mack shook off the jokes and the criticism. He still had his supporters, not all of them hometown hypers like Richter. In August a *New York Evening Journal* writer commented:

Connie Mack was great in victory and he is great in defeat. There is that same unconventional disregard of common practice to the Mack system now as there was then. We admire him for it. There is something majestic in the quiet, unostentatious way he goes about patiently building up his newest machine. Other managers may fuss and fret when a pitcher appears to be imminently going into the air. Relief men are rushed to the "bull pen" and all is confusion. When one of Mack's youngsters begins wavering, the lanky Connie sits silently by, observing everything without so much as lifting a finger to another pitcher.

He is teaching his youngsters how to go through fire. Victory is to be desired if possible, but the lesson in defeat may be greater than victory. Many a ballplayer who is now young will look back some day and say that Mack was the greatest teacher of them all.

But as the dreary 1916 season ground on, Connie Mack changed. He still had the courage, but he no longer had the convictions. For two years he had enrolled hundreds of candidates in his baseball school, and almost all of them had flunked. He was disappointed, disillusioned by what he saw. For whatever reason, the raw material just wasn't there to suit the schoolmaster of Shibe Park. He became convinced that he could not duplicate his earlier success with the same methods that had built his 1910–1914 machine.

Not that he would abandon his youth movement altogether. He would never stop searching for uncut, unpolished gems. He just couldn't build an entire new crown out of youngsters who didn't pack a shaving kit. The days of importing students by the carloads to Shibe Park were over. In a few years the ranks of the auditioners would shrink to a dozen or fewer. They would be older, many from higher minor leagues, and have briefer trials.

In August Mack sent Ira Thomas on a scouting trip to the West Coast. Adhering to his policy of never tipping his thinking to the public, Mack astounded fans and writers with the announcement that the A's had purchased outfielder Ping Bodie from the San Francisco Seals. The announcement on August 20 by Seals owner Harry Wolverton mentioned no price; it was said to be five figures. (It was $3,500.) Bodie, who was batting .300

and would wind up with 30 home runs, had expected to go to the Cardinals. For some reason that deal fell through, and Mack told Thomas to negotiate the purchase,

All of Philadelphia balldom was amazed. Connie Mack, the bargain-hunting cradle robber, paying five figures for a cumbersome, 5-foot-8, 200-pound, twenty-nine-year-old retread who had been turned back to the minors after four years patrolling the gardens of the White Sox, where he had earned more ink as colorful rainy-day feature material than for game-winning exploits? Bodie was just the kind of player Mack had disdained in the past: physical, not mental, schooled—if at all—by somebody else. Contenders bought experienced sluggers like Bodie to help them finish first. He had some power and a good arm, but the reversal of form on the part of the fifty-three-year-old keeper of the White Elephants boggled the sporting mind.

When they recovered from the shock, some writers found it impossible to reconcile the deal with Mack's frequently avowed philosophy of rebuilding and called it indefensible. But others cheered the acquisition.

Acknowledging Bodie's Chicago reputation for being "not dependable," Jim Nasium (pen name of Edgar Wolfe of the *Inquirer*) added, "but players who've seen him in the Pacific Coast League say he's much improved."

And Random of the *Press* wrote, "There have been many unfavorable comments on the move, but all lost track of the realities of the move. With the White Sox [Bodie] never was coached in proper form. So when he slumped and lost a certain amount of interest in his work he was shipped away to the PCL. Mack's scouts have found that he still slugs as of old, is fast and has all his latent strength. With all his natural advantages Bodie ought to be a valuable man with the proper coaching and that he will get with Connie Mack."

Mack didn't stop there. Thomas's scouting resulted in the purchase of second baseman Roy Grover, twenty-four, from Tacoma, and the drafting of three twenty-seven-year-olds: third baseman Ray Bates from Vernon, infielder Pete Johns from Columbus, and pitcher Winfield Noyes from Portland. He drafted one of John McGraw's discards, Rube Schauer, from Louisville. The twenty-five-year-old Russian-born Schauer, a one-time seminary student, had been primarily a relief pitcher for the Giants since his purchase from Superior of the Northern League after a 20-10 season in 1913. Schauer had provided more comedic than pitching relief, as the *New York Times* reported on his debut August 27, 1913:

Schauer was bought out in the Wisconsin cornstalks on the "what-do-we-care-for-expenses" plan. He cost anywhere from $1.98 to $15,000.

Schauer pronounces his name "Shower" and all the merry wags took occasion to perpetrate sparkling quips about the young man's title. Some said his first name is April, but it isn't; it's Rube.

When Schauer began to pitch in the ninth inning, rain began to fall, so somebody said that it never Schauers but it pours. As there seems to be no law against this sort of thing, there is no telling where the comedy will end.

It seemed as though Connie Mack had settled on twenty-seven as a more suitable age for rebuilding than seventeen. He paid $2,000 and several players to obtain .337-hitting outfielder, Frank Thrasher, also twenty-seven, from Atlanta. Thrasher had a big day September 30, banging out 3 doubles, a triple, and a single in a doubleheader at Washington.

All together Mack put in for twenty-six minor leaguers in the draft and obtained twelve from AA and A ranks. From the lower minors he drafted Walter "Lefty" Anderson from South Bend and right-hander Rollie Naylor, a 19-game winner at McAllister in the Western Association. Naylor was twenty-four, a little old for Class D competition.

These were not the stuff of which "greatest ever" championship teams were likely to be built, but Philadelphia fans applauded Mack's aggressive efforts to put a presentable lineup on the field, one that might even ascend from the cellar. They were losing patience with his trying to grow a victory garden from seeds.

Connie Mack, it seemed, had lost some patience as well.

The Athletics actually improved a little in September, winning 8 of their last 27 games. Well, for them that was an improvement. Stuffy McInnis batted almost .500 during the second half of the season, and his average climbed to .295. More than four thousand of the faithful turned out on a cold September 30 to witness the closing home doubleheader. When the A's won the second game, 10–9, in the ninth inning, the crowd celebrated so long and loud you'd have thought the home team had just clinched the pennant.

And when they closed the season by taking two in Boston, with the rookies Whitey Witt and Roy Grover collecting 11 hits between them, it was as if everybody had forgotten they had lost a league record 117 games, what with all the predictions that the A's would be back in the pennant race in 1917, just as Connie Mack had promised.

Was Connie Mack the best judge of young players in the game? Even if he was—and he never claimed he was—the best doesn't mean infallible. It just means making the fewest mistakes. Every manager cut loose players who later made it elsewhere. But none of the prospects Connie Mack rejected at this time became stars somewhere else.

Connie Mack would not disagree with the contention that nobody really knew who would become a star and who wouldn't, despite the ballyhoo they all blew. He knew that sandlots, colleges, and minor leagues were full of youngsters who looked "can't miss" and missed. (The records of future number-one amateur draft picks bear that out.) An experienced scout or manager could tell a "possible" from an out-and-out dud and even then be proven wrong. How would a rookie act under big league pressure? Nobody knew. And Connie Mack never did and never would pretend otherwise.

Mack had tasted the lemonade of paying a big price for a minor league star who wasn't worth it. Since then, he'd shied away, leaving McGraw, Comiskey, Dreyfuss, and the rest of the best of baseball brains to pay dearly for disappointments. The great Marty O'Toole, who had cost Dreyfuss a record $22,500 in 1911, was back in the Western League. New Cubs owner Charles Weeghman claimed he had paid more than that for shortstop Chuck Wortman, who wouldn't have hit his weight if he'd been a little heavier than 150.

Connie Mack's reputation as a brilliant discoverer and developer of raw young talent took some tarnishing as his club showed no signs of fulfilling his vow of a greater-than-ever champion by 1917. His lack of progress fanned discussions of whether the discovery and development of stars was really just luck and that Mack had been very lucky to come up with his 1910–1914 champions. A Philadelphia column signed only "Shortstop" concluded as much.

J. Ed Wray of the *St. Louis Post-Dispatch* wrote:

Mr. Mack's kindergarten is sickly and unpromising. . . . Time was when slim Mr. McGillicuddy was supposed to be just a long filament, topped by a big bulb of 99 44/100 pure gray matter. He essayed no trace of bone.

Therefore when Connie said he would cast aside his star hitters and pitchers and rebuild a pennant winner in three years we all kow-towed and sat down to watch this future giant grow.

But the cramps have seized it. If anything, Mack now has a worse club than ever. His veterans are slipping and his newcomers haven't come—and show little prospect of coming up to anything like a title class.

All of which brings us to the conclusion that managers are creatures, not creators. Players are born, not made, when it comes to world's championship caliber.

Mack's history in the matter of rebuilding proves that he was lucky in the past to get star pitchers and he will have to be lucky in the future to get the same essentials to success. They cannot be made to order.

Mack will win a pennant just as soon as he stumbles across another trio of Planks, Coombses or Benders—and not before.

Perhaps it had been just luck after all. Or maybe the country had changed in the last ten years and the youth of the nation had changed too.

When a *Sporting News* editorial wondered why there were so few young players, a newspaper in Uniontown, Pennsylvania, responded:

The reason is that the youngsters of twelve to fourteen are gradually los-ing their interest in baseball. There isn't one boy playing ball regularly in this city of 21,000 [for every] ten that played consistently twenty years ago when the population was about 8,000. Not long ago I gave two youngsters a dime each to attend a ball game for some little service they had done for me. Neither one of them showed up for the game, both hustling to a movie as soon as they got their hands on the money. Ty Cobb, Tris Speaker, Grover Alexander, et al aren't the heroes of youngsters anymore. Charlie Chaplin, Buster Farnham and the rest of the screen gods having superseded the men of the diamond in this respect.

If it isn't one thing hastening baseball's demise, it's always something else.

At the age of fifty-three, Connie Mack became a father again when a daughter, Rita, was born on November 21, 1916. His second family now included three girls and a boy. Another daughter, Elizabeth, would come along four years later. He had one grandchild, Peggy's year-old son, Robert McCambridge. A second, Cornelius, would be born to her in 1917. Earle Jr. would become the third, born in 1918, while Earle Mack was working in a shipyard in Philadelphia and living with his Uncle Dennis's widow, Annie, and her family.

The McGillicuddy clan had outgrown the narrow house (the lot was 16 x 120) at 2119 Ontario. In February 1916 they had found a large, three-story house at 604 W. Cliveden, on the corner of Lincoln Drive, adjacent to Fairmount Park in the Germantown section. They didn't actually buy the house; like swapping pitchers, they made a trade. Connie Mack signed over the house on Ontario and a 16 x 81 lot on Oxford Street (near the A's first grounds, Columbia Park) in exchange for 604 W. Cliveden. The Macks' new home was assessed at $9,000. When the indenture granting the deed was signed on March 10, it listed only Katherine as the buyer; she was the only one available to sign the necessary papers. Mr. Mack was in Jacksonville awaiting the arrival of his pitchers and catchers. Later the property was transferred into both names. It would be their home for twenty-five years.

It was left to Katherine, the baseball wife, to deal with the chaos of moving. It didn't help her disposition that two-year-old Ruth had the measles.

A three-car garage was under the house on the Lincoln Drive side. A long porch ran around three sides of the house. The front door opened to a large vestibule. On the left was a spacious, heavily draped parlor, in which a Steinway baby grand piano occupied one corner, and a living room where they spent most evenings, playing bridge or whist and entertaining guests. When Ruth learned to play the piano and sang along with it, she drove her brother Connie out of the house. It was also a player piano; they had rolls of classical and show tunes. Straight ahead was a dining room with a fireplace and a table that seated at least twelve when fully extended. A pantry on the right led to a kitchen and breakfast room.

A door in the hallway led down to the basement, which had a laundry room, bathroom, coal bin, and furnace. On the right as you entered was the staircase leading up to the second floor: three large bedrooms with spacious walk-in closets, two baths, a sitting room, sewing room, and enclosed porch. There were four more bedrooms on the third floor. One was used for storage, and one became a bright corner playroom where "Mother would sit each of us in a different corner," Ruth recalled.

Betty, the youngest, born in 1920, said, "The happiest time I can remember I was about six and it was Christmas Eve and my sisters and brother knocked on my door and took me crawling down the steps to the living room to see the tree all lit up and to get the stuff out of our stockings. Usually, they were all going in different directions, but that was one time there was unity. Oh, it was beautiful."

The presents were all in the third-floor playroom. "It looked like a department store," Ruth said, "and you'd be so excited, yelling, 'Which one's mine?'"

The neighborhood had a private night watchman service, but Connie Mack was prepared to defend his own castle. "Late one night Mother and Dad heard a noise," Ruth recalled with a laugh. "The commotion woke all of us. Dad got a golf ball and threw it out the window onto the porch to scare off any intruders."

There was never any doubt as to who was in charge. Katherine Mack had grown up taking charge in the Holahan household. She wasn't the oldest of her ten siblings, but she was the one who had gone to work and brought home the most income when their father deposited more money in his saloon's till than the household accounts.

The words most often used by her children and grandchildren to describe her were "dominant" and "capable." She handled all the money, dealt with the help, was a good cook and seamstress, and worked long hours raising five children. When something needed fixing around the house, she saw to it without her husband's help, for Connie Mack was no handyman. The only tools he was familiar with were bats and mitts and shin guards. She made the doll clothes for her four daughters at Christmastime and christening gowns when they became mothers.

Some of her brothers owned a grocery store that delivered. She was a regular customer, but that didn't mean she was a satisfied customer.

"One time she telephoned and laid it into them about something," one of her children recalled, "then she went to the store and let them have it some more."

Katherine ran everything. While a junior at Chestnut Hill College, Ruth, twenty-one, was dating Frank Cunningham. Ruth never finished her senior year; Katherine insisted they get married, then did all the planning, and even bought a house for them. Said Betty, "My sisters didn't have big weddings because she felt that their husbands needed the money more than to spend it that way. She was very practical. I was the only one who had a big wedding."

Betty's wedding in 1940 would be a gala event at the Philadelphia Country Club. But Mother was still in charge. Betty continued: "[The bridesmaids] usually get their own dresses. Well, Mother wouldn't have any of that. She had to take care of everything. She said, 'Get their sizes and I'll get the dresses.' And she did. She took me to South Street and let me be part of it. But she took care of the menu and the arrangements."

Ruth's son, Frank, said, "I got along with her okay, but sometimes she was a bulldozer. We'd go shopping and she'd say, 'Frank, I'm going to buy you a suit.' So we'd go into a store and she'd drive the guys crazy—and me too. And I'd be thinking, 'Man, I don't really want this suit.' And after a while it would be, 'How do you like that?' and I'd say, 'Terrific,' and she'd say, 'No, I don't like it.' She called the shots."

At the supper table Connie Mack always cleaned his plate. He ate slowly; arthritis was beginning to bend his fingers—not to the sides like many old catchers' digits, but straight down. In time it would force him to slide a knife and fork off the table to get hold of them and use them. Katherine kept pushing more food at everybody. Any of the girls who didn't finish it all were brusquely dispatched from the table. There was rarely a meal where somebody didn't leave in tears.

Otherwise there was little conversation at the table. "We ate pretty much in silence," Betty recalled, "never discussing things that were going on in the world." Baseball talk was banned by Katherine.

There was some concern on Connie Mack's part that his wife's controlling behavior was a sign of some mental health problems. He confided in his closest cousin, Nora, who often came for the weekend and read the comics to the kids on Sunday mornings. Nora made some inquiries about seeking help on his behalf. When Katherine found out about it, Nora was no longer welcome at 604 W. Cliveden. Connie Mack visited Nora at her apartment whenever he could. When his children were old enough to drive, he would ask one of them to take him to see her. The children remained fond of her. When Nora was dying in the 1930s, Roy's wife Margaret took Ruth to see her. Nora gave her some personal possessions she wanted Ruth to have.

All the kids loved their half-sister Peggy, Connie Mack's daughter from his first marriage. Peggy's health was as fragile as her mother's had been. Years later they remembered her always sitting on a radiator to stay warm. But there was a frost between Katherine and her stepdaughter. "She didn't like my mother," said Peggy's son Connie McCambridge. "When we lived near Philadelphia, we used to go there quite often for Sunday dinners, but it was Katie bar the door. You could feel the tension. She never cottoned to us." Connie McCambridge remembered her as a "tough cat."

Katherine called her husband "Con," and he addressed her as "Katherine." The children called them Dad and Mother. Later, Connie Jr.'s children called Mack "Pop-Pop" and Katherine "Nanny" or "Granny." Roy's and Earle's children called him Pa-Pa. The McCambridge boys called her Aunt Katherine. Their father died when they were very young; they looked on Connie Mack as a father and called him Dad.

It was evident to the girls that their parents were devoted to each other. Con often had his arm around Katherine. Arguments occurred but were rare, at least within the children's hearing. Katherine was diligent about looking after his welfare, sometimes to his annoyance. On cold, damp days she would insulate him with sheets of newspaper under his shirt before he headed for the office at Shibe Park. It was embarrassing to him, but he deferred to her rather than argue. "I'm sure he hated it," Ruth said, "but he always told us Mother knew best."

He didn't like being fussed over by anybody. Once in 1940, when the A's were training in California, Philadelphia writers Red Smith and Stan Baumgartner were riding in a car with him in San Francisco to a game at San Quentin. Mack was nearing eighty. Lena Blackburne, a longtime coach for him, was left behind in bed with a leg infection. Somebody asked Mack if he wanted the car window closed against the chilly morning air.

"Dammittohell," Connie exploded. "I'm all right, don't worry about me. Everybody's always fussing about me. Mrs. Mack says, 'Con, wear your rubbers. Con, put on your overcoat.' So I put on my coat and rubbers and go out to buy medicine for her.

"And that Blackburne," he sputtered. "It's 'Boss, are you warm enough? Boss, are you comfortable? Boss, you better come inside and rest.' And where is Blackburne? Lying down there in Anaheim on his tail, dammit."

Betty recalled, "When Dad would come home after a game, Mother would always go upstairs and put a shot of whiskey on top of his chest of drawers, and she would no sooner go back down than he would take it into the bathroom I used and dump it in the sink. She was probably right that it was good for him. But he didn't want it."

Perhaps the photograph of his mother sitting on the dresser reminded him of how she had had to cope with his heavy-drinking father.

As in most baseball families, with the father away much of the time, Mother was the disciplinarian, the one who washed Ruth's mouth out with brown laundry soap when Ruth sassed the help. "I had overheard someone say hell, and that night when we were told to go to bed, I said, 'The hell we will.' When she heard about it, Mother did the soap bit and made me stay in my room for the day." Mack impressed on his children that they had a wonderful mother who was always to be obeyed. He knew there were times when they didn't get along with their mother. He would stay out of it, telling them, "I wish I could do something about it, but I can't."

But that didn't mean he ducked all the child-rearing duties. His style was different. Connie Mack never yelled at anybody, anywhere. When he raised his voice in anger, it went from soft to sharp, not loud. They never heard him swear or saw him lose his temper. (Family members were shocked and disbelieving when, years later, anyone tried to tell them, "You should have heard him in the dugout sometimes.")

Connie Jr. could remember only one time his father hit him: "I was about ten. I was sprawled out on the living room floor one evening with some papers strewn around. He told me to pick them up. I didn't pick them up. He gave me a slap and sent me up to bed. Later he came up and told me, 'You'd better mind me.' I always did after that."

With the girls, whom he addressed as "Girlie," when he had a point to make or a lesson to impart, he talked the same way he would talk to a player who had made a mental error in a game.

Ruth said, "I was so unaccustomed to Dad's even looking cross about anything that I was crushed on the three occasions when he blew up over something I did, and all he said was 'Why did you do this?' or 'Why didn't you do that?'

"One of those times occurred when I was married and had driven him to a game. There was a big crowd that day, and he wanted the car brought around to a certain gate to wait for us after the game. He sent a man to where I was sitting to get the car keys. The man asked me for my license plate number, and I said I didn't know it. I told him what the car looked like.

"Later, in the car, Dad told me, 'Girlie, don't tell me you didn't know your license plate number.' I said, 'No, I didn't.' And he said, 'Well, you should have.' And I felt very chastised."

Mack felt very strongly about cigarettes and urged all his children to avoid them, sometimes granting something they wanted on the provision that they would quit. His players did their smoking out of his presence.

There was always live-in help in the house. The Macks had become acquainted with Maggie Page's cooking when they stayed at an Atlantic City hotel owned by their friends, John and Ellen Burke. When the Burkes gave up the hotel business, Connie Mack hired Maggie, a jolly, rotund exemplar of the Southern Mammy, "the only employee we ever had who made Mother happy," said Ruth. Connie Mack had a sweet tooth, and he would be disappointed if there wasn't something sweet to finish a meal. Blueberry pie was his favorite, but he was just as happy with the chocolate cake Maggie baked every weekend. The kids adored her. When their parents were out for the evening, Maggie and the girls would make fudge or pull taffy.

"She was part of the family," Ruth said. "Every once in a while we would give a play for Mother and Dad, and of course Maggie had to be the center of the play. We used the drapes between the parlor and living room for the curtain. Mother and Dad would sit in straight-backed chairs and listen to the show, and after it was over they very dutifully clapped for us."

A girl named Katie Logan, wearing a small, round hat and tight-waisted floor-length dress, did the housework, sometimes helped by a girl named Fudgie. But neither one satisfied Katherine, and they didn't last long.

About ten years later Maggie became mortally ill. The girls were at boarding school and were called home to say goodbye to her before Connie Mack granted her wish to go home to the South to die. She was replaced by a Miss Gearhart, who was so immense she had to turn sideways to get through the front vestibule. Then Annie Boykin arrived to take charge of the kitchen with her two daughters, Mamie and Biddie, who helped with the housework. They occupied the third floor bedrooms.

"I was in high school," Betty said. "Mamie was about two years older than I was and Biddie about four years older. Mamie and I were the best of friends. I used to lock her in the closet and do terrible things." In 1934 Annie's husband James moved in.

"James loved Dad," Ruth recalled. "He cooked, drove Betty to school, did all kinds of odd jobs."

"James was a little man," Betty said, "very quiet, very smart. He was there until the house was sold in 1941."

Mack was always protective of his girlies. While Roy was working for the American Thread Company and going with his future wife, Margaret Mayo, he lived with them. Ruth was about seven. "We used to play awful tricks on him," she said. "Once he was getting ready to go out, and to avoid us he stepped into a stall shower to hide. We knew where he was and turned on the shower. He ran after us and I slid under a bed, but my feet were sticking out. Roy was just about to grab them when Dad came up the stairs and said, 'What are you doing to that girl?' Roy told Dad what we had done. Dad told him to leave us alone."

Connie Mack was now a commuter. He could no longer walk to the office. During the season he went to Shibe Park every day they were at home, even on Sundays when there was no game. He hated driving. "I don't know why anybody needs an automobile," he would mutter. Later, when Mack was in his sixties, they bought Buicks from Davis Buick. The salesman, Tom Carroll, gave the Macks driving lessons. Mrs. Mack took to it, although every time she went up a hill, it was an adventure. She didn't give it enough gas or shift gears in time, and the car would stall. Mr. Mack tried it and soon gave it up. He was critical of other drivers; he had his own ideas of how a machine should be driven properly, ideas that seemed to differ with those of every other driver on the road. (He may have been right; in 1925 there would be 1,272 people killed by cars in New York City alone.) It made him nervous, and anybody else in the car too.

Perhaps his attitude stemmed from the day in 1910 when John Shibe had taken him and Harry Davis to the Fairmount Park Motor Race practices. Mack had watched with interest how the drivers took the sharp turns at high speed without crashing. Shibe introduced them to one of the drivers, Len Zengle, who invited Mack to take a spin with him. Spectators who recognized the Athletics' leader were astounded to see him whizzing around the track at eighty miles an hour.

When nobody was available to drive him, Connie Mack was happy to walk a hundred yards to the number 53 trolley stop on Wayne Avenue and change to the number 33, which took him to Twenty-second and Lehigh, a block from Shibe Park. Later, when the routes changed, he would change to the 21 line down Seventeenth Street to Lehigh and walk three blocks or change again to the number 54, which went past Shibe Park. The fare was fifteen cents for two tokens good for two rides. The journey took him about an hour, less if he used the Broad Street subway after it opened in 1928. Earle joined the team as a coach in 1924 and Roy moved into the front office in 1936; they sometimes came by for him. Ruth obtained a driving license at sixteen, and when she was home from school, she would take him in the morning, then return for the game. She sat behind the A's dugout and kept score the way her dad had taught her. The players and coaches knew her and waved to her. After the game she took him home.

"His demeanor was the same, win or lose," Ruth said of those postgame rides home. "He might comment on a good or poor pitching performance, maybe a mental mistake that had cost the A's the game, but never in anger or detail. One time I was upset because an error cost us the game. Dad said, 'Girlie, the players are human and they will make mistakes.' I always thought to myself how brave he was to be just himself whether they won or lost, and I know at times he had to have felt bad."

Eventually Mack hired a full-time chauffeur, Chuck Roberts.

Connie Mack's routine at home rarely varied. He was usually in bed by eleven and rose early. He slept soundly on his back, his arms at his sides, and awoke in the same position. Every morning at 6:45 he knocked on doors and roused the children. He ate a big breakfast: orange juice, oatmeal or cream of wheat, sometimes bacon and eggs and toast, and his one cup of coffee for the day. In later years he ate meat—liver, bacon, a chop—for breakfast every day. He read the morning newspapers thoroughly, without glasses. Mary learned to read at an earlier age than her siblings; Dad would put her on his lap and read the paper to her.

On Sunday mornings they all walked a half mile to St. Madeleine Sophie Church on Greene Street for nine o'clock Mass, the girls in hats and gloves. Both their parents walked with long, rapid strides. The kids had to hustle to keep up with them. Later, when the older ones were away at camp or school and Betty was the only one at home, she and her dad would walk to church. They were often invited by a passing motorist to hop in for a ride. Mack preferred to walk, but, as Betty recalled, "It could be a car or a truck, and we'd always get in. Dad did it just to be nice."

Sunday dinners were usually a rib roast or lamb or turkey. In summer they bought corn and vegetables from country farm stands. The good china came out: Limoges white plates with gold rims and gold and blue circles. The gatherings might include Dennis's widow and her girls, Hazel and Mary; Katherine's sisters: the heavyset Aunt Rose, twice-widowed Aunt Margaret (considered the beauty of the family), and spinster Aunt Nan, so quiet you barely knew she was there; Roy and Earle and Peggy McCambridge and their families; Connie Mack's brothers; cousins, nephews, nieces, and sometimes students from nearby boarding schools where Mack had given a talk and invited them to dinner; his coaches and their wives; out of town visitors: insurance man Parker Woods from St. Louis, banker Hyman Pearlstone from Texas, screenwriter Shannon Fife from upstate New York, and Philadelphia friends, the Jacoby and Hollinger and Lyons families. Woods's daughter Jean and George Jacoby were the Macks' best friends. Local Republican power Judge Harry McDevitt—known as "20 to 40 McDevitt" because that was his favorite sentence to hand down—might be found at the breakfast or dinner table or sitting on the porch chatting with Connie Mack.

Later, Sundays and holidays found the Macks at Ruth's or Connie Jr.'s house for dinner. Junior's wife, Sue, was never comfortable in her mother-in-law's presence, and she and Junior rarely went to the Cliveden Street house. Wherever they were, Katherine took charge. They would arrive at Ruth's about three, dine at five, and leave around eight. Connie Mack sat at the head of the table. Ruth's son Frank sat at his right. "He liked to salt his food," Frank recalled. "He would pick up the salt shaker by the bottom and flip it over and over so it flew all over his food and onto mine too. I got enough of the residue so that I wouldn't salt anything because I knew eventually it would get salted."

Many motion picture and show business people were avid baseball fans. Hughie Dougherty, a veteran minstrel and burlesque performer, was honored by the A's and Phillies as Philadelphia's number one baseball fan. When the Athletics trained in California, Mack attracted new, lasting friendships among the movie crowd. One family story, handed down with a moral by Betty to her children, involved a house guest in the 1930s she remembered as actor Robert Young. "He kept checking Hedda Hopper's newspaper column for a review of a film," she recalled. One day at breakfast the toast was burned.

"Mother said, 'Do you like your toast burned?'

"The guest, being polite, said, 'Oh, yes.'

"Mother was sure to serve him burnt toast for the next three days," Betty told her children. "The moral of the story is always say what you mean."

From waking to bedtime Connie Mack wore a suit and tie. Even when he visited his brother Tom's summer place on the lake in Paxton, near Worcester, he was always in suit and tie, never went near the water, never picked up a fishing pole, occasionally picked up a bat and swung as Tom tossed them in.

In the evenings Mack would read the afternoon papers. He enjoyed going to the theater and movies—action pictures were his favorites.

Sometimes in the evening Mack would walk to a drugstore on Wayne Avenue accompanied by one of his girls. "We usually went a certain way," Ruth recalled. "One evening when we started out on our jaunt, he said to me, 'Girlie, I'm not going to go that way tonight. We're going to take a different route. It's better that you don't form a habit, cause if you do, you may have trouble breaking it.' That has always stayed with me."

When Ruth was a teenager, he would take her to the movies on a Saturday night.

Connie Mack enjoyed being with his children and grandchildren, though when they were little, he didn't see much of them during the season. They were put to bed before he arrived home after a game so they wouldn't disturb him.

In the 1920s Ruth, Rita, and Betty went to camps in the Poconos or Adirondacks. Other years he rented a house for them on the Jersey shore for two or three months, or they stayed at the Flanders Hotel in Ocean City.

On winter evenings Mack enjoyed entertaining the children with stories of Rube Waddell's escapades and how many glasses of ginger ale he'd consumed going from bar to bar looking for the wayward Rube. No matter how many times they heard it, the girls always giggled; picturing their tall, dignified, white-haired father in his stiff collar making the rounds of saloons tickled their imagination.

Mack told yarns about the hazing rookies would take in the old days, how they'd be talked into sleeping on trains with an arm in the little hammock beside the berth, and other pranks. He talked about his mother, whose photograph sat on his bureau, but never about his father or his first wife. In that respect Connie Mack fit the perceived penchant of the Irish to avoid mention of unpleasant family skeletons or emotional situations.

The children went to Catholic day schools at first. Later, with their parents away at the World Series every fall, then traveling to California or heading for Florida in January, it became difficult to find someone to look after five children and a big house—anyone who could please Katherine, anyhow. They went to boarding schools in the area: Sacred Heart, Cecilian, Chestnut Hill (now Millrose), Mt. St. Joseph's. Mary and Ruth were tall, built like their dad, and played basketball on school teams. Connie Jr. went to Germantown Academy, where he pitched and played football and basketball.

Although the family's legal name remained McGillicuddy, the children never thought of themselves as anything but Mack. When Ruth started school and the teacher called her Ruth McGillicuddy, Ruth hotly denied that was her name. Not until her mother assured her that it was true did she believe it.

At the start of Betty's freshman year at Cecilian Academy, the teacher, Sr. Jane Frances, asked all the new students to write their last names and bring them to her desk.

"She said, 'I want your real last name,' Betty recalled. "I didn't know what to do. I was always Betty Mack. So I raised my hand and asked, 'Sister Jane Frances, how do you spell McGillicuddy?' The class roared with laughter, and she was ready to get out the ruler and let me have it. She thought I was pulling her leg. I think I just wrote down Mack anyhow."

Connie Mack's office was on the third floor of the Shibe Park tower. His high-backed black chair sat behind a massive oak desk facing the windows. His back was to the door. A ball made of a lump of coal was one of the few coal-based gifts Mack kept on his desk. He received many such items, like a checkerboard made of coal from fans in Slatington. Among the porcelain white elephants on his desk was one of white jade brought to him by one of his closest friends, Dr. James H. Penniman, from the Orient. At this time the walls were covered with action photos of his past and present stars. There was a bench made entirely of bats that had been given to Mack by a Pennsylvania group. To his left was a small alcove with a couch for a quick nap before a game. To the right another door opened to a small office used by Earle. There were no nameplates on any of the doors. Until an elevator was installed in 1938, the only way to reach Mack's office was by climbing two flights of stairs or crossing a catwalk extending from the upper deck. Miss Lally, who took dictation and sometimes signed letters for Mack, was on the second floor, where John Shibe had his office.

As long as Connie Mack managed the Athletics, any of his children could walk into his office at any time, even when he was with someone, and never be made to feel they were intruding or out of place. One day during World War II, Ruth went up to give him a message from Katherine. "I knocked on the door and he said, 'Come in.' I saw he had company and started to back out, saying, 'I'll be back later.' But he told me to come in. 'I'm never too busy for one of my girlies.'

"His company happened to be Jack Dempsey in a navy uniform."

The myths of Connie Mack's skinflint reputation bear no resemblance to the Connie Mack his friends and family knew. He was the patriarch and benefactor of a large family: brothers (all of whom he outlived), his brothers' widows and their families, children, grandchildren, nephews, nieces, cousins, in-laws. Until the end of his life he corresponded with them, remained solicitous of their welfare, supported those who needed it, found them jobs, invited them to come and see him. And nonfamily too. After Mass on Sundays or on the way to the ballpark Ruth would drive him around the neighborhood of Shibe Park. "Stop here," he would say, get out, and go up the steps to a front door.

"A lady would appear and Dad would give her an envelope," Ruth said. "Then we'd go to another address, and he'd do the same. He'd tell me they needed coal or food or the rent or whatever."

He preferred his charity to be quiet, personal, rather than ostentatious donations to organizations. He also had an envelope for each of the park guards in Fairmount Park for Christmas.

"It's better to deal with an individual when you want to give money to help," he said.

No old-time ballplayer down on his luck ever went away from Mack's office empty-handed. Checks went out regularly for old-timers' benefits, testimonials, memorials, and funerals; homes for nurses, orphans, and the aged; and campaigns to save this or that. In that regard and in supporting extensive families and sending nephews and nieces to college or business school and helping them find employment, he and his oldest baseball friend, Clark Griffith, were alike. Today, under the patchwork tent of conventional wisdom, they share an ill-fitting reputation for tightness. But it was never so for either of them.

In a 1930 *American Magazine* profile, writer William S. Dutton described "old Connie's private payroll":

There are old ballplayers on this payroll, men who have been "up there" and have gone down through misfortune or mistake. Widows are on it. Report says that it has sent boys back to school from the streets.

What the names are on this "payroll" nobody but Mack knows, and he does not choose to say. Never has he even admitted that it exists. How much he has paid out is also his secret, though I have heard guesses that run into six figures.

A week never goes by without its quota of boys in the right-field grandstand of Shibe Park. They come from schools, from hospitals, from orphans' homes, from the Boy Scouts and other organizations. It always has been so under Mack's management.

One of his retainers on the payroll was Nelly Franklin, a holdover from the days when Mack had employed him for his valiant but too often vain attempts to shepherd the wandering Rube Waddell. After Waddell was gone, Mack kept Franklin, described years later by *New York Evening Journal* columnist Ford C. Frick as "old and bent and worn," to guard the press box and do related chores.

When his former players managed in the minor leagues and needed uniforms or practice balls, Mack sent them. He sent balls and other equipment to schools, Indian reservations, prisons, military bases, and youth and semi-pro leagues. He took his team to play exhibition games for charities, church fundraisers, player benefits, and financially strapped minor league clubs, charging nothing but his traveling expenses and taking none of the receipts.

Mack was always comfortable with youngsters, his own or visitors. He teased the little ones by locking them between his long extended legs as he sat in an easy chair and urged them to try to get out. Or he would put them on his knee and bounce them gently. He asked the older ones about their schoolwork.

Ruth's son Frank Cunningham said:

He treated every little kid he met like a grandson. My cousin Connie had a friend who was about twelve, but he was little and looked about six. One day grandfather was there and Connie introduced his friend to him, and Pop-Pop picked up the kid and put him on his lap and the kid was embarrassed, but he did look about six. Kids knew who Pop-Pop was, but they were very comfortable around him. There was a lot of energy, not only physical. Sometimes that energy could reflect itself even if he was sitting there calmly. His presence was serene, but his eyes sparkled; there was an aliveness in his countenance. He never got engrossed in small problems that some people make a big deal out of.

Baseball fans who picture Connie Mack as a staid, humorless old man dipped in starch would be astounded by this scene described by Ruth: "One day, when my oldest children were about five and six, Mother and Dad were at our house for Sunday dinner. Mother was in the kitchen, and I was in the living room with Dad and the kids. There was music playing on the radio. Dad pulled aside a throw rug and began tap dancing. The kids were laughing. He was about eighty at the time."

Well into his eighties Mack still put on a glove and joined his grandchildren in tossing a ball around in the yard, playing "stealing bases" or "pickle" before Sunday dinner.

"In the side yard we had two bases," recalled Frank Cunningham. "One player was on first base and Pop-Pop was at second, and the player would try to steal second base. Pop-Pop was okay. He could handle it. He wore a glove and could throw."

Connie Mack was close to seventy when his daughters were teenagers, but they never saw him as an old man. "He was always so young in spirit," said Ruth. "I think it was his players, his teams, that kept him that way."

And they never thought of him as a celebrity. Shibe Park was where he worked; away from it he was just Dad or Granddad or Pop-Pop to them.

Betty said, "When we went out to dinner, he was constantly approached for a handshake or autograph. After he was gone, I had people say to me, 'Do you realize what a wonderful man your father was?' A friend told me, 'I had an uncle who absolutely worshiped the ground that man walked on.' But I had no real idea of his fame when I was growing up."

6 | A DIFFERENT KIND OF WAR

When Connie Mack had vowed that come one more war, he would quit baseball, the only Kaiser Wilhelm he knew anything about was a pitcher for the Baltimore Federal League club. Now, as 1917 dawned, that name had become connected with a different kind of war, one that made news on the front pages, not the sports pages. Other unfamiliar words also entered the public vocabulary: conscription, inflation, diplomatic relations.

In addition to the usual smorgasbord of rumors—the A's would move to Brooklyn; Connie Mack would buy and manage the Red Sox, whose owner was looking to sell—some old words still dominated the off-season sporting sections: money and strike. Players talked about striking if salaries were cut and other demands weren't met: continued salaries for injured players, travel expenses from home to spring training. Most clubs already provided those things. But Christy Mathewson, now managing the Cincinnati Reds, said the situation was more serious than the magnates believed. Dave Fultz, president of the Players Fraternity, talked about calling mass meetings of fans to back the players. Considering baseball as an amusement, the White Rats—the vaudeville unit of the American Federation of Labor—invited the players to join their union. Fultz took them up on it, applying to AFL president Samuel Gompers for a charter.

In the league meeting on February 15, 1917, a motion by Tom Shibe that all relations with the Players Fraternity be terminated in view of its frequent violation of the letter and spirit of the January 6, 1914, agreement was carried unanimously. Ban Johnson called Fultz's group "a conspiracy hatched to throttle the business of club owners. Experience has taught us there is no cohesion in a society of ball players. They are too greatly diversified."

He was right—for a long time.

Connie Mack's take on all this?

"It would cause quite a lot of trouble if the players refused to sign their contracts, though really I cannot see what they're complaining about. Ball players are getting mighty good salaries, it seems to me. [Veteran players earned about $4,000 a season, more than double what the average private industry clerical job paid for twelve months' work.] The minor leagues have made little or no money for two years. Minor league clubs would not care much if they had to keep their parks closed this summer. As for the big leagues, I guess they would worry along somehow."

In November 1916 Oscar C. Reichow of the *Chicago Daily News* had reflected on the lingering effects of the Federal League war:

Ball players were spoiled by the Federal League. They were offered such enormous salaries and bonuses that they lost sight of the game itself, and thought only of the big stipends. Conversation on the ball field, instead of concerning the contest itself, was on money, automobiles, or farms. The players had their minds elsewhere instead of on the battle. As a result the game lost its punch and the interests that made it the finest of all sports.

The time has come . . . when the players will have to think of their work on the field. Magnates are again in power. They have not been getting what has been due them, although they have paid tremendously for it. They have their money invested and have not been getting the expected returns. Now they will reform the sport and put it back on the old basis. Big salaries will not be paid anymore. There will be much slicing done this year.

"Players have squeezed the magnates almost to death," wrote Joe Vila in New York. "They have been pampered . . . and incurred heavy losses for their employers."

Among the Athletics, Joe Bush, Wally Schang, and Amos Strunk were reported to be uniting in their quest for raises. Strunk was the most voluble. At first he said he'd be satisfied with a $500 raise to $3,500. Mack said okay. Then Strunk decided that wasn't enough; he'd hold out for $5,000 or quit and go into business while playing for Upland on weekends à la Frank Baker.

"There are fifteen major league clubs willing to pay me $5,000 a year," Amos told reporters. "If Connie Mack won't do it, I don't see why he shouldn't trade me."

Strunk's estimate of the demand for his services was off by fifteen clubs.

Mack was unperturbed by it all. If any of his players chose not to sign, he'd get along without them. In the end, they all signed. Mack gave Strunk a $1,000 raise, to $4,000. Schang signed for the same amount. Bush settled for a $200 bonus instead of a raise.

To the guy in the bleachers, life in the big leagues was a dream he would give anything to enjoy. For many a country kid who made it to the majors it was a life beyond his imagination: showers (however weak and tepid) in the clubhouses (however small and cramped); sleeping in comfortable beds between clean sheets in high-class hotels; eating all the steak and potatoes they wanted (a steak dinner in New York went for seventy-five cents) or more exotic edibles they'd never seen before, like Boston's lobsters and clam chowder. Men bought them drinks. Good-looking women gazed awestruck at them, craving a wink or a nod or a date.

Connie Mack knew his ballplayers. He knew that some of them would eat or drink or wench themselves back to the farm or mine or factory. He knew he couldn't stop them, just try to temper their behavior and see that the older players didn't take the younger ones with them. "If you can't find what you're looking for by eleven o'clock," he'd say, "forget it and go to sleep." Or "You wouldn't bring a slut into your home, would you? Your hotel room is your home on the road. Keep it clean." He had no fines unless they fell so far out of condition they couldn't do their jobs.

The public was more concerned with prices and peace. People in every walk of life were learning about inflation. There hadn't been any such thing since the Civil War. Prices until now had generally been lower than fifty years earlier, when Connie Mack was four years old. When the government announced that the cost of living had jumped 7.6 percent in 1916, it only confirmed what housewives were finding in the stores. Prices of bread, milk, and coal continued to rise in January 1917. Bread went from five cents to six; by summer it would be ten cents a loaf. Milk at fourteen cents a quart drew a headline in the *New York Times*. Beer was a nickel a bucket.

Pressure to lift wages, which had also remained stable for a half century, was both a cause and effect of the rising prices. By 1918 Henry Ford would raise the bar; his assembly line workers could earn $1,800 a year, the highest factory wage in the nation. At the same time teachers' salaries soared 16 percent in three years to an average of $630.64. Coal miners won raises of 19–39 percent. The highest-paid were up to two dollars a day for a six-day week—$600 a year. The pay of breaker boys, slate pickers, water boys, and jig runners went from $1 to $1.30 a day. Within a few months the price of coal would double to ten dollars a ton.

The A. J. Reach Company tried to calm worried club owners by announcing that the price of baseballs would remain at $1.25. They were making their own yarn; horsehide supplies on hand were enough for the year. The price of cork imported from Spain and Portugal had not gone up. Foul balls hit into the seats were still considered club property, and park police wrestled with the customers to retrieve them.

Connie Mack held the line on ticket prices at Shibe Park and didn't reduce the number of twenty-five-cent bleacher seats.

Saloons selling hard liquor were gradually disappearing from ballparks. But beer was still widely sold, along with a variety of items: hot dogs, peanuts, sandwiches, pies, cheese, tripe, candy, planked onions, ice cream, and chewing tobacco.

Until now the war in Europe had been "their problem" over there. Most of the time, a glance at the front page headlines with the strange-sounding names of faraway cities and forests and battlegrounds only briefly detained baseball fans from turning to the box scores. The United States was officially neutral, but American lives had been lost at sea when German U-boats had sunk the British luxury liner *Lusitania* on May 7, 1915. In April 1916 the Germans had promised that passenger ships would no longer be attacked and due warning would be issued to all cargo vessels, armed or not, that offered no resistance. Before a ship was sunk, crew members would be given a chance to cast off in open boats that would not be fired upon.

That all changed on February 1, 1917. The United States broke off diplomatic relations when Germany served notice that its submarines would sink any vessel, freight or passenger, without warning, that was headed for the ports of Western Europe. "Armed neutrality," President Wilson told the Congress, "it seems, is impracticable."

But Wilson remained reluctant to get the United States into the European war, still hoping to mediate a peace between England and Germany. Maybe the Germans wouldn't carry through on their threat. Even as more ships with Americans aboard were sunk, most of the nation backed him. Freedom of the seas was a vague concept to the millions of farmers and small-town residents far removed from the coasts.

Then, on March 1, the American people learned that Germany had secretly proposed a military alliance with Japan and Mexico, offering to help the Mexicans take back Texas, New Mexico, and Arizona. That brought the war to their backyard and Americans were now fighting mad.

War sentiment swept the country like a tidal wave. A huge throng gathered in Philadelphia's Independence Square on Saturday, March 31. The next night a U-boat sank the *Aztec*, the first gun-bearing ship sailing under the American flag to be lost.

Woodrow Wilson had run out of time. Reluctantly he went before Congress and asked for a declaration of war. On April 4 the Senate declared war on Germany. The next day the House did the same. Mothers who had been singing "I Didn't Raise My Boy to Be a Soldier" would soon change their tune to "Over There." Men left their jobs and went to work in shipyards and were not called slackers—not yet. Nobody but radicals and Reds protested when Congress passed a law making it a crime to speak out against the war or criticize the government.

Registration day for the draft was set for May 31. Every man registering would be given a number. Single men between nineteen and twenty-five would be called first.

This gave Ring Lardner the inspiration for his preseason doping of the A's in the pennant race: "When conscription comes, it will most affect the Athletics, a club made up to a great extent of young unmarried men. Should all Connie Mack's youngsters be called away for military training, the team would be vastly improved, and even the loss of half the regulars should make the Philadelphia outfit strong enough to run away with the title. It is worth calling to the attention of the Philadelphia fans that even though the Mackmen failed to cop last year, they were far and away the most consistent club in the league."

There was talk of a moratorium on baseball. Nobody knew how many players would be marching off to war. The minor leagues were sure to be hit the hardest. Attendance was bound to drop, how much nobody could guess. Barney Dreyfuss said he was willing to shut down for the year. "Our club has not made any money for three years. We would not have all the expenses and we get enough outside income to take care of the interest on our investment."

Rumors of shortages of food and fuel sent prices soaring. Congress declared war taxes on postage, sugar, tea, coffee, ice—and baseball tickets. Ban Johnson declared that a 10 percent admission tax, if borne by the clubs, would cost them $250,000. They might as well shut down.

But they didn't. And nobody in Washington asked them to shut down. They would, as Connie Mack said, "worry along somehow."

Business was anything but normal, although in the baseball business, it seemed as though chaos had become the norm. If they were going to play out the season, then Connie Mack had to conduct business as usually as possible. He began by paring Rube Bressler and Tom Sheehan from the payroll, sending them to Atlanta, no strings attached. Mack was especially disappointed in Bressler, who, he said, had a world of stuff but never took his job seriously enough.

Mack had turned down the overtures of a group of businessmen in Natchez, Mississippi, to train there. Spring games never drew much of a crowd in Florida, but the city of Jacksonville had built a new field for the A's, the weather was good, and there were plenty of other clubs for tuneup games. For the first time since 1909, Ira Thomas was not in camp. He had signed a five-year deal at $5,000 a year to coach the Williams College nine and would do some scouting when school was out. To replace Thomas as pitching coach, Mack hired Pat Flaherty, a forty-year-old onetime 20-game-winning southpaw, primarily to teach the young pitchers how to field their position and hold runners on base.

Another familiar face missing from the big league scene was Nap Lajoie. After the 1916 season Mack had told him he was free to go wherever it suited him. Lajoie chose to become manager and part owner of the Toronto club.

There was one unexpected newcomer at the camp. The military spirit was in the air. Soldiers put on drill demonstrations at exhibition games. The army gave a plum assignment to fifteen drill sergeants (the Phillies did not participate). One was assigned to each major league club for the entire season to lead the players in pregame drills. Sergeant W. E. Smart arrived in Jacksonville in the middle of March and took charge of the Athletics' maneuvers. Charles Comiskey outfitted his men in army uniforms for the daily exercises. Ban Johnson and John Tener urged all clubs to include one hour of drill a day, using bats for rifles. The American League put up a $500 prize for the smartest-looking drill team. The St. Louis Browns won. The A's finished last.

Clark Griffith launched a bat and ball fund to provide baseball equipment to every military camp at home and overseas. Collections were taken up at games; one day in June, 25 percent of the receipts of every game went into the fund. (The first shipment to France was sunk by a German U-boat.)

The Athletics' outfield lined up with Bodie, Strunk, and the rookie Frank Thrasher. Mack knew Thrasher was only a fair fielder; some unkind pundits called him "miserable" in the field. But Mack believed he "will be a star because he can hit so well."

Stuffy McInnis, who became more of a magician around first base as the rest of the infield became more scatter-armed, was a fixture. Second base was up for grabs between Otis Lawry, who was doing "everything that Eddie Collins could do" in Jacksonville, and Roy Grover, once described by Ira Thomas as "a bundle of electricity." Whitey Witt was the shortstop. Ray Bates, said Mack, was "my best third baseman since Baker."

Mack intended to keep Wally Schang behind the plate, sharing the load with Bill Meyer, who was Joe Bush's personal catcher.

Mack's fortunes were, as always, at the mercy of his pitchers. "If I had the Yankees' pitching," he said, "I might be able to talk about winning the American League pennant this year." He predicted that the A's would score more runs and win more games than last year. They might even lead the league in hitting, maybe hit .275 as a team, not counting the pitchers. "We'll be a tough club to beat, with Bush or Myers hurling," Mack told a St. Louis visitor.

Beyond Bush and Myers, the pitching staff was an unknown. In Florida Mack devoted most of his time to working with the young ones, learning them while teaching them.

"He took an interest in each one of us," recalled Lefty Anderson. "The first thing he did with me was change my landing. I wasn't coming down with my front foot in front of me, but off to the side, and he corrected it."

Veterans never gave rookies a rough time in an Athletics training camp. They were more likely to take a hand in the teaching. Anderson remembered Joe Bush teaching him how to throw a better curve.

Mack was impressed with Wynn Noyes, Harry Seibold, and Jing Johnson, dubious about Rube Schauer, and concerned about having only one left-hander. He would take fifteen pitchers home and see who could do the job.

(It's a good thing some of Mack's players had shed their original names. Over the years he had problems, though they've been exaggerated, with some tongue twisters. He would have tripped over Francesco Pezzelo—Ping Bodie was easier. Witt fit better on the lineup card than Wittkowski. And Rube Schauer might have never gotten into a game if Mack had to tell Dimitri Dimitrihoff to warm up.)

As for the ancient "boy wonder," Jack Nabors, Mack wrote him off. "I am not counting on him." Still Mack hedged, "Jack may come back suddenly and prove a star. In fact I look for him to come through as he has every attribute." Whatever he thought of Nabors's prospects, Mack rarely bad-mouthed a player he might shed and would never undercut a man's confidence.

Why, then, did Mack give up so early on a big, strong, supposedly twenty-one-year-old who had worked more than 200 innings for him and been no less effective than Elmer Myers?

My guess is that Mack either suspected or learned that Nabors was a heavy shaver of both whiskers and years and was closer to thirty than twenty. Photos of Nabors at the time don't show him looking like the flower of youth.

Connie Mack was a shrewd, perceptive judge of players as people, not just athletes. When he made a mistake, it was usually one of expecting more from players than they ultimately produced or failing to tame a known bad actor as well as he had hoped he could. Mack never completely conquered the hot temper of his youth. When the temperature rose under his stiff collar, he could sound off with biting sarcasm on the bench. And when he was really teed off by a player's conduct or attitude, his legendary patience would pop, and he would air his irritation to the press. As much as he despised players carrying contract negotiations to the newspapers, nothing stopped him from blasting a player publicly when he was really riled, nor praising the same fellow with equal fervor after his cannon had cooled.

Such an incident occurred on the way north from Jacksonville. Amos Strunk had been one of Mack's original kiddie corps, making his debut with the A's in 1908 at the age of eighteen. Throughout the championship years he had been a dependable center fielder. During the last-place years he had never stopped hustling. Strunk was in good shape in Jacksonville but apparently picked up a bug of some kind that upset his stomach just before they headed north. He told the trainer and some of the players that he was not well. It is unfathomable by today's standards, when trainers routinely report players' physical complaints to managers, that nobody told Mack of Strunk's illness.

Some days Strunk felt well enough to play his usual stellar game. Other days he appeared indifferent, sulking on the field. In Atlanta he failed to run out a few ground balls, which was in no way typical of Amos Strunk. Off the field he acted as though he was trying to avoid Connie Mack. When they arrived in Charlotte to play Earle Mack's team, Strunk sat in the hotel and didn't go to the ballpark at all.

Connie Mack took it as the behavior of a player unhappy over his salary, even though Mack had given him more than his original demands.

Why didn't Mack call Strunk to his room and ask him what was bothering him? Or did he? A few days later, after learning that Strunk was ill, Mack said, "I went out of my way to find out what was wrong, but he never offered any explanation. Therefore I concluded that he was loafing and naturally would not stand for it." Either Mack didn't go out of his way enough to ask the trainer, or Strunk had asked that his condition be kept a secret, which is possible, given the attitude in those days of veteran players afraid of losing their jobs if they were too sick to play.

At any rate, after the game in Charlotte Mack told Rudy Ohl to give Strunk a railroad ticket and send him home. When Amos said goodbye to some of the players, they thought he was being sent home to see a doctor. The team went on to Rocky Mount, where the writers asked Mack why Strunk was missing. Mack's reply, wrote the *Inquirer*'s "war correspondent," came like "a bolt from a clear sky":

> You can just state that I am through with this player until he explains the cause of his actions against me. I cannot understand why he acted so indifferently toward me by not speaking to me for the last ten days. His actions have been noticeable for the past two weeks and if they were caused by illness, I fail to see why he did not make it known instead of making us look ridiculous at times on the ball field. He was one of the first to get into first-class physical condition in Jacksonville. We will have no disgruntled stars on our team, and if any players are dissatisfied they can go at once. In conclusion I will say that this man will not play another game for me until he reasonably adjusts matters.

Even if Mack's words were not transcribed verbatim, their gist conveyed Mack's suspicion that he had a dissatisfied player, not a sick one, on his hands. He might also have been embarrassed at being the last to learn that the player was ill. But his attitude was consistent with his determination to keep his team free of the infection of soldiering or disgruntled influences, no matter how long or distinguished a player's past service.

The Athletics arrived home in a snowstorm on April 8 and spent the next two days burning oil, spreading sawdust, and mopping up to get ready for the opener. The first chance he had, Mack went out of his way to repair the impressions he had made in his Rocky Mount outburst.

"I want to say I expect to have Strunk in the game and I look for him to play wonderful ball. This is one season that Strunk must show what is in him because my team is coming."

Strunk, now twenty-seven, had batted .297 and .316 for the two last-place finishers. Mack was referring to his attitude, not his ability.

"I can't have a man around who is not willing to hustle," Mack went on, "and Strunk knows this. I sent him home because I did not think he was hustling. I did not know he was sick until after I had sent him home. That was his own fault. . . . It's probably just a misunderstanding and I don't expect to have any trouble with Amos. He is a splendid boy and has been with me long enough to know that I must have discipline. There is no cause for worry as far as Strunk is concerned. He will play great ball this year."

Somewhere along the line, probably after reading this in the *Inquirer*, Strunk apologized to Mack and was in center field on opening day. With Ping Bodie dropping fly balls in each of the first two games and slow-footed Frank Thrasher in right, it quickly became obvious that Strunk would be covering most of the outer real estate in all directions.

Mack gave Otis Lawry the first shot at replacing Lajoie at second base. The rabbit from Maine quickly demonstrated the eternal adage that starring in the minor leagues and scintillating in spring training ain't the same as playing in the big leagues when it counts. All managers live with the knowledge that projections are just that—nothing more—as ephemeral as slides projected onto clouds. No law of nature, no principle of logic, says a .330 minor league hitter will be a .330 major league hitter.

On a cold opening day the A's ran into Walter Johnson at his best. Before an enthusiastic Shibe Park turnout of twelve thousand—double the 1916 opener's crowd—Johnson struck out 11 and shut the A's out with 3 hits. Johnson so overpowered Lawry that two weeks later Mack said, "Down south Lawry made me believe he was another Eddie Collins. But after facing Walter Johnson in the opener he went all to pieces." The twenty-three-year-old Lawry batted .164 in 55 at bats, his last in the big leagues. The only way he surpassed Eddie Collins was by outliving him.

The A's woke up in the third game and banged out 20 hits in a 16–4 rout of Washington. Ray Bates drove in 5 runs in one inning with a double and triple, and Connie Mack felt confident that he had filled the third base chasm at last. Then they outhit the Red Sox in 4 games but won only 1 of them, on a twelfth-inning home run by Ping Bodie, whose slugging and colorful swagger had made him an immediate Shibe Park favorite, despite his limited range in the outfield. Connie Mack made as much effort to boost Bodie's confidence as he would with a raw rookie. If Ping struck out on three vicious swings with the bases loaded, Mack would chirp, "It did me good to see you swing, Ping." But Bodie didn't really need any ego boosting. When anyone joshed him about his fielding, he would say, "If you folks don't want me here I will go back to that old Coast League. I am the Ty Cobb of that bunch."

A week later Frank Thrasher failed to duck out of the way of a Carl Mays sidearm fastball. The beaning made him gun-shy at the plate. He began bailing out and drove in only 2 runs in 23 games. The disheartened Mack had to send his prized hitter back to Atlanta. Thrasher, too, had played his last major league game.

The wartime atmosphere was on full display when the A's opened Washington's home season on April 20. Assistant Secretary of the Navy Franklin Roosevelt marched to center field and raised the flag. British and French flags flew, the Senators put on a snappy exhibition of military drill, and Vice-President Marshall threw out the first ball.

Outside of the pitching, Connie Mack liked what he saw. Athletics fans did too. Attendance for the first seven home dates was up 11 percent over the same time last year.

Sizing up his team, Mack said, "I have discovered that I have a better team than I had figured at the start of the campaign. Now I am sure the entire outfit will come along very fast. . . . We're going through a constructive season and I am convinced it's going to be exactly that. . . . I have watched the team very carefully in action and I am convinced that we have plenty of baseball brains."

National baseball writer Hugh Fullerton was impressed with Mack's improvements, predicting the A's would win 20 more games than last year.

The Yankees' beat writer for the *Evening Journal* commented that both the fans and other club owners had "renewed faith in Mack."

After sweeping a pair in New York, the A's were 6-7. But they were never that close to .500 again, losing 11 of the next 12 before splitting 4 in Cleveland and taking 2 of 3 in Detroit, giving them more victories in the west than they had had all of last year.

They were playing hard, spraying line drives to all fields, pulling squeeze plays, running the bases aggressively. Mack urged them to try to score from first on a hit and run if the ball was dumped into the outfield. They succeeded more than once.

Mack was right about one thing: they were hitting. They just didn't do much of it when Joe Bush was on the mound. In his first 9 starts they scored a total of 13 runs. And they didn't do enough of it with men on base. They were second in batting but sixth in runs scored. Led by McInnis, Strunk, Bates, and Bodie, they were first or second in the league all season, finishing at .254 in another pitchers' year. There were six no-hitters in April and May—two in one game.

The widespread use of the shine ball, in place of the banished emery ball, was partly responsible. Applying a shiny dark spot to the ball made it harder to follow out of the pitcher's hand. Pitchers who didn't use it encouraged stories that they did. Making batters think you threw it was just as effective as the doctoring itself.

Eddie Cicotte rode the shine ball to a 28-12 season. The A's were 2-4 against him, about as well as anybody did that year. Connie Mack, who favored outlawing all trick deliveries, exhorted his hitters to ignore the pitch's ballyhoo. "Shine ball or no shine ball," he told them, "go up there with the intention of hitting the ball, not seeking an alibi for your failure."

In the ongoing debate over how to boost offense, National League president John Tener offered several suggestions: a walk on ball 3, move the pitcher back, abolish the foul strike, put more rubber in the ball.

That last suggestion brought this reaction from one infielder: "I remember that lively ball and I don't want to see any more of it. You could knock a man down with an ordinary drive. Put more rubber in the ball and your infielders cease to be players and become heroes."

Cap Anson said, "Cut out the fielders' gloves. Those huge pillows they wear cut down many a drive that would have been a hit in the old days. I played first base for twenty years and never wore a glove and I don't see why they're necessary now except for catchers."

But if hitting had fallen off, it wasn't due to Mack's crop of young pitchers. Elmer Myers looked nothing like the budding star of 1916. He cut down his walks, but his strikes were eminently hittable. He would be Mack's biggest disappointment, suffering the league's highest ERA: 4.42. Noyes had some good outings, but Jing Johnson wasn't getting the job done. And Harry Seibold pitched better in the wine and women league. On April 16 Jack Barry came back for the first time as manager of the Red Sox, who drove Seibold out in the third inning. Whitey Witt recalled that when Connie Mack yanked him, Seibold stormed in and threw his glove against the back of the dugout. "Mr. Mack says to him, 'Keep on going and don't come back.'" Seibold didn't start again for almost eight weeks.

Connie Mack's goals for 1917 had undergone some shrinkage in the two years since he had predicted another winner by that time. He was now aiming for sixth place and a .400 winning percentage. But to achieve even that much and to show his customers that he was doing all he could to improve his product, he had to find some consistent pitching—fast. What he did astonished his customers and fellow magnates even more than the purchase of

Ping Bodie. He sent Jack Nabors and $5,000 to Indianapolis for a thirty-six-year-old retread, Fred "Cy" Falkenberg. This was the 6-foot-5 right-hander's third trip to the major leagues. Washington had given up on him and sold him to Cleveland. He had been up and down with a sore arm that had been given the last rites. But armed with an emery ball and fadeaway, he had come back to win 23 for Cleveland in 1913 before jumping to the Federal League, where he won 25 for Indianapolis. His arm was healthy enough to work almost 600 innings in two years. Falkenberg had been one of the surplus Federal League pitchers offered for sale when the Feds folded. Mack and everybody else had turned him down. He signed with Indianapolis in the American Association, won 19 games, pitched 291 innings, and had a 1.83 ERA. So he was hardly the broken-down, sore-armed pitcher some look-back critics label him in assessing Connie Mack's transactions.

Mack and Harry Davis had watched Falkenberg pitch a 3–1 win over the A's in Albany, Georgia, on the way home in the spring. They had been trying to obtain him ever since, but Indianapolis held out for a player as well as cash. Mack finally sent them Nabors with no strings. (The *Indianapolis News* said Falkenberg was nearly thirty-nine and Nabors "only twenty-two" at the time.)

The deal surprised Falkenberg as much as it did the followers of the Athletics who thought they knew Connie Mack's thinking. "I never had an idea for a minute I'd be back in the majors," Falkenberg said, "and never figured for a minute it would be with Mack, for Connie generally passes us old birds up." While Falkenberg had once relied on a variety of spitters, emery balls, and other trick deliveries, he was now depending on brains and control. "It's an old saying among ballplayers that a pitcher never knows how to pitch until he begins to lose a lot of his natural ability," he said, "and I guess it holds good in my case."

Connie Mack was holding court in the lobby of the Copley Plaza in Boston when Falkenberg reported on a rain-soaked May 2. Writers looking for rainy-day copy were told by Mack, "I want the Philadelphia fans to know I have secured Falkenberg merely to round out my staff. I shall still continue my campaign to develop young pitchers. Falk is a seasoned veteran, and in good shape, and will step in and keep the boat from rocking."

Translation: I need somebody who knows how to pitch and can throw strikes and win some games until some of these young fellows start showing me something.

But Falk turned out to be what was commonly called a "flivver." He lost his first start, 9–4, in New York, though 6 errors didn't help. The only team he could beat was Cleveland, twice. He lost 5 more starts and 1 in relief, and by July he was back in Indianapolis.

A week later, sitting in the grandstand in St. Louis before a game, Mack told the *Inquirer's* correspondent, "The collapse of Fred Falkenberg was a sore disappointment to me. If he had come through as I expected, I am positive I would have made the first division before another September."

Connie Mack's capacity for absorbing disappointments seemed limitless. If he could only find two more dependable pitchers. Mack looked at his bench. Maybe the answer was Rube Schauer, who had started only 11 of the 60 games he appeared in for the Giants over four years. He was big—6-foot-2—and husky. Why not?

Schauer lost his first start, 3–1, in Cleveland on May 20. On the afternoon of Memorial Day, before a crowd of twelve thousand, he hooked up with New York rookie Slim Love in a 15-inning battle won by the Yankees, 2–0. That day also marked Harry Davis's last appearance as a player. Pinch-hitting in the thirteenth, Davis hit a hot grounder to third that started a double play.

As a starter and reliever, Schauer worked 215 innings. He was often the victim of poor fielding support and pitched better than his 7-16 record indicates. Better, but not good enough to be the answer to Mack's needs.

In June the latest "another Eddie Collins" made Philadelphia headlines. Joe Dugan was an infielder at Holy Cross. The twenty-year-old freshman (he later claimed he was eighteen at the time) was considered the top college infielder in the nation. His coach, former major leaguer Jesse Burkett, tried to persuade him to sign with the Red Sox. But scouts who went to his parents' home in New Haven to get a signature on a contract for their minor son were told, "Sorry, Joe is promised to Connie Mack." Once again they were too late.

Contrary to some accounts, Joe Dugan knew all along that he was headed for the Athletics. Mack, tipped off by a bird dog or a friend or his brother Tom, who went to the Holy Cross games in Worcester, had had an eye and a tie on Dugan for at least two years. Ira Thomas later said that Mack sent him to New Haven to check out the high school junior in 1915. Learning that Dugan's parents wanted him to go to college, Thomas told them that Connie Mack would come to see them and arrange for Joe to go to Holy Cross.

As Dugan later recounted it (with some variations in each telling), Mack did show up at their house. "My father, mother, brothers and sisters, and myself were sitting down to eat one night when the doorbell rang. My mother answered the door and said, 'There's a man for you, Joseph.' I got up from the table and almost fainted. It was Connie Mack. Connie said he wanted to sit down with my father and mother and me for a few minutes.

"'Mr. Dugan,' said Connie, 'I hear your boy is quite a ballplayer.' And my old man replied, 'I hear tell he's pretty good.'

"'Well,' continued Connie, 'I've got a train to catch to Philadelphia and I'll make it brief.' Mack reached into his pocket and put five one hundred dollar bills on the table in front of my father, a poor working man who had never seen a sawbuck in his life.

"'I want you to promise me,' said Mack, 'when Joseph comes of age and decides to go into organized baseball you'll let him come to the Philadelphia Athletics.'

"My father looked at the money, then glanced at my seven brothers and two sisters. He couldn't contain himself. He said, 'For five hundred dollars you can take the whole family.'"

In 1922 Dugan told the *Boston Post* that Mack had gone to see his mother one afternoon and persuaded her to promise that if her son ever wanted to play professional baseball, it would be with the Athletics. "After high school I went to Holy Cross and got six major league offers in one year, all better than the A's offer. But I turned them down and kept my mother's promise."

However accurate or embellished these tales, Joe Dugan was committed to the Athletics and it was a well-kept secret until the Crusaders' season ended. No entry for $500 to the Dugans was found, but Mack did send Joe $350 while he was at Holy Cross in the spring of 1917 and gave him another $200 when he reported.

Dugan broke in at second base in the first game of a July 5 doubleheader, a 4–3 loss to the Red Sox (Joe Bush's record-tying fourteenth consecutive loss to Boston). Looking nervous, he made 1 error and 1 hit. Three days later Whitey Witt made 3 errors that helped the White Sox to an 8–4 win. When Witt was hurt, Mack gave Dugan a shot at shortstop and decided that Joe was a better shortstop than Whitey. But Dugan was struggling at the plate.

The Athletics climbed within 1½ games of sixth place after July 4. When they started a western trip winning 5 of the first 7 games, the goals of a .400 season and a sixth-place finish seemed within reach. They actually won 4 in a row, and that hadn't happened for a few years. They kept hitting; even the slumping Wally Schang, who had shown up at spring training sporting a much-ridiculed moustache and woke up with the bat when he was persuaded to shave it off.

Mack still had problems at second base and in right field, where he had found no acceptable replacement for Frank Thrasher. On July 17 he claimed Charlie Jamieson off waivers from Washington. A left-handed batter, Jamieson, twenty-four, had been purchased with Joe Judge from Buffalo for $8,000 in 1915. He hadn't shown Clark Griffith enough in three trials to win a regular job. He had no power and was hitting only .171. But Mack's right fielders weren't doing any better.

On July 20, 687,000 numbers were drawn in the army draft. Suddenly ballplayers were reading something besides the sports pages. Wynn Noyes was the first of Mack's boys to receive greetings from his hometown exemption board, as the draft board was called. Whitey Witt, Rube Schauer, and Ray Bates received notices to report. Once again outside forces were laying land mines in Connie Mack's rebuilding path. When the Russian Army collapsed, all talk of a short war disappeared with it. The government said 2 million men would be needed. Ban Johnson declared the season would end early if the president requested or ordered it, and there might not be any World Series, a statement that further eroded Charles Comiskey's esteem for his longtime comrade in arms. Comiskey had spent a lot of money buying a collection of stars to dethrone the Red Sox. The two teams were running neck-and-neck in the race. He was already steamed at Johnson for ordering the umpires to keep a close eye on Chicago's pitchers to prevent them from using the now-banned shine ball. When Johnson suggested the league would shut down and the World Series be canceled if President Wilson thought they should, the sports editor of the *Chicago Herald* wrote to Wilson and asked him what he thought of Johnson's suggestions.

Back came a letter signed by the president's secretary, Joseph P. Tumulty, saying the president "sees no necessity at all for stopping or curtailing the baseball schedule."

Attendance was down throughout the league, except in Philadelphia. Washington was the weakest club at the gate as well as the plate. The Senators would draw under ninety thousand for the season. There was talk of moving them to Brooklyn or Baltimore. Detroit was also in trouble. On May 24 the A's had played there before 597 paying customers, the smallest turnout in Tiger history.

It was even worse in the minor leagues, which were beginning to shut down. The North Carolina League was among the earliest to disband, taking

Earle Mack's Charlotte club with it. Earle moved on to Hagerstown, then to Hanover in the Blue Ridge League. By mid-July eight minor leagues had closed. At Gettysburg the players hadn't been paid for two months. Jimmie Dykes was living on the thirty dollars a month that came from the Athletics. The team also owed the league. The players went on strike. Dykes and a teammate went to Hagerstown to pick up some money playing for a semipro team. Earle Mack saw them and gave them fifteen dollars each to get by on until the league took over the team.

With fewer minor league and college players to scout, Connie Mack's rebuilding efforts were hobbled.

Players receiving draft notices wanted to go home immediately and take a few weeks off before reporting for duty. Trying to keep his team together, Connie Mack explained to them that appearing before the exemption board did not necessarily mean immediate induction. It might be months before they were called up for duty. So they stayed, but their thoughts were not entirely on baseball.

The A's returned home from the west on Wednesday, July 25, and a rejuvenated Elmer Myers beat Detroit, 8–3. That evening lights were installed at Shibe Park for a much-ballyhooed match between the lightweight and featherweight champs, Benny Leonard and Johnny Kilbane. Connie Mack was probably on hand for the brief bout in which Leonard beat the daylights out of Kilbane before the loser's handlers threw in the towel after three rounds.

A late July record heat wave pushed Philadelphia temperatures over 100. One sweltering day the fans turned ugly. They took exception to some of umpire Harry McCormick's decisions and showered the field with pop bottles. While deploring their behavior, Mack appreciated that they were once again interested enough to make an emotional investment in the team's fate.

Grantland Rice, pointing out that no other sport allowed players and managers to argue with game officials, advocated a rule banning anyone from speaking to an umpire and umpires from speaking to a player or manager during a game. Connie Mack, while urging his players to refrain from complaining, would not have gone so far. He wanted to reserve the right to point out when an umpire got a rule wrong, which happened occasionally.

Connie Mack felt like a cross-eyed safecracker. Every time he thought he had the combination right to make a run for the pennant, the tumblers wouldn't click. He had put together a powerful lineup, but the defense was poor and the pitchers too generous with free passes. Despite some brief spells of success, intermittent 6- and 7-game losing streaks sank them. They clung to seventh place as sixth began to rise out of reach.

Unlike some managers, Mack slept soundly and never skipped a meal while enduring the mounting losses. He projected dignity even in failure, a rare art. Like other managers of last-place teams, he could put aside the standings, the losses—on the field and financial—when the first pitch was thrown. Every game was a separate challenge, opportunity, battle of strategy and observation. There was a special joy in developing young players, watching one grow and improve, that outweighed the heartache when the many failed and had to be cut loose. Any game might be a breakthrough for a youngster. He might learn something, achieve something he had been working on. A young pitcher might suddenly "get it."

This is what kept Connie Mack going, kept him young, just as it has always sustained managers of hopeless teams.

To keep his benchwarmers' heads in the game, he designated a different one to flash the signs each day. The fellow might be sitting two or three or four men away from Mack, who would tell him what to signal while going through a series of wiggles and gestures himself. It also made it harder for the other side to pick up the signs.

Boston and Chicago were fighting for first place. The Athletics had 10 games against Boston in three weeks and 6 against Chicago, half of them in September. Mack considered it important to field the same lineup against both contenders to avoid the appearance of favoring either one. He urged his players to do their best at all times, regardless of whether they had friends on other teams or favored one team over another in the race. Even before John McGraw's accusations that his Giants had deliberately swooned against the Dodgers at the end of the 1916 season, Mack had cautioned his boys against letting up when they played one of that season's three contenders—Detroit, Chicago, and Boston.

"I pointed out that should my team let up against Boston, it would be like sneaking up behind the Detroit players and stealing their purse. If they let up against Detroit, it would be like climbing Chicago's porch and robbing the White Sox while they slept. My advice fortunately prevailed. We had no scandals."

They had indeed shown no favorites down the stretch that year, going 1-7 against Boston and Chicago and 0-6 against Detroit.

Safeguarding the integrity of the game was paramount to Mack. Win or lose, it was crucial that the fans believed in the honesty of what they watched on the field. Without that trust, the business, in which his life and fortune were invested, would be jeopardized. He was aware of the talk going around the league now that the Browns and Tigers had been "laying down" to the White Sox, preferring to see Comiskey's team beat out the Red Sox.

Before the season ended, Connie Mack had one more hot potato to handle, one that would lead to another uproar-causing trade.

Joe Bush found life in baseball's nether lands insufficiently stimulating. There was more excitement to be found in the evenings than in the afternoon activities. His work on the mound became inconsistent. On July 22 in Cleveland he was hit hard, leaving in the fourth inning of a 20–6 loss.

Six days later at home against the Tigers, Bush had a 3–0 lead in the ninth. An error by Bates seemed to upset him, though he was no longer an inexperienced pitcher. Three hits, 3 walks, and 2 wild pitches led to 5 runs and another loss. Bush then complained of a sore arm and took off for four days. There were hints that he was trying elbow-bending exercises to cure it. Mack didn't use him again until August 9. He pitched well in his next few outings, including a relief stint in Chicago on August 17.

Connie Mack had noticed that Chicago and Cleveland were sitting on Bush's fastball. Before his next start in Cleveland on August 22, Mack told Bush to use his fastball sparingly. Bush disagreed and ignored the order. Pitching in a steady drizzle, he gave up only 1 hit in 4 innings. Smiling smugly, he kept throwing his fastball. In the fifth the Indians teed off on it: single, sacrifice bunt (that Bush threw away), single, double, single, single, sacrifice, single. Five runs scored before Mack could yank him and rush in Jing Johnson.

Mack was furious. When Bush reached the dugout, Mack lit into him for disobeying orders. "Pack up and go home," he told the pitcher and fined him $200 for being out of condition. Relying on Myers, Noyes, Schauer, and Seibold, the A's won 2 and lost 8 the rest of the trip.

But there was more to it than that. The day after the blowup in Cleveland, Mack ripped into Bush in the *Press*:

> I'm through with him for good. He has been out of condition for weeks and has been breaking training right along. His conduct has been such that I don't want him with my ball club.
>
> Bush was spoiled by that one game he won back in the last World Series played by the Athletics. He got the idea he was a great pitcher.

Then he couldn't understand it when he began going bad the next season. I told him the trouble was he figured himself to be a great pitcher.

And he owned up that I was right. I told him he had the makings of a great pitcher if he'd only buckle down and tend to business. For the rest of that season he did so, and he went great.

He earned a raise and he got it. But he hasn't kept in shape this season, and the result is that instead of being a help to the ball club, he has been exactly the opposite.

I talked to him several times but it did no good. So I have sent him home.

He was my one big worry this season, and it's a big relief to get him off my mind.

Mack misspoke or was misquoted in this interview. It's unclear if he was referring to Bush's 8–2 win in the 1913 Series or his 12-inning 5–4 loss in 1914, the last Series played by the Athletics, followed by Bush's subsequent flop in 1915.

Meanwhile, Joe Bush popped off and said he'd never pitch for a club as rotten as Mack's again. So when the Yankees arrived in Philadelphia on September 10, manager Bill Donovan asked Mack how much he wanted for Bush, McInnis, and Strunk. He didn't expect to land the latter two; it was Bush he was after. He was surprised when *New York Globe* writer Harry Schumacher quoted Mack's reaction to the proposal: "Never again will I either trade or sell a ball player while he is still at the top of his career. . . . I've learned my little lesson with that sort of thing. Good ball players are scarce, especially in this part of the neighborhood. The few I've got I'll keep and it's no use trying to tempt me with more money."

What Donovan didn't know was that Mack and Bush had both cooled off by the time the A's returned home. To stay in shape, Bush had been pitching batting practice for the Phillies. He admitted that he had disobeyed orders in Cleveland and was in the wrong. And Connie Mack was not through with him after all. Bush started on Labor Day, was wild, and lasted 3 innings. Rube Schauer relieved him, and the A's went on to win. Bush may have asked for the ball the next day to redeem himself and did—temporarily—defeating Washington, 2–1. But he was inconsistent the rest of the way, finishing with an 11-17 record, though his 2.47 ERA was the lowest on the A's staff.

Connie Mack had broken tradition on Labor Day, scheduling an afternoon twin bill instead of the usual morning/afternoon split, and drew his largest crowd in over three years—nineteen thousand—who enjoyed a sweep of the Senators. The Athletics finished strong, winning 5 of 8 in the last week. Mack brought up right-hander Rollie Naylor, one of his $500 Class D bargains he had farmed out to New Haven. Naylor impressed everybody by throwing strikes and pitching 3 complete games.

On September 27 only about four hundred showed up to watch the A's defeat seventh-place St. Louis. Connie Mack wasn't one of them. He was in Boston to manage an All-Star team in a game against the Red Sox for the benefit of the family of Tim Murnane, his longtime friend. The first professional player to become a sportswriter, Murnane was sports editor of the *Boston Globe* when he died in February. As a lifelong boxing fan, Mack enjoyed the rare chance to visit with former heavyweight champion John L. Sullivan, who coached first base for the All-Stars. The event raised a reported $14,000 for Murnane's widow and four children.

The Athletics closed the home season by taking two from Detroit, the nightcap with a rousing 6-run ninth for a 12–11 victory, a teaser to buoy the hopes that better days lay just ahead—again. The A's played the Seventh Infantry team in Gettysburg on October 1, Eddie Plank doing the umpiring, before closing out the year in New York, where the sixth-place Yankees could draw no more than five hundred for a Tuesday game.

Despite slim turnouts in September, attendance was up by thirty-seven thousand at Shibe Park, still not enough to avoid a $25,000 operating loss. They had failed to reach Connie Mack's goals, but they had won 17 more games than the year before. They missed climbing out of the cellar by 1½ games, and .400 by 41 points. Had they not lost third baseman Ray Bates to the army and Joe Dugan with a sprained ankle in September, they might have made it to seventh.

Billy Weart had replaced Chandler Richter as the lead cheerleader for the A's. *The Sporting News* correspondent wrote in September, "As a team builder Connie Mack has certainly come through with the goods this season. . . . The individual improvement in the Athletics has been remarkable. All of the Athletics' opponents respected the team this year. Next year they will not only have respect but also fear when they have to face the White Elephants, or the writer is a very bad prophet."

Given the state of the world, it was not a good time for prophesying. The loss of players to the military service—how many and for how long, nobody knew; the deepening red ink—a majority of clubs in both leagues had lost money; rising prices and taxes; the public mood as the casualty lists began coming back from France—all gave no reason for confidence in the outlook for the baseball business, in Philadelphia or anywhere else.

7 | CUTTING BACK

Nineteen eighteen began with the coldest January in Philadelphia history. By the end of the month a deep blanket of snow covered the city. A shortage of coal forced the federal government to shut down all manufacturing for five days, idling 560,000 workers in Philadelphia. Department stores closed on Mondays. When a small shipment of coal arrived, riots broke out as people stormed the railroad yards to fill sacks and wagons.

For baseball fans, who subsisted on tidbits of trade rumors until box scores reappeared in the papers, the winter served up a rare feast of controversial fare.

Phillies owner William F. Baker had rocked the city on December 11, 1917, with the announcement that he had sold his star pitcher, Grover Alexander, and catcher Bill Killefer to the Cubs for $55,000; Mike Prendergast, a 3-6 pitcher; and a .126-hitting catcher named Pickles Dillhoefer. The deal made bigger headlines than the sale of Eddie Collins had done three years earlier. Alexander had won 30 or more games for three years, pitching over a thousand innings. After winning the 1915 pennant, the Phillies had finished second the next two years. They wouldn't see the first division again for fifteen years.

There was speculation that the National League was eager to build up the second-division Cubs to compete with the world champion White Sox, as the American League had hoped to do for the Yankees against the dominant New York Giants.

The second shock wave hit the city in the morning papers on Saturday, December 15. At the American League meeting in Chicago, Connie Mack sent Joe Bush, Wally Schang, and Amos Strunk to the Red Sox for $60,000, catcher Chet "Pinch" Thomas, rookie outfielder Merlin Kopp, and retread left-hander Vean Gregg. Mack rarely revealed the amount of money involved in any player purchase or sale; any figures would come either from the other party or reporters' guesses. When a writer for the *Boston Herald* asked Mack to confirm the figure, Mack just smiled. So it is surprising that an unsigned account in the *Public Ledger* said that Mack "displayed the agreement," which showed the sum of $60,000 in black and white. The *Record* more accurately reported, "To prove that $60,000 was the actual sum involved, Frazee exhibited the agreement signed by himself and Mack."

To the old-time baseball men, only a bushwhacker would have done that, to show off for the home folks how free-spending he was.

Asked by the *Herald* what the fans of Philadelphia would think of the sales, Mack was quoted: "It is up to me to replace the aggregation with a winner and I guess all my past errors in the estimation of the fans will be forgotten. A manager is like a player. When he is good, he is real good. When he is bad, he's rotten."

While the Phillies management felt the brunt of the slings from writers and arrows from fans, the two trades were widely condemned in tandem. William H. Rocap, sports editor of the *Public Ledger*, blasted both: "Do the BUSINESS MEN who control the great American game of baseball in Philadelphia intend to erase the sport as a major athletic activity in this city? In the face of the scandalous pair of actions there appears to be only one answer: yes."

The paper's editorial board took time out from directing how the Great War should be fought to condemning Baker and Mack for turning Philadelphia into a minor league city.

The consensus was that Baker had thumbed his nose at Phillies followers and Mack had booted a chance to woo the disenchanted National League patrons to Shibe Park. One paper editorialized:

> It is beyond our comprehension that Mack could have thought by any possible means he could have justified the disposal of the three stars and very backbone of his club. By no other reason than the fact that he had already experienced the heavy displeasure of Quaker fandom by similar acts of disposing of local favorites to the highest bidder, it seems to us that he would have thought twice before making his latest deal which has cost the club so dearly in public esteem. Connie had ringing in his ears the righteous indignation incident to the explosion from the sale of Alexander and Killefer. He certainly knew that the wrath that was being vented upon the head of the executive of the

Phillies club would be visited upon him in turn. Why he could not have profited by his previous experience and the lesson exemplified by the sale of the two star Phillies is inconceivable to us. It should have been a tremendous thing for Connie Mack. How he could have overlooked that fact is a source of amazement and wonder. Fans were ready to transfer their entire sympathies to the Athletics. Mack would have profited immeasurably by the bone pulled by the management of the Phillies, had he not gone them one better.

The Sporting News trilled the same theme, asserting that Mack had "booted a chance to get big gates when he brought down the wrath of fans on his head by the sale. Philadelphia has always been a National League town. Fans said harsh things when Baker got rid of Alexander and Killefer. Instead of Connie Mack taking the hint and spending money to bolster his team, figuring he would get those foreheads, he followed Baker's lead and now the rooters have lost all interest."

Connie Mack considered it unlikely he would have seen any increased patronage from resentful Phillies fans. As Fred Lieb pointed out, the more "moneyed" fans followed the Phillies. The A's were the favorites of the mill workers from the Kensington district of the city. Mack would have to put a better team on the field to reap a richer reward at the gate. And he knew it. He didn't expect any more support until then and did what he thought was best for the team, "even though it placed me in a bad light with the baseball fans."

Why were the deals made? Baker was looking short term; Mack was looking both short and long term. Baker said he needed the money, but he didn't. Mack never said he needed the money, but he did. The war was a factor in both cases. Baker suspected that Alexander might be drafted into the army; nobody knew for how long or how it might affect him by the time he came back. Might as well cash him in now. Baker was right—for one year. Both deals had clauses that would trigger some form of compensation if any players involved were drafted before April 1, 1918. Alexander started 3 games for the Cubs in April before his induction ended his season.

While cutting his payroll in highly uncertain times, Connie Mack sincerely believed he was improving his team, and that took priority for him over the fans' reactions or some temporary gate-boosting shot at the Phillies. Besides, the heart of Mack's rebuilding plan had already been cut out, and not by his hand. Fourteen of his most promising players were now in the armed forces, including Ray Bates, his solution to the third base problem;

Whitey Witt; and three-fourths of the young pitching staff he had been counting on. Who knew how many more would be called up—or even if there would be a 1918 season?

"I fully expected to be the surprise of the 1918 race," Mack told James Isaminger. "The team I finished last season with had untold possibilities. Nearly all our prospects were caught in the first draft, and I saw the handwriting on the wall. That's one reason I let go of Schang, Bush, and Strunk."

There was plenty of evidence to support his thinking at the time. And what he knew without benefit of a crystal ball or the historians' rearview mirror was all he had to go on.

As for the players involved, the *Public Ledger's* correspondent wrote, "Mack refused to discuss the trade at length, other than to say that he had long contemplated getting rid of the players."

All three had been holdouts a year ago. Dissatisfaction over salaries, coupled with dwelling in the cellar, could corrode a player's disposition like inflation eats a dollar. They would likely be among the players who were already balking at talk of further pay cuts, which were being proposed throughout baseball.

But there was more to it.

Connie Mack appreciated Wally Schang's hustling for a losing team. But Schang had too many deficiencies as an outfielder or third baseman. His sidearm throwing motion made him prone to erratic throws from either position, and a few incidents had soured Mack on him as a catcher.

On July 26, 1917, against Detroit, Donie Bush was on third with 2 out in the sixth inning. Rube Schauer was pitching. On a short passed ball, Bush raced for the plate. Schauer came down to cover home. Instead of throwing, Schang held the ball and dove for the plate. Bush beat the tag but would not have beaten a throw, and the tying run scored. The Tigers won in the twelfth.

A month later the A's were tied in the eleventh inning in St. Louis. Schauer, who had less support than if he'd been a private in the Russian Army, was on the mound. With a man on third, Mack ordered George Sisler walked. Schauer then threw two wide ones to the next batter, Del Pratt. Mack decided to walk him intentionally. He moved up to the edge of the dugout and called to Schang, who turned toward him—without calling time—as Schauer began to pitch. When Schauer stopped, the umpire called a balk and the winning run scored.

Joe Bush had moped through the season. Mack was fed up with his attitude, his refusal to follow orders, and his lapses in condition.

Mack did not intend to part with Amos Strunk. He had resisted efforts by Red Sox manager Jack Barry to obtain Strunk throughout the 1917 season. Now he was the key to the entire trade. Barry insisted he be included or it was no deal.

Overlooked in all the uproar was—and is—the fact that the players Mack received in return were no second-raters. At the time—the only honest way to evaluate them—Pinch Thomas was considered by some observers a better catcher than Schang. Burt Whitman of the *Boston Herald* called the curly-haired fan favorite more combative and peppier. Jim Nasium had named Ray Schalk and Thomas as his American League All-Star catchers.

The A's needed an experienced left-handed pitcher. Vean Gregg's name is usually preceded by "the sore-armed" in later accounts. It's true that he had a history of arm trouble. After winning 63 games in three years for the Indians, he had been traded to Boston in August 1914 and suffered arm problems the next two years. With a reported salary of $5,000 a year plus two World Series shares in Boston, he had earned almost $17,000 for pitching a total of 153 innings—about twenty hours of work. At that point he could have retired to his eight-hundred-acre ranch in Alberta. Instead he went down to the minor leagues, won 21 games for Providence in 1917, and, at thirty-three, seemed sound again. While some writers pronounced Gregg's left arm "as dead as a mackerel in a barrel," lobby chatter when the deal was announced said that Gregg was still a big league pitcher who would beat the Red Sox more often than Joe Bush would beat the Athletics. (They were right; Gregg shut out the Red Sox three times. Bush was 1-2 against the A's.)

Merlin Kopp, twenty-five, had batted .292 at Buffalo and led the International League with 57 stolen bases.

An unsigned item in *The Sporting News* opined that Mack "got a better catcher in Thomas than he gave the Red Sox in Schang. He got a good prospect in Kopp, and if Gregg's work in the International League last year is any criterion he struck near a balance for Bush."

Isaminger's reaction to the trade was as scathing as that of the rest of the local press corps, predicting the A's would open the season "with something like a Delaware County League lineup." But a few months later he changed his tune. "The outgoing crew was dissatisfied with conditions here. [They] are great ballplayers but the one truth is they kept the Mackmen in last place for three straight years, or at least helped to do so. In justice to them, perhaps they may be excused for not showing more ambition after the partition of the team."

Certainly the cash was a factor. In addition to three years of operating losses, the Athletics were still responsible for their share of the payments to Federal League clubs under the peace settlement. Given the plight of the depleted roster and the uncertainties of the year ahead, the A's needed the money more than they needed Amos Strunk. Cash could keep them in business; Strunk couldn't keep them in the pennant race.

Connie Mack refused to be drawn into a public needle-swapping when the *New York American* carried a story in which Jake Ruppert accused Mack of going back on his word. The Yankees owner claimed that at a private meeting in Trenton, Mack had promised the Yankees the first chance to buy Amos Strunk for $30,000, or Strunk, Bush, and Schang for $75,000. When the players went to Boston, Ruppert felt he had been double-crossed. He was quoted as saying he was off Mack for life, and hereafter if he had any dealings with him, he would have witnesses.

Reporters then as now thrived on conflict. That afternoon Isaminger hurried out to Shibe Park with the story. "Mack smiled a calm smile," Isaminger wrote. "'I have nothing to say,' he said. 'I have too much on my skull to deny newspaper articles. I will say that if anybody pledged me a player I wanted and he didn't make good, I would get hot under the collar too.'"

Stuffy McInnis was the last survivor from the glory years. His three-year contract at $4,000 a year was up. A pay cut was inevitable.

On the evening of Friday, January 4, Mack told Isaminger:

We're lucky to be alive. Players can no longer expect to make unreasonable demands. We can't pay the salaries we paid last year. McInnis, like the rest, will have to stand for a cut. I want to keep McInnis and will do as much as I can for him, but it is out of the question for me to think of paying him as much money as we did in 1917. . . .

If McInnis becomes balky he would also become worthless to me and the only thing left for me to do would be to put him on the market. I want to say that McInnis has been fairer with me than any player I ever had. He's always been satisfied and worked his hardest even when we were shot to pieces. I hope he agrees to my terms.

Isaminger estimated that the superlative first baseman would bring $50,000–$75,000 in the marketplace. There were also reports that McInnis would soon enlist in the navy, if he hadn't already done so. (He didn't.)

McInnis did balk at Mack's salary offer and requested that he be dealt to Boston to be near his home, as Jack Barry had done. On Thursday night, January 10, traveling secretary Rudy Ohl telephoned the morning papers with the word that Stuffy McInnis had been traded to the Red Sox (where he would earn the same $4,000 a year for the next four years). No terms were announced. Mr. Mack was not available; he was on a train to Jacksonville to check out the feasibility of sharing his spring training accommodations with the Pirates, who had expressed an interest in such an arrangement.

"There was sentiment, lots of sentiment, in sending Stuffy to Boston," Mack told syndicated columnist Hugh Fullerton a few months later. "He wanted to play near his home town. That wasn't what made me agree to part with him. It also was a question of paying him a big salary. He wanted and is worth a salary that I figured I possibly could not pay him. If I had been able to pay him the money he wanted I feel quite sure he would have played for me. . . . A more loyal player than Stuffy never has been on my club. I figured I owed it to him to let him go where he wished to play in the event I could not keep him on account of the salary question."

Public reaction to the departure of the popular McInnis was full of fury, but it was muted somewhat because nobody knew who or what the A's had obtained in return. At least one paper ran a contest to guess what players the A's would receive.

The immediate speculation was that a bundle of cash and some bench-warmers were all they could expect. When Connie Mack returned, he wouldn't comment on the deal. The fact was he didn't know who he was getting any more than the least curious fan.

There were complications. The Red Sox had no manager. Jack Barry had enlisted in the navy. Harry Frazee had not yet chosen his replacement. Mack had been given a list of players from which to choose three or four, but the list was shrinking. First baseman Del Gainer was on it. The navy took him. Herb Pennock, still a bullpen resident, was on it. Into the military he went. Another player was withdrawn because of physical problems. By the time Frazee named Ed Barrow to manage the team, the list was so depleted that Barrow said they might have to go out and buy some players to complete the deal.

At no time did Connie Mack ask for any cash.

Finally, after seven weeks, the deal was done. The A's received outfielder Tilly Walker, third baseman Larry Gardner, and catcher Forrest "Hick" Cady. The thirty-year-old Walker was fleet of foot with a strong, accurate arm and what passed for power at a time when his 6 home runs in 1914 tied him for third in the league. The Yankees, who even then believed that every good player should belong to them, had been after Walker for some time. The New York papers predicted that Mack would quickly pass Walker on to new Yankees manager Miller Huggins. It didn't happen.

Gardner, a ten-year man with the Red Sox, was second to Frank Baker as the top-hitting third baseman in the league. At thirty-one, he was, Mack said, "the youngest thirty-year-old in the league." Gardner and Hick Cady, a backup catcher near the end of the line, had been in three World Series with Boston, Walker in one.

The Athletics still needed a first baseman to replace McInnis. The Yankees still craved an outfielder. Mack had one he'd be happy to let them have: Ping Bodie. With all the old stars gone, the redoubtable Mr. Bodie boasted, "I and the Liberty Bell are the only attractions left in Philadelphia." He proclaimed that his .291 batting average and 7 home runs—one more than the mighty Home Run Baker had hit—deserved a raise, a big one, not a cut. The Yankees wanted Bodie, but they wouldn't part with Wally Pipp, who had led the league with 9 home runs.

"Lookit," said Mack to Huggins, "there's a first baseman named Burns at Detroit that I understand the Tigers are willing to deal. You buy him and swap him to me and Bodie is yours."

The Yankees paid $6,000 for George Burns and the trade was made on March 7.

Was Connie Mack shrewd, or was he the bonehead businessman portrayed by the papers? Suddenly all the jokes about the Athletics disappeared along with Mack's public relations problems. Gardner and Walker were over the draft age. Burns, though only twenty-five, had a low priority number in the draft and would not likely be called for a year or more. The acquisition of Burns was so popular it wiped out all remnants of resentment over the departure of McInnis and the rest because George Burns was a hometown boy.

Mack had kept an eye on Burns for six years, since the nineteen-year-old had arrived at Shibe Park for a tryout with a $150-a-month minor league offer in his pocket. "I told Connie of the offer," Burns said after his acquisition, "and he said I'd better take it and he would follow my career. Detroit scouts got busy and I was sold to Hugh Jennings."

Burns hit .291 in his rookie year in 1914, slumped the next year when appendicitis sidelined him until June, had another good year in 1916, then fell to .226 in 1917. He never got along with Jennings. Philadelphia fans remembered his hitting a home run off Eddie Plank in his first time at bat in Shibe Park and his 6 hits in those first 2 games in 1914.

Before the 1918 season was a month old, if Mack had returned Burns and brought back Stuffy McInnis, the fans would have torn down Shibe Park.

As harsh as the attacks might be on his home turf, Connie Mack had his supporters among objective observers in other big league cities. Hugh Fullerton wrote, "In spite of the howl that has gone up in the Quaker City, it looks as if Mack knew exactly what he was doing and that, from the standpoint of useful material, he got more than he gave—and coin to make up the deficit."

This unsigned commentary appeared in *The Sporting News*:

Much has been written about how Connie Mack wrecked the Athletics and put the pennant with the Boston Red Sox. There is one critic, Ed Wray of the *St. Louis Post-Dispatch*, who begins to see a great light, and now implies that Connie hasn't done so badly in his deals with Harry Frazee. He sees it this way: Mack has given up Bush, Schang, Strunk, and McInnis. He gets in exchange Gregg, Chet Thomas, Kopp, Walker, Gardner and Cady and $60,000 to boot. Taking it all in all, Wray figures that Mack hasn't been so badly worsted, that he is a good deal of an old fox yet. The conclusion is that, not trades or sales but the war has hit Mack hardest, and had army demands not been made on his ball team he might yet be able to show other ball clubs in the American League a few tricks. It is quite a relief to see someone coming to Mack's defense, for he has been subjected to some pretty severe panning this past winter.

Mack expected criticism, shrugged it off, and rarely responded. When his five-year-old son, Connie Jr., sat behind the A's dugout and had his young ears blistered by the fans around him booing his dad, Connie Sr. smiled and told him, "Lookit, young fellow, when you play for the public, you are king when you are right and a bum when you do badly. You have to learn how to take the good with the bad."

Years later, when Mack was once again under attack for selling his stars, his angry daughter Ruth told him she was going to write to the papers and defend him. "No, girlie," Mack said, "don't bother. They've made up their minds that's the way it is."

His insistence on putting harmony first, even ahead of winning, had led to player moves that brought heavy censure down on him from press and public. Still he told Hugh Fullerton, "To be candid about it, the critics have not panned me [in the past three years] as much as I expected to be panned."

It's easy for historians, operating in a vacuum devoid of context, to lump together Connie Mack's breaking up of the 1914 team and ascribe it all to avarice and cheapness. But the transactions had occurred over a tumultuous three-year span and for reasons far more varied and complex than the basic economics of cutting payroll and replenishing the bank account. Mack had made the mistakes and suffered the disappointments that every baseball genius experiences. There would be more of each. But Mack was at heart a builder of teams, not a merchant of flesh. Unlike Branch Rickey, who pocketed a percentage of every dollar collected from selling players, Connie Mack didn't personally profit from these sales.

On a Sunday afternoon in January Harry Davis walked into the tower office. As they looked out over the snow-covered field, Davis told Connie Mack he was quitting baseball. He owned a prosperous scrap metal business that demanded so much of his time that he had missed the last two western trips of the season. Since then he had been elected to the Philadelphia Common Council by an overwhelming majority. Respected by players and fans throughout baseball, Jasper, as the players called him, had been coaxed by Connie Mack out of an early baseball retirement at the age of twenty-eight in 1901. He had been with Mack ever since—as first baseman, scout, captain, coach, assistant manager, and friend—except for one unhappy season managing the Indians. Four times he had led the league in home runs; four times he had led the A's to a pennant. When his legs began to go, he had taught his replacement, Stuffy McInnis, the art of playing first base.

"I'm sorry to see you go," said Mack, "but you must consider your own interests first."

Davis told reporters, "I am forty-five years old. While I feel like a two-year-old, I know I am beyond the age for baseball. I enjoyed every minute I was connected with the Athletics and I think Connie Mack is the best fellow I ever met."

When the Philadelphia members of the Baseball Writers Association made their annual visit to the grave sites of their departed colleagues on the Sunday before Memorial Day, they would have two more wreaths to leave. On December 7, 1917, Billy Weart, who had kept to his beat despite heart problems in recent years, passed at forty-five. The *Evening Telegraph* writer and *Sporting News* correspondent had chronicled Connie Mack's ups and downs with the Athletics as thoroughly and even-handedly as any of the city's reporters. The A's and Phillies scheduled a spring exhibition game for the benefit of his widow.

In January 1918 Mack's harshest critic, A. M. Gillam, died after more than twenty-five years as sports editor of the *Record*. The death of Gillam did not mean that Mack now had a free ride with the press. The days when writers owned a piece of the team and promoted the A's were long gone. The new Philadelphia *Sporting News* correspondent, James Isaminger, could be supportive or critical and was given to the satirical, cynical approach. He was fond of applying alliterative appellations to Mack: tall tactician, tall Tiogan, tall tutor, lean leader, gaunt general.

Connie Mack had a lot on his skull. He was a half-owner of a business facing another season of red ink—if they had a season at all. In years past Connie Mack would have put on the field a team of no-names, confident that he could discover enough nuggets of gold to develop into stars and championships. No more. The war had forced him to postpone his rebuilding plans. For 1918 he would have a veteran lineup of familiar names, with a few rookies and second-year men, a lineup respectable by anyone's standards.

Except for the pitching. Alas, the pitching, that 70 or 80 or whatever percent of baseball.

With it all, Mack looked forward, always forward, to a new season, and always with optimism.

8 | 1918

"Baseball is selling its product too cheap. No park with a lot of twenty-five-cent seats can make money."

So said Boston theatrical/baseball producer Harry Frazee.

Tickets for plays and musical comedies ranged from fifty cents to two dollars. Baseball should charge the same, Frazee argued. Cheaper seats were appropriate for the old wooden ballparks but not for today's modern facilities. The new parks required three times the staff of twenty years ago. Salaries were higher. Clubs now had full-time trainers, assistant managers, even pitching coaches. Players traveled first class, one man to a bed.

Inflation had risen to 17.4 percent in 1917. It would rise the same amount in 1918. Postage stamps went from two cents to three. Peanuts doubled in price. *The Sporting News* reluctantly went from five cents to seven. Railroad fares rose 30 percent; Pullman cars, 50 percent. When a team rode the rails for more than one hundred thousand miles a year, that added up. Instead of two sleeping cars using only lower berths, some clubs cut back to one car, putting the rookies in the uppers.

Connie Mack and Ben Shibe raised their ticket prices only because of the 10 percent war tax, rounded up so the ticket sellers didn't have to deal with pennies. The new scale was thirty cents for bleachers to $1.10 for box seats. (League meetings sometimes bogged down in the kind of endless discussions familiar to members of nonprofit boards and committees. It took forever—or so it seemed—for them to figure out how to collect the war tax on passes. They finally decided the easiest way was for each holder of a pass to drop a dime in a box when he went through the pass gate.)

In holding the line on salaries, Connie Mack was no exception. At the annual meeting in December 1917 every club had agreed to limit its payroll to about $70,000 while maintaining the twenty-five-player limit. They did it not to increase profits, but to cut losses. Clark Griffith needed a loan to keep going; the league agreed to lend him $30,000 at 6 percent interest, Charles Comiskey casting the only No vote.

Most of the actions taken in the winter meetings caused little stir: ten-year players must clear waivers and agree before being sent to the minors; teams must pay all traveling expenses to spring training; no more than eight players may be out on option at one time. Another routine action that went unremarked at the time would reap a whirlwind: disputes between major league and minor league clubs would be heard by an expanded commission, including the secretary of the National Association of Professional Baseball Leagues—the minor leagues—and the president of the league involved.

The American Association banned the spitball, a movement that was growing, with Connie Mack's enthusiastic support.

Ban Johnson had long advocated a 140-game schedule as the ideal length for a season. But he failed to persuade anyone to go along with it. Despite April's usual cold, wet conditions, Mack was against a later start. May, he said, was often worse than April. It had been so in 1917. If the season was to be shorter, he preferred an earlier finish.

Johnson saw the uncertainty of the times as an opportunity to push his plan again. When he brought it up at the December league meeting, his club owners rejected it again. The whole question might become moot anyhow. In February the National Commission advised all clubs to wait before spending money to print tickets. There might not be a 1918 season.

Another movement was making its way through the country's legislative grinder: Prohibition. Connie Mack did not support that one, though it would have no effect on his own way of life. He held no brief for drinking; he had seen its effects on his father's wasted body and the careers of ballplayers. But he had a keener insight into human nature than the Prohibitionists. He saw nothing wrong with men relaxing over a beer or two and knew that drinkers, undeterred by any laws, would find the stuff like a French pig sniffing truffles. Wood or denatured alcohol would become the cheapest substitute among the poor and middle class. The unintended result: cheap, poisonous hooch would kill more people quicker than the real thing.

Mack refused to give out a list of players he would take to spring training, partly because he preferred to wait until they had signed. As it turned out, he had little trouble signing his players. Two who balked were new acquisitions. Catcher Chet Thomas didn't like the terms. He thought maybe he'd stay in California and try his hand at playing cowboy roles for Farnum

Films. Mack told Thomas to go trade himself. He wound up in Cleveland. The other balker was first baseman Jake Munch, purchased from Atlanta. Mack offered him seventy-five dollars a month more than his minor league salary. Not interested, said Munch. Same to you, said Mack, and returned him to Atlanta.

Rube Schauer was the lone holdover who returned his contract unsigned. No great loss, Mack shrugged. "If Schauer studied batsmen more he could become a good pitcher," he told the *North American*. "He will pitch nine innings and not know one hitter from another. I don't know what I will do with him, but I've erased him from my mind as far as a place on the A's is concerned. Were he to report tomorrow he wouldn't get as good a contract as the one I sent him."

Schauer didn't report tomorrow or any other day. He went to work in a shipyard. At twenty-seven, his big league career was over.

Mack denied as "absurd" a story that he had set a $2,000-per-man salary limit but added, "The public probably realizes that the days of six-, seven-, and eight-thousand dollar salaries for ordinary players have gone forever."

Equally absurd is the tale that Mack asked his players to share in the club's profits in lieu of any salary. Neither Mack nor any other club owner expected to see a profit in 1918. What he said was that in the unlikely event the Athletics showed a profit, he would gladly distribute it among the players. Some contracts—Joe Dugan's for one—did contain a bonus clause based on net profits. In Dugan's case, he would receive $100 for each $1,000 up to $5,000 of profits after all expenses, in addition to his $1,800 salary.

This year Connie Mack had another reason for remaining silent about his plans. Nobody knew who would still be a civilian come March, who would be available on opening day or a month later.

The A's left for Jacksonville on March 16. Riding through the night, Connie Mack may have thought of more tranquil times, when he had first made this journey thirty-one years earlier as a rookie with the Washington Nationals. Or maybe not. Like the rest of the nation, he may have been more preoccupied with the daily reports of the brutal stalemate on the battlefields of France and Belgium. The wartime pall hung like a shroud over the country. Tommy Rice noted in the *Brooklyn Eagle*, "It seems empty to write about heroes on the diamond when there are heroes on the battlefield."

In addition to Rudy Ohl, Tom Shibe, trainer Doc Ebling, and a dozen players, Mack was accompanied by a friend, John P. McCoy, a Philadelphia manufacturer whose son was stationed at Camp Johnston, near Jacksonville.

Mack promised to bring his team to the camp for a game and arranged for the city to waive its ban on Sunday baseball so the camp team could play the A's and Pirates in town. Thousands of soldiers turned out for the free games, reminding Mack and his players how much it meant to be able to help the boys in khaki forget for a few hours why they were where they were.

The sharing of the facilities with the Pirates worked well. Hotel rooms—prices jacked up to ten or fifteen dollars a week per man plus three dollars a day for meals—were in short supply. But there were two fields. The Pirates used Barrs Field; the A's had a new park, Rose Field, on the other side of the St. John's River. At noon the A's rode the ferry and went back to town for lunch. Mack believed the rest and respite from the training grounds was good for them.

The Athletics didn't look like a last-place team, and they didn't feel like one. Only five of them had been with the cellar dwellers of 1917. There was speed and agility that had been missing. "Last year those who could hit couldn't field or were slow," Mack said. "The fast ones couldn't hit. This year they're all fast. The slowest is Burns and he's faster than McInnis." Even the veteran Larry Gardner cavorted like a rookie.

One member of Mack's championship teams returned. Rube Oldring had sold his farm—couldn't get any hired help, he said—and moved back to the city. At thirty-six, he would pinch-hit, play a little outfield, fill in here and there.

They were short of catchers. Chet Thomas was in California blasting Mack for not considering him indispensable. Forrest Cady, who had come over in the McInnis trade, had spent the winter recuperating from two broken shoulders, suffered in an automobile accident in which his wife had been badly injured. Cady went to Jacksonville but hadn't recovered enough to play that year. Mack brought back Jim McAvoy, who had hit .313 for Baltimore. He and Cy Perkins would share the load.

The pitching was a big unknown. Most of the 1917 prospects were in the armed forces. Mack counted on big things from Elmer Myers and hoped for big things from the veteran Vean Gregg. After that it was rookie, rookie, rookie.

Someone in the Milwaukee chapter of Connie Mack's Volunteer Bird Dogs of America had written to Mack about a skinny nineteen-year-old semipro pitcher named Joe Hauser. The young left-hander had been pitching area teams to state championships for five years. Mack sent him a railroad ticket and invited him to spring training. No contract, just an invitation.

Joe arrived around March 21. Although the squad was the smallest Mack had taken south in years, nobody paid any attention to him for about a week. Then one day Connie Mack said to him, "Joe, let's go out to the park. I want to see you throw."

"Forrest Cady was the catcher," Joe recalled seventy years later. "I was scared to death, so wild I couldn't throw a ball he could catch."

Connie Mack handed him a hundred dollars and a ticket home.

One day Cy Perkins made a suggestion to Connie Mack that would lead to the biggest fracas between the leagues since the 1901–1903 war.

Perkins had caught a big, burly right-hander named Scott Perry in Atlanta in 1916. Perry had won 23 games for the fifth-place Crackers. "He throws as hard as anybody," Perkins said, "and has a sharp curve and good control." Perkins didn't know where he was, but he thought Perry still belonged to Atlanta.

Connie Mack had seen Perry once, when the Browns bought him on trial from Louisville in 1915 and gave him a start against the Athletics on May 13. He gave up 4 runs in 2 innings, and the Browns sent him back to Louisville, which sold him to Atlanta. Since then he had been up and down like a yo-yo. In August 1916 Atlanta manager Charlie Frank sold him to the Cubs for $6,000, with a down payment of $2,000 and the balance if they kept him past April 10, 1917.

Perry made his first start for the Cubs on September 14, an 11-inning 2–0 win over George Stallings's Boston Braves. James Crusinberry of the *Chicago Tribune* described the swarthy, powerfully built Perry as looking like "he might have trailed a plow and pitched bundles into a thrashing machine for several summers, then chopped wood all winter just to pay for his board. There are a few tricks about pitching he may not have learned yet, but he showed a big free arm delivery that at times looked like the movement of Walter Johnson. He has just about as much speed, too, as the great Walter, and early in the game one of those fast ones went awfully close to the head of Fred Snodgrass. The latter dropped to earth and he nor any one else didn't hug the plate quite so closely from then on."

During the winter the Cubs changed managers. The new boss, Fred Mitchell, didn't think Perry was worth the rest of the purchase price and notified Atlanta on the April 10 deadline.

Perry refused to go back to Atlanta. Cincinnati bought him, apparently also on a trial basis, although words like "outright" were used in the stories.

On May 3, 1917, he gave up 6 runs in 4 innings of relief. He showed "a world of speed and elegant curves," wrote W. A. Phelon, "but he fields his position like Tseng Tsu, the Chinese god of war. . . . Nevertheless, the boys think that Mr. Perry can pitch good ball."

Given a start two weeks later in Brooklyn, Perry was battered for 10 runs before being yanked in the eighth. Reds manager Christy Mathewson disagreed with "the boys" and sent Perry back to Atlanta. Again Perry refused to go. The sixth-place Boston Braves then inquired about Perry. Atlanta said it wanted $3,000 for him. Stallings offered Atlanta $500 down for a thirty-day look and another $2,000 if they kept him. Charlie Frank agreed.

There was something about the swarthy Texan they called "Rope" that managers didn't like. As far back as Louisville in 1914, hints of "dissension" had appeared in stories about him. Whatever the reason, he apparently ticked off Stallings from the start. Perry reported to the Braves at the Metropole Hotel in Cincinnati on June 1, sat on the bench for seventeen days, and never threw a pitch. There were rumors that Perry claimed he had a sore arm, that he and Stallings had had a run-in, that the manager had called him a lazy so-and-so whose absence would be appreciated—or words to that effect. Perry obliged by departing for Chicago, where he drove a truck and pitched semipro ball, reportedly racking up a 27-1 record.

Two days after Perry left, Braves secretary Walter Hapgood wrote to Charlie Frank, "The Boston club is *no longer interested* in the player *in any way* and because of his desertion feels in no way obligated to the Atlanta club" (emphasis added).

There was not a word about the thirteen days still left on the trial meter. As far as the Boston club was concerned, it had never owned Perry and didn't want him. The next day Frank sent Hapgood a telegram: "Where is Perry?"

Hapgood didn't know and didn't care. He inquired of league secretary John Heydler if it was appropriate to ask for waivers on Perry, "fearing that such action would indicate that the Boston club still claimed control of the player and that such asking of waivers might weaken the cause of the Boston club." It was clear that the Braves didn't want to give anybody cause to think they owned the pitcher; nor did they have any interest in paying the $500 for another thirteen days of Perry's time. Heydler replied that waivers should be asked "so the records in the National League office would be complete."

Whatever that meant.

National League president John Tener thought Perry belonged on Boston's ineligible list as a result of his desertion. National Commission chairman Garry Herrmann disagreed. "*The Boston club does not want to exercise their option on the player,*" he wrote Tener on June 28. "That being the case, they had better notify the Atlanta club that the player is released back to that club and should be placed on its ineligible list and this way there will be no contention about the Boston club's liability to make a second payment" (emphasis added).

Obviously, the Boston Braves were trying to wash their hands of Perry as desperately as Lady MacBeth trying to out that "damned spot."

Meanwhile, the Atlanta club, which had been paying its bills by selling and reselling Scott Perry, had received nothing from the Braves—no official paperwork and no money, not even the $500 take-a-look payment. In July Charlie Frank asked the National Commission to compel the Braves to pay the full $2,500 for Perry since they hadn't returned him within the thirty days. "If I don't get the pitcher back, I should get the money," Frank said.

Charlie Frank's complaint was the seed that would grow into a file of letters, telegrams, and court documents several inches thick.

On August 1, 1917, Garry Herrmann unofficially offered the Braves his opinion that if Perry ever decided to return to organized baseball, they still would have thirteen days to decide if they wanted him enough to pay the remaining $2,000. At the same time, Herrmann advised the Atlanta club that it was "authorized to use or *dispose* of the pitcher pending the adjustment of the 1917 controversy over this player"(emphasis added).

Ten months later, at the height of the ensuing imbroglio, the inherent absurdity of Herrmann's actions would be pointed out by Ban Johnson, who wrote to Herrmann: "In connection with the Perry case your correspondence is absolutely contradictory. In one letter you make certain promises to the Boston Club, and in a communication to the officials of the Atlanta Club, you advise them to play Perry or dispose of his services. How are you going to make those two propositions dove-tail?"

On August 6, 1917, the un-Solomon-like National Commission, aware of Herrmann's convoluted curbside opinions but unable to cut Perry in half, ruled that the Crackers were entitled to the $500 down payment but not the additional $2,000, as Perry had jumped the Braves before the thirty-day trial period had expired. "The commission disallows the claim of the Atlanta club for the deferred payment of $2,000 on the grounds that the Boston club did not formally or informally perfect its title to the player beyond the trial terms."

The baseball writer for the *Atlanta Constitution* voiced the minor leagues' general dislike of the commission setup: "When it's a question between a minor and major league team, the National Commission always decides for major league clubs regardless of the merits of the case."

The Braves squawked, claiming that Perry's desertion had completely nullified the deal, and asked the commission to reconsider its decision. On August 30 the commission affirmed its decision. The Braves paid the $500. The commission said nothing to clarify the pitcher's status.

After the 1917 season Boston listed Perry on its ineligible list, based on Herrmann's August 1 letter.

Wrong, said John Heydler; Perry is not the property of your club. You never completed the purchase. He belongs on Atlanta's suspended list. The *Constitution* showed Perry on the Crackers' reserve list for 1918, not its suspended list.

Perry was playing for a semipro team in Joliet, Illinois, when the *Constitution* reported his signing an Atlanta contract on March 21, 1918, adding that "Frank will believe Scotty's promises of reporting only when he sees him on the grounds."

So when Connie Mack called his old friend Charlie Frank on Monday morning, March 25, and asked if Scott Perry was available, Frank said, "Sure." He didn't say anything about that "pending" stuff that Herrmann had written to the Braves. Mack sent Atlanta catcher Val Picinich and outfielder Lee Strait in exchange. Frank told Mack where Perry could be found. Mack wired the pitcher an offer of $1,800 for the season. Perry said fine and headed for Jacksonville.

Scott Perry backed up everything Cy Perkins had said about him. Batters couldn't hit him in batting practice. Catchers couldn't hold onto his pitches in practice games. Isaminger waxed rhapsodic: Perry's fastball was faster than Walter Johnson's; he had a hopping curve and baffling slowball and control the equal of Grover Alexander.

The only time the Braves and A's were in the same place on the same day was March 31 in Jacksonville. George Stallings had left Miami ahead of his team and was there on Saturday, March 30, when the A's played Pittsburgh. In June Connie Mack would be quoted as saying he had seen Stallings in the grandstand at Jacksonville, where Stallings "watched Perry pitch for us."

Shown the article quoting Mack, Stallings called it "absolutely untrue." In a letter to Garry Herrmann, he admitted being there with Buck Herzog on March 30 but said, "It was a bitter cold day and we remained at the game just three innings. Perry did not show on the grounds during the time I was there and if he was at the park he remained undercover."

Stallings was correct. Mack had seen him on Saturday, but it was Sunday that Perry pitched against a military team from Camp Johnston. The soldiers played the Pirates in the second game that afternoon. The Boston team had arrived in town Sunday morning and had the day off before heading for Dublin, Georgia, to join the Yankees on the way north. Most of the Braves players went to Barrs Field to see the games. They saw Perry pitch and had plenty of opportunity to visit with him if they wanted to. But Stallings may not have been there.

Burt Whitman, the Boston correspondent for *The Sporting News*, later wrote, "I was with the Braves in the south and I can vouch that in all that time I did not hear Stallings make any statement about Perry. I am morally certain the manager would have made some remark, some comment in my hearing if he had known that his old rival of 1914, Connie Mack, had taken up with the erratic Scott."

But that was after the fact. It was more likely indifference, not ignorance, on Stallings's part. Mack's purchase of Perry was reported in the papers. Stallings didn't care where Scott Perry was pitching. The Braves had made no effort to contact him during the winter or spring to collect the additional thirteen days' look they had purchased. If Stallings had been interested, surely some players or writers would have told the manager when they saw him pitching that day in Jacksonville.

Connie Mack didn't talk about building a champion. He was just trying to field a respectable team until things returned to normal. The Athletics were no longer a joke. Nobody was calling them the worst collection of nondescripts the league had ever seen. Back home the fans read the dispatches from the south and believed their cellar days were over "if the pitching comes through." The perennial "if."

The Pirates and A's traveled north together. They arrived home in a snowstorm, after rain and snow had washed out every game during the last week, wiping out the results of the weeks of conditioning and any chance the clubs had of recovering spring training expenses.

The nation inaugurated daylight saving time on March 31. An extra hour of evening sunshine would enable the games to start later and draw more businessmen. Mack announced that after opening day, games at Shibe Park would begin thirty minutes later, at four o'clock. The afternoon papers booed the move; they were used to getting the complete play-by-play and line score in their late sporting editions. The morning papers didn't care. The cooks on the home front complained the loudest, as suppers would be delayed. In a compromise, Mack moved the first pitch back to 3:45. The complaints continued. He surrendered and went back to 3:30.

The A's opened in Boston and lost 3 in a row, went to Washington and lost again before they won a pair. They opened at home on a brisk 54-degree afternoon before an enthusiastic crowd of seven thousand eager for their first look at seven new players in the lineup. Vean Gregg and Babe Ruth matched zeroes for 7 innings. In the eighth, with two on, George Burns hit Ruth's first pitch into the bleachers for the 3–0 win. Anyone passing by Shibe Park would have thought a pennant-clinching celebration was going on.

Despite a 3-8 start, Mack remained optimistic. After Gregg lost 2–0 in New York, Mack told New York writer Sid Mercer, "Despite what the critics say, I still contend that the Athletics are not a tail-end team." He conceded that he had realized two years ago that "a team of youngsters, no matter how promising, could not compete with seasoned opponents." Now he had mixed his prospects with veterans like Gardner and Jamieson and Tilly Walker.

"I am not discouraged," he concluded. "On the contrary, I think our prospects are very good."

Scott Perry pitched 3 complete games in April. He lost 1–0 to Carl Mays on April 16 in Boston, an eighth-inning infield hit by Joe Dugan the only safety they could manage off Mays. Stallings must have read about it in the Philadelphia papers; the Braves were playing at Baker Bowl. Perry beat Walter Johnson, 5–1, then lost a 4-hitter, 2–1, to Boston at home on April 26. Stallings read about that one in the Boston papers.

With Perry, Gregg, and Myers doing most of the pitching, the A's broke even in a three-week home stand. In his first 8 games, Perry threw a 1-hitter, 3-hitter, and 4-hitter and 2 shutouts. He gave up 10 runs in 58 innings. He pitched often on two days rest and beat the Yankees twice in one week—a lineup of Peckinpaugh, Baker, Pratt, Pipp, and Bodie that Sid Mercer dubbed Murderers' Row. On May 3 the A's leaped into fifth place with an 8–6 win sparked by Burns's two triples. The next day Perry shut out the Senators, 1–0, in 11 innings, Johnson taking the loss in relief.

Scott Perry and George Burns had become the Shibe Park fans' favorites.

Of the three pitchers, Myers was the least consistent. For every good outing, he was bombarded in two. The war might have been on his mind; his draft number had risen on the list. On June 13 Myers started his last game before going off to war. He was soon followed by rookie pitcher Bob Geary, who had been Mack's bullpen strength.

The military atmosphere overlay the ballparks. Drilling and martial music and flag-raising rites preceded games. Liberty bonds were sold at booths throughout the grandstand. Bat and ball days raised thousands of dollars to buy equipment for camps at home and overseas. The A's made Shibe Park available to service teams on Sundays. They played an exhibition game at Fort Meade before twenty-four thousand soldiers, their biggest crowd of the year.

In Washington, where war workers and soldiers stationed in the area had little to do on Sundays but roam the streets and get drunk, the DC commissioners approved Sunday baseball. Connie Mack could only note with envy the crowd—more than fifteen thousand paid plus two thousand soldiers admitted free—that turned out on May 19 for the Senators' first Sunday home game.

On May 23 there came a thunderbolt out of Washington. Provost Marshal Enoch Crowder wiped out almost all draft exemptions, except for men doing "essential" work. Baseball players were considered non-essential, along with idlers, bartenders, gamblers, and clerks. For the first time married men were no longer exempt. All men between twenty-one and thirty-one were told, in effect, "Work or fight." The deadline was July 1. Since 90 percent of the players in all leagues were affected, all of professional baseball could be shut down by that date. There weren't enough teenagers and over-thirties to go around. The Athletics had only four players outside the new draft range.

Players began leaving their clubs to go to work at munitions plants, steel mills, and shipyards, playing ball for company teams, in hopes of avoiding the draft. Hotel lobbies and ballparks swarmed with employment agents trying to lure top stars with offers of $50 a week for soft jobs and $100 for weekend games in the industrial leagues that were flourishing. Plant owners built new ballparks or expanded their old ones. With most minor leagues shut down for the duration, scouts checked out the Bethlehem Steel, Delaware Shipbuilding, and Triangle Factory Leagues. Criticized for sheltering "shirkers," the steel leagues passed a rule requiring players to be on the job for thirty days before they could play for the company team. The shipyards had no such rule and attracted the most players. By the end of July some industrial teams were stronger than some major league lineups.

Connie Mack was kept busy swatting away these pesky gnats who waved less money but were just as annoying as the Federal League promoters of a few years ago. He talked several of his boys into staying with the A's and taking their chances with the draft and was aided in that effort when draft boards began to call up men classed as A-One even if they were working in shipyards.

Hugh Fullerton wrote, "It is hard to estimate to what extent the game will develop after the war. While the professional game is going back and the business end of the game is wrecked for the period of the war, at least the sport itself never was so big, or so widely played."

This was true. Industrial leagues drew large crowds to their games. The Bethlehem Steel League championships attracted as many fans as the World Series opener in Chicago. The popularity of these leagues inspired companies to step up the competition for players, offering light workloads and big salaries to professionals who would play for the company team even after the war.

Just about every hamlet containing at least nine male adults had a town team. Rivalries with neighboring towns were as heated as tribal feuds. Men who had never seen the inside of a betting parlor left their milking parlors to put down a dollar on the local lads. Baseball didn't need the major leagues to remain the national pastime.

What really shocked the baseball magnates was the exemption granted to movie and stage actors, with its implication that these forms of entertainment were somehow more essential to public morale than baseball. Their eyes told them differently. The thousands of servicemen in their grandstands testified otherwise. Secretary of War Newton D. Baker rubbed salt in the wound, saying of actors, "People cannot do without all amusement in wartime."

Might as well say that vaudeville, not baseball, was the national pastime. (Baker didn't say it, but one reason for his position on actors' exemptions was that more liberty bonds were being sold in theaters across the country than in ballparks. That was only because there were more theaters. Teams raised thousands of dollars for the Red Cross and other war charities. Players, officials, and umpires would subscribe to more than $8 million in liberty bonds. Baker later canceled the actors' exemptions.)

President Woodrow Wilson didn't think baseball was too non-essential for him to take in a Senators game the day after the work-or-fight edict was issued. He and eight thousand other fans saw a 16-inning 2–2 tie with Detroit in a benefit for the Red Cross. A ball signed by the president raised $3,500.

Washington catcher Eddie Ainsmith had been ordered to find work in essential industry or be drafted. Relying on his contacts in Washington, Clark Griffith appealed Ainsmith's case directly to Secretary of War Baker. But Baker turned him down. That brought a hailstorm of criticism on Griffith's head for going off on his own instead of joining a united plea by organized baseball for a blanket policy from Marshal Crowder.

Claiming there were only 258 men on major league rosters, the National Commission appealed to Crowder to reconsider his edict. Crowder backtracked a little and vaguely left the door open for specific appeals by athletes before a final decision would be made on their status. He left it to individual draft boards to handle individual cases, resulting, not surprisingly, in mixed results. Boston catcher John Henry lost his case when his Massachusetts draft board said baseball was not essential. Joe Finneran, a Yankees pitcher, earned a "baseball is essential" verdict from his New Jersey board. And so it went.

While some baseball people raised umbrellas against the falling sky, Connie Mack remained calm, stoic, philosophical. "I don't like to talk about it because it isn't clear to me, and I've not read the full details," he said of the "work or fight" edict. "I don't think our parks are going to be closed all over the country on July First. Whatever we are asked to do we will do ungrudgingly. I will not cross a bridge until I come to it. It seems to me that the news from Washington is vague and indefinite so far as it affects baseball."

When asked what he intended to do, Mack said he would "keep on smiling."

"But what if your players leave you and get into essential industry right away?"

"Well," Mack replied, "I believe they'll be here for tomorrow's doubleheader. I cannot say anything about my plans, for I haven't any for the present. As for the future. . . ." He waved a hand and shrugged.

Connie Mack retained his confidence and optimism that things would work out. He'd been through plenty of triumphs and troubles in his thirty-four years in baseball—and he was still in business. If his roster was depleted, his plans wrecked by desertions or wars of whatever kind, he would keep going, keep trying, keep moving toward his goal. It wasn't an act, nor mere buncombe for public consumption.

Connie Mack didn't read many books. Most of his library consisted of baseball-related publications. Twenty years earlier a visitor to his room at the Republican House Hotel in Milwaukee had observed his collection of "baseball lore and correspondence to a sufficient extent to fill a city library."

He never discarded any of it. When a young fan, Howard Ballard, wrote to him from Hale Center, Texas, in 1932, offering Mack a 1914 rule book he had come upon, Mack responded that he had the book. "In fact, I have all the rule books from the time our league opened up to the present time."

Dr. James H. Penniman was one of Connie Mack's eclectic covey of close friends. A professor of literature at Penn, a wealthy collector of rare books, and a fixture at every A's home game, Penniman said that Mack was an avid reader of the works of Orison Swett Marden, one of the early self-help authors. A hotel operator until the 1892 depression, Marden became a publisher of Success publications. In 1897 his *Success* magazine had a circulation of a half million, enormous for the population of the time. He wrote dozens of books on the theme. *The Secret of Achievement*, published in 1898, was a compilation of anecdotes, quotations, and fables pounding away at themes indicated by some of the chapter titles: Moral Sunshine, Blessed Be Drudgery, Honesty as Principle and as Policy, Courage, Self-Control, The School of Life, Tenacity of Purpose, The Art of Keeping Well. A 1911 expanded edition of *Pushing to the Front* consisted of almost nine hundred pages of examples from Horatius at the bridge through Caesar, Washington, Nelson, Napoleon, Grant, Lincoln, and hundreds of others whose lives demonstrated "perseverance and will over seemingly insuperable difficulties" and success "by dint of indomitable will and inflexible purpose."

How early in life Connie Mack began reading Marden's works is impossible to say, but their aphorisms are consistent with the views he expressed about life and the singular course he took in pursuit of victory. At the age of seventy-seven, his reading would still pursue the secrets of success: Walter West Tomlinson's *Time Out to Live, A Guide to Personal Success*.

Mastering worry kept him young. And in times like these, that kind of attitude helped a man survive. That spirit, his children said, made the fifty-year difference between his age and theirs insignificant to them.

As was so often true in the past and would be in the future, major league baseball didn't make a very good case for itself, this time with the War Department. Instead of playing on its strengths—the game's contribution and importance to the morale of the nation—it pleaded an economic case: $10–15 million was invested in plants that would be idle if the season ended early.

Newton Baker was unimpressed. The war had affected a lot of private businesses, and baseball was no exception.

When Ban Johnson proposed that major league teams be granted exemptions for eighteen players per team to keep the game going, some politicians and baseball men—led by John Tener—questioned his patriotism and blasted him for promoting shirking by ballplayers

Connie Mack's temper flared up. He fired back in support of "Friend Ban":

The men who are blistering Ban Johnson make me tired. Johnson has more patriotism in his right foot than many of them have in their hearts. Johnson offered his services to his country in any capacity without any conditions. How many of those who are now criticizing him have been near a recruiting office?

Johnson made the suggestion of the exemption plan to see how it would be received. Now he is being called every name in the calendar by persons who are too cowardly to say a word till they have felt public opinion. Johnson would be the last person in the world to embarrass the administration on the war in Germany. If the game is allowed to die the nation will make a colossal mistake. Just like England did at the start of the war when it abolished its favorite sports, it so affected the morale of the country, the leaders saw light and were forced to restore them.

If the administration does not take kindly to Johnson's suggestion that is all right. At all times we will bow to superior judgment. What I object to is innuendo from people who think there is something wrong with Johnson's patriotism.

Minor league parks were closing, squeezed by higher costs and lower attendance and the depletion of their rosters. Of the ten that started the season, only one, the International League, would finish, cutting short its schedule and starting its playoffs September 2.

Ban Johnson said it was up to the government whether the season would be cut short. But it wasn't. At no time did the War Department or anyone else order major league clubs to close their parks. Baseball had no leadership, no unity. National League president John Tener declared they'd probably have to close down immediately. His secretary, John Heydler, disagreed; they would get players wherever they could and play out the schedule.

The entire baseball business was day to day.

There was never any uncertainty in the mind of the chairman of the Philadelphia draft board, Dr. John A. Boger, who happened to be the Phillies' longtime physician. Dr. Boger considered the ruling as settling things.

"Next week we will start to call in ballplayers and ask if they are in essential industry," he said. "If not, they will be ordered into one."

Joe Dugan was high on Dr. Boger's list. His number had been the 496th drawn out of the bowl. Jittery Joe went home, returned, took off to a steel mill, came back, disappeared to see about getting into the shipbuilding trade, reappeared. It wasn't fun turning twenty-one on May 12, 1918.

From one week to the next nobody knew who would be in the clubhouse. On May 20 Mack's speedy young outfielder Merlin Kopp thrilled the home fans by stealing home with the winning run in the fourteenth inning against Detroit. Five days later he left to report to his draft board in Toledo. They told him to come back in a month. When he did, they told him they didn't need him yet.

Mack never knew when Dugan or Kopp would show up. On Friday, June 28, Dugan struck out twice with men on base, once with the bases loaded, against the Yankees. The Philly fans let him know they noticed. Saturday morning he didn't show up. Claude Davidson took his place and drove in the winning runs that day. On Monday Davidson went to Mack and said he was quitting the game. He felt that he would never be a star and baseball had no future for him. He went to work at a shipyard. Mack had to put old man Rube Oldring at second until Dugan returned on Tuesday. Then shortstop Maurice "Red" Shannon enlisted.

Mack was playing pitchers in the outfield. He picked up a little-used out-fielder, Merito Acosta, on waivers from Washington. Acosta's primary asset was that he was Cuban and exempt from the draft. He surprised everybody by batting .302 and playing a sprightly outfield.

On April 27, the morning after Scott Perry had lost 2–1 to the Red Sox, George Stallings, whose Braves were in seventh place with a 2-7 record, was suddenly cured of his Scott Perry antipathy. He told club president Percy Haughton he wanted Perry. Haughton sent a telegram to the National Commission: "Have just learned pitcher Scott Perry is playing with Philadelphia American League club."

Percy Haughton may have just learned it. There was no way it was news to George Stallings, whose superstitions did not include refraining from reading the sports pages.

Connie Mack received notice of the claim from the National Commission on May 11.

The Boston claim on Perry set off a flurry of telegrams and letters, some of them irreparably caustic, among the parties involved. Garry Herrmann tried to extricate his foot from his mouth by wiring Charlie Frank that his telegram of last August had meant that Atlanta was "allowed to dispose of player Perry temporary."

Frank fired back: "That must be some new law in baseball that I have failed to hear of. When you decided last year that our case ended with the payment of $500, where did you think then that you would reopen the case? Your decision I believe gave this association the absolute title of the player Perry, hence were we not right to place player on the reserve list? Had we not done so, you could say that our right was lost, when we failed to reserve the player."

Frank's attorney, Charles Jacobson, wrote to Herrmann: "The Boston club was relieved from all further liability, the player necessarily reverting to the Atlanta club. This inference is indisputable, either logically or legally. Services of the player have been reverted to the selling club. That club under baseball law was compelled to place him on its reserve list, otherwise he was a free agent. Title to the player had never passed out of the Atlanta club. It had a right to dispose of his services as it saw fit."

Charlie Frank had told Herrmann that Perry had signed a 1918 Atlanta contract, but the National Association office notified Herrmann that no such contract had been recorded.

John Tener defended the Braves' position. "The Boston club had the right to say if they wished to complete the deal by making the final payment."

No mention of the half dozen ways they had made it clear they *didn't want* to complete the deal.

Ban Johnson asked Connie Mack for his version of the facts. The A's were on the road on June 1 when Mack dictated his reply, describing the meeting of Perry in Jacksonville with some Braves players and Boston newspaper-men: "Manager Stallings undoubtedly knew of his presence with my club, but he seemed in no manner interested in the player, for the reason he considered him a bum and a poor pitcher. Why did they make such a vigorous protest on paying the preliminary five hundred dollars for Perry, if they had any further thought of continuing with the player?"

Johnson forwarded Mack's letter to Herrmann, adding his own opinion:

[Mack] brings out the salient feature the Boston Club made no effort this spring to secure and tryout the player at its training camp.

It is plain from the facts submitted, the Boston Club would never have considered this player again, had it not been he was taken up and his value demonstrated by Connie Mack. The player's name did not appear on the reserve list of the Boston Club. He was purchased in a regular way from Atlanta. It is the height of folly and injustice to contemplate the taking away of Perry from the Philadelphia Club.

Herrmann's reply to Johnson, defending his earlier ill-advised assurances to the Braves, drew this scathing response:

I must again draw your attention to the fact the Boston Club made no effort to try this player out in the early spring, and did not communicate with the Atlanta Club relative to his address and intentions. Further than this the Boston Club did not carry the player on its reserve list. [Never mind that the National League told them not to list him.]

Some years ago [Nap] Rucker was taken away from the Athletics on a technicality. Mr. Mack is entitled to the utmost consideration. We would be lacking in our duty if the interests of the Philadelphia American League Club were not thoroughly safeguarded.

Then came Johnson's zinger:

I regard your position in this matter as absolutely absurd and unfair. If Organized Base Ball is to be conducted on the lines you indicate, we might as well have a reconstruction that will guarantee to the clubs a stronger safeguarding of their financial interests. I am amazed members of the National League should have the effrontery to try to push a case of this sort to a conclusion.

Every response from Herrmann was sent on to Mack, still on the road. On June 8 Mack turned from legalisms and logic to sentiment when he wrote to "Friend Ban":

I would like to call your attention to the fact Mr. Herrmann is overlooking one of the most important points in this case. That is, owing to Perry being allowed to play with our club for a month or more, and after he has made an excellent record and has become a strong favorite with the Philadelphia fans, that to deprive the Philadelphia Club of his services at this time would mean that we would lose every admirer of our National Game in Philadelphia. Under the circumstances can the

National Commission award this player to the Boston Club? It would certainly mean Philadelphia would be eliminated from the baseball map for the balance of this season. On the other hand, how much of a benefit would this player be to the Boston Club? In the first place I doubt very much if the player would return to Boston under any consideration, and in the second place Boston has not had this player, and therefore will lose nothing by his not returning there.

I have always considered Mr. Herrmann as a fair and upright man, and always thought he would do the right thing by every one connected with the game.

I cannot help but feel the Boston Club made a serious mistake in not claiming this player when he first joined our club. This was a most grievous blunder on the part of that club. Are we to suffer on account of their negligence? I am not going to believe Mr. Herrmann under the conditions that now exist in baseball, is going to still further injure the game and embarrass the Philadelphia Club by granting Boston's unreasonable request.

But they were preaching to each other. Unjust or not, Garry Herrmann was stuck in defense of his own contradictory original sin. Mack's arguments cut no ice with John Tener. In a final salvo at both of them, Ban Johnson fired, "If the interests of the American League are to be crucified in this manner, we want no more of the Commission. The action of yourself and President Tener in the conduct of this case is positively reprehensible."

The commission stood 2–1 for the Boston claim. But the rules now called for an expanded panel when a minor league team was involved, giving votes to the secretary-treasurer of the National Association, J. H. Farrell, and the president of the Southern Association, R. H. Baugh.

The Athletics were in Detroit on June 12, playing on a raw day before fewer than 250 paid customers, the smallest gathering ever at Navin Field, when a small shot was fired. It wasn't heard round the world, not even the baseball world—not yet. But it triggered an explosion that rocked baseball more than anything the War Department could throw at the game.

The expanded National Commission, on a 3–2 vote, upheld the Boston Braves' claim to pitcher Scott Perry and nullified the A's purchase from Atlanta. Garry Herrmann, John Tener, and J. H. Farrell voted yes; Ban Johnson and R. H. Baugh dissented. They ordered the Athletics to send Perry to Boston forthwith.

When, a year earlier, they had declared the Boston trial purchase null and void after Perry left the club, the commission members now said they hadn't really voided the deal. The Braves still had an equity in Perry until their thirty-day trial period ended. Herrmann's letter to them, copies of which had gone to the rest of the commission, assured them of a prior right to Perry in organized baseball. At the time, however, there was no reason to think George Stallings had any desire ever to see Scott Perry again. Nor did he, until Perry started winning for the Athletics.

As of the morning of June 12, Perry had won 5 and lost 10, but that belied how well he had been pitching. The Athletics had scored a total of 28 runs in 14 starts.

The commission concluded that the Athletics were "an innocent purchaser" but ordered Perry to report to Boston immediately.

As Connie Mack expected, Perry said no way; he'd go back to driving a truck before he'd pitch for George Stallings.

"They didn't give me a square deal when they had me," he said. "They bought me on trial from the Atlanta club last year and then let me sit on the bench till I got good and tired of it and left them in disgust. They didn't want me when they had me, they fought to prevent paying for me, and now that Mack has given me a chance to make good they're trying to steal me."

Connie Mack didn't go so far as to say he'd drive a truck first, but his reaction was as blunt and uncomplicated as Perry's. The stubbornness that was as much a part of his character as his kindness had been spurred. He declared the decision the rankest injustice he had ever heard of. He refused to send Scott Perry to Boston or anywhere else.

To the baseball establishment, Connie Mack's position was like an enlisted man refusing a general's direct order. Those who thought they knew him were stunned by his stance.

Outside of the official ruling, a strange comment was attributed to Garry Herrmann. Apparently the paperwork required by baseball's rules when a player is transferred had never been filed on the A's purchase of Perry. According to *The Sporting News*, "The chairman states had it been presented, probably the whole controversy could have been avoided. The National Commission would have halted the deal right there until agreement had been reached by all parties."

If the National Commission had in fact allowed a pitcher to work regularly for half a season without noticing that it had no record of his belonging to the team he was pitching for, what did that say about the way the business of baseball was being conducted?

It was common practice for Mack and other managers to throw an amateur player into a game on a trial basis without bothering with the formalities of signed contracts, much less filing them with any office. Under the rules they had ten days to do so after a player agreed to terms and could use the player in the meantime. But it's very unlikely that Mack would have gone into the season without ever notifying anybody that he had bought Perry from Atlanta. Nor was any such thing cited in the decision to void the purchase. Technically Mack may have violated baseball rules by negotiating with a contract jumper, although Atlanta had never suspended Perry and Mack had Charlie Frank's permission to do so. Garry Herrmann cited this point as the basis for the commission's decision, even though it was not mentioned in the decision. He chastised Mack for signing a "player who had left his ball club flat. Having done that, and having been shown that the man was a jumper, and having been impressed with the desire of the Boston club to recover the player, under the majority decision of the board which decided the case, the Philadelphia club should have retired in good order."

Despite the technicalities, *The Sporting News* agreed with Connie Mack. The decision showed "a lamentable lack of sportsmanship on the part of the Boston magnates, surprising lack of sense of logic and justice by a majority of the commission membership."

The paper's editorial writer, Earl Obenshain, told Garry Herrmann the more he studied the decision, the more he was inclined to question the worth of Boston's technical pleas. "It's ridiculous that Boston wouldn't know until April 27 about Perry's pitching when everybody knew about it."

Joe Vila in the *New York Sun* expressed surprise at the decision. He had thought Stallings's actions were so "raw" the commission would censure him for lack of fair play.

Some writers called it no big deal, a trivial matter between two teams over a rookie pitcher of unstable reputation who had recently lost seven of his last eight starts. Surely organized baseball would have enough sense to arbitrate a solution.

Meanwhile in Boston, Stallings was all sweetness, oozing compromise. He appreciated Connie Mack's awkward situation. If Mack was responsible for Perry's developing into a winning pitcher, the Braves wouldn't insist on taking Perry away. Nor did he want to do anything that might hurt Connie Mack and the Athletics financially. Heaven forbid. So he sent Mack a friendly telegram saying he would accept other players in place of Perry, and that would settle everything.

Connie Mack was not receptive. "I see where reporters quote Stallings as saying he would try to help me out," Mack told Philadelphia writers. "Stallings positively is no friend of mine. I don't want him for a friend. He is not the kind of a man that I want to make a friend of. The friends I want must be aboveboard in their dealings and loyal."

The Athletics then went on to Cleveland without Perry, who had gone home to Oklahoma to be with his ailing father. On arriving, Mack told the *Plain Dealer*:

> There was no fairness in Boston's claim. Generally, when one club discovers a player to whom it has a right has joined another club, it makes its claim for the player to the National Commission at once. But the Braves did nothing of the kind. They did not want Perry. They did not want him when we picked him up. He was with us on the training trip and the Boston players saw him pitch a game at Jacksonville, so it scarcely can be said Stallings was in ignorance that we had him. But, twelve days after the season opened and Perry had pitched three good games, Boston discovers Perry is with us and wants him. Is there any justice in such a claim?
>
> If Boston had any right to Perry, I would give him up in a minute. But it has not and I intend to keep him.

On Friday, June 14, after the Indians had beaten the A's, 4–2, Mack heard from the Braves: "The decision of the National Commission makes Scott Perry the property of this club. Can you suggest a trade that would be agreeable to you and us whereby you can retain Perry's services. Otherwise please have Perry report to us at Boston at once."

Mack ignored it. He wasn't about to offer any players to the Braves.

Like a merchant eagerly awaiting merchandise he had ordered, Braves president Percy Haughton kept after Mack, asking when the pitcher would be delivered. Mack didn't reply.

Ban Johnson backed Mack's defiance from the day the decision was announced. Even before that, he had warned the other members of the commission that "under no circumstances or conditions will Perry be turned over to the Boston club." That was like one dissenting justice of the Supreme Court advising a losing appellant to ignore the court's adverse ruling.

Whatever animosity had been simmering among Herrmann, Tener, and Johnson now boiled over into public view. The break could jeopardize the playing of the World Series.

"The entire fabric of organized baseball, the national agreement, is in danger of being abrogated," wrote Ed Bang of the *Cleveland News*. "Unless the National Leaguers back up, the national agreement may be abrogated, which would mean that the American and National Leagues would go their separate ways, and the world's series, balldom's blue ribbon classic, would be a thing of the past."

Others allowed as how that wouldn't be such a bad thing; the Series had taken on too much importance for the good of the game, what with teams spending fortunes on players just to get in on the October jackpot and scandals of ticket scalpers and speculators who never went to a game during the season buying up blocks of tickets.

Connie Mack could have applied for a rehearing of the case before the commission. But he didn't. Instead he threw the bomb that shook baseball's feckless foundation more than any anarchist's bomb could topple Wall Street. Perry rejoined the team on Sunday night. First thing Monday morning, June 17, he, Mack, and Luther Day of the law firm of Gage, Day, Wilkin and Wachner were in Common Pleas Court in Cleveland asking for a temporary injunction against the commission's enforcing its order. They got it, and that afternoon Perry pitched at League Park and lost his fifth in a row.

It was like the day a bar of Ivory soap sank at Procter & Gamble. Connie Mack had broken baseball's holiest commandment: no club shall appeal a league or commission decision in a civil court. He was the first. Those club owners who had pledged to punish sinners severely would now be put to a test they didn't want to face.

Ban Johnson may not have actively encouraged Connie Mack to go to court, but he now said that Mack had every right to do so. In effect Johnson was undermining the institutional structure for which he had been a pillar since its creation fifteen years earlier.

The first fallout was the secession of National League president John Tener from the commission. In a letter to his club owners, he blasted Connie Mack:

In my opinion, the defiance of our laws by the Philadelphia club of the American League constitutes such a breach of the agreement and good faith that this league can no longer, with honor, continue its representative on the National Commission. . . . I beg leave, therefore, to advise you that hereafter I will give no attention or consideration to any cases submitted to which the American League is a party. We cannot continue to maintain our honor and self-respect by dealing with those who consider our agreements and base ball law as mere "scraps of paper."

Tener made it clear what he thought of Ban Johnson: "The American League has been unsportsmanlike in its attitude," he told the *North American*. "There are two National League men on the commission and one American League man, yet the latter has won virtually every case submitted to the body. Yet the first time a decision is against the American League club, he refuses to abide by it, but goes to court and wants to upset baseball."

To Garry Herrmann he fired this missile: "For the information of our club owners, please advise me whether or not the American League proposes to abide by the decisions of the National Commission, or must we try our cases in the civil courts."

The animosity genie was now really uncorked. Barney Dreyfuss said he disagreed with Tener's stance, and he didn't have much use for the rest of the commission either.

Other owners voiced their long-muffled unhappiness over a club owner, Herrmann, serving as the chairman of the adjudicating body. As for the National Commission, ideas for reorganizing it, and prominent names to head it, began floating in the papers.

Connie Mack received another telegram from George Stallings, withdrawing his offer to compromise. Mack paid no more attention to it than he had to the others. "The courts have the matter in hand now and the right party will be protected. Under no circumstances will I ever surrender Scott Perry to the Braves. That's final."

Whatever doubts they had about the National Commission, nobody in baseball except Ban Johnson supported Mack's actions. All were scared of the courts, and with good reason. They knew that many of their internal laws and rules would never withstand legal scrutiny. Going to court could expose their practices to a spotlight they might not survive. Only through expensive settlements had they dodged more searching litigation in the Federal League suits, and one of those—Baltimore's claim for compensation—was still sitting in Judge Landis's court.

While most writers were sympathetic to Mack's position, they did not approve of the course he had taken. The entire structure of the industry was threatened. All it would take to settle it, they chorused, would be admissions by both Mack and Stallings that they had been remiss in their methods. But Connie Mack was not about to admit to any such thing. Hadn't the commission found the Athletics to be "innocent purchasers"? What was there for him to admit?

Years later Mack confessed that he knew all along the laws of baseball were on Boston's side. It was Stallings's waiting until Perry began to win for the A's before trying to claim him that riled Mack. And when Connie Mack was riled, he dug in—always had, always would. And had it been anybody else except the one man he most disliked in baseball, he probably would have been more gracious about it. Probably. Maybe.

Arriving in Boston the day after he had gone to court, Mack said, "I won't back down in my fight to the end for Scott Perry. I wouldn't dare to. I might as well under the present conditions close my park as to allow Perry to go to the National League. I would lose my reputation as a manager if I did not fight to protect the rights of my town and its fans. I have great respect for the National Commission but none at all for this decision."

Some writers thought it strange that "the most peaceful manager" would be the one to pull down the rotting pillars and bring down the temple on his own head as well as his fellow magnates'.

But this was the same Connie Mack who, thirty years earlier, had been a leader in the players' revolt against the National League's tyranny. Now, as then, he believed his cause was just and he had no recourse but to fight to the last. If that meant destroying the way the game was run, maybe it was time for a new way to run it.

At the same time, this was a mellower Connie Mack than the twenty-five-year-old hothead he had been. At a league meeting in Cleveland's Hollenden Hotel on July 22 he told his peers if it was the judgment of the members of the league not to press the matter so as not to hurt the game, he would bow to their will and do nothing.

In effect, that's what he did—nothing.

He did not withdraw the suit, nor did he press it. The next court date was set for July 29. A few days before the hearing, Mack hinted that "something might happen" to postpone it. He wouldn't elaborate. What might happen? A compromise with Stallings? A withdrawal of the Boston claim? Pressure from the league to drop the case? Mack wouldn't say. When the date came, attorney George S. Wachner was granted a postponement to September 23.

Scott Perry continued to pitch for the Athletics. In one stretch in July, Perry started 7 games in seventeen days, including a 1-hitter against the Phillies in the game that raised $3,700 for Billy Weart's widow and two children.

Perry and Vean Gregg, sometimes both in the same game, carried the load, with guys named Bill Pierson and Willie Adams and John "Mule" Watson filling in. (Only Watson, called up from New Haven when the Eastern League shut down July 1, would be heard from again.)

Connie Mack was scrounging for pitchers. One day in early July a tall, slender young man of twenty-two wandered into Shibe Park and asked to see Mr. Mack. Directed to the office, he introduced himself as Tom Zachary. Or did he? What happened after that has often been portrayed with a sprinkling of facts in a stew of fantasy. Connie Mack never talked about it. Zachary's version of what happened was told—with a few "misrememberings"—forty-three years later to Irwin Smallwood of the *Greensboro (NC) Daily News*.

Zachary was the son of a Quaker minister in North Carolina, a student and star left-handed pitcher at Guilford College. He had registered as a conscientious objector and volunteered for relief work in France. He was stationed with a Red Cross unit outside Philadelphia waiting to go overseas.

"I guess I kinda bragged on myself," Zachary told Smallwood. "Mr. Mack told me to go to the clubhouse and put on a uniform. He said he'd come down and watch me throw. After I had thrown a while, he said that was enough.

"'We'll pay you $250 a month, starting now,' he said to me. I was sort of stunned. I had never seen $250. But I wasn't sure I wanted to sign a baseball contract. I thought I might want to pitch again for Guilford College. I told him that wasn't enough. I said I wanted $300. He said no, but that I was welcome to stick around for a few weeks and that if I could pitch I might get as much as $500. We shook hands and I stayed."

A few days later, on Thursday, July 11, Mack told Zachary he could start against the Browns.

"I was shocked. I still didn't know if I wanted to play pro baseball. I told him I'd prefer not to play under my right name. 'That's all right,' he said. 'Today you'll be Zach Walton.'"

Either Zachary suggested the name and Mack agreed, or he had introduced himself as Zach Walton from the start and this conversation never took place, or he had introduced himself as Jonathan Thompson Walton Zachary, his full name, which is the only—and least likely—way Connie Mack could have come up with Zach Walton.

When Babe O'Rourke, the megaphone man, announced the battery of Walton and Perkins, men in the press box asked each other, "Who is this guy? Anybody ever heard of him?" Nobody had. They hollered down to batboy Hughie McLoon to ask about him. All they got back was that he was from Alabama, which he wasn't; he just sounded like he was. Somebody spotted the veteran Cardinals scout Pop Kelchner and asked him. Kelchner said he never heard of him. Nobody was surprised. They were used to a parade of sandlotters and semipros who were seen once or twice and nevermore.

Walton pitched 3 innings, giving up 3 runs and 4 hits, before Mack pinch-hit for him. Walton left the premises before the game ended but was credited with the 8–5 win. (There was no starters' minimum innings requirement at the time.)

"He has more stuff than he showed me today," Mack told the writers after the game. "In fact, he was not himself this afternoon, but you can look for him to pitch some good ball later."

On Saturday, July 20, the largest crowd of the season, about fourteen thousand, turned out for a doubleheader with Cleveland. Walton started the first game, pitched 5 innings and had 2 hits in the A's 10–4 victory.

He still had not signed a contract.

Right after the second game, the A's headed west. Zachary/Walton told Mack he couldn't go with them; he didn't know when he was going to ship out.

"[Mack] said he was sorry, that he understood about the war and all, but that when I got back from France to get in touch with him. He gave me $200 for my work—I figured a hundred a victory wasn't bad."

Zach Walton disappeared from baseball, but Tom Zachary reappeared in 1919. After the Americans marched into Paris, *Excelsior*, an illustrated French daily, ran a picture of a baseball game between teams of American ambulance drivers. Zachary may have pitched in that game. It's not clear if somebody tipped off Clark Griffith about Zachary or if Zachary decided to write to Griffith in hopes of pitching for Washington, which was the closest big league club to his home in North Carolina. There was correspondence between them.

Zachary landed back in New York on Sunday, June 22, 1919. He found the A's were in New York for the next few days and called Connie Mack at his hotel. Mack told him the A's would be back home on Saturday; come and see him. Zachary also contacted Griffith, who told him to come and see him in Philadelphia on the same Saturday. The Senators would be there for a doubleheader.

"I called on Mr. Griffith soon after the sun came up that Saturday," Zachary continued. "I remember him coming to the door in his long night gown and peering out at me. We talked a while. I told him I wanted $300 a month but he balked. He asked me if I was talking with somebody else and I said yes, with Mr. Mack. He said he didn't do business that way. He asked me if I did or didn't want to play for him. Finally, I said yes, I'd play out that season for $1,000. He said okay, and I signed a contract."

It bothered Zachary that Connie Mack was expecting him. Riding to Shibe Park on the streetcar with Griffith, Zachary voiced his uneasiness about having stood up Mr. Mack.

"But Mr. Griffith said he'd talk with Mr. Mack and straighten it out. As far as I know, he did."

Zachary placed his next meeting with Connie Mack on April 20, 1920, when he beat the A's at Shibe Park, 8–5. But he had actually faced them a month after signing, on July 27, in his first start for Washington. On whichever occasion it was, Connie Mack had not forgotten him.

"You never came back to see me," Mack said to him.

Zachary said, "Aw, Mr. Mack, you didn't need me."

According to Zachary, that was the end of it.

(Zachary pitched until 1936 and was 3-0 in three World Series. He is best remembered for throwing the pitch that became Babe Ruth's sixtieth home run in 1927. When reminded of it, he would tartly reply, "Nobody asks me how many times I struck out Ruth.")

Ban Johnson declared that the 1918 season would end after the games of Sunday, July 21, and called a league meeting for the twenty-second to formally take action. Mack didn't think such a drastic move was necessary and remained optimistic that "a way out will be found." It wasn't a matter of money. The confusion, the casualty lists, the uncertainty of when the season might end and who would be in anybody's lineup from day to day virtually guaranteed that nobody would make expenses in August or September. And not even watching a rookie pitcher issue 8 free passes to the sixth-place Browns on a hot day was enough to make Connie Mack wish the plug would be pulled early on the dismal season.

The leagues estimated that only thirty-nine players were outside the draft age in the AL and thirty-four in the NL. If necessary, said Mack, "I can get a team together in twenty-four hours that will furnish a pretty good article of baseball."

Philadelphia fans probably wouldn't notice the difference.

About twelve thousand showed up at Shibe Park on Saturday for what they feared would be the last baseball action they'd see until the war ended. They grew restless with the home team losing, 9–1, in the eighth inning, and, with no police on duty in the park (the result of a tiff when a plainclothesman was denied entry through the press gate for refusing to pay the war tax required of off-duty policemen), the crowd poured out of the stands and down the foul lines. They began to throw cushions at each other. With no hope of restoring order, umpire Dick Nallin forfeited the game to the Indians.

Mack took one pitcher, John Watson, to Cleveland for the announced doubleheader season finale. Watson lost the first game, 3–2, in 11 innings and pitched the second game, a 5–5 tie called after 8 innings, so the A's could catch the train back home.

Mack remained in Cleveland for the meeting on Monday, July 22. He didn't agree with Johnson, but he wouldn't oppose him publicly. Not so his old friend Clark Griffith, who was furious at Johnson's panic. The meeting produced nothing but a wait-and-see attitude.

The National League was also divided. John Tener said they should close down immediately. Secretary John Heydler said they should try to complete the season. Ebbets and Dreyfuss agreed with Heydler. Dreyfuss was most emphatic that "Ban Johnson is not going to tell me when I should close shop. Neither is he going to dictate to the National League." Charles Weeghman backed Tener. They met the day after the American League at the Schenley Hotel in Pittsburgh and decided to appeal to Washington for an extension of the work or fight deadline until October 15. The American League agreed.

The three members of the National Commission headed to Washington to present baseball's case to Crowder and Baker.

Newton D. Baker, who had the final say, was a baseball fan. He knew the importance of the game to the morale of the men in the service, as it was expressed in a letter to the *Cincinnati Enquirer* from a soldier in the tank corps at Camp Colt in Gettysburg: "I am hoping they will not knock out baseball for this work or fight order. There is no reason why they should. There are plenty of boys in these camps without drawing on a few hundred ballplayers. The first thing these boys turn to when they see a paper is the sport page and they can tell you how many hits so and so got yesterday and who pitched for the various teams. Baseball is the one thing back home that they can all follow."

(Despite the boys' intense interest in the game, *Stars & Stripes*, their main source of information, had ceased carrying baseball news earlier in the season.)

Citing the relatively small number of men (now 237) involved, Baker announced on July 26 that the order would not be enforced for ballplayers until

September 1. That slowed the exodus to the shipyards and steel mills, but it left major league baseball with a new dilemma: when to end the season, and when—or if—to play a World Series.

Ban Johnson proclaimed the season would end on August 20 so the Series could be played before the deadline. That's what the government wanted—though Baker had said no such thing—and it was baseball's patriotic duty to obey.

An editorial in the *New York Sun* chided the big leaguers for panicking. Nobody in Washington, it reminded them, had ever ordered them to stop the game. President Wilson, in a letter to a Chicago newspaper, had said he saw no necessity for cutting short the season. If a player was called up by his draft board, an appeal would delay things for weeks, maybe until October.

John Tener said there should be no World Series. But when Tener looked behind him, nobody in the National League was following him. At a meeting on August 2, a majority favored playing out the entire schedule. But they knew Ban Johnson wouldn't go along with that, and Johnson was the American League. At least he always had been. They were adamantly opposed to closing early to get the Series in by September 1, no matter what Johnson wanted. And since September 1 was a Sunday and the next day was Labor Day, why stop short of a big holiday gate? So they voted to end the season September 2 and start the World Series two days later. Since players would have ten days grace in which to find jobs after September 1, the chance of the pennant winners losing the bulk of their lineups before the Series could be completed seemed remote.

The American League and National Commission were meeting separately in Cleveland on August 3. John Tener refused to have anything to do with Ban Johnson, so the Nationals sent Heydler to the commission meeting and Barney Dreyfuss to negotiate with the American League.

Ban Johnson was confident that his club owners would "unanimously approve my view after the situation is thoroughly discussed. . . . The government gave us our orders in declaring baseball non-essential. We are duty bound to carry them out." Any action would have to be by unanimous vote.

He was wrong. He went into the meeting with maybe five votes—Griffith, Comiskey, and Frazee against him—and came out of it with none. Griffith argued passionately and persuasively to continue at least until September 2. Stopping play on August 20 meant that the fourteen clubs not in the World Series would have to pay their players for another ten days with no income. (Contracts had a war clause that cut off a player's salary if the war shortened the season. But that may have applied only if the government ordered the season curtailed. Whether or not Griffith's interpretation was correct is moot; he prevailed.) The eastern clubs were in the west; they wanted one more home stand. And while the Cubs had the National flag pretty much in hand, Boston, Cleveland, and Washington were still in a close race. Griffith wanted the extra two weeks to try to catch the first-place Red Sox. (The Senators won 9 of their last 13 but failed to catch Boston. The Indians were eliminated on August 31. With second place clinched and industrial jobs already lined up, the Cleveland players refused to go to St. Louis for the Labor Day doubleheader. Both games were forfeited.)

"I believe a majority of us favored Johnson's view," Mack said later. "But when we learned that the club owners having chances to compete in the World Series were satisfied to keep on playing until September 2 and take a chance on having the big games prevented, that let us out."

Mack was especially sympathetic to his longtime ally, Griffith, who faced the loss of two big Sunday gates plus Labor Day. "Griffith has suffered grievously for two or three years and has lost money. He was angry . . . therefore, at the thought that he might miss this last chance to get some cash back in the treasury."

In the end, it was the Nationals' insistence that under no circumstances would they take part in a World Series unless it started after Labor Day that cost Ban Johnson the rest of his support. The majority, said Mack, thought Ban Johnson was right, but for the sake of harmony, they went along with the Nationals.

John Tener had had enough. Three days later he asked the National League owners to accept his resignation, which he had submitted eight months earlier. They took him up on it and named John Heydler acting president.

Ban Johnson had been repudiated by his club owners for the first time. After the meeting he said peevishly, "If the club owners wish to take a chance with the government, that is their business," an uncharacteristic comment from the autocrat of the American League, whose club owners' business had been very much *his* business for eighteen years.

Was Ban Johnson nervous about the government's reaction to playing the World Series after September 1? Did he fear the War Department would swoop down on the Cubs and Red Sox on September 3 and swear them all into the army? Or did he hope to be vindicated by an official frown on the proceedings? We don't know if he was relieved or disappointed when

Baker saw no problem in extending the September 1 deadline for the two teams in the Series until September 15: "The boys over there are so intensely interested in the game and the number of men who are involved here so small in comparison that there is no reason why it should not be played out."

The present discord, coming on the heels of the still unresolved Scott Perry imbroglio, led Johnson to talk of the need "to clean house in [base-ball's] business methods and in the membership of some of its present family." He still thought like the autocrat of yore, purging those who opposed him. "Major league clubs must be better governed."

Not major league baseball, just its member clubs. Ban Johnson wasn't a well man, and his stature in the game had diminished. But Johnson saw himself as part of the solution, not the problem.

Others saw him differently. The National Leaguers believed that Johnson pulled Garry Herrmann's strings and dominated the commission. He was rarely on the losing side of a vote. In 1910, when they had intended to elect John Montgomery Ward as the NL president, Johnson had declared that he would not serve on the commission with Ward and cowed them into backing down. They chose Tom Lynch instead. They never really liked Lynch and liked Johnson even less because of it.

Johnson was now under fire from some of his own magnates. Harry Frazee fired a blast at Johnson, citing—without their permission—Charles Comiskey and Clark Griffith as his allies. He accused Johnson of "bungling the affairs of the American League" in urging them to end the season on August 20. "From now on Johnson is through spending our money. The club owners are going to run the American League in the future. His policy of rule or ruin is shelved."

Connie Mack, who maintained his roseate "we'll find a way" composure throughout the bickering, told James Isaminger, "Griffith was wrought up and Frazee does not know Johnson very well as yet. . . . When we line up next winter Griffith will be strong for Johnson as he has always been. I told Frazee that he, too, would be for Johnson when he knew Ban as well as we did. Next December everything will be lovely."

If Ban Johnson had been dictatorial in his running of the league, it was because from the start the owners had gladly heaped every responsibility and decision on his plate: travel arrangements, schedules, Western Union contracts, finding buyers and financial backing and players and managers for struggling franchises, even who should receive season passes. Those who had started out with him—Griffith, Comiskey, Mack—knew how much they owed him for the strength and success of their enterprise.

Now there was no leadership, or when the elected leaders tried to lead, they were ignored. Club owners were castigated by the press for not backing their presidents. They were condemned for trying to stretch the government's generosity beyond its limits. Work or fight meant just that. They had wheedled a two-month extension and were trying to push it another two weeks just to get in what some writers called the "Slackers Series."

On August 3 in Chicago, Vean Gregg, who had been working with an aching back all summer, hurt his arm and went home to his ranch in Alberta and retired. (He came back as a forty-year-old reliever for the 1925 champion Senators.) Mack's pitching staff became John Watson, Jing Johnson, and Perry. Watson, a sturdy farm boy from Homer, Louisiana, started 10 of the last 32 games, including 3 complete games in the last three days. Perry started 7 more and relieved often. On August 24 he earned a $500 bonus for winning his twentieth. He finished with 30 complete games, a league-leading 331 innings pitched, and a 21-19 record, one of five 20-game winners in both leagues. His 1.98 ERA was fourth in the league.

What Connie Mack would have done for pitchers had the season gone on to October is a good question. After a 7-game losing streak in a heat wave at home that hit a record 106 on August 8, the A's actually won 10 of their last 18 games and finished 4 games back of seventh-place Detroit. If Perry and Watson could have lasted another 26 games, who knows how high the A's might have ascended?

The season had begun in the shadow of enemy armies slogging and slaughtering each other back and forth over the same few miles of bleak terrain, producing headlines like these:

WORLD'S GREATEST BATTLE:
A MILLION HUNS IN COMBAT
BRITISH IN RETREAT

At first baseball had benefited from the need for escape among the population. "America uses sport to forget its troubles," Isaminger wrote. "In the present dark hours we embrace baseball to get away from casualty lists." But in July and August, as the casualty lists had grown longer amid the squabbling among the game's custodians, enthusiasm had withered.

Shibe Park closed until the end of the war before a small Wednesday gathering of mostly men in uniform on August 28. John Watson dispatched the Indians, 1–0, in seventy-nine minutes. The two teams marched to the center-field flagpole while Kummel's Veteran Corps band played "The Star Spangled Banner." They lowered the flag and the White Elephant banner that had flown at home games since 1902. The band then played "Auld Lang Syne" as the players returned to the dugouts. Many fans lingered, as did Connie Mack, who shook hands with all those who approached him before he went up to his tower office.

"It is a period to test the character of men in all lines of endeavor," he told Francis Richter of the *Philadelphia Press*. "I think we all have underestimated the war's immediate necessities."

Despite the disruptions that were beyond his control, Connie Mack looked back at the 1918 season with some satisfaction. He had given the fans the best Athletics team they had seen since the glory days. They had gained 20½ games in the standings and were only 10½ games out of the first division.

The trades for which he had been panned had proved him right. Ping Bodie hit .254 in New York; George Burns batted .352 and was among the top three in all offensive stats, leading with 236 total bases. Strunk hadn't produced in Boston. McInnis had dropped to .272; both Tilly Walker and Larry Gardner outhit him. Tilly Walker tied Babe Ruth for home run honors with 11 (the A's led the league with 22). Gardner had played as hard for the last-place A's as he had for the pennant-winning Red Sox two years before, leading all third basemen in assists. Merlin Kopp, distracted all year going back and forth to his draft board in Toledo, never got started at the plate. Joe Dugan hit a league-low .195, but he was young, immature, impatient, and high-strung.

Pitching continued to plague the A's. The team's 4.36 ERA was the worst in either league. With it all, and despite the previous winter's chorus that the 1918 A's would be worse than the 1917 club, they had risen from .359 to .406 for the shortened season.

Mack's efforts to improve his product had been well received by the fans. The A's outdrew the last-place Phillies, whose do-nothing ownership was fast losing customers. For the year the Athletics averaged about three thousand per game on their fifty-nine home dates, close to the 1917 attendance. Mack had his share of vocal critics, but there was also a silent core of Philadelphians who respected him and rooted not for the team, but for the man, to return to the top.

A dozen years later William S. Dutton wrote in the *American Magazine*:

I know a businessman who for years kept away from Shibe Park—he told me he couldn't bear to see Mack's team lose. But he never failed to buy a season ticket, which somebody used in his stead.

"I've got to do that much for Mack," he told me. "As he sits out there day after day, come what may, he is an inspiration to every man or woman who has an uphill fight. He's the underdog now, but you don't hear him whine. He was humble in victory, and now he is showing what it means to have courage and guts in defeat. The ticket is my bit toward keeping Connie out there. I give it to fellows who I know can shout for him."

But the view ahead was murky. Joe Vila estimated that a majority of major league clubs had lost money in 1918. (The Athletics showed a small profit, but only after they booked receipt of the $30,000 second payment for the 1917 sale of Bush, Schang, and Strunk.) The National Commission predicted a two-year hiatus before major league baseball would reopen its gates. Even if the war ended before the following spring, it would be months before enough players were mustered out to get in a 1919 season. Mack conceded there was no way he or anyone else could now put together a draft-proof team. Only seven players were selected in the minor league draft, none by Mack. But his near-term pessimism didn't dampen his long-term outlook.

"Some of the club owners will be hard hit," he said, "but I doubt if it will be fatally. The only chance for big changes to result in baseball is if the war lasts two or more years. In that case, all the well-known stars will have passed on. Certain owners will probably have withdrawn under the financial strain. The country may have suffered so greatly that the men and means to carry the game on might not be at once available. As far as permanently hurting the game is concerned, war in the long run will boom it. The cantonments are developing hundreds of thousands of fans."

At fifty-six, with four years of red ink behind him and the prospect of no income for the next year or two, Connie Mack never gave a thought to his being one of those who might withdraw under the financial strain—not even if he had to carry the $40,000 fixed overhead each year with only the occasional $1,500 rental for boxing matches at Shibe Park.

Some club owners planned to lease their ballparks for storage to cover expenses. Mack never considered it. He and Comiskey and Griffith would never quit, no matter how rough the going. It was the outsiders, the bush-whackers, who would cut and run. As Louis A. Dougher of the *Washington Times* wrote, "During the attack upon organized baseball by the Federal League, Clark Griffith once remarked to me, 'They'll fail because they can't take a beating. I'd rather string along with a man like Connie Mack, for instance, who is willing to play it out, even if he hasn't a cent, than with a millionaire who never played ball.'"

The National Commission had met in Cincinnati on August 20 to try to work out a compromise that would keep the Scott Perry case from going to a full court hearing, which might lead to places the owners didn't want to go. They had reason to be nervous about any legal exploration into the way they did business, like their recent agreement—collusion—to "release" all the players to avoid paying them after September 2 but still reserve them to their 1918 clubs.

In the meeting Ban Johnson had proposed several options for disposing of the dispute outside of the courts. The way John Heydler remembered it in an October 10 letter to Herrmann, the choice that met with the Braves' approval was a cash settlement, "the American League to pay whatever sum you and I agreed upon as fair compensation. The Boston Club elected to accept the cash proposition, and we fixed the price of $2,500—a most rea-sonable figure considering the worth of the player and the loss sustained by the Boston Club."

Nothing happened. Negotiations went on between John Heydler and the Braves, who wanted some traveling and incidental expenses covered as well.

At the World Series in Boston September 9, Ban Johnson talked to Tom Shibe, who agreed to settle for $1,000 to cover the original $500 outlay by the Braves and their lawyers' fees. For the sake of peace they might go another $500 "to meet the traveling and incidental expenses mentioned by Secretary Hapgood." That's as far as Connie Mack would go.

On October 1 Ban Johnson passed that information along to Garry Her-rmann: "To make a payment of twenty-five hundred dollars would concede the Philadelphia club was wrong in principle, and Mr. Mack is very much opposed to such an adjustment. Few, if any, could be found who would grant there was justice in the decision," Johnson added.

John Heydler's patience had dissolved into peevishness, and the feud played on. His October 10 letter to Herrmann continued:

After nearly six weeks of delay, we find not only that our award is not accepted, but that the suit has not been withdrawn from the Cleveland courts, as promised.

I entered into this arbitration agreement in good faith, and confident that our finding would be promptly complied with.

It is because of the unexpected attitude taken by the American League, that the Boston Club is now compelled to reassert its baseball rights to the services of Perry by placing his name on its reserve list, and thus protect the title vested in it by the original ruling of the National Commission.

I have forwarded to President Johnson a revised National League reserve list to which the name of Scott Perry has been added.

Well. That gave Ban Johnson another opportunity to let them know that as far as he was concerned, he was saddled with dealing with nitwits. On October 12 he wrote to Herrmann:

I have your letter relating to the Perry case. I received a communication from Mr. Heydler this morning on the subject. It is quite evident to me your minds are both befogged.

You refer in your letter to the American League and that this organization will take care of the matter. That positively is not the case. It is purely an affair of the Philadelphia American League Club, and any settlement that is made will come from that source.

You and Mr. Heydler both intimated I agreed to abide by any price you might fix. The fact remains you and Mr. Heydler did not agree upon a figure. It was named by Secretary Hapgood, of the Boston Club.

I can recall no understanding that the case was to be immediately withdrawn from the Cleveland courts. Mr. Mack was prepared to take that course at the time you and Mr. Dreyfuss were at the Hollenden Hotel in that city. At your joint requests the case was allowed to continue on the calendar.

Connie Mack was ready to be done with the matter. To settle it while still preserving his point, he agreed to pay the Braves $2,500, which would include the expenses and incidentals. On October 17 George Wachner asked the presiding judge in Cleveland to dissolve the injunction that had been granted back in June, as the matter had been settled out of court.

On receipt of the check, John Heydler wrote to Herrmann:

I agree with you that no undue publicity should be given this matter, except that it will be necessary to say that Perry is to remain with the Athletics, the Boston Club having agreed to a cash settlement. The Boston Club will be so advised.

The satisfactory termination of this case without a court decree will prove a great thing for Organized Baseball, and will be especially gratifying to all those who will face the adjustment problems of baseball after the war, and who are working for the joint success of the two major leagues.

The collective sigh of relief heaved by all of organized baseball caused enough of an upper air disturbance to spawn tornado watches across the country.

But there was one man to whom the termination of the case was not satisfactory: Charlie Frank. As he saw it, the National Commission had awarded Perry to the Braves, who then sold him to the Athletics for $2,500. So didn't the Braves owe Atlanta the $2,000 due if they owned him beyond the original thirty-day trial period? On October 30 in Atlanta he pecked out a letter to Garry Herrmann asking "if we are not entitled to this amount from the BOSTON NATIONAL LEAGUE BASE BALL CLUB."

Either Herrmann appealed to Connie Mack for help or Mack volunteered to relieve him of dealing with Frank. On February 17, 1919, eleven months after Mack's initial inquiry into the availability of Scott Perry, Mack wrote to Garry Herrmann: "Have this day received letter from Chas. Frank, President Atlanta Club, saying he would settle the Perry case with me. No doubt you have heard the last of this case."

The Reach Guide said of the compromise, "The National Commission decision was, in effect, pronounced legal; the Athletic club admitted its error of taking the case into court; and the Boston club admitted it had no moral claim to the player by accepting a comparatively small sum for a valuable player [Isaminger priced Perry at $30,000]—all for the sake of harmony in the face of the many adverse conditions pressing upon baseball."

Connie Mack certainly didn't see it as admitting any error on his part. Harmony was all he agreed to. "I don't believe that Boston had any moral or legal claim to Perry," he maintained. "The bargain was a good one for the Athletics for I wouldn't let him go for triple the amount we paid to Boston."

If there could be peace between Connie Mack and George Stallings, why not in Europe? Peace rumors filled the November headlines. The Allies had the Hun on the run, across the Marne and the Somme Rivers. German soldiers surrendered by the thousands. On the morning of November 11 an armistice was signed and the guns were silent.

Three days later the minor leagues met in Peoria and demanded that the majors relinquish all drafting rights and quit farming out players on option.

Baseball was back to normal, squabbling over how to operate its business.

9 | THE SOLDIERS' RETURN

In the unaccustomed quiet of the premature 1918 off-season, Connie Mack gave some lengthy interviews. He had never hesitated to speak his mind in defense of others and preferred discussing ideas to improve the game over talking about himself or his business. A year earlier, when Ban Johnson had asked for a broad ruling on the draft status of ballplayers, Johnson had been accused of seeking a blanket exemption for them. Mack had defended Johnson's motives and patriotism at great length and with strong condemnation of his critics.

Now he was incensed by those who impugned the reputations of players who were working in defense plants and shipyards after the season ended. They were not draft dodgers. They were all Class 3 or 4 in the draft, unlikely to be called.

"Yet some persons insinuate that a ball player who abandons all the comforts of life to put on overalls at five in the morning is unpatriotic," he said in an interview that was picked up by papers everywhere. "I am particularly pained that insinuations have been made against members of the Athletics. These men [Scott Perry, Rube Oldring, Cy Perkins] stayed with me until the season closed and then went to the shipyards."

Mack took exception to remarks by Johnny Evers, who was in France conducting baseball clinics. Evers had called players working in essential industries "loafers" and "draft dodgers."

"Baseball has been very kind to Evers," said Mack, "and it does not become him to condemn class 3 or class 4 men who are working hard to support their wives and children. All this derogatory comment is unfair to the ballplayers."

In another widely distributed interview, Mack drew gasps and chuckles by advocating a ban on the sale of players. Anticipating the "look who's talking" reaction his words evoked, he said, "Some fans might smile when I say so, but I say it. There should be no more sales of a player. If a manager wants to get rid of a player, he should release him outright or ask for waivers and turn him over to the club making application and charge the usual waiver price of $2,500. But there should be no spectacular sales of stars for fabulous sums. These sales have hurt baseball more than anything else. They have caused inflated salaries, made players discontented and the fans dissatisfied. I hope the leagues get together and pass a rule prohibiting any more transferring of players for money considerations."

Mack was especially against the sale of veteran players to contending teams late in the season.

Despite the expected scoffing Mack's comments received, he had some supporters. Hugh Fullerton wrote, "Connie Mack has given the baseball world a big laugh, but at the same time he has sprung an idea which, if adopted, would be a tremendous move to return baseball to a decent basis. Connie knew the baseball world would laugh, since he has been the biggest dealer in baseball livestock. Yet he advanced the suggestion sincerely and he is right."

Francis Richter agreed: "This man, who in the past four years has sold over $100,000 worth of ballplayers, now frankly admits that this player-selling custom . . . is radically wrong. It should be eliminated from the game."

Was Mack being hypocritical? He was not alone in condemning the practice of wealthy clubs trying to buy pennants, as exemplified by the White Sox, Red Sox, and Giants, and now the new owners of the Yankees. Longtime manager Fielder Jones was quoted: "Championships should not be purchased as a number have been in recent years. This is one of the greatest evils which can befall baseball. It is a fact that few clubs ever make any money, aside from world championship aggregations, with possibly two exceptions in the past five years. It is really hard for a city like St. Louis, which has two clubs, to compete financially with a club like the New York Nationals, when it comes to purchasing men to bolster up a team."

Connie Mack meant what he said. He knew he was unable to compete with the deep pockets of some clubs. He was confident that if every franchise had to develop its own talent, he could more than hold his own. He was willing to forgo the money from player sales. More than once he had maintained that he was not in the baseball business to buy and sell "livestock." (Mack was about to be surpassed in that department by a buyer-turned-seller, Harry Frazee.)

None of his colleagues backed Mack's idea, though in 1920 the American League would ban the sale or trade of players without waivers after July 1.

Mack also expounded at length on the need for reforms regarding team roster and payroll limits. He told Richter:

> It is likely that when the game resumes there will be an ironclad agreement among the magnates not to pay even the biggest star in the game more than $5,000 a year. No ballplayer who ever lived is worth more than that amount for a season's work. Inflated salaries have done more to hurt the game than anything else. There is no other work in the world where a man receives greater compensation for less effort than he does in baseball. But the end has come. I have contended for years that $5,000 for six months of play should be top money. And this proposition will be put up to club owners when the next meeting of the league is held.

Players' complaints about impending pay cuts ran through all of baseball. Even the "wealthy dabblers" were balking at some of the demands of their stars.

And the press backed them. Ed Wray, for example, in the *St. Louis Post-Dispatch*: "Baseball has to retrench and all salaries should be cut."

Baseball's postwar boom, which the magnates did not foresee coming so soon; the onset of the Roaring Twenties; and Babe Ruth would make short work of any notions of salary caps.

Connie Mack was no longer the twenty-seven-year-old catcher who had been among the leaders of the players' rebellion against the 1890s owners' collusion on salary structures and limits. He had been on the ownership side for twenty-two years, going back to Milwaukee in 1897. He had learned how difficult it was to operate a baseball team at a profit. He was now a businessman and not a wealthy hobbyist dabbling in the game. Clark Griffith and Charles Comiskey fit the same description, though Comiskey's White Sox, with the aid of Sunday baseball from the start, had prospered the most of the three.

But there is no evidence to indicate that Mack or Griffith or Comiskey were painted as misers or more tight-fisted than other club owners at that time, either by players or the press.

Typical was Louis Dougher's comment in the *Washington Times*: "Clark

Griffith's reputation is excellent when it comes to generosity toward his players. However[,] the halcyon days of fat contracts forced by the ever-present shadow of the independent circuit have gone."

Were the writers buttering up the home clubs that paid reporters' travel expenses and allowed them to work out with the teams and room with players? Were they all in the owners' pockets? No. There are as many words in newspaper archives blasting the owners for incompetence and greed as there are in support of them. In Philadelphia, Isaminger and others could—and did—rip Connie Mack for some of his player sales and trades and silences as readily as they praised the "slim schemer."

And Mack didn't mind it; in fact he welcomed it if it was justified. "It's better if there's a touch of bad in even the best of notices," he said. "Then people are more likely to believe the good things that are said."

A story told by Isaminger about one player belies the myth that the supposedly "notoriously parsimonious" Connie Mack's salary scale was skimpier than other clubs. The player—not identified in the story—was Amos Strunk. During the 1918 World Series, Isaminger was on the train carrying the Red Sox from Chicago to Boston.

I sat down to chat with this player and started the conversation with something like this: "It's pretty soft for you to be with a team where you get a lot of salary and win the pennant besides."

"Say, nix on that stuff," replied the player. "I am working with the biggest hard-boiled egg in baseball. As for getting a big salary I want to tell you that I am getting the same money [$4,000] that I did from Mack. When the trade was made I thought I would get a big advance. But my new owner declared he was astounded when he heard what Mack had been paying me. He said that if he knew what my salary had been he never would have got me. Since I was with his team he would give me the same salary, although he hated to do it. He talked to me about three hours and he made me feel like Jesse James. As a matter of fact, I am worse off than in Philadelphia, for I have a house there and I have to pay rent where I am now.

"Say, when you see Connie Mack, will you tell him to get me back?"

Wally Schang had received the same treatment in Boston: no raise over the $4,000 he had drawn with the Athletics.

Connie Mack often had fewer holdouts or contract squawkers than most other club owners. He took a personal interest in his boys and they felt it. He had some players he didn't like, but that didn't affect his judgment of their ability or the way he treated them. There was a mutual respect that went beyond the ordinary employer-employee relationship. The list of his former players, even those who played for him when he was in his eighties, who later volunteered, "He was the greatest-finest-kindest man I ever knew," was astonishingly long. On the road he was a soft-spoken but in-control surrogate father to the youngsters. The wayward among them didn't get away with much.

On Sunday mornings if Mack saw any of them hanging around the hotel lobby, he would wiggle a finger at them, say, "Come here, boys," and off they'd go to the nearest Catholic church. It didn't matter what their religion was, if any. Nor was he trying to convert anyone. He just thought a church was a good place for them to be on a Sunday morning.

If a player on the trading block had a preference for where he wanted to go, Mack would try to accommodate him.

The esteem in which his players held him comes through in letters they wrote to him from overseas. The letters reveal the genuine fondness for him that existed among his past and present players, stars and one-game wishfuls alike. They also destroy the myth that his boys always addressed him as Mr. Mack, never as Connie. That may have been true in his later years, when he became more of a surrogate grandfather to them, but it was not so at this time.

Ray Bates, Mack's 1917 third base hopeful, wrote on September 21 from "somewhere in France" (Villers-en-Haye) with the 153rd artillery brigade of the 78th division:

> Dear Connie:
>
> Just a few lines to say hello and let you know I am still alive and enjoying myself. Surely was sorry to see the team finished in last place again. When I was there they surely were going great and looked like a first division team. Presume baseball is over now and will not continue until after the war. Suppose it was a bad year financially for both leagues, for everybody is too interested in this league over here to have time to bother with baseball. Believe me, Connie, this is certainly some fast league, and a person has to be on his toes all the time, or you will get "canned." This is one league

where a "slump" does not figure, for if a person gets in a slump over here there is only one answer, and the same is "he is out of luck."

Connie, I always felt Walter Johnson had a fast one that was great, but Fritz has beaten him. When Fritz cuts loose his fast one, it makes Walter's look like a slow one. And talk about a break. Fritz surely has one. If a person isn't always on his toes, and don't do some fast thinking and ducking, he is out of luck, for Fritz will surely bean him. The other evening Fritz gave us a fine reception, but it didn't do any harm. It wasn't his fault he didn't. He cut loose a couple of fast ones, and when I saw the break on the first one, I decided it was move. Before I could move, he shot a second one right at my bean. Believe me, I surely did get out of the way of it. Before he could send over his third strike, I made a pretty 20-foot dive which landed me behind a tree, which afterwards proved a very fortunate position.

At the present time I am hitting about .400, but I can't say so much for my fielding. Fritz is hitting them down to me so fast that I have all I can do to duck them. However, we should worry. The Allies are going to win this pennant. No doubt about it. Noyes and Alexander are over here somewhere but I haven't seen them, nor do I know where their sector is. I saw their pictures in a paper. They are pitching for a regimental team.

Well, Connie, I think I'll say adios. Would like to hear from you when convenient. I hope the war is over soon and that baseball will be going full speed again next summer.

Yours sincerely, Ray Bates

As a lifelong letter writer, Connie Mack doubtless found it convenient to reply to Ray Bates.

Mack received a long, chatty letter from right-hander Elmer Myers. It was written at Evacuation Hospital 15 on November 25.

Dear Mr. Mack:

Well, at last it is all over and I think that no one is happier than I am. The next question is, when will we get back?

Some will be lucky and get back soon, but I don't know about our company, as our commander wants us to go to Germany. I hope we don't, as now, with the fighting at an end, I would prefer to get home without delay.

We have been stationed at Verdun for quite a long time and have been under shellfire all the time. But I escaped unscratched, though was pretty lucky at times.

I certainly have learned many a lesson over here, and when I get back I will appreciate things more than I did before, as I never realized how easy I had it.

I used to kick about sleeping in an upper berth, but will not do it anymore after sleeping in a French box car. Forty-three of us traveled in a box car, about half the size of an American freight car, for four days and nights. I stood up all the time and virtually had nothing to eat. If that doesn't teach you a lesson, nothing will.

And talk about work, we have plenty of that. Twenty-four hours at a stretch was nothing. Even now I have plenty to do, cleaning up the dirt made by the war.

Sometimes we have plenty to eat and sometimes we don't. But through it all I have gained in weight. How I did will always be a mystery to me. I see by the papers that baseball will be resumed next spring. I believe it will be a great year, as all the boys say they won't work when they return home, but enjoy themselves and take in all the amusements.

I can't say when I will get back, but as Secretary Baker always wanted baseball to go on, it may be that he will make arrangements for all ballplayers to return. So if he does I will certainly appreciate anything you can do for me and will never forget it.

I feel that I can deliver better than I ever did for you, and hope to be with your team next spring. This should be a wonderful Christmas back home on account of victory, and I hope you and your family will enjoy it to their fullest extent.

Sincerely yours, Elmer Myers

Mack heard from another of his pitchers, Rollie Naylor, who had enlisted at the end of the 1917 season. Naylor had been at the front in France for a year when the armistice was signed and hadn't touched a baseball. He was among the troops who joined the "lost battalion" just after Giants infielder Eddie Grant had been killed in the Argonne.

"He told me that he had a half-minute's conversation with Anderson, the lefthander who had been with the team in 1917," Mack said, "but they had barely the chance to greet each other, Anderson's company being under marching orders for another point. He asked me if there would be any baseball in 1919 and whether I wanted him back. I replied immediately that baseball would be bigger than ever next season and I banked on his being back with the Athletics. I want Naylor and will make every effort to have him in Philadelphia by the first of April."

Mack even received a long letter from Lt. Thomas L. Turner, who had made one start for the A's in 1915, after which he and Mack had briefly discussed a scouting job. That had been their only contact, yet here he was, three years later, taking the time to write to Connie Mack from the front.

There was general agreement among interested parties that the National Commission, baseball's governing body, was a shambles. Comments by I. E. Sanborn in the *Chicago Tribune* were typical: "War or no war, professional baseball is due for an early collapse, unless reorganized and new principles put to the fore. Even if there had been no European war, baseball could not have survived many years without going to pieces of its own weaknesses. Commercialism, typified by the growth in size of the dollar sign, was sapping the sporting foundations so fast there would have been none of them left in another year or two at most."

The more things change, etc. etc.

As it did—and always would—in many ways, baseball's methods of operation reflected the American society in which it was embedded. William Pinkerton of the detective agency complained, "Inefficiency, incompetence, a lack of centralization, and jealousy between federal agencies had often spoiled important cases of espionage" during the war. Although "we're no worse than anybody else" is a weak defense, the camouflage of commonness dampened baseball's reform efforts.

Enforcement of the rules of the business of baseball was inconsistent. Paperwork was slipshod. The lending of players between clubs was open and unimpeded. The minor leagues were convinced that they would never be treated justly in disputes with major league clubs. Some of the commission's decisions were ignored. Others, while obeyed, gave the impression that the triumvirate didn't know what they were doing. Three cases in particular—George Sisler, Scott Perry, and John Picus Quinn—had cost the commission the support of key leaders among the owners.

Barney Dreyfuss had distrusted the commission ever since it voided his claim to George Sisler in favor of the Browns. In 1911 Sisler, a pitcher at the University of Michigan, had signed a minor league contract but never played professionally. The contract changed hands a few times while Sisler starred at Michigan, playing for coach Branch Rickey. Barney Dreyfuss bought Sisler's contract from Columbus in 1915. Rickey was managing the St. Louis Browns when Sisler graduated. Rickey persuaded the National Commission to nullify the original contract signed by Sisler, a minor at the time, wiping out the Pittsburgh club's claim to him. Ty Cobb, in a letter to Connie Mack, later claimed that Rickey and a regent of the university, Judge James O. Murfin, had threatened the commission to "bust baseball wide open in the court on their contract and reserve clause" unless Sisler was turned loose. Declared a free agent, Sisler signed with the Browns. As he watched Sisler become a star first baseman, Dreyfuss's digestion deteriorated. His resentment at what he considered a raw deal had simmered ever since. He was ready to dump the whole commission setup.

The divided decision in the Scott Perry case and Ban Johnson's backing of Connie Mack's going to court to overrule it further weakened the tottering structure.

A concurrent case involving the White Sox cost the commission Charles Comiskey's support. It exposed the incompetence and inefficiency of the three-headed body whose days were numbered long before the White Sox turned black. The folding of minor leagues in 1918 raised the question of the status of the players involved. The National Commission decided that when a league disbanded, players in that league became, in effect, free agents. Any club they signed with could reserve them for 1919 upon payment of the draft price.

The Pacific Coast League voted on July 12, 1918, to disband after the games of Sunday, July 14. The Vernon club had a thirty-five-year-old pitcher, John Picus "Jack" Quinn. After seven big league years, including two in the Federal League, Quinn had been toiling in the minors. On July 15 Comiskey sent a telegram to the National Commission asking if major league clubs had the authority to deal directly with PCL players "both for balance of this season and for future."

The chairman, Garry Herrmann, informed Comiskey that major league clubs did indeed have that authority. Comiskey then contacted Quinn, who agreed to sign for $500 a month for the rest of the season. On July 18 Comiskey so notified the commission "for the record." On that same day the commission was advised that despite the PCL's having disbanded, Los Angeles and Vernon had decided to play a 9-game series to decide the pennant winner. Until that series ended on July 22, those clubs insisted they retained the right to dispose of their players as they saw fit.

Garry Herrmann then sent Comiskey a cryptic telegram: "Question rights of Coast clubs to sell any players now."

Confused, Comiskey immediately called Herrmann, who told him to go ahead and deal directly with Quinn "and pay no attention to the owners for the present as an adjustment with the owners could be made later on if the latter had any right to the player's services."

As if that made everything clear.

So, acting on Herrmann's advice, Comiskey sent for Quinn to come to Chicago. What none of them, including Quinn, knew was that Vernon, believing it still owned the pitcher, had sold him to the Yankees on July 18. Quinn pitched that day and again three days later for Vernon.

(Ten years later Quinn told his version of the story. After the game at Salt Lake City on July 14 manager Bill Essick told the team the season was over and they were disbanding. "That night Essick got a telegram from Los Angeles telling him to keep the team together for a championship series, as two teams were tied." During the series Quinn received wires of offers from shipyards, independent ball clubs, and five major league clubs. Essick told him to make a good deal for himself. "The Braves made the best offer, but then a White Sox scout said he'd ask Comiskey to match it. Comiskey did. I was then living in Chicago, so I accepted it. On the bench that afternoon I told Essick about my break of luck. He congratulated me. But after the game, while I was changing my clothes, I received a note to stop in the office before I left the grounds. When I got there, Essick said, 'Jack, you're sold to the New York Americans.'")

Quinn angrily protested. Essick ordered him to report to New York. Quinn said he wouldn't; he had already signed with Chicago. He decided to go to Chicago and tell Ban Johnson the story, but he went directly to the ballpark instead and told Comiskey the situation. Comiskey said he'd straighten it out.

That was Quinn's story. He remained in Chicago and won 5 and lost 1 between then and the end of the season.

Of course the Yankees immediately filed a claim on Quinn. It's not known when they had notified the commission of the purchase. (The official records are such a mess, they show Chicago's terms accepted by Quinn "8/7/18";

Quinn on the Vernon reserve list "10/21/18" and the Yankees' reserve list "11/1/18"; the "Agreement for purchase from Vernon 2/20/19 filed with Commission"; and "Released by Vernon to New York: 4/29/18"—the "18" apparently a typo.) Anyhow, Quinn continued to pitch for Chicago while the commission dithered over the dilemma. On August 26 it awarded Quinn to the Yankees and sent Quinn a wire advising him of it. In their ruling, the commissioners fell all over themselves apologizing to Comiskey, admitting implicitly in convoluted language that they had blundered, while hedging that their advice would have been different if they had known another American League club was negotiating with the Vernon club for Quinn. They now concluded that Vernon did have the right to dispose of players until its last series was over.

Another detail of the ruling points up the sloppy way in which the business of baseball was being administered, what Warren Brown in his history of the White Sox called "the most glaring pair of errors ever recorded in an official baseball ruling." Twice in the ruling the commission refers to the Los Angeles club as the one involved in the Quinn controversy. Not then, not ever, did John Picus Quinn pitch for Los Angeles. Yet nobody picked it up at the time. They all apparently had a "whatever" attitude toward baseball's "we can run our own business" administrators.

Comiskey hit the roof. He made noises about following Connie Mack's tracks to the courthouse but didn't pursue that route. He was furious with his old comrade in arms Ban Johnson, who had gone along with the unanimous verdict, in contrast to his vigorous dissent in Mack's case.

The commission called the situation "unfortunate."

There were too many such peculiar and unfortunate situations that illuminated the state of baseball's governance. Things had been chaotic all year. Nobody knew from one day to the next what the game's official position would be regarding the continuing of the season, whether the commission even had one, or what it ought to be. The three members of the commission often took different public stances on matters affecting the game. They had been roundly and regularly roasted in the press for not knowing what they were doing.

Organized baseball was as disorganized as it had been back when two National League factions had elected two league presidents at the same time.

The game's government needed repairing. But there was no agreement on how to fix it: expand it, abolish it, replace it with one czar, name a baseball magnate, or bring in an outside person of noble reputation to rule alone or as chairman. They were all embarrassed when they learned that Harry Frazee and Giants owner Harry Hempstead had approached former president William Howard Taft about accepting the position of commissioner of baseball. So was Taft, when he learned they had no authority to offer him the job.

Connie Mack ripped into Frazee. "I regret deeply that a former president of the country should be placed in an embarrassing position by Frazee of Boston, who is acting on his own initiative." Mack called Frazee a "limelighter who gives the American League a black eye by his irresponsible and unjustifiable action. . . . Frazee is the last man in the world we would select to speak for us."

Phil Ball described Frazee as a "postage stamp" magnate.

Frazee's colleagues watched hopefully as he and George M. Cohan and theatrical producer Sam Harris tried to buy the Giants, which meant he'd have to sell the Red Sox. (Wouldn't *that* have changed baseball history!) But a group headed by John McGraw, Charles Stoneham, and Judge Francis X. McQuade bought the Giants, and Frazee could find no buyers at his asking price—a reported $1.5 million—for the Red Sox.

That was the atmosphere when the league meetings began in December 1918. The Quinn fiasco had been an eye-opener for newly elected NL president John Heydler. The Scott Perry squabble disturbed him. The bumbling manner in which the threatened 1918 World Series strike by the Cubs and Red Sox had been resolved had appalled him. Years later he said, "I decided after that spectacle in the umpires' room that the old National Commission form of baseball government was outmoded, and we needed a strong one-man administrator to run our game." That's what the National League voted for, and the one man in charge wouldn't be Garry Herrmann or Ban Johnson. The Americans, with Mack in agreement, saw no alternative but to keep the National Commission as it was. "If that's what happens," the Nationals told Heydler, "do not vote for Johnson as a member of the commission." Whereupon the Americans huffed that the Nationals weren't going to tell them who could represent them. They'd choose their own man, and it would be Ban Johnson.

No "interests of harmony" persuaded either side to budge. In the January 1919 joint meetings, the NL was opposed to Herrmann continuing as chairman. Four AL clubs wanted him to continue. Mack and Frazee favored a neutral chairman. Seeing no progress, Mack moved that the commission be continued for another year until various problems were disposed of. The AL said yes by a 6–1 vote, the NL said no by the same count. They finally named a committee of two from each league to come up with a new chairman acceptable to both leagues. Committees—especially baseball committees—being what they are, that meant nothing would change for another year.

The minor leagues were also fed up with the way the game was being run. They wanted nothing more to do with the National Agreement. "Leave us alone to run our own affairs," was their plea. "No more player draft. No more options."

Browns general manager Bob Quinn agreed with them. So did Charles Ebbets, Harry Frazee, and William Veeck. Connie Mack said, "The majors should be able to help the minors if possible, otherwise they should be free to manage their own affairs."

The strongest opposition came from Branch Rickey, who saw the threat to his visions of a farm system. Jake Ruppert also disagreed. No action was taken.

The flu epidemic of 1918–1919 first hit the East in October. Among the early victims was Chandler Richter, son of the *Sporting Life* founder and a former sports editor. Connie Mack's family in Philadelphia escaped the wave but not his brother Tom in Worcester. He and Tom, forty-five, were the closest of the Mack brothers, though their personalities were unalike. Connie had a dry wit and responded to humor with a smile or gentle chuckle. Tom was an outgoing innkeeper, telling Irish dialect jokes and laughing heartily.

On the evening of January 6 Mack received a phone call from Tom's wife Alice, telling him that Tom was near death. Mack took the midnight train to Boston.

"My dad was delirious," Tom's daughter Helen recalled, "but when Uncle Connie came he straightened up and they talked about family and business and baseball clearly. They spent the last few hours together before my father died. Uncle Connie was very shaken."

Mack took care of the funeral arrangements and thereafter sent a check every year for the grave site maintenance. Tom's wife suffered a nervous breakdown and spent some months in a sanitarium. She later remarried, but Connie Mack remained a surrogate father for Helen and her brother Tom. Tom went to Bowdoin College, where he formed a band and later had a career in the music business in Hollywood. Whenever the A's were in Boston, Helen and her mother were always greeted with a hug and a kiss on the cheek, invited to stay in Mack's suite at the Copley, go to the game, and have dinner with him that evening. When they left, Mack always put a hundred dollar bill in Helen's hand. His letters to Tom's family were always signed "Love to all, Con."

In 1927 Helen wanted to marry Henry Thomas. Her mother didn't think Thomas would amount to anything. She wrote to Mack to ask his help in breaking it up. The young couple went to New York and were married.

"I wrote to Uncle Connie and tried to explain everything," Helen said. "He wrote back and said not to worry. He was always supportive. Like my dad, Uncle Connie was a kind, loving, warm person."

The end of the war in Europe lifted national spirits, employment, and the economy. But not for long. Returning soldiers found few jobs. Layoffs by the war industries and the emigration of blacks from the South added to the joblessness. A red scare swept the nation. In April there was a wave of letter bombs. On the evening of June 2 eight bombs went off in eight cities. Race riots exploded in twenty-five cities during what was called the "bloody summer." Eighty-three lynchings were reported.

The moguls of baseball, still suffering from wartime jitters and uncertainties, remained in a retrenching mood. More clubs had operated at a loss than a profit for several years. Until they saw the predicted prosperity, they remained cautious. For the first time, most player contracts were written in monthly salary terms, not for the season. They approved a twenty-one-player limit, with returning servicemen exempt for thirty days.

Mack and Frazee agreed on one thing: they wanted to go back to the 154-game schedule. Ban Johnson argued again for 140 games, which would eliminate the piling up of doubleheaders that seemed to occur every year. In the last complete season—1917—the A's had played twenty-four twin bills, including holiday split games. This time Johnson prevailed. Mack voted with the 6–2 majority; Boston and Chicago dissenting. The National League went along with it, the season to open May 1 (later moved up to April 23). When the timorous Nationals passed a monthly salary limit, the American Leaguers refused to go along, and the Nationals quickly reversed that move under a barrage of public ridicule and criticism.

If the season was going to start that late, Connie Mack reasoned, the Athletics might as well do their training at home. His team usually spent the last three weeks traveling north anyhow, often in rain and snow. There was room for twenty pitchers to work out under the roof of the Shibe Park pavilion if the weather was bad.

Denied their annual sojourn to the south, the correspondents warned Mack that he would get less publicity by staying home. Bosh, Mack replied. They could write as much about the players at home as in Florida.

Baseball continued to wrestle with how to cut up the World Series melon. A motion by Mack at the annual meeting to double from 25 percent to 50 percent the American League pennant winner's share of the receipts going into the league treasury was approved 6–2, Frazee and Ruppert voting no. But the two leagues couldn't agree on the best way to include all four first-division teams in the pot. In a joint meeting in January, the AL voted to limit the players' shares to the two World Series teams; the NL said no. Mack proposed a compromise: the winning players would receive $2,000 each, the losers $1,400; second-place teams would cut up $10,000 each, third-place $7,500, and fourth-place $5,000. It was seconded by Charles Ebbets. The Nationals approved it, 5–3; the Americans turned it down, 3–5. Another proposal to allot 55 percent of the players' share to the two participants and the rest to the runners-up was okayed by the Nationals, turned down by the Americans.

The returning servicemen meant competition for playing time, so even with widespread salary cuts, there were few holdouts. Mack had one: outfielder Charlie Jamieson, who balked at being cut from $425 a month to $375. Jamieson had joined a steel league team after the season and threatened to stay there rather than play for the A's. He had been in the game as a pitcher and outfielder for seven years without making much headway. Mack was not interested in placating a dissatisfied twenty-six-year-old .202 hitter who had driven in only 11 runs and shown no particular improvement in the outfield.

At the annual Philadelphia writers' dinner at the Wolcott Hotel in February, Mack was his usual optimistic self. He told the gathering of four hundred that with the war over, he could see a clear road ahead. "Things look rosy now, and I will never again sell a player, though I am willing to make an advantageous deal. The policy of the Athletics is to acquire strength rather than take it away. I will also say I am going to have a team that will surprise the fans."

Despite having heard those unfulfilled promises before, his audience cheered him heartily. They were with him; they *wanted* to believe. Mack's team was still in last place, but the man himself was still tops in the hearts of all who knew him. They appreciated that he had never quit trying to improve his team, in contrast to the Phillies' do-nothing owner William F. Baker. (Baker tried to recapture some following by signing former A's ace

Jack Coombs to manage the Phillies in 1919. That ended in a messy divorce when he fired Coombs in July.) Since the Phils' 1915 pennant winner, Mack had regained the ascendancy among the public, if not in the standings.

The bleaker the picture, it seemed, the more the fans' hearts went out to this man who worked so hard to bring renewed glory to Shibe Park. Just as the will to win is what counts in war, so it was the will to win that drove him on, in hotel corridor huddles, through endless letters and phone calls, during thousands of miles of train travel, and nights in sleeper cars and small-town hotel rooms. Those four hundred who gave him a standing ovation that night were showing their recognition and appreciation of his spirit and his efforts.

Connie Mack planned to move Whitey Witt to the outfield, alongside Tilly Walker. He needed another outfielder. The Indians had the man Mack wanted and were eager to be rid of him. Bobby "Braggo" Roth could do it all. He had Deadball Era power, leading the league in home runs with 7 in 1915. He was usually among the leaders in triples and stolen bases and was adept at stealing home. And he hit well at Shibe Park. Half his 14 career home runs had been hit there, including 2 in a game in 1916 in which he had also stolen home. Mack had seen him go 7 for 10 in a doubleheader and bat .348 in Shibe Park in 1918. Roth covered the outfield with unrestrained enthusiasm, which could be hazardous to his fellow fly chasers.

But Roth was a troublemaker, a bad actor often in hot water. He had been suspended on August 15 by Cleveland manager Lee Fohl for "indifferent play." Cleveland writers were on him. Ed Bang wrote, "He didn't play heads-up ball" and might have cost them the pennant they lost by 2½ games. Henry P. Edwards branded him "temperamentally unable to play his best for Cleveland last season," whatever that meant.

One veteran American Leaguer described Roth as having "an unconscionable temper and general combative nature toward teammates. The latter then banded against him and he found himself ostracized." Sounds like he tried to pattern himself after Ty Cobb, on and off the field.

Connie Mack knew all about Roth's reputation. He liked that kind of player on the field. He'd take his chances with a knockoff Ty Cobb any day. Besides, he'd had that kind of malcontent before and thought he could handle him. Sometimes a change of scenery or a lighter managerial hand made a difference.

Mack had spoken to Cleveland owner James Dunn at the winter meetings, where Roth patrolled the lobby expecting to hear some news about himself. Mack offered the Indians Larry Gardner and Elmer Myers. Dunn wanted Tilly Walker. Mack said no.

The negotiations continued, Indians captain Tris Speaker sitting in on them with Fohl and Dunn. Throughout February almost daily reports had Gardner, Myers, and the holdout Jamieson going for Roth, although Isaminger insisted all along that Gardner would not be part of the deal. Thirty years later both Speaker and Mack remembered it this way: It was Gardner and Myers for Roth. Then Speaker asked Mack to "throw in" Charlie Jamieson. Not counting on Jamieson, Mack agreed. Looking back, Speaker called it one of his best deals ever, and Mack told Fred Lieb it was "a bad mistake." But at the time neither man had reason to think that was the case. Jamieson was considered just a benchwarmer who might not even report to the A's, and in 1919 he would bat only 20 times for the Indians before morphing into their star leadoff man for the next eleven years.

Several newspapers said the A's received pitcher Walt Kinney and third baseman Fred Thomas in the deal, but both were with the Red Sox at the time. Mack claimed Kinney on waivers and asked Jim Dunn to pay Boston for him as part of the Roth deal. Mack paid $1,500 for Thomas.

Some critics said giving up Gardner was too much for Roth. Mack admitted that he expected the men he had given up to do good work where they were going, but he said that about every player he traded or released. He saw nothing wrong with a trade that helped both teams.

The trade gave the A's their most potent outfield in years, moving Isaminger to applaud the team's strong lineup as a sure ticket out of the cellar. (Fallibility is endemic to spring prophecies. Cleveland sage Henry P. Edwards declared the Indians' pitching staff the best in the league; by June it would be the worst.)

Mack applied some psychology on Roth, naming him the A's captain. The prestige and responsibility might mature him, turn his aggressiveness into leadership. Mack also gave him an injection of confidence. Right field is yours, he told Braggo, even if you don't get a hit for the first ten games.

The army issued orders to give soldiers immediate discharges if they had a job waiting for them and applied for early release. Mack looked forward to the return of the nineteen boys he had lost to the armed forces, but with some apprehension. He had no idea how their overseas duties and absence from baseball might have affected them. Just a few years earlier he had predicted that Frank Baker would not be the same after his year-long layoff in 1915.

The servicemen began returning in December. Bob Geary, John Watson, and Lefty Anderson were the first A's pitchers back. Connie Mack quickly found his apprehensions had some basis. A 1,400-pound bomb had fallen off a loading tray and pinned Anderson against a railing, dislocating a vertebra. That cost him his fastball. He would pick up a win in relief in the second game of the season, then go down to Louisville and never make it back. Geary, "an unusually bright chap," according to Mack, had lost his compass and couldn't find the strike zone. Watson, the workhorse of late 1918, couldn't get himself into condition nor anybody out and wound up in Baltimore.

Jimmie Dykes came back with a wider rear end than ever. Mack sent him to Atlanta to work off the fat.

Ray Bates, Mack's 1917 third baseman of the future, wasn't discharged until May. Now twenty-nine, the year away had set him back too much. Mack sent him to Los Angeles; he never returned to the major leagues.

Mack eagerly but nervously awaited the return of Rollie Naylor and Wynn Noyes. Naylor had won 18 games at New Haven in 1917 and impressed Mack by pitching three "elegant games" before enlisting. "Naylor is an artist," he enthused, "one of the most finished youths that ever broke into the swift set. He has what I call a great delivery. He puts stuff on every ball he pitches, but has the style of Walter Johnson. His arm will never wear out. He has as much smoke as I have ever seen, as good a curve as any American League pitcher."

But Naylor hadn't picked up a baseball in over a year. He needed at least a month to get into shape. And Noyes wouldn't be discharged until the middle of July.

Short of pitchers—a condition that had become so chronic it would have been appropriate for his epitaph: "Here lies Connie Mack, still short of pitchers"—Mack sent letters and telegrams to Vean Gregg at his ranch in Alberta. He received no reply.

The Athletics opened in Washington with Tilly Walker hobbled by a sprained ankle and Roth a sore shoulder. For the first time Mack had no veteran coaches or players—no Ira Thomas or Harry Davis—who knew how to man the coaching lines, read opposing pitchers, pick up signs.

The 1919 season began like a continuation of 1918. Scott Perry lost, 1–0, in 13 innings to Walter Johnson. The next day they won in 13 innings, then they went to New York, where Perry pitched 12 innings and lost, 3–2.

For the home opener on May 1, Mack planned a salute to the military and lined up an admiral to throw out the first pitch. But it rained, and the admiral wasn't available the next day. So Mrs. Mack was drafted to do the first-ball honors before an enthusiastic crowd of about twelve thousand who saw them lose, 7–2.

They were 2-2, then bade farewell to .500 for the season. Then they were 2-3 and bade farewell to .400. Then they were 2-5 and never saw .300 again. They played at a .266 pace the rest of the way, never winning as many as three in a row.

Mack began his improvising and juggling acts early. Nobody was hitting but Whitey Witt. He had a second baseman playing third, a pitcher in the outfield. The pitching was lousy most of the time. When it was good, they didn't hit. They were shut out three times in Scott Perry's first seven starts and scored 11 runs in all. On May 2 and 5 Washington pitcher Jim Shaw hit a total of 3 home runs off A's pitching. He would hit only 4 in 287 games.

Mack gave the Browns $2,000 for right-hander Tom Rogers, who pitched one good game—including the team's only shutout—for every two poor outings. Rogers became the third A's pitcher in three years to post the highest earned run average in the league.

The infield was a disaster. George Burns, the hot-hitting hometown hero of 1918, was off to a slow start that affected his fielding. One day he muffed two pop flies in one inning. It's not always a joy to play in your hometown, especially in Philadelphia. The more pop-ups Burns dropped, the more they rode him. One of the rare times they cheered him came on a hit that didn't appear in the box score; after dropping a foul pop-up, Burns reached into the stands and slapped a heckler.

Meanwhile, a twenty-one-year-old left-handed first baseman, Maurice Burrus, was attracting scouts in Columbia, South Carolina. Mack went down to look him over and came back lauding him as "can't miss. The day I saw him he made five hits. I still would have gone to just as much effort to get him if he hadn't made a hit that day." Mack outbid seven other clubs for Burrus, paying $4,500 plus a few players. He immediately installed him at first base and moved Burns to the relative quiet of the outfield.

Mo Shannon was not getting the job done at second base and was also drawing the hecklers' aim. Scott Perry publicly said he wouldn't pitch with "that guy" playing second. Mack tried Roy Grover, who couldn't do anything right and was peddled to Washington for $5,000. He was forced to move Whitey Witt to second, where Whitey didn't want to be, Connie Mack didn't really want him to be, and the heckling fans loudly didn't want him to be.

It got so bad Mack had his best catcher, Cy Perkins, filling in at shortstop. But Perkins wasn't hitting. He had no power but was trying to pull everything to left field. One day the A's had the tying run on second with nobody out late in the game. Perkins was up. He hit an easy fly ball to left. The base runner never scored. After the game somebody told Perkins, "Mr. Mack wants to see you in the dugout." He went out and saw a pitcher on the mound and a catcher behind the plate. Mack said, "I want you to learn to hit to right field" and stayed out there watching while Perkins worked on hitting to right. After twenty minutes, Mack said, "That's enough for today. I never want to see you hit to left field with a man on second again." And he never did.

Joe Dugan remained an enigmatic, erratic shortstop. On the field he made spectacular plays, then booted routine ones. Off the field he harkened to his own sirens, jumping the team to go home with undisclosed ailments or to hear what an industrial league agent had to offer. At the end of the season he told a Boston writer he would quit baseball if Connie Mack didn't trade him. To which Mack replied, "I guess he'll have to quit."

Mack had counted on Ray Bates or Fred Thomas at third, but Bates was finished and Thomas wasn't hitting a lick. Mack admitted he had made a mistake in acquiring him from Boston.

In desperation Mack picked up infielder Terry Turner from the Indians, who said he was out of shape. He was. He was also thirty-eight, on his way out. Turner, the only player active throughout the entire 1901–1919 Deadball Era, filled in as needed at second, third, and short.

The outfield was described by Isaminger as "a slovenly, witless combination." Syndicated humorist Bugs Baer quipped, "Can't say Connie Mack's outfield is contagious. It ain't very catching." Tilly Walker's range had shrunk to "not quite far enough." They played all hitters alike, not that the pitchers were dependable enough for Mack to bother waving the fielders into position.

And the fundamentals weren't there. Pitchers didn't back up infielders or cover first. They cut off throws to home they should have let go through. The stoic Mack may have winced inside at what he saw. Perhaps it had been a mistake to cut short spring training. There had been little time to work on the routine plays. Or perhaps he had believed he had an experienced team that didn't need elementary drills.

A veteran player once described Philadelphia fans of the 1910s: "It takes something mighty classy to get them excited. Unless a pennant is depending on the result of the game, they will sit there and cheer perfunctorily.

But once they get going, look out. Then they are the wildest crowd that one could care to meet."

When something got them going, it was the custom of the fans sitting behind the visitors' dugout to bang away on the tin roof, to the annoyance of the players trapped beneath it.

On the afternoon of May 30 the Red Sox were in town. The defending champions, an uptight, cliquish bunch, were struggling in sixth place. Babe Ruth was giving manager Ed Barrow fits with his after-hours activities and complaints about being used as both a pitcher and outfielder. Carl Mays was griping about Jack Barry's sore-legged play and was suspicious that his teammates let up when he pitched because they didn't like him. He had lost 5 in a row before beating the A's (Mays made a career of beating the A's) the day before.

Scott Perry and Herb Pennock were locked in a 1–1 tie after 7. In the eighth with a man on base Babe Ruth awed the crowd of fourteen thousand with the mightiest home run shot they'd ever seen hit out of Shibe Park. The ball bounced off the roof of a house on the other side of Twentieth Street. The crowd saluted the Babe with a chorus of cheers when he trotted out to left field after the inning.

In the ninth hands and feet and vocal chords came alive when Braggo Roth tripled—his third hit of the game—Burns singled, and Dugan doubled to tie the score 3–3.

In the tenth, the tinny tom-tom on the dugout roof began to rattle the Red Sox cage as reliever Al Dumont started the inning by walking Witt. When he walked Shannon, the fans behind the dugout banged away with hands and feet and whatever weapons they could improvise. While Bill James was coming in to relieve Dumont, the irritable Carl Mays jumped out of the dugout and fired a ball at the drummers. It grazed a woman's head and knocked the straw hat off a customs house worker named Bryan Hayes. Another Sox player came out of the dugout, reached into the stands, and punched a fan sitting next to Hayes, judiciously bypassing Hayes, who, it turned out, was an amateur boxing instructor. The clatter crescendoed when Roth beat out an infield hit to load the bases and erupted when the jittery James hit Burns with a pitch to force in the winning run.

Ban Johnson fined Mays $100. The club's refusal to pay it for him became a factor in subsequent events that tore apart the American League.

The A's couldn't buy a hit in a pinch. One day they had 18 hits and lost, 12–6, tying a league record with 17 left on base. On their first western trip they were outhit only 84 to 75 but outscored 43 to 19. Witt and Roth were batting over .300. Walker and Burns began to wake up at the plate. They had some good stretches, winning 4 or 5 in a week. But the bad stretches lasted longer—5, 6, 7 losses in a row.

"They play championship ball one day and like bushers or worse the next," Mack complained. "I want some new ball players."

In early June they lost 5 in a row at home. Mack was eager to get away to do more scouting. His front office duties were claiming more of his time. He had carried the load of manager, general manager, chief scout, and club spokesman in duties if not in title for nineteen years without complaint. Negotiating salaries with players, then managing them in the dugout, presented awkward situations that club owners like Frank Navin, Comiskey, Frazee, and Ruppert didn't face.

Mack persuaded Harry Davis to come back as assistant manager and Paddy Livingston to return as pitching coach. It was a good move. Both were well liked. If Connie Mack was a father figure to his players, then Harry Davis was their favorite uncle. On his fiftieth birthday they would throw him a surprise party. Honest, warm, open, gracious, Jasper was "the squarest man I ever knew," said Mack. Davis could be closer to the men in the clubhouse, a venue that Mack usually stayed away from, not always to his team's benefit. Players would approach Davis with questions or problems or complaints when they might hesitate to bother Mr. Mack.

Sporting News columnist John B. Sheridan congratulated Mack for benching himself. "Maybe Mack has just gone stale."

Maybe he had. Maybe he needed a break after sitting through so many bad ball games, watching so many failed prospects. "You know," he admitted years later, "I never was a good manager of a bad ball club. Probably the worst." He knew that he was not at his best dealing with men who didn't learn, didn't hustle, didn't seem to care. Despite his outward calm, Mack had not become inured to bad baseball. The same traits that had led to success—patience, accent on youth, developing his own players—were now leading to failure.

James Isaminger coined another alliterative title for Mack: the haggard helmsman.

Thomas Hardy wrote, "More life may trickle out of a man through thought than through a gaping wound." Life was trickling out of Connie Mack. He never stopped thinking, working to improve his team. Suffering through the worst years of his career since 1915 had not affected his health, his appetite, his sleep, his optimism—until now.

Now, in his fifth year of losing three games for every one he won, seemingly on an eternal treadmill to oblivion, even Connie Mack's iron will and perseverance cracked.

Sitting in his office on a rainy afternoon seventeen years later, Mack admitted to *Baseball Magazine* editor F. C. Lane that during this time his optimism had dissolved into hopelessness:

> For a week or more I did not sleep well and found myself feeling thoroughly discouraged. The job was getting on my nerves. I was tempted, strongly tempted, to chuck it all and quit. But then one day I took myself to task. I faced the situation squarely. What was there to do? What could anyone do? The answer was simple. A manager can but do his best. If he does that, why worry? Whatever happened, I was doing my best. I could do no more. It would not help the Athletics and certainly would not help me to buckle under the strain and give up. So I snapped out of it and have never sunk so low again.

For his 1944 book *How to Stop Worrying and Start Living*, Dale Carnegie asked Mack if he ever worried over games that were lost.

"Oh yes I used to," Mack was quoted, "but I got over that foolishness long years ago. I found out it didn't get me anywhere at all. You can't grind any grain with water that has already gone down the creek."

From that experience was born the philosophy he impressed on Connie Jr.: "Son, there is never a worry worth taking to bed with you. When you look back on any worry, you will always wonder why you took it so seriously in the first place."

His serenity restored, one day he said to Cy Perkins, "Some day you'll see me have a good ball club and I'll show you how to handle it."

In New York at the end of June, Connie Mack told Joe Vila of the *Sun* that he had allowed things to slide during the war, but now he intended to provide his fans with a winner regardless of expense: "I'll get more first class players just as I dug up Collins, Baker, McInnis, and others. In my new first baseman Burrus I have a man who looks like another Sisler. All I really need is pitching material and in due time I'll get that too. I do not intend to give up the management of the A's as reported, but I've engaged Harry Davis to look after things while I'm scouting now and then. I'm not a bit discouraged but just a bit disappointed over the way things have been breaking for us all season."

He was more than a bit disappointed. Most clubs have four or five men playing above their normal level, some below, and some performing as expected. In Mack's view, every man on the Athletics was playing below expectations, a malady that has struck baseball managers and club owners from the beginning of time.

Rumors that Braggo Roth was on the trading block began to appear. The Red Sox were said to be eager to have him. Isaminger, who for all his close contact with Mack was often out of touch with the tall tactician's thinking, said rumors of a Roth-for-Barry trade were nonsense. "The A's need Roth and don't need Barry."

Despite the rumors, Roth was doing what he had been obtained to do—hitting, hustling, stealing bases with flair and bravado. On June 9 he provided all the offense to beat Cleveland 3–1. The next day he tripled with three on to beat the Browns. Braggo was aces with the Shibe Park constituents, who cheered him lustily, leading Isaminger again to pooh-pooh the trade rumors. "It would cause an explosion worse than any Mayday terrorist could pull off."

Wrong again. Harmony still meant more to Mack than fan favoritism. Braggo Roth had not grown with the captaincy. He was still the same old unlikable Braggo. Now, with Harry Davis in charge in the clubhouse, his captaincy was hollow. Roth's attitude was getting on everybody's nerves.

Admitting that the reclamation of Braggo Roth had been a failure, at the end of June Mack sent Roth and Shannon to Boston for two old favorites, Amos Strunk and Jack Barry. (Braggo bounced from Boston to Washington to New York and was out of the big leagues before he was thirty.)

Strunk had begun with Mack in 1908 and was overjoyed to be back. Barry had also broken in with the A's in 1908 and was not happy to be back. He had a business in Worcester that he could keep an eye on when the Red Sox were at home. The prospect of returning to life in a hotel in Philadelphia did not appeal to him and his wife. Barry's legs had lost the range of his youth, but his brain still worked, and Mack wanted him between Burrus and Dugan to steady the infield. The A's were in Boston July 4–8; Mack and Barry met a few times, but Mack was unable to persuade him to return. Barry retired from baseball and would soon begin a forty-year career as baseball coach at Holy Cross College in Worcester.

Connie Mack's pitching hopes rose with the return of Rollie Naylor and Wynn Noyes. But Naylor, rusty from his layoff, was inconsistent until he suddenly found consistency—losing 9 in a row. And Noyes was now thirty. It would take him a month to get ready to pitch, and when he did, the promise of 1917 had been lost somewhere in France. He won 1 game, was sold to the White Sox for $2,500, and never won another.

After the A's lost 2 games at Boston on July 4, their record was 15-43. They went west and won 2 out of 16. But they were in most of them; 7 of the losses were by 1 run.

Scott Perry began to feel the burden of being overworked in a lost cause. He lost 1-run games; he lost by close scores and not-so-close scores. He lost almost every time he pitched. By August 9 he had won only 4 and lost 17. It was enough to drive a man to drink. And Scott Perry didn't need a ride.

Some major league club owners, for all their decrying of Federal League and industrial league tactics, were not above using the same methods to raid their colleagues' rosters. They secretly contacted disgruntled players and urged them to "play for your release"—dogging it—while letting the player's club know they were interested in trading for the player. It was tampering pure and simple, and Connie Mack knew it was going on, who was doing it, and which of his players were the targets. Scott Perry was one, Joe Dugan another.

In Boston, Carl Mays, who looked as unhappy as Hamlet, knew that three teams in the pennant race—Cleveland, Chicago, and New York—wanted him, and he wanted to go, preferably to New York. He continued to sound off about Frazee's refusal to back his players by not paying his $100 fine for throwing a ball at an A's fan. His mood didn't improve when he lost a 3–0 game in St. Louis on July 9, his tenth loss in 15 decisions. Four days later he started in Chicago. In the first inning shortstop Mo Shannon pulled a rock that led to 4 runs. Mays's internal weather grew fouler in the second, when Eddie Collins set out to steal second and catcher Wally Schang's throw was low and glanced off the back of Mays's head. When the inning was over, Mays stormed into the dugout and kept going, muttering, "I'll never pitch for this ball club again."

And he never did. He went home.

The appropriate procedure was to suspend a player who left the team, but a suspended player couldn't be traded or sold, so Frazee told Barrow not to suspend Mays. "I can get a lot of money for him."

He was right. The bidding began. Comiskey went as high as $30,000, but Barrow wanted pitchers in addition to cash. The Yankees threw in Allen Russell (younger brother of Mack's $11,000 Lefty lemon of 1910) and Bob

McGraw, along with probably $40,000. To create the appearance that a repentant Mays had returned to the fold, the pitcher finally paid his $100 fine and showed up at Frazee's office on Tuesday, July 29. He had been AWOL for sixteen days. The next day the deal was made, and Mays left for New York ready to pitch.

When Ban Johnson heard about it, he immediately voided the deal and suspended Mays for the rest of the season. The Yankees partners, Ruppert and Huston, were dumbfounded by Johnson's action. Despite widespread press reports that three of his teams were dickering for Mays, Johnson declared himself shocked—shocked!—that any club owner would consider buying a player who had jumped his team. "Baseball cannot tolerate such a breach of discipline," he said. Since the Boston club had not suspended Mays for breaking his contract, "it was my duty as head of the American League to act."

Johnson believed he was in the right, like the man who insists from his hospital bed that "I had the right of way." A year earlier, when Johnson had voted to award Jack Quinn to New York, the colonels had applauded his wisdom. Now they decided he wasn't so wise any more.

Ruppert fired off a telegram reminding Johnson that he had to have been aware of the Yankees' interest in Mays—Huston claimed he had told Johnson in Chicago on July 21—and asking why he had waited for two weeks before he acted. There were hints, accusations really, that Johnson would not have suspended Mays if his old crony Comiskey, whom he was trying to appease, or the Indians, in which Johnson was said to have a financial interest, had landed the prize. The Yankees claimed that Johnson was trying to prevent them from improving their team, which was absurd. He had long favored strengthening the Yankees to combat the Giants' hold on New York fans. The Indians matter was neither a secret nor new. Over the years both Johnson and Comiskey had put up money to facilitate sales of teams that needed bailing out. Half of the loan to Jim Dunn, backed by Indians' shares as collateral, had been repaid.

Charles Comiskey, though he lost out on Mays, also thought Ban Johnson had gone too far. He would be allied with Frazee and Ruppert from then on.

Johnson's actions in the wake of his backing of Connie Mack in the case of another suspended player, Scott Perry, worked against him as well. He went to New York on August 4 to try to convince the colonels that he had done the right thing, to no avail. Citing Mack's actions in the Perry case as precedent, the Yankees went before Judge Robert F. Wagner of the New York Supreme Court and obtained an injunction against the suspension of Mays.

That was just the beginning. Knowing that Johnson had the backing of St. Louis, Cleveland, Philadelphia, and Washington, the trio of Frazee, Ruppert/ Huston, and Comiskey appealed to the league's board of directors to overturn Johnson's decision voiding the sale. Conveniently, the board consisted of Frazee, Ruppert, Comiskey, and Jim Dunn. By a 3–1 vote, they lifted the suspension and approved the trade, and Carl Mays went to the Polo Grounds and beat the Browns, 8–2.

Connie Mack, conceding that Ban Johnson "like all the rest of us, is not infallible, and makes some mistakes," told the *Atlanta Constitution* that in this case he backed Johnson's position all the way: "This situation is a great mistake for baseball . . . and if this is allowed to go through, it will hurt American League baseball inconceivably. The players, very much interested in the case themselves, are asking, 'If one player pitching for a club that is relegated to a second division berth can become dissatisfied and ask to be exchanged to some other club that has a chance to get in on the world's series money, why don't we do the same thing?"

Mack took a swipe at New York teams and fans, who "seem to think that because they represent New York, they can just take money and buy valuable players from any other club in the league. All the other seven teams in the American League go out of the league and get their players for the pennant fight and there is no reason why the New York club should not follow that course."

Scott Perry was one of the players following the Mays developments with great interest. The White Sox had made no secret of their desire to acquire him. Some reports put their offer at $20,000, others as high as $35,000. Connie Mack had assured his patrons that he was through selling players, no matter how much money was waved at him. He would not go back on that. He told Comiskey Perry was not for sale.

Perry was peeved. His chance to go to a contender, as Mays had done, was gone. He took another 1-run loss at home on August 9, and when the A's headed west, he and another disgruntled pitcher, Tom Rogers (4-12), missed the train. Connie Mack was not surprised; he had already suspended Perry for "breaking training." Rogers had been assigned to Baltimore and refused to report.

Umpire Billy Evans was traveling with the Athletics. He asked Mack what he intended to do about the White Sox offer.

"It would be a good trade for me," Mack said. "I am refusing a lot of money and some good players, but there are certain principles involved that must be upheld, hence I refuse to give the deal a thought. Perry can do all the worrying."

Perry didn't worry. He said, "No more big league stuff for me," and he and Rogers joined an independent team in Franklin, Pennsylvania.

Francis Richter wagged a reproving finger at Mack. It served him right for signing a contract jumper in the first place, then going to court over him. "Going to court is a baseball sin and be sure your sin will find you out," Richter preached.

So the Athletics showed up in St. Louis with four pitchers. It was Noyes and Naylor and Johnson and Kinney on the 1-11 swing through hostile territory.

Meanwhile, in Atlanta, Mack's friend Charlie Frank was in a hot pennant race and needed an outfielder. Mack sent him Merlin Kopp. When Frank became ill, Ira Thomas filled in for the manager. The Crackers went on a 30-3 rampage and came from fifth place to win the Southern Association pennant. The grateful Charlie Frank granted Mack first call on anybody and everybody on the Atlanta roster—even the entire Atlanta franchise if Mack wanted it.

Taking advantage of Harry Davis's presence, Mack slipped away to Atlanta to look over the team. He watched them play the Nashville Vols August 7 and 8 and liked what he saw.

Sitting in the stands behind first base, Mack and Ira Thomas gave a group of army officers seated around them and an eavesdropping *Constitution* reporter named Wheatley an unforgettable Thursday afternoon at Ponce de Leon Park.

When the Atlanta first baseman stretched to catch a wide throw, Mack asked Thomas his name. Told it was Ivy Griffin, Mack said, "That kid seems all right. He has confidence and he sure can field a ball. He is a natural first baseman and if he can hit at all, he will surely go up."

Mack was pleased to see the slimmed-down Jimmie Dykes. He admired the shortstop play of Chick Galloway—"a natural ballplayer"—and the Crackers' veteran catcher Bob Higgins. But when the crowd broke out in hearty applause for a running catch by outfielder Hardin Herndon, Mack shook his head in dissent. "He might catch a whole lot that way," he told those around him, "but unless he learns to catch close to his body instead of in the air he will lose out. He is young and ought to learn at once. Herndon is fast and must overcome this difficulty before he looks promising."

Herndon never did.

When he returned home, Mack announced that he would take nine Crackers, in addition to Dykes, to report after the Southern Association season ended in September. One of them, pitcher Bob Hasty, caused him some legal headaches similar to those in the Scott Perry squabble. It seems that Charlie Frank had loaned Hasty to Mobile in July, provided that the right-hander not pitch against Atlanta—a good deed that did not go unpunished. At the end of the season, Frank sold Hasty to Mack. The Mobile president, John Logan, claimed Hasty belonged to Mobile and put him on the Mobile reserved list. When Hasty started two games for the A's in September, Logan threatened to sue Mack for $10,000. Frank took his case to the league president and saved the pitcher for Mack.

On Sundays when the A's were idle, Mack often took the train to Newark to look over the International League teams. On August 3 he watched a young Newark spitballer, Eddie Rommel, give up 5 runs in 3 innings in the first game, then pitch the second game, giving up 12 hits in a 10–6 win. None of that put Mack off. He noticed that Rommel was breaking his curve inside to all the hitters, an easily corrected fault. He was impressed with the pitcher's easy motion and delivery and the way he fielded his position, handling 1 putout and 6 assists in the second game. Before he went home that day, Mack bought Eddie Rommel, a John McGraw reject, for $2,500, to report in 1920.

Mack liked a young Buffalo second baseman and offered $5,000 for Stanley "Bucky" Harris. The Giants and Washington liked Harris too and matched Mack's bid. Buffalo manager George "Hooks" Wiltse asked Harris where he preferred to go. Harris considered: the Giants have Larry Doyle with Frank Frisch coming up. The Athletics are a last-place team; no thanks. Washington had finished third in 1918, and he wouldn't have to face Walter Johnson. The Nationals got him.

Mack continued to audition walk-ons; by year's end forty-nine would wear the uniform with the white elephant. Many of them were on hand on September 5 to see Babe Ruth hit his twenty-fifth home run, tying Buck Freeman's record, 1 of 5 hits for Ruth that day. It would be the biggest—in some cases the only—thrill of their big league minute. Some of them appeared in one or two games without ever signing a contract. Or if they did, Mack never filed them. Nobody noticed. Nobody cared. Paperwork was not the National Commission's thing.

The A's were at home for all but two days in September. Attendance, which was booming in both leagues, held up as curious fans turned out to see the new faces even though they won only 6 of the 26 games. Five of the ex-Crackers—Dykes, Galloway, Griffin, catcher Lena Styles, and pitcher James Boone—were among six rookies in the starting lineup on September 10 when they took their second straight from the pennant-hopeful Tigers, 6–5, with a 6-run rally in the last of the ninth. The *Public Ledger* said of Galloway and Griffin, "Both boys gave a most promising exhibition," handling themselves "like real 100 percent prospects."

The season ended with five games against the Yankees, who were battling Detroit for the third-place piece of the World Series pie. Mack used his regulars, such as they were, to avoid the appearance of favoring the Yankees, but they still lost all five. The Tigers won their last five, but three straight losses to New York in the preceding week had done them in. They finished a half game back in fourth place.

Or did they?

Carl Mays had won 9 and lost 3 for New York. Detroit president Frank Navin, a staunch Ban Johnson supporter, protested that the games Mays pitched for the Yankees should be thrown out and third-place money awarded to the Tigers. Turned down by the league directors, Navin appealed to the National Commission, which agreed to hold up the payment until the courts or the league resolved the matter. Ban Johnson had two sets of final standings prepared, one counting Mays's New York record and one omitting it. Neither one was considered official. Confident of vindication, the Yankee colonels advanced the third-place money to their players.

Baseball's ticky-tacky house creaked and sagged a little more, and the sound of the boards splintering under Ban Johnson's throne were heard throughout the land.

10 | BIG BUSINESS—BIG FIGHT

In the National League the Cincinnati Reds had clinched the 1919 pennant by defeating the second-place Giants in 8 of their last 11 meetings. The Reds' pitching was rated better than the White Sox, who had the heaviest hitters. The Sox were early favorites to win the World Series, but the Reds were no flukes, winning 96 games in the 140-game schedule. They were picked to win by Cincinnati beat writers Tom Swope and Jack Ryder, among others, even before the odds later shifted dramatically.

Rumors of a fix began before the Series had gone three games, based on reports of heavy betting on the Reds, suspicious phone calls and telegrams, and some rank-looking actions on the field. After the Sox lost Game 4, 2–0, manager Kid Gleason called the Reds "the luckiest team I ever saw in my life. . . . Cicotte was good and they went out in order in eight of the nine innings, and yet they were able to win on a couple of errors [Cicotte] would not make again in 40 games."

But Gleason knew better. So did other Chicago players. There were reports that catcher Ray Schalk knew something was wrong in the first two games and had fought in the clubhouse with the players he suspected. Schalk never denied it.

After the Reds won the championship, 5 games to 3, writers who saw nothing amiss chalked up the Chicago loss to overconfidence: "too cocksure . . . too careless . . . believed in themselves too much . . . didn't look like the same team they did a month ago. . . ."

Many of the experts who were there either could not or chose not to believe there was any explanation hinting at dishonesty. Robert J. Casey, later a noted war correspondent, and Joe Foley covered the Series for the *Chicago Journal*. Casey later wrote about Game 3:

I marveled at the way fly balls bounced out of the glove of Shoeless Joe Jackson and I wrote down the White Sox as a fourth-rate baseball team. . . . But I saw no evil.

Along about the fourth inning of that game, Foley and I got duplicate telegrams from [*Journal* owner] John Eastman who was doing something in Cincinnati: "Have incontrovertible evidence this series fixed stop what about it question."

I don't know what Foley said but my reply was a fine tribute to my innocence and credulity: "Such things are not done in the big leagues."

"If ever a Series was full on the level it was this one," wrote W. A. Phelon. Hugh Fullerton, who according to Fred Lieb "early smelled something ratty," afterward refused to countenance the "scandalous rumors." Henry P. Edwards unwittingly provided the most ironic comment when he said of the "off-form" White Sox: "They beat themselves."

Connie Mack and other baseball men conceded that a bad apple may turn up here or there, but it was inconceivable that enough players could be reached to throw an entire World Series. If the fix was in, nobody tipped off Ty Cobb. He later admitted losing $150 on the White Sox in the first two games, the only time, he said, he ever bet on a game.

White Sox owner Charles Comiskey offered a reward for information proving the Series was rigged. Nobody collected. He knew it was, but who could prove it?

The National Commission made a few inquiries but found nothing to substantiate the rumors and punted the responsibility back to Comiskey.

Unresolved, the story died, overtaken in the mostly male sporting world by more scurrilous realities, like Prohibition and women gaining the right to vote.

Baseball had become a major industry. *The Nation* observed, "The sport has grown to vast dimensions, involving an amount of money and time and emotion that hardly any other institution in the United States can equal." Total big league attendance more than doubled. Thanks to Sunday baseball and the Yankees being in the pennant race for the first time in fifteen years, the two New York clubs drew more than 1,300,000 fans to the Polo Grounds. Attendance more than tripled for the White Sox and Tigers and rose almost as much in St. Louis. But the postwar boom in attendance had done little more than burp at Shibe Park. The Athletics and Senators had the smallest gains, less than 30 percent. With rising expenses, profits for both Mack and Griffith remained as elusive as victories.

For the first time since 1906, both leagues' cellar dwellers resided in the same city, not the last time Philadelphia would earn that honor. When Connie Mack surveyed the wreckage of what J. V. Fitz Gerald of the *Washington Post* called his "Apathetics," he was not encouraged. They had lost 104 games, plummeting 149 points from the year before, landing 20 games below seventh place.

A lot of it was due to the pitching. They recorded only one shutout, walked more batters and gave up more runs than any team in either league. But it was a total team effort. They had the lowest batting average, made the most errors, and scored the fewest runs of all but the National's third-place Cubs.

The availability of high-grade Australian wool yarn and the Shibes' improved yarn-winding and cover-sewing machines had given the ball more spring—more liveliness—in 1919. The Deadball Era was over. American League run production leaped almost 25 percent, substantial even allowing for the 10 percent longer schedule. But it didn't leap for the Athletics, whose scoring increased just 10 percent. The league earned run average rose .44; the A's was up 1.04.

Disappointing seasons turned in by proven performers are part of baseball. Always have been. So are first-year rockets who fizzle the next season. Why a man can hit anybody one year and nobody the next year is beyond explanation. Pitchers are as delicate as Swiss watches. Anything can throw them off, physically or mentally, for a month, a year, forever.

Connie Mack had seen it all in the five years of his three-year rebuilding plan. Winning is addictive; losing is habit-forming. A pall of resignation seemed to have taken over among his boys. Prospects who looked like worldbeaters flivvered with stultifying frequency. Proven hitters quit hitting. They would all come and go, while Connie Mack stayed and endured. He knew that shooting high in his expectations made him vulnerable to disappointment and frustration. But he could never be content to aim low. He knew what it took to put together a winning team, had done it more than once. But it had never taken him this long. It had been an ugly stretch. And his team was still not good.

Departing from his custom of predicting the Athletics would surprise in the coming year, Mack sounded discouraged when he sat for an interview following the 1919 World Series. His unflagging optimism had flagged. He had never believed in his own infallibility or genius. But he had always believed that he could build another championship team.

"I'm not going to say wait until next year. I'm not going to predict the Athletics will do better in the coming season. To tell the truth I don't see how they can."

Or was he being foxy, laying the groundwork to spring a real surprise instead of a predicted one?

"There's no use disguising the fact that I have a bad team, one that is fit only for last place."

He seemed as bent on squelching any hope as he had been in espousing it in the past. Was he letting his boys know that they were expendable in case they had ideas of asking for raises?

"I won't get out of the cellar until I get some new talent. The team that I have at the present time is not a good one. I have only two or three good players on it and they might be better. I'm not laboring under any false hopes for anything of the sort. As I look at the situation now, there isn't a chance for me to get out of the cellar. No man can do any more with the material that I have than I have done. The only way for me to get better results is to get new men who have the goods."

Any manager who so openly put the blame for his team's sad showing on the front office would be out of a job in a hurry for his honesty. But Connie Mack was his own front office.

"I believe when I get the material . . . the Athletics will be up there battling for the lead. I look for many stars to be developed in the next two to three years. Few players have come up since the Federal League trouble. The war also put the business to the players. But now the minor leagues will be full of stars and that is where I expect to get my players. I can't get any players from the American League. There are no stars to be spared in the circuit. The only way I will get a team is by developing one."

Mack had a few players to build with: Joe Dugan, if he ever matured; Whitey Witt; Cy Perkins, considered the best catcher in the league; Jimmie Dykes, when he got back into shape; Rollie Naylor, when he recovered from a year in the trenches; Scott Perry—maybe.

But they were not enough.

For the rest of the year Connie Mack logged more Pullman and hotel time than evenings at home. He decided to forsake Florida for spring training and set out for Texas to find a new site. He found one but not in Texas. Stopping off in Lake Charles, Louisiana, he sat in the Majestic Hotel waiting out a downpour. The proprietor, Lem Calvert, used the opportunity to show Mack his clean spacious rooms and feed him a bountiful dinner. When the rain stopped, Mack inspected the ball field and was surprised to find the rain had soaked right through, leaving not a puddle or muddy spot. "A game could have been played on it," he said. "That is one reason I picked this spot."

Mack went on to Dallas, where he announced an agreement with Cardinals manager Branch Rickey to barnstorm together through Texas.

Mack had barely returned home when the American League blew up. Frazee, Ruppert, and Comiskey had been plotting to overthrow Ban Johnson since the Carl Mays incident in August. Comiskey had lost out in the bidding for Mays, but that was just part of the game. He believed that Johnson should have left the suspension of Mays and blocking of the sale up to the league's board of directors instead of acting on his own—even if his decision was the right one. It was all part of the complaint that Johnson had become a dictator who ran the league as he pleased.

Was there anything to that charge? Was Johnson too possessive of his "baby," which he had created and nurtured? Where was the gratitude for the prosperity the venture had brought to those who had gone in with him at the start?

But Johnson's baby was now nineteen years old. It had grown into a big business and had more big businessmen than unsophisticated former ballplayers among its ownership. Papa Ban was still trying to run everything, and it didn't work any more.

Ruppert brought up the old claim that Johnson was influenced by his financial interest in the Cleveland club, which had tried unsuccessfully to buy Mays in August. But most of the $100,000 loan from Johnson enabling Dunn to buy the Indians in 1916 had been repaid by now; besides, Comiskey had backed Jim Dunn in the purchase as well, and it took him until December to find a buyer for the Indians stock he had acquired in lieu of repayment of his loan.

As usual, Connie Mack considered the entire fracas trivial. It would be quickly settled. He was loyal to Ban Johnson and would remain so. And what, he asked, had Johnson done that was detrimental to anybody's interests? Mack bypassed the similarity between his action in the Scott Perry case and the Yankees going to court for relief from what they considered an unjust decision. As for buying and signing a suspended player, hadn't he done the same thing, albeit unknowingly? With Mack loyalty came before logic or legalisms.

Mack understood Comiskey's personal grudges against Johnson. But

Frazee, Ruppert, and Huston were not baseball men. They knew nothing of the struggles to launch the American League. They had no appreciation of Johnson's dedicated leadership in the assault on the National League monopoly.

The strategic maneuvering began when Johnson called the annual league meeting for December 10 in Chicago, where they had been meeting since 1912. The three rebels knew they were outnumbered and the loyal five were immovable. But the board of directors consisted of Comiskey, Frazee, Ruppert, and Dunn. They wanted a showdown to determine where the power lay. The league constitution fixed the time of the annual meeting but not the place or the authority to call the meeting. If they could get a court to give the board that right, then they would try to assert the right to overturn the Mays suspension and the blocking of the sale and go on to oust Ban Johnson as president.

The Yankees went before Judge Robert F. Wagner and obtained a temporary injunction against the Chicago meeting on the grounds that only the directors could determine the meeting place, and they wanted it in New York. The status of Carl Mays remained before the court.

Three directors—Dunn refused to participate—met in New York on December 2 and called the league meeting for December 10 in New York. They passed resolutions recommending to the league the rescinding of the Mays suspension, the awarding of third place to the Yankees, an investigation of Johnson's handling of league funds and the Western Union contract, and a show of proof of Johnson's alleged twenty-year contract.

They raised the possibility that they might secede from the American League and start a third league. Or maybe they'd find buyers for the two weakest clubs, Washington and Philadelphia, thus taking control of the league. Just before the new year, Clark Griffith had joined his closest baseball friend Connie Mack as a club owner. Griffith had been searching for a wealthy partner to join him in buying control of the underfunded, debt-ridden Washington franchise. Mack and Ben Shibe found him an angel in William Richardson, a Philadelphia grain broker. Unable to obtain the kind of assistance that Johnson and Comiskey had provided Jim Dunn for the Cleveland purchase, Griffith mortgaged his Montana ranch to come up with his share of the $175,000 price. Like Shibe, Richardson preferred to leave all the baseball business to his partner. Griffith would carry both the manager's and president's duties for the 1920 season before leaving the dugout.

Clark Griffith said nothing in response to the directors' proposal to find a buyer for his team. But Connie Mack was irate. Just the suggestion that the Athletics might be acquired by some baseball upstarts infuriated him.

Referring to the Yankees' status as tenants of the Giants at the Polo Grounds, he said, "The Yankees' owners are making a lot of trouble for a club which has no ball park." As for their threat to break away and start a new league, he said, "The American League would be better off without them."

Mack left himself wide open for retaliation. The volleys he took were predictable and some of them deserved. Newspaper columns were the talk shows of the time. J. V. Fitz Gerald took a "look who's talking" poke at Mack: "So it appears that Connie laid himself open to a paralyzing counter by taking a slap at a third-place club and one of the biggest money-makers of the late season, without having any real cause to do so. Mack's position in the present matter is hardly an enviable one. He was the first magnate to question the rulings of the national commission."

Col. Huston fired a lengthy barrage at Mack, a scathing denunciation worthy of political campaign rhetoric:

Out of pity for poor old Connie Mack, we would rather not notice his humorous remarks to the effect that it would be a good thing for baseball if the New York Yankees would get out of it. But the idea of Connie reading anybody out of anything is so humorous that we just can't resist the temptation to say that the Yankees have been traveling to Philadelphia during the five years Colonel Ruppert and I have owned the club, and on few trips have we ever received enough, as the visiting club's share of the receipts, to pay hotel bills and car fare.

[New York American humorist] Bugs Baer is authority for the statement that Connie Mack has the only ball park in the world where the turnstiles register fractions. One day the total receipts [were] doubtless the lowest amount ever taken in by a major league club. We were paid for twenty-one people, grand total of $4.11. Connie has run last consistently—almost dropped out of the league without any other club to read him out.

It is only a question of time when our league will raise the question of the propriety of a share of ownership in the Athletics. That club for a long term of years has not contributed to the prosperity of the league in proportion to the population of Philadelphia. Philadelphia has shown itself in the past to be one of the best baseball cities in America, and the poor management in the last few years has made it the worst.

Too much praise must have made Connie think himself a genius. So great grew his opinion of his own ability that he broke up the greatest ball club in history, thinking, of course, he could build another at odd moments. But somehow it didn't work. Like the small boy with the watch apart, he couldn't put it together again. And now Connie is trying to read us out. He says we have a ball club but no ball park. All right. He has a ball park but no ball club, making it fifty-fifty. We can stand for criticism from a man whose ball club lost 504 ball games in five years.

Connie Mack is a nice old man whom the procession has passed. In this regard there is a strong bond of sympathy between himself and Ban Johnson. They are both in the good old boat has-been, floating down the river of time into oblivion.

Yes, of all men in baseball, it ill becomes Connie Mack to criticize another club in the American League, or to question its desirability as a member.

Fans well remember this same old Connie was the first man in base-ball to bolt a ruling of the National Commission and drag the sport into the courts. For fifteen years the commission had regulated baseball and everything was running smoothly. Suddenly the Supreme Court of the game made a ruling against Connie Mack in the Scott Perry case. He refused to abide by the ruling and rushed for a court injunction. That was the precedent for succeeding injunctions.

Newspapers across the country played up one quote in particular: "[Mack] says we have a ball club but no ball park. He has a ball park but no ball club."

The blast was fired by Huston alone. This was not Jake Ruppert's style. It's possible that Mack's and Philadelphia fans' antipathy toward the Yankees (which never prevented him from rooting for them as the American League's champion in the World Series) began at this time. Philadelphians had long resented the Big Apple's denigrating their home as "sleepy town." But the fans' enmity had always been aimed at the Detroit Tigers. The Yankees had been weaklings for years.

Connie Mack had no interest in responding. Asked for his reaction, he said only, "I had my say and I expected Col. Huston to reply in the vein he did."

Connie Mack, Tom Shibe, and Clark Griffith left for Chicago on Sunday, December 7. Meanwhile, Tigers president Frank Navin was in New York to try to mediate the dispute. He met with Huston and Frazee at the Engineers' Club and began by suggesting a split of the third-place money between the Tigers and Yankees. That went nowhere.

Huston and Frazee then proposed their own compromise:

- A new board of directors consisting of Ruppert, Comiskey, Navin, and Connie Mack
- A promise by Navin that he would prevent a quorum by not attending the Chicago meeting on December 10
- The league to conduct routine business only, then adjourn and work out their differences informally
- All the rulings by the outgoing board to be honored and the Mays case considered closed
- Legal immunity to be granted to Ban Johnson and the loyal five if they came to New York for the meeting and agreed to everything on this list

Navin took the night train to Chicago and conveyed the offer to the others on Monday. There were more lawyers than club owners at the meeting. They considered moving the meeting to New York as a gesture to pacify the minority and, not incidentally, to avoid what Johnson's attorney, George W. Miller, called "further litigation to embarrass the league." They decided to go to New York but rejected everything else on the list.

So they all boarded a train that night. Arriving in New York the next morning, Johnson spoke of naught but peace and goodwill. "We came to New York because we didn't want this case to drag through the courts for what remains of the winter and perhaps a good part of the spring and summer. The thing to do is to settle it in a league meeting and that is the object we will try to attain tomorrow. I have no personal fight with the board of directors or any club owners. We have made no plans and we have had no overtures. We are for a peaceful adjustment of things unless unpleasantness is forced upon us. Five sensible men came on the train with me."

In other words, if the rebels are sensible men and see things our way, the doves will fly.

Questioned about the final standings of the pennant race, Johnson said he had them in his pocket but would not reveal them before the meeting. Asked if the games pitched by Mays for New York were included in the official averages, he said, "I believe they are."

Johnson was dissembling. He had a plan.

The three rebels were confident that the agreement to meet in New York was a sign of conciliation. They were quickly disabused. While Johnson huddled with his lawyers at the Holland House and Connie Mack smiled and told reporters that he was sure everything would be patched up satisfactorily the next day, Frank Navin went to the Biltmore Hotel to inform Comiskey that there would be no compromise. The majority intended to replace Comiskey as vice-president and vote in an all-new board of directors, who would then reverse every action the old board had taken a week earlier.

These steamroller tactics were conveyed to Frazee and the colonels, and the doves of peace remained caged.

The next morning Huston, sounding like the Sons of Liberty in 1776, vowed, "The three clubs constituting the minority will take such measures as will demonstrate that they will not submit to the tyranny of those who merely reflect the will of this discredited man Johnson."

The hostilities began immediately at the Wednesday morning board meeting. For the first time since the Mays suspension, Johnson and Jim Dunn were in the same room with Comiskey, Ruppert, and Frazee. Johnson assumed the chairman's role. The trio elected Comiskey to chair the meeting. After consulting his lawyer, Johnson stood up and walked out, followed by Dunn. The trio conferred with their lawyers, who told them Johnson had the constitutional right to preside. They asked Ban to come back. Ban refused. The three went on with their agenda, awarding third place to New York, banning suspensions without a hearing, and passing restrictions on Johnson's authority.

The full league meeting began at noon, Ban Johnson presiding, with bitter, nasty tirades against Johnson by Comiskey and Ruppert. J. V. Fitz Gerald reported that they roared so loudly they could be overheard by reporters waiting outside the closed doors. After Comiskey denounced Johnson as a menace to the best interests of the league and the club owners, Ruppert said, "I want to tell you, Ban Johnson, before all the club owners, that you are not going to force me or any of my friends out of baseball. If anyone goes it will be you, and we will devote every effort and our last penny to putting you out."

Ruppert rehashed the Mays case and accused Johnson of trying to undermine the Yankees by urging the Giants to evict them from the Polo Grounds (which wasn't true). He laid the blame for all the league's problems on Johnson's head. "Without Johnson this league would be run as smoothly as a well-organized business firm."

Ruppert then appealed to the owners "to meet without Johnson, without attorneys, without stenographers, and have a heart-to-heart talk. I am sure we can bring quiet out of chaos."

There was a long silence. Then they proceeded to the business of the day.

Ruppert moved the election of a president. He was ruled out of order; Johnson was in the middle of a twenty-year term. Ruppert asked to see documentation of this. Johnson said all the papers were in Chicago. Ruppert attempted to overrule the chair and was defeated, 5–3. Next he moved to elect a secretary. He was told Johnson was the secretary. Ruppert moved to elect a treasurer. Same answer. Ruppert demanded the league award the third-place money to the Yankees. Johnson said they couldn't do that because the Yankees' lawsuit involving Mays was still in court.

Every resolution introduced by the board of directors was tabled, including one that declared Johnson "not only had not performed, but had broken the conditions of his employment, that he forfeited all right to compensation and that steps be taken preventing the use of funds to pay for his supposed services and that his accounts be audited."

It became obvious that no motions from anybody, friend or foe, would be acted upon. Clark Griffith and Connie Mack had each come with a pet peeve. Griffith argued that the entire Mays flap could have been avoided if there had been a ban on all sales or trades of players once the season started. His motion to enact such a ban was tabled.

Connie Mack was still angry at rival managers and their agents who had dogged his team all season, telling his players they could make more money with other clubs and urging them to soldier the manager so they'd be traded or released. He was determined to stop it. He had already put his players on notice that jaking or easing up to promote a trade wouldn't work:

Hereafter we will not sell or trade any player who is of use to us or any other big league club. If I get a player we want or any other club wants, he is going to stick with us. If he doesn't want to play with us, then he can retire, but he will never be sold or traded to another club. Our players will know this, and then they will realize that their future is with the Athletics and will always give us their best efforts, and the rivals who practice this insidious device to undermine our players will be balked. I have proofs in my possession to show that this tampering has been carried on. I know exactly who the guilty parties are and am in a position to expose them if I care to do so.

Whether or not the players believed it, the other club owners did. Mack had received no inquiries from anybody about Scott Perry or Joe Dugan or anybody else all winter. But that wasn't enough. He introduced a motion that called for a $1,000 fine for any manager or club official caught tampering with a player on another team. The penalty for a second offense would be expulsion from the league.

This, too, was tabled.

From the start, Johnson intended to carry out only one piece of business: the purging of the board of directors. In rapid order, Frank Navin was elected vice-president. He and Phil Ball of St. Louis, Ben Minor of Washington, and Tom Shibe were elected to the board. (Newspaper accounts name Ben Shibe, but his declining health had made him inactive for some time.)

The meeting then adjourned. Comiskey left immediately for Chicago. He told reporters who met him at the station, "Conditions in the American League are awful, terrible." The three wealthiest clubs—Chicago, Boston, and New York—were considering withholding revenue from the league unless Johnson was removed and a new National Commission chairman could be found. Otherwise, said Comiskey, "the league may not last beyond July Fourth."

The rebels had not been idle. Their lawyers had been busy that morning. Before the new board could meet, all five of the loyalists were served with papers in three lawsuits. One was for $500,000 damages for Johnson's public assertion that the Yankees did not belong in the league. One challenged the legality of Johnson's presidency. The third concerned money allegedly owed a Cincinnati lawyer for work investigating Western Union's operations in the league's ballparks.

At ten thirty that night the new board met. It rescinded everything the previous board had done since August. It was a complete, if temporary, victory for Ban Johnson. But not for the business of baseball. All the disputes would simmer in limbo until they met again in February.

The National Commission met the next day and took no action on the third-place controversy. Garry Herrmann said he'd had enough and would not continue as chairman beyond thirty days, even if they hadn't found anybody to replace him. He meant it. He went home and packed all the records in boxes and crates, ready to be sent to the new chairman, and took off for Miami. The National League wanted him out, but Ban Johnson wanted him to stay and had dragged his feet in appointing anybody to a joint search committee for a new chairman.

Griffith and Mack stayed in New York to try to act as peacemakers. According to the *Times*, Mack did some fence mending by telling Huston, "Colonel, you said one thing about me that was true when you said I didn't have a ball club. I guess I haven't one, but I hope to get one together before the season is over."

Mack's friendly gesture bounced right off Huston. At the February Philadelphia writers' dinner Mack said, "If we are to believe what we hear from certain members of our league, we may not have an American League this year."

Huston swatted away what he called "this latest ebullition of Connie Mack": "Mack hints that there will be no American League this year. Well, that should make no difference to him, for, from the way the Athletics played ball the last few years, they weren't in any particular league. The clubs opposing Johnson are going to play ball if the other five teams draw off by themselves under some other name. If such is the case, then Connie and his Athletics cannot finish worse than fifth, which will be a big improvement over their positions in the last five years of play."

For all the fiery verbiage, efforts to resolve—or at least paper over—the schism continued. Ruppert received a telegram from an undisclosed Chicago reporter proposing a solution: submit the controversy to binding arbitration before Judge Landis. Suspecting that Johnson was behind it, Ruppert conferred with his allies by telephone. They agreed to the plan, provided that Landis would also rule on the fitness of Johnson to remain as league president. Those terms were wired to the Chicago newspaper. There was no reply.

So the legal papers and lawyers' billing time continued to mount like slag at a smelting plant.

The game's rebound at the gate did not go unnoticed by the players. Holding the line on salaries in 1920 would go out the window. The contracts sent out by the clubs brought a flood of unsigned returns. Stars and rookies alike wanted a piece of the postwar boom. There was talk of reviving the Players' Association. Labor unrest was in the air; there had been 2,600 work stoppages involving 4 million workers in 1919. Inflation had driven the average annual wage up to $1,400. Since 1914 the price of steak had gone up 50 percent, butter and eggs had almost doubled, and milk had risen from nine to fifteen cents a quart. Players were paying up to twenty dollars for new shoes that had cost twelve dollars a year ago. Gloves had almost doubled in price to fourteen dollars.

Despite the club owners' talk of cutting back during the Great War, there had been no real retrenchment. Salaries had been rising steadily for years. Connie Mack blamed it on fears of having too many malcontents on the teams, a carryover from the dissension sown by the Federal League. He offered an interviewer a lesson in Baseball Economics 101:

Club owners fear a discontented baseball player on the team. He's like a blight on a peach. Unless thrown out, he contaminates others in a short time. For that reason many club owners yielded to pressure and gave in to keep their men healthy-minded during the past few years, when there was every reason for retrenchment.

And now there comes a boost to keep up with the times. This situation is really unfortunate because under ordinary conditions it is impossible for eight baseball clubs, averaging an investment of $500,000 each, to make money on such a capitalization with the overhead involved. But ballplayers have no heart. I asked one where he thought I would get the money from to pay salaries such as he demanded. "That's your affair," was his answer, which was illustration enough of the general attitude of the ball player. Baseball players after a good year will demand and get a raise. If they fall down the succeeding season they won't stand for a cut. Fearing a sorehead on the team, most club owners consent to the holdup. There you are with a deteriorating man and his salary fixed a notch higher than wartime prices. I do not think a wage scale based on performance will ever be adopted. It would affect the playing of the men whose minds would be on their record and not on teamwork.

I have fought the salary holdup for years. I have battled against the long-term contract, which was the worst disaster in the financial heart of baseball. I have argued against paying $15,000 and $20,000 salaries, as they would wound the vanity as well as the pocketbooks of other players almost as good as the fortunate contract holder. But I have not succeeded in breaking the backbone of high salaries, nor in checking unreasonable players' demands. I am still fighting but I must have a real ball club and they are hard to find unless you meet the market price.

The terms "large and small markets" were not used, but baseball already had its haves and have-nots. St. Louis was the smallest two-club city and supported neither. Frazee's resources were being drained by non-baseball activities. The Boston Nationals were a threadbare operation. Washington had limped along from payday to payday and was in hock to the league for $30,000. The deep pockets were in New York, Chicago, Detroit, Cincinnati, and Pittsburgh.

Where did the Athletics fit? They were in a large market but had been losing money for the past five years, eating into the profits from the pennant-winning days. Attendance had been up in 1919, but their share of home gate receipts that went to the league had been the lowest of any club—$5,630.24. Connie Mack had no outside resources. Ben Shibe was not looking to make money from the club, but he was a businessman, not interested in subsidizing a baseball team to boost his ego. Both he and Mack knew it was up to them to improve their product to bring back the customers and the profits, whatever the cost.

Still, Connie Mack would not be bulldozed into paying more than he thought a player was worth just to keep him happy. The youngsters on the lower end of the Athletics' pay scale—Dugan, Witt, Perkins, Naylor—received raises. When pitcher Jing Johnson complained that he could make more money outside of baseball, Mack readily asked waivers on him and released him. He was never one to stand in anyone's way of bettering himself.

In March 1919 Harry Frazee had gleefully signed Babe Ruth to a three-year contract at $10,000 a year. Now Ruth was a star, the new home run record holder. Unlike Home Run Baker in 1915, there was nothing coy about Ruth. He demanded that his contract be torn up and a new one with bigger numbers replace it. Buck Weaver was in the same situation in Chicago and made the same demands.

Some players criticized them; a deal was a deal. If their numbers had fallen off, they wouldn't be asking for a pay cut. Other club owners with players on long-term contracts watched nervously to see how Frazee and Comiskey would handle it.

Frazee handled it by selling the troublesome slugger to the Yankees for more than $100,000, a price the editor of the *Reach Guide* considered justified "only in conformity with the depreciated value of the dollar, which has raised the price of all commodities more than 100 percent."

Ruth would undoubtedly boost attendance for the Yankees, but even with his unprecedented slugging the Red Sox had finished sixth. Would he be enough to turn the Yankees into pennant winners?

Reach was dubious. "It will take more than a mere slugger like Ruth to make the Yankees a pennant winner in the future, even though Ruth should lend his best efforts—and that is by no means assured, judging from his Boston record."

Practically everybody who was anybody in the baseball business was headed for the Congress Hotel in Chicago on Sunday night, February 8, 1920. In addition to the major league meetings, three top minor leagues were meeting. (In Kansas City, Rube Foster was organizing the Negro National League at the same time.)

Connie Mack arrived on Sunday afternoon and immediately went into the joint rules committee meeting. He and Griffith were the American reps; the National had picked William Veeck of the Cubs and Pirates owner Barney Dreyfuss. Umpires and writers sat in on the discussions. They met for four hours and another three hours on Monday. And they changed the game.

The American League and National Commission were not the only messes in baseball. The playing rules needed overhauling. Official scorers had their own individual notions of stolen bases, earned runs, winning and losing pitchers. The writers' association had been trying to enforce uniform rules for years with little success. The rules committee invited players, owners, and managers to submit suggestions. A majority of the managers, including Mack, favored a designated hitter for the pitcher. There was broad support for abolishing the spitball and all other "freak" pitches.

Cubs manager Fred Mitchell proposed that fly balls caught in foul territory should not count as outs. That one didn't fly.

Connie Mack suggested a scoring change. He never believed in the sacrifice fly rule, maintaining that the batter was sacrificing nothing in trying for a base hit. But if a batter was ordered to bunt with a slow runner on base, and he put down a perfect bunt but the base runner was out—where an ordinary runner would have been safe—the batter should get credit for a sacrifice. In rejecting that idea, one writer said the manager should be penalized for ordering a bunt with "an ice wagon" on base in the first place.

The most hotly debated issue was an attempt to abolish the intentional walk. It had long been an accepted but little used part of the game. Until now the top sluggers had been threats to hit fewer than a dozen home runs, most of them inside the park. Babe Ruth had catapulted the home run into prominence by hitting a record 29 of them. Like the Pied Piper, he had led other players into sliding their hands down toward the knob of the bat and swinging for the fences. Managers began ordering free passes in unprecedented numbers, especially to Ruth. Fans booed when they saw catchers move away from the plate to provide a wide target before the pitch was thrown.

Clark Griffith was the most outspoken critic of the deliberate base on balls. He proposed that all men on base advance one base on an intentional walk, two bases on the second in an inning. He suggested leaving it to the umpire to decide if a pitcher had intentionally thrown a wide one. Veteran umpires Bill Klem and Hank O'Day didn't want any part of that. "You'll get us all killed," they yelped, "if the crowds don't like the call."

It took until the second day for the committee to agree on a compromise suggested by Bob Quinn of the Browns: make the catcher remain in his crouch behind the plate until the pitch was thrown. If he stepped to the side before the ball left the pitcher's hand, all base runners would advance one base. Even that, protested O'Day, would produce a riot if a vital run scored as a result of an umpire's call.

The *Reach Guide*, with its usual faulty vision, pronounced the intentional pass a thing of the past.

A proposal by Fred Lieb that was approved increased future home run totals by counting game-ending homers regardless of the final score. In the past, for example, a batter hitting a home run with a man on third that ended a tie game was credited only with a single and one run batted in. The only dissenter was Hank O'Day, who maintained that you can't count runs that cross the plate after the winning run has scored and the game is over. The irascible Hank O'Day remained a stalwart purist killjoy.

In other rule changes, umpires were given sole authority to stop and re-start games because of rain, rather than the home team manager. Home runs would be judged fair or foul according to where they left the playing area, not where they were last seen, a rule that had cost sluggers like Baker and Ruth an unknown number of homers. Oddly, this rule would be rescinded in June after umpires complained that it was too difficult to tell where a ball was when it went over the fence or the roof. The "last seen" rule, although not uniformly followed by all umpires, would remain in effect until 1931.

A few hours were consumed trying to come to some agreement on the wording of the balk rules. They never did agree; the umpires were urged to enforce the ones on the books more strictly.

The most important change took the least time: the abolition of freak pitches, which some minor leagues had already banned. Connie Mack and Clark Griffith had argued for a ban on the spitter for years. Mack never thought much of pitchers who relied on it. "Ed Walsh was the only man who could win with it consistently," he once said, "and he didn't last as long as he would have if he had developed a so-called natural line."

Banning the use of any foreign substance or the discoloring or marring of the ball was unanimously applauded, except by some pitchers. Infielders who had to grip and throw the moist ball cheered the loudest. A limited number of pitchers who were already using the spitter were exempt for the 1920 season, a grace period that was later amended to allow them to use it until their careers ended.

As the delegates and onlookers arrived, the lobby of the Congress Hotel buzzed with speculation as to who would be the new chairman of the National Commission. Dozens of names were floated. There didn't seem to be a favorite. The rumor given most credence was that the search committee of Ruppert, Navin, Baker, and Veeck would recommend Judge Landis. That was hooted down by reminders that the final selection would be up to the two league presidents, and Ban Johnson would never go for Landis.

Another hot topic was the fireworks that were expected when the fractious American League met on Tuesday. There was no aroma of reconciliation in the smoke-filled air. In his remarks at the Philadelphia writers' annual dinner just before leaving for Chicago, Mack had said that Ban Johnson would never resign.

Clark Griffith's new partner, William Richardson, was new to the scrap and eager to learn. When he inquired what the fight was all about, Phil Ball said it was all over a third-rate pitcher named Mays. To which Jake Ruppert reportedly replied, "You have a third-rate club." Quoted verbatim or not, it was indicative of the kind of juvenile sniping that was going on.

Monday afternoon the two camps met in separate confabs, the five Johnsonites in the league office, the three dissenters in Comiskey's ballpark office. At noon on Tuesday it was freezing outside and not much warmer in the AL meeting room. The three sat at one side of the table, the five opposite them. Ruppert set the tone for much of the meeting when he moved that reporters be allowed to be present and was voted down 5–3. One after another his motions were defeated by the same score. Once, when he asked Johnson to report on the season just past, including the final standings—a routine item in past annual meetings—the bullheaded Ban said he was not required to submit such a report and would not do so.

Connie Mack brought up his anti-tampering motion again: any owner, agent, manager, or player had to get the consent in writing from the club owning a player before talking to that player. Penalty for the first offense would be a fine of $1,000, for a second offense, expulsion from the league. Clark Griffith seconded it. Col. Huston, with the Carl Mays incident in mind, offered an amendment to make it retroactive to include the 1919 season. Only Ruppert, Frazee, and Comiskey voted for the amendment. Mack's resolution then passed, 8–0.

Clark Griffith argued for a June 1 trading deadline. Ruppert argued for September 1. The consensus compromised on July 1. (The National voted for August 15.) Rules on the rescheduling of postponed games were clarified.

There was a brief bit of levity when, to the exaggerated surprise of Ruppert, Frazee, and Comiskey, a motion by Ruppert dealing with the withdrawing of waivers was approved unanimously. But another by Ruppert, to adjourn for thirty minutes to allow the club presidents to go into executive session without Ban Johnson present, went down to the usual 5–3 defeat.

Ruppert's wish list was not yet exhausted when Ban Johnson abruptly adjourned the meeting and left the room. Nobody else moved. Declaring himself neutral in the divisive feud, the newcomer William Richardson pleaded for the two sides to make an effort to end the fighting without further drawn-out litigation. Ruppert, having spent upwards of $60,000 on lawyers in the Mays case, renewed his request for an informal discussion in which they could freely exchange views, charges, insults—whatever was on their minds—with no rules of procedure, no note taking, and no chairman. He was confident that they could resolve their differences that way. The loyalists, equally weary of the battle (the American League had spent $18,315.66 on legal and other expenses), agreed. It was past seven; they adjourned for an hour. Comiskey, Ruppert, and Frazee went out to dinner. The other five stayed in the meeting room and ordered sandwiches. Some reports have Ban Johnson in the hotel but are silent on what he was doing for the rest of the evening.

Although reporters were not present when the club owners reconvened, an unnamed *New York Times* correspondent either had a reliable informant or a vivid imagination. Or perhaps the exchanges were so boisterous it didn't take much eavesdropping to overhear what was happening. "The club owners merrily assaulted one another's ball club," he reported. "There were many times when all were talking at once. If the tense atmosphere of the meeting had not been broken often with bits of humor, it would have developed into a Donnybrook affair. . . . There were times when the club owners threatened each other. At one time Colonel Ruppert of New York and Phil Ball of St. Louis arose and faced each other and seemed all set for a passage at fisticuffs. Then they quieted down for a while when cooler heads prevailed."

Every description of the heavyset, urbane, socialite Ruppert is at odds with any picture of his engaging in a "passage of fisticuffs." Still, none of the three rebels was reticent about airing his opinion of Ban Johnson. Nor was any of the five hesitant in defending him.

Since it all began, it seemed as though they had been playing a variation on Zeno's Paradox—an infinite number of meetings ultimately winding down to a conclusion in a finite time.

In the end, though it took until close to two o'clock in the morning, the cooler heads did prevail. They arrived at a truce that enabled both sides to claim victory. A few dozen sleepy reporters were lounging in the corridor when the combatants, appearing subdued but satisfied, straggled silently out of the meeting room. One carried two pages of hotel stationery with the handwritten agreement on it, which he summarized for the writers:

Ban Johnson would remain in office with clipped authority. A two-man arbitration committee of Griffith and Ruppert would serve for two years to hear appeals from decisions of the president. If they were unable to agree, the matter would be put to a Chicago federal judge. (Landis was undoubtedly in their minds.) Any member of the league could appeal any act that he felt affected his constitutional rights as a member. Carl Mays was reinstated, a moot point since his suspension did not carry over into the 1920 season. New York was awarded third place.

In return, the rebellious trio agreed to drop all litigation against Ban Johnson and his five supporters.

The *Times* predicted that Ban Johnson would retire rather than be subjected to the new restrictions. It didn't know Ban. He still controlled the National Commission by blocking any nominated chairman he couldn't influence. The National League was adamant for a one-man commission. That was okay with the Johnson loyalists, as long as the one man was Ban Johnson. They knew that would never happen, so they voted to retain the troublesome troika arrangement.

The committee in search of a new chairman was unable to agree on one choice. From a list of fifteen they had come down to five: Landis; New York state senator James J. Walker, who had sponsored the 1919 bill permitting Sunday baseball in the state; New York Internal Revenue Collector William Edwards; New York attorney John Conway Toole; and Harvey T. Woodruff, sports editor of the *Chicago Tribune*. As a sentimental gesture, Garry Herrmann introduced the name of Cap Anson, having promised Anson that he would.

Landis asked that his name be withdrawn, leaving four finalists.

Informal polling by the *Times* found Walker and Woodruff the favorites. Walker, who became mayor of New York before he sailed away to stay out of jail, was the choice of some easterners. Woodruff had the backing of the westerners, including Herrmann. Everybody was confident that Ban Johnson and NL president John Heydler would settle on someone within a few days.

They didn't. Johnson okayed Woodruff. Heydler had nothing against him but believed it should be someone with more national recognition. If Johnson couldn't have his way, he'd rather have nobody than somebody too independent. So he stalled. The National League threatened to break the National Agreement and go its own way if he didn't act. John Heydler kept after Johnson for months, even proposing they flip a coin, the winner choosing the new chairman. Johnson refused. That would be—gasp—gambling.

So they went through the 1920 season without a chairman, the two presidents running things as best they could.

With the air cleared of controversy if not smoke, the joint meeting of the two leagues on Wednesday was peaceful. Johnson greeted Frazee and Ruppert with a handshake and smile—how hearty a handshake was not reported. The leagues split on whether to abolish inter-league waivers. The American, with Mack's support, voted yes. The Nationals rejected it. They discussed the final payments yet to be made to Harry Sinclair and the estate of the late owner of the Brooklyn Federal League club, Robert Ward, in the seemingly endless Federal League settlement. The 1920 schedules were approved. The Yankees were given twelve Sunday dates at home, the Giants thirteen, and the Dodgers nineteen.

Without the Yankees sharing the Polo Grounds, the Giants would have had as many Sunday dates as the Dodgers. This was the sole reason the Giants wanted to evict their tenants. It had nothing to do with the arrival of Babe Ruth in New York. As far back as August 2, 1919, when Ruth was still in Boston, the Giants' new owners had notified the Yankees that their 1920 lease, which had a one-year option for 1921, would not be renewed. As Tommy Rice pointed out in the *Brooklyn Eagle*, "Six more Sundays at the Polo Grounds for the Giants would be worth more than the $50,000 or so the Yanks are paying."

The Giants doubled the rent for 1920 and ultimately agreed to extend the lease through 1922, while Yankee Stadium was being built.

Citing rising expenses, the leagues raised ticket prices. Gone was the twenty-five-cent bleacher bargain. The new scale began at fifty cents, seventy-five for pavilion seats, and one dollar for grandstands. Prices of box and reserved seats were left up to the individual clubs. Two alleged skinflints, Clark Griffith and Branch Rickey, pleaded successfully to allow clubs to have special low-price seats at fifteen and twenty-five cents for kids under fourteen.

Connie Mack went along with it. The Shibe Park cheap seats were now in line with the forty-four cents charged by the city's silent picture shows. Besides, the booming economy had changed the spending habits of many fans. "The bleachers are being deserted in favor of the grandstands due to higher wages," Mack said. "The bleacher patron of other days is now an occupant of the pavilion or the grandstand."

In the National Commission's last meeting, Scott Perry was reinstated from the suspended list. Connie Mack went home and mailed a $5,000 contract to Perry's tailor shop in Franklin, Pennsylvania. Maybe, with Prohibition in force, the prodigal Perry might regain his 1918 form, stick around, and earn it.

11 | THE BABE RUTH ERA BEGINS

Connie Mack was home for one week before he headed for Lake Charles with the pitchers and catchers, business manager Bob Schroeder, and trainer Doc Ebling. He also hired Charles "Shots" Monaghan to assist Ebling and, during the season, provide a trainer's ministrations to visiting clubs at Shibe Park. Like Schroeder and Ebling, Monaghan became one of Mack's lifers, remaining in his post until he died when the Athletics left Philadelphia in 1954.

Mack may have felt ten years younger when the rest of the squad joined them on March 1. They reminded him of his kiddie corps of 1908 and 1909. There wasn't a Collins or Barry or Baker among them. But they were as young and green as those colts had been. Of the thirty-three players in camp, two-thirds were rookies. They were the youngest bunch in the big leagues. The oldest was Tilly Walker, thirty-two; the youngest, Robert McCann, not yet eighteen. Connie Mack was always happiest when he had youngsters to teach. They gave him hope, as essential to any manager as air.

Mack had beefed up his offense in the past few years, but the defense had become shoddy. Now he had to find a way to stop the leaks without giving up too much punch. He considered Atlanta recruit Ivy Griffin at first base and Joe Dugan at second as good as any in the league. Chick Galloway at short had the glove but not the bat. At third Jimmie Dykes had baseball smarts and a rifle arm but was not showing much at the plate.

"That boy is a wonder," Mack described Dykes to Tiny Maxwell of the *Public Ledger*. "Nobody can field the position any better, but fielding is only one-half of the job. If he could hit my worries would be over but he can't hit."

Mack had enough outfielders to platoon them, but Walker and Strunk were gimpy-legged. George Burns had no speed. Whitey Witt was the only one who could cover more than his shadow.

Visitors considered Mack's pitchers his best-looking crop in years. The mound staff was the tallest Mack had ever assembled. Six of them stood over six feet, topped by the 6-foot-6 left-hander William Jennings Bryan "Slim" Harriss, who was born in 1896 in Brownwood, Texas, when the Populist orator William Jennings Bryan had a large following in that part of the country. The whole team was big. In a team photo taken in Lake Charles, a half dozen of the players seem to tower over the 6-foot-2½ Mack, black derby and all.

A dozen scouts had passed on Harriss, who had won 21 at Houston. Mack's agents thought he had a chance, so the boss paid $2,500 for him. He had a smooth windup and sharp curve to go with his fastball. His odd-for-a-southpaw sidearm delivery left him in an awkward position to handle bunts. Mack ordered intensive fielding drills for him.

Two other tall left-handers, Walt Kinney, with a full big league season behind him, and twenty-one-year-old rookie Roy Moore, up from Waco, might bloom into consistent winners. A chastened Scott Perry was working as hard as anybody. Dave Keefe, after three years of seasoning, looked ready to join the starting rotation.

The presence of one not-so-young prospect, twenty-five-year-old lefty Pat Martin, illustrates how Connie Mack did business with minor league club owners and why his reputation was tops with them. Whenever he offered players in a transaction, Mack usually provided a sort of warranty: if a player he sent proved unsatisfactory, he would take the player back and send a replacement until the other party was satisfied. It also depicts an unusually generous club owner, shoe company executive George Johnson, president of the Binghamton Bingoes in the AA International League. Several scouts and managers had shown interest in Martin, a winning pitcher in the minors for five years, who had a 17-6 record and a $5,000 price tag in August 1919. Clark Griffith had gone to Jersey City to see him work but was more impressed with the Jersey City pitcher, Al Schacht, and bought him instead.

On August 4, 1919 Mack sent a special delivery letter to Johnson:

Will give you twenty-five hundred cash for pitcher Martin, and two pitchers, one of the pitchers Robert Geary, now pitching for Columbia in South Atlantic League. I loaned this pitcher to that club for balance of season. Geary has been with me for two seasons. In 1918, just before he went into the Army, he shut out Boston and New York. Would class him with Seibold, now with Baltimore. A number of my players consider him better than Seibold. I feel positive that this player can win in your league.

The other pitcher I will send you on trial and if he does not come up to expectations will then send you another man whom I feel can win. Grevell has been with me all season; has great curve ball and may develop into a first class pitcher. I will keep my promise to send you another pitcher in the event of Grevell not making good and will continue to send someone till I satisfy you.

It is agreed that Martin will remain with you until the end of your championship season. As I am going away in the next few days to Atlanta, Ga., would like to have you wire me after you have thought the matter over. With kind regards, I remain,

Very truly yours.

When he received no reply, Mack wrote again, telling Johnson where he would be in the west for the next week and assuring the club owner that he would pay Martin "a salary that you feel that he should have in case you would part with the player."

A week later, for unspecified reasons, Mack withdrew his offer. Perhaps he had been unable to deliver the other pitchers he had promised. Johnson notified Pat Martin on August 19 that "there is today no offers for your services from any source, which means that probably they have decided that you were not quite ripe for faster company. Am afraid you will be disappointed, but there is nothing I can do except to furnish you with the facts. Wish we might have placed you, for your sake. I had in mind, if we should make a deal, to split the price between you and the Club, which I think would have pleased you. Now this has fallen through, of course, and am very sorry."

Sometime between then and mid-September, again without explanation, the deal was back on, and Mack sent Binghamton a check for $2,500, asking Martin to report immediately. Johnson endorsed the check over to Pat Martin, with this note:

Now, this transaction is closed, after considerable correspondence and some little delay. I have understood that you preferred to go to Chicago, but as a matter of fact, these Chicago people were too slow. They had ample time to secure you, but they had a lot of haggling and a lot of talk, and wasted a lot of time, and wanted to see you pitch game after game, and never seemed to be satisfied that they were willing to pay for you, but wanted you on trial, or something of that sort. Now, I have been able to get real money for your services, and it is one of the greatest pleasures that I have had in Baseball, to be able to turn this money over to you, to whom it rightfully belongs, and to say to you, Mr. Martin put this money away. Don't fool it away. Hang on to it. You may not make good with Philadelphia, but you have made good with Binghamton, and have cleaned up a good clean twenty-five hundred dollars, all "velvet." Now take care of it, like a good boy.

My kindest regards to you, and best wishes for your future good luck.

Your friend,
George F. Johnson

Martin had fared well in his debut at Shibe Park on September 20, though he lost to the Browns, 4–0, 3 of the runs scoring on his own wild throw with the bases loaded. A week later the Yankees had driven him out after 2 innings.

Martin had good stuff, said Mack, but forgot everything he was told as soon as the game began. He was 1-4 when Mack sent him back to the minors.

The hardest worker in camp was Eddie Rommel. The tall, blond, twenty-two-year-old had won 23 at Newark, relying on a spitball. Now that the wet one had been banned, he had to come up with another pitch. Lacking speed, he turned to the knuckleball. He came in loaded with confidence, which came across as a fresh busher. When batters complained about swinging against a knuckler in practice, he told them where to get off. Rommel had been down with appendicitis during the winter and reported twenty pounds underweight. He had to go slow to build his stamina while working on his new pitch, his fielding, and his pickoff move. He had filled in at every position except catcher while at Newark, so taking ground balls was no novelty for him. He hopped on them like a jackrabbit and stayed out there as long as anyone would hit them to him.

Rollie Naylor was now one year removed from his army service. Mack turned down a cash offer for him from Comiskey. He said he was through selling players and he meant it.

For all their youth, most of Mack's rookies had performed well in the higher minors. He had .350 hitters and 20-game winners. But a manager or scout could have a hundred years of experience, and he would still be wise to count a minor league star as an unknown quantity. Pitchers, especially, might shine in the minors, where inexperienced batters took good pitches and swung at bad ones. Until they were tested under fire, you just never knew. There wasn't a genius in baseball—Mack, McGraw, Rickey, Comiskey—who hadn't spent a bundle to buy some can't-miss who missed or rejected a future star.

Mack named Amos Strunk his captain. He brought back Danny Murphy to man the coaching lines. Whatever cross words may have passed between them when Murphy had gone to the Federal League were forgotten. Murphy was a sharp sign stealer. He could pick up a hit-and-run sign between a batter and base runner with uncanny success and call for a pitchout from the bench.

The rawest rookie in camp was Bob McCann, the son of a friend of Mack's in Philadelphia. Mack had sent him to play for Rube Oldring at Suffolk in the Virginia League. McCann resembled Rogers Hornsby in appearance, so the players called him Hornsby. The resemblance ended there.

Mack had given up on his prewar hopefuls Ray Bates and Merlin Kopp. He sent them with pitcher Bob Geary to Seattle for right-hander Lyle Bigbee, who would have more home runs (1) than wins (0) in the big leagues.

During the weeks the Athletics and Cardinals barnstormed together around Texas, Branch Rickey and Connie Mack cemented a friendship that lasted a lifetime. Sharing long talks in Pullman drawing rooms and hotel lobbies, Rickey, thirty-eight, was doing more learning than teaching. He had adapted Mack's use of pregame meetings to his own use and expanded on them. Years later Rickey recalled, "I'd known Mack since my American League playing days, but I saw him in a new light. We would talk together about our players, about trades, coaches and tactics, and team building."

Rickey was intrigued by Danny Murphy describing the arts of stealing and relaying signs and picking up catchers' signals to pitchers. Mack rarely flashed any signs himself. He gave them to a player on the bench, who relayed them to the coach.

"It was in these talks that I got my first idea on how to get, but more particularly how to give, signals," Rickey said.

He learned about the handling of men from Mack's tales of Rube Waddell and Osee Schrecongost, citing one as an example:

In complaining about a ten-dollar fine Mr. Mack had assessed on Osee for his second late arrival for a meeting, the famous catcher, who was

Rube Waddell's roommate, said, "Rube didn't come to the meeting at all, and you didn't fine him."

"Now, lookit, Osee," Mr. Mack replied, "if you want me to treat you as we do George Edward, we will do just that."

"Oh no, no, Mr. Mack," Osee exclaimed. "I don't want that." And Osee left, penitent and satisfied.

This was one of many examples of how Mr. Mack would exercise his marvelous control and guidance of diversified personalities. He wanted his men to have such regard for physical fitness that they would impose upon themselves those restrictions or practices that kept them at top condition for winning games. He believed that no real discipline was obtained unless it was self-imposed and voluntary. Here was Mr. Mack's highest contribution to team morale. Every man was his own manager in his desire for knowledge and physical fitness. That was, and still is, the uncharted but everlasting influence of Mr. Mack's teaching. This is his immortality. I understand why he was so different from McGraw but equally successful in handling men. We owe so much to many, but to some like Mr. Mack we owe more than others.

Another friendship developed during those barnstorming weeks, between Joe Dugan and Cardinals second baseman Rogers Hornsby. The jumpy youngster was plagued with insecurity and wide mood swings. If everything didn't go just right for him or the fans got on him, he was liable to go home or go somewhere, anywhere. Once he disappeared from Lake Charles for a few days. When he returned, he said he'd been to visit a friend in Beaumont, probably Hornsby. Though only a year older than Joe, Hornsby tried to steady him and help with his hitting.

"I get tempted to do something foolish, I get so sore and disgusted," Dugan told a writer. "Nobody will ever know how much help Hornsby has been to me. I listen to him like a father."

Hornsby proved to be a better hitter than counselor.

When Mack's giant pitchers left the practice field and began to face Cardinals hitters, they didn't look like world-beaters. They lost by scores of 7–6, 12–7, 8–6, 9–8. Before the barnstorming tour was over, Mack concluded that it had been a mistake. The daily hops had cost him the morning practices he valued. Next year he would do things differently.

The Athletics were the beneficiaries of Babe Ruth's debut in Yankee pinstripes. They opened at home on a chilly Wednesday afternoon before an enthusiastic crowd wrapped in furs and overcoats. Ruth drew a big ovation when he appeared in the on-deck circle in the first inning. He had 2 singles for the day but wound up as the goat of the game. In the eighth inning, the score tied 1–1, with Walker and Griffin on base, Joe Dugan hit a fly ball that landed in Ruth's glove and fell out. Two runs scored and the A's, behind Scott Perry, won 3–1.

The New York papers played up Ruth's error as if it was the turning point of a World Series. The *Times* portrayed him as a caricature of a mercurial-tempered overgrown kid: "The petted Babe of the New York Yankees appeared today in the role of the enfant terrible, when with two of the Athletics retired in the final half of the eighth inning, the score tied at one run each, Ruth gracefully stumbled backward and raised his capacious cupped hands heavenward for Joe Dugan's long fly, only to fluff the catch. 12,000 Philadelphians arose and volubly criticized New York's methods of raising children."

The paper conceded that Ruth "is only human, if that."

The next day as Ruth went up to bat for the first time, a small boy came out of the stands carrying a big box and handed it to Ruth. It was common for fans to present gifts to players on their first plate appearance of the afternoon; nobody tried to stop the lad. The players gathered around while Ruth untied the string and ribbons, opened the box, and pulled out a small brown derby. Grinning broadly, he waved it in the air and perched it on his large head. The players and fans recognized it as a vaudeville symbol of a dunce cap and laughed with Ruth.

The Bambino, as Damon Runyon dubbed him, struck out three times, once with the bases loaded. But the Yankees beat Rollie Naylor, 4–1, on cheap hits in the seventh and ninth.

The Athletics played well at times but were often tripped up by untimely slips. They might hit for 27 total bases, as they did on April 20, and still lose, 8–5. "The Philadelphia flinging was a nightmare," wrote Fitz Gerald in the *Washington Post*, "and the fielding was of an order to make a man less accustomed to punishment than Connie Mack do a Brodie [jump] into the Schuylkill."

They made 11 errors in a series against the Red Sox and as many mental mistakes.

Their 7-13 record in the first three weeks was a 3-game improvement over the year before. But they lacked the pep and aggressiveness of Mack teams of yore. When a writer implied that the modern players cared for nothing but their pay envelopes, Connie Mack didn't disagree. He knew it had always been about money with the players. His own leadership in the 1890 players' rebellion was evidence that he had no illusions on that score. Even so, it had not been *all* about money in those days, as it seemed to be now.

"Baseball has suffered because of the listlessness of players," he said. "I would like to see the players as much interested in winning a game as the fans. They have not been showing much spirit."

For one thing, they never kicked about a close call. Mack didn't want them to carry on so much that they'd be thrown out of a game, but he didn't want them to be docile when they had a gripe coming. He wasn't.

In the early weeks of the season Mack focused on the enigmatic Jimmie Dykes. He loved the fire and hustle of the Bryn Mawr boy. But Dykes couldn't buy a base hit. At the plate his head was steady, eye on the ball, his swing smooth. He made contact but produced only weak grounders and pop-ups. Puzzled, Mack studied him in morning practice and every time at bat. After about three weeks, he thought he had the answer: Dykes was not completing his swing. He was chopping at the ball. Mack had corrected the same flaw in Joe Dugan when he was hitting under .200 a few years ago. He showed Dykes how he was pulling back as soon as the bat connected with the ball, stopping the swing in the middle instead of following through.

On May 12 Dykes hit his first big league home run. With new confidence, he launched a hitting streak and wound up hitting .256. Only once in the next eighteen years would he hit for a lower average.

Frank "Bug" Welch, the twenty-two-year-old outfielder bought for $1,000 from the Norfolk Mary Janes, had a different problem. His swing was complete but he swung too fast. Mack kept after him to tone it down.

The A's opened the Yankees' home season before a crowd of twenty-five thousand who screamed for Babe Ruth to hit one out in batting practice. Trying to oblige, the Babe strained a muscle in his right side and had to leave the game after 1 inning.

The phenomenon of Babe Ruth had taken over baseball. Jacob Ruppert predicted that Ruth would hit 51 home runs. The Yankees drew huge crowds wherever they went.

The whole country went gaga over Ruth. It has become generic for writers to portray Ruth as saving baseball following the Black Sox scandal. But Ruth was a nationwide craze when the 1920 season opened, five months before the fixed World Series would make headlines. The game was prospering and didn't need saving. Some writers have also given Ruth credit for expanding baseball's audience from mere followers to real fans. It was the opposite. Like the World Series, which brought out many once-a-year patrons, Ruth attracted thousands, especially women, who were curious to see what this "rare slugging curio" was all about. Some may have become hooked and turned into scorekeepers in the stands, but it's not accurate to depict baseball's earlier addicts, many of whom disdained the new slugging game, as "mere followers" instead of the diehard fans and students of the game that they were before Babe Ruth came along.

Ruth was seen as bigger than life as soon as he entered the New York hype circus. He became beloved by millions of men and women who had never cared about baseball. Women who tut-tutted over his peccadilloes did so with a smile: the Babe was just a good-natured, not-a-bad-bone-in-his-body overgrown scamp. Kids adored him because he was genuinely one of them. One Boswell went galactic, extolling him as "in reality a Martian," the "super-slugger on the interplanetary league," using "the parallax of Jupiter for a bat and the Pleiades for batting pills. Those shooting stars we used to look at with such awe when we were kids—what were they but 'Babe's' long hits?"

Whenever somebody in the minor leagues hit a few home runs, he was now tagged "the Babe Ruth" of that league. Six clubs, including the A's, were said to be after "the Babe Ruth of the minors," first baseman Frank Brower, who had hit 22 home runs at Reading. Washington won him with a package of cash and three players. The first Frank Brower never became the second Babe Ruth; he hit 30 home runs in five years.

The word "Ruthian" entered the cliché ranks. His influence was so ubiquitous one writer quipped, "They will soon be calling John D. Rockefeller the Babe Ruth of the gasoline world."

Everywhere Ruth went, everything he did—in public—was news. He signed to star in a movie for $100,000. The Central AAU Track and Field Championships put on by the Knights of Columbus obtained the bat he used to hit his fifty-third home run of the season as the prize for the mile relay. Baseballs signed by Ruth were in great demand for charity auctions.

Applicants for jobs as physical education instructors in Philadelphia found this question on the exam: "Is Babe Ruth a tennis player or a boxer?" Anyone demonstrating so little knowledge of the current sporting scene as to circle either choice was eliminated from consideration.

Ruth even inspired at least one robbery attempt. The ailing Charles Comiskey was not allowed by his physician to watch White Sox games. He would sit in the box office during the game. A gang planning to steal the gate receipts at Comiskey Park decided the biggest haul would be when the Yankees were in town on September 16. Comiskey had a bad scare, but the gang was nabbed and the caper failed.

Ruth's biggest impact was on other players. Everybody stopped what they were doing and watched when Ruth took batting practice. They saw where the money was and would be. Until now bats were thick-handled, slightly tapered. Hitting was done with the forearms to drive the ball through the infield. Ruth used long bats that weighed up to fifty-two ounces. Hitters began asking for longer bats with thinner handles and more weight at the flying end to whip it for distance.

Ruth also ushered in the tape measure era. Distance estimates of his clouts became news. In July he hit one in St. Louis that was estimated to have traveled five hundred feet. Even his infield pop-ups went higher than anyone else's, so high that when Jimmie Dykes staggered around under one in the Polo Grounds one day, Ruth was on second base when Dykes dropped it.

"Connie Mack had a rule that the first infielder to call for a pop-up had to catch it," Dykes told Arthur Daley of the *Times* forty years later. "When Ruth was at bat, this meant an awfully silent infield. No one wanted any part of him."

Various theories were put forth for the increase in hitting in 1920. The abolition of freak pitches and the frequent introduction of new balls (whose seams were flatter than before, making it harder to throw a curve) had more to do with the changed game than any so-called "juice" in the ball. Tom Shibe confirmed that the ball was unchanged from 1919: "Same yarn, same size and weight of rubber, same core, same horsehide."

One veteran player told Hugh Fullerton, "Stopping the spitter and the freak pitches gave a bunch of weak hitters confidence in themselves. Not so many are guessing and very few are stepping back. They're standing up to pitching 'cause they aren't afraid of being hit by some freak shoot."

Connie Mack agreed that banning freak pitches made all the difference. "Now the batter knows about what can be expected and can stand up there with more confidence. It's better. The public likes it."

It took longer for the home run numbers to jump in the National League. Joe Vila asked Ban Johnson if the American League ball was livelier. "The Spalding and Reach balls are made by the same concern," Johnson said, "and the same material is used in both. The only difference is the color of the stitching."

Some Yankee fans were unconvinced. They collected home run balls and sent them to the Bureau of Standards in Washington. The balls were tested and compared to some made in 1919 before being cut open. Conclusion: no difference that would cause the newer balls to go farther when hit.

Even Prohibition was credited with lifting batting averages. Players found it harder to find a few beers after a game, so they lost weight and gained some speed and could beat out more infield hits. Or so the theory went.

Whatever, the days of the stained, scuffed, loaded, shined balls were over. Hit-filled baseball was in. One coach said, "I've been knocked down twice by drives on the third base line. In one game I saw two drives go by pitchers and I doubt whether they ever saw the ball."

Thirteen home runs were hit at Shibe Park in five days in May. One Saturday in St. Louis the Senators lost by scores of 13–6 and 17–2. Even the losers had 21 hits. In June the A's were hitting 20 points higher than they had in 1919, and they were still the lowest in the league.

The fans, especially the new "Ruthian" ones, loved it. The magnates noticed. They began looking for sluggers. "The next Ruth" replaced "the next Cobb" or "the next Mathewson" in scouts' reports.

For the first six weeks of the 1920 season the A's pitching was a nightmare. Naylor, Perry, Kinney, and Keefe did most of the work. All were inconsistent. Kinney pitched well in some losing efforts, then took two drubbings in four days at home in May and left the team for Franklin in the Oil and Steel League, a mecca for discontented players. Jing Johnson soon followed him. The press jumped on Connie Mack for paying such low salaries that a promising young player would prefer to play in an industrial league. Stung by the criticism, Mack abandoned his principle of not responding about or discussing private personnel matters in public. He revealed that Kinney had signed for $2,500. After Kinney had taken two tough extra-inning losses, Mack had raised him to $4,000. Mack also said he had given Kinney $1,000 in advances over the winter and the player still owed him $900 when he left.

Mack suggested that Kinney didn't have the heart for pitching in the big leagues. He was the kind of player who would rather pitch in obscurity. Though he had vowed that Kinney would never pitch for the A's again, Mack offered to give him another chance. It took Kinney until July to decide he wanted to come back. By that time Mack was fed up. Sorry, he said. Too late. I don't want you any more.

Concluded James Isaminger, "The good treatment Kinney received from Mack belies the general impression that the Athletics do not pay real salaries."

Try as he might and erroneous as it was, once that reputation was hung on Connie Mack, repetition etched it into stone. It has outlived Mack by sixty years and counting.

After a month-long trip around the circuit, in which they won 5 and lost 24, Mack surveyed his predicament. "Out west the pitching was all that could be expected. Not world beating, you understand, but all I expected from my staff. The trouble was with the rest of the team. Men playing out of their customary positions couldn't get all the drives they are supposed to handle. Such lobs get scored as hits and rightly so, but it makes the pitcher's record for the day look worse than it deserves."

When they hit and caught the ball, they still lost. Their first day back home on June 30 was typical. In a doubleheader against the Yankees, what the *Times* called the "poor, helpless, hapless Athletics" made 26 hits for 44 total bases. New York had 27 hits for 43 total bases and won both games. From June 3 through July 6 the Athletics won 2 games and lost 31.

After losing two on July 5, the Philadelphia "Strangers," as Fitz Gerald dubbed them, had a 17-55 record. They "improved" from there, actually playing .500 ball for a month before going 5-22 the last month, and finished 50 games out of first place, a gain of 2 games over 1919.

Connie Mack brought Eddie Rommel along slowly, using him solely in relief for the first three months. This was partly because the pitcher's winter illness had delayed his getting into top condition, and partly to give him time to adapt to major league hitters while relying on the knuckleball. Once Rommel had demonstrated that he could control the unpredictable pitch by averaging fewer than 3 walks per 9 innings, his relief stints became longer. But for three months he had no decisions.

On the other hand, Dave Keefe was a model of inconsistency. On July 7 at home he shut out the Red Sox on 2 hits. Six days later he started against Cleveland and was hammered for 3 runs and 4 hits in the first inning. With one out, Mack sent in Rommel. The A's tied the score. Rommel gave up 1 run and 4 hits the rest of the way, but the 1 hit was a tie-breaking home run by Ray Chapman.

After the game a writer asked Mack, "Why did you put Keefe in the box to start the game instead of Rommel?"

Mack had no more (and maybe less) patience with writers' dumb questions than today's managers. The *Philadelphia Bulletin* described the effects of his response: "A patrol wagon gathered up the remains."

The press box denizens persuaded the official scorer that Keefe deserved the loss, not Rommel, despite Ban Johnson's guidelines. The scorer agreed and sent in his report, charging Keefe with the loss and suggesting the guidelines be waived in such cases.

Rommel earned his first decision on July 19, again relieving Keefe in the second inning of a 9–4 victory. "I'm in there at last," he beamed. "First time I've either won or lost a game all season. Now I'll feel like I'm in the league when I read the pitching averages on Saturdays. I was getting desperate. I would just as soon have been charged with that Cleveland defeat instead of Keefe to get my name in the records, so I could prove to folks at home I had a job with a big league club."

(Ban Johnson later reversed the July 13 scorer's decision and pinned the Cleveland loss on Rommel.)

In June Scott Perry had pitched 40 innings without allowing an earned run, but by mid-August he was 9-19, Naylor 7-19. As Mack pointed out, a lot of their hits should have been charged to the fielders behind them. Mack had counted on Roy Moore, who won his first start and didn't win again, finishing 1-13.

The infield was a mess. At one point Dykes, Galloway, and Dugan were all out of the lineup. First base, which had looked so clogged with outstanding candidates, became a problem. When he had bought Maurice Burrus in 1919, Mack told reporters, "I have bought the greatest young player in the country. Burrus is no experiment. He would make good even if he didn't want to."

Apparently he *really* didn't want to. Mack gave up on him and tagged him one of his bigger disappointments. (Burrus spent four years in the minors before turning in a few good years with the Boston Braves.)

George Burns was hounded out of town by the hecklers, those early-morning hawkers of fish and produce who exercised their leather lungs at Shibe Park every afternoon, forcing nearby fans to cover their ears and rabbit-eared players to fidget away their focus on the job at hand. Mack tried him in right field. That didn't help. He knew Burns was good enough to play regularly somewhere else and sold him to Cleveland for $10,000. Burns thrived away from Shibe Park.

Ivy Griffin was a puzzle. The previous September he had come up hitting all kinds of pitching. Now he couldn't hit any kind of pitching. All the ability he had shown in Atlanta he left there. He didn't seem to care and didn't stay in shape.

Mack tried to beef up his offense by benching Galloway, moving Dugan to shortstop and Dykes to second. Dugan was batting .300 but remained a pain in the neck. He went home for his brother's funeral. He went home to see his sick mother. He went home because he wasn't feeling well but didn't tell anybody. Recruiters from the industrial leagues buzzed around like cheetahs preying on the laggards in a herd of livestock. Oil City, Franklin, Lebanon, and other Pennsylvania boom towns in the oil fields had money to spend and civic pride to feed. They had signed so many ineligible and suspended players, major league clubs were warned by the National Commission against playing any exhibition games against any teams that played Oil City or Franklin. Dugan and Whitey Witt took off one Wednesday to check out Lebanon. Cy Perkins told the *Bulletin*, "I don't believe Dugan is going to sign with the steel league. I room with him and I didn't know he was going to hop out. He's a funny fellow. You can never tell what he'll do next. I wouldn't be surprised if he tried to jump back next week."

Dugan and Witt were back on Saturday.

Joe might have been the inspiration for the Jimmy Durante song, "Did you ever get the feeling that you wanted to go, then you get the feeling that you wanted to stay?" The fans were fed up with him. As good as he was on the field, they would just as soon see him jump and stay jumped.

When Mack moved him to shortstop, Dugan didn't like it. He cleaned out his locker and went home. "He doesn't like it," Mack explained, "because of the long hard throw, which tears him apart. His heart isn't in his work when he is on that side of second base and too many get by him."

They needed his bat in the lineup, so Mack promised Dugan he could play second. He put Thomas at short and Dykes on third. Dykes would play anywhere. Mack would have swapped ten Dugans for one more Dykes if he could find one more.

Looking for a shortstop who could hit, Mack took another chance on Mo Shannon, giving Washington $2,500 for him. Shannon had all the tools to be a star except the head and the heart. He was an enigma to Mack and to himself. Mack had first signed him in 1917, gave up on him in 1919, and sent him to the Red Sox, who passed him on to Washington. Wherever he played, Shannon's careless fielding and indifference in running out ground balls brought down the wrath of the fans. When Mack asked him why he had such a nonchalant attitude, Shannon said he didn't know. "I mean to run out all hits but, somehow, something I can't explain happens and I don't run them out."

Mack was stumped. Shannon was only twenty-three and "ought to be one of the best shortstops in the country. But he kills himself by his methods.

He gets himself in bad all over the circuit. The razzing he has received here lately isn't new."

Mack gave up on him on August 31, suspended him without pay, and sent him home. "I won't sell him or release him," he said. "If he wants to play here he has to make peace with me before we go south next spring." Shannon made one pinch-hitting appearance in 1921 before Mack cut him loose, and he disappeared from the majors except for a brief stint with the Cubs in 1926.

The outfield became a patchwork quilt that couldn't cover a baby's crib. Amos Strunk was limping. Mack asked waivers on him. Only thirty, Amos seemed to have been around forever. Like Rube Oldring, Strunk could have been great, but he lacked the combativeness of the stars of his era. The White Sox claimed him, and Strunk became a pinch-hitting specialist for the rest of his career.

The heavyset Frank Welch had a bad ankle. Witt, Mack's only .300-hitting outfielder, suffered a plague of abscesses and spent weeks in the hospital. So Mack paid the Rocky Mount Tar Heels $7,500 for Frank Walker, who had been up once with Detroit. Walker looked and moved like Tris Speaker and started out hitting like him. But it didn't last. The son of a cotton mill millionaire from South Carolina, Walker turned out to be as jumpy as Joe Dugan. He went home once because of illness in the family and again when his ulcer acted up and he wanted to see his family doctor.

Mack continued his juggling act, which over the years had developed into a routine worthy of W. C. Fields. At times he had a catcher, pitcher, and first baseman in the outfield. Pop flies fell between them when they weren't running into each other. There were times when Mack may have considered using a Ouija board, the latest craze for drawing guidance from the spirit world.

Branch Rickey once distilled the art of managing to: "Get the players and the rest is a lead-pipe cinch." Connie Mack amended it to: "Get the players and keep them all in the game all the time, then all you have to do is wave your scorecard."

The tryouts went on. Mack had more scouts out than he had ever dispatched. It was like rolling dice. On Tom Turner's advice he bought a nineteen-year-old left-hander, Fred Heimach, from Raleigh. Turner had seen him pitch in the army during the war in France, according to one version, or as a semipro in Heimach's home town (Camden, New Jersey), according to another. Nor is there any evidence to support the account that Turner told Heimach to see Connie Mack after he got out of the army and that Mack signed him and farmed him out. Heimach's 11-18 record with the Capitals was less important than his 1.83 earned run average and exceptional control.

First time out, Heimach was shelled for 9 runs in 5 innings. Another stranger, Bill Shanner, surrendered 4 runs in 4 innings. Jack Slappey, famed for pitching a perfect game against some college all-stars, gave up 6 runs, none earned, in his trial.

Shanner and Slappey were never seen again. Heimach stuck around for twelve years.

Meanwhile, Elmer Myers, who had returned from the war and couldn't win in Philadelphia or Cleveland, went to Boston and won 9 in a row in five weeks. You never knew.

Cy Perkins found a silver lining in catching the parade of wild young pitchers. "I had to protect myself or get killed," he recalled. "I caught so many bad pitchers that it helped me to be a good catcher."

Mack considered Dykes, Perkins, Witt, and Dugan the stars to build on, Rommel, Perry, and Harriss the core of his future pitching staff.

On August 16 in New York, Indians shortstop Ray Chapman, crowding the plate, was unable to move out of the way of a pitch thrown by Carl Mays. Mays threw a deep underhand fastball with a hop that carried it high and inside to right-handed batters. The pitch hit Chapman in the head and killed him. Mays denied that he had thrown at Chapman. But Mays was a surly, unpopular person who had earned a reputation for throwing at batters in the past. He didn't mind that; even if it wasn't true, it was to his advantage if hitters went up to bat against him with that thought nagging at them. Any pitcher would welcome that edge. Mays was known to scrape the ball to rough up the surface before the new rule banning such practices. But he was far from alone in that practice.

Connie Mack had no love for Carl Mays. In 1914 Mays's dusters had infuriated the Athletics. Frank Baker had once retaliated by letting the bat fly out of his hands with Mays as his target. A year ago, when Mays had thrown a ball into the box seats behind the visitors' dugout at Shibe Park and hit Bryan Hayes, Hayes had sworn out a warrant for assault. Just six weeks ago Mack had persuaded Hayes to withdraw the warrant and brought the two men together in his office, where Mays apologized, then went out and shut out the A's 5–0.

But Connie Mack was the first baseball man outside of New York to defend Mays:

Outside of Chapman's immediate family, nobody deserves more sympathy than Carl Mays. Nobody is sorrier for Chapman's death. I have nothing for him but sympathy, and the Athletics take that stand, whatever be the actions of other teams. To my mind Mays has been an exemplary ball player this year. I think digging up his past to blacken his name is nearly an outrage. I don't think Mays should be made the goat for this accident. Since the protests against Mays hitting batsmen a few years ago, he has been more than careful not to hit batsmen, and knowledge that his peculiar underhand delivery is especially hard to get away from has caused him to be especially careful in this respect.

The records supported Mack. Since 1915 Mays had hit 55 batters; forty-four pitchers had hit more over the same period. Mays had led the league once, in 1917, with 14. Had the universally admired Walter Johnson thrown the fatal pitch, there would have been no protests against him. Yet over one six-year span, Johnson had hit 86 batters.

Eddie Collins, in Philadelphia with the White Sox at the time, acknowledged that "dusting 'em off was [Mays's] favorite pastime back in the old days," but Collins considered the beaning of Chapman "purely accidental."

Ray Chapman's teammates sent a letter to every other club asking each to refuse to play if Mays was scheduled to pitch. Cy Perkins received the letter, but all the Athletics agreed that they would not go along with any strike or boycott of Mays. They were the first team to take that public stand.

If any team refused to take the field with Mays pitching, all the Yankees had to do was announce Mays as the starting pitcher and go home with a forfeit win. There would also be heavy fines involved. Concerned that such actions would "place our league in a very embarrassing position," Connie Mack dictated a letter to Ban Johnson on August 28. Addressed to "Friend Ban," the letter suggested a compromise:

> Should it come to the point where the [striking] players are bound to win, before preventing any games from being played would it be possible to assure the players that if they will continue to play out the present season schedule that the league will take up the Mays case in the Fall[?]
>
> I have in mind that the League should demand or request that the New York Club dispose of Mays. No doubt a National League Club would pay a big price for Mays. If it was the opinion of the American

League Club owners that Mays should be dropped from base ball then the eight clubs are to make up the sum that the New York Club paid for the pitcher or any sum that the New York Club may lose by disposing of Mays to some other league. Mays should not be allowed to play against Cleveland in case an agreement of this kind should be feasible.

Ban Johnson's only public comment was, "It would be inadvisable for Mays to pitch again this year."

The strike talk ended. Mays continued to pitch—though not against Cleveland—and win; he was 8-2 the rest of the year.

Two weeks after Chapman's death the Indians acquired Walter Mails from Seattle. Nicknamed "Duster" for his reputation of throwing at batters, he was 7-0 to help the Indians win their first pennant.

New York, Chicago, and Cleveland battled for the pennant. In the National League it was New York, Brooklyn, and Cincinnati. On July 19 Babe Ruth broke his own home run record. The slugging curio and tight pennant races produced record attendance in both leagues. The Yankees often turned away thousands from the Polo Grounds, especially on weekends.

As far back as February 1917 the American League had considered it desirable for its New York club to have its own grounds. A committee appointed to consult with Ruppert and Huston on their plans reported in December that the league should be willing to render some financial assistance toward the project. There was unanimous agreement. Nothing happened during the war, and everyone had moved cautiously during the 1919 season. Then along came Ruth, and the colonels were as eager to build a bigger stage for the Bambino as the Giants wanted them to move out. But Manhattan land was expensive. Construction costs had gone up in the postwar boom. With the Yankees now baseball's biggest attraction, they were helping to keep the weaker clubs, if not the entire league, afloat. Ruppert thought it only right that the other clubs back up their earlier words of support with a pledge to contribute to the cost of a new stadium.

At Ruppert's request, Ban Johnson called a special meeting for Tuesday, August 24, in Philadelphia. Since it was just one week after the death of Ray Chapman, it was widely believed that the purpose of the meeting was the disciplining of Carl Mays. But Mays was not on the agenda. The meeting began at eleven o'clock at the Bellevue-Stratford. Ruppert outlined his plans for a stadium that would hold at least sixty thousand. He had three sites in mind, all within a short subway ride of Times Square. With the Polo Grounds lease expiring after the 1921 season, it would have to be ready by opening day 1922. Ruppert asked the other club owners to bear some of the cost of the new building, since all of them would benefit. Whatever estimates he presented, the ultimate cost would be $2.5 million.

Tom Shibe and Connie Mack were present, and Mack carried the proxies of Detroit, St. Louis, and Cleveland. Whichever way he went, the league would go. After obtaining an agreement that the league would have some say in the location and final plans, Mack and the rest agreed to help with the financing. No specific commitment was made. Clark Griffith was appointed to inspect the proposed sites and report on them.

As if to underline Ruppert's case, the following weekend the White Sox drew 129,000 over four days at the Polo Grounds, despite rain delays on two days. The Yankees became the first to top 1 million attendance for a season.

As the crowds grew larger, they became rowdier too. A wave of hurling soda bottles and cushions onto the field broke out. During an August game in New York the Braves were forced to huddle around second base to escape the shower of bottles. Charles Ebbets began selling soda pop in paper cups only. Maybe it was a reflection of the rowdiness in the world around them. Russia had invaded Poland and made threats against England, France, Germany, and America. The Red scare unnerved the population. On September 16 a bomb exploded on Wall Street killing twenty-nine people.

Baseball was a form of escape, but the fans carried the viruses of the world with them.

During the season expressions of concern surfaced about players associating with gamblers in the Pacific Coast League. This was nothing new. Players had been involved in fixing and betting on games since the nineteenth century. Players and umpires occasionally reported "propositions" made to them by gamblers and players on other teams.

One player blamed bonus clauses for some of these activities. "When a pitcher is in for a bonus for winning 20 games and he has 19 and the club he is pitching against is out of the running, players who would like to see him get his bonus would let up on him. A few players started getting involved in the betting end of it. That was the opening wedge."

Hugh Fullerton had hammered away on the subject for years. There were stories of managers suspecting players' World Series performances that drew no publicity or questions from the press. Fullerton alluded to players offered bribes or rewards to throw games, often by players on other teams to help their chances for the pennant; club owners getting to players on other teams to "come up injured" when their teams met. Recent rumors had Brooklyn players offering the second-division Cardinals a $1,000 incentive to beat the Giants, a reversal of the "easing up" approach. Usually the players kept quiet about these overtures, and club owners preferred it that way.

Fullerton, like Ban Johnson and Connie Mack, wanted to believe that the game was beyond the reach of fixers.

Players were reported hanging around with gamblers, notably in Boston, Pittsburgh, and Detroit. For the most part, ballplayers were basically honest men. But "the most part" was not the same as 100 percent, so it was never enough.

Ban Johnson had crusaded against gambling from the founding of the American League. He constantly badgered his club owners to stamp it out. In 1918 it was so rampant at Fenway Park that he had hired detectives to investigate the wagering activity in the grandstand. He read their report at a league meeting, which did not endear him to Harry Frazee.

But in fact gambling at ballparks had declined. There were always some members of the sporting crowd who would bet on the outcome of every pitch—penny ante stuff. It was outside the parks where the betting had boomed. And not just among professional gamblers. It seemed that every office and factory had somebody who was operating a betting pool. The game lent itself to a variety of chance-taking, from the number of runs that would be scored in a week to daily odds on Babe Ruth's hitting a home run. It had become a big business built on small bets. Newspapers quoted odds. Banners strung across the houses overlooking Shibe Park openly invited customers to "Make Your Bets." Wagering was no more prohibitable than drinking. It was as true now as it had been in the Old West, when a Texas prosecutor had said it was "impossible to enforce Texas's gambling statutes without arresting the entire populace."

Connie Mack had backed Ban Johnson's campaign against gamblers from the start. In 1911 a Newport, Kentucky, syndicate had schemed to form a nationwide betting pool on the pennant races. Connie Mack thought anybody would be a sucker to put up any money in April and hope to collect in October:

Apart from that, it's bound to hurt the game. The league had one taste of the harm that gambling does to the game years ago [in 1877 four

Louisville players had been kicked out of the National League for throwing games] and that ought to be enough. You take the betting that is done on the grounds even now. There are bets made on the spot and even those have a bad effect on the baseball.

Here's an illustration. Suppose those Kentucky fellows bet tons of money around the country. A good earnest ballplayer is playing his best. He makes an error at a critical time. There would be hundreds of people in any city that would swear he did it purposely. This talk might ruin one of the kids for life and break his heart. Personally, I haven't any objection to a man's betting if he wants to. But gambling as a side issue in baseball cannot fail to harm the game.

The fans didn't seem to mind players betting on games as long as they were honest about it. Published reports of players betting on World Series in which they were not involved evoked no outcries from the public or club owners. In a 1955 letter to Connie Mack, Ty Cobb mentioned that betting on one's own team had gone on openly for twenty years prior to 1919. "For instance," he wrote, "two times Boston and Washington wagered on their pitchers, Johnson and Wood, in a game. The papers were full of it. Then pitchers who knew they would win more than they lost would wager on themselves for extra pocket money."

Most of the Pacific Coast League action now centered around the Vernon club and its first baseman, Hal Chase, who had been under suspicion for years and epitomized the do-nothing attitude that prevailed. In 1914 Yankees manager Frank Chance had been sure that Chase was throwing games. When Christy Mathewson became the Reds manager in 1916, he inherited Chase. By 1918 he had come to the same conclusion as Chance. Matty obtained affidavits from three Giants players charging that Chase, Lee Magee, and Heinie Zimmerman were involved in trying to fix games. Zimmerman was suspended for "breaking training," a coverup. Matty gave the statements to league president John Heydler, who did nothing about it until late in the 1919 season, when he arranged for all three to be quietly released. That's all.

Now here was Chase doing business as usual in Vernon. On August 3 he was expelled from the league along with a few other players (two of whom were immediately signed by a club in the Southern Association). Chase joined a San Jose semipro team until that league kicked him out.

The 1920 papers were full of the "peculiarities" of the White Sox pattern of performance. On July 31 they lost to the A's 5–1 despite making 9 hits. The

Inquirer observed that they ran the bases "stupidly." At the end of August, after a 16–5 win in New York, they lost 5 in a row to New York and Boston. Yankees shortstop Roger Peckinpaugh later said, "You never knew whether they were going to go out there and beat your brains out or roll over and play dead. Somebody was betting on those games, that's a cinch."

At the time one unnamed Sox player said, "Jackson, Felsch, and [Swede] Risberg began dumping the ball to the infield every time we had a chance to score runs. Some of us always had believed we were sold out in the World Series. When the players showed they meant to beat us out of getting in on this one, we decided to act. Cicotte was told he would have to win a certain game or he'd be mobbed on the field by the honest players on the team. He won it."

Other Chicago players weren't shy about being quoted. Utility men Byrd Lynn and Harvey McClellan told reporters they were convinced that errors were made that cost them games in New York and Boston.

Eddie Collins smelled it too. He told a Philadelphia paper that he had gone to Comiskey right after the Boston series and told him his players were throwing away games. He demanded that something be done about it. Nothing happened. Neither Collins nor Comiskey ever denied the story after it appeared. Collins later told his son he played alongside Swede Risberg all year and never spoke to him.

The public believed the rumors: "where there's smoke," etc. But it didn't keep people away from the games or stop them from playing the pools. Identify the few bad apples and run them out of baseball, that's all they asked.

As Isaminger wrote, "If there are any crooks in baseball, throw 'em out. The time is past when anybody's reputation should be spared."

Other writers thought the few crooks should be quietly let go. That was the nervous magnates' attitude too. Don't stir up anything. The less publicity the better. When John McGraw suspected a player of dishonesty, his silent method for disposing of him was to send him a contract for such a ridiculously low salary, he knew the player would not sign it

That was the kind of gab that was blowing in the breeze when, on the night of August 30, the odds on the next day's Phillies-Cubs game suddenly changed from 2–1 Cubs to 6–5 Phillies. Tipoffs went out from the heavy betting centers in Cincinnati, Detroit, and Chicago. A Kansas City writer later reported that a wire to a KC gambler from the Cubs' scheduled starting pitcher Claude Hendrix said, "Bet $5,000 on opposition." Another wire from Hal Chase confirmed the fix.

The next day at two o'clock Cubs president William Veeck received a telegram, then a long distance call, then another. Within an hour five more telegrams arrived. All carried the same message: heavy betting on the Phillies; the fix is in. One named Hendrix.

Veeck took all such tips seriously. He called in his manager, Fred Mitchell. They decided to ask Grover Alexander to start. They promised him a $500 bonus if he won. Despite his best efforts, the Cubs lost 3–0.

When the story broke four days later, Phillies manager Gavvy Cravath said of his last-place team, "There's nothing to it. We're liable to win a ball game most any time." Fred Mitchell said he knew nothing about anything. Veeck asked three Chicago baseball writers to investigate.

Cook County Judge Charles A. McDonald didn't wait for any more reports. He ordered the grand jury to look into any possible conspiracy between any players and gamblers to throw the August 31 game. And while they were at it, he suggested, they might take a look at "every form of baseball gambling in this city, including the baseball pools and lotteries being operated outside the ballparks, to preserve and restore the integrity of the game."

Maybe this put a little scare into some of the White Sox. Prior to September 4 they had lost 6 in a row. From then until the grand jury began its hearings on September 22, they went 14-5, all at home. At that point Cleveland and Chicago each had 91 wins; the Sox had lost 3 more than the Indians.

Connie Mack was skeptical that any more could be done to stop people from betting on baseball than could be done to stop them from drinking, unless somebody passed laws making it a felony and then enforced them. As for the players, he knew that unless they were all honest, there was no way to guarantee against future attempts to fix games. Only the honesty of the players could prevent it.

The grand jury decided to widen its scope to include any suspicious games in the past eighteen months. It listed players, writers, owners, and league officials to testify. Among the players was Giants pitcher Rube Benton, who had accused the Cubs' Buck Herzog of offering him a bribe to throw a game late in the 1919 season.

The Cubs sent Herzog and Hendrix home from Boston to testify. Herzog brought with him affidavits from two Boston players swearing that Benton had told them he had won $3,000 betting on the 1919 World Series because he knew it was fixed. Herzog also told the press he had been in John Heydler's office in June when Benton admitted he had been tipped off to the fix and won $1,500. Apparently Heydler never told Comiskey or anybody else.

Suddenly the transgressions of Claude Hendrix and Buck Herzog were forgotten. The World Series took over the headlines. (Herzog and Hendrix were quietly released after the season as part of the Cubs' "disposal of veteran material.") Ban Johnson, Comiskey, Veeck, and some Chicago writers testified behind closed doors on the first day of the hearings. As a result, assistant state's attorney Hartley Replogle announced, "The World Series was not on the square. From five to seven Sox players were involved."

In Boston, Connie Mack read the story in the Shelby Hotel before Elmer Myers beat the A's 9–2.

The next day Rube Benton named names. None of it seemed to bother the White Sox. They took 2 of 3 from the Indians and swept a pair in Detroit before returning home. Replogle said he wouldn't interfere with the pennant race by calling them to testify until they had a day off on September 28.

Everybody claimed to be the most eager to expose the plot or blame somebody else for doing nothing. Comiskey told one story, Sox manager Kid Gleason another. John Heydler told half a dozen flip-flopping versions, blaming Ban Johnson one day for doing nothing after Heydler had told him of White Sox officials' suspicions during the Series, pooh-poohing the stories another day as a bunch of lies written by Fullerton and the rest of the "muckrakers," and finally declaring the whole thing could have been avoided if Kid Gleason had taken prompt action.

Comiskey testified that he had held up the Series checks for eight of his players, but not for long. He didn't say why. (The *Chicago Tribune* reported on October 5 that when the White Sox returned from their final series in St. Louis and picked up their last paychecks, all but the eight received an extra $1,500, the difference between the World Series winners' and losers' shares.) Comiskey hammered away at Johnson. "At no time since the World Series have I had the cooperation of Ban Johnson or anyone at the National Commission," which was only Johnson and Heydler. Comiskey now accused Johnson of trying to prevent Chicago from winning the 1920 pennant. "The whole effort looks to me like an effort to break our team morale and cause the Sox to lose the pennant race."

Johnson replied that Comiskey's charges were the "vaporing" of a vindictive man. Besides, Comiskey had known about the rottenness on his club at the time and had suppressed it because many of the suspected players had cost him a lot of money.

Comiskey's attorney, Arthur Austrian, who had dismissed all the evidence brought to him a year ago as hearsay, said he and Comiskey had been working on the case for a year, then boasted, "Because of our investigation the lid has been blown off this scandal."

Hugh Fullerton maintained that Comiskey knew who the eight were at the time of the Series and had assured him that they would not be back with the Sox in 1920, but his attorney had advised him to take no such action against them.

Johnson's antipathy for both gambling and Comiskey had probably been equal motivations for his having launched his own investigation and hiring his own detectives after the Series. Johnson had turned up an East St. Louis theater owner who had testified that he knew about the fix and, at the request of Johnson and Gleason, had told White Sox vice-president/secretary Harry Grabiner and Comiskey what he knew. He had been brushed off as a rumor peddler.

When Connie Mack read the attacks on Ban Johnson, he could not remain silent. He knew that nobody had been more diligent in combating gambling.

Back in Philadelphia on the Sunday after Benton's testimony, Mack told Isaminger, "I just looked in my safe and found letters dating as far back as eight years ago in which Johnson implored club owners to stop gambling at the parks. Since that time I don't believe there has been an American League meeting in which Mr. Johnson has not brought this subject up. But he never received encouragement from the owners. Johnson has been grossly maligned in connection with gambling exposure. His every act as head of the American League has been to stop it."

When Mack's remarks were circulated, they were blasted as "hokum" by some New York writers. Hyatt Daab of the *Evening Telegram* hopped on "the long, lean, cadaverous individual whose chief claim to distinction is the fact he has kept the once great Athletics in the cellar for six straight terms and ruined Philadelphia as a major league baseball town." Hadn't John Heydler tipped off Johnson to the crookedness of the Series, only to be dismissed with a curt answer? "Johnson took no more action than an ailing goose about to pass into the next world. Certainly the inaction could not have been due to lack of support by fellow club owners."

Mack understood that if Johnson had suspended even a single Chicago player in the fall of 1919, when he was scrapping with Comiskey, Ruppert, and Frazee over the Carl Mays sale, everybody would have accused the league president of the vengeful wrecking of Comiskey's expensive team. Besides, nobody could produce any evidence at the time.

On Tuesday, September 28, Eddie Cicotte and Joe Jackson entered the Criminal Court Building in Chicago and admitted that it was all true; eight of them had thrown the World Series. Comiskey immediately suspended the seven still with the team. That evening the honest Sox held a celebration dinner.

Connie Mack was in his office that afternoon, watching the rain that had washed out the game with the Yankees, when the news came from Chicago over the teletype at the *Bulletin*. A reporter called him for a comment.

"I don't know anything about it personally," Mack said, "so do not care to discuss it. It's an unsavory mess. I am sure it is for the best interests of baseball to have it all cleared away. A thorough housecleaning will do the game a world of good. It will freshen the air, so to speak, and arouse even greater interest in the national pastime. I did not see the last World Series and do not consider it advisable for me to comment on the reports I received at second hand."

Mack tried to put a "for the best" spin on it, but his heart was heavy. For the past year his world had been poisoned by turmoil, personal feuds, and arguments. It had been more unpleasant off the field than sitting in the dugout watching his team lose 104 games.

In the years to come, Connie Mack would often recall the morning of Wednesday, September 29, as the darkest beginning of a day he had ever had in baseball. His bacon and eggs didn't go down easily as he read the front page headlines of the *Inquirer*:

WHITE SOX STARS CONFESS THEY "THREW"
LAST YEAR'S WORLD SERIES FOR MONEY

EDDIE CICOTTE WILTS AND BARES BETRAYAL
FOR GAMBLERS' GOLD

EIGHT PLAYERS OF CHICAGO
AMERICAN LEAGUE CLUB
INDICTED FOLLOWING
DRAMATIC CONFESSIONS

CICOTTE AND JACKSON ARRESTED FOR CONSPIRACY;
GOT THOUSANDS FOR "THROWING" GAMES TO REDS

COMISKEY SCRAPS PENNANT-WINNING CLUB
IMMEDIATELY TO PURGE BASEBALL OF
WORST SCANDAL IN ITS HISTORY;
ANNOUNCES HE WILL DRIVE EVERY
GUILTY MAN OUT OF THE GAME FOREVER

"I PLAYED CROOKED AND LOST,"
CICOTTE CONFESSES WITH TEARS

A doubleheader against the Yankees at Shibe Park was scheduled that afternoon. Usually the appearance of Babe Ruth promised an exciting afternoon before a big, noisy crowd. But with the papers declaring the public was through with baseball, Mack anticipated rows and rows of empty seats. The Yankees were all but eliminated from the pennant race, 3½ games behind the Indians.

For the first time in his life, Connie Mack was not eager to get to the ballpark.

"I felt very blue," he later told Ed Pollock of the *Evening Ledger*. "My world was falling in on me. We had tried hard to keep baseball honest and here was this terrible scandal. I hated to go down to the bench. I thought there would be only a handful of fans there."

He expected raw displays of rancor from the disillusioned fans. In a small gathering you could hear every word. Mack put on his derby and solemnly went to work. "I came down to the office early and just sat around," he said. "I was sick at heart."

When he entered the dugout from under the stands just before the first game, he was stunned to find the grandstand nearly full. About fifteen thousand people awaited him. As soon as they spotted him in the dugout, they stood and gave him the kind of ovation usually reserved for a game-winning hero.

"I couldn't understand it at first and then I realized they were telling me they still believed in baseball. That was a wonderful thrill."

He was heartened to see that the fans were focusing more on the house-cleaning than what had caused the need for it. "It seemed," he said, "that people wanted to show their confidence in the integrity of the game."

What had started out as the saddest day of his career turned into one of the happiest. Never mind that his Athletics lost both games with sloppy fielding. The fans marveled at Babe Ruth's fifty-fourth and last home run of the season, a blast over the right-field fence that was picked up by a passerby who turned it over to press gate custodian George Brand, who gave it to Ruth. The Babe signed it to be auctioned off for the fund to replace a building that had burned down at his old school, St. Mary's Industrial Home in Baltimore.

Mack was even more uplifted in Washington on Sunday when the final game of the season, a meaningless contest between his last-place Athletics and the sixth-place Senators, drew eight thousand customers. Had the Black Sox scandal really killed baseball, there would have been more like eight hundred present for the funeral.

When he had read the headlines out of Chicago, Mack groaned for another reason. He knew he'd be in for another round of explanations about the 1914 World Series and the breaking up of his team. He was right. As though the heavens were weeping over baseball's woes, every game was rained out on Thursday, September 30. Mack was sitting in his tower office when a writer for the *Bulletin* came looking for a story. As Mack anticipated, the writer brought up the A's loss to the Braves in 1914 and Mack's subsequent sale of some players. Mack sighed:

> I almost wish that team had never been broken up. Every time there's a gambling scandal or a League of Nations or a poor wheat crop, sure enough they ask me whether that wasn't the reason I broke up the 1914 team. I've given out enough statements on why I dismantled that team to paper our grandstand. Lookit, I can convince any man or any body of men from the United States Supreme Court down just why I sold and traded those ballplayers, and gambling had nothing at all to do with it. It would take me about twenty minutes, I guess, at the most to make it absolutely clear to anyone. Surely the fact that Eddie Collins and Eddie Murphy acted as they did throughout this White Sox expose shows what kind of men I had on my club. I want to say that I am as sure as I am of my own life that no member of that team ever stooped to anything like crookedness in ball games. I think Philadelphia should be proud that such a taint never came to its teams but every time any writer wants to sit down and throw dark hints and suspicions at anything, he at least considers the 1914 World Series. I guess they'll go on doing it on and on, as long as there are any Athletics.

Good guess.

After rehashing the effects of the Federal League and falling attendance,

Mack added, "I've explained this thing a hundred times since 1914 and, by George, a couple of weeks and months later the same fellows I explained the thing to come back and ask me something different about it. You better keep your copy of these remarks, next time you want my explanation of the 1914 World Series, and why I broke up my club."

It had been a long, hard, bitter, angry, vexing, disappointing year for Connie Mack. He was entitled to vent some frustration.

The World Series played to capacity crowds in Brooklyn and Cleveland. The purge of the White Sox left the game more free of suspicion, not more suspect. The grand jury's final report concluded that the problem was not widespread and had been confined to a few players. The public agreed. But it had not been just an aberration brought on by a tightfisted owner, as it has been made out to be. It was a dormant volcano that had finally erupted.

In addition to the eight players, the grand jury indicted five other men involved in the fix and three operators of baseball pools.

Babe Ruth had become a huge attraction before the Chicago grand jury hearings. The major leagues had prospered beyond all expectations in 1919, and the 1920 season turned out to be the most profitable to date. Even the Athletics showed a profit of $61,701.14.

Ruth didn't save baseball. Neither would Kenesaw Mountain Landis.

Baseball didn't need saving. The game itself was its own salvation.

12 | JUDGE LANDIS PRESIDING

Albert D. Lasker was a successful businessman and a major stockholder in the Chicago Cubs. Aloof from the personality conflicts, old grudges, and resentments behind baseball's ongoing conflicts, Lasker deplored the unbusinesslike way in which the business was run. Picking up on Georges Clemenceau's postwar observation that "war is too important to be left to the generals," Lasker declared that baseball was too important to be left to baseball men to run. It needed a commission of three outsiders of prominence who had no financial stake in the business. Men like General John J. Pershing, Judge Charles McDonald, ex-president Taft, Judge Landis—all "civilians" in baseball jargon.

The Lasker plan had the support of the eight National League clubs and the Red Sox, White Sox, and Yankees. Ban Johnson and his loyal five knew that the plan's basic motive was to get rid of Johnson or at least strip him of power. John McGraw and Barney Dreyfuss admitted as much. It didn't matter how far back their grievances went. They were like bulldogs who bit into an ankle and held on for years.

Ban Johnson was not alone in believing that baseball was best left to baseball men to clean out the undesirables, who in his mind included club owners who allowed open gambling in their ballparks and who did not acknowledge his benevolent suzerainty.

Connie Mack saw nothing wrong with the old setup. The issue as he saw it was that the American League didn't want the National choosing the new commission chairman, and the National didn't want Ban Johnson choosing him.

Before the 1920 World Series began, a letter went out to every club, asking each to sign on to the Lasker plan and inviting them to a meeting in Chicago on October 10.

Mack was in Brooklyn for the Series, where he predicted a Cleveland victory. "Coveleski will be unhittable by Brooklyn, and Mails is the best lefthand pitcher in the American League." Coveleski won 3 games, Mails 1 in their 7-game victory. Covey's success led to the extension of the grandfathered spitballers' use of the pitch to the end of their careers.

Asked to comment on the Lasker plan, Mack said he didn't see the need for such a drastic change. "This is not the time for baseball owners to lose their heads. For that reason I will not sign such a petition. The gambling cases are now in the hands of the Chicago grand jury. No move along such revolutionary lines should be taken by organized baseball until the grand jury makes its findings and then the criminal court finds the players guilty or not guilty. When such a decision is made, it will be time for baseball to change its front. But I feel sure it would be a very tactless procedure just now."

Mack evaded the central issue and emphasized the timing of taking any action. His comments fell far short of a ringing endorsement of the continuation of business as usual. He did not attend the October 10 meeting. Nor did the other Johnson backers, which astonished Giants owner Charles Stoneham: "How men who had fortunes invested in this game could afford to remain away from a meeting whose only aim was to safeguard the big investments in baseball and protect the sport is beyond me."

The Laskerites gave the five Johnson loyalists until November 1 to submit a reform plan of their own. Otherwise they would form a twelve-team New National League, inviting the first of the five who wished to join them to become the twelfth team. If nobody crossed over, they would invade one of the five cities.

Connie Mack scoffed at that idea. He had been in the old twelve-team National League in the 1890s, had seen it collapse under its unwieldy bulk, saved only by the amputation of four members. No matter how much Johnson blustered about putting new teams in the seceding cities, Mack never took any of it seriously. When Johnson said, "War, in my judgment, is the best cleanser," Mack shivered. "I am for it," Johnson went on, "as I believe it will clean up baseball like it cleans up everything else." No "War is not the answer" bumper stickers for Big Ban.

Connie Mack wanted nothing to do with another war. His previously unwavering support for Ban Johnson began to waver.

In Baltimore the mayor and leading businessmen had dreamed of returning to the major leagues ever since Ban Johnson had, in their minds, stolen their team and moved it to New York in 1903. They announced an interest in buying the Athletics and moving them to Baltimore. Mack brushed them off like dandruff, telling a Baltimore paper the A's were not for sale "in a voice, accents and manner which left no mistake as to his meaning," the reporter noted.

Not that the National League was solidly behind the twelve-team idea. The Phillies, for one, weren't crazy about the prospect of finishing twelfth instead of eighth.

Ban Johnson kept up the attack. At one point he was quoted, "What baseball needs is to get rid of some of its recalcitrant club owners." In other sources, "recalcitrant" was reported as "undesirable."

Mack also took some gratuitous swipes at the Laskerites:

It's not quite clear to me what they are driving at. I'm not so sure that some of the National League clubs represented at the meeting do not need a housecleaning. No one in or out of baseball can point a finger at the five American League clubs not represented at the meeting. They are all clean. Not one of them had ever caused any trouble. The club that came nearest to it was our own in the Scott Perry case. [*Came nearest to it?* The Perry case had caused the most trouble since the war of 1901–1903.] When we knew we were right and threatened to take the decision of the National Commission into court, we were urged by Comiskey not to do it. I stood up at our meeting and said if it were the judgment of the members of the league not to press the matter so as not to hurt the game, I bowed to their will and did nothing. And yet six months later when Comiskey's interests were threatened, he tried to start trouble in attempting to get pitcher Jack Quinn from New York.

Here Mack is dancing around his actions in the Perry case. He may be referring to his finally settling with the Braves and dropping the lawsuit before the hearing to make the temporary injunction permanent. But by saying he "threatened" to take the matter into court, he made it sound as if he had never done so. And of course he had. Comiskey had not. Nor had Comiskey attempted to "get" Quinn from New York. Comiskey had signed Quinn before the commission awarded the pitcher to the Yankees.

Reading Johnson's and Mack's comments, Cubs owner William Wrigley said he had never been so insulted.

Whatever arguments raged within baseball, Connie Mack always believed things would work out and everybody would be friends again. On November 6 he told the *Bulletin*, "Personally I think we are all going to get together peacefully. . . . It is only my personal opinion, but I think if each league is given a just and equitable choice in the reorganization, everything will come off all right."

Mack was whistling; Ban Johnson was not about to go for any chairman, from in or out of baseball, that he couldn't dominate, and the Nationals would never accept anybody they thought could be influenced by Ban. It was all politics, which Mack knew. He also knew the fans couldn't care less about all this. Besides, it was autumn and their attention had turned to football.

Both sides gathered at the Congress Hotel in Chicago on the morning of November 8, the Laskerites in one room and the Johnson five in another. The five's idea of a reform plan was a committee of nine—three from each league and three from the minors—to work out a reorganization. The eleven wasted little time electing Judge Landis chairman of a new commission at a salary of $50,000 a year. Landis said he'd let them know.

Clark Griffith and attorney George Miller then went to the Lasker meeting to try to sell their committee plan. The eleven didn't buy it. Instead they invited the five to meet with them to iron out their differences. They gave Griffith until four o'clock to respond.

Everybody left for Kansas City to present their cases to the minor league clubs meeting there. The Lasker plan met strong opposition among minor league owners.

Through it all Connie Mack continued to declare there would be peace. After all, even the Vatican and Switzerland had resumed diplomatic relations after forty-seven years. Anything was possible. But Ban Johnson remained belligerent. He even blamed former National League president John Tener for ruining the old commission because he "couldn't get along with chairman Herrmann" when it was Tener and Herrmann who had agreed in the Scott Perry decision. Tener had been a vocal critic of Johnson, not Herrmann.

But Mack was right in predicting peace. Weary of the fighting, the five put aside their loyalty to Ban Johnson—"threw Ban Johnson down," according to some commentators—and agreed to an informal meeting of just the club owners. They gathered at noon on Friday, November 12, in room 1102 of the Congress Hotel. The meeting quickly became stuck in a procedural stalemate. The Laskerites insisted that the new chairman be elected by a vote of the sixteen clubs. The five wanted to continue voting by leagues. The eleven also wanted all disputes settled by majority vote, not by league votes. So they compromised. The new chairman would be elected by a majority vote of the sixteen owners. Other matters would be voted on by the leagues. If the leagues failed to agree, the new chairman would cast the deciding vote.

They unanimously elected Judge Landis to chair the commission. (Phil Ball of St. Louis was opposed, but he allowed his representative, Bob Quinn, to vote for the judge.) Then eight of them went to Landis's courtroom, where he was presiding over a trial involving a $15,000 bribe in an income tax case. Landis's first ruling over baseball's club owners was to order them to be quiet and wait for him in his chambers. Three more, including Mack, arrived while Landis was airing some blistering comments about men who falsified their income tax returns.

In his chambers Landis at first turned down the job; he loved being a federal judge and didn't want to give it up. Assured that they had no objection to his holding both positions, he agreed, asking that his salary be reduced by the $7,500 judicial stipend. They all posed for a photograph around the judge seated at his desk. Connie Mack towered behind the 5-foot-4 Barney Dreyfuss.

Mack was pleased to have the bickering behind them. He was more of a peacemaker than an ideologue, loyal to Ban Johnson but not to the old way of doing business, which had produced so many squabbles. He may have been persuaded that nobody with a financial interest should adjudicate disputes, though he never voiced any reservations about the integrity of Garry Herrmann. Nobody did. They would really miss the lavish spreads he had put on at special events like the World Series.

Mack was solidly behind the choice of Judge Landis:

He does not own a dollar's worth of stock in any club and . . . he comes in from the outside without any of us having any claims on him, [and] he is a brainy man and is [as] well versed in the science of finding the right or wrong in a claim as any other man in America. We know that Judge Landis will have to decide issues and his decisions will favor one man and be against another. While the defeated claimant may feel a tinge of discomfiture, he will know his case was decided by an honest, scholarly man on its merits without any outside influence. We baseball owners have been accused of being bad sports, but I don't think you will find many rows on decisions that Judge Landis will make next season.

On December 8 an appellate court dismissed the Baltimore Feds' case charging the national agreement violated antitrust laws. "Fine news," said Mack, "the best I've heard in years. I expected the decision, because I always knew the foundation of organized baseball was clean, legal, and entirely aboveboard. Had the court ruled otherwise we were ready to change our laws governing baseball, but I take it the court upholds our contention."

(The Supreme Court would finally close the book on the Federal League after hearing the case in April 1922, ruling that putting on an exhibition of baseball was not commerce as the word was defined in the antitrust laws, and players traveling to another state to give such an exhibition did not make it interstate commerce. The Court never said, "Baseball is not a business." The decision was in line with earlier cases in which the staging of plays and operas was held to be "not commerce.")

The club owners didn't wait for the Supreme Court to hear that case. They immediately set about writing a new national agreement to govern the game, and it included the role of Kenesaw Mountain Landis. Tom Shibe was a member of the committee that met in New York on December 11 to write the new agreement. Landis did not really want to be chairman of any three-man commission. He wanted unquestioned authority. He insisted on one change in the committee's draft: all his decisions would be final, not just recommendations. And so it was written

The major leagues had been operating with no written agreement with the minors pending the outcome of the Baltimore Feds' appeal. The drafting of players by major league clubs, long a bone of contention, had been suspended, although the minor leagues could still draft from lower leagues. A lot of business was being conducted by "gentlemen's agreements." There was plenty of winking and nodding going on among the gentlemen: the courtesy granting of waivers; phantom or conditional purchases of minor league players to keep them from being drafted, then their return; agreements to draft a lesser player from a team that could lose only one man under the rules to protect a star from being taken.

In September 1920 Connie Mack bought a rookie outfielder, nineteen-year-old Leon Goslin, from Columbia in the Class c Sally League. Goslin, known as "Goose" or "Geese," had hit .317. Ordinarily this was the kind of youngster Mack craved. But he never took a look at him. In December Goslin cleared interleague waivers and was returned to Columbia, to be sold to Washington for $7,000 during the 1921 season. The Red Sox bought the top three pitchers from the Texas League champion Fort Worth Cats and returned them all the following February, also without a trial. What other explanation for these series of events can there be except that major league clubs were doing favors for minor league clubs to protect their stars from being drafted?

Branch Rickey took a different tack. He was about to launch his farm system, buying interests in minor league clubs and controlling the careers of hundreds of young players.

The new commissioner abhorred all these practices. In his first year in office he would fine clubs, declare players free agents, and nullify deals. Proper paperwork and procedures mattered. Landis would soon have other clashes with his employers over his novel approach to baseball's rules—enforcing them. That's why he insisted that players be allowed to appeal directly to him if they thought they were being unfairly treated.

Outfielder Greasy Neale was one who took him at his word. In the spring of 1921 Neale signed a secret agreement with the Phillies calling for him to be paid $6,000 at the end of the season. Cincinnati claimed him on waivers but was told nothing about the secret agreement at the time. When the Reds learned of it, they refused to pay it. Neale appealed to Landis, who allowed his claim, at the same time fining the Phillies $200 and Neale $100 for making the secret deal.

Landis also had old business to clear up, unresolved grievances that had been gathering dust. Back in 1917 the White Sox had bought pitcher Charley Robertson from the Sherman, Texas, club for $250 down and another $1,750 if they kept him past May 15, 1918. Instead of returning him before that date, they optioned Robertson to Minneapolis and never paid the balance. Landis ruled in the Sherman club's favor.

Yet a year later, when Detroit recalled shortstop Rabbit Tavernor from Fort Worth before the draft, then returned him to the Cats, no fines were levied. An unsigned comment in *The Sporting News* declared, "The Commissioner is becoming more of a practical baseball man as time passes." Or maybe his dogmatic antagonism toward the practice of keeping players down on the farms had become tempered by Justice Oliver Wendell Holmes's dictum that "general propositions do not decide concrete issues."

But nobody was betting on it.

Ban Johnson put on a smiley front. "I am for Judge Landis," he said, "and I think these club owners have acted wisely. Baseball will be placed on the highest possible standard now and there will be no more fights. I am well satisfied with everything that took place."

Nobody was betting on *that* either.

In Chicago the prosecutor of the suspended White Sox players had a case of the slows, and the disappearance of alleged players' confessions from the files resulted in the indictments being dismissed by the new state's attorney. Landis rebuffed Johnson's pleas to pursue the case. He wasn't about to wait for any indictments or trials. On March 12 Landis suspended the eight players from baseball for life: "Regardless of the verdict of juries, baseball is entirely competent to protect itself against the crooks both inside and outside the game."

The players were tried in a Chicago courtroom in July and found not guilty. Landis's ban remained.

13 | THE TWENTIES' CURTAIN GOES UP

War may or may not cleanse things, as Ban Johnson once asserted. But it sure changes things.

Once the war was over over there and the world was safe for democracy, it was time to get ahead, make money, party. From 1916 to 1921 the number of automobiles in the nation tripled, to 10.5 million, making the feast of the '20s the most moveable in history.

Historians disagree over just when what Westbrook Pegler called "the era of wonderful nonsense" had begun. Some dated it from November 7, 1918, the day the United Press flashed an erroneous bulletin proclaiming the war was over, which triggered a wild celebration that turned into a store-front-smashing riot when the wire service recanted the story. Others paired its beginnings with the start of Prohibition in July 1919. Whenever it was, the old values went out the window. Taboos were now taboo. Backseat sex, campus "necking parties," bathtub gin, short skirts, bobbed hair, cigarettes, jazz, and limb-flapping dancing were in. Not even Prohibition could stifle the fun. If anything, it stimulated more raucous living, adding an extra thrill to the now illegal liquid part of the partying. Breaking the law without really harming anybody and getting away with it was an exciting adventure, even if you didn't like the watered-down whiskey.

Fads became rages, rages became crazes: crossword puzzles, mah-jongg, flagpole sitting. Hand-wringers had a field day worrying about the ruination of the nation. Newspapers devoted acres of newsprint to such questions as, "Is jazz corrupting us?" Sports idols Babe Ruth, Jack Dempsey, Red Grange, Bobby Jones—all were ballyhooed. Even the nineteen-year-old swimmer of the English Channel, Gertrude Ederle, would have her splash of fame. The public couldn't get enough of them, and that sold papers. So the papers went all out to feed the demand. The race to be the first to hit the streets with scoops, exclusive interviews, scores, photos, race results, or round-by-round fight reports was as hectic and competitive as the contests themselves.

Sportswriters began to invest the events they were covering with all the grandeur of the Creation or an equally significant occurrence. Sports heroes were enshrined in purple prose. The baseball business benefited by the gobs of free publicity. One-third of the front page might be covered with the latest scores and play-by-play in the afternoon final editions in big league cities. At one point the *New York Press* had four sports pages daily and eight on Sunday, a lot of space for the thinner papers of the time.

And baseball helped sell papers. Before radio, daily and weekly newspapers were the only ways the public could keep up with the teams and players. Westbrook Pegler, later known for his vitriolic political columns, was acknowledged by many of his contemporaries as the best in the business. No sentimentalist like Grantland Rice, he knocked those he thought deserved it and had a well-earned reputation for raking con artists, phonies, and mountebanks.

Writers had always been divided between the "gee-whiz" and "aw-nuts" schools. Paul Gallico of the *New York Daily News* admitted to being in the "gee-whiz" group. Pegler was the "aw-nuts." The "gee-whiz" school built up players into heroic stature. *New York Herald-Tribune* sports editor Stanley Woodward called it "godding them."

Among managers, Connie Mack got the most "godding" treatment, even from the acerbic Pegler. In an effort to emphasize Mack's uncommon civility in a tobacco-chewing environment, wrote Joe Williams of the *New York World-Telegram*, the press "created an image that made him seem like a cross between a professional greeter and the granddaddy of the Rover Boys." Mack wasn't profane, but he wasn't all "goodness gracious" by any means. The press created and perpetuated the myth. Mack, always conscious of his public image, did nothing to correct it. Once on a radio program a youngster asked him, "I've heard that whenever you do get mad and swear, the worst thing you say is 'my gracious.' Is that true?"

"I guess that's pretty near true," Mack said, "because I don't like to hear the swearing. Tell [the boys] that swearing never helped any ballplayer's success."

It was common for writers and hangers-on to work out with the clubs in spring training. They went out on the field in any kind of uniform or attire and took grounders in the infield or shagged flies.

By 1924 the radio would become another megaphone of ballyhoo. Football games and the World Series joined political addresses, book reviews, and studio sopranos on the air. Secretary of Commerce Herbert Hoover proposed a national hookup. Scientists at Princeton would express alarm over national "ear exhaustion" from listening to the radio too much. Baseball managers were talking into microphones with no wordsmiths to repair their grammar or embellish their stories. The media was born.

The Babe with his big salary was a role model for the times; he had made it big despite his humble origins. The same was true of Jack Dempsey.

New York hadn't legalized boxing until 1919. Then Tex Rickard took it uptown to Madison Square Garden, and the sports and swanks swarmed to the high-priced ringside seats with their blond trophies on their arms, and the million-dollar gate was inaugurated.

Knute Rockne brought his Fighting Irish to New York to play Army and turned millions of non-Irish non-Catholics into Notre Dame subway alumni.

Sports became big business. But the age of cynicism had not dawned. The public genuinely cared about their heroes. It was that caring, that emotional investment, that made them count, and endure, not their statistics. Roger Maris and Barry Bonds and a dozen more might surpass Babe Ruth's stats but never his stature.

Even the staid British press took notice. The *Manchester Guardian* commented in June, "The average player in the major leagues makes 28 singles for every home run he hits. Babe Ruth is hitting 4 singles to every 3 home runs."

Pitchers were also walking him with uncommon frequency, inspiring loud choruses of boos from the fans.

Connie Mack never seemed to fit, yet always seemed to transcend, the different eras in which he occupied the sports stage. He didn't reflect the early roughneck, brawling, society-shunned world of baseball any more than he fit in or reflected the circus of the '20s that would roar for a decade before burning out like a fizzling meteor. And yet Connie Mack, who hadn't had a winner since 1914, had acquired a status beyond the sporting pages. When child movie star Jackie Coogan went on a tour in May 1921 to promote his new film, *Peck's Bad Boy*, Mack was among the celebrities—along with Babe Ruth, Enrico Caruso, and the mayor of New York—asked to be photographed with him.

New York became the capital of baseball in the early 1920s. John McGraw ruled the National League, winning four straight pennants, 1921–1924. Jake Ruppert and Ed Barrow finally turned the Yankees into American League champions in 1921–1923, world champions in '23.

As this era of wonderful nonsense began, baseball fans took little notice of Philadelphia, where the last-place residents of both leagues slept, except as the butt of jokes. Spotlights don't shine in cellars.

In Chicago Mack's daughter Marguerite and her family were living a happy, prosperous life. Her husband, Bob McCambridge, was the head of bond sales at the Sheridan Trust & Savings Bank. Three of his brothers worked for him. Peggy's son Connie recalled, "My dad bought a Packard and drove it so fast he blew the motor out. The next day he bought another one. Later we had a Ford touring car with isinglass windows." A sportsman and gambler, Bob took over sponsorship of an amateur girls' basketball team, the Uptown Brownies, who would win Central AAU tournaments in 1922 and 1923. He was an avid poker player and, according to one family story, once won $25,000 in a crap game in Boston.

When the Athletics were in town, Peggy had lunch or dinner with her father at the Cooper-Carlton Hotel (renamed the Del Prado in 1930), went to the games, and kept score the way her father had taught her. "She knew baseball," her son Connie recalled.

It all came to an end in 1924, when Bob McCambridge fell off a horse in a riding accident and broke his leg. He developed tuberculosis. The doctor advised him to go to the southwest to recover. He and Peggy left their two sons with his parents in Chicago for a year and went to New Mexico. When the A's were in Chicago, Mack invited the boys to eat with him and go to the games as their mother had done. Then they joined their parents in Albuquerque. Once in 1926, when the team was in St. Louis, Peggy came to see her dad for a few days.

Bob McCambridge died in Albuquerque on March 21, 1928. He was thirty-three.

Connie Mack's reputation for scouring the sandlots, giving youngsters tryouts, and answering every letter he received went back to his earliest managing days in the 1890s. With his early successes in Philadelphia it had become common knowledge. His cradle robbing and kindergartens were sometimes respectfully lampooned by writers like L. C. Davis of the *St. Louis Post-Dispatch*, who in 1921 contrasted John McGraw, "the champion checkbook manager," and Connie Mack, who "made his reputation by despoiling cradles of infant prodigies."

In 1917 Hugh Fullerton had commented on Mack's "marvelous connections and machinery for finding promising young ballplayers. If they exist any-where, he seems to know about them, and he turns up each spring with the most amazing number of promising youngsters that have been raked in from unheard-of corners of the earth, from colleges, Class z leagues, and the lots."

One reason for this was the army of volunteer scouts—former players, businessmen, priests and nuns, salesmen, coaches, merchants—who, from personal acquaintance with Mack or just what they read about him, thought of him first when they saw a sandlot, college, or minor league player they thought he might be interested in. What's more, they knew their tips would not be ignored.

Example: Otto Schomberg.

Schomberg had been a first baseman in the National League in 1887, when Mack was a catcher for Washington. A native of Milwaukee, he was in the lumber business there when Mack managed the Brewers for four years at the end of the nineteenth century. Until Schomberg's death in 1927, they corresponded regularly. Mack's letters chatted about his team's outlook and fortunes, invited Schomberg to visit when the Athletics were in Chicago, commented about players Schomberg had recommended in his travels: "Af-ter giving the matter further thought, I am rather inclined now to gamble on the young player out on the Coast. If you can possibly arrange with him to join our club wish you would do so. From what you say he will not do anything this year, but we will probably be able to do something with him in another year so if you can do anything with him or the coaches, on behalf of our club, will certainly appreciate it."

And: "Note that you will look over that young pitcher and first baseman and will be pleased to hear further from you in regard to them."

Mack's reputation was taken seriously by young hopefuls. Over the past six years he had given hundreds of them a look, even a big league cup of coffee. Between 1915 and 1925 it would be estimated that more than five hundred players wore an Athletics uniform, if only for a workout. Through it all, he never got used to giving a youngster the heart-breaking news that the kid wasn't good enough.

That's why one day in 1910 Stanley Baumgartner, a fifteen-year-old Chi-cagoan eager to make his high school team as a pitcher, waited until the Athletics were in town to seek some advice. He found Connie Mack on the boardwalk outside the Chicago Beach Hotel, easily recognized in his three-inch high white collar and dark blue suit. The youngster hesitated to approach him. Mr. Mack turned and smiled at him.

Encouraged, he approached. "Mr. Mack," he said, "could you tell me the secret of pitching?"

Mack put his arm around the boy's shoulder. "Get the ball over the plate," he said. "Don't be afraid to let the other fellow hit it. Remember, you have eight men to help you out."

Fourteen years later the boy would be pitching for Mr. Mack.

Scouts working for pennant winners and last-place teams had disparate advantages over clubs in the middle of the pack. The front-runners could use the promise of frequent World Series payoffs to lure a prospect. The trailers could offer a faster track to the big leagues because of their teams' needs. But that basement bargaining didn't always work for Connie Mack.

In the spring of 1920 Mack had sent Harry Davis to Texas to look at a freshman pitcher at Baylor University. Ted Lyons had been 10-2 in the Southwest Conference. He told Davis he was interested in going to law school. Davis said the Athletics would pay for his education. Lyons said he didn't want to jeopardize his amateur standing. What he didn't tell Davis was that he had been pitching for semipro teams and had less concern about his own standing than that of the lowly Athletics. He didn't want any part of a perennial last-place team.

Two years later Lyons pitched the Baylor Bears to the conference championship. The A's were still last. Davis renewed his offer and Lyons repeated his bogus concerns about his amateur status. (The following year Lyons signed with the fifth-place White Sox. He pitched for Chicago for twenty years; it took them thirteen years to finish in the first division. Lyons never made it to a World Series.)

James T. Farrell was a young White Sox fan who later said he was among the gang of kids in the parking lot outside Comiskey Park when Happy Felsch and Joe Jackson were supposedly asked if it was so that they had thrown the World Series. Twenty years later, in his largely autobiographical Danny O'Neill novels, Farrell described the fifteen-year-old would-be ballplayer writing a letter in 1919 to Connie Mack seeking a tryout. Why Connie Mack? Because, Farrell wrote, "Connie Mack was known above all other managers as the man to pick promising players off the sand lots and develop them into stars."

Danny mails the letter, confident that he will hear from Connie Mack.

So it wasn't unusual that in 1921 a semipro outfielder in Milwaukee named Aloysius Szymanski, who had adopted the name Simmons from a billboard advertising hardware, would choose Connie Mack to write to for the same reason. Al had an odd batting stance that he was comfortable with, wide open, close to the plate, with his left foot pointing toward third base. He had also read that Mr. Mack never tried to change the style of a player as long as it worked for him.

But the letter came at a time when Mack had abandoned his futile effort to mold a championship team out of green recruits. Besides, the new commissioner, Judge Landis, was committed to stamping out the practice of major league clubs controlling hundreds of young players through phantom options and phony sales with buy-back "understandings."

Connie Mack received many such letters. But for all the hundreds of tryouts he offered, they were always based on a scout's report or a tip from someone who had actually seen the player in action. All letters received directly from young players were answered the same way: "Kind of you to let me hear from you. Very sorry but my team is already made up. Wish you all the success in the world and many thanks."

That's the reply Al Simmons received. He received a tryout offer from the Giants' affiliate in Toledo, but they wouldn't send him the train fare, So Al signed with the hometown Milwaukee Brewers.

The world had changed; Connie Mack had not. At fifty-eight he was still full of energy, optimism, and expectations for himself and his players. When his old friend Clark Griffith stepped down as manager of the Senators after the 1920 season to concentrate on front-office matters, Mack chided his fifty-one-year-old colleague. "I gave him the old Harry," he said. "A man shouldn't quit in his prime."

The war had set back Mack's rebuilding plans for a few years. But he was not prepared for the effects of the peace, as though ballplayers ought to be immune from the rest of society's carryings-on. When they weren't, when that happy-go-lucky joy-ride attitude showed up on the Athletics, it puzzled him.

"This ball team I have now, the one I finished the 1920 season with, is the queerest one I ever heard of," he admitted soon after arriving in Lake Charles for spring training. "There is more natural ability concealed about that team than any ball club in the country. But it is a question of getting it out of the men."

They had none of the fighting spirit of the old days, he lamented, and he didn't know how—or if—he could instill it in them. When Connie Mack talked about the old days, he went back to the 1890s, when his Pittsburgh

Pirates were known for "Mack's dirty play," when a third base coach would run interference for a base runner and charge into the catcher so the man could score, as Mack himself had done. The rules didn't permit that anymore of course, but "men used to fight about their base hits and their being safe on a base"—and they could still do that.

"They would go to the mat if necessary," Mack said of the old days, "and a bloody nose was the sign of a brave fighter who was willing to go the limit to win a game, yet who was a true sport and a gentleman."

Last year it hadn't seemed to matter to the players whether they won or lost. Well, you might say, they were a last-place team. But to Mack, that's *why* they were a last-place team.

"There isn't enough of that old spirit left," he said. "Or maybe it is merely lying dormant. If that is the case I hope to bring it out of my men. If I can do that I will be happy. The men have the talent and with a little perking up here and there will have all that any other team can boast of. Put the fight into 'em and they'll be up in the first division fighting and if the chance presents itself, maybe battling for the top, though that is a long distance wish, but figuring just the same."

Mack conceded that he had a weak-hitting lineup, but he refused to bow to his critics' howling at him to buy a few high-priced stars. He saw no point in laying out big money for a temporary patch that might move them up a few notches in the standings. Once he had a solid core of players—with some fight in them—then it would be time to open the purse strings and spend whatever it took for the last pieces that would carry them to the top. In the meantime he would stand pat. He had culled what he considered the best available men the minors and colleges had to offer. He didn't believe his ability to find and assay talent had diminished. Discerning what was inside a young player was the eternal challenge.

Jimmie Dykes was one who had that old fighting spirit. He never shut up, on the field, on the bench, or in the clubhouse. He rode the rabbit ears on other teams and got on teammates who didn't hustle to suit him. He was quick to jump on umpires when he didn't like a call, a practice Connie Mack tried to curb.

"Jimmie," he said, "you're no good to the club sitting in the grandstand. Don't let yourself be thrown out of games." Dykes took the advice and began to intercede with teammates to keep them in the game when they started to kick about calls. But he never fully tamped his own fire.

Dykes had finished strong and was full of confidence. But he wasn't a complete ballplayer yet, and Connie Mack let him know it when Dykes showed up at Shibe Park to talk contract. Dykes had prepared a speech outlining why he deserved so much money.

"[Mack] listened to me for about fifteen minutes," Dykes recalled to Joe McGuff of the *Kansas City Star*. "'Young man,' he said when I had finished, 'everything you say is true. But you're still lucky to be in the major leagues.' Then he proceeded to tell me all the things I was doing wrong. By the time he finished I was reaching for that contract before he changed his mind."

Joe Dugan was full of fight too. Trouble was, he was fighting himself. But he had led the A's with a .322 average, and Mack needed all the hitting he could get. Miller Huggins had been after him all winter to sell or trade Dugan to the Yankees, offering first baseman Wally Pipp and cash. Dugan was not for sale. Mack was interested in Pipp but refused to part with Dugan and gave jittery Joe a raise to $5,000, making him one of the higher-paid Athletics.

Chick Galloway was everything Mack wanted in a shortstop, but he was light with the bat.

A year of catching a bunch of wild pitchers who couldn't hold runners on first base had made a keener catcher out of Cy Perkins. Most bases are stolen on the pitcher; when a runner got too big a jump, a catcher could have a cannon for an arm and still not throw him out. Perkins had been forced to study runners' mannerisms for signs of when their feet itched too much to stay put. After that he had the edge on them.

Mack thought he had three or four genuine big league hitters, but the rest he rated as "mediocre." At one point in spring training the tall, lean gentleman in the dark suit became so frustrated he grabbed a bat and went up to the plate to demonstrate how it ought to be done. Damon Runyon was there and commented that "old men trying to show young men how to do things they were not able to do themselves would get better results by advising."

Scott Perry reported ten pounds lighter. Even young infielder Frank Brazill, bought from Brooklyn for $2,500 and farmed out to Atlanta last year, was behaving. In his short career he had gained a reputation for believing he knew more than any manager he played for and letting them know it. "A disorganizer, a baseball Bolshevik," Charlie Frank had called him. But wherever he played, he had been among the league's batting leaders.

The A's went to Texas and won 5 of 6 from the Cardinals. They began to show some fight. Cullen Cain of the *Public Ledger* called them a cocky, happy team full of pep and ginger. "Connie Mack told me a month ago it was not lack of mechanical skill that kept his team in last place the last two years. It was the lack of spirit. Well, he had the spirit this spring."

Then they beat the Giants 8–6, and McGraw told Mack he had a "real team" at last.

Spring training visitors lauded the A's. Joe Vila of the *Sun* said, "Mack has a dangerous ball club. If he gets a fair share of the luck, the Athletics will finish within striking distance of the first division."

Sid Mercer of the *New York Evening Journal* saw "wonderful possibilities" in the pitching staff and predicted a first-division finish with "a little luck."

So Connie Mack went to New York to open the season with high hopes and new road uniforms: gray with blue cap, elephant, and trimmings. A good start would give his boys a big dose of confidence and enthusiasm.

Hours before the three thirty game time it was apparent that there was no hangover among the fans from the Black Sox scandal. Thousands milled around the outside of the Polo Grounds, unable to get in. In the florid journalistic style of the day, the *Times* account led: "The baseball season of 1921 burst into being full-panoplied, like Minerva emerging from the cracked brow of Jove, yesterday afternoon at the Polo Grounds, and 37,000 persons, drenched in sunshine and joy, declared themselves in on the initiation ceremonies. That constitutes a record-breaking throng for opening day in New York, which is to say, it's a record for all the wide, whirling globe."

Connie Mack would remember that opening day eighteen years later, when a birthday interviewer asked him about his worst teams. "Well, I can't say exactly," Mack said. "But I've had some birds. There was one of my teams in those dark days that was terrible. We opened the season in New York and I wanted to win that first game in the worst way. But the Yankees murdered us. I almost cried, but I left the bench smiling and one of the New Yorkers couldn't understand how I could smile when I was licked so bad. I didn't feel much like smiling, I'll tell you that. But during all those terrible days, I knew we'd come through."

The A's had run into an old nemesis, Carl Mays, and a new one, Babe Ruth. Mays held them to 3 hits, and Ruth had 5 but no home runs. Scott Perry held the Yankees down to a 5–1 lead until the eighth, when Bob Hasty was slammed for 6 runs.

The A's looked more like what Connie Mack was hoping for the next day, when they rallied for 2 runs in the ninth and a 4–3 win. Brazill tripled and stole home, Jimmie Dykes drove in the winning run, and Eddie Rommel went the distance.

It turned out to be the last day the Athletics saw .500 for the year.

What happened?

For one thing, though they finished last again, they weren't really that bad. Almost one-third of their 100 losses were by 1 run—the most in either league; 49 of the 100 were by 1 or 2 runs. They had the spirit to stage late rallies, usually falling just short. They could hit, but then everybody could hit. Four teams batted .300 or over. Home runs were up 30 percent.

They would play winning ball for a while then go into a tailspin, and before they could pull out of it, they were in a deeper hole. They went west in May and lost 8 in a row; played .500 ball then lost 7 in a row; won a few and lost 6 in a row. And so it went. Their longest slump was 10 games in September. They ended the season the same way, winning 5 out of 6 before dropping their last 6.

The infield had the most problems.

When Frank Brazill wasn't injured, he was sick. He turned out be one of those players who thrive only in the minor leagues, which he did for the next seventeen years.

Ivy Griffin had more good times off the field than on it and didn't care. Johnny Walker, a journeyman first baseman up from Akron, wound up with the first base job.

Third base was in turmoil. Joe Dugan would go off to New York or Atlantic City until his money ran out and then come back. Or sometimes he'd just go home. Tiny Maxwell tagged him "Jumping Joe." Connie Mack honed an automatic comment: "Dugan will never be sold or traded. He will play here or nowhere."

Dugan liked Connie Mack but not Philadelphia. The first time Dugan came back, the hecklers got on him. The next time not just the hawkers but the usually quiet fans chimed in. When he went 0 for 4 in a 9–2 loss to Detroit in the second game of a doubleheader on July 28, a sizable ensemble of the Dugan Choral Society serenaded him, and they weren't singing Hallelujah.

"I can't play where the fans don't like me," he told Mack after the game. "My heart isn't in it. You'll have to trade me."

Apparently Dugan didn't read the papers. He wasn't aware that there was a new sheriff named Landis in town. Landis didn't like the practice of the rich clubs sowing dissatisfaction among the players they coveted. It was common knowledge that John McGraw had been after chronic Cincinnati holdout Heinie Groh, and the star third baseman wanted to heed the Giants' siren.

But in June Landis had ruled that Groh would have to remain with the Reds for the entire season.(The Giants won without him but reeled him in after the season.) Mack told Dugan he would play for the Athletics or nobody. Dugan went home anyway.

When he came back a week later, the subject was moot; the trading deadline without waivers had passed.

Hugh Fullerton saw Joe Dugan as an example of the "great trouble with baseball," which, he wrote, "lies in the spirit of discontent and dissatisfaction among the ball players. Whether owners or players are responsible or whether it is due to conditions neither can control is not for me to decide."

Fullerton then decided to blame the prosperity that had led to the commercialism of what had been a sport and was now "an amusement enterprise."

Nobody, Fullerton went on, wants to play on a last-place team, but the resultant wish to be traded to a winner leads to a lack of hustle and giving of players' best efforts that keeps them in the cellar. His solution: ban all trades or sales during the season so everybody knows the team they signed with is the team they'll be stuck with all year.

Jimmie Dykes was a rock at second base. His batting average improved, and his home run production doubled. And Mack was pleased with Chick Galloway at shortstop, when he wasn't filling in at third.

In the outfield Frank Welch, Whitey Witt, and Tilly Walker weren't the spriest flychasers in the business, but they could hit, though Welch missed a month with a torn tendon.

Cy Perkins had developed into a steady hitter and sturdy catcher—he caught 141 games—and had become the best catcher in the league.

The pitching?

Bob Hasty was built like Walter Johnson and had a grip like a steel vise. His fastball set up a devastating change-up. A clumsy fielder whose composure was shot when the other team started bunting on him, he was working on that part of the game. But he forgot everything he was told as soon as he reached the mound.

Roy Moore was out for weeks at a time with injuries. He won 10 but control problems kept him in trouble.

Rollie Naylor could pitch—9 of his 13 losses were by 1 run—but wasn't always in condition to do so.

Mack had learned the knack of using humor to belay stress. To be sure, it often had a sharp edge to it, but it helped him maintain his composure and prolong his life.

Slim Harriss knew only one pitch: hard. Make that two: hard and harder. In the third game of the season he threw an 0-2 pitch that Babe Ruth crushed for his first home run of the new year. Back in the dugout Connie Mack asked Slim, "What was the idea of giving him a fast one?"

Harriss said, "I tried to slip it past him."

With a line that could have been uttered by W. C. Fields, Mack muttered, "How marvelously you succeeded."

But Harriss was capable of learning and in midseason would win 7 in a row.

And Scott Perry? Called by some writers Mack's cross to bear for sinning against baseball by going to court over him, Perry had a lot of friends who knew where the better speakeasies were. In early May Mack fined and suspended him for ten days. "If he's not in shape after the ten days, another fine and suspension will be handed out." He turned down a Cleveland offer of cash and players for Perry, vowing not to trade or sell him.

Perry came back, beat Detroit May 25 and Boston May 30, lost to Boston June 1. Then he decided he'd had enough of the big time. Back he went to Franklin, Pennsylvania. The industrial leagues were in decline; he knew it but went anyhow. There was always the tailor shop. He knew he would be automatically suspended for five years and didn't care. Thus ended the saga of Scott Perry.

Connie Mack was out whatever he might have gotten for him, but he didn't care either. He had stuck to his principles, which were not for sale.

Eddie Rommel was a bright spot. Steady Eddie had kept them in the league, earning 6 of the team's first 11 wins. He took his knuckler and his heart to the mound 46 times—only 3 fewer than the league's busiest pitcher, Carl Mays. It didn't matter if he lost 23. He won 16; only eleven AL pitchers won more.

Two of Connie Mack's sons, Earle and Roy, were in baseball that year. Earle Mack was going nowhere as a player. He was still a .250-hitting first baseman, but he had two things going for him as a manager: a record of helping young players develop and a dad who would send him players.

Warren Giles, an astute young resident of Moline, Illinois, came back from the war and took an interest in the affairs of the local community-owned club. The Plowboys had finished last in the III League in 1919 and were in bad financial shape. When Giles spoke up at a meeting, he was invited to see if he could do a better job running the team.

Giles knew of Connie Mack's reputation as a square dealer with minor league owners. He appealed to Mack for players and a manager. Mack sent him Earle and some prospects. The Plowboys finished fourth in 1920 and won the pennant in 1921. Giles went on to become general manager of the Cincinnati Reds and president of the National League—and another of Connie Mack's lifelong admirers.

Roy Mack, fronting for a group of Baltimore Orioles officials, bought the Akron franchise in the International League for $25,000 and moved it to Newark. The Akron owners had agreed to sell the club to Montreal buyers for $40,000, but Jack Dunn squelched that, persuading the IL directors that it would add at least $25,000 to their travel costs. Roy was named the Newark president.

One day Connie Mack heard that Frank Gilmore, his old battery mate and roommate in Hartford and Washington thirty-five years earlier, was in "poor circumstances." The beanpole pitcher and catcher had been tagged the "bones battery" in those days. Gilmore's baseball days had ended in 1891. Now fifty-seven, he was living in Hartford, in poor health. Mack contacted the owner of the Hartford club to arrange an exhibition game for Gilmore's benefit. On August 31 the A's stopped in Hartford for the benefit game. The A's half of the receipts were to go to Gilmore. Before an enthusiastic crowd of 3,500, Mack and Gilmore appeared in Hartford uniforms and took their places on the field to start the game. The spry Mack drew a big hand when he lunged to his left to stop one of Gilmore's errant pitches. The pair then watched from behind the press box as the A's regulars defeated the host Senators, 8–3. Thereafter, every time Mack brought his team to Hartford, he turned over the team's guarantee to Gilmore. When Gilmore died July 21, 1929, Mack sent the local sports editor $500 for the widow.

Over the years the Athletics played frequent exhibition games in minor league towns for a variety of causes. Connie Mack found it hard to turn down Catholic priests in Pennsylvania or New England. With a couple days off traveling from St. Louis to Boston, they had played in Johnstown, New York, the day before their Hartford stop. The A's share of the receipts usually went to a local cause: a church or school building fund, a workingmen's free bed fund, the Knights of Columbus, an old teammate or a deceased player's family, a minor league club in distress. The players didn't mind; they were paid extra, even if the club didn't share in the receipts.

Other teams did the same. The Yankees, with Babe Ruth the biggest draw in the game, played the most extra games in the 1920s. Ruth's contracts stipulated how much he would receive for each appearance.

Umpire Billy Evans wrote, "Mack is the only developer of players in the major leagues. Other managers buy stars; Mack makes them."

That was about to change.

After seven years in the wilderness Connie Mack concluded that he could no longer grow stars from seedlings. The soil of American society had changed. The players had changed. Old-timers complained that kids refused to take orders and ignored signs that wouldn't benefit their own stats. But since it had become a business baseball had always embodied the split personality of a collective enterprise whose players expect to be paid on the basis of their individual skills and stats—win or lose. The pace of life was faster and Mack's patrons expected—and deserved—more results than his kindergartens had produced. If a youngster looked like a future star, Mack's philosophy was, "Give a player every chance, then give him two or three more." He had done that for three years while developing his 1910–1914 machine. But it hadn't worked since then.

And the game had changed. Babe Ruth, not A. J. Reach, had changed it. The emphasis was more on slugging than brains. The Reach Company, maker of the balls used in both leagues, denied that the balls were intentionally injected with "eau de lapin" but were livelier only because the postwar wool yarn was of a higher quality and new machinery wound it tighter. But that had been true since 1919, when the live-ball era had really begun and the deadball died. Hugh Fullerton maintained that "every player knows that it is a livelier ball than the ball in use in the pre–Babe Ruth days." Which also happened to be the wartime days. In 1921 and again in 1922 the Reach Company would send out letters to its big league customers swearing that the ball was unchanged, to no avail.

Fifteen years later, in another hitters' era, George Reach would still be maintaining that "Collins and Cobb batted against a ball that was as lively if not livelier than the ball that is in use today. The liveliest baseball ever made was used during the 1910 World Series and the first six months of 1911. It was made of Australian wool and it traveled like a bullet. The deadest ball on the other hand was made during the war years when the government requisitioned all the best wool."

It didn't matter whether Ty Cobb liked it or not. The home run was here to stay. And Connie Mack was never one to be stuck in the past. He appreciated that the level of talent was better than it had been in his playing days, even if the spirit wasn't the same. He once told Cy Perkins, "Class D catchers today are better players than I ever was."

Not everybody appreciated the new game. Some writers were chronic bemoaners. They had formerly lamented the lack of scoring; now they decried the increase. In a four-game series at Philadelphia in early June, the Tigers and A's hit a combined 15 home runs and scored a total of 65 runs. The A's scored 32 of them but lost 3 of the 4. On June 3 the A's set AL records, hitting 3 home runs in the first inning and 7 in their 15–9 win. It helped that Danny Murphy was reading the Detroit catcher's signs and tipping the A's batters to what was coming. Except once, when pitcher Carl Holling missed Johnny Bassler's sign but Murphy didn't, and Cy Perkins wound up hitting the dirt. Detroit writer H. G. Salsinger blamed the home run derby on the intentionally juiced ball. "This series is the best argument this year against the lively ball now in use. Undoubtedly the magnates arranged for the lively ball in order to help batting, figuring that batting was what the public wanted because everybody flocked to the park to see Babe Ruth bat. The Bambino's swatting performance made batting the predominant feature of baseball as far as crowds are concerned. But the profusion of hits this season is hurting baseball. There is too much batting."

Perhaps the Detroit pitching contributed to Salsinger's dyspepsia. On September 9 they would join the White Sox in setting a record for total runs (35) and hits (42) in a 20–15 White Sox win.

Salsinger claimed he heard plenty of criticism of the "pneumatic" balls among Shibe Park spectators. But the Shibeshire fans were enjoying the hitting circus as much as anybody. A's attendance was up almost 20 percent, although the last-place Phillies' gate was down by about the same amount. They didn't care what was in the ball when Babe Ruth came to town and tied his 1920 record by launching his fifty-fourth homer on September 9. It cleared the center-field wall, later measured at 500 feet, crashed through a tree on Somerset Street, and bounded away. It probably went as far as a 585-foot shot Ruth had hit in Detroit.

Isaminger, with his usual myopia, claimed the fans were already tired of home runs, high scores, and long, drawn-out games. "If the baseball czarists think the public visits major league parks to see the kind of a game the leans and fats play at the boilermakers' picnic they are mistaken." He decried the parade of batters taking toeholds at the plate trying for homers, turning pitchers into "toy soldiers in front of a machine gun."

Looking back on these early days of the home run craze, a 1929 *Sporting News* editorial recalled, "Managing editors were daffy about home runs because they thought that they bore the same resemblance to a ball game that an elephant bears to a circus. The pages of the sports departments were forced to engage special home run editors."

Sam Crane of the *New York Journal* was more on the mark in gauging the 1920s public appetite for action. "Fans want to see swats sent over the fences. The year of the home run appeals to the present day fans. The days when small scores and pitchers' battles were popular have come and gone."

Connie Mack would always be open to looking at youngsters. (On September 15 he gave a semipro left-hander, Arlas Taylor, a chance to start against Cleveland. His 2-inning cup of coffee was stirred by 5 runs and 7 hits—and 1 strikeout of Joe Sewell. Not many pitchers could boast of executing one of Sewell's 114 lifetime strikeouts.)

But it took years of experience to turn a good young ballplayer into a pennant winner. Seven years of that were enough. Mack had made his optimistic preseason predictions for so many years that he had begun to sound like the Bellman in Lewis Carroll's *Hunting of the Snark*: "I have said it thrice. What I tell you three times is true."

Just as the press had poked fun at his green recruits of 1907 and 1908, expert carvers like Westbrook Pegler were calling his current crop a bunch of clowns dressed up as ballplayers.

Gordon Mackay of the *Inquirer* wrote that out of the hundreds of prospects who had paraded on the field at Shibe Park over the past seven years, "only eight . . . have proved they act, hit, field, and run like ballplayers." He added what many were thinking: either Connie Mack had lost it as a manager or his scouts were not doing their job.

Different eyes may look at the same picture and see different truths.

Connie Mack looked at his roster and saw the nucleus he needed to build a winner: Dykes and Galloway in the infield, Cy Perkins, Slim Harriss and Eddie Rommel. Maybe Whitey Witt. Tilly Walker might have one more good year in him. The old redhead would be thirty-five by then, more of the past than the future. One or two key additions could turn twenty of those 1-run losses into victories, and you'd be fighting for a first-division finish.

What the scoffers and skeptics didn't know was that Connie Mack was through trying to grow big leaguers out of bush league phenoms like Jack Nabors and Maurice Burrus. His next champions would be built by purchasing players in the top minor leagues who were ready to bloom in the majors. He had a few years of profits to spend.

Aided by the good-times mood of the country, the drawing power of Babe Ruth, and the emergence of the Yankees as pennant winners, attendance was booming. Despite two more last-place finishes, the Athletics' home and road receipts had doubled in the past two years, producing almost $150,000 in operating profits. Connie Mack might be outbid by the money-pots in New York and Chicago, but he was ready to take them on, whatever the cost. Given the laws of supply and demand, it would not be easy. There were only so many who looked ready to produce. And it was always a gamble.

At the top of Connie Mack's shopping list was an outfielder. He began by calling his good friend Jack Dunn in Baltimore. Jack Dunn was the most successful minor league operator in the business. Like Mack, he was an owner and manager. As shrewd a judge and developer of raw young talent as anyone in the major leagues, Dunn held on to his players while they grew and ripened, paid them well, built winning teams with them, and sold them when they had matured and would bring peak prices. During the 1920–1921 winter meetings he had led the fight to allow the top minor leagues to opt out of the draft so they wouldn't be forced to sell players before they wanted to lest they be taken at the $5,000 draft price. The International League had been one of the three Class AA leagues (along with the III and Western Leagues) to drop out of the draft system. They may have regretted it. The Orioles ran up a 27-game winning streak that made a shambles of the 1921 pennant race. The winning pitcher in the last game of the streak was a rookie left-hander, Bob Groves.

For Dunn it was the second of seven consecutive pennants. There were stories all summer that the rest of the league was trying to oust Dunn; that he was going to buy the Phillies and move the team to Baltimore; that he was going to sell his stars to the Giants, then sell the Orioles and become the Phillies' manager—all as full of hot air as the shores of the Chesapeake Bay in August.

If anybody deserved to be called the Babe Ruth of the minor leagues, it was the Orioles' Jack Bentley. The twenty-five-year-old not only pitched like Ruth, winning 16 against 3 losses, but he also hit like Ruth, batting .371 with 20 home runs, playing the outfield when he wasn't pitching. Mack—as well as the Giants and other deep pockets—wanted him.

"Name your price," said Mack in his New England twang.

"He's not for sale," said Dunn in his high, piping voice.

(When Bentley was for sale a year later, he refused to go to a second-division team, so the Giants reeled him in instead of the A's.)

Next on Mack's shopping list was a first baseman. For that he called Otto Borchert, the brewery magnate who owned the Milwaukee Brewers.

Joe Hauser, the young pitcher from Milwaukee Mack had invited to spring training for a look in 1918, had not been forgotten by Mack. Joe had gone home and signed with the Brewers. They sent him to Providence, where he had become an outfielder. After a year in the outfield in Milwaukee, manager Jack Egan had told Joe to buy himself a first baseman's mitt and he'd be up in the big leagues in a year.

Hauser was popular with the German-speaking crowd back of first base. Whenever fans booed him for striking out or making an error, his supporters would yell, "Leaf him alone—dot's Unser Choe"—our Joe. During the 1921 season, when the manager heard a rumor that Hauser had offers from an industrial league, he considered trading him to Kansas City. The fans got wind of it and blew up such a storm that the talks were called off.

Harry Davis scouted Hauser and reported that Unser Choe, who batted .316 and lined out 20 home runs, was ready for the big leagues. Otto Borchert was always more interested in obtaining players than cash. Connie Mack had a list of expendables ready: first baseman Ivy Griffin, outfielder Paul Johnson, catcher Glenn Myatt, and pitcher Dave Keefe. The A's ledgers show no cash involved. (Borchert wanted Keefe especially, but when Mack asked waivers on him, Cleveland claimed him. The deal went through anyhow. In August Mack bought Keefe back from Cleveland for $4,000 and gave him to Milwaukee.)

Connie Mack decided reluctantly to give up on Joe Dugan, who might be a great third baseman, but never in Philadelphia. The boy had all the stuff of stardom, but he had not responded to Mack's handling.

"I've never found it paid to drive a player," Mack later told Alan J. Gould of the Associated Press, "no matter how unruly he might be. He will not do his best. Players require different types of handling. . . . Some need persuasion, even coaxing. Others need a pat on the back or encouraging, or to be taken aside and given proper advice like a son. I always try to study each man and suit my actions or words to what I think he requires to produce his best."

But Joe Dugan had tested Mack's belief that any player would respond to "kindly treatment." Mack's father-son talks every time Joe returned from a French leave had had no effect. The fans were fed up with him; his teammates were disgusted at his lack of effort when he was in the lineup and Mack's coddling of him.

Detroit was said to be offering $50,000 cash for Dugan. Connie Mack thought he could do better than that. He wanted players in addition. Miller Huggins was interested. There was speculation that Dugan would go to Washington in exchange for first baseman Joe Judge. Somehow Harry Frazee in Boston entered the picture.

Mack's December huddles with Frazee, Griffith, and Huggins resulted in a complex web of deals. Before the end of the year the Yankees sent two young pitchers, Rip Collins and Bill Piercy, and an old one, Jack Quinn, and veteran shortstop Roger Peckinpaugh to the Red Sox in exchange for shortstop Everett Scott and pitchers Sad Sam Jones and Joe Bush. Mack was supposed to send Dugan to Clark Griffith, who would pass Dugan along to Frazee in exchange for Peckinpaugh, the man Griffith really wanted. But the deal stalled in early January when Frazee asked Griffith for more than Dugan. Griffith balked. Mack was in Texas. Telephone calls went back and forth. Griffith agreed to add infielder Frank O'Rourke. Three weeks after the negotiations had begun, step two was completed. Mack sent Joe Dugan to Washington for second-year outfielder Bing Miller and Cuban pitcher Jose Acosta. Dugan kept on going to Boston, and Peckinpaugh went to Washington.

Boston fans were fed up with Harry Frazee, condemning him as a toady and talent supplier for the Yankees. The new Red Sox manager, Hugh Duffy, found it necessary to deny reports, generally believed, that the Yankees were really Dugan's destination in all this. Joe would be happy playing in his native New England, Duffy claimed, and would not be harassed by the more sedate Boston fans. Whatever. Six months later Dugan was a Yankee.

It was fitting that Jumping Joe should bounce among three different clubs in six months.

There were denials all around that any cash was involved, but that didn't stop speculation as to how much and from whom. One writer said that if Connie Mack hadn't received any money in addition to Miller and Acosta, he had really been suckered.

In the Clark Griffith scrapbooks in the home of Calvin Griffith's ex-wife Natalie, there was a picture of a check dated June 29, 1922, from the Washington club, countersigned by Griffith, made out to the Philadelphia American League Club for $50,000 as "settlement in full for player Dugan." That's the date the check's receipt was entered on the books of the A's. Where did this money come from, and why was it paid five months after the deal was made? Perhaps Mack had given Griffith until June 30 to come up with the money, a common arrangement. Or perhaps this was the $50,000 that reportedly went from the Yankees to the Red Sox along with several players for Dugan in July. It's possible the entire chain of events was based on the Yankees providing the cash to Griffith to finance his initial purchase of Dugan and the money went around the horn like a triple play—Ruppert to Frazee to Griffith to Mack.

Some New York writers, always looking for a chance to aim a zinger at Connie Mack, claimed the Dugan trade raised despairing wails from Philadelphia fans. But in fact A's fans were delighted at his departure. Mack said he was sorry to see Dugan go, but he had reluctantly concluded that a trade was in the best interests of all concerned. Mack's critics didn't think much of the players he received in return (Acosta would be sold to the White Sox in February). Bing Miller had been scouted by Ira Thomas when the teenager and his brothers were playing on a homemade ball field on the farm in Vinton, Iowa. The Tigers bought him for $600 from Clinton in the Central Association in 1917, but he remained in the minor leagues with a year in the military until 1921. Mack considered him a solid outfielder. "I have always liked Miller's play. He is young and a good outfielder." Besides, Miller had "a fine disposition."

They were singing Jerome Kern's new hit, "Look for the Silver Lining" on the radio these days. Connie Mack believed he could see it.

14 | OUT OF THE BASEMENT

Money was on everybody's mind in the winter of 1921–1922.

The new commissioner had some reservations about the state of the game. The *Boston Globe* on October 18, citing "persons he has expressed himself to," attributed to Landis a distaste for the conduct of the Giants in the dugout toward the umpires and the Yankees during the World Series and the large amount of money involved (a record $900,233 for the eight games).

"The money divided between the two New York clubs from the World Series is greater than the profits of the Cubs for the past three years," the unsigned article said. "It is greater than the profits of the Cardinals, Browns, or Athletics for the past two years. This incentive for clubs to get into the World Series is breeding discontent, especially as the majority of clubs cannot swing the money necessary to get the players that the New York clubs can."

The Giants were reported to have spent $75,000 for a San Francisco outfielder, Jimmy O'Connell, and $150,000 and two players for Cincinnati third baseman Heinie Groh. In July 1922 John McGraw would buy more pennant insurance, sending three players and $100,000 to the Braves for right-hander Hugh McQuillan. The outcries over these ridiculous prices ranged from Branch Rickey's cry of unsportsmanlike conduct in using players the Giants didn't develop to writers' fears that players seeing these huge sums being paid for minor leaguers would figure they deserved higher salaries and that would be the end of the sport of baseball, dissolved in the acid of commercialism.

In Detroit H. G. Salsinger predicted the largest list of holdouts in history. "It's only natural that the players demand huge salaries. . . . They say if a busher is worth $50,000 cash I ought to be worth at least half of that. They know that I can do it and they don't know what this new bird will do."

In New York Joe Vila was condemning the "greedy players conspiring to mulct magnates of their hard-earned receipts."

And Frank Graham of the *New York Sun* was sounding the tocsin against everybody:

There must be not only a stabilizing of the players' salaries but a return to sport and sanity on the part of club owners. Should the magnates through sheer compulsive measures derived from laws drafted by themselves stamp out the present agitation on the part of the players and then stop right there, they will establish a basis which may for the present be satisfactory to themselves, but they will be piling up trouble for the future. They must go further than that, but they must purge themselves of money madness or stand convicted of hypocrisy and open to attack from the public as well as from the player.

Some lessons, it would seem, can never be learned.

The Athletics generally had fewer holdout problems than most other teams. Mack's players knew he was fair and did the best his finances would justify. He was open with them about the club's financial situation, good times and bad. Toward the close of the 1921 season he had called each of them into his office and inquired into what they would expect next year, given their last place finish. To his surprise he found that none of them would admit to having had anything to do with the team finishing last. But the A's had shown a profit, and several of them wound up with raises. Cy Perkins became the highest paid at $7,000.

"I have been a ballplayer myself and try to see their side of it," Mack told Tiny Maxwell. "I am willing to go along with them and when they make good I am the first to pay them for it. But they can't be satisfied. I have two worries in my life. One is to sign a ballplayer and the other is to release him. In regard to salaries, despite reports to the contrary, I know that considering their ability the Athletics are better paid than any other club. Considering their ability."

James Isaminger agreed. "The Athletics pay as big salaries as any clubs in the two leagues," he wrote. "Only one man [Rollie Naylor] on the 1921 team was cut and he was a man who drew an exceptional salary last year in the hope he would do good work, but he did not do as well as he did in 1920. Yet even with a cut his '22 salary will by no means be out of major league tune. While I don't expect everybody to believe it, nevertheless it is the truth that if the salaries of all clubs in the two leagues were made public, the Athletics would be proved to be as liberal as any of the first division clubs." Conceding that "there is no doubt that the owners of the Athletics have the reputation of being poor payers," Isaminger declared that "there is likewise no doubt there isn't a scintilla of truth in the charge. Connie Mack is getting justly indignant at this story and he would willingly vote at any baseball meeting to make salaries public, so that the impression wouldn't go around the players get nickels in Philadelphia and dollars in other cities."

The Athletics' payroll for 1922 would reach $112,000, almost double that of three years ago.

During the December meetings Tom Turner, the world's most traveled scout, who thought nothing of crossing the country several times each season, resigned as an A's scout to become the manager of the Portland club in the Pacific Coast League. Mack immediately began supplying him with players. Before the season was over Turner would have enough of managing and go back to scouting for the Beavers. He continued to maintain close ties to Connie Mack.

After several years of declining health, Ben Shibe died on January 14, 1922, two weeks short of his seventy-fourth birthday. The pioneer innovator in the manufacture of baseballs and sporting equipment left not a single enemy behind. The pristine reputation he brought to the American League's new franchise in his home city had been worth more than his financial investment in the successful launching of the Athletics.

No more perfect union has ever been forged than the partnership of Ben Shibe and his sons and Connie Mack. Everything they had done as 50-50 partners had been 100 percent backed by both. All the baseball decisions had been willingly left to Mack. But no major moves had been made without the agreement of both. Not even seven consecutive last-place finishes had rocked the tranquility of their working relationship. Ben Shibe's confidence in Connie Mack had never wavered.

"Every ball player knows he was a great man for the game," Mack said of Shibe. "While he was quiet and never impressed himself on people, yet his advice was always good and was invariably taken by those who sought it. He was a wonderful character. Everyone in baseball will miss him."

It might be said that Ben Shibe's death ended a perfect partnership, but in fact the Athletics had always been more of a family business, equally divided between the Mack family and the Shibes. There had been no behind-the-scenes plotting, no infighting. Connie Mack once described their working relationship: "When I had decided to buy a player and obtained the details for the transaction, I went to my partners and told them I'd like to obtain the player in question. I told them the terms and explained why I thought the deal would benefit us. I did this whether the amount of cash involved was $10,000 or $100,000. And the Shibes so respected my judgment that not once did they object."

Tom Shibe became the club president; his brother John, the vice-president and secretary. Connie Mack remained the treasurer.

Both Ben Shibe and Connie Mack had from time to time transferred shares in the Athletics to their sons. Of Ben Shibe's remaining holdings, 141 shares now went to Tom, 126 to John, 141 each to Ben's daughters Elfrida S. Macfarland and Mary S. Reach.

Often this spreading of ownership in a business among a wider circle of the next generation begets quarrels and feuds, but never was heard a discordant word among the Shibe heirs until many years later, when Connie Mack's sons had a falling out. Ben's son-in-law, Dr. Frank Macfarland, was the team physician; later Ben Shibe's grandson, Benny Macfarland, would become the traveling secretary. Eventually all of Connie Mack's sons would be employed by the club.

Tom and John Shibe were Mack's friends as well as business associates, although their personalities were markedly different. Tom and Mack traveled, went on spring training camp searches, and attended sporting events together. Tom served on the league's board of directors and was active in drawing up the new national agreement. He often worked out with the players. His wife, known affectionately as Aunt Ida, was the A's number one rooter. She went to spring training every year, missing only one because of a fall. Ida owned a large collection of jewelry and objects in the form of white elephants with their trunks turned upward for luck. But Tom could be gruff and short-tempered and left all the public relations glad-handing to Mr. Mack.

John Shibe was a different piece of work. He was a nervous wreck rooting for his team. When a pitcher was wild, he could be heard muttering, "Get it over . . . throw strikes . . . make 'em hit it." He followed the games on the road by a ticker tape in his office. Matt Kilroy, a former pitcher who owned a saloon in the neighborhood, said that John Shibe would rather win one with two hundred people in the stands than lose one with thirty thousand pouring dollars in his pockets.

John would hole up in his office playing solitaire on a cold winter's day, and a visitor who looked over his shoulder and suggested a move would, as

Bing Miller learned, "see cards and table go flying across the room." John never smiled, refused to answer the telephone—according to Art Morrow of the *Inquirer*, more than once he ripped the telephones from the wall in his office, knocking the ballpark out of the Bell system so nobody could get through to them—and had no use for reporters. One November morning Paul Gallico of the *New York Daily News* was in Philadelphia for a football game. He went to Shibe Park looking for news about the A's and found John Shibe playing solitaire. Gallico asked to see Mr. Mack. John responded with a sound approaching a grunt. When Gallico asked again, John grabbed him and pushed him toward the stairway. In the scuffle some books Gallico was carrying went tumbling down the stairs. "It was a very messy affair," he wrote in a column headed "Welcome to Philadelphia." Nobody who knew John Shibe doubted it for a minute.

One thing the Shibes and Connie Mack had in common, in addition to their commitment to the success of the Athletics, was a perverse generosity they didn't want anybody to know about.

The ill-tempered John Shibe's private side in particular has gone unrecognized. A fight fan like Connie Mack, he heard about a prelim fighter who had been blinded by blows taken in the ring. Shibe arranged for an operation and a long recovery at a resort hotel—and paid for all of it. And nobody knew about it until after his death, when the fighter, sworn to secrecy by Shibe, told his story.

As Art Morrow, who covered the team for twenty-five years, put it, "The Shibes loved nothing better than to twist an arm while slipping a buck into somebody's pocket, or angrily slam the phone or the door on anyone trying to express thanks for a ton of coal."

John was devoted to maintaining and improving the baseball palace that bore the family name. He had refused to rent the ballpark to professional football teams because he didn't want the grass torn up. The football games were played at rundown Baker Bowl, which was falling apart, rusting, and in danger of being condemned by building inspectors. John was busy supervising the painting of the grandstand and the installation of a screen in front of the press box, to the relief of less than agile writers who had been dodging foul balls lined back into their work space for thirteen years. The only fatalities had been a few typewriters. John was also contemplating erecting a screen in front of the left-field bleachers to prevent fans from reaching down and interfering with a ball in play.

John Shibe was active in Democratic Party politics and had been leading the long fight to legalize Sunday baseball in the state.

The optimism that bubbled throughout the country was reflected in the annual winter meetings of the moguls. The scandal that had rocked the national pastime in 1920 was forgotten. Attendance in 1921 had boomed; minor league attendance set records. Prohibition was given credit for part of it; most of the saloons were boarded up.

When it came to spring training sites, Connie Mack was the wandering Irishman. He couldn't seem to find the perfect place. No matter where he went, there was always something that didn't suit him—the weather, the distance from Philadelphia, the lack of major league practice competition. He liked the people, the Majestic Hotel, and the climate in Lake Charles, but he wasn't happy with the field and clubhouse. He wrote to the chamber of commerce in Montgomery, Alabama, to see what they would do for him, but they showed no interest in meeting the attendance guarantees or the expense of building the ballpark and adequate clubhouse facilities he asked for.

Then he received a letter from the mayor of Eagle Pass, Texas. There were five other Texas cities hosting big league teams, and the mayor was eager to join them. He invited Mack to come down and look over his town. Two days after Christmas, that's just what Connie Mack did. For all his vowing to shorten the distance between training camps and Shibe Park, it's incongruous that he would endure a three-day train ride of 2,014 miles to check out a small town on the Mexican border. It's equally strange that for all his emphasis on daily practice games, he would consider a location almost 500 miles from the Cardinals, the only team he would meet in five exhibition games.

Most of the six thousand residents of Eagle Pass were Mexicans. Signs and street names were in Spanish. Youngsters played at bullfighting in the streets. When he arrived, Mack found the town fathers congenial, eager to please and make him welcome. They loved *beisbol*.

On Sunday a local booster, Leonard Brooks, took Mr. Mack to his first bullfight in Piedras Negras. Brooks wrote to the *Evening Public Ledger*, "If his players throughout the season show as much pep as he did during the fight the Athletics will win the pennant."

After the bull was dispatched, the banderillero pulled one of the decorated spears from the neck of the bull and presented it to Mack from the arena, to great applause from the crowd.

The ballpark was three miles from the Eagle Hotel. Fine, said Mr. Mack, the boys will walk in the morning and afternoon. It'll do them good. We'll use jitneys to go back to the hotel for lunch and a break. The grounds were the reverse of most amateur fields: a skin outfield and grass infield. The city fathers promised to build a clubhouse. It was a five-minute walk across the International Bridge over the Rio Grande to Piedras Negras, a wide-open town where there was no prohibition—of anything. That's okay, Mr. Mack said, my boys are all good boys. They'll like it here. Oh, and Sunday games would have to be played in the mornings, so that everybody could go to the bull fights in the afternoon. No problem.

There was at least one Chinese family in Eagle Pass, proprietors of a restaurant. The owner's son, Chuck Fonn, was an outfielder on the high school team. Mack invited him to work out with the A's.

So Connie Mack brought his team to Eagle Pass, where they found more excitement than they expected. What Texans call a blue norther—a blast of cold air siphoned out of Canada—blew through the state and cost all the Texas camps three days of workouts. The clubhouse stove froze and cracked; there was no way to heat water until Harry Davis and Danny Murphy scoured the town for a new stove. The boys played dominoes and billiards and saw the sights in Piedras Negras. When it warmed up, the wind kicked up biting sandstorms, forcing the players to wear goggles to keep the sand out of their eyes.

Then Ban Johnson blew into town with a military escort on his way home from a hunting trip to Mexico and threw a banquet in Piedras Negras for his favorite Mexican colonel. Army officers and bigwigs from both sides of the border were there, along with Mack, Tom Shibe, Harry Davis, and Danny Murphy, and writers from Chicago and Philadelphia papers. Johnson announced that as a goodwill gesture he would provide a bronze trophy to be awarded to the Mexican baseball champions each year.

The sandstorms made some of Connie Mack's boys too thirsty to be satisfied by Eagle Pass soda pop. Whitey Witt and Cy Perkins were roommates. Witt later said the stories about him "being ashamed of being associated with the A's and getting drunk and hiring some guitar players to help me serenade Connie Mack to goad him into trading me are all bunk."

What happened, he said, was this:

I checked into the hotel and Isaminger liked me for some reason and he came over and wrapped his arms around me—half-drunk—and Connie

Mack and everybody's watching. That night we went over to Mexico and Perkins and Isaminger and I came back singing some song and we woke up Mr. Mack. My room was two or three rooms away from his. The next morning Mack was there when I came down to the lobby and Mack tells the clerk, "There's Witt, you give him another room away from me."

I think it had something to do with my being traded, though. I was nonchalant in spring training and I told some of the players and Mack that I didn't want to play there any more, so that must have been the starting of it.

The ending of it came in a game against the Cardinals played in the rain. Witt continued:

I'm standing in water in right field. Man on first. Ball hit to me. Instead of throwing to third base I throw it over the catcher's head up against the grandstand. After the game we come back to the hotel and Connie Mack is talking with Branch Rickey and Hornsby and Mack says, "Whitey, come here. I want to talk to you. I'm going to get rid of you. I'm going to send you back to Philadelphia and you stay there until further notice. Do you have any idea where you would like to go?"

I found out there were a lot of clubs wanted me, but the Yankees needed an outfielder because Ruth and Bob Meusel had been suspended for barnstorming and Bob Shawkey was a friend from the A's and he talked to Huggins.

So the Yankees bought him for $7,500.

Witt's reference to the suspension of Ruth and Meusel referred to Judge Landis's enforcement of a rule that had been written back in 1910 after the world champion Athletics had gone to Cuba and larked through a series of games in which the Cubans won all but one. The embarrassed magnates decided that no member of a World Series team may barnstorm after the season. Ruth and Meusel (and pitcher Bill Piercy) had ignored the rule after the 1921 Series. Landis fined and suspended them until May 20. Clark Griffith complained that suspending the game's biggest attraction would hurt the American League clubs more than Ruth, but Landis held firm. (Despite a section of the new agreement prohibiting club officials from publicly criticizing the new commissioner, the crusty Griffith would also accuse Landis of "insulting 98 percent of the ballplayers who conduct themselves like gentlemen" when the judge held a clubhouse meeting in June and lectured the Yankees and Red Sox on the evils of gambling, bootlegging, and carousing.) Ruth was so popular throughout the nation, the rule was soon changed to allow no more than two members of a World Series team to barnstorm together, paving the way for Ruth and Meusel, and later Ruth and Gehrig, to thrill thousands of fans in the hinterlands each fall.

Three of the Athletics missed most of the fun at Eagle Pass. Newly acquired outfielder Bing Miller had been given permission by Mack to report late. Miller was in good shape from husking five thousand bushels of corn and raising grain for the livestock on his farm in Vinton, Iowa. To him the baseball season was a vacation. Joe Hauser was a holdout. It wasn't that he objected to the $3,000 contract Connie Mack had sent him. It turned out that Hauser was looking for a hundred dollar bonus the Brewers had promised to anyone who hit a home run for them in Minneapolis, and Unser Choe had hit one. Mack told him his argument was with the Brewers, not the Athletics. Mack's old partner in Milwaukee, Henry Killilea, advised Hauser to forget the bonus and sign or he'd be out of baseball. Meanwhile three weeks went by. As insurance, Mack claimed veteran first baseman Doc Johnston on waivers from Cleveland. When Hauser showed up, he was not ready to play and Johnston had the first base job.

Except for pinch-hitting duties, Hauser would sit on the bench for two and a half months before starting a game.

The third case was Eddie Rommel. His first contract in 1920 had been for $2,100. The next year he received a raise to $3,500. His 1922 contract called for $4,500. Rommel wanted $5,000. Mack considered Rommel a good pitcher but not a great one—not yet.

In dealing with players asking for more money, Mack sometimes said that what he was offering was all he could pay. Sometimes he gave in. Mack told Eddie if he believed he was being treated unfairly, he should accept the commissioner's invitation to players to send him their grievances. Rommel did—Rollie Naylor did too—and the judge prudently declared that he would not get involved in salary disputes; that was between the players and their employers.

But Eddie Rommel did something no player had ever done to Mack. He showed Mack's letter that had accompanied the contract to a Baltimore newspaper. That breach of confidence peeved Mack.

When he received an inquiry from Landis about the Rommel matter, Connie Mack sat in the Eagle Hotel on March 7 and dictated this letter:

Dear Judge Landis,

Your's of March 4th, pertaining to pitcher Rommel, received. When I sent this player his contract some time ago he took the letter I inclosed with it to the office of a Baltimore newspaper the very first thing and had the letter published in full. In all my experience in base ball that is the very first time I ever heard of a player taking his manager's letter to a newspaper office for publication. I regret that I haven't a copy of this newspaper with me, it is now at our Philadelphia office.

Rommel commented at the time that the salary offered him was a minor league salary. Some time ago I sent you a letter in which I gave you some facts in regards to our club's dealing with Rommel.

At our recent American League meeting the salary question was discussed rather freely by the league members and I talked for some little time in regards to the demands that were being made by the Philadelphia players. I brought the Rommel case before the members and gave them an outline on our club's treatment of Rommel from the time he joined our club and told them the salary offered him for the coming season, which was forty-five hundred dollars. They all seemed to think that Rommel was very fairly treated.

If Rommel had not gone with his grievance to the newspapers but had followed my instructions that if not satisfied with the salary offered him to take the matter up with you I would then have been more than willing to have done something better for him after receiving your letter.

As the case stands now if our club should concede to Rommel's demands or give him a better contract he is going to come to our club and let every player on the team know that he won by holding out. This would have a bad effect on the other players of the club at the present time, for our players now realize that there was a lot of propaganda handed them the past season in order to keep them from doing their best work. While I cannot now go into details with you concerning this latter condition will do so at the first opportunity.

One of our newspaper reporters has received today a dispatch from Baltimore which says that Mack, according to Rommel, wants to drive him, Rommel, out of base ball. He fails to remember that our club sent him five hundred dollars about the middle of December when he was hard pressed for money, which does not prove that Mack wants to drive him out of base ball. This player could live a cleaner life and if he did so would not require an advance of five hundred dollars two months after the close of the season.

On the whole I feel that Rommel has been badly advised and he should have realized that when in 1921 we raised his salary one thousand dollars over the previous season in spite of the fact that he had been ill most of that season that it was the intention of our club to treat the player in the right manner.

While I regret that Rommel is still dissatisfied with his salary I do not feel that our club would be doing the right thing at this time by giving in to the player. If the player comes to our club and shows an inclination to do the right thing and has a good year in 1922 our club will surely satisfy him in the way of a contract for 1923.

Very truly your's,
/s/ Connie Mack

In the meantime Mack had made some caustic comments about Rommel's behavior. Feeling unjustly maligned, the pitcher sent the clippings to the commissioner, asking for his advice.

Landis's answer, according to the *Washington Post*: "Replying to your letter of March 8 with inclosure, I have no desire to contribute anything to that cruel newspaper war."

Mack actually offered to submit the $500 salary difference to a board of arbitrators; he would choose one, Rommel one, and those two would choose the third, perhaps the first such offer of arbitration in baseball history. But before that could happen, a contrite Rommel arrived in Eagle Pass and signed the $4,500 contract. Mack, having fined Rommel for each day away from camp, canceled the fine. Rommel had been working out in Baltimore and was ready to pitch.

Mack had added to his infield by claiming veteran second baseman Ralph Young on waivers from Detroit and paying Hartford $5,000 for Heinie Scheer. He sent Johnny Walker to Newark for Frank McGowan, a leading slugger of the International League.

With more than his usual confidence Connie Mack bid adios to the mayor and the Chinese outfielder and the other good citizens of Eagle Pass and went to Galveston to start a five-game series with the Cardinals. The A's were soundly thrashed in all five games.

Last place, here we come again, Isaminger lamented.

But this was no lackadaisical, dispirited team. Through May the A's showed they were not the same old losers. They were full of confidence, hustle, never-give-upness. And they were a lethal lineup. At the time of the Dugan trade, A's fans thought old Connie had been euchered again, getting a nobody named Miller in return. But Bing Miller quickly became a fan favorite, hitting in 26 of the first 29 games, batting around the .400 mark, and taking charge in the outfield. Crow was now in the bleacher experts' diets.

On May 2 Tilly Walker, Perkins, and Miller hit back-to-back-to-back home runs. A week later they rapped out a record-tying 42 total bases in a 15–4 rout of Cleveland. The outfield of Miller, Walker, and Welch were all long-ball threats.

They may not have been a murderers' row yet, but they were at least an assault and battery row. Jimmie Dykes hit 5 home runs in two weeks in May and began swinging for the fences. But his batting average fell and Connie Mack had to persuade him that if he tried to make the fans forget Babe Ruth, they would soon forget Jimmie Dykes. Still, he contributed 12 to the team's league-leading 111 homers for the year.

Tilly Walker would beat out the short-seasoned Babe Ruth with 37 home runs, second to the Browns' Ken Williams.

They rambled around the .500 mark into June, never far from second place, never far from eighth. In the middle of May they won two series in a row against western teams at home, something they hadn't done since 1914. Then they went west, graveyard of past Athletics' dreams, lost 11 of 15, and came home battling the Red Sox to stay out of the cellar for the rest of the season.

And the jokes continued. In the June 1 issue of *Life*, a humor magazine, *Life*'s Historical Calendar for June by playwrights Marc Connelly and George S. Kaufman included this entry: "23-F[riday] William Penn acquires Pennsylvania from the Indians, thereby making himself responsible for the Philadelphia Athletics, 1683."

In May Connie Mack lost a close baseball friend when Charlie Frank, the longtime Southern Association manager, died. Frank had been a constant, true gentleman in their many player agreements of the pre-Landis days. A month later Tiny Maxwell, the erudite sports editor of the *Public Ledger*, was killed in an automobile accident. A renowned football field official, Maxwell was the most learned sportswriter of his time, well-versed in as varied fields of knowledge as John Kieran of the *New York Times* would be.

When Doc Johnston's aging legs finally gave out at the end of June, Joe Hauser took over at first base and added another potent bat to the lineup. Mack didn't release Johnston, who remained the team's leading cheerleader from the bench. That made him worth his salary to Mack.

With only one year's experience at the position, Joe Hauser was far from a finished glove man. But he studied the stars—George Sisler, Stuffy McInnis, Joe Judge—and listened to Connie Mack. When he picked up a bunt and touched the runner with the ball, Connie Mack suggested he hold it in his glove to make the tag so they wouldn't knock it out of his hand.

From the time he began playing regularly, Hauser's exploits were head-lined in the Milwaukee papers, which referred to him as "Zip." When the A's played an exhibition game in Milwaukee on September 25, it was Joe Hauser Day. His friends gave him a bowling ball and shoes and other gifts.

Hauser was popular with his teammates and in the Shibe Park neighbor-hood. They called him Dutch, more for his "Ja Ja" accent than his favorite Dutch Masters cigars. Until Eddie Rommel married Emma Fahey in Balti-more on September 13, he and Hauser shared a room in the Truitts' home at 2535 Lehigh, two blocks from the ballpark, for ten dollars a week each. Mr. Truitt worked at Strawbridge & Clothier department store and managed a West Philadelphia team. Other single players had rooms nearby. They all ate their meals a block away at Mrs. Devlin's boarding house—all you can eat for a dollar a day. And they could eat; Hauser remembered Rommel regularly putting away five or six ears of corn. In the evenings they played pinochle or bridge, sometimes gathered around the player piano for a sing-along, or sat on the porch smoking cigars and talking with whoever passed by.

Everybody in the neighborhood rooted for them. Unser Choe recalled the Truitts' Irish cleaning lady. "She was very pious. Religious. You know the type. But one day when a base runner spiked me on the foot, she said to me, 'That sonofabitch.' Ja ja."

Every day at home the team reported for an hour workout at ten o'clock. Connie Mack would sit in the grandstand watching. If somebody had been invited for a look, that's when it would take place. Then back at one for stretching, pepper, and batting practice. Before the start of a series they had a meeting to go over the opposition, in the clubhouse at home, Mack's hotel room on the road.

By midseason Mack had a line on which players were quitting on themselves and on the team, who would go and who would stay. McGowan and Welch were adequate but still unproven. Ralph Young, Doc Johnston, and Tilly Walker were giving 100 percent, but they were on their last legs.

Chick Galloway would hit .324, far above anything he had previously done with the bat. He wouldn't reach that level again, but he had learned to hit to all fields, pull a line drive or dump a Texas Leaguer, bunt, and hit behind a runner—a versatile, reliable .270s hitter, which was all that was looked for from shortstops of the time.

The nucleus for the future was a little stronger with the addition of Joe Hauser and Bing Miller. "When Joe joined us," Mack said, "he was shaky and uncertain. But the rest of the boys took a liking to Dutch and they have served to instill confidence in him. He is full of life and possesses that supreme confidence in himself."

In September a *St. Louis Post-Dispatch* writer noted, "[Hauser] is one of the leading hitters in the league and unlike McInnis, he is a free hitter who is liable to drive the ball to any field. He has nerve and intelligence."

The A's were fifth in the league in scoring runs, but once again they gave up more runs than anybody.

The pitching was in-and-out except for Rollie Naylor and the untiring Eddie Rommel. Young pitchers who shone in the spring dimmed in the summer. Roy Moore was going back after his 10-10 season in 1921. Only twenty-three, he had all the physical equipment to be a winning pitcher, but not the mental. In July Mack sold him to Detroit for the waiver price; Moore never won another game.

Byron Yarrison, a twenty-six-year-old $1,500 pickup from Class D Hanover, came from Eddie Plank's neighborhood and had been coached by Plank. A Carl Mays–type submarine pitcher, he had a devastating sidearm curve, control, and pitching sense. He had shone in the practice games against the Cardinals, giving up 1 hit in 5 innings. Once the gong sounded, he couldn't get anybody out.

What happened?

"I don't know," Mack told Cullen Cain of the *Ledger*. "He ought to be a great pitcher but he's not. That's all there is to it."

Mack sent him to Portland, and Yarrison found a home in the Pacific Coast League.

Jim Sullivan was a product of Jack Dunn's Orioles. He hadn't been a big winner in Baltimore, but Mack had looked him over the year before and gave him another chance. The young right-hander was remembered by other players more for the rare sight of Connie Mack ripping into a player in front of the rest of the team than for anything else he did. Ed Rommel recalled, "One day [Sullivan] had a ball hit back to him and threw to the wrong base.

"'Why did you do that?' Mack asked him.

"'I don't know,' he said.

"'Well, don't ever do it again.'

"In the very next inning a ball was hit back to the pitcher again and he made a wrong throw again.

"'Sullivan, you're the dumbest player I've ever seen in my life,' Mr. Mack said in front of the club. As soon as I heard him say that I told the rest of the boys that Sullivan was a goner."

Sullivan went to Portland too.

Mack had counted on Slim Harriss to be a winning pitcher. Had he fulfilled Mack's expectations, the Athletics might have finished in the first division. But Harriss was hit hard in several early starts and gave up on himself. Pitchers will tell you when they lose their confidence, they lose everything. But Connie Mack refused to give up on him and kept running him out there, starting and relieving, a total of 47 games, fourth in the league. Six of his 20 losses came in relief.

Bob Hasty, who was built like Walter Johnson, could throw strikes with his fastball and devastating change-of-pace. He had not overcome his awkwardness at fielding bunts, which frazzled his composure.

Fred Heimach started and relieved without complaint. But Heimach had the highest earned run average in the league.

Rollie Naylor was not a quitter. Mack would have liked to have an entire roster as conscientious and team-spirited as the army veteran. He lost more close low-scoring games than anybody in the league.

Eddie Rommel had emerged as the rock on which Connie Mack would build his staff. Seldom has a third-year pitcher—or any pitcher—had a comparable season. His large hands and long fingers enabled him to throw a knuckleball with amazing control; pitching almost 300 innings, he averaged under 2 walks per 9 innings. He worked in turn, out of turn, starting the first game of a doubleheader and relieving in the second. Twice in a two-week span he picked up double wins that way. Some days he never used the knuckler. His fastball and curve were good enough, and he knew that every hitter went up to bat looking for the floater, so he could keep them off balance all day. His 27 wins were 42 percent of the team's 65 that enabled them to climb out of last place.

In the American League's new system of two writers from each city selecting a most valuable player, Rommel finished second to George Sisler, who led the Browns to within one game of their first pennant.

"He deserves all the credit that can be given him," Mack said. "I worked harder this year to avoid last position than I ever did to win world's championships, and Rommel was the one who helped me most."

Nobody ever confused Eddie Rommel with the terrible-tempered Lefty Grove, but as was true of many pitchers of that era, he hated to come out of a game. One day he was starting to get roughed up, and Connie Mack waved for a new pitcher. Rommel let it be known that he didn't agree with that maneuver. Mack didn't change his mind. When Rommel came into the dugout, he threw his glove and it landed right beside Mr. Mack. "Go in the clubhouse," Mack said, "take a shower and cool down, then come up to the office after the game and I'll talk to you."

The New York Yankees had the Philadelphia Athletics to thank for their 1-game pennant margin over the St. Louis Browns—for two reasons. They won 17 of the 22 games between the two teams, thanks in part to some intelligence on the part of Joe Bush. His days with the Athletics had taught Bush how to look for tics and signs that might give away a pitcher's or catcher's intentions. He noticed that Cy Perkins moved his legs upward when he called for a curve and didn't move them when he gave the fastball sign.

"I passed that along to our hitters," Bush said, "and we had little trouble beating them. Connie Mack knew I was reading Perkins for pitches but neither he nor Cy knew what was giving it to me."

The other reason was the result of Connie Mack's—what: Curiosity? Kindness? Undying dream that one day one of the oddball characters who had the guts and bravado to make his way to Mack's office and pass himself off as a pitcher might actually turn out to be the genuine article?

What follows is a blend of accounts at the time and recollections as best they could be authenticated.

First of all, Adolph John "Otto" Rettig was no youngster. He was twenty-eight. He had pitched in the minor leagues for a few years before returning to his home in Newark, New Jersey, where he had starred in semipro circles since 1917 while working as a theater manager.

The house at 604 West Cliveden that was home to the Mack family for twenty-five years. *Courtesy of the Philadelphia Athletics Historical Society.*

(ABOVE) The Mack family in 1926:
(from left) Betty, 6; Mr. Mack; Connie
Jr., 14; Mary, 15; Rita, 10; Ruth 12; Mrs.
Mack. *From the collection of Connie
Mack Jr. / Courtesy of Connie Mack III.*

(OPPOSITE) Jack Nabors (seated),
hailed as a twenty-year-old sensation
when Mack bought him in 1915, was
really twenty-nine when this photo was
taken in spring training 1917. Mack's
older brother, Michael, is standing in the
doorway, with trainer Doc Ebling on the
right. *Courtesy of Robert Warrington.*

(ABOVE) Bench made of bats that stood in Connie Mack's office. *Courtesy of the author.*

(OPPOSITE TOP) Branch Rickey. A lifetime friendship between him and Connie Mack began when Rickey's Cardinals and the Athletics traveled together around Texas during spring training in 1920. Rickey was the Browns manager prior to crossing over to the Cardinals in 1919. *Courtesy of the Library of Congress, Call No. LC-F81-1264.*

(OPPOSITE BOTTOM) Commissioner Kenesaw Mountain Landis with Reds manager Jack Hendricks in the mid-1920s. The scowl and the unruly white hair were Landis trademarks. *Courtesy of the author.*

(OPPOSITE TOP) Earle Mack takes infield practice at first base wearing a catcher's mitt. *Courtesy of the Library of Congress, Call No. LC-H261-4420.*

(OPPOSITE BOTTOM) Managing last-place teams for six years hadn't yet turned Connie Mack's hair gray by 1921. *Courtesy of Robert Warrington.*

(ABOVE) As the youngest manager in the league, Stanley "Bucky" Harris had led the Washington Senators to the 1924 and 1925 pennants when he greeted the league's oldest manager on opening day 1926. *Courtesy of the Library of Congress, Reproduction No. LC-USZ62-103758.*

(LEFT) Al Simmons surprised the batting-stance purists when he batted .308 and drove in 102 runs in his rookie year 1924. *Courtesy of the Library of Congress, Call # LC-F8-29789, Reproduction #LC-DIG-npcg-10883.*

(BELOW) Connie Mack looked every bit the successful businessman during the Roaring Twenties. *Courtesy of Robert Warrington.*

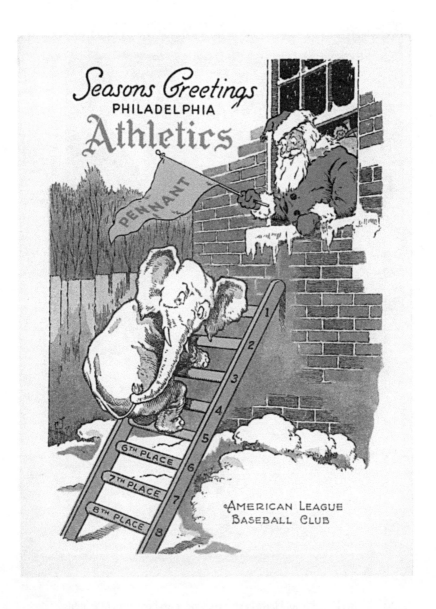

(ABOVE) This 1924 Christmas card shows the A's rung-by-rung climb out of the cellar beginning in 1922. *From the collection of Connie Mack Jr. / Courtesy of Connie Mack III.*

(ABOVE) Joe Hauser could have been a contender for home run titles if his knee hadn't disintegrated in 1925. *Courtesy of the author.*

(OPPOSITE) Dick Richards, who brought Connie Mack and the Athletics to Fort Myers in 1925, and Mr. Mack. *Courtesy of Frank Richards.*

The A's are welcomed to the first spring training in Fort Myers by a local Kiwanian named McCabe, with Connie Mack in an unaccustomed place in the driver's seat of a 1925 Buick. Seated on the front bumper are Sammy Gray and Bing Miller. McCabe is shaking hands with Ira Thomas. Behind Thomas are, from left, Lefty Grove, Fred Heimach, Mickey Cochrane, Walter French, and Slim Harriss. On the ground, from left, Jimmy Foxx, Joe Hauser, Al Simmons, and Cy Perkins. Three future Hall of Famers were among the rookies: Grove, Cochrane, and Foxx. *Courtesy of Connie Mack III.*

THOMAS   MACK   HEIMACH   COCHRANE   FRENCH   HARRIS   PERKINS
GROVES   HAUSER   SIMMONS
FOX

(OPPOSITE TOP) Mr. Mack stands beside Dick Richards in the Royal Palm Pharmacy in Fort Myers. Al Simmons is at the left. Mack's spring training office was on the balcony in the rear. *Courtesy of Frank Richards.*

(OPPOSITE BOTTOM) The Athletics in front of Thomas Edison's home in Fort Myers in 1926. Edison is in the center of the front row. Mack's daughter Betty is at Edison's right hand, with her mother behind her; Ida Shibe is at his left. *Courtesy of Frank Richards.*

(ABOVE) Thomas Edison, a frequent visitor to the A's spring training practice, at bat, with Connie Mack behind the plate in 1927 at Fort Myers. Ty Cobb was lobbing in the pitches. *Courtesy of Edison & Ford Winter Estates, Fort Myers FL.*

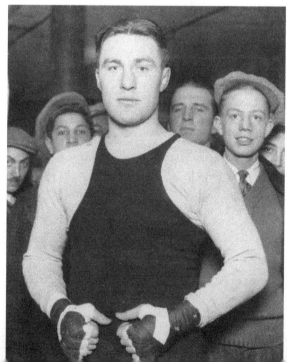

(ABOVE) Connie Mack watches batting practice behind the batting cage in Fort Myers, ca. 1925–1930. *Courtesy of Hugh Richards.*

(RIGHT) Light-heavyweight champion (1927–1929) Tommy Loughran, Connie Mack's close friend and favorite prizefighter. *Courtesy of John DiSanto/ www.phillyboxinghistory.com.*

(LEFT) Connie Mack in Fort Myers, ca. 1925–1930. *Courtesy of Frank Richards.*

(BELOW) On April 15, 1927, Eddie Collins, Ty Cobb, and Connie Mack (left to right, foreground) visited the A. J. Reach baseball factory. Here they watch a machine smoothing the seams. *Courtesy of Robert Warrington.*

Sheet music cover for "The Galloping A's," celebrating
the 1929 world champions. *Origin: Pennant Music Co.*

"I'm interested in results" - CONNIE MACK

(LEFT) Connie Mack was featured on the cover of lesson #13, dated May 2, 1930, of a "Practical Selling" correspondence course for improving selling skills. Inside the lesson Mack was extolled for "getting results." *Courtesy of Robert Warrington.*

(BELOW LEFT) John McGraw and Connie Mack confer in the Biltmore Hotel lobby during the December 12, 1929, major league meeting in New York. *Courtesy of Robert Warrington.*

(BELOW) Connie Mack had plenty to smile about by 1930. *Courtesy of Robert Warrington.*

(OPPOSITE TOP) From (left) Bing Miller, Connie Mack, Ira Thomas, and Jimmie Dykes at the home of Dr. Walter Grier in Milford, Delaware. *Courtesy of William Grier.*

(OPPOSITE BOTTOM) The A's pose at Dr. Walter Grier's home before playing a benefit game for the Milford hospital. The players loaned to the local team have a Milford banner pinned to their uniforms. *Courtesy of William Grier.*

(BELOW) The Connie Smack candy bar was well received in Fort Myers in 1930 but never reached national distribution. *Courtesy of the author.*

(BELOW RIGHT) Baseball lifer Kid Gleason was among the most popular men in the game throughout his forty-five-year career, which ended as a coach for the Athletics. He managed the 1919 Chicago Black Sox. *Courtesy of the Library of Congress, Call #LC-F8-5271, Reproduction #LC-DIG-npc-00472.*

(ABOVE) Lefty Grove with some young admirers. Contrary to accounts depicting his surly nature, Grove was congenial with other players, youngsters, and everybody but newspapermen he didn't know. *Courtesy of Gil Dunn.*

(OPPOSITE TOP LEFT) George "Mule" Haas was the steady center fielder for the 1929–1931 pennant winners. *Courtesy of the author.*

(OPPOSITE TOP RIGHT) A dapper Mickey Cochrane waits by the team bus in Fort Myers in 1930. *Courtesy of Hugh Richards.*

(OPPOSITE BOTTOM) Four of the lesser-known but key players for the 1930–1931 AL champs: (from left) Roy Mahaffey, Eric McNair, Dib Williams, and Jim Moore. McNair had the longest career: fourteen years. *Courtesy of the author.*

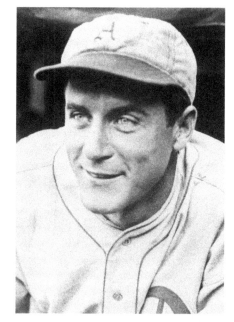

(ABOVE) Young Jimmy Foxx and his first automobile, a 1931 Studebaker President Brougham, purchased with about $2,000 of his 1930 World Series share. *Courtesy of Gil Dunn.*

(RIGHT) Jim Moore, remembered best as the man who misjudged the fly ball that led to Lefty Grove's 1–0 loss after winning sixteen in a row in 1931. *Courtesy of the author.*

(RIGHT) Connie Mack's scorecard for Game 1 of the 1930 World Series, won by Lefty Grove 5–2. Mack marked hits with a cross; dots indicate a run scored. Thus we can tell that Simmons homered in the fourth and Cochrane in the eighth. A walk was represented by a "B." Mack did not write in pinch hitters' names. *Courtesy of the author.*

(BELOW) 1931 Athletics: (Top row from left) Roy Mahaffey, Dib Williams, Roger Cramer, Waite Hoyt, Mule Haas, Hank McDonald, Lew Krausse, Joe Heving, Jim Peterson. (Middle row from left) Lefty Grove, Bing Miller, Mickey Cochrane, Eddie Collins, Connie Mack, Kid Gleason, Ed Rommel, Al Simmons, Max Bishop, Jim Moore, Jimmie Dykes. (Bottom row from left) Joe Palmisano, Eric McNair, Jimmy Foxx, Rube Walberg, Marcucci (batboy), Doc Ebling (trainer), Joe Boley, Phil Todt, Earle Mack. *Courtesy of the author.*

Not even a stock market collapse could erase Connie Mack's optimism.
Courtesy of Robert Warrington.

The Athletics' second-string catcher, Frank Bruggy, lived in nearby Eliza-beth and was aware of Rettig's pitching exploits for the Montclair Athletic Club for the past five years. Bruggy might have thought Rettig could help the A's, or Rettig might have asked the catcher to arrange a tryout for him. Whichever way it happened, accounts at the time cite Bruggy as bringing him to Connie Mack's attention. On Wednesday morning, July 19, Rettig and a friend, H. Russ Van Vleck, boarded a train for Philadelphia.

Six months later, in reply to an inquiry about Rettig from Reds' president Garry Herrmann, St. Louis Browns general manager Bob Quinn wrote: "I will give you the story as it was related to me by Connie: This young fellow blew into Philadelphia and asked for a chance to show what he could do. After joking with him a while, Connie told him to come out and work out. He said, no he did not want to do that, he wanted to pitch a regular game and show him what he could do; he did not want a contract until after he proved himself. Connie said to him, the "Browns" are in town today and Shocker is going to pitch for them. The player said that is just the club I want to work against."

That's the way Quinn relayed the conversation. Five years later Connie Mack confirmed it to Westbrook Pegler, adding, "Of course that was very strange, but so was my ball club, and I figured we would probably lose the ball game anyway." Mack sent Rettig down to get a uniform. Then, he told Pegler, he looked in his baseball guides and couldn't find any Rettig. "I decided if he was a pitcher his name was not Rettig, and if he was Rettig, he was not a pitcher." Mack did not watch Rettig warm up before the game.

It's not likely that the Browns were Rettig's first choice to pitch against. They were the strongest team that ever would wear a Browns uniform, led by .420-hitting George Sisler and Ken Williams, AL home run and RBI leader. As a team they would lead the league in batting, slugging, runs, and stolen bases. That morning they were in first place with a 1½ game lead over the Yankees. But after the St. Louis series the A's would be on the road for almost a month, and Mack didn't want to keep Rettig waiting for his big chance.

The Athletics won, 6–3. Rettig gave up a run in the first, another in the fourth, and 1 in the ninth. The A's were scoreless until the sixth, when Tilly Walker hit a 2-run homer. Walker hit another one in a 4-run eighth.

How did Rettig do it?

After the game William E. Brandt of the *Bulletin* went into the clubhouse and put that question to catcher Cy Perkins.

"He took me to a corner," Brandt wrote, "and whispered, 'Listen, I'm not knocking this guy. He certainly made those Browns look silly. He was great. But just for your own information, just so you don't turn too many somersaults in your paper, what he has is as nearly nothing as any pitcher I ever saw. No speed, no curve, no slowball, except that some were slow and some hardly moved. Nothing at all.'

"'Then how come?'

"Perk's view was that Rettig took the Browns out of stride. Their batting eyes and swings attuned to sizzling and darting curves and erratic knucklers, they swung way ahead of the Rettig zero ball."

Out of stride or not, the Browns didn't exactly look foolish. They made 9 hits. Rettig walked 5. They had him in trouble often but left 13 stranded. Many of their outs were line drives hit straight into a glove.

After the game Mack walked into the office, where John and Tom Shibe asked him who this fellow Rettig was. Mack laughed and said they had all just seen a miracle. If he had seen Rettig warm up, he never would have pitched him.

Bob Quinn told Garry Herrmann, "I made it my business to ask not only one but a dozen players what was the matter with this fellow and they said he hadn't a thing; couldn't pitch up an alley. However, there have been several of those fellows who have gotten by and we sometimes make a mistake by not giving them a look, although in this fellow's case everyone that I have talked with gives him the laugh."

George Sisler told Quinn he was willing to bet Rettig would never win another game from St. Louis or anybody else.

But this fellow had won his game, and the press got after Mack to sign him, and he had to go as high as $1,000 a month to do it, against his better judgment. The A's went west, where on July 26 Rettig's zero ball fooled the Indians, although George Uhle shut out the A's, 2–0. Five days later in Detroit the Tigers timed his nothing ball for 6 runs in 2⅓ innings. On August 5 Adolph Rettig closed out his career as he started it, against the Browns. This time he walked the first two batters, and Connie Mack cried, "Enough." Reliever Charlie Eckert's third pitch to Sisler was lined to Galloway to start a triple play. That night Connie Mack released Rettig and sent him home.

Bob Quinn offered this advice to Herrmann: "Permit me to suggest, however, that if you decide to take [Rettig] South, have a definite understanding with him before he goes, for if he pitched a couple of good games during the spring training trip, you like Connie, might be compelled to do something rash to keep him, where if you had a definite understanding with him before he started, you would know what you would have to give him. From all the information I have, he is a hundred to one shot."

Adolph Rettig went back to managing theaters in northern New Jersey. The 1922 Browns never forgot him.

The A's came home on August 15 and were 6-2, including 3 out of 4 from the Browns—without the aid of Adolph Rettig's zero ball. It was like old times at Shibe Park. Nobody was dogging it; spirits were high. No more settling torpidly into the basement; they were looking up, eyeing the sixth-place Senators only 4½ games ahead.

They looked so good that some out-of-town writers wondered in print why they were in seventh place.

And the fans were back. For a Tuesday doubleheader against Detroit, concessions manager Bob Schroeder ordered rolls and hot dogs and lunch meat and Goldenberg's Peanut Chews for about eight thousand. Almost twenty thousand showed up. And they didn't fill up the cheap seats anymore either. The one-dollar seats sold out quickly, then the seventy-five-cent seats in the grandstands. Some fans left rather than settle for the bleachers. Philadelphia was no longer a twenty-five-cent town.

It was time to expand the pavilions and double deck them. It was also time to put up the screen in front of the left-field bleachers, after a fan reached out and scooped up a ball hit by Tigers first baseman Lu Blue and the umpire gave Blue a home run and Cy Perkins squawked so loud he was thrown out of the game. When it happened a second time that day, John Shibe said the screen would go up next year.

In the spring Ban Johnson had urged fiscal caution, based on economists' predicting low crop prices for farmers, industrial stagnation, labor troubles in coal and railroads, and rising unemployment. But you couldn't tell it by the way people seemed to have money to spend. The stock market was going up, the start of a 500 percent run from 63 on the Dow to a peak of 381 in 1929, a winning streak as long as that of Jack Dunn's Orioles. Attendance was down in some cities, up in others—up 23 percent at Shibe Park. The A's net cast flow, including the sale of Dugan, topped $75,000.

Probably no other manager in history has been as pleased about finishing seventh in an eight-team league as Connie Mack was in 1922. Umpire Billy Evans worked an intense series between the Browns and Yankees in New York August 25–28, the last an 11-inning battle that put the Yankees a game and a half up in first place. Then Evans went down to Philadelphia for a series between the seventh-place A's and eighth-place Red Sox. When he came into the A's dugout before the first game, Connie Mack smiled and said, "Well, you're in for another crucial series."

A player on the bench commented, "From the sublime to the ridiculous."

Mack's smile disappeared. "Finishing in seventh place this year will be as pleasing to me as winning pennants in the old days," he snapped. It meant progress at last and better days ahead.

"The Athletics must be rated as a joke aggregation no longer," he told Evans. "My team has passed out of that class. I want to finish seventh this year. Next year I will be aiming a notch or two higher."

And they did, finishing 4 games ahead of the Red Sox. (Both Philadelphia teams rose to seventh; both Boston teams sank to eighth.) They were only 13 games behind fourth-place Cleveland.

If only Slim Harriss had lived up to expectations. . . .

15 | ON THE RISE

After five years of red ink, the Athletics had made enough money in the last three years to declare dividends totaling $150,000, half of which went to Connie Mack, and most of that into the booming stock market. Attendance was the highest since 1913. The seventh-place A's had actually outdrawn the 1914 pennant winners by 25 percent. Of course the times were as different as the two versions of the Athletics, and that helped. But some light—even a five-watt bulb—at the end of the tunnel was greeted enthusiastically by Philadelphia's American League fans. Connie Mack was ready to spend those profits—and more—to build his next champions. He was in the market as a buyer, not a seller, and the fans and the other clubs knew it.

After Eddie Rommel had won 5 in a row in May 1922, the rumor mills began reporting big cash offers dangled before Mack. There was press speculation on how much more Rommel might earn in New York or Chicago. Mack knew it for what it was: "propaganda to get the player dissatisfied."

The stories bothered Rommel. During the winter he went to see Mack. "I was worried because I had just gotten married only a few months before and I wanted to know if I should bring my wife to Philadelphia," Rommel recalled. "'You can stay here as long as you want,' he told me.

"I asked him, 'What about all those newspaper stories?' I had one sportswriter in mind particularly."

"'Pay absolutely no attention to him,' Mr. Mack said. 'He goes home to sleep every night and dreams those things. Don't let his dreams disturb you.'"

Mack was true to his word. Eddie Rommel was not for sale, would never be for sale. And now that Mack considered Rommel a great pitcher, he rewarded him by doubling his salary to $9,000.

The Athletics had no holdouts in 1923. Joe Hauser received a 50 percent raise to $4,500. Even the disappointing Slim Harriss was bumped up $500.

During the winter there was talk of the players forming a union, led by Milwaukee lawyer Raymond J. Cannon. Asked about it, Mack said, "I have no official knowledge but heard indirectly some are working in the National League toward that end. If any American League players have been approached I am unable to say one way or another." Nothing came of it.

Players complained that the top stars were getting a disproportionate amount of the total payrolls. Club owners liked publicity that showed they were paying high salaries in an effort to provide winning teams, but seeing those big numbers disturbed the lesser-paid players. That's why some owners, like Mack, never gave out salary information. He didn't care about the publicity. His customers already appreciated his efforts to build another winner.

Prices of minor league stars were going up like General Motors and RCA shares on the stock market. If you wanted to play, you had to pay. Mack didn't draft any minor leaguers in the fall of 1922. The higher classification minors had opted out of the draft, and he wasn't going grazing in the bushes. He did more business with Otto Borchert in Milwaukee, paying $7,000 and infielder Frank Callaway for center fielder Wid Matthews, a leadoff man who could bunt, run, and hit .350.

His greatest need, in addition to the perennial pitching search, was for a second baseman. Heinie Scheer didn't hit enough. When rumors circulated in New York that Mack had bought or traded for a star second baseman he remarked, "No such luck. This is one report it pains me to deny." He took a $5,000 chance on Henry Riconda, a .335-hitting second baseman from New Haven. He could move Dykes to second, but then he'd have to fill the gap at third.

Tom Turner, as much a traveling salesman as a scout for Portland, had made a trip to the East in September, promoting some merchandise. He had a third baseman for sale—Sammy Hale. The twenty-six-year-old Texan had been up with the Tigers in 1920 but was used almost entirely (52 times) as a pinch hitter. He had small hands and was considered a liability in the field. But he had batted .358 at Portland, and Turner maintained that Hale's defense had improved 100 percent since his time at Detroit. *Sporting News* Portland correspondent Lou M. Kennedy called him "the best-looking piece of baseball furniture in the league." There was a story that the Portland club had taken out a $50,000 life insurance policy on him.

According to Joe Vila, the Beavers had offered Hale to several National League clubs for $25,000 and a few players during the summer with no takers. Maybe so. It is a fact that Turner was in Philadelphia in September, and by then other clubs, said to be the White Sox and Tigers, were reportedly bidding $50,000 for Hale. Writers speculated that Mack wanted him and went higher than he had intended in order to land him—$75,000, including a few players. Mack, as usual, wouldn't discuss the financial terms of this or any deal. He considered any reported figure that included players as basically flawed. "Any player who goes to the minors in a trade has to clear waivers. That means any other major league club could have bought him for $4,000. Yet the papers might assign as much as $10,000 value to such a player who could have been bought for $4,000 by anybody."

Club secretary Bob Schroeder entered the Hale purchase in his ledger at $24,000 and two players.

Mack did not go to the second all–New York World Series. He played golf and relaxed. But he went to the minor league meetings in Louisville in early December, where Pacific Coast League managers assured him he had bought himself a real star in Hale.

Turner also had a left-handed pitcher, Rube Walberg, for sale. The twenty-six-year-old Walberg—also known as "Swede"—grew up in Pine City, Minnesota, where there was more ice fishing than baseball. He had never pitched in organized baseball before 1922. Turner rejected a Cubs bid because it didn't include enough players. Washington scout Joe Engle was interested in him. Connie Mack apparently was not. Turner went on to New York, where John McGraw, on the advice of Al Demaree, a former Giants pitcher who had briefly managed Walberg in Portland, paid "a goodly sum," said to include six players (later reported as a down payment of $15,000 and two players) for a conditional purchase with a May 15 deadline. McGraw asked Turner not to reveal the amount of cash involved. Apparently the publicity over the $75,000 he had paid for Jimmy O'Connell, added to the $65,000 plus three players valued at $2,500 each he had paid Baltimore for Jack Bentley, had proved awkward for him. When McGraw said that playing up the amount of money paid for players was "bad for the game," he may have been thinking not of the fans' reactions but his veteran players, who saw the numbers and raised their salary demands accordingly.

The American League held its February winter meeting in Philadelphia for the first time. Two items on the light agenda were voted down. Putting numbers on the uniforms was nixed because, they said, scorecards were already being printed. Posting of scorers' hit or error decisions on the score-board was turned down because it would give the gamblers one more thing to bet on. That's the reason they gave.

At the annual writers' dinner that followed, Ban Johnson introduced Ty Cobb as "the greatest ballplayer the country had ever produced," and the Detroit star who had been reviled for wreaking havoc on past A's contenders received a standing ovation, proving that bygones can sometimes really have gone by. Cobb announced that he had named one of his prized hunting dogs Connie Mack and boasted like a proud father that the dog had won the recent field trials in Augusta.

One spring in Eagle Pass, Texas, was enough for Connie Mack. He went to Montgomery, Alabama, and was so happy with the training facilities and brand new concrete enclosure, called Cramton Bowl, he quickly signed a two-year agreement. He was also enthusiastic about the condition of his youngsters, who exemplified what he called the new attitude of the modern ballplayer. "Instead of debauching and growing fat he lives a clean life and does some kind of indoor or outdoor work to keep in shape. . . . It was not that way in the old days. Then nearly everybody reported hog fat and it was June before most players were in proper shape."

Mack also declared his days of experimenting were over. He would always be willing to take a look at recommended prospects, but no longer by the dozens. There would be no more splitting of his troops into regulars and Yannigans, the two squads taking different paths north. In fact, he said, there would be no more lengthy trekking through the tank towns of the South. They would play their practice games in Montgomery and go home from there.

Clarence "Pants" Rowland, who had managed the White Sox for four years, won a world championship in 1917, and manned the first league scouting bureau, acting out of Ban Johnson's office on behalf of any American League club requesting his services, had been hired by Johnson to be an umpire. At Mack's invitation, Rowland was in Montgomery breaking in by working the A's exhibition games.

The biggest object of curiosity in camp was the size of Sammy Hale's hands. The knock on him was that they were too small. But everybody who studied his so-called "dainty fins" considered them no smaller than those of Eddie Collins or Chick Galloway.

In February Mack had signed Walter French, star halfback at West Point who was the fastest runner in college football. In 1920 against Notre Dame French had galloped 40 yards to set up a touchdown, returned a punt 60 yards for another touchdown, and kicked a field goal. But he had been outshone by George Gipp, who ran wild and threw passes and kicked extra points in Notre Dame's 27–17 win. For two years French had ripped through the Navy defense. French had been baseball coach Hans Lobert's leading hitter. But he would have been more at home in the game of twenty years earlier: a productive singles hitter, he had zero power.

French was dropped from the military academy for academic reasons, then enlisted in the army in hopes of seeking a commission through other routes. When Mack offered him $500 to sign a contract for $400 a month, he obtained a discharge from the army. In spring training French hit well, but his fielding needed improving. Mack told him, "Throw away your bat and learn to field," and sent him to Williamsport, where he would hit .363 and play alongside another rookie, George "Mule" Haas, a .342 hitter.

For the first time in a long time, the A's had a little bench strength: Riconda and Scheer could fill in at any infield post but first base; Walker, Welch, and McGowan were available for pinch-hitting and outfield duty. Visiting writers left with the impression that Mack had put together a team that would be a factor in the pennant race.

Connie Mack was a hunch player. He had one ace in Rommel, but the rest of his pitchers were a "pick-'em" group of "vergers"—always on the verge of stardom. As he doodled with his list, he noticed that three of them were H's: Hasty, Harriss, and Heimach. On a whim he decided to bypass his logical opening day pitcher—Rommel—and start the three H's in the first three games against Washington, "for no reason at all," he later told Al Horwits.

They won all three.

Rommel started the next two games and lost them both.

In their first visit to Jake Ruppert's palatial new Yankee Stadium in the Bronx the A's won 2 out of 3, the finale a 5–1 Rommel masterpiece before a Sunday crowd of 55,000, capping a record 3-game turnout of 110,000. The *Times* man, getting his first look at the "lowly Mackmen," was so impressed by the "unheralded and unknown" Wid Matthews, he gushed, "Wid ranged the outfield yesterday as if he were another Tris Speaker, lined out a clean single after the manner of George Sisler, and ran the bases like Ty Cobb," although Matthews was nipped in his Cobbian attempt to stretch a single into a double. Connie Mack demonstrated that he was still one of the league's best outfielders; in the seventh he stood up in his dark blue suit and conducted a long, methodical this-way-now-that-way maneuvering to place Matthews where he wanted him before Aaron Ward lifted a fly ball directly to where Matthews stood.

Then for the first time in eons they went west and didn't swoon. From May 12 to 20 they won 7 of 8, the pitchers averaging 1 run a game. They were giving the Yankees their only competition, and thousands of Yankee haters were rooting for them, even in New York.

John McGraw gave Rube Walberg two brief looks in relief and by May 15 decided the rookie needed more experience, and he wasn't going to get it with the Giants. McGraw was not a builder; he preferred veterans who could win now. Still, the *Times* beat writer expressed surprise that McGraw was returning the big lefty with the "frying pan" hands and speculated that some sort of "gentlemen's agreement" must have been arranged: "It seems unlikely that the Giants would not keep a string on a youngster who cost them as much as $15,000 and two other players. In any event the Giants would do well to keep an eye on this young lefthander. The Yankees were after him last year and thought they had him at one time. Here is one pitcher who will be back beneath the big tent."

In fact McGraw wanted to keep a string on Walberg. The leagues had passed a resolution in December prohibiting the release of players to any minor league that did not accept the draft, effective January 15, unless those players were declared draftable at the end of the season. The AA leagues refused to go along with the draft. The Giants asked Judge Landis if the rule applied even if the deals had been made before January 15. Landis said it did. That meant McGraw would have to come up with additional cash in lieu of the players he had intended to send in the deals for Walberg, O'Connell, and Bentley. In Walberg's case, he would have to pony up the rest of the purchase price, characterized by Portland reporter Lou M. Kennedy as "a big bundle of cash," as well. Instead he tried to skimp on the deal by returning Walberg to Portland with no further outlay and an "understood" string to pull him back, which would have been an end run around the rules. Tom Turner said no dice (well, in those gambling-sensitive days he probably said nothing doing); you either buy Walberg outright and pay for him or return him outright. McGraw sent him back stringless.

Turner immediately called Connie Mack, who was in Cleveland. Mack had no qualms about keeping Walberg with the A's and bought him for $10,000. Turner wound up with more cash and clear title to Sullivan and Yarrison, the pitchers Mack had sent to Portland. Turner found it very profitable dealing with Connie Mack. In September he sold Yarrison and shortstop Binky Jones to Brooklyn; Yarrison never won a game for the Dodgers.

Mack didn't hesitate to use Walberg starting and relieving. Rube had some wild streaks, but he also turned in some strong performances. On June 8 against the Browns he relieved Hasty in the third and held St. Louis scoreless the rest of the way, enabling the A's to come back for a ninth-inning 6–5 win. (In a rare gesture of old-fashioned gallantry, Connie Mack allowed a courtesy runner, Pat Collins, for third baseman Homer Ezzell in the second inning. Ezzell stayed in the game. In the ninth Collins pinch-hit for the pitcher and walked and was replaced by a pinch runner.) A week later Walberg gave up 1 run in 8 innings of relief in a 4–3 win over Cleveland.

Philadelphia was an Athletics town again. The papers gave front page headlines to their exploits. Connie Mack was spending money to build a winner and beginning to show results, while the product the Phillies put on the field was as shabby as their ballpark, and they sank back into the cellar.

The jokesters were quiet as the A's kept pace with the favored Yankees for the first two months. The addition of Wid Matthews and Bing Miller had made all the pitchers better; fewer balls fell safely in the outfield. The infield was tight. Six weeks into the season Christy Walsh, syndicator of ghostwritten articles for sports stars, put Babe Ruth's name to a column speculating on whether the A's had the experience to pull off a miracle. "Will their amazing enthusiasm and team morale make up for what defects they may have?"

Suddenly Connie Mack was no longer an old man who had lost it. Allusions to Mack and King Tut's tomb, which had been discovered in February, disappeared. The New York papers were full of praise for Mack's "comeback" and resurrected developing skills, predicting at least a third-place finish for the A's.

On the morning of May 26, after Rommel and Naylor had shut down the Yankees the previous two days, Frank P. O'Neill of the *New York Sun* called the ascent of the Athletics the talk of the baseball world and "the best thing that has happened in the national game in a long, long time. . . . They are young, exuberant players who thrill to the last nerve with the fierce thrill of victory."

O'Neill asked Connie Mack to explain their sudden rise:

I would first state that the pitchers are learning how to pitch. I contend that no pitcher, however great his ability, really learns his craft until he has had several seasons of big league baseball under his belt. There are men who make reputations, of course, but I exclude the comets of the game. My boys started when young and they were hammered all over for a couple of seasons but now they can play ball. . . .

I needed a third baseman last season and now I have two of them. Hale is a great ballplayer right now and Harry Riconda is but a step behind him. As long as the Athletics have Riconda they are well fortified. And Joe Hauser, the first baseman, has developed wonderfully for me. He is playing better baseball right now than ever in his life and he will not fade out. There are certain natural moves that identify the ballplayer. Joe makes these moves instinctively. I think Chick Galloway ranks with any shortstop in the business.

And another need was filled when we acquired Matthews from Milwaukee. . . Matthews is not the greatest thrower in the game but he is the best hustler, or one of the best I ever saw. He plays ball because he loves to play ball, and that kind always wins fame.

Mack was not predicting any pennants. "We'll just play the best ball we have in us and never stop trying."

Rollie Naylor was finally showing Mack the winning form he had been looking for since signing the big Texan before the Great War. Naylor was 8-1 on Saturday, June 16. That morning he was shagging flies in the outfield, where ropes had been put up in anticipation of an overflow crowd. He tripped over a rope, sprained his left leg, and was on crutches for the next five weeks. He never regained the same form, going 4-6 the rest of the year.

On June 28 the A's were 5 games back in second place. They went to New York for four games with Hale, Hauser, Miller, and Naylor all on the injured list. Freddie Heimach was playing first base, or Frank Bruggy was when he wasn't catching Rommel's knuckler. They put up a game fight, but gameness alone wasn't enough. They lost all four games and left New York still in second but 9 games out. They held second until July 7. A week later they were tied for fourth with Detroit and St. Louis. Beginning July 21 they lost 12 in a row, 10 of them at home. They broke the losing streak with a 14-4 outburst against the White Sox. Hale, Hauser, and Miller were 3-4-5 in the lineup and collected 13 hits in 15 at bats. The fans had been on Sammy Hale when he did not live up to his big price tag at first, but he broke out in this series and quieted the hecklers. But their 4-19 stretch sank them to seventh and killed attendance.

There was no single direction to point a finger of blame—no defensive lapses, severe batting slumps, or pitching collapses. Jimmie Dykes was carrying too much weight and his bat slowed. Rommel's knuckler didn't behave as tamely as last year. When injured players returned, the ones who had stepped it up fell back on their heels. They just weren't strong enough to climb any higher.

During the July–August tailspin Connie Mack blew up at Wid Matthews.

They called Matthews "Spark Plug" after a racehorse in the popular comic strip *Barney Google*. He was an aggressive base runner—sometimes unwisely so, at a time when the stolen base had been replaced by the long ball in most teams' arsenals—and a wide-ranging center fielder. But he was also truculent, hot-tempered, a clubhouse lawyer who irritated his teammates and occasionally ignored Connie Mack's directions. It all came to a head on August 2 in a game at home against Detroit that ended in the A's eleventh straight loss, 6–5. Matthews pulled a base-running boner that cost the A's a chance to win it. He came back to the bench and Mack tore into him in a tirade described by Isaminger as "remarkable for choice of words as well as length." Those who had been around Mr. Mack long enough knew that when he was really sore, the damns and hells would fly. Matthews didn't know Mack well enough to know that respect and discipline were paramount. He talked back. The next day and for four weeks thereafter McGowan was in center field.

What prompted such an unexpected outburst? Not the losing of a ball game. Matthews was a thorn of dissonance among the players. Mack knew it. Perhaps that had eroded Mack's patience, and this was his way of setting the cocky youngster back a notch.

It didn't put a damper on Spark Plug. Matthews went to the coaching lines, where, to his credit, he didn't sulk but continued to be a live wire.

President Warren G. Harding was the most avid, knowledgeable baseball fan to ever occupy the White House. A stockholder active in the management of the Marion, Ohio, club in the years before the Great War, he loved to talk about how he had promoted the sale of Jake Daubert and Wilbur Cooper to higher clubs. When winter meetings were held in Washington, the magnates were all invited to the White House. The old first baseman enjoyed visiting with players and managers at the ballpark. Ty Cobb was a special favorite. Cobb treasured a signed photo of himself and the president. He was in Philadelphia with the Tigers at the Aldine Hotel when he received a phone call from the White House notifying him of the president's death on August 2. Ban Johnson and John Heydler canceled all games the next day and the day of the funeral, August 10.

In September the A's suffered the humiliation of being no-hit twice in a week at home, on the fourth by New York's Sam Jones and on the seventh by Howard Ehmke of the Red Sox. (They really had 1 hit, a double by Harriss, against Ehmke, but Slim, unfamiliar with the intricacies of running the bases, failed to touch first and was caught in that omission. In the eighth a knee-high line drive to left that Mike Menosky dropped was called a hit; after the game the official scorer conferred with the players and changed it to an error. Four days later Ehmke almost pitched another no-hitter; a grounder by Witt, leading off the first for the Yankees, hit third baseman Howard Shanks in the chest and was called a hit. Had it happened in the ninth it would have been called an error.)

But the new improved Athletics never gave up. Unlike the cellar dwellers of the past, this was a spirited crew that did not believe in the inevitability of failure. They bounced back, won 16 of their last 26, and finished sixth—only 5½ games out of the first division.

The most satisfying victory of the waning days came on Wednesday, October 4, in New York. In front of an estimated sixty-two thousand empty seats they finally chased Carl Mays and beat him, 7–6, ending a run of 23 consecutive losses to the dour submariner.

Connie Mack wasn't on hand to see Howard Ehmke no-hit the A's on September 7. He was in Martinsburg, West Virginia, for the opening game of the Five-States Series between the pennant winners of the Blue Ridge and Eastern Shore Leagues. Mack's son Earle was the Martinsburg manager. The Dover Senators had won 24 of their last 26 to capture the Eastern Shore pennant.

Mack kept tabs on everybody and everything that was happening in the minor leagues, especially the nearby Tri-State, Blue Ridge, and Eastern Shore Leagues. He knew the Dover catcher, Frank King, had hit .322 and had a reputation as a speedy, fiery hustler but was not much with the glove. It surprised nobody when King took a swing at an umpire during an argument over a strike call and was ejected from one of the games.

Mack sat with Eddie Plank, Ban Johnson, and Tom Turner. Mack's scout Mike Drennan might well have seen King play during the season and recommended him. Tom Turner, scouting for Portland, had seen him. So had Cardinals scout Pop Kelchner, who had offered $1,500 for him and been turned down. The A's and Cardinals and at least two other clubs had him on their draft list.

What none of them except Tom Turner knew was that King was the alias of a student at Boston University who didn't want to be a catcher. He wanted to remain eligible for the football, basketball, ice hockey, baseball, and boxing teams in his senior year. His contract with Dover had guaranteed him his release at the end of the season. He had vetoed the Cardinals' purchase, turning down the Dover club's offer of half the sale price for himself. He had obtained his release on September 1, two days before the season ended—though he kept on playing because Dover needed two wins to clinch the pennant—and that same day had met Turner at the Hotel Richardson and agreed to play for Portland in 1924 for $325 a month and a $1,000 bonus. He signed the sheet of hotel stationery on which the agreement was written: Gordon S. Cochrane.

(It isn't clear why he had used a pseudonym; the previous summer he had played for Saranac Lake with other collegians in a semipro league under his real name. Maybe academia tolerated the summer college leagues as "pro lite.")

They called him Kid Cochrane at BU, but according to Cochrane's account, Tom Turner dubbed the black-haired Irishman Mickey before they parted.

Connie Mack had adapted to the slugging game. "The days when a club could squeeze or double-squeeze a team into a victory are gone forever," he said. Spotty pitching had beleaguered the A's, but too many prolonged batting slumps had kept them from a first-division finish. "It takes hitting and that is what I am after," he declared.

In November 1922 Ira Thomas had led a group that bought the last-place Shreveport Gassers in the Class A Texas League for $75,000. The Texas League was a pitchers' league, where all kinds of trick and "doctored" pitches were still legal. Thomas would manage the team as well as run the business end of it. He was also interested in getting in on the new boom, drilling for oil in East Texas. Buying leases on what might lie under a farmer's cotton field was a hotter gamble than buying a farmer's boy who could throw a ball through the side of a barn. Some of them would pay off for Thomas—fifty years later his heirs were still receiving checks from them—but the leases he got Connie Mack into never produced anything but dry holes.

A letter Thomas wrote to Connie Mack gives us some insight into the operation of an independent minor league club in those days:

Very busy with my baseball team getting the business end fixed up. We bought the club for $75,000 which included the grounds and a big piece of ground outside the park facing the street. I consider this piece of ground to be worth some money someday the way Shreveport is growing. Mr. Nelson, our secretary, and his brother took a $50,000 mortgage on the grounds. They thought I should divide up my stock to make it equal but I showed them this was wrong. I have to devote all my time to the business while they had other lines of business to make money. I own a one-third interest and had to put up my share of the balance of the $25,000, or $8,333. I got the bank here to loan me the $8,000 on my note bearing 8 percent.

The draft took Felix, our outfielder, Boston getting him. We received $2,000. We expect the player back in the spring. Now I am working on the concessions. The Coca-Cola people paid me $500 a year for two years for exclusive rights of their goods to be sold at the ballpark. I am closing a deal with a party whereby he pays me $5,000 a year subject to the Coke contract for the concessions. This concession doesn't give the scorecards. I have the Memphis card and the prices they get for space. I will start out after the first of the year to sell my scorecards. Memphis made $2,900 in ads. The fence ads were sold out last year to a baseball system for $1,200. I haven't decided whether to sell the ads myself or let them have it at the same price.

The team has one infielder, a shortstop, and three outfielders, one good one. The pitching staff is not strong made up of young players although they might be better next year. Others I have an old man and a young player.

You can see how I am sitting right now and can imagine how I feel. Still I could be worse off. I have a meeting in Louisville the 5th of December and will try to get some players.

I will stop on my way to Louisville at Grenada, Mississippi to see the pitcher that is ineligible and try to get his case before the board. I feel sure he will be reinstated. I will attend the meeting in New York and do my hardest to get some players from the majors. I have written them all a letter asking them to send me a player that needs to be developed and I will teach him the game as it is played in the majors and return them a ballplayer. I don't suppose you can help me much because you don't have many players, but I sure would appreciate whatever you can do for me. I will take anything you have and develop the players for you. I feel sure you can help me get some players from the other clubs in the American League. I have done all I could for the AL in my years as a player and since, always trying to boost the American League. I will see you in Philadelphia before the meeting as I will leave Louisville for home.

One of the club owners who sent Ira Thomas a player to be developed was Otto Borchert of Milwaukee. Al Simmons, the young Milwaukee outfielder who had written to Connie Mack seeking a tryout, had signed with the Brewers in 1922 and been farmed out to Aberdeen in the Class D Dakota League, where he hit .365. When the Brewers brought him up in September, Harry Davis was in Milwaukee negotiating the purchase of Wid Matthews. He saw Simmons in a few games and offered to buy him. Simmons was still too green for American Association pitching, but Borchert wasn't ready to part with him.

"I kept him in mind all winter," Davis told Gordon Mackay of the *Inquirer*. "In 1923 in Montgomery I asked Wid about him. He said in Milwaukee they didn't think he could hit. I got hold of Ira Thomas and told him there's a whale of a ballplayer in Milwaukee and I'm told they don't think he can hit. Grab him and take him to Shreveport."

Thomas asked for Simmons, and Borchert sent him to Shreveport. Simmons arrived on April 13 and was immediately loaned to a short-handed Bastrop team for an exhibition game. After singling as a pinch hitter in the season opener, Simmons started in left field and had 3 hits including 2 home runs. A few days later he held onto a fly ball as he crashed into the wall and fell to the ground and received a big ovation as he headed in to the dugout. When he made 3 more hits the next day, he was clearly the Gassers fans' favorite player. He cooled off at the plate, but by the end of July he was batting fourth, hitting .348. Sometimes he was joined in the outfield by a big slugger from Arkansas, Smead Jolley, who was primarily a pitcher in those days.

Ira Thomas saw greatness in the twenty-one-year-old Simmons and worked with him. When Simmons fell into the inevitable slump, Thomas told him, "A slump is just a short circuit in your nervous system. Do not play ball on your nerves."

Other lessons addressed attitude, which Thomas knew could turn average talent into a star or scuttle a superbly fitted athlete: "I have no use for a so-called good loser. A sportsman, yes, but a good loser is seldom a hard fighter."

When Simmons jogged after a ball in the outfield, Thomas told him, "A mediocre player who tries hard is more effective than a star who loafs."

Ira Thomas was a scout at heart. He wrote often to Connie Mack during the summer, reporting on his own players and others he saw in the league. In every letter he lauded Simmons, urging Mack to acquire him: "This fellow Simmons can put a kick in your team," Thomas wrote. "He can hit anything and everything, big leagues or minors. He can field, he can throw, and he's going to climb to the very top. You can't go wrong on him. If he isn't what I say about him, I'll never recommend another ballplayer."

At the same time Thomas implored Otto Borchert to give Connie Mack the first chance to buy the young outfielder. Mack sent Mike Drennan to look him over. Drennan seconded Thomas's opinion.

Thomas was a disciple of Connie Mack. He saw a natural hitter and did nothing to change him. In fact, there may not have been all that much to change. Simmons was a loose-jointed free swinger from the right side. Despite the enduring myth, Simmons was never a "foot-in-the-bucket" hitter, as the term is defined: a timid batter who bails out of the way of a curve and is likely to be curved out of any league. It certainly didn't happen in the Texas League. There was nothing timid about Al Simmons with a bat in his hands. Pitch him inside, he lined it to left. Pitch him outside, he lined it to center or right. Players who later played with him and against him, including Joe Hauser and Bill Werber, testified that Simmons "murdered the high outside fastball."

Simmons's approach to hitting was similar to that of Rogers Hornsby, who stood deep in the batters box and moved according to the pitch. Hornsby told umpire Billy Evans:

My style enables me to meet all the different pitches. The toughest pitch for any batter is the tight pitch—high or low and inside. My position takes the dynamite out of the tight pitch, and to hit the low pitch on the outside, curve or fastball, you take a full stride in the direction of the plate as the pitch is started, which brings you pretty much on a line with the plate and enables you to either push the ball to right field or drive it for distance depending on the power you put behind the effort. I have always felt that my style at the plate immediately created a hazard for the smart pitcher by practically eliminating his having a chance to pitch to your stance and make you hit the ball that he wants you to hit.

Al Simmons may not have analyzed it that way, but it worked about as well for him as it did for Hornsby over twenty-plus years. You can look it up.

No reference to any "peculiar" batting stance was found in the *Shreveport Times*, nor, for that matter, in either the *Sentinel* or *Journal* during his two September call-ups in Milwaukee. After batting .361 at Shreveport, Simmons joined the Brewers in Louisville, where Harry Bloom of the *Louisville Post* observed simply, "He looks like a dependable clubber." No feet in buckets.

Otto Borchert went to Louisville to see for himself and told the *Milwaukee Journal*, "Al had the southern folks buzzing after his first game last Thursday. He showed them that he will hit any sort of pitching."

Harry Davis went to Louisville too and followed Simmons the rest of the season. "He had improved so much he didn't look like the same player. The Yankees had just paid $50,000 for Earle Combs in Louisville and I wouldn't take him over Simmons any day."

In 24 games Simmons hit .398. The Milwaukee papers told their readers to look for the handsome, dark-haired kid they called Sheik to be in the Brewers' outfield in 1924.

Shibe Park attendance climbed another one hundred thousand in 1923. The magnificent new Yankee Stadium had produced generous checks for visiting teams. Connie Mack's boys had drawn well on the road, posting a 35-42 record, their best away from home in nine years. Connie Mack was smelling pennant, and he'd spend whatever it took for those last few pieces. As early as July he had zeroed in on his top priority: a big bat in the middle of the lineup.

Connie Mack knew Milwaukee fans, and he knew Borchert wasn't about to let a hometown hero get away without a year or two of playing for them. So, as he related it in his 1930 serialized biography, he wasn't surprised when he brought up the subject of Al Simmons to Borchert and was told, "Listen, I wouldn't part with this Milwaukee kid for all the money in the world. Think what he will mean to our gate. Born right here in Milwaukee, he will make our followers wild with his base hits. Now if there is anybody else. . . ."

Mack also knew that money was less important to Borchert than obtaining players who would help his team. Not that he would turn down cash. But he would rather get a good year or two out of a player, then sell him for a big price. He had done that with catcher Glenn Myatt, part of the Joe Hauser deal. After Myatt hit .370 in 1922, Cleveland had paid $50,000—maybe more—for him.

So Mack studied his roster, decided who was expendable and figured to be successful in the American Association, and came up with six players. They included Spark Plug Matthews, who had been a favorite in Milwaukee, was a discordant presence on the A's, and could be replaced by Simmons.

Meanwhile somebody reportedly had put a bug in Borchert's ear that Simmons would be curved out of the American Association. That might have made the Brewers' owner more receptive to Mack's next call. When he heard Mack's list of players included the popular Wid Matthews, that clinched the deal.

Al Simmons came to Philadelphia for Matthews, Frank McGowan (on option), Heinie Scheer, and $40,000, payable over two years.

There must have been "cooperation" for three players as highly regarded as Matthews, McGowan, and Scheer to clear waivers and be dealt to the minors. The aging "gentlemen" still employed the winks and nods of their younger days in the game. Judge Landis would have a devil of a time stamping it out.

A *Washington Post* column, "In the Press Box with Baxter," on December 17 surmised as much:

This means that not a club in the American League thought there was enough in [Matthews] to give him another trial in fast company. Or else Matthews did something else for which he is being severely disciplined. Several clubs in this circuit could have used him, unless there is some basic fault in his makeup. Washington, for instance, could have done worse than to give Matthews a trial, for he might easily have proven to be a more valuable man than either Leibold or Goslin. Several other clubs in the league could use some new outfield material, but for some reason every one of them fought shy of Matthews.

During the winter the *Inquirer* asked Matthews for his version of his problems with Connie Mack. This time Spark Plug was diplomatically evasive: "I will say that the season 1923 is a closed chapter as far as I am concerned. I have no alibi to offer, or suggestions to make. I will give to the Milwaukee baseball club my best this season, my very best efforts, and I hope these efforts will again place me in the major league."

(Six months later Clark Griffith would pay "a big bundle" more than the waiver price for Matthews, who would bat .302 before he was sent in August, with $35,000, to Sacramento for outfielder Earl McNeely. Again nobody claimed him on waivers. Griffith later bought him back for $5,000, but by the middle of 1925 the sparky fan favorite would be out of the major leagues for good at twenty-eight. Matthews went on to a long career as a scout.)

The Pacific Coast League was a unique circuit. The clubs played a 200-game schedule. Monday was usually a travel day, followed by a six-day stay in one city that ended with a Sunday doubleheader, often a morning and afternoon game. The arid air and short fences in Salt Lake City—306 feet down the left-field line—produced an abundance of scoring there. In 199 games the Bees scored 1,303 runs. Their team batting average was .327, slugging average .499. Not even the 1927 Yankees would reach those levels.

On May 11, 1923, Pete Schneider hit 5 home runs and a double and drove in 14 runs in Vernon's 35–11 win at Salt Lake City. Schneider, a lame-armed ex-pitcher for the Reds, was 6 for 8. Four other players hit home runs in that game: Ping Bodie and Andy High for Vernon and first baseman Sam Leslie and outfielder Paul Strand for the Bees.

Five days later the two teams hit 11 home runs in a 14–11 Vernon victory. This time Schneider was schneidered.

Players and magnates discounted Salt Lake batting averages by at least thirty points. Perhaps that's why outfielder Paul Strand could hit .384 with 28 home runs in 1922 and nobody in the major leagues bought him. Strand said that none of the conditions in Utah worked in his favor; he was a line drive hitter, not a lofter, and many of his home runs were inside the park. Or maybe it was that Bees owner William H. Lane put a $100,000 price tag on Strand and nobody was willing to pay it. Or maybe Paul Strand was a "troublemaker." When he had arrived in Salt Lake in 1921, it was his seventh team in five years. But the six-foot, round-faced twenty-nine-year-old was described at the time as a "cheery chap."

Who was Paul Strand? An anomaly who did everything left-handed but batted from the right side, he was a schoolboy pitching ace from a small town near Tacoma, Washington. He signed with Spokane in 1911 at seventeen and was drafted by the Boston Braves in 1912. He won 5 and lost 1 in relief work in 1914 and expected to pitch in the Braves' sweep of the Athletics in the 1914 World Series. But George Stallings had used only four pitchers. By 1916 Strand was in Toledo, dividing his time between pitching and the outfield until a sore arm led him to give up the toe plate in 1919. He was a slow outfielder with a fair arm, but he had been a .300 hitter before he got to Salt Lake. In 1920 at Yakima his .339 led the Western International League. The next year his Salt Lake manager, veteran outfielder Gavvy Cravath, worked on his biggest weakness, shoulder-high fastballs that had been getting him out. That led to 289 hits and a .384 average in 1922.

Connie Mack sent Harry Davis to take a look at Strand. The Salt Lake manager was Duffy Lewis, one of the peerless outfield trio of the Red Sox championship years. Lewis told Davis that Strand wouldn't make it as an outfielder, pointing out how the former pitcher still used a modified windup before he made a throw from the outfield. But Davis was looking for a hitter, not another Duffy Lewis. His report led Mack to go see for himself. When the A's left Detroit to go to Cleveland on August 17, Mack went west. He arrived in time to see Salt Lake City baseball for himself. The Bees scored 16 runs in the sixth inning of a 25–12 victory, won two the next day, 11–10 and 7–2, lost an 8–6 pitchers' duel, then won 18–16. The Bees' management said Strand was in a slump; he had only 2 or 3 hits a game.

"What impressed me about his hitting," Mack said later, "was this: if he was fooled by a curved ball the first time, he was not caught again on the same pitch for a number of times. That proved the batter."

Mack quickly spotted the flaw that Lewis was talking about and another one he considered serious but correctable. "He hesitates when about to throw and at times when on the bases." He realized that Strand would never be a good outfielder, but he could cover ground and his hitting would make up for his weaknesses. So Mack was willing to peel off the bankroll, offering an additional $10,000 if Strand would join the A's by Labor Day. Lane said no; he wanted players too. Mack had none he was ready to part with, so he rejoined the A's in Chicago without Strand.

Strand went on to bat .394 with an unprecedented 325 hits, which included 66 doubles and 43 home runs.

It took until December for Mack and Lane to agree on Hank Hulvey, a 16-7 pitcher for Martinsburg; Harry O'Neill, 10-4 for Ira Thomas at Shreveport; and infielder Pinky Pittenger, claimed by Mack on waivers from the Red Sox, and $32,500 cash. The exaggerated figures usually attached to the deal—up to $100,000—include inflated values for the three players.

In the wake of the big splash made by the purchase of Paul Strand, Connie Mack quietly bought a second baseman. Signed by Jack Dunn in 1918, Max Bishop had been with the Orioles for six years. Now twenty-four, he had batted a career-high .333 with 22 home runs. Dunn decided it was time to sell him. He had another, stronger-hitting Maryland youngster to take his place. In an unusual cash-only deal, Mack paid $20,000 for Bishop. He knew

Bishop would never be a big league slugger. He also knew he was getting his smartest player since the days of Barry and Collins.

Jack Dunn had effectively controlled both the Baltimore and Newark clubs since 1921. Some International League directors, led by Buffalo manager George Stallings, accused Dunn of syndicate baseball. When they heard that Judge Landis would be in Buffalo on May 31 for the opening of the Bisons' new stadium, the Buffalo management talked him into arranging a meeting to investigate the charges. One thing Landis learned was that not all minor league club owners were as subservient to authority as their big league counterparts.

Buffalo reporter Carl W. Chester wrote that when the subject of the Orioles' interest in other clubs in the league came up in the meeting, "it was reported that Jack Dunn put in a vigorous denial, so vigorous and so fraught with language that wouldn't sound good in church, that the walls fairly shook, and almost precipitated a riot, after which the owners of the Newark and Jersey City clubs, accompanied by Dunn, indignantly left the meeting."

No action was taken then. But at the end of the season Dunn's Baltimore partners sold their Orioles interests and openly took over the Newark club. When they denied Roy Mack a chance to buy at least 25 percent of the franchise, he resigned.

Connie Mack had no World Series jackpots to spend, but that didn't stop him from spending whatever was in the club's bank account. Once he had made up his mind to abandon the pick-'em-green approach that had worked fifteen years ago in favor of harvesting the ready-to-bloom best of the minors, he pursued his new plans with the same dedication and enthusiasm he had given to growing his own. Since 1921 he had spent about $200,000 along with players, two of whom had cost him at least $20,000 each. His critics, Joe Vila said, who had called him a tightwad, had been forced to "take to the tall timber." He was now being classed with the lavish spenders in New York and Chicago.

And he wasn't selling. Harry Schumacher of the *New York Evening Mail* reported a story of Red Sox manager Frank Chance pursuing one of Mack's players at the December New York meetings.

"The player I have in mind," Chance said, "would just about make the Sox, and if money can buy him he will be my man within another day or two. It is possible, however, that Connie won't want to sell. In that case, I will try to maneuver him into putting a seemingly exorbitant price on his man, in order to convince me that the player isn't for sale. Then I'll hand him a check for whatever amount he names and make him go through with the deal."

Mack refused to name any price.

More important than Mack's determination not to be a seller is the fact that he at last had more than one player who could make such stories credible.

16 | "HEY, BIG SPENDER"

Connie Mack regretted signing a two-year contract to train in Montgomery, Alabama. He had no complaint about the grounds or the hotel, but it was too remote from other teams' spring headquarters. All the National League teams were in California and Florida. He had been unable to persuade any of those in Florida to make the trek to Alabama. Except for a few games with the Baltimore Orioles, his Athletics had only local high school and college teams and their own Yannigans for practice games before a five-game city series with the Phillies. It wasn't enough. Spring training expenses ran to $10,000 or more; receipts from exhibition games rarely covered them all, but they helped. More important, the lack of big league competition in tune-up games hampered the honing of baseball's particular skills. That would become evident in the A's ragged start of the season.

Paul Strand reported over a week late. Strand had married during the winter and intended to bring his wife to camp. Maybe she needed longer to pack. It took them seven days to travel from eastern Washington to Montgomery.

"I was beginning to believe everything I read about myself," Strand was quoted, "and held out for $5,000 salary. I didn't get it." The reporter got it wrong or made it up; league records show Strand signed for $6,000. Mack said, "I met his terms and sent transportation money."

Most of the writers' attention focused on Al Simmons. Mack had seen Strand; he had not seen Simmons. According to the *Ledger*, "Mack does not doubt that Strand will deliver. It is Simmons who is the doubtful person." It didn't take long for Mack to change his tune. After watching Simmons run down everything in the outfield and hit line drives in all directions, he began predicting that Simmons would be the most talked-about player in the league by midseason. Little was made of Connie Mack's supposed warning for everybody to "leave Simmons alone and let him hit however he's comfortable." Mack probably never said it because nobody really tried to change the youngster. What everybody noticed was that Simmons stood straight up, his body almost facing the pitcher, squeezed his 36-inch bat at the end, swung from the tail, and seemed to throw the barrel of the bat at the pitch. On an inside pitch, he might take a small step to the left, not a big one, really more of a step forward than away, hardly a step toward the dugout like a true bucketfoot. Sometimes he made that move after the pitch went by him, not before. Standing in the corner away from the plate, he looked as if he could never reach an outside pitch, especially swinging one of the heaviest bats in the league. But his stride toward the pitch was so fast and his bat two inches longer than most, so he was hitting all kinds of pitching. (Shibe Park groundskeeper Bill McCalley said Simmons "always had me cut one-eighth inch off his new bats." But McCalley never knew why. "Superstition, I guess," he said.)

One practice pitcher said, "I tried [Simmons] on every kind of pitch, straight balls of course, but he whacked them all, especially those on the outside. Takes a good two-handed hold of the bat. Stands back a bit in the box, and then steps up to meet the ball. He also has the arms and wrists of a good hard-hitting batsman. He looks good to me."

Isaminger called him "one of the sweetest hitters Mack ever revealed on a training trip."

There are too many game accounts over the years describing his hitting high outside pitches for doubles, triples, and home runs against and over right-field fences to believe that Simmons ever "bailed out" at the plate. (Later Simmons said, "I studied movies of myself. Although my left foot would stab out toward third base, the rest of me, from the belt up, especially my wrists, arms, and shoulders, was swinging in a proper line over the plate.") Over the years whenever he went into a rare slump, he would change his stance and choke up on the bat until he came out of it.

His stance wasn't orthodox, but as Isaminger pointed out, there were golfers who ignored all the form books and still shot low scores. S. O. (Stephen) Grauley mentioned other good hitters—Bug Holliday, Gavvy Cravath, Heinie Groh, Larry Lajoie—who had peculiar stances and still did the job. Lajoie in fact had no stance at all. He stood any which way on any pitch and did all right.

American League pitchers who thought the rookie's deep unorthodox stance made him an easy out on an outside pitch soon learned their mistake. What few of them tried, to Simmons's delight, was pitching him high and tight. Sam Gibson, a 1926–1928 Detroit right-hander, was one who took that route; Simmons hated to face him and took some collars against him.

According to Simmons's recollections, Connie Mack had given him a big injection of confidence even before spring training. Impressed by the big price that had been paid for him, he decided not to sign the first contract that came in the mail.

"Mr. Mack sent me a telegram to come to Philadelphia. I walked into the deserted stands at Shibe Park, strolled to the upper section. Mr. Mack put his arm around my shoulders, looked down to left field, and said quietly, 'There's where you're going to play. Some great men have played that position and I know you can fill the job.' Right then and there I would have signed an Athletics contract for nothing, but actually he gave me exactly what I asked. [It was probably a little more: $4,125.] He showed me pictures of all his great championship teams and players. It was quite a thrill for a youngster."

Joe Hauser was now married; he and "Mama" took an apartment near Shibe Park. Simmons took a room in the neighborhood. Mack knew that Unser Choe was no chaser or drinker and paired Simmons with him on the road. Neither one could be called a big spender. Simmons early gained a reputation and some ribbing for not believing in tipping anybody for anything. He would carry his own bags on and off the trains and in the hotels. Hauser didn't teach him anything in that department but remembered counseling Simmons "not to show off out there as a rookie." He also introduced the rookie to the pleasure of smoking cigars.

Missing for the first time in six years was the thirty-six-year-old slugger Tilly Walker, released by Mack in December. Only Cy Perkins remained of the band that had wandered in the wilderness for seven years. Coach Danny Murphy was the only reminder of the good old championship days until Mack brought back Amos Strunk for pinch-hitting duties after the veteran outfielder was released by the White Sox in May.

Earle Mack joined the A's coaching staff. A playing manager in the lower minors for most of the past ten years, Earle would remain on the payroll for the next thirty years. Never a commanding presence, tolerated as an errand boy for "Daddy" more than respected by the players, Earle would often be mentioned, sometimes by his father, as the heir apparent to the managership. But it's doubtful that Connie Mack ever seriously considered it. Besides, like Queen Elizabeth II, "Daddy" had no intention of retiring until the heir apparent would be an old man himself.

As for the pitching staff, Mack was determined to shore up the weakness in his bullpen. He had fifteen pitchers in camp, including the usual allotment of amateurs and college boys whose names would appear in print but never in box scores. He hoped to carry ten of them north. Eddie Rommel was elated to discover that his knuckler, which had gone astray too often in 1923, had now returned. Bob Hasty had worked out all winter. Rollie Naylor had recovered from his knee injury when he had tripped over a rope on the field in 1923 and was working harder than anybody.

The magnet of attention among the new pitchers was Sam Gray, drafted from Fort Worth for $4,000 on Ira Thomas's recommendation. The right-hander from Texas, twenty-three, had been bought by Cleveland for a look last year and returned on June 1 without pitching an inning for the Indians. According to Thomas, Gray threw a fastball that sailed unlike any he had seen. But too often it sailed clear out of the strike zone. Gray had grown up throwing rocks at a knothole in the side of a barn. He had never pitched before he joined the army prior to the Great War and never outside of Texas since his 1921 debut in the Class D Texas-Oklahoma League.

The Athletics rode the trolley to Cramton Bowl, where Danny Murphy ran the two-a-day workouts. Most of the players were in good condition. Simmons and Hauser had played indoor baseball in Milwaukee all winter. Dykes was goaded into working harder by the arrival of Max Bishop. Connie Mack missed nothing on the field, from Rommel's throwing to Walberg's practicing his pickoff move to first while shagging flies in the outfield. Mack and Murphy worked with the pitchers, Murphy lecturing on how to cover up their pitches and not tip off what they were going to throw. Mack concentrated on their fielding. The loss of games because of pitchers' sloppy handling of bunts had always irritated him. And he knew how fragile pitchers are, especially in the early weeks of spring. A false move fielding a bunt or a hurried throw from an unnatural position and an arm may not be right for a week.

"First principle is to finish your follow-through so you can go either left or right for a ball," Mack lectured. "Second is to get to the ball as fast as you can and then get into position to throw from a natural position, so you will always have your eye on the runner as well as the ball."

When the pitchers made hasty, wild throws, he stopped the action. "Not too fast, boys. Make sure of that peg. All of your other work is lost if that throw is not true."

They experimented with the new ball with raised seams being given a trial in various camps. The pitchers liked the better grip and increased movement. They were also cheered by Ban Johnson's edict to keep balls in play longer and not throw them out because of minor marring or discoloration.

Connie Mack disagreed with that decision. He told Will Wedge of the *New York Sun* in May:

> I think that our league has made a serious mistake in letting our pitchers go as far as they have with the balls. The league thought we were using too many balls. That is wrong. I am not in favor of using balls when they get soiled or marred. There will be unavoidable "cheating" by some of the pitchers—that is, nicking and manipulating balls so that they become "sailers."
>
> No pitchers cheated last year. They all worked on their merits, which is what I prefer to see. The pitchers are only just beginning to "work" on the balls—dirty 'em up and rough 'em, that is. It is the smart pitchers who will do it. My pitchers are not doing it now, but I suppose they will unknown to me. No orders will prevent the wise ones doing it and getting away with it. Of course the new rule doesn't seem to have cut down the batting very much or cause any trouble, but my personal opinion is that it is bad policy to arm the pitchers with this potential advantage.

In the evenings Mack relaxed in the Exchange Hotel lobby and enjoyed talking about the old days. After forty years in the game he had a lot of them to remember. Asked to name the best shortstops he had seen, he chose Herman Long and Hughie Jennings as the best he had seen on a regular basis, pointing out that he had seldom seen Honus Wagner.

One night George Stallings and his Rochester club stopped at the Exchange on their way to Mobile. Stallings was seen huddling with his 1914 pitcher, Paul Strand, for an hour but seems not to have crossed paths with Mr. Mack, who never shed his dislike for the man.

As usual, they had the kind of cold wet weather the natives allowed they hadn't seen in twenty years. On March 10 they woke up to snow flurries and had to haul out the overcoats to walk the half block to the cafeteria for breakfast. Back at the hotel they sat in the lobby fanning, mostly about hitting. Puffing on his first cigar of the day, Joe Hauser claimed that Hornsby was the best hitter of them all. "We played the Cards in Galveston two years ago. Just before the game Hornsby came up to me and said, 'Joe, today I'm going to drive a base hit through each of your infielders in turn.'" He then related how Hornsby had done just that.

There was a penny weighing machine in the lobby. After Rommel discovered the idleness had caused him to gain five pounds, they coaxed Connie Mack to step on the scale. He had lost seven pounds. He probably didn't tell Mrs. Mack, who was there with her friend Mrs. Jacoby and Ida Shibe.

Some managers—McGraw and Cobb among them—had banned golf once spring training began. Mack did not. He had always left his players to condition themselves at their own pace, and if they wanted to play golf, that was okay with him, as long as they didn't overdo it and got the job done on the field. Mack and Dykes and Bruggy and Perkins enjoyed the local links more than once.

The A's did no barnstorming north. Half the team made one stop, at the Marine camp in Quantico, Virginia, for a game against the Devil Dogs as a favor to Mack's friend General Smedley Butler, who had taken a one-year leave from the Marines to head Prohibition enforcement in Philadelphia. Mack and his boys stayed for dinner and an evening of boxing matches, Frank Bruggy refereeing.

An astounding baseball-starved mob upwards of twenty-five thousand stormed Shibe Park on Saturday, April 5, to see the first game of the city series. They weren't there to see the new Phillies; there weren't any. Connie Mack's expensive new sluggers were the big attraction. Every seat was taken; every rooftop in the neighborhood was filled. Rarely would the A's draw as big a crowd during the season.

The Phillies won the game, but the fans were more interested in seeing the wonder man, the batter who stepped in the bucket and still hit the ball over the fence. At first some in the stands gave him the "Bucketfoot" business, but after he hit one into the street in the eighth inning, he didn't hear from them anymore.

In the next game Simmons made believers of everybody when he hit 2 home runs over the right-field fence in his first 2 times at bat. No right-handed hitter had ever done that in Shibe Park. Said S. O. Grauley, sports editor of the *Inquirer* known for his unembroidered accuracy, "Simmons took that one left side step from the plate when he hit those balls but if there was any weakness in this alleged 'toward-the-bucket-step,' it certainly was not apparent in the way Al met that ball."

Gordon Mackay summed him up: "Sure Simmons won't hit. Only like Dempsey."

Connie Mack said, "All that talk about his stance at the plate is rot. Simmons stands up at the plate all right to suit me, and he'll hit to any field, too.

Of course he'll be fooled, just like all of them are. But when you fool him on a bad one he'll come right back again and hit that same bad one. He suits me right down to the ground."

Harry Davis said, "He always hits that way. He'll take that step and he'll hit one into right field. Then he'll poke another into left. He'll lash the next into center field. He's a natural hitter and as soon as that boy gets a little more experience in this league and has been around a little longer, he'll have 'em all talking about him. He's a ball player."

It was one time a scout's hype would prove to be an understatement.

High hopes rode with the Athletics into Washington for the opener April 15. In February Mack had told a Knights of Columbus luncheon, "I look for the Athletics to finish second and expect to see one of the best and closest races ever held in the American League. We'll fight the Yankees tooth and nail, but I think the Yanks will win the pennant."

The players believed they could hold their own with anybody in the league if Hasty and Harriss could "find themselves" and the pitching held up. Nobody questioned Connie Mack's belief that he had the batting order of a contender: Bishop, Hale, Strand, Hauser, Simmons, Miller, Galloway, and Perkins, with Welch and Dykes in reserve. All were right-handed batters except Bishop and Hauser.

Even higher hopes reigned in the capital, where Clark Griffith had surprised all of baseball by appointing his twenty-seven-year-old second baseman Stanley "Bucky" Harris as the new manager. After three years of chasing the Yankees, the Senators and Tigers each believed they could topple the champs, Babe Ruth and all. Calvin Coolidge and his wife, Grace, a lifelong Red Sox fan, were among the Washington turnout of twenty-six thousand who watched Walter Johnson pitch his fifteenth opener. He was never better, blanking the A's 4–0, striking out 8.

Undaunted, the A's came back to take the next 2, Hauser scoring the winning run in the last game with some aggressive base running. With 2 out, Simmons and Hauser on first and third, Mack called for a double steal. While the Washington pitcher, Paul Zahniser, held the ball, Simmons broke from first and Hauser from third. The pitcher hesitated, then threw to second. Simmons was tagged for the third out but not before Unser Choe had chugged across the plate.

On Sunday, April 20, the A's traveled from Boston to New Haven to honor the late Bill Donovan, who had been killed in a train wreck in December.

Despite a steady rain, five thousand people, including Judge Landis, turned out to see the unveiling of a memorial plaque, and the Athletics defeat the Eastern League nine, 11–4. All the receipts went to the family of the Philadelphia-born Tigers' pitching mainstay and nemesis of Connie Mack's up-and-coming young teams of fifteen years earlier.

The A's won 5 of 7 from the ambitious Senators, who rode Simmons for his unusual stance. The *Post* joined the chorus, stating that "Simmons stands at the plate with one foot in the bucket." Two months into the season they would still be referring to him as "Water Bucket" Al Simmons. Even the Philadelphia papers routinely called him Bucketfoot Simmons. It was true; that's the way he stood facing the pitcher—until the pitcher threw the ball. Unlike most sluggers who kept the bat on their shoulder until the pitcher threw, he was what Clark Griffith called a "double swinger," a hitter who held the bat out in front of him, bringing it back while the pitch was coming toward him, then slapping back at it. Griffith believed such hitters never hit well in the spring; it took them longer to get their timing right against fastball pitchers.

Simmons's response: on April 25 he hit a 3-run home run "against a stiff breeze into the left field bleachers" off Walter Johnson, and the next day hit another one, then capped his day with a long running catch of a foul ball and "rolled up against the concrete amid cheers. It was some catch," said the *Post*.

The riding bothered Simmons at first, but a bigger problem for him was the white shirts worn by bleacher fans in Griffith Stadium and Fenway Park. When he complained about it one day on the bench in Boston, Connie Mack told him to forget the excuses; just concentrate on what you're up at bat to do. He never forgot that admonition.

The A's then went into New York, where rookie Dennis Burns, up from Shreveport, suffered a case of stage fright in front of fifty thousand spectators and failed to record an out in the first inning of an 11–2 defeat, the first of 12 in a row that buried them in the basement like a vampire at noon.

Fred Lieb watched them lose to the Yankees—number 7 in the streak—and wrote them off, calling Connie Mack "the tragedian of the ball field":

Tall, thin and sorrowful, he peered out of the Athletics' dugout at the Yankee Stadium yesterday. He stood on the front door stoop, bent over in an angle of seventy-five degrees, waving instructions to his gray clad gladiators with a score card.

Already those same players have taken on the apathetic attitude of a Philadelphia tailender. Mack stuck there, as though rooted to the concrete, for six and a half innings, and then a Yankee fusillade, in which four former Athletics drove out scorching hits, sent him into the seclusion of the innermost recesses of his cavern.

The morning after the Yankees pinned loss number 9 on them, 7–4, Ford C. Frick wrote off the A's in a column headlined "Connie Mack Seems Doomed to Disappointment":

> For ten years, since 1914, each season has found Connie sitting there in the dugout, watching and hoping—hoping for the thrill of another winner, hoping for the breaks that never come.
>
> And each year has seen his vision fade away into the mist of disappointment, and his hopes die before the specter of a tail-end aggregation. Connie has not complained. He is too wise in the ways of baseball for that. But hiding his regret he has gone out to build anew.
>
> This year he thought he had succeeded. His hopes, his ambitions and his dollars had gone into the building of his club. And Connie looked upon his work and was satisfied. But when the season opened it was the same story. Unexpected weakness developed in a defense that was supposedly impregnable. Pitchers, supposedly good, weakened, and hitters, nominally powerful, slumped at moments when hits meant runs and ball games. . . .
>
> What thoughts went shooting through Connie's agile mind and what bitterness was hidden there behind the quiet mask of his face as he watched? It would be interesting to know—and it would be interesting to know, too, what dreams have been shattered by the slump that has been as startling as it was unexpected. Interesting but pathetic! . . .
>
> Today Connie Mack will be down there in the dugout again, his face set, his eyes somber—watching and waiting and hoping, even as he has waited and hoped through ten long seasons of disappointment.

From what we know of the man, we can guess that he was not wasting his strength with anger or regret or frustration but was intently assessing the men he had, thinking, as always, of where improvement was needed and how best to accomplish it. And those who knew him day in and day out at the time, knew that even seven years in the cellar had not wilted his spirit nor dulled his agile mind, and today's setbacks wouldn't either.

Mack took the blame for the poor start. "You can be an old timer but still learn in baseball. I learned that good practice games down South are more important than training weather. . . . When the real thing was on, my men did not measure up to the competition."

Max Bishop was in poor health and never played up to form. Hauser, Hale, Simmons, and Dykes were the only ones hitting. Mack dropped Strand to seventh, then benched him and put Bug Welch in the outfield. The pitching was terrible, the bats dead with men on base, costing them frequent 1-run losses. Mack gave Rube Walberg two starts; he didn't get out of the second inning in either one. Red Smith later wrote that after Mack yanked Walberg on May 15, the manager told him to "keep on going, out of the dugout and out of my sight." Rube kept going, farmed out to Milwaukee.

Joe Vila resurrected the rumors that a discouraged Mack was seriously thinking of retiring in favor of a younger man. Vila's latest imaginative fling at forecasting in the *New York Sun* on May 26 concluded: "The Athletics have broken Mack's heart this year. Instead of battling among the first-division contenders, the Mackmen are deeply submerged in last place and their future seems hopeless. American League men have been slow to arrive at the conclusion that Mack is too old to stand the wear and tear of a pennant campaign, but now they are hoping that Connie will see the light and select a successor for 1925."

So much written, so little known.

Once again the A's were the butt of jokes. On May 27 *You Know Me, Al*, a comic strip written by Ring Lardner, featured two card-playing ballplayers and the following dialogue:

> "*How long since the Athaletics win a pennant?*"
> "*They win their last pennant in 1914. That's when they had Collins and Baker and McInnis and Bush and that bunch.*"
> "*Why did they let go all them stars?*"
> "*They were too good. The Philadelphia fans wouldn't come out no more. They were tired of seein' the home team win.*"
> "*They must be rested up by this time!!*"

Stan Baumgartner worked at the *Public Ledger* covering football during the off-season. The football, baseball, and basketball star at the University of Chicago had had five brief discouraging trials with the Phillies, the last in 1922. Every manager the southpaw played for tried to change his delivery and he never pitched his own way—an underhand crossfire motion—until he was sent down to New Haven in 1923. He credited manager Bill Donovan with building his confidence. "He would shoot me in against a club," Baumgartner told Gordon Mackay, "and when he felt that I might wobble, he would take me out. In other words, he never let me get lambasted so that I would lose confidence in my own ability." Baumgartner won 23 and lost 10. But he was twenty-nine, and the scouts ignored him. Given permission to negotiate his own sale, he went first to John McGraw, who told him the Giants had all the pitchers they needed. Then he persuaded Connie Mack to take a chance on him, harking back to their meeting in 1910, when he was a struggling high school pitcher seeking advice. Mack agreed to give him a trial—Baumgartner said until May 31—and sent pitcher Frank Loftus to New Haven.

Mack handled Baumgartner the same as Donovan had done. He slipped him into the opener in Washington to mop up in the last inning of the loss to Walter Johnson. Two days later Baumgartner relieved Fred Heimach in the fourth and blanked the Senators until the A's took a 4–3 lead in the eighth. When Baumgartner walked the lead-off man in the bottom of the eighth, Mack immediately sent in Harriss. He knew what blowing the lead would do to what former Cubbie Del Howard called "the old con-fee-dence." Harriss preserved Baumgartner's first win.

On May 14 Mack let Baumgartner stay in to finish 4 scoreless innings against Detroit in a 5–4 win that ended the A's 12-game losing streak. After the game the manager said, "Go downtown to Wanamaker's tomorrow and get yourself a suit of clothes and charge it to me."

"What kind of suit?"

"A real good suit," Mack said.

The next day the pitcher picked out the best English tweed in the store with two pairs of pants—a $150 job. The first time he wore it, Mack looked it over. "That is a good suit," he said.

But Baumgartner was still on the fringe as the deadline neared. With a poor memory for most of the details, Baumgartner recalled the events of May 30 in a 1945 column. Lightly edited, it went something like this:

The A's were in New York for a Memorial Day doubleheader. Herb Pennock shut them out in the opener, in which Ruth hit his 250th home run. Between games Baumgartner found a railroad ticket to New Haven in his locker.

As Eddie Rommel started the nightcap for the A's, Connie Mack tapped Baumgartner on the shoulder. "You're the relief pitcher."

The Yankees led 4–2 when Mack sent up a pinch hitter for Rommel in the seventh. Baumgartner relieved. Frank Bruggy was the catcher. In the eighth Bing Miller hit a 3-run home run and the A's took the lead 5–4. The closer hadn't been invented yet. Baumgartner took the lead into the last of the ninth. After two men went out, Baumgartner faced three ex-A's. Bush pinch-hit and legged out an infield single. Schang pinch-hit and walked. Dugan was hit by a pitch.

The bases were loaded and Babe Ruth was up, and the fifty thousand fans were on their feet in full throat.

Bruggy looked at Connie Mack for the signal for a new pitcher. Mack got to his feet. Instead of waving in a new pitcher, Mack shook his fist at Ruth.

"The pitcher watched that fist and a wave of confidence surged up within him," Baumgartner wrote.

Up in the press box, an old-timer commented, "[Ruth]'ll swing at anything."

Bruggy called for nothing but curves.

The New York Times account said, "Ruth swung at one fairly near the plate and missed. He couldn't have reached the second pitch with an oar, and he would have needed both an oar and a shovel to reach the third one, which almost tore up the turf two feet outside the plate. . . . Connie Mack himself could have fanned the big slugger at that moment."

"Connie Mack draped an arm around Stan Baumgartner's shoulder," the pitcher recalled. "'Give me that ticket to New Haven,' he whispered. 'You won't need it now.'"

At the end of the season Mack sent a check for $4,000 to New Haven owner George Weiss.

After three weeks of bullpen duty, Baumgartner asked for a start.

"Do you really want to start?" Mack asked.

Baumgartner nodded.

Mack smiled. "How about tomorrow against Walter Johnson?"

It was June 26 at Washington. Before a big-for-Washington crowd of twenty-three thousand, which included President Coolidge and his family and a lady in Section D of the upper tier who was seen smoking a cigarette—an act considered scandalous enough to warrant a mention in the game coverage—the A's ran into Walter Johnson in top form and lost, 5–0.

Baumgartner had to wait until July 4 for his first complete game win. He went on to his biggest season in the sun. He wound up 13-6 with the best earned run average—2.88—on the staff, then went back to writing football for the Ledger in the fall.

Mack brought along Sam Gray the same way. He waited until May 31 to give him his first big league start. Despite the shock of seeing Babe Ruth hit one of his sailing fastballs halfway up Yankee Stadium's expansive center-field bleachers, Gray won, 5–3. After a few rocky outings when he escaped the decisions, Gray beat the Yankees at home, 10–5, giving up another Ruth homer. He followed that with back-to-back shutouts, and Mack proclaimed him a surefire star of the future.

Another rookie traveled with the A's that summer—eleven-year-old Connie Mack Jr. For the next five years the manager's son would realize most any boy's dream, traveling with a big league club. "I was just like a member of the team," he later recalled. "The Athletics just loved to play cards. When a game was rained out, the word quickly spread about whose room the game was in. I think they taught me to play fantan just so they could take my meal money. Even then, Dad always treated me like an equal. After the games, he would talk to me like I was a man. Over dinner, he would discuss the day's game, the strategy that worked and the things that didn't. He would talk over one particular play in great detail and, always, the talk was about baseball."

Connie also remembered that he was free to order an ice cream sundae with chocolate syrup every night on the road.

"After dinner, we would go to the movies. Dad liked rough, tough action pictures, and Charles Bickford was his favorite actor."

At the end of June the A's were still in last place. On the morning of June 30 only 6 games separated the first-place Yankees and seventh-place Indians. The A's lagged 8 games behind Cleveland. They looked forward to an extended 30-game home stand to move up.

Paul Strand had been benched again. The joke making the rounds was, "He couldn't hit the ground if he jumped off the roof of the dugout." Connie Mack had joined the crowd he hadn't particularly cared to join—clubs paying big bucks for big stars from the Pacific Coast League and watching them bomb. It was no consolation that he wasn't alone: McGraw's high-priced Jimmy O'Connell had done nothing; Comiskey's $100,000 third baseman, Willie Kamm, was hitting .250.

They were all gamblers, Mack as much as any of them. You had to be if you were in this business of dealing in human potential. They all made mistakes, the same kind that would be made three generations later by geniuses with computers. Mack wasn't a gambler in the usual sense. The last time he had bet on a horse was in 1905 in New Orleans, where, he later told Westbrook Pegler, he lost $300 and never bet again. But when it came to putting together a championship club, he would rather make the bet and lose than not make the bet at all. He would be that way as long as he was in the game.

Injuries forced Mack into another juggling routine. He moved Simmons to center field. Miller switched to left field. Frank Welch was in right. When Miller, Dykes, and Galloway were sidelined, Mack put Sammy Hale in left, Riconda on third, and John Chapman at short—not the lineup he had envisioned. One day he was reduced to using a semipro pickup, Joe Green, as a pinch hitter, the only at bat Green would see in the big leagues. After catching almost every game for the past four years, Cy Perkins was slowing down although he was only twenty-eight.

Rommel's knuckler was behaving. On May 26 he dispatched the Browns, 2–1, in a seventy-two-minute game. Gray and Baumgartner were pitching well. Heimach and Harriss were in and out, more often out than in. Warming up in the bullpen before a game, Harriss had all the stuff in the world, but he seemed to leave it there when the game began. He never learned how to hold men on base. He would stare at a runner on first but never move his right foot off the rubber, even when the runner took off for second. And there were mental lapses. "Slim usually beats himself," Mack said. "He gets in a pinch and lays in a ball which defeats him." One day Harriss was being hit hard. Mack pulled him in the third inning, even though the A's were leading. Harriss stormed into the dugout complaining about being taken out. Instead of pointing a bony index finger at the 6-foot-6 pitcher, Mack picked up a fungo bat and chased him off the bench. Hasty and Naylor were being battered. Bob Hasty was a mystery; he worked hard, had plenty of stuff, took care of himself, but couldn't win.

And now nobody was hitting except Simmons. They were shut out 10 times by July 1, most in the league. Their .243 batting average was 30 points lower than the next lowest in the league.

Joe Hauser was hitting the long ball but little else, batting around .250. Mack saw a flaw in his swing. "Joe," he said, "when you go up to bat, leave the bat on your shoulder and swing from there. Don't wiggle it or move it before you swing."

Unser Choe listened. In one week he raised his batting average 30 points to .280. He began hitting lefties and righties alike. He would hit as many home runs (3) off lefty Joe Shaute as he did against Walter Johnson.

Paul Strand was batting .228 and had yet to hit a home run. Strand seemed to be the epitome of the minor league mentality. With no pressure he could hit any old apple. In the big leagues he couldn't hit a grapefruit. He was a

consistent .300 hitter in the minors before Mack bought him and after Mack
sent him back, never to return to the big time. On June 28 Mack gave up
on him and offered him with $10,000 to Toledo for outfielder Bill Lamar.
Toledo said no; Lamar was batting .364 and they didn't want to part with
him. However, if Mack could spare a pitcher. . . .

Mack added Rollie Naylor.

Isaminger said the next day he found a disconsolate Connie Mack in the
parlor car of a New York–bound train. "I am through paying skyscraper
prices for minor league players," he quoted Mack. "I am going back to my
old policy of getting players off the independent or college diamonds and
developing them myself."

Maybe, in a funk of disappointment over the failure of Strand, he put
voice to his thoughts of those good old Collins-Barry-McInnis days. But
he didn't mean it. He was on his way to Jersey City to watch Lefty Groves
pitch for Baltimore.

Bill Lamar was also a bit of a retread with a big reputation in the minor
and after-hours leagues that earned him the nickname Good Time Bill.
Mack was taking a chance bringing him to Philadelphia, considered a wide
open town that took Prohibition lightly. Arms control talks proposed in
Geneva would have been more appropriate for Philadelphia, where the
gangland murder rate was second only to Chicago. No matter how often
the speakeasies were raided, they reopened the next day. Judges handed out
light fines. There were plenty of drugstore oases offering poisonous libations,
and empathetic physicians willing to prescribe a 40 proof remedy for a dry
throat condition.

Bill Lamar had broken in with the Yankees at twenty in 1917, was shunted to
the Red Sox in May 1919 and to Brooklyn in March 1920 without impressing
anybody. He had led the American Association at .391 in 1923 and nobody
bought him, maybe because his arm was lame. After a winter of treatments,
his wing was strong again. He would add another bat from the left side.

Lamar jump-started the offense. He joined the team July 2 and led the
attack in winning 4 of the next 5. He and Hauser both hit home runs in the
morning game of July 4, a day of triumphs for Baumgartner and Rommel.

But the best they could do on their lengthy home stand was break even
in 30 games, and they left town July 25 still in the cellar with the hecklers
riding them and the *Evening Ledger* printing letters from fans seeking Connie Mack's scalp. For all the money he had spent, there seemed to be little
to show for it.

Mack didn't complain, but he did crack the veneer that covered his feelings enough to let the public know that losing got to him too: "You can't blame a patron for kicking when we don't win, but I wish he realized that failure hurts me worse than anybody else. I have been too long in baseball to object to criticism, and my only answer is to get the team out of the cellar rather than to resent it with words."

Just before they left town, Connie Mack made a small purchase. Frank Baker, the home run hero of Mack's 1910–1914 machine, had really finally retired after the 1922 season. He'd been persuaded to manage the Easton, Maryland, team in the Class D Eastern Shore League, about ten miles from his home. Baker had signed a sixteen-year-old catcher, a farm boy from a tiny town up the road called Sudlersville. His name was Jimmy Foxx. He had played infield and outfield, pitched, and caught for his high school and town teams, had bulging forearms and biceps built by lifting milk cans and heaving hay bales, wrists stronger even than Baker's, a cannon for an arm, and the fastest legs in state high school track competition.

Easton needed a catcher and that's where Jimmy played. The moon-faced, blue-eyed, sweet-tempered kid with the ever-ready smile became the fans' favorite, hitting longer wallops than anybody in Easton could remember. Baker later said he saw the youngster was a natural hitter and he never offered any hitting advice except "to bust away at the first one that looked good."

According to Bill Werber, who shared many a duck blind and goose pit hunting with Baker on the Choptank River in later years, Baker said he first offered Foxx to his last team, the Yankees, when they were at Shibe Park. Miller Huggins was in a tight battle for his fourth straight pennant and wasn't thinking about schoolboys. He told Baker he couldn't use the lad. Baker said he then walked across the field to the A's dugout and told Connie Mack about Foxx. The only time this could have happened was June 30–July 3, although Easton played every day the Yankees were at Shibe Park.

If Baker went to see Connie Mack about Foxx, it probably happened on July 14, when Detroit was at Philadelphia and Easton had the day off. Connie Mack, for all his immediate needs, was always looking a few years ahead. Ever the teacher, he had not lost—would never lose—his love for finding raw, unpolished youths with natural ability and slowly developing them into champions. The story, as often told, is that Mack said, "Bake, if he's as good as you say, I'll take him. Go up to the office and get a check."

It's most likely that Mack's chief scout, Mike Drennan, saw Foxx in Easton. The Eastern Shore League, just south of Philadelphia, was part of his regular beat. There were reports in a few papers that Drennan had watched Foxx in several games in July and advised Mack to grab him. Other scouts prowled the small towns of Maryland, Virginia, and Delaware, where rivalries among town teams manned by brawny farmers were fierce. Nobody knows how many scouts' reports might have been filed on Foxx.

However Baker remembered it twenty-five years later or Bill Werber remembered it forty years after that, Washington and Baltimore papers reported the sale as taking place on July 30, negotiated by Drennan in Easton. The A's had left Philadelphia July 25 and were in Cleveland at the time. The commissioner's office recorded the agreement on August 1.

The price was $2,000.

After the Five-States championship series, in which Foxx hit 4 home runs, Mack invited him to join the A's for the last western swing of the season and put him in the care of Cy Perkins.

The A's emerged from the basement temporarily on August 8 on the wings of their third straight win over St. Louis. The offense was finally clicking the way Connie Mack had expected. Six hitters would finish over .300, Joe Hauser at .288. On August 2 Hauser hit 3 home runs in Cleveland; a fourth drive just missed, hitting the top of the screen in right-center and bouncing back for a double. His 27 home runs (the record for a Philadelphia Athletics left-handed batter) were second to Ruth's 46, and his 115 runs batted in were fourth in the league. There was plenty of life and chatter on the bench, led by Jimmie Dykes, who never shut up before, during, or after a game. A story he told Arthur Daley of the *Times* thirty-seven years later is credible:

> One day in Philadelphia I backed into right field with the Babe at bat and the bases full. So did Joe Hauser, our first baseman. Then I noticed Connie gesturing with his scorecard, pulling me in. I gave him the "Who, me?" business but he brought me in on the dirt. Then he did the same to Hauser. I cupped my glove and shouted to Hauser.
>
> "Hey, Dutchman," I said. "Which one of us does Connie want to get killed?"
>
> Fortunately for Joe and me, the Babe flied out. I asked Connie about it later.
>
> "I just had a hunch that he might hit a grounder," he said.

"But did you ever think how hard he might have hit it?" I said politely "He could have torn either of us apart."

Connie Mack appreciated Jimmie Dykes's spirit, but when Dykes got out of line, the Old Man didn't hesitate to put him in his place. On August 15 against Detroit, the hot-tempered Connie Mack of the nineteenth century erupted. The Athletics were trailing 4–2 in the ninth. Syl Johnson was pitching for the Tigers. Al Simmons led off with a double. Dykes was up next. Connie Mack called on Joe Hauser to pinch-hit for him. Dykes, red with anger, slung his bat. It sailed into the dugout and landed near enough to Mack to make him jump out of the way. Dykes stormed into the clubhouse, showered and dressed, and waited for the game to end (they lost 4–3).

"That was one of the biggest mistakes I ever made," he told Ed Pollock almost forty years later. "I should have left the park right away. . . . When the game was over, in he came. Wow. Did he ever let me have it. He really gave it to me. . . . When he got mad, I don't know anyone who could handle him."

Even Mr. Mack was rekindling that old excitement from the days when his team was playing well and there was something at stake. Unser Choe recalled, "One day an ump was missing a lot of balls and strikes, and I heard Connie Mack mutter, 'Goddammit, those are terrible calls.' I heard him say it. Ja ja."

On August 16 they won two from Cleveland and evacuated the basement for good. Ed Rommel started both games but had to be rescued in the second by Sammy Gray, who got the win. Mack had his sights on fifth place and better than the .454 of 1923.

On the last long home stand in August they were 10-5. They had their most successful western trip in years, winning 9 of 12, including a sweep of the Tigers that knocked Detroit out of the race, and they came home for a final series against the Yankees in fifth place, only 3 games out of the first division. That's where they finished: 71-81, .467. The failure of Hasty and Harriss had cost them a shot at a slice of the World Series pie.

There were plenty of reasons for a capacity crowd to turn out on Saturday, September 27. For one thing, the A's had a chance to be the spoilers against the hated Yankees. The day before Herb Pennock had defeated them, 7–1, while the Red Sox stopped Walter Johnson's 14-game winning streak, 2–1. Washington now led New York by 1 game with 3 to play.

For another, it was Boosters Association Day to honor the home team's most valuable player, selected by the city's sportswriters. Joe Hauser was the fans' favorite. The six writers met and cast their ballots just before the game. Using a point system, the results were Dykes 22, Simmons 20, Hauser 19. The versatile Dykes had taken over for Bishop at second base and done a bang-up job, batting .312. When a gray Flint sedan was wheeled out to home plate and Jimmie Dykes was announced as the winner, some boos, not all with German accents, were heard among the twenty-five thousand spectators. Connie Mack was also presented a $500 platinum watch by the Boosters.

Not since the 1913 World Series, when they had routed John McGraw's Giants, had Shibe Park been rocked by so boisterous a gathering. When Babe Ruth beat out a bunt in the first inning, they whistled and applauded almost as enthusiastically as if he had hit one over the neighborhood streets and houses. They hollered themselves hoarse when the A's unloaded on Joe Bush for 3 runs in the bottom of the first and cheered when the scoreboard showed Washington had scored 2 in the first at Boston and again when the Senators scored in the fifth and sixth to lead 7–5. They laughed and hooted when Ruth took a called third strike in the eighth and tossed his bat almost as high in the air as one of his skyscraper pop-ups. They relaxed as Rommel took a 4–1 lead into the ninth, then grew quiet and tense as the Yankees scored twice. With runners on first and third and 2 outs, Whitey Witt's grounder ended the game and uncorked the kind of celebration that championships inspire.

At the end of the day the Senators had a 2-game lead with two to play. When they won the next day, Washington clinched its first pennant. The town where politics was the primary industry celebrated its heroes with as much civic pride as any "normal" city in the country. President Coolidge made more lengthy statements about the team and the World Series than he did on any other subject all year.

Nobody in baseball was happier over Clark Griffith's success than his oldest and closest friend, Connie Mack. In a way, Mack had aided the Senators more than just by beating the Yankees in the last game of the season (the last two at Philadelphia were rained out).

Back in 1921 a Philadelphia scout had secured an option to buy a young shortstop in Peoria named Ossie Bluege. When Bluege went out with an ankle injury, the scout let the option expire. A Washington scout later was convinced the injury had healed, and the Senators bought him. Bluege became their regular third baseman in 1923 and remained for the next sixteen years.

In 1923 Mike Drennan was in Little Rock to look over a big right-hander, Fred Marberry. On that particular day Marberry's teammates made a bunch of errors behind him. The pitcher walked off the field after the fifth inning and refused to continue. Drennan crossed him off as too temperamental. Senators scout Joe Engle recommended Marberry to Griffith. Nicknamed Firpo, he became an early relief specialist while starting frequently as well.

The chain begun by Mack's return of Wid Matthews to Milwaukee the previous year had led to Washington's midseason acquisition of Earl McNeely, who hit .330 for the Senators and would drive in the winning run in Game 7 of the World Series.

In 1922 Harry Davis scouted two sophomore pitchers at Swarthmore, Curly Ogden and George Earnshaw. Mack looked them over, signed Ogden, and advised Earnshaw to finish his education. Ogden spent parts of two seasons with the A's before starting the 1924 season with them. He was 0-3 in May, when Mack asked waivers on him to farm him out. Griffith claimed him. The Senators were 9-1 in his first 10 starts, including three shutouts. (Earnshaw eventually signed with Baltimore but didn't join them until 1924.)

Ogden's explanation for the sudden turnaround in his performance is a lesson in why pitchers give managers gray hairs. Ogden was Connie Mack's kind of player, a college man who brought mental and physical strengths to the task. In his morning meetings Mack went over the opposing batters' weaknesses, what they liked, and what gave them the most trouble. To Mack's dismay Ogden ignored it all. He went out and tried to throw everything past the hitters as hard as he could. The balls came back at him just as fast.

"I wanted to win for Connie," Ogden told Gordon Mackay of the *Inquirer*. "I tried too hard and that's what ruined me."

It wasn't until Curly Ogden was on the train to Washington that he realized maybe Mr. Mack knew what he was talking about. "I took out an old envelope and jotted down the names of six or seven players on each club and the weakness of each man." He became a pitcher, not a thrower, mixing speeds and locations "instead of trying to stick everything past the batters and putting all that I had on each ball."

But he never had another year like this one.

While Connie Mack relaxed and played golf at Pine Valley, Ed Rommel led a barnstorming tour through New Jersey and Pennsylvania, clearing better than $100 a day for each player. After years of saying no, the A's allowed football on the field at Shibe Park, permitting Villanova to play there.

Anticipating an end to the A's pennant drought, John Shibe was busy adding upper decks to the pavilions on the left and right sides and left-field bleachers, at a cost of more than $600,000 borrowed from banks. The expanded capacity of thirty-eight thousand made it the largest American League ballpark except for Yankee Stadium until Comiskey completely double-decked his Chicago park. Shibe's project raised a ruckus with the labor unions that generated more phone calls, correspondence, councils, and meetings than an international peace conference and almost led to a national union boycott of the Athletics.

On June 6, 1910, the league had entered into an agreement with the American Federation of Labor that all future stadium building projects would be done by union labor. John Shibe never heard of it. Besides, the only steel works in the city that could make the necessary support beams were all open non-union shops. And they wouldn't make the beams unless they could also erect them. Shibe contracted with Belmont Iron Works to do the job beginning with the right-field stands. He agreed that union men could do all the rest of the work.

The unions apparently said okay, but only if Belmont's non-union hoisting engineers were prohibited from finishing their part of the job. Belmont said it would sue for breach of contract. Shibe's lawyers said Belmont would win. The meetings, phone calls, and letters continued from January into April, with Ban Johnson in the middle of it all. The local unions agreed to finish the job, then didn't show up because central headquarters said no. So Shibe, with Ban Johnson's assurance that AFL president William Green would see that no boycott was voted, finished the job with non-union labor.

Ford was producing 7,000 cars and trucks and 450 tractors a day to keep up with the demand. The automobile enabled more fans to come to games from out of town, where there was no train service. (It worked two ways; people could drive to Shibe Park, but they could also drive out of the city to the Jersey shore.)

With more people arriving in automobiles, parking became scarce on the streets around the grounds. Shibe built a parking garage, complete with service station (and room for his racing boats) under the stands. He did it all with non-union labor; union councils would picket wherever the A's played throughout the 1925 season. A few years later Shibe would add 750 reserved seats by inserting a mezzanine level under the upper deck behind home plate. But its occupants couldn't see balls hit into the air, and it was rarely used. By 1929 the grandstand would be enlarged by another 3,500 seats. They had no more room to expand on the city block they occupied.

"What are you going to do when this site gets too small?" Isaminger asked him.

"Find a bigger site in the outskirts of the city," Shibe replied.

John Shibe built a new press box on the roof—a climb of 147 steps—with good views from all seats, a workroom, showers, and a locker room. Anticipating a deal whereby the Phillies would move to Shibe Park, he built a clubhouse for them under the left-field stands and elaborate offices where a furniture store had been on the Lehigh Avenue side. But he died before the Phillies would occupy them a dozen years later.

For the first time, the word "rebuilding" in *Sporting News* headlines jumped from the Philadelphia to the New York column. Connie Mack considered the Yankees on the decline. Of the eight pitchers in the league who had been active ten years earlier, the Yankees had started the season with four of them: Bob Shawkey, Herb Pennock, Joe Bush, and Sam Jones.

In August Connie Mack told Sid C. Keener of the *St. Louis Times* that he was satisfied with everything else but needed "one powerful pitcher. If I can find one this winter I may be closer to the 1925 pennant than people expect me to be."

For a few years he had been prodding Jack Dunn to part with his fireballing strikeout king, Robert Moses "Lefty" Groves. (Connie Mack was later lampooned for referring to Lefty as "Groves." In fact, the pitcher's real name *was* Groves, and he had pitched for six years as Groves before the spring of 1926, when he announced, for unknown reasons, that he wished to be known as Grove.) But Dunn knew the pitcher wasn't ripe enough yet to command a big price. In January 1923, when a reporter asked Dunn to name the six best pitchers he had ever managed, Grove was not among them. "His best work is still ahead of him," Dunn said. His smoke ball was just about as fast as Walter Johnson's at his best, but he was "wild as a hawk sometimes."

Dunn was right. In 1922 Grove had averaged more than 6 walks per 9 innings. The next year he struck out 330 and walked 186 in 303 innings, while winning 27 and losing 10.

Connie Mack had seen plenty of Grove in 1924, beginning in Montgomery. In 2 innings Grove had given up 4 hits and 2 walks and struck out nobody. When the A's were home or in the east, Mack often took in International League games on Sundays and other days off, riding the train to

Baltimore, Newark, or Jersey City. Mack and Jack Dunn were close enough that Mack would let Dunn know when he would be watching the Orioles play, and Dunn would start Grove that day. Grove was willing to pitch any time without complaint. He finished the 1924 season 26-6, with almost 9 strikeouts and only 4 walks per game. In one stretch of 27 innings in September he had not issued a base on balls. He was not charged with a single wild pitch all year and hit only five batters. On June 29 Mack watched Grove walk only one batter in a 5-1 win over the Jersey City Skeeters. The A's went to Baltimore for an exhibition game on September 3; Grove shut them out on 2 hits, striking out 13 and walking none. Mack and Brooklyn manager Wilbert Robinson were in Baltimore for the first game of the Junior World Series against St. Paul on October 2. Grove struck out 11 and walked 3 in a 4–3 win.

Of course every other team's scouts had been watching Grove too. He had been pitching against major league teams in exhibition games since 1921. John McGraw saw him on one of Lefty's wilder days and wrote him off. But it was no surprise that when Dunn was ready to sell, the A's would wind up with the prize.

Piecing together disparate accounts by Dunn and Mack, it's impossible to pin down the exact timing of the deal. Some reports say that Mack made his offer after the game against the A's on September 3. But there were no reports of a meeting after the game—the Orioles left immediately by train to Kingston, New York, for an exhibition game—and it would have meant the story was leakproof for over a month. Not likely. It was probably after the game against St. Paul on October 2 that Mack went to Dunn's office and said, "Name your price."

Dunn said, "$100,000."

It may have crossed Mack's mind that he could recall the days when that amount of money could buy an entire minor league and all the players in it. But he didn't hesitate. They shook hands on it, Dunn agreeing to four annual payments of $25,000 through 1927. At Dunn's request, they agreed to keep it quiet until after the Junior World Series was over and the papers were signed.

A short time later, it occurred to Dunn that he could score some publicity and boost Grove's reputation as the best pitcher in baseball if he could sell Grove for more than the record price the Yankees had paid for Babe Ruth. He made some inquiries among his well-placed baseball contacts and was told Ruth's price tag was $100,500.

Dunn called Mack. "I've overlooked a bet, Connie," he said. "Remember when all the papers were full of the story about the record price paid when the Red Sox sold Ruth to the Yankees? I understand the actual price was $100,500. How about adding six hundred to the Grove price so we can beat that record by a hundred? I'll give the $600 along with some more to Grove."

Connie Mack readily agreed.

The story didn't break; it just sort of dribbled out. Perhaps the timing, coincident with an exciting New York–Washington World Series that blanketed sports pages, had something to do with it. An unsigned item in the October 8 *Baltimore Sun* was the first to report a rumor "emanating from the outskirts of inside circles here" that Grove had been sold to Mack and shortstop Joe Boley to Brooklyn. (The Dodgers were said to have offered $100,000 for Boley a year earlier, but Dunn hadn't been ready to sell. Now he was. But that sale didn't happen.) "It is said the transaction will be announced shortly, the *Sun* noted. "Along with the news of the double sale has come on the tongue of court gossip the reported price involved in the Grove transaction. The figure is set at a cool $100,000."

Other papers picked up the story, giving it small play while embroidering unlikely details, setting the price at $105,000 or $106,000, and alluding to a record price, "with the possible exception of the Babe Ruth deal."

On October 16 *The Sporting News* buried it at the bottom of page 5, as if it was a trade between two Class C clubs. Under a whispering headline in small caps, "MACK BUYS LEFTY GROVES," the story, dated October 12, was tentatively worded:

Connie Mack of the Philadelphia Athletics is reported to have purchased Pitcher Bob (Lefty) Groves from Baltimore of the International League for a price given as $106,000. The previous record price for a player was set when Babe Ruth was sold by the Boston Americans to the New York Yankees for $105,000 cash and pitcher Ernie Shore, who was valued at $30,000 in the statements given out about the deal. [That's what the story said. Shore remained with the Yankees.]

Groves has set a remarkable record during his five years' service with Baltimore. He has won 108 games and lost only 36 for a percentage of .750.

He has been the strikeout sensation of minor league baseball. He led the International League in 1922 and in 1923, striking out 330 batters in 1923. He worked in only 303 innings that season and thus he fanned batters at an average greater than one per inning for the entire season.

He won 26 and lost 6 this year and had a winning streak of ten games. He is 25 years old.

Jack Dunn and the Orioles were in St. Paul at the time. When *Sun* beat writer Don Riley asked Dunn about the reports, he received an emphatic denial that anybody had been sold: "They must be picking these stories out of the air," said Dunn.

When the Orioles returned home on October 15, Dunn again denied that anybody had been sold. But the next day, with the Junior Series over, Riley was in Dunn's office when the sale was confirmed. Grove had stayed over in Baltimore before returning home to Lonaconing in western Maryland. Dunn had asked him to come by Orioles Park in the morning.

Dunn called Mack to tell him that he was officially announcing the sale.

"After a telephone conversation with Mack," Riley reported, "Dunn declared Grove sold." Dunn admitted that he had withheld the announcement until the Junior World Series was over. Then he called Grove into the office.

"I've sold you to the Athletics, Lefty," said Dunn.

"Anything you say goes with me," answered Grove.

Dunn had a 1925 Athletics contract on his desk and asked Grove to sign it. The southpaw glanced at the figure and grabbed a pen and signed. Neither one would say what the amount was. (It was $6,500.)

Riley wrote, "Grove thought the interview was over, but Dunn had other plans. 'How many games did you win for me?' Dunn asked Grove.

"'I think it was 108.'

"'Well, I am not going to let you go without a remembrance, and here is something else for you.'"

Neither man disclosed what the "something else" amounted to, but Lefty departed "all smiles."

Asked why the price wound up at $100,600, Dunn said he understood from "unimpeachable authority" that Babe Ruth had been sold for $100,500 and he demanded and received the extra $100 "to justify my claim that Grove is the best pitcher in baseball today."

When New York general manager Ed Barrow heard the news, he fired off a telegram to the *Sun* declaring that Ruth had really cost the Yankees "approximately $135,000." Barrow was including the supposed "value" of Ernie Shore, who probably wouldn't have drawn a waiver claim at this stage of his career.

(Federal tax reports showed that New York paid $100,000 over two years for Ruth. Interest payments might account for the $500.)

On the evening the deal was announced, Bill Duncan of the *Public Ledger* happened to be seated near John Shibe at a restaurant they both frequented. Shibe was normally a man of few words, even fewer where the press was concerned. Duncan said to him, "Well, I see you have purchased Groves at last."

"Yes," said Shibe, "we bought him and for plenty. It's a big gamble for us. All I hope is that he'll be a second Eddie Plank. That'll be good enough. And if he ever gets control he'll be a wonder, because he's got nearly as much speed as Rube Waddell."

On November 6 the A's sent Dunn a down payment of $25,600. The balance was paid by annual checks for $25,000 on July 1 of each of the next three years.

It's difficult to discern just what went on with Portland scout Tom Turner, Connie Mack, Mickey Cochrane, and the purchase of the Portland Beavers in 1924. This is what we know:

In 1922 Portland Beavers owner William Klepper and his partner, infielder Duke Kenworthy, had been reprimanded by Commissioner Landis for tampering with a San Francisco player. Klepper was barred from all baseball activity except the administration of the club's financial business. Kenworthy was barred from playing or managing in the PCL until 1924. Now they wanted to sell.

Tom Turner and incoming manager Duffy Lewis wanted to buy the Beavers. But Turner didn't have the money.

Klepper and Tom Turner came to Philadelphia just before the World Series. Turner and John Shibe went to the first two games in Washington, then took the train to Portland, where, according to Isaminger, John Shibe and Turner "signed the papers" to buy the Beavers. Connie Mack denied that he had any interest in the deal. The Beavers' official history has John and Tom *Shibe* buying the club, "with Thomas L Turner their representative here as club president."

On his return to Philadelphia to resume his favorite activity—renovating and expanding Shibe Park—John Shibe denied he was an officer or stockholder; he had merely "helped finance the deal" that enabled Turner to buy control. Nor would the Beavers be a farm club of the A's. Turner was free to hire his own manager, make trades, and buy or sell players not on option from the A's, on his own. Acting for the Beavers in the past, he had made several satisfactory deals with the Dodgers, who expected to retain some form of "working agreement" with him. Roy Mack, stymied in his efforts to buy into the Newark or Reading clubs, went to Portland as the business manager.

The official transfer of the team took place on November 8, 1924. The minutes of the PCL meeting of November 24 mention no selling price but list all the owners: Turner, Lewis, Phil Metscham, and Harry Fisher, directors, and twelve other minority stockholders, including Mrs. Duffy Lewis. No Shibes. Yet ten years later, a December 13, 1934, story that Turner had sold his "heavy interest" in the club included this statement: "In 1924 Turner in association with John D. Shibe bought the club. Last spring he greatly increased his baseball investment by buying the entire stock interest of Shibe." In his 1937 obituary of John Shibe, Gordon Mackay detailed that stock interest as 882½ shares.

There is no record of Tom Shibe's ever owning any part of the Portland club.

Here's what the Athletics' ledgers show:

On November 1, 1924, the Athletics initiated a loan of $129,725 from the First National Bank of Philadelphia. On June 30, 1925, a $15,000 payment was made on the note. The Athletics continued to pay the interest on the "Portland note" until it was paid off on November 13, 1933.

During that time, according to the Bills Receivable, the club advanced the Beavers chunks of money between $8,000 and $50,000. Some of these notes were repaid; some were forgiven as payment for players bought by the A's.

In 1936 and 1937 Tom Turner repaid the Athletics $115,844.

Despite a Pacific Coast League rule barring major league clubs from owning any part of a PCL club, the Athletics' books show the receipt of dividends from Portland of $5,289 in 1926 and $8,815 in 1927. There is also a 1933 entry: "Loss, Sale of Portland Stock 107,225."

The Shibes apparently continued to "aid in the financing" of Turner. That's the way a March 28, 1926, story put it when Turner announced the construction of a new ballpark, which became Multnomah Stadium. Tom Shibe reportedly had bought the property "a little over a year ago" with a mortgage for which the Athletics made the payments.

So, did the Athletics buy the Portland club to get Mickey Cochrane, as legend has it?

Even murkier is the trail leading up to the purchase of Mickey Cochrane. Tom Turner was under no pressure to dispose of Cochrane. The PCL had opted back into the draft, but it applied only to players who had advanced from another minor league club. Since Cochrane had been signed as a free agent, he was exempt from the draft.

In October Isaminger wrote, "Turner, acting on behalf of [William] Klepper former owner of Portland, made a special trip [last summer] across the continent to sell Cochrane to Mack, who demurred and wanted more time." A month later, after Turner bought the club, Isaminger wrote a contradictory version, "Tom Turner last summer made a hurried trip to Philadelphia and was button-holed by Mack on Cochrane. He had been sought by five major league clubs."

Maybe both of Isaminger's accounts are correct and there were two different cross-country journeys by Turner. And maybe Mack and John Shibe told Turner they would finance his purchase of the Beavers only if he guaranteed that Cochrane would wind up with the Athletics, an agreement that morphed over time into the legend that "we bought the entire team to get the catcher."

If you believe Cochrane's account of his sale, there was never any understanding that the Athletics had an inside track to get him. Four years after the sale he told Bill Dooly of the *Record* that Tom Turner had said to him, "I have three offers for you. One from the St. Louis Cardinals, one from the New York Giants, and one from the Athletics. Which club would you rather be sold to?"

Cochrane said to Turner, "Sell me to the Athletics."

When Bill Dooly asked him why, Cochrane said, "Well, up in our part of the country [Massachusetts], we had always heard a lot about Connie Mack. He comes from around there, you know, and the people think there's nobody like him. Another thing, I knew the Athletics were a coming ball club, a team of young fellows that were up there and were due to stay up for eight or nine years. That's the kind of a team I wanted to play with."

When he read of the deal in a Los Angeles paper, Cochrane said, "I was so happy about it I could have done a war dance. The next day I hopped a train for home."

Mack announced the purchase on the night of November 17. Reports from Portland put the price for Cochrane at $50,000 and five players: infielder Henry Riconda, pitchers Bob Hasty and Dennis Burns, catcher Chuck Rowland, and outfielder Ed Sherling. Other accounts list the $50,000 as a total of cash and players' value. This was accurate; the cash was $35,000 and the five players were valued at $3,000 each.

In assessing Connie Mack's first forty years in baseball, Gordon Mackay wrote:

His principal asset has been his uncanny skill in choosing young players and molding them into stars. . . . But that method apparently has died away now, and Connie himself has come to believe that the only way in which to win pennants and prosper financially is to go out to the minors and buy the stars who have been developed.

Hence his policy was completely changed. While it has only been within the past two or three years that he has been reconciled to the fact that he must discard past ideas and meet modern foes in a modern manner, he has been a plunger in tremendous fashion.

No leader in the game during the past two years has obtained more stars through the bankroll than has Connie, and no pilot has been willing to spend the money faster and oftener.

Connie Mack's buying of players like Simmons, Grove, and Cochrane on the installment plan was in line with the latest trend in American life. Time payment was fast becoming a national habit. Will Rogers commented that the whole country was now on a dollar down and dollar a week basis. There were more mortgages than votes.

Rogers continued: "It ain't taxes that are hurting this country; it's interest. The only way to solve the traffic problems of this country is to pass a law that only paid-for cars are allowed to use the highways. That would make traffic so scarce we could use our boulevards for children's playgrounds."

Main Street had fallen in love with Wall Street. Everybody was playing the stock market. The Dow would soon hit a record 125 and keep on going. Steel and concrete skyscrapers were rising everywhere.

In Philadelphia there were forty-two theaters—stage, screen, vaudeville—doing big business. Sportswriters complained that pursuit of the almighty dollar was the major sport in society, and baseball was on a strictly commercial basis.

Bethlehem Steel magnate Charles M. Schwab declared, "I believe the next twenty years will see the greatest expansion and the greatest accomplishment American industry has ever known." To which the *Inquirer* added, "Thinking persons must agree with Mr. Schwab that only wild speculation can halt two or more decades of continued prosperity."

The Teapot Dome scandal in Washington caused few ripples throughout the country, not enough for the Democrats to oust Calvin Coolidge from the White House. Coolidge was preaching economy and nobody was listening, including Connie Mack.

17 | JOHNSON V. LANDIS

The stage revolved. Exit John McGraw, who had won the last of his ten National League pennants and lost his sixth and last World Series in 1924. He would come close again, but coming close was nowhere for McGraw. No longer would the Giants dominate baseball with him at the helm. He had been a big league manager almost as long as Connie Mack—twenty-five years. Ten years younger than Mack, his health had begun to decline.

Enter, or rather reenter, Connie Mack. As hale as ever at sixty-two, his fortunes were on the rise. For the first time in more than ten years, the Athletics and the pennant were being mentioned in the same sentence.

As unalike as they were in methods and mien, Mack and McGraw shared genuine respect for each other as baseball men. Oddly, their assessment of the best in the game was so similar that their all-time all-star teams, given in separate interviews in 1922 and 1923, disagreed in only two positions. Both chose Buck Ewing, catcher; Mathewson and Waddell, pitchers; and an infield of Sisler, Eddie Collins, Jimmy Collins, and Honus Wagner. Mack put Cobb, Speaker, and Fred Clarke in the outfield. McGraw named Cobb, Hugh Duffy, and Willie Keeler.

A changing of the guard had taken place in the leadership of baseball too. When Judge Landis had taken the commissioner's position, everybody had agreed to refrain from public criticism of the judge or his decisions. Ban Johnson had never been able to bring himself to accept the presence of a commissioner, especially one determined to be supreme and independent. Be it resentment, jealousy, senility, declining physical health, ego, or any or all of the above, Johnson found it impossible to let any action by Landis go by without criticizing it. The sun and the moon could tolerate being eclipsed once in a while. Ban Johnson could not.

Technically Landis was the chairman of an advisory council including the two league presidents. If this was some sort of power-sharing arrangement, it was doomed. Ban Johnson and Kenesaw Mountain Landis could no more share power than could Henry VIII and the Pope. Landis wasn't interested in any advice. When, for example, the umpires had prematurely called Game 2 of the 1922 World Series, tied 3–3 after 10 innings, on account of darkness at 4:45 on a clear day, the public and press cried foul. Landis donated the $120,000 receipts to soldiers' hospitals and other charities without consulting the league presidents. Landis worked harmoniously for the most part with NL president John Heydler, but if any advisory council meetings were ever called, Ban Johnson's invitations were lost in the mail.

The purging of the Black Sox didn't stop the rumors and charges of gambling in baseball. Baseball pools, based on such detailed action as the number of runs scored by a team, or all teams, in a week, continued to thrive openly. Landis considered the policing of the game his bailiwick now. When John Heydler investigated charges against former Giants pitcher Rube Benton and the National League backed him in banning Benton from the league, Landis overruled them and allowed the Cincinnati Reds to purchase Benton from St. Paul. When a gambling ring was uncovered in the Pacific Coast League, Ban Johnson launched his own investigation. Landis fumed; Johnson had no business getting involved in anything outside his own league, and the AL's directors agreed it was out of their jurisdiction.

The last straw came just before the 1924 World Series. The story was that New York outfielder Jimmy O'Connell had offered a $500 bribe to Phillies shortstop Heinie Sand to ease up against the Giants in their September 27 game. The Giants won the game, 5–1, clinching their fourth straight pennant by 1½ games over Brooklyn. When the incident was reported to Landis and he questioned O'Connell, the young outfielder not only admitted it, but he also implicated a Giants coach, Cozy Dolan, and three of McGraw's stars. Acting alone, Landis questioned everybody involved. Then, with John Heydler's concurrence, he banned O'Connell and Dolan for life and exonerated the rest.

Ban Johnson knew nothing about all this until he read it in the papers like everybody else. He immediately announced that Brooklyn should be declared the pennant winner and meet the Senators in the World Series, or the Series should be canceled. "From the evidence before me I think the entire New York National League team should have been disqualified and the Brooklyn team substituted in their place to play Washington," Johnson told Chicago reporters. "It looks like the corruption had gone clear through the entire team."

The Washington papers picked up the story the day before Game 1. That night some of the incensed Giants called on Landis at the Willard Hotel and asked him to squeeze an apology out of Johnson. Landis wasn't about to squeeze Johnson for any reason. "I make my own decisions," he told the press.

Reported the *Baltimore Sun*, "Smashing his fist on a table when pressed by newspapermen to comment on the day's developments, the Commissioner declared, 'It seems to me to be time for those persons not clothed with responsibility to keep their shirts on. There was a clear case of bribery; it proved abortive. The guilty men have been punished. Why call off the series?'"

Johnson called for a federal investigation and sent his attorney, Henry Killilea, to Washington, where New York Congressman Sol Bloom called for federal regulation of baseball as a form of interstate commerce.

That did it. Landis made it clear that he'd had enough interference from Ban Johnson. If the American League didn't do something to shut him up and make him mind his business, they could have his job.

But Johnson didn't shut up. On October 7 he was quoted in Kansas City accusing Landis of being "too close to the National League and the New York Giants. There is a whole lot of crookedness in the game and Judge Landis will not or cannot ferret it out." Johnson still nursed his hatred of John McGraw twenty-two years after McGraw had jumped the AL's Baltimore club for the Giants, taking several Orioles stars with him. Calling Landis a "wild-eyed, crazy nut," Johnson proposed that Landis quit or be compelled to drive the Giants' owners out of baseball. Johnson never denied saying any of it.

National League magnates never liked Ban Johnson. Those who had been in the game since 1901 still resented having lost the war against the AL invaders. John McGraw never had any use for Johnson, even when they were on the same side. Barney Dreyfuss still bristled every time George Sisler made a base hit for the Browns instead of the Pirates. Others were fed up with Johnson's criticisms of how they ran their business and let Connie Mack and the rest of Johnson's loyalists know it, offering enough examples to draw nods of understanding. Whatever their reservations about some of the commissioner's ideas and decisions, they were solidly behind him.

The American League owners panicked. They were scared to death of the public reaction if they were seen as responsible for Landis's quitting. At the same time, they were not happy about repudiating the man who had fathered, nurtured, and built their league into the prosperous business that it was.

There is something about baseball that seems to turn successful business-men in other fields into bumbling fools when they become baseball club owners forced to take collective action. Maybe there's an irreconcilable clash between the traits of the successful individual and the need to act in concert with partners who are also competitors. Whatever it is, in Isaminger's opinion, "They handled a delicate matter with the finesse of a Missouri mule going through a mud hole."

Meeting in New York on December 10, 1924, the league magnates tried to avoid a showdown that would require them to do something. James Crusinberry of the *Chicago Tribune* compiled an account of what went on behind the closed doors that day. Charles Comiskey, whose health had kept him from attending meetings in the past few years, led the recitation of charges against Ban Johnson. Comiskey explained at length and in great detail the events surrounding the investigation into the 1919 World Series, pointing out several examples of how Johnson, rather than deserving credit for uncovering the scandal, had actually impeded the White Sox' efforts. He accused Johnson of spending $37,500 of league funds—"of which I paid one-eighth"—to acquire evidence against the eight accused players, yet neither Comiskey nor anyone else had ever seen any of that evidence "When some of those blacklisted ballplayers sued the White Sox club, I asked Johnson to bring that $37,500 worth of evidence to Milwaukee where the trial was held and offer it in testimony for the defense, but he would not come the distance of eighty-seven miles to appear. On the other hand, President Heydler of the National League, though ill at the time, traveled one thousand miles to testify."

According to the writer's sources, Comiskey concluded along these lines: "The public likes to see you drive crooks out of the game, but what will the public think if you drive honest men out of the game?"

In other words, condone Ban Johnson's conduct and we'll lose Judge Landis.

Ban Johnson, it was said, sat through the entire volley of charges and made no reply, then or later.

Connie Mack and Tom Shibe had gone to the meeting standing "four square behind Ban Johnson," as they had done almost without exception from year one of the American League. Throughout the Carl Mays controversy of 1919 and its aftermath, which almost blew up the league, Mack had been steadfast among the Johnson "loyalists." He had "bent"—broken is too strong a word—with Johnson in December 1922, when Johnson had petulantly insisted on holding the league meeting in Chicago after reportedly agreeing to move it to New York at Landis's request.

But after Comiskey's plea, Mack said, "We learned much from Comiskey that we had never known before."

Clark Griffith had it in for Johnson for trying to cancel the World Series and discredit it while it was being played.

The AL magnates passed a unanimous resolution that reaffirmed publicly "our continued faith and confidence in the integrity and ability of" Judge Landis; urged cooperation between the two major leagues and the commissioner; and appointed a committee of Jake Ruppert, Ernest Barnard, and Tom Shibe "to wait upon Judge Landis to the end that full harmony may be restored and full cooperation obtained under the present agreement under which major and minor leagues are now operating." The committee sought to assure Landis that it would "persuade" Johnson to stifle his views and harmony would be restored.

It didn't work. Ruppert's attempt to "make nice" by issuing a public statement calling on the two men to work in harmony only riled Landis that much more by implying that he bore part of the blame for the discord. Landis wouldn't budge. "It's him or me," he told the committee.

The press concluded that either Ban Johnson would have to resign or Judge Landis would quit.

The thought of forcing Ban Johnson's resignation caused an epidemic of dyspepsia among the American Leaguers when both leagues met again in Chicago on December 17. What could they do that would appease Landis without impeaching Johnson? They had faced a similar situation a year ago when Landis had complained about public criticism by Johnson and others, and they had assured the judge it wouldn't happen again. But of course it had.

In a supplication addressed to Landis and approved, if not dictated, by him, they scolded and punished Ban Johnson like a misbehaving schoolboy: "We recognize that conditions have arisen that are gravely harmful to baseball and that must be intolerable to you and that these conditions have been created by the activities of the president of the American League."

The resolution went on in that vein for three paragraphs, then promised:

1. That his misconduct will cease or his immediate removal from office will follow.
2. That legislation will be adopted that will limit his activities to internal affairs.
3. That any and all measures which you may deem advisable to secure the above will be adopted.

It all sounded like a craven appeal on bended knees before his royal majesty and could not have elevated Landis's disdainful opinion of the lords of baseball.

The resolution was announced as unanimous, but in fact it had only seven signatures. Phil Ball of the Browns was in a hospital in St. Louis, but he had instructed his attorney to be there and oppose anything critical of Johnson, who had made Ball's entry into the league possible as part of the Federal League settlement.

In a gesture similar to yanking the brass buttons off the uniform of a discredited army officer, the nabobs replaced Johnson on the advisory council with Frank Navin. This had little practical effect; the council rarely counseled, and Navin's views were the same as Johnson's in most matters.

Mack, Shibe, and Griffith went to see Johnson in his office the next morning "to pay our respects and express our support for him." Ban wasn't there to thank them for their "support." His only public comment was uncharacteristically mild and muddled: "I am sorry that the American League club owners could not conceive their faithful and exact duty to the public. I have no criticism to make."

The press just about everywhere ripped the "ingrates" for humiliating the man who had done so much for baseball and their personal fortunes. "Free speech has been sacrificed to Landis's ego," was a common refrain.

Connie Mack replied, "Events have been misunderstood and misinterpreted. No attempt was made to force Ban Johnson to resign." The action taken was for the good of baseball, and "everything will turn out all right." It made for a lot of "sound and fury" copy over the winter doldrums, but it signified little to the public, which was more interested in player deals.

Ban Johnson was relatively quiet for a while, though he continued his own investigations into gambling in baseball. Perhaps he was biding his time until Landis's term was up and the judge might be replaced by someone more "in harmony." After all, he, not Landis, was the one who had been crowned "Mr. Baseball" for twenty years. He was the one who had routed the rowdies from the game, backed his umpires, fought the good fight for clean baseball and against the gamblers. His was the voice of the best interests of the game, not some newcomer with a fancy title, crown of white hair, and majestic scowl.

In the end, Judge Landis would outlast him by seventeen years.

18 | FORT MYERS

Stan Baumgartner had had a good year, winning 13 games. Years later Baumgartner recalled Jimmie Dykes's warning not to go to Mack's office to ask for a raise. "Don't go up to his office and cross that bridge of sighs [the runway connecting the main grandstand with his tower office]. You'll come out without a raise and thankful you have a contract," he quoted Dykes.

"Ignoring the advice," Baumgartner wrote, "I knocked on the door, entered the office. Connie smiled affably. Before I could say a word he remarked, 'Son, you had a splendid year, won a lot of games for us. But do you know I got the surprise of my life a few days ago. When I asked for waivers on you, fifteen clubs passed you up.'

"He stopped. I reached for my hat and said, 'I just thought I'd stop by to see how your health was. Goodbye.'"

Baumgartner was pleasantly surprised when his contract arrived giving him a 50 percent raise to $6,000.

Mack had a different kind of problem with his prized new catcher from Portland.

On November 4, 1924, he wrote to Mr. Gordon C. [*sic*] Cochrane in Los Angeles, enclosing two copies of a 1925 contract for $4,500. On receiving them, Mack said, he would send them to the American League office for Ban Johnson to sign and return them, after which Cochrane would receive a signed copy. In his letter Mack wrote, "In the agreement you signed with Mr. Turner I note that our club is to pay the transportation of yourself and wife from Los Angeles to Boston. Whenever you are ready to receive this you can notify me and I will be pleased to see that this matter is attended to."

Mack added that he intended for pitchers and catchers to leave Philadelphia for Fort Myers about February 20.

Cochrane signed and returned the contracts. "I know Mike would have signed no matter what the salary was," his wife, Mary, recalled seventy-one years later. "At twenty-one, he was so glad to be going with the A's."

In July 1924 John Shibe and Connie Mack had recommended that whenever a minor league player was sold to a big league club, 10 percent of the purchase price—if at least $10,000—should go to the player. Since the transactions went through the commissioner's office, there would be no question of the bonus being paid. Players sometimes claimed that clubs made such promises and didn't keep them, causing the buyer to have a disgruntled player on his hands through no fault of his own. In fairness to minor league club owners, there may have been instances where no such promises had been made. Some club owners willingly shared the purchase price with the player. The higher the sale price, the more likely the controversy. Jack Bentley, McGraw's $65,000 prize (Bentley later claimed it was $72,500), had demanded a piece of the money from either Jack Dunn or the Giants all winter before giving up and signing his 1923 contract with the Giants. More than once the A's had purchased players who balked at reporting because of an alleged broken promise that they would share in the sale money. Sometimes the A's and other clubs had to fulfill somebody else's promises to satisfy a player they needed.

When Mack had brought up the idea in the December 1924 league meeting, nobody supported it.

After returning to New England, where he worked in his father-in-law's shoe factory, Cochrane either read about Mack's views or some friends informed him of them and urged him to claim 10 percent of his reported sale price. If Tom Turner had made any such promises, they weren't in writing, and Cochrane had not brought the subject up before signing the Athletics contract.

On December 31 Cochrane sat down and wrote to Mr. Mack, declaring that he would not report to the A's until he received 10 percent of the purchase price from the Portland club. Otherwise he would play in some independent league somewhere.

Returning two weeks later from a trip to Fort Myers, Mack found the letter and fired off a reply that would have struck terror in the heart of any young rookie aspiring to a big league career.

Cochrane would receive many handwritten letters of a fatherly nature from Mr. Mack, but not this time. No "Dear Mike" or even "Dear Mr. Cochrane." It was addressed to Mr. Gordon S. Cochrane (this time he got the middle initial right) c/o Rice & Hutchins, Factory B., Windsor, Vt. One can imagine a fuming Connie Mack seated in his high-backed office chair dictating a frosty "Dear Sir" to Miss Lally. After explaining the reason for his delayed response, Mack fired away:

Am not altogether satisfied with the manner in which you express yourself in regard to your contract with our club. From what you say everything relating to what our club has done in the way of contract, etc. has been satisfactory to you but you are taking the stand that unless the Portland Club does something for you you will not carry out your agreement with our club. That is what I take from your letter of December 31st.

As our contract with you was made in good faith and as the contract has been promulgated by the American League Office it is now your duty to see that your agreement with our club is carried out but in order that we may understand each other thoroughly will say that on or before February 20th our club will send you transportation from Windsor, Vt. to this City and on your arrival here you will receive transportation with the other players to Fort Myers, Fla.

In the event that you should fail to report to our club as per your contract then it will be necessary for us to deduct, as a penalty for failure to live up to your contract, the sum of fifty dollars per day for each day you are absent from our club.

Now this is not going to be a pleasant thing for our club to do but if you insist upon taking this stand you are taking you can plainly see there is nothing else for us to do.

Then again, on account of your contract having already been promulgated, if you fail to fulfill the agreement it is possible Mr. Landis, Commissioner of baseball, might have something to say as to whether you could play with our club, even if you reported at a later date. I dislike very much to bring the Commissioner's name into this matter at this time but thought it well for you to know what the consequences might be, so that in the event of your persisting in your intention not to carry out your contract you will be made aware of what might take place.

Again I say, I trust you will give this your earnest consideration, before making what might prove to be a fatal mistake.

Very truly yours,
Connie Mack

Cochrane made no further demands. He showed up at the North Philadelphia station on February 20. There he met another rookie, Jimmy Foxx. One day the seventeen-year-old farm boy had come home from school and found a contract for $2,000 and an invitation to spring training. His mother wanted him to finish school, but Jimmy couldn't wait.

When the Athletics' train stopped in Washington, Bob Grove, also on his way to his first big league training camp, joined them.

Fort Myers, on the southwest coast of Florida, had begun as an army base during the Seminole Indian wars and was expanded to supply beef to federal gunboats patrolling the Gulf of Mexico during the Civil War. The building of the Royal Palm Hotel in 1898 attracted some well-heeled tourists. A grand plan to build a country club never got much beyond a clubhouse and rudimentary nine-hole golf course. The one-hour trek through the sand to reach it doomed it to an early demise. A more accessible golf course was built in the early 1920s.

Thomas Edison had built a winter home and laboratory there in 1886. Thirty years later Henry Ford bought the house next door. In 1925 Harvey Firestone brought Edison a four-foot high Banyan tree from India. Edison planted it in the yard of his workshop. It stands there today, 62 feet high with a spreading canopy of 191 feet.

But in 1923 Fort Myers was still a quiet, sandy town of about 1,200 population, a good hundred miles south of the nearest big league training camps in Sarasota, St. Petersburg, and Bradenton, and an equal distance from Miami.

Led by an energetic go-getter, Richard Q. Richards, owner of the Royal Palm Pharmacy, the Kiwanis Club set out to put Fort Myers on the tourist map. If they could entice a major league team to train there, the writers' dispatches would give them publicity to draw the sporting crowd. Richards wrote to all the major league clubs, inviting them to come and look over the town. Those who came considered it Fort Wilderness. When Richards went to Philadelphia in late 1923 to plead his case, Connie Mack said he was bound to Montgomery for another year. He liked the facilities in Alabama, he told Richards. He didn't tell Richards that he had become discouraged by the lack of major league opposition for practice games.

On Monday morning, January 21, 1924, Richards almost fainted when Connie Mack walked into his pharmacy in Fort Myers. Mack had arrived unannounced at noon the day before and checked into the Royal Palm Hotel. Richards showed him around downtown, which didn't take long. Although he barely came up to Mack's shoulder, Richards was as fast a walker as Connie Mack, and there wasn't a lot of downtown to cover. There was no hotel big enough to accommodate an entire team, but Richards pointed out several small hotels along First Street, near the pharmacy. They drove the mile to Terry Park, the Lee County fairgrounds. There was the original clubhouse from the early golf club that had failed and a few small fair buildings and an oval race track, but no baseball field or grandstand. The only clearing big enough would be the race track infield, a sand dune with occasional palmettos and pine trees. They discussed whether that might work. In the afternoon Richards took him to the Fort Myers Yacht and Golf Club, where Mack was much taken with the "greens as smooth as major league diamonds."

Two other things pleased him: the weather, which was as warm as a June day, and the absence of unwholesome distractions for his boys in training.

Richards hastily arranged a meeting that evening of the Kiwanis board of directors at his office, on the balcony overlooking the ground floor of the pharmacy. Mack expressed his pleasure at everything he had seen and set out his terms: a suitable field and grandstand, a cash guarantee for exhibition games, railroad fare for away games. All gate receipts, ads, and scorecards would be handled by the city. The Athletics would pay their own hotel expenses. He concluded with an admonition that he did not want them to accept the deal if it would mean a financial hardship to them, then left them to their deliberations.

The next day Mack enjoyed eighteen holes of golf, played, the *Ft. Myers Press* reported, in just under 100.

"It would be fine if Fort Myers wants us bad enough to hook us for next spring," he told the *Press*. "But if that cannot be arranged satisfactorily to all concerned I'll leave in a good humor and I'll tell the world just the same that Fort Myers is the prettiest city in all of Florida. I've been coming to Florida since 1888, so I should know it fairly well."

Added the reporter, "Mr. Mack is a regular guy who has made a lot of good friends since his arrival here Sunday noon. He leaves here tomorrow after the luncheon meeting of the Kiwanis club."

At the meeting "Connie Mack, amid great applause, took the floor. He made a corking good talk and likewise a fine impression." He estimated it would cost $20,000 to bring the A's to Fort Myers. The club then "unanimously and enthusiastically agreed by rising vote to accept Mr. Mack's proposition" of a $6,000 guarantee.

Dick Richards offered him the use of the pharmacy's office as the club's headquarters during their stay each spring. In the years to come he and his sons were often guests at the homes of Connie and Earle Mack. Years later his son Joe said, "I think Mr. Mack looked at my father almost like his son."

In January 1925 Mack went back to Fort Myers. He drew up the design for the ball grounds and grandstand. That's where he had been when Cochrane's letter had arrived in Philadelphia. By this time a road between Tampa and Fort Myers, which turned east to Miami, was nearing completion, making it possible to line up other big league clubs for exhibition games.

A brass band and hundreds of people greeted the Athletics when they arrived on Sunday, February 22. After checking into their hotels, the players were taken by bus to the beach. The local Lincoln dealer drove the visiting writers, the Macks, and the Shibes. The wide-eyed players gaped at Thomas Edison standing on his front lawn, the bathing beauties at the beach, the cars and buses driving on the hard-packed sand.

The Macks and Shibes and other club officials and coaches stayed at the Royal Palm. The players were housed at the Grand Central and Bradford Hotels. That caused a problem. The Grand Central had no dining room. Clubs preferred that players eat in the hotel and sign the checks. The players preferred meal money. There were two reasons for this. First, with cash in hand—say three dollars a day—a player could skimp on the calories, or search out a diner where the cuisine wasn't so haute, or drink his dinner, or treat himself to a malted milk on the management and pocket the change each day. Also, the heavy hitters in the knife and fork league, faced with an opulent hotel menu, had to make deals with the waiters to falsify the tabs so the manager wouldn't know a "double salad" had been a double pie à la mode.

Make that three reasons. It was hard to get out of leaving that quarter tip in the hotel dining room, lest you risk being ignored the next day. And some players would sooner hit a foul tip off their big toe than tip a waiter.

So Connie Mack had a crisis on his hands. The players at the Grand Central had to be given meal money. The others complained. Mack compromised; he gave the hotel diners tip money. It was a precedent; the A's became the first to make tip money an annual protocol. Concerned that some players, especially the rookies, might gamble away their money in the casino or dice games and go hungry, Mack doled out the meal and tip money daily at his office on the pharmacy mezzanine.

In the evenings before his nightly bridge game Mack would walk to the players' hotels and sit outside in front for a while, but that was the extent of his checking on them.

Mack knew which players were using the back entrances to duck out. And gradually they came to realize that he knew it too. But fines weren't Connie Mack's way of managing men.

Eddie Collins once described Mack's style to Westbrook Pegler: "Sometimes he lets fellows get away with things when they aren't kidding him at all, merely because he thinks it is better to rely on a fellow to do the right thing in the long run than to expose him in something he shouldn't have done, which would only upset the player and perhaps make him sulky. He just tells them what the club rules are and if they simply won't live by the rules, he won't have them."

The daily schedule was:

8—breakfast
10–12—practice
12–2—lunch and rest
2–4—practice
6—dinner
11—in bed

In the evenings the players gathered on the benches along First Street or hung out at the Royal Palm Pharmacy soda fountain or took in the show at the Arcade Theater. On Saturday nights the town scattered corn meal on the Main Square for a street dance. Sundays they had off; some were up early to go fishing or swimming, go to church, or play golf. High socks and knickers were the latest in men's fashions, on the streets and golf courses. One Sunday they were all invited for a sail down the Caloosahatchee River to Lake Okeechobee. The local citizens couldn't do enough to make them feel welcome.

The biggest distraction was the hordes of real estate salesmen who had descended on the quiet town. Florida was in the midst of a historic land boom. On both coasts remote acreage had gone up 50, 100, even 150 times its value of just a few years ago. Not 150 percent, but 150 *times*. Lots in Miami were being flipped as often as ten times a *day*. Some of it, sold sight unseen to buyers up north, was under water. A standard vaudeville joke went, "Congratulations. They found land on your land in Florida."

Pitchmen hawking lots lined the sidewalks on First Street. Unaware of the cynicism of the visiting scribes, developers took them on tours of the proposed developments, hoping for free publicity. They were dismayed when

Bill Dooly of the *Record* reported to Philadelphia readers, "The houses are stucco, and so are the purchasers."

At some point in the next few years Connie Mack bought two lots in Fort Myers. The records show that in 1932 he paid $3.04 in taxes on them.

John McGraw had been persuaded to front for a development near Bradenton he called Pennant Park. When the A's traveled in private automobiles over the rough, bone-jarring road to Sarasota to play the Giants, all the talk in the hotel lobby was about land and money. Frank Frisch and Hugh Jennings weren't talking inside baseball but "How much should we sell for? . . . What will they charge us to clear those palmettos? . . . How much is the first payment?" Giants catcher Grover Hartley claimed he had made more money in real estate that winter than he had playing ball for the past four years.

Ira Thomas, who had made a lot of money buying and selling oil leases in the new East Texas oil fields before selling his interest in the Shreveport club at the end of 1924, was back as Connie Mack's pitching coach. Along with half the population, Thomas took out a Florida realtor's license and was trying to talk the A's players into forming a syndicate to buy ten acres of land six miles out of town at a bargain price of $1,000 an acre. The fact that it had sold for $50 an acre a few years ago was evidence of how rich you could get. If you were lucky. Thomas had no more success with them than he did trying to sell Lefty Grove on throwing a change-of-pace.

When the Athletics returned to Fort Myers a year later, the bubble had burst. Everybody wanted to unload; buyers were as scarce as little Foxxes.

The first day the bus took the A's to Terry Park, they discovered that the county fair was under way. They passed through a carnival midway advertising acrobats, high-diving dogs, and contortionists. In the afternoon horses galloped around the track that encircled the ball grounds. The infield was sandy and uneven, making traction difficult. There were dips and dunes in the outfield

But there were no complaints. Enthusiasm was evident in every workout. Mack wanted to instill a winning spirit from the start. They played—and Mack managed—every exhibition game as if it would count in the standings. The sun shone almost every day. Unlike the last several years, there were no cold, wet interludes that rusted them and set back the pitchers' conditioning. To the contrary, toward the end of their stay it seemed as though the daily hot sunshine was beginning to sap their strength.

They were all in good shape. Some were athletes, not just ballplayers.

Walter French had been a halfback at West Point. Kid Cochrane had won ten letters at Boston University in football, basketball, baseball, hockey, and boxing. He was the leading runner, passer, punter, drop kicker, and tackler on the football team. In January 1923 while ice skating, he had saved the life of a boy who had fallen through a patch of thin ice. Sudlersville had no football team, but Jimmy Foxx had been captain of the basketball and soccer teams and held eight state titles in sprints, high jump, and broad jump.

Lefty Grove was described by Westbrook Pegler as "long and tough and wide and thick as six feet six of lynching rope." He could walk all day over the mountain trails with a shotgun on his arm. Bing Miller worked the farm between seasons. Simmons and Hauser were always in condition. Even Jimmie Dykes had shown up without too much excess baggage.

Like a kid at a circus, Connie Mack didn't know which dazzling performer to gaze at next. It was the greatest collection of genuine young darbs he had seen since the days of Collins and Barry and Baker and McInnis and Bender and Plank.

Al Simmons was old news to the visiting reporters. He'd hit .308 in his rookie year. Nobody made a big deal about "Bucketfoot Al" anymore. But they gushed over Grove and Mack agreed, though he winced when they started predicting a 20-win season for him. Lefty's long, flat, supple arm muscles promised plenty of work, but his Indian club windup and delivery from three different positions was not conducive to control, as his record demonstrated. For all Grove's spectacular numbers at Baltimore, there was still a gap between minor league stardom and making it in the big leagues. Nobody knew that better than Connie Mack, who had painful memories of too many Paul Strands in his life. He didn't want Lefty burdened with expectations that he was going to pitch the A's into the pennant. That's why he had been eager to add a veteran right-hander over the winter to anchor the staff. But he hadn't found one. Both Joe Bush of the Yankees and the Browns' Urban Shocker were available, but Mack was not willing to give up the players either team asked for in return. The two veterans wound up being traded for each other.

Everybody raved about Cochrane and Mack agreed. The fiery catcher was already shouting at infielders and pitchers in practice games as if the pennant was on the line. He chattered at batters, which Ira Thomas considered an asset. But as a catcher, Cochrane was a great halfback. In college Cochrane had fancied himself another Ty Cobb or maybe a third baseman. He didn't want to be a catcher, didn't want, as Connie Mack put it, "to carry all that 'truck' that catchers wear." But Mack wasn't about to waste that spirit and leadership by sticking it out in the pasture. He humored Cochrane by giving him some time at third, where the Kid stopped more line drives with his chest than his glove. Like it or not, Cochrane was turned over to Cy Perkins to make a catcher out of him.

Perkins was prepared to catch every game but was happy to help train his fellow New Englander. And the new kid needed it. Perkins worked with him on everything: footwork, pop fouls, throwing, working with pitchers.

Every time he caught a pitch, Cochrane went down on his knees. Perkins cured that. Cochrane's mitt had little padding at the top, none in the palm. Many old catchers' knuckles resembled burls on a bonsai tree. Ira Thomas's fingertips looked like flags in a stiff breeze. Cy Perkins had never suffered a broken finger with the A's. He taught Cochrane how to catch one-handed, keeping his right fist away from the ball until it hit the glove. "He never did learn to one-hand the pitch like I did," Perkins later told Shirley Povich of the *Washington Post*, "and sometimes he got banged up. But he had guts. When he did hurt a finger he'd say, 'So what? I've got nine others.'"

Cochrane learned that he had to have a different set of signals for each pitcher; what was easy for one to follow was like Greek to another.

Pop-ups drove him crazy, always had. He improved with practice but still shied away when he got close to the grandstand. Every morning he went out early and had a young pitcher hit him pop flies in back of second base. He would turn his back to the infield and catch them.

What Cochrane didn't need was injections of attitude. He was all fight and determination.

None of the writers paid much attention to Mack's favorite newcomer, the seventeen-year-old catcher warming up pitchers, until Mack pointed to "Jimmy Fawks."

"There's the boy that attracts my eye," he told them. "He's the dandy of them all. He's going to be the greatest player in the land someday. He may not look like so much to you fellows now. He's green and lacks experience, and he doesn't know how to handle himself. But if I ever saw a diamond in the rough, it's that lad. There's a great deal of power in him. He takes a free swing with the bat. There is no halting cut at the ball. And he is fast. He looks like a little truck, but he gets over the ground."

Jimmy Foxx later said it was days before he got up the nerve to approach batting practice, and then Connie Mack led him to it and handed him a bat. But once he showed them what he could do, the shyness disappeared. Always cheerful and friendly, he had no brashness about him.

Foxx's speed made them all gape. Charlie Paddock—the world's fastest human—not Babe Ruth, was his idol. In one practice game Foxx hit a fly ball into the pine trees in center field. As one writer described it, "Foxx crossed home plate and was studying the dinner menu before Al Simmons caught up with it."

Once they took notice, the writers gushed over him too. "Foxx shapes up as a gem of purest ray serene," cliched the *Evening Ledger*. "Jimmy's confidence, polish, and action behind the bat are more sensational than Cochrane because Jimmy wasn't heralded far and wide. He hasn't been tested but has the look of a catcher who will be there for fifteen years to come."

After a disappointing debut season interrupted by illness and injuries, Max Bishop appeared fully recovered. The A's smartest player since Collins, Bishop had some weaknesses as a lead-off man that Connie Mack set about correcting. With six .300 hitters behind him he had scored only 52 runs in 91 games.

"You need to get on base more often," Mack told him. "You are going after too many bad balls. From now on I want you to go down the line with the pitcher. You must make him pitch, make him go the limit."

Bishop heeded Mack's advice and learned the strike zone so well that he acquired the nickname "Camera Eye" while drawing more than 100 walks in each of seven seasons although never playing a full schedule.

The left-handed hitting Bishop had a tendency to pull too many line drives foul down the right-field line. The previous year he had resisted Mack's efforts to get him to move his feet three or four inches forward in the batter's box and hit to all fields. Now, with the manager's renewed urging, he moved up, choked up on the bat, and was working on hitting to left.

From the right-handed side, Jimmie Dykes was practicing his footwork to hit behind the runner to right field.

Joe Hauser, like Frank Baker, could hibernate all winter and wake up and hit line drives against and over the fences. But he was still an inexperienced first baseman; he'd had trouble making an accurate throw around the base runner on a 3-6-3 double play. He was working on his footwork to correct it.

The outfield of Lamar, Simmons, and Miller was good enough to squeeze Frank "Bug" Welch out of a regular role. And they had to be good to do that. A strong-armed, reliable run-producer, Welch had the promise of stardom but after five years had never quite fulfilled Mack's expectations. He seemed to lack baseball intelligence, was prone to making the wrong play. But as a fourth outfielder he was as good as any in the league.

Mack also had time for the youngsters who had no chance to make the team. He put them at unfamiliar positions for a while before switching them to their normal positions. Asked why, he replied, "I believe in playing a youngster breaking in in a place unfamiliar to him. Then when I shift him to his regular place he goes at it with a new confidence."

Years later Jimmy Foxx remembered this side of Mr. Mack. "The greatest thing he did for me and young players was give us confidence. He explained things, never raised his voice." The only time Foxx could recall him bawling anybody out was when a player was thrown out of a game for arguing with an umpire. "As he started toward the tunnel to the clubhouse, Mr. Mack called him over. He told him, 'It's perfectly all right to argue when you think you're right, but there's also a time to stop. Don't ever let me see you get thrown out of a ball game again because I want you to know you're of no value to me whatsoever in the clubhouse.'"

That lesson stuck; Jimmy Foxx was never thrown out of a game.

Ed Rommel was the rock of the pitching staff. Starting and relieving, he would appear in 52 games.

Sammy Gray reported in midseason shape after a winter of doing farm chores and hunting rabbits by running them down. After he had beaten the Yankees twice the past year, veteran shortstop Everett Scott said of him, "I never saw a kid pitcher deliver a more bewildering curve ball. He has everything, and his control is amazing. He knows how to pitch to each hitter, and, at the same time, he depends on his support to carry him along. Gray has a brilliant future."

Slim Harriss also reported in midseason condition, determined to achieve that breakthrough season Mack was looking for after five patient years of losing records.

Mack now had four experienced left-handers for the first time. He looked for a big year from Fred Heimach, but when Heimach tripped shagging flies and dislocated his left shoulder, sidelining him for most of the year, it was not the devastating blow that it would have been in previous years. Besides Grove and Stan Baumgartner, Rube Walberg was ready for regular work. He still had a tendency to be wild at times, perhaps because of the contortions he went through in his corkscrew windup. But he had won 18 games at Milwaukee and was a workhorse. Mack would use him in 53 games, starting and relieving.

"Give him one more year," said Mack, "and he'll be the equal of Waddell."

The Yankees were the biggest attraction in Florida, but they were not scheduled to play in Fort Myers. The locals wanted to see Babe Ruth. The

Kiwanians asked Connie Mack to ask Miller Huggins if he would lend Ruth to the A's for a day. Mack obliged them with a note to Huggins, who replied that if Ruth didn't object to riding the hundred miles to Fort Myers, it was okay with the Yankees. Other more temperamental stars would have refused, but Ruth didn't mind. They settled on March 13 for a game against the Phillies. But Ruth hurt a finger, and they had to put it off. Ruth didn't forget. Ten days later Huggins notified Mack that he would be there on the twenty-fifth.

Every business in Fort Myers closed at noon on March 25 so everybody could go to the game against Milwaukee. And it seemed that literally everybody was there. According to the historical society, five thousand fans—almost 80 percent of Lee County's entire population—showed up. People always felt a little lighter at heart in the Babe's cheerful, carefree presence. Bug Welch greeted him, "Hello busher. I thought from the newspaper reports you weighed a ton. You don't weigh a ton. You weigh a ton and a half." Ruth laughed, put on an A's uniform, and signed six dozen baseballs. He batted third, Hauser fourth. The Babe didn't get a ball out of the infield; Hauser had a single, double, and triple.

Connie Mack, the spring training nomad, had found a home for the next dozen years and a host of new lifelong friends. Before the Athletics headed north, the Kiwanians promised to plant grass, put up a fence, build individual lockers in the clubhouse, and improve the press facilities. Connie Mack signed a five-year contract.

An upbeat Mack told the Rotary Club, "Don't count the A's out of the pennant race. At the same time don't count us in. But any team training in Fort Myers should make the other teams sit up and take notice."

In describing how Scotland Yard had gone through more than ten thousand men in its first eight years trying to build a team of three thousand, Yard historian Belton Cobb wrote, "Success requires a large element of luck and good luck only comes to those who are ready to receive it, while better luck comes to those who actually look for it." Ed Bang estimated in *Collyer's Eye* (a racing sheet) that Connie Mack had looked for that "better luck" by going through more than six hundred recruits since 1918 trying to put together a winning combination of twenty.

Connie Mack believed he had found it, despite the many skeptics who put his team down for another sixth or seventh place season. Maybe too much sun shining on all those glittering gems on the fairgrounds field had made Mack giddy. If so, after suffering through the grim years of the past decade, he was entitled.

19 | IN THE RACE AGAIN

Philadelphia fans had their first look at Lefty Grove in an A's uniform on Saturday, April 4, 1925, at Baker Bowl. The Shibe Park renovations wouldn't be finished until sometime in May so the city series was played at the Phillies' yard. The old park couldn't begin to hold the crowd that turned out to see the world's most expensive ballplayer. They saw exactly what they had been told to expect. They gasped in awe at his blinding speed, and he walked 6 in 5 innings, 2 in the ninth who scored the only runs in the Phils' 2–1 win.

The series resumed on Tuesday. In the bottom of the first, with Eddie Rommel pitching, lead-off batter George Burns hit a ground ball to Galloway at short. Joe Hauser started toward first as Galloway threw. A sharp pain shot through Hauser's right knee and he fell to the ground as the ball flew over first base. Rommel and Perkins chased the ball and Burns raced toward second while Hauser lay writhing in agony.

They carried him into the clubhouse and put him on the trainer's table. Phillies trainer Red Miller gave him some spirits of ammonia to revive him. When he came to, Unser Choe saw John Shibe standing nearby and asked him for a cigar.

"It's hard to say how it happened," Joe said. "My knee gave me some trouble Monday but I thought nothing of it. Doc Ebling gave me a treatment and I felt much better. In fact I did not feel any pain today and had no inkling of any trouble until my knee gave way and I sprawled in the dirt. I hope I can get back in the game in a couple of weeks."

When the tearful Mrs. Hauser came in she saw a cloud of smoke hovering over her husband and knew he was okay. But he wasn't. An ambulance took him to Medico-Chirurgical Hospital. His kneecap had cracked. The next morning Dr. John B. Carnett drilled two holes in it, wired it together with gold wire, and put a cast on it. Hauser remained upbeat. That evening he devoured two porterhouse steaks and six eggs. When Connie Mack and some of the players visited him the next day, Unser Choe was joking and feeling no pain, confident he would play again that year. The doctors doubted it. Some of them said he might never play again.

Connie Mack believed Unser Choe was finished, telling J. Roy Stockton in St. Louis a month later that "it will be very remarkable if he ever comes back and plays major league baseball."

Even if he did, the doctors said his leg would be stiff and he would always have to favor the knee. The wire remained in his knee for the rest of his life. (Ten years later the other kneecap would shatter while he was running the bases with Minneapolis.) Hauser stayed on the payroll in Philadelphia all season. Once the cast was off he did what he could to stay in shape. When the A's played exhibition games in nearby cities, Joe went along and received the same twenty-five dollars the active players earned. Occasionally Mack sent him to Federalsburg on the Eastern Shore to help coach the younger players and do a little scouting.

Connie Mack was downcast but not discouraged despite the loss of his most dangerous batter. "Accidents will happen in baseball and we have to take the bad with the good. We may be handicapped by these accidents, but the team has the spirit."

It may have reminded him of the time twenty-three years earlier when an opening day court decision had cost him Larry Lajoie and three other players he had been counting on. He had done perhaps the finest managing job of his career in overcoming that blow and winning the 1902 pennant. Once again he had lost his premier slugger just before the season started.

The entire American League suffered a different kind of blow the same day Joe Hauser's knee collapsed: all of Babe Ruth collapsed at noon in the rail-road station in Asheville, North Carolina. For the past five years Ruth had been hit with flu bugs every spring. He insisted on playing every exhibition game, no matter how wet and cold it was, because he knew he was the one people came out to see. The day before he had thrilled them with a home run in Knoxville, despite feeling ill.

The Yankees brushed it off as nothing more than acute indigestion, but when he fainted and hit his head on a wash basin as the train arrived in New York and had to be carried out a window on a stretcher, the rumor spread that Ruth was dead. He wasn't but the Yankees were. Ruth would be out until June and the Yankees would finish seventh.

Whoever Connie Mack had in mind to replace Joe Hauser, he wasn't saying. "I have several plans in mind, but not for publication." He had a capable replacement in Bing Miller and Bug Welch to replace Miller in the outfield. Stuffy McInnis had been released by the Braves, but Mack did not consider him an everyday player at thirty-five. (McInnis signed with Pittsburgh and played in his fifth World Series.) Portland first baseman Jim Poole, a veteran Pacific Coast League slugger, was sitting at home in North Carolina, holding out for more money from the Beavers. Considering Mack's ties with Tom Turner in Portland, the press expected him to acquire Poole. On April 8 Mack called the story "bunk," his usual response to rumors, even if they were true. Three days later Poole showed up at Shibe Park. Mack may have become skeptical of PCL .350 hitters who hit 38 home runs, but Poole would cost him only a few players who didn't figure in his future plans, and he preferred not to disrupt his outfield if he could avoid it.

With the unfinished left-field stands roped off, only twenty-five thousand could squeeze in on opening day to see what Connie Mack's fighting new Athletics had in store for them. The A's wore new yellow leather warmup jackets over their white uniforms with black trim. They sat gloomily while an edgy Lefty Grove didn't survive the fourth inning, walking 4 and striking out nobody. Slim Harriss left his stuff in the bullpen again as the Red Sox ran up a 6–0 lead. But the jeers gradually turned to applause, then cheers, and finally pandemonium as the A's scored 2 in the seventh, 4 in the eighth, 2 in the ninth to tie it, and 1 in the tenth to win it, 9–8. Mack used three pinch hitters and five pitchers. There were plenty of heroes. Poole, Miller, and Welch homered; the last was a 3-run pinch hit in the eighth. Lamar drove in the tying run in the ninth. Cochrane pinch-hit for Perkins in the eighth and had to handle Rommel's knuckler and catch a pop foul with two men on in the tenth. In the last of the tenth Poole, Cochrane, and Hale singled to win it and send the exuberant crowd home happy. They didn't know that they had seen something that has never been seen since—two future Hall of Fame players making their debuts in the same game.

Lefty Grove seemed to be trying too hard to justify his big price tag. Three days later he again failed to make it out of the fourth, and four days after that he walked 6 in a 6–2 loss. Grove got off to such a rocky start, Mack inquired about buying veteran catcher Lew McCarty from Reading. McCarty had caught Grove at Baltimore in 1924. But Reading had pennant aspirations and didn't want to part with McCarty. Later in the season, when they were out of the race, they were willing to sell. But by that time Mack wasn't interested.

The first appearance of the defending champion Senators brought out the largest baseball crowd in the city's history on Saturday, April 18. Occupants of the rooftop bleachers looked down on a sea of caps and derbies and fedoras in the streets around Shibe Park as thousands tried vainly to push their way inside. More than thirty-five thousand, many of them swarming into the roped-off unfinished left-field upper deck, watched Slim Harriss demonstrate why Connie Mack had continued to carry him through five losing seasons, outpitching Walter Johnson, 3–0.

Through the early weeks Mack was using Walberg, Rommel, Grove, and Baumgartner in relief with all but Walberg also starting. By the time they headed west for the first time, they were tied with Washington for the lead at 12-5. They won 9 in a row, Rommel and Gray winning 3 each. When they came home on May 27 to a gala opening of the new double-decked grandstand, which left only center and right fields without seats, they had built a 72-point lead over the Nats. Neither Harriss nor Walter Johnson survived a sluggers' duel that day, won by Washington. Both pitchers came back in the next day's doubleheader; Harriss and Walberg won; Johnson was routed before thirty-three thousand. The A's turned 7 double plays.

Then, gushed *Times* man James R. Harrison, "Sweeping on like a mountain torrent, the mad Mackmen of McGillicuddy" won 3 in a row from New York, including a Memorial Day split doubleheader that drew over sixty thousand for the day.

"At last," wrote Grantland Rice, "the ten-year span of taking Mr. Mack's Athletics as the closing word in jokes is about over."

They had the pitching, although Grove was erratic and a discouraged Baumgartner had been able to finish only one of his five starts. One day in the dugout he muttered, "If I could get a job for forty bucks a week I'd give up this lousy game."

Connie Mack heard the remark. "I've got just such a job in the office," he said. "Do you want it?"

Baumgartner picked up his glove and sauntered to the bullpen.

They had the tight defense that had been missing all those years. The outfield of Miller, Simmons, and Lamar could all play in close, the way Mack preferred, and go back to the fences when necessary. "No more than one or two out of fifty will go over your head where you can't get it," he told them.

Chick Galloway was playing the best ball of his career. Always a light hitter, he had become a deft bunter, pushing the ball past the pitcher, and a reliable right-handed batter who could punch the ball behind a runner at first. As a keystone combination, he and Bishop were the best the A's had seen since Collins and Barry.

Connie Mack later admitted that his boys' fast start fooled him. "Philadelphia's fans were wild about my team," he recalled thirteen years later to Bob Paul of the *Philadelphia Daily News*. "So were folks in every other city. Sports writers began to hail the club as a sure winner."

They didn't fade. Through June they kept a step ahead of Washington in a two-team race. They did it with one spectacular comeback after another. Example: probably as a favor to somebody, Mack was giving a look-over to Tom Glass, a twenty-seven-year-old right-hander who had pitched the year before for the Cambridge Canners in the Class D Eastern Shore League. On June 15 Rommel started against Cleveland. The knuckler didn't dance that day. Cleveland led 12–2 when Mack sent Glass in in the sixth. By the last of the eighth it was 15–4. Many of the disconsolate viewers headed for the exits and missed the parade of 3 walks and 9 hits in the A's 13-run eighth inning. When Al Simmons hit a 3-run home run onto the left-field roof to make it 17–15, Connie Mack threw his scorecard in the air along with the straw hats and cushions sailing out of the stands. He shook the hand of every jubilant player he could reach, while Earle Mack turned flips in front of the dugout. Rube Walberg pitched a scoreless ninth. Tom Glass soon went home with a 1–0 lifetime record.

The next day they piled up 10 runs in the first 2 inning, but Grove's wildness forced Rommel to rescue him in the eighth to preserve a 12–7 win.

And they had done it all so far despite injuries that would have finished them in former years. The starting infield was seldom together in a game. Sammy Gray and his mystifying curve, and not Lefty Grove and his speed, were the talk of baseball. Grove had yet to win a start. Gray was 8–0 when he was hit by a pitch on May 21 that broke his thumb and sidelined him for a month. A line drive split Rube Walberg's finger. Dykes had pulled up lame with a charley horse in the second game of the season.

It had been a long time since Connie Mack had had so strong a bench to call on. Hale, Bishop, Dykes, Lamar, and Miller each would miss thirty to fifty games with injuries. Dykes was a one-man bench. He played second when Bishop broke a bone in his foot and third when Hale went down.

The injuries forced Mack to juggle his batting order: eighteen variations by mid-August. Hale, Dykes, and Bishop took turns leading off. Cochrane was all over the lineup, even leading off a dozen times—something no catcher had done since Roger Bresnahan of the Giants twenty years earlier.

Mickey Cochrane had a strained back but kept on playing. Seemingly indestructible, he would catch 133 games and hit .331. On May 21 he hit 3 home runs in a game at St. Louis. He might have hit more but for Connie Mack's mental lapse. After Cochrane hit his third in the seventh inning, the A's led 15–2. Mack felt that Mickey could use a rest. He took him out and Perkins went in. The A's scored 5 more runs and Perkins batted twice. Mack's decision had cost Cochrane a chance to hit one or two more over the fence.

"After I sent Perkins in the game, I saw what I had done," Mack admitted to Sid. C. Keener of the *St. Louis Times.* "I went into the clubhouse when the game was over and told the boy I was sorry about what I had done when it came to my mind.

"'Don't you worry about me, Mr. Mack, it's the game that counts' was what young Cochrane handed back to me. Wasn't that a fine spirit? Well, that's just what you find on this club."

With Cochrane, Perkins, and newcomer Charlie Berry to do the catching, Jimmy Foxx was unlikely to see any action. In batting practice the muscular seventeen-year-old was already hitting balls into the upper decks in ball-parks that had them and clear out of those that didn't. He made his debut on May 1, singling as a pinch hitter for Grove. In 9 pinch-hitting appearances, he had 6 hits. But sitting on the bench, he gained weight. Mack thought he would be better off playing every day and optioned him to Providence in the International League, where he caught in only 17 games, pinch-hit in 24, and batted .327 with 1 home run.

They were winning and they were having fun. They rode each other as well as the opposition and umpires. They had what the British Navy under Lord Nelson was known for—a "bloody-mindedness." Connie Mack had to keep after them to lay off stars like Ty Cobb. "Don't get him mad," he reminded them whenever they played Detroit. After they won their first five meetings with the Tigers, it wasn't easy to stifle them. Cochrane later said he got on Cobb at the plate and it cost them a game.

When they were hit by a pitch, they didn't charge the mound. Just the opposite; they did nothing to give the pitcher the satisfaction of knowing they might be hurting or upset. Before his injury Joe Hauser would taunt the pitcher as he trotted to first base, "Hey, pitch, if that ball left a mark I'll buy you dinner."

To intimidate a batter, especially when Lefty Grove was pitching, they'd holler, "Let him smell a little leather," or "Let's see how he hits lying on his back." And Lefty wasn't reluctant to oblige. If a batter dug a hole to get a foothold in the batter's box, the next pitch would be high and inside—not too high but a little too inside. If Grove wanted to hit a batter, he aimed at the man's back, not his head.

"I was a rookie. I was wild," Grove told his hometown friend Judge Jim Getty. The first time Grove faced Ty Cobb, he walked him. "When he was going down to first base, he yelled over at me, 'What's the matter, busher? You afraid to toss it across the plate?'

"I thought, 'I'll show you if I'm afraid to throw it across the plate or not.' The next time he came up he was standing there with his two hands five inches apart on the bat. I threw as hard as I could inside and it hit between his hands before he had time to drop the bat. He never called me busher again."

Max Bishop said, "When Grove pitched, I would say to myself, 'Dear God, thank you for allowing me to be on the same team with him.'" But Bishop also knew what it was like to play behind Lefty. "If somebody hit a shot through the infield off him, Grove thought it should have been caught, no matter how hard it was hit. He'd give the infielders a black look, glower at them like, 'You shoulda had it.'"

Jimmie Dykes would get on anybody he thought wasn't hustling or thinking on a play. He and Simmons barked back and forth at each other like a vaudeville act, sometimes moving Mr. Mack to tell them both to shut up. Once when Dykes was on the bench and Simmons made an error, Dykes hollered, "Take him out of there." Mack said to him, "Mr. Dykes, would you really want me to take Mr. Simmons out of the game?" Mr. Dykes said nothing.

The players called Grove Mose. The quiet Max Bishop was "Tillie" because he was an immaculate dresser like a little guy named Max in the comic strip *Tillie the Toiler*. Cochrane was Mike or Black Mike because of his inky-black hair, "Grumpy" for his early-morning disposition. (He and his wife disliked "Mickey." She called him Mike. But to writers and baseball fans he would indelibly be known as Mickey, so Mickey he will be in these pages, except when a player is being quoted.) Jimmie Dykes was "Pudgy." Bing Miller was "the black boy" or "Blackfolks" because of his dark complexion from year-round exposure to the sun.

Cochrane, Miller, and Dykes were chatterboxes. Eddie Rommel was an energetic bench jockey. Walter French had the most powerful voice of them all. "When he shouted, you could hear him all over the park," Mack said, "and he often troubled the opposing pitcher with his ironical comments that they would not fail to hear."

Even the rejuvenated sixty-two-year-old Connie Mack got into the spirit. When they objected to an umpire's decision, Mack would often join the chattering, arm-waving chorus.

It soon became apparent that Mickey Cochrane was the most fiery field leader Mack had ever managed. Sparks flew when he was on the field, gabbing at batters, barking encouraging pep talk at his pitcher and infielders, or shooting black looks and blue language at anybody who wasn't wide awake out there. Play out of position, throw to the wrong base, pull any kind of rock, and Cochrane let the offender know before Mack had a chance to say anything.

"That Mike was on you all the time," Al Simmons recalled. "Make one little mistake or don't get that ball in as fast as you might have and he'd step out in front of the plate and glare at you. No matter how deep you retreated into the outfield, you could feel that stare."

Later Mack would single him out as the difference-maker in the team's success.

Cochrane was a music lover. He had played the saxophone in a band in college. He carried a portable phonograph to spring training, and his sax on the road, playing it enthusiastically to the dismay of his roommate, Stan Baumgartner. He strung the room with radio antennas to pick up musical broadcasts. When he went to the theater and saw an act he liked, he'd go backstage to meet them, sometimes inviting them to visit the A's clubhouse. That's how popular performers like the Ink Spots and the Mills Brothers wound up entertaining the players before games.

Connie Mack was shrewd enough to realize that Lefty Grove wasn't ready for Cochrane's incendiary brand of leadership. Mack had more patience with Lefty's wildness than Cochrane would have. One day Grove missed a curve sign and threw a fastball. Cochrane was furious. After the inning, they barked at each other and almost came to blows. Mack said to Cochrane, "Be quiet," and sent him to the clubhouse. Almost every time Grove started, Cy Perkins caught him. When Grove relieved, Perkins replaced Cochrane behind the plate.

Lefty Grove hated to lose. No professional athlete *likes* to lose, but Mose Grove took the art to volcanic heights. He blew and then it was over. In the evening he'd sit in the lobby or at home on the front porch, smoke his one cigar of the day, retire by nine with a western pulp magazine. He had one drink a day, a shot from a miniature bottle of scotch or a beer. That didn't bother Mack. One day somebody saw Grove carrying a case of beer out of a speakeasy in Philadelphia to take home. Connie Mack heard about it. He called Grove into the office and said, "I'll have that delivered to your house from now on. We don't want anybody to think you're drinking."

Grove picked up an early reputation for being gruff, rude, and unapproachable. The press created it. Connie Mack had plenty of experience with writers' misquotes, distortions, and inventions to create a better story, usually at the subject's expense. "They write what they want to write," he often said. Once his friend Walter Grier read a quote of Mack in a Philadelphia paper that didn't sound like the Connie Mack he knew. When he asked his friend about it, Mack chuckled. "I haven't seen that writer for more than a month," he said. "They make up things like that all the time." He understood that it was part of the tradition of journalism that remains to this day. The story was everything. The subject had to be made "colorful," even if he wasn't. Over the years this journalistic tradition would result in many players distrusting writers. But it was all new to Lefty Grove, a hardscrabble mountaineer from a coal mining family, who had not gone beyond the fifth grade.

According to Judge Getty: "[Lefty] told me his difficulty in getting along with the press originated when he was first with the Athletics and on the train ride to Detroit he got into a long conversation with a sportswriter, and a lot of things he said and a lot that may have been misinterpreted appeared in the Philadelphia newspaper. Mack called him in and advised him against being too available for extended interviews or long discussions, especially with writers that he didn't know well. Lefty was so shocked by his failure to understand these facts of baseball life, he was probably very aloof to all reporters from that time on."

Grantland Rice told the story of a St. Louis reporter during the 1930 World Series who went into the hotel looking for Grove.

"To his joy," wrote Rice, "an elevator door opened and Grove, long cigar in his mouth, stepped out. The reporter rushed up to his hero and began, 'Mr. Grove, I would like to do a story about you and . . .' Grove scowled and said, 'I knew I shouldn't have come downstairs,' stepped back into the elevator and the door closed as the reporter stood open-mouthed."

When Ed Rumill retired after forty years at the *Christian Science Monitor*, his farewell column began with an account of his first assignment in 1932—interviewing Lefty Grove when the Athletics were in Boston.

When the reporter walked into the Brunswick lobby, the temperamental Grove was sitting near the door, staring into space.

"Mr. Grove," the youngster began, "I'm with the *Christian Science Monitor* and I wonder if I could talk to you for a few minutes?"

The reaction was shattering to an already terrified writer. Grove stared coldly for most of half a minute, let out a grunt, bounded up out of the chair, and disappeared into an elevator.

Alone in the middle of the lobby, the completely demoralized young scribe, tears welling in his eyes, had just one overwhelming desire—to get out of there as quickly as possible.

But at that instant, a slender gentleman came out of nowhere to take the boy's arm, lead him to one side of the lobby and say in a soft, kindly voice, "I'm Connie Mack. Is there something I could help you with?"

Just two short sentences, hardly spoken above a whisper, but they salvaged what was to become a long, exciting, and gratifying sports writing career.

Connie Mack often came to the rescue of a bewildered writer. "Don't pay any attention to Lefty," he might say. "He just doesn't feel like talking this morning." And Mr. Mack would provide the scribe with a story. Despite his peevishness over their misquotes and speculations, Mack appreciated the free publicity they gave baseball. Over the years he came to tolerate the inaccuracies that appeared in print. In 1933 a fan sent him an article about Mack's first major league game in Washington on September 11, 1886. In a letter thanking the fan for the article, he wrote: "There have been many articles published in regards to this game, but none of them have had the correct score or the correct date that the game was played. . . . Naturally, I remember this game very well and have told many newspaper reporters that the game was played in Washington, but they will have it that my first game was either played in Philadelphia or New York."

Mack understood that the writers had a job to do, filling a given space each day with something new in the face of severe competition. He was always good for a story, a reminiscence, an analysis of a pennant race to fill a column. Perhaps that's one reason a 1944 poll of sportswriters named him the manager most liked by writers and players.

As for Grove, he mellowed after his playing days were over. Years later, at a Hall of Fame induction weekend in Cooperstown, Ed Rumill reminded Grove of the incident in Boston.

"You're kidding me," Lefty said. "Did I really do that? Boy, I must have been something. Well, I'll tell you what I'll do. Just to show you how sorry I am, I'll let you buy my lunch."

"He did, too," wrote Rumill.

But the players never saw Mose that way. Sure, he sulked when he lost, threw some furniture around in the clubhouse, popped the buttons tearing off his uniform. They just kept out of his way until it was over. Jimmie Dykes could get his goat by needling him. Otherwise they loved and respected him. He was easygoing, roughly greeting them with a slap on the back or a playful poke in the stomach. He enjoyed a good prank. In his later years when he went up to Connie Mack's office to visit, he might grab Mack's high-backed chair from behind and give it a spin.

Ira Thomas's nephew, Jim Morrow, was a clubhouse boy in those days. He recalled, "Grove used to stand against the third base line wall beside the A's dugout and throw baseballs over the right field roof onto Twentieth Street. Just took one step and threw it. He was doing that one morning and Connie Mack unexpectedly showed up. Mack went up to him and said, 'You do that one more time and I'll ban you from baseball.' It wasn't the cost of the balls. Mack had just paid over $100,000 for him and he was afraid Grove would throw his arm out pegging the ball like that."

Trainer Doc Ebling said, "He was inclined to be retiring, sometimes morose, but a heart of gold, generous, and a likable chap once he became friendly."

Grove's generosity was unsung and unnoticed, and that's the way he wanted it. He bought uniforms, dozens of baseballs, and other equipment for kids he saw playing on sandlots on his way to Shibe Park and swore his suppliers to secrecy. He supported his mother and father, a retired coal miner.

Jim Morrow had a different view of Grove's generosity from Doc Ebling's or the boys on the city lots for whom Lefty bought bats and balls. "I think Lefty had the first nickel he ever made," he recalled. "When he was in the bullpen he'd send me up to get an ice cream or candy bar. No tips."

Mose never went big city, couldn't wait after the season to get back to his bowling alley and Elks Club in Lonaconing, where he could live comfortably on eight dollars a week.

The public never knew the sentimental Lefty Grove, who had bought a round-trip ticket to Martinsburg to try out for the team in 1920 and carried the unused return ticket in his wallet until the day he died.

Al Simmons hated pitchers. They were the enemy, out to take his money. Bill Lamar had a reputation of being "too passionate" when he failed to hit in the pinch. That's the kind of passion Mack wanted to see.

They were full of ginger off the field too. On the night of June 8 Ira Thomas, Perkins, Cochrane, and Rommel went to the Lew Tendler–Jack Zivic fight at Shibe Park. When Rommel made some disparaging comment about preliminary fighter Benny Bass, a Bass admirer took offense. Rommel took a poke at the man, who ducked. Rommel's fist landed on the man's brother's eye. They were all hauled into court, where Rommel was bound over for trial. A crowd gathered outside the courthouse and booed the players as they left. Thomas knew this was prime material for the Shibe Park hecklers and appealed to them not to use the incident to ride the players.

For Connie Mack the pennant ride was exhilarating. He felt younger than he had in a decade. He was at his best with this kind of young, smart, hungry team. When the A's were in Boston in early June, one of Mack's literary friends, Samuel Merwin, editor of *Success* magazine, came to see him at Fenway Park. Merwin told Isaminger, "I consider Mack one of the most remarkable figures in sport today. Just think of a man in the mid-sixties with his enthusiasm, imagination, and perseverance. There is no parallel anywhere in sport."

Connie Mack was what they call a players' manager. Do your job, and he left you alone. Need a shot of confidence, and he'd find the right time and the right words. Pull a bonehead play, and he'd call you aside the next day and suggest you try it a different way. He shook off physical errors. If an outfielder dropped a fly ball after a long run, Mack would tell him few outfielders could have even reached the ball. Boot a grounder? "This game would be altogether too easy if such things didn't happen." But grouse or complain or argue with him or talk back to him, and he wouldn't hesitate to snap at you with a barb as sharp as an arrowhead. Stir up trouble in the clubhouse, and it didn't matter what you were hitting, you'd be gone. He managed men with consideration and kindness but left no uncertainty as to who was the boss.

Like most managers, Mack played the percentages. But he was not bound by "the book" and was indifferent to being criticized if he played a hunch and it backfired. When Jimmie Dykes became a manager in 1934, Mack's advice to him included, "Always play your hunches, no matter how unorthodox they are. Whether or not they work, don't second-guess yourself."

Mack's pregame meetings were always open to those who had a comment about an unfamiliar pitcher or batter they may have seen in the minors or anything they might have noticed about the day's opponent. Bing Miller recalled, "In sizing up an opposing team, ballplayers are inclined to pick the key men, the fellows who are likely to do the damage, the players who must be stopped. But Connie used to emphasize the other men in the line-up, the weaker hitters that you would be inclined to ignore. 'It's the short hits from the weak batters that ruin you,' Connie would say."

There was not much talk about reading pitchers or trying to steal catchers' signs anymore, although a base runner on second might pick up the catcher's signs and relay them to the bench or the batter—for example, by holding his hands straight down for a fastball, curved for a hook. Most players didn't want to know what was coming. Some were afraid of being crossed up. Signs could be changed with a man on second. Others tended to overswing if they were counting on a particular pitch. Instead Mack had them watching for tipoffs that enabled them to read the signs for the hit and run, steal, and sacrifice bunt.

Mack let Cochrane call his own game. If the rookie looked over to the bench for help, Mack would shake his head and let him call the pitch. It wasn't just because it was Cochrane. Mack had always been that way, wanting his players to have the confidence to think for themselves. When Cy Perkins was a rookie, Mack had told him, "If you're ever in a spot where you don't know what pitch to call, just look over at me." One day the count was 2-2 in a close game, and Perkins looked over to the Athletics dugout. Mr. Mack just shrugged his shoulders. And they knew he wouldn't second-guess them.

Connie Mack was not only easy to play for, he was easy to work for. He had very few rules. He believed it intrigued ball players to figure out a way to break rules if given too many.

He didn't need private detectives, matchsticks on top of the hotel room doors, or spies among the desk clerks, bellboys, and telephone operators to tip him off to curfew violators. He knew all the tricks.

Make a big show of saying goodnight to him in the lobby at eight o'clock, and you might find him waiting for you at the back stairs or the freight elevator when you tried to duck out.

The A's were staying at the Buckingham Hotel in St. Louis that year. "The players often sat around after dinner," Baumgartner said, "their feet resting on a low wall facing the street. As it got dark, they yawned, said, 'I guess I'll go to bed,' excused themselves. Then they eased out the side entrance. I was alone one night with Mr. Mack. Finally I yawned, said, 'Well, I guess I'll turn in'—and started toward the door. Mr. Mack looked up, smiled. 'You, too?' he asked."

And he knew who were the fun-loving players who needed closer watching. He never went to night clubs, but he seemed to know who did. If he said something to them, it was more to let them know that he knew what they were up to.

Once in spring training he was sitting in the hotel lobby when a rookie plopped down beside him. "Do you mind if I sit next to you and think with you?" the rookie said.

"Not at all, son," said Mack. "You better start thinking right now about getting in shape."

Sometimes he didn't even have to say anything. A player who had pulled an all-nighter might enter the elevator from the lobby at seven in the morning just as Mr. Mack was getting off to go to breakfast. The manager would walk right past him without a word. The night owl just *knew* that Mack knew. Jimmie Dykes recalled:

> Connie wasn't strict with us. I can't ever remember him fining anybody. We had a midnight curfew. If you were going to stay out late, he insisted you tell him about it beforehand. It was a good idea to tell him, too, because he'd find out about it. I don't know what his sources of information were, but he always knew. If he accused you of something and you were guilty, the thing to do was own up. Then he'd say, "All right, I just wanted to let you know that I knew." But if you denied something, if you tried to lie your way out of it, then he'd lay you out. So we all got the idea pretty quick: Plead guilty.

"Big league ballplayers are no children," Mack told Sid Keener. "There are times when we are invited out by friends—myself and the boys. And when I'm out do you think I want to be looking at my watch every second waiting for quarter of eleven so I can run back to the hotel by eleven? I don't and I don't want the boys [to do so], either. I tell them to make it as close to twelve o'clock and to let their own conscience be their guide. A bit of recreation is good for anybody, ballplayers who are nervous and going through the strain of a pennant ball club in particular."

But let your drinking or late-night carousing affect your play on the field, and you'd hear it from him, privately but firmly. There'd be a lecture on how you owed it to yourself, your family, your teammates, the fans who paid the fare, and your employers to be in shape to give your best every day. And if that didn't work, you'd be gone. Unless, of course, you were another Rube

Waddell. But Connie Mack hadn't seen the likes of Rube Waddell for going on twenty years now.

In July Mack saw an opportunity to pick up the veteran pitcher he had been looking for since January. The Red Sox asked for waivers on Jack Quinn. Mack claimed him. A Slovakia-born right-hander named John Quinn Picus who preferred to be thought of as an Irishman named John Picus Quinn, he was forty-two and knew everything there was to know about pitching. He was 3-0 in his first 4 starts for the A's.

So they rode merrily on their way, surprising everybody as they ran neck-and-neck with the Senators. Bill Lamar hit in 28 straight games; Al Simmons had a 23-game streak. As a rookie, Simmons had not gotten his bat around quick enough against right-handers' fastballs and was hitting them to right field. He had corrected that and was now pulling those pitches. He hit three balls onto the roof of the new second tier in left field within ten days in June. One day Isaminger asked Mack if he would swap Simmons for Babe Ruth.

"Not in a thousand years," Mack replied.

The pitching staff had the fewest complete games in the league, but that was because Mack didn't hesitate to use his starters as relievers. Stan Baumgartner told Ed Pollock of the *Ledger*:

> The boys go in there and pitch their heads off. They don't have to worry whether they'll be able to last the whole game or not. That's not the idea.
>
> They pitch as hard as they can as long as they can. If they weaken along the way they know some one else is ready to go in and pitch his head off to save the game for him.
>
> There's not so much talk about games won and lost as you think there is. If the club wins the ball game, what difference does it make who gets credit for it? We're all shooting for the pennant. The boys are inning pitchers. They work to win each inning and the ball game takes care of itself.

While maintaining his public optimism, privately Connie Mack questioned whether his young team had the experience to hold off the defending champions for an entire season. "They were tired and near the point of exhaustion," Mack later told Bob Paul. "So long as they were winning, however, they felt fresh and strong. Some of the boys hadn't been through a major league grind, and what a grind it becomes in the dog days of August."

It was as if he was waiting for the inevitable. He didn't have long to wait.

On August 15 they led by a game and a half.

On the twenty-eighth they were a half-game back.

Ten days later they were 9 games out.

It began in Boston on August 15, when Red Ruffing shut them out after Slim Harriss had one of his good outings. They headed west, and it must have seemed to Connie Mack as if he was reliving the days when they rarely won a game on the road. They opened in St. Louis with a 2-game lead, still cocky as ever. Ignoring Connie Mack's cautions about firing up opponents like George Sisler, they started riding the fourth-place Browns before the game. St. Louis jumped on Jack Quinn for 5 in the first, and though the A's tied it, the Browns came back and beat them 7–6.

That night Connie Mack had a feeling the worst was yet to come. He was right.

The next day the Athletics put on another of their garrison finishes. Trailing 6–2 in the ninth, they scored 6 runs, but the fired-up Browns did their own rallying and won in the last of the ninth, 9–8, when the usually sure-handed Rommel made an error. Mack again used five pitchers, twenty players all together. The Browns swept the series when Sisler drove in the winning run with a triple off Grove in the ninth, 7–6.

Mack's boys left St. Louis in second place and not so confident.

"Suddenly everything went wrong," Mack said. "Tired players became aware of sagging muscles. Their work became listless. Others tried to overcome this by seeking to force the breaks. They pressed too hard. The entire team lost its naturalness. I'm telling you it was a painful experience."

After 5 losses in a row, they won 2, then lost another 6 and went into Washington for an old-fashioned "crooshul" series down by 3½ games. On September 1 a howling mob filled every inch of Griffith Stadium, shouting down the thousand A's fans who had come on special trains, and razzing the 6-foot-6 Slim Harriss about his Washington Monument build until he pulled an ascension act in the third, failing to cover first on a drag bunt, walking a batter, and hitting another as 4 runs scored. When he came out of the game in the seventh, he thumbed his nose at the hooting rooters and was shooed off the premises by one of the four umpires. Meanwhile the A's could do little with Walter Johnson.

The next day they made 4 errors, ran into each other chasing pop flies, and let others fall between them. Their defense had fallen apart but the fight was still there. Down 7–0 after 4 innings, they scored 5 runs but fell short.

They continued to lose and were 7 games back when they came home for a do-or-die Labor Day doubleheader against Washington.

More than thirty thousand fans jammed Shibe Park for the morning duel between Lefty Grove and Walter Johnson. Grove, who preferred pitching morning games, had yet to win a game against the Senators and would never beat Johnson in their three meetings. The crowd gave the Senators a taste of the razzberries—except for Johnson, who was cheered when the public address barker, Babe O'Rourke, announced the starting battery and every time he came up to bat. Johnson outpitched Grove, but the way the A's saw it, a spectacular play by shortstop Roger Peckinpaugh did them in. With men on second and third and 2 out, Bill Lamar lined a shot over second base. Peckinpaugh lunged through the air and snared it, saving 2 runs. So Johnson took a 2–1 lead into the ninth, when these new, exciting Athletics rapidly pumped up, then deflated the crowd, threatening but failing to score when Miller overran third base and was tagged for the game-ending out.

Down 5–0 in the afternoon game, Mack's boys again thrilled their followers, this time a record-breaking throng of thirty-eight thousand, by coming back to tie it in the seventh before losing, 7–6. Jack Quinn lasted only 5 innings, and Stan Baumgartner couldn't hold off Bucky Harris's crew. It was the seventh 1-run loss in their 2-17 swoon.

The next day, aided by the lively antics of a pair of little black mascots, they broke the 12-game losing streak as Slim Harriss, rescued in the ninth by Sam Gray, held the Nats, 6–4. The lead was down to 8 games, and that's about where it ended.

They closed out the home schedule on a high note. Connie Mack had been after Jimmie Dykes about taking too many good pitches. He urged Dykes to become a first-pitch hitter. Dykes decided to try it. On October 2 against the Yankees he hit 3 singles, a triple, and a home run—all on first pitches. Stan Baumgartner pitched his only shutout of the year, 10–0.

Ed Rommel had been the workhorse again, appearing in 52 games, winning 21. Part of his effectiveness lay in his foolproof delivery; nobody could detect when anything other than a knuckleball was coming. Walberg was in 53, mostly in relief, and was still learning. At this stage of their careers, Walberg was more of a pitcher than Grove, but he wouldn't pitch inside—wouldn't "make 'em smell leather"—and everybody around the league knew it. They also knew that he was among the easiest pitchers in the league to read; he telegraphed his fastball with a straight wrist, his curve with a bent one. It was a tribute to his stuff that he would become a winning pitcher without ever perfecting the art of concealment.

Sammy Gray had two seasons in one. He came back from his broken thumb in May to win his ninth without a loss. Then, a week after he took a 1–0 loss in New York on July 3, his young wife died in Texas. Three weeks later he began a 5-game winning streak but was 2-6 in August and September, finishing 16-8.

Slim Harriss, though sometimes very good and sometimes very bad, had learned the value of changing speeds to go with his fastball and curve and won 19.

Grove was a thrower. None of that change-of-pace stuff. On June 26 against Washington, Goose Goslin had been up with men on first and second. Goslin tried twice to bunt but fouled off Grove's fastballs. Goslin swung and fouled off the next one. Philadelphia writers in the press box were begging for a curve. Grove fired another fastball over the plate and Goslin hit it out of the park. Grove had relieved twice as often as he had started and was more effective in that role, though he didn't like it. Erratic in the early going, he occasionally showed hints of things to come. On July 4 before fifty thousand in New York he battled Herb Pennock for 15 innings, striking out 10 and walking only 5 before losing, 1–0. In the thirteenth he pitched out of a three on, no out situation His strikeout ratio of 5.27 per 9 innings was the highest in the league in a decade. He also led the league in walks.

Led by Simmons's .384 with 253 hits and a league-leading 392 total bases, they batted a league-best .307 as a team. Hale, Cochrane, Lamar, and Dykes all hit well over .300. Walter French pinch-hit 37 times and hit .351 in that role.

(The Pottsville [PA] Maroons joined the National Football League that fall. They wanted French to play for them. When he approached Mack about it, French later told Frank Graham, "He didn't like the idea very much at first." French had a young wife and baby daughter to support and he really needed the money, "and [Mack] gave in after a while."

French and catcher Charlie Berry, an All-American end at Lafayette who had played for Pottsville in 1924, led the Maroons to the NFL championship and played again in 1926.)

They were the youngest team in the major leagues and their inexperience cost them. They finished the year 7-13 against the defending champion Senators. When they began to lose, they were at full strength, free of the injuries that had handicapped them at the start of the season. Mack lamented the breaks that went against them, the untimely double plays—even one triple play—that snuffed out rallies. It got so that whenever they had men on base, somebody on the bench would mutter, "I suppose we'll hit into a double play now"—and they would. An exasperated Mack told them to shut up.

"It just seemed that fate was against us," Mack said.

In fact, they were up against themselves. "Slovenly" was the word Mack later used to describe their late-season performance. They had tightened up, making costly mental and physical errors. They were neither the first nor last young team to wilt in the late August heat of a pennant race.

The 1926 *Spalding Guide* summed it up: "The breaks went against them. When a team begins to feel that the breaks are going against it, it must have two qualities, one of them fight and the other no regard for what happened the day before. The Athletics had not been through the pennant mill long enough to have either and they began to worry. From then they began to lose, and the first thing they knew the possibility of winning the pennant had slipped away from them like oil from the bung of a barrel and was floating away down South toward Washington."

Looking back, Mack admitted to Bob Paul, "That team wasn't of championship caliber. There were too many young men on the club. [Lefty Grove] hadn't settled down. We had played fine ball on the first two western trips, but it wasn't in the wood for us to hold our fast pace. Some of the players were tired from the hard grind."

Connie Mack hoped that his boys had learned from the experience. The old man had learned something too: it was much tougher to win a pennant today than it used to be. Gone were the days when the brainy Jack Barry and Eddie Collins could invent plays that might take a whole season for somebody else to work out and emulate—if they had the men who could do it. Players and coaches and managers were smarter than ever.

"Baseball has changed since the days of that Athletic team," Mack told St. Louis writer J. Roy Stockton in May. Now, he said, "your individual stuff is no longer your individual property. In the old days we could perfect a few plays and use them over and over before they became common property. Now everybody has their eyes open and if you devise a play and use it on Monday the other fellow will try to beat you with the same play on Tuesday. They throw your stuff right back at you."

The season had turned into a two-team race. Next year Mack expected the competition would be tougher, with three or four more teams in contention.

The rise to a second-place finish was gratifying, but it was still disappointing that they had come so close before fading. One consolation was the second-place shares of the World Series gate. When it came time for Judge

Landis to send out the checks, Mack requested that his share be included in the players' pot. Twenty-eight players, Doc Ebling, and Earle Mack each received $904.40. When Jim Poole was injured, Mack had bought veteran first baseman Red Holt from Jersey City. Holt had batted .273 in 27 games but was sidelined with a pulled groin muscle in September and was left off the list submitted to the commissioner's office. Landis, scrupulous about things like that, checked his record and sent him $150 from the pot.

Many fans outside of Washington were also disappointed for Connie Mack, "who, when all is said and done, is a genuinely esteemed gentleman the baseball world over," wrote Will Wedge in the *New York Sun*. In May Grantland Rice had written, "No leader in baseball has a greater number pulling for him to win than the angular Connie Mack. [White Sox manager] Eddie Collins and Bucky Harris are popular in every city, with multitudes of friendly supporters, but there is something appealing in the eleven-year patient vigil of Mack searching for the lost trail back to glory."

Rice called Mack "a great example for those easily discouraged. He has shown that it is worthwhile to keep an uphill battle against the odds going on for eleven years to land among the elect. He has faced enough tough breaks to discourage a rhinoceros. It is no easy matter to buck fate two or three years without making any headway. To keep hammering for more than a decade without an alibi or complaint deserves all the reward there is. The willowy Mr. McGillicuddy has shown more in almost unending defeat than he showed in victory, so far as inspirational fiber is concerned."

The close pennant race, despite the late-season collapse, and the scrappy, heavy-hitting team that Mack had patiently assembled paid off at the gate. The A's shattered all Philadelphia records, drawing almost 870,000, nearly three times the sixth-place Phillies' attendance. It would be twenty-two years before the A's would reach that level again. Home and road receipts topped $1 million for the first time, net income after $30,000 depreciation and $70,000 of player purchase payments, exceeded $350,000. The directors declared another $50,000 dividend.

It was more than just winning that did it. Fans had a hard time trying to pick a favorite player. Al Simmons drove off with the new Buick awarded to the team's MVP chosen by the writers. Unlike the businesslike, near-perfect champions of the 1910–1914 era, this edition of the Athletics was a collection of colorful characters. They were loud and brash and made good copy.

They had their superstitions. When he was pitching, Sammy Gray went into a rage if anyone picked up his glove where he had left it on the ground between innings. Eddie Rommel considered it good luck if he saw the 6777 trolley go by Shibe Park on Lehigh Avenue before a game, an ill omen if he didn't. Jimmie Dykes considered a certain traffic light outside the hotel they used in Detroit as an omen of good or bad luck, depending on what color it was when he saw it on the way to Navin Field.

Even Mr. Mack had his quirks. Woe be to anyone who borrowed his score-keeping pencil between games of a doubleheader if the A's had won the first game. Mack's longtime scholarly friend James Penniman, who had rarely missed a game since the Athletics' debut in 1901, told Will Wedge, "Sometimes to break a losing streak he will wear odd shoes, one tan and one black, or two left shoes. He'll give himself any discomfort if he thinks it will help his team. He's very superstitious about the side of the plate on which the umpire's whiskbroom is tossed. If it is on the off side, all is well with the A's. If it is not, then Connie sneaks a player up to the plate to toss the whisk in the lucky position."

On Saturdays, Mack's children, sometimes his late brother Dennis's daughters, and other relatives sat behind the A's dugout, drawing winks from some of the players. They joined the players' wives in crossing their fingers, sitting immobile lest a movement kill a rally, or turning their thumbs down when the visitors were at bat.

It had been a long time since it was so much fun to go to a ball game at Shibe Park.

20 | HERE COME THE YANKEES

Nineteen twenty-five had been a strenuous year for Connie Mack. After a decade of sitting through abysmal ball games while patiently trying to put together another winner, he had been energized but enervated by the tension and excitement of once again being in the thick of a pennant race.

He skipped the World Series between Washington and Pittsburgh—the only game he planned to attend in Washington was rained out—and relaxed at Pine Valley golf course and at football games.

The Red Grange mania began in the fall of 1925. The Galloping Ghost signed a contract with the Chicago Bears that paid him a piece of the gate in their exhibition and NFL games, an amount that exceeded $20,000 several times. On Saturday, December 5, a capacity crowd sat in a freezing rain in Shibe Park to see Grange score twice in the Bears' 14–7 win over the Frank-ford Yellow Jackets. The Athletics' 20 percent of the gate—$16,214—made up for Grange's tearing up John Shibe's muddy field. The next day the Bears attracted more than sixty-five thousand to the Polo Grounds in New York. They played 19 games in eleven weeks.

On December 24 *The Sporting News*'s cracked crystal ball predicted the Grange craze wouldn't last and "professional football will never become the national game."

In the days of rudimentary conditioning methods and unschooled trainers who used rolling pins on knotted muscles; when batters went up to the plate with no armor shielding their hands, arms, shins, or heads; when almost all games were played in the glaring heat and humidity of late afternoon by men wearing heavy woollen uniforms; when collisions were common between base runners and guardians of the bases; when they played with broken bones and charley horses; when catchers debated whether plain dirt or tobacco juice was the better treatment for split fingers—and the lucky ones endured all that for eight, ten, maybe fifteen years—the wear and tear on ballplayers' bodies often left them with arthritic joints and scarred legs for the rest of their lives.

There was another toll to pay: the emotional toll of the frustration of frequent failure, of inexplicable slumps that could grip a man at any time. A loss of confidence could end a career as suddenly as stepping into quicksand could snuff out a life. The biggest mental challenge for anyone in the game was maintaining an even keel, enjoying the good days and years without getting too high, and suffering through the slumps and losing years without sinking too low. Every team went into each season knowing it would lose anywhere from three to six games out of every ten. Most batters knew they would be defeated by a pitcher at least 70 percent of the time. Pitchers knew that a good year meant losing only 40 percent of their decisions; even the best might lose a 1–0 heartbreaker or be ignominiously routed on any given day.

Every player had his own demons to deal with. For Connie Mack, squirming on the pine boards of the dugout every day for six months, his only physical hazard was splinters penetrating the shiny seat of his pants. But behind his stoic facade, like any manager he had to deal with the demons of each of his men in addition to his own. During his years in Philadelphia he had swung from exhilaration to humiliation. He had won six pennants and known only one losing season in his first fourteen, then had been plagued by ten losing years until 1925. After twenty-five years on this roller coaster, his Athletics had won 1,838 games and lost 1,865.

The fact was, Connie Mack was tired. One writer described him in the spring of 1926 as "gaunt, wrinkled and gray." At sixty-three, he had been a manager for over thirty years, after a dozen years as a catcher.

Perhaps that's why, when Mack signed Kid Gleason as a coach, speculation began that Gleason would succeed Mack as the A's manager in a year.

William "Kid" Gleason was 67 inches and 158 pounds of pure rawhide. Four years younger than Mack, Gleason was born across the river from Philadelphia in Camden, New Jersey, and lived there all his life. A teammate of John McGraw and Hughie Jennings on the 1895 Baltimore Orioles, he was a charter member of the creators of the old school of baseball. Breaking in as a pitcher with the Phillies in 1888, he had switched to second base when he joined the Orioles. He became the Giants' captain in 1896 and may have been the first to order a batter intentionally walked. He jumped to the new American League in 1901 and back to the Phillies in 1903.

Gleason played his last game at the age of forty-five in his first year as a coach for the White Sox in 1912. Seven years later he became the White Sox manager and was the innocent victim of the men who sold the 1919 World Series out from under him. His heart was broken but not his spirit. He remained with the depleted Sox through 1923 and had been sidelined by illness for the past two years.

"I feel sure that 'Kid' Gleason will help the team as a coach," Mack told Joe Vila of the *New York Sun* on December 11 in New York. "I am glad to have him with me. The Athletics, under his influence, will fight harder and longer. Gleason is one of the best posted men in the game."

Gleason was a tough disciplinarian whose feisty attitude and sharp tongue could be caustic as well as comic and might have earned a less respected man a lot of enemies. He had a reputation for whipping any man of any size he thought deserved whipping. Veteran Philadelphia writers enjoyed telling the story of Gleason's role as enforcer of club curfews in 1907. Pitcher Frank "Fiddler" Corridon was rooming with a reporter in spring training in Savannah. One night at curfew time Gleason looked for the pitcher.

"He's around the hotel," said the reporter-roommate.

Gleason went to his room, picked up a shaving strop, and returned to the lobby to wait. When Corridon came in, the forty-year-old Gleason grabbed the six-footer, bent him over his knee, and whaled him with the strop.

Jimmie Dykes, who sometimes misplaced the details around the kernels of truths in his many yarns, was the source of a story describing Gleason's role of seeing that his young Athletics charges behaved.

One day in a Pullman diner there were two good-looking girls seated nearby. The players started to show off. Dykes was slurping his soup and giggling. The players sitting with him did the same.

"That will do," snapped Gleason, seated nearby.

When they kept it up, Gleason picked up a soup spoon and rapped Dykes on the head. "Let that be a lesson to you."

He then turned to the girls and said, "Ladies, pay no attention to these rowdies. It will not happen again."

With it all, Kid Gleason was liked and respected throughout baseball. Umpire/columnist Billy Evans said that as a manager, "Gleason was more of a father to them. To a man they say they would play their heads off for him. In the evening he was in the midst of them discussing the game of the day."

Early in the 1926 season, when the A's got off to a slow start, one writer tried to pin the blame on the players' resentment of Gleason's cracking the whip in practice. The A's all laughed at the idea and shook their heads at the inane stuff reporters came up with.

The latest flap to divide the leagues and add to the bitterness between Ban Johnson and Judge Landis involved the use of the resin bag. Technically banned since 1920, caches of resin had been kept on or near the benches for years. Between innings pitchers would dip their fingers into it and apply a dab to their gloves and uniforms to apply while on the mound. At its December meeting the NL proposed to make it legal. The American League, led by Mack and Clark Griffith, who believed it would be a step backward toward the return of the days of the doctored balls, opposed it.

The joint rules committee met at the Hotel Roosevelt in New York on January 29, 1926, to consider the proposed rule: "Provided, that under the supervision of the umpire the pitcher may use to dry his hands a small, finely meshed, sealed bag containing powdered resin, furnished by the league, to be put near the pitcher's box." The pitcher had to request it.

Mack, umpire Tom Connolly, and former Chicago writer I. E. Sanborn, representing the AL, voted no. Pirates representative Fred Clarke, Cardinals owner Sam Breadon, and William Wrigley voted yes for the NL. Dale Gear, president of the Western League, represented the minor leagues. Judge Landis, as chairman, and Dale Gear broke the tie by voting yes.

As far as Judge Landis was concerned, decisions of the joint rules committee became law, not just recommendations. It didn't matter if the league delegations were split and he had to break the tie. It wasn't the first time he had decided things when the two leagues disagreed. He had done so twice in the very first joint meeting he had presided over, on January 12, 1921. The AL had voted for a thirty-player limit; the NL for twenty-five. Landis voted for twenty-five. The AL wanted a trading deadline of July 15, the NL August 1. Landis sided with the NL.

Ban Johnson didn't see the joint rules committee's recommendations as law. Nobody was going to tell his league what to do. On February 9 his club owners backed him with a unanimous vote to reject the rules committee's recommendation on the resin bag. This action was seen as a slap at Landis, and it wasn't the only one delivered by the AL that winter. The Nationals, eager to show their support for Landis, had voted on December 9 to extend the commissioner's contract by ten years when his original seven-year term expired. The Americans, meeting at the same time, didn't even discuss it. Instead, conceding that they had treated their leader shabbily while caving in to the glare-down with Landis a year earlier, they gave Johnson a $10,000 raise and a new contract through 1935.

"But we didn't give him the new contract wholly as a balm to assuage injured feelings," one unnamed owner felt obliged to explain. "We did this because the organizer and lifelong head of our organization was entitled to it."

Maybe it wasn't wholly a balm. Just mostly.

No American League umpires were issued resin bags for spring training. While touring the training camps, Judge Landis conducted an informal survey of pitchers, asking them if they had been using it in the past and become dependent on it to keep their hands dry. Some admitted they had.

The possibility that the two leagues would operate under different rules wouldn't necessarily compromise the game until it came to the World Series, which was played under the commissioner's supervision. But Landis wasn't about to let the matter simmer until then.

Once again Ban Johnson forced the issue. Ten days after the season opened, he sent out a notice reminding all managers that the use of resin, or even its presence on the field or in the dugout, was forbidden in the AL. Managers and pitchers would be suspended indefinitely for violating the order.

"Nonsense," thundered the judge. "Any rule approved by the joint rules committee applies to both leagues, in fact, to all leagues." Eight minor leagues had also voted to continue the ban on resin. Landis reminded them that under the major–minor league agreement, all rule changes passed by the joint rules committee were effective immediately, everywhere.

That judicial thunderclap scared the AL owners. At a meeting originally called for the Hotel Belmont in New York on April 28 to adopt a new league constitution, they repudiated Johnson, their "lifelong head," and caved in to the commissioner. The vote was 6–2. Clark Griffith remained adamant in opposing the use of resin by pitchers. Phil Ball of St. Louis didn't care about any resin bags. He was enraged that Landis was telling them what they had to do. Then they hedged by passing a resolution urging all managers to request their pitchers not to ask for the foul substance.

Revising the constitution, which had been amended so many times over the past fourteen years that nobody really knew what was in it, was postponed again.

From time to time the two leagues had been appealed to for financial aid by indigent former players and their families. They had been generous in their responses. In 1922 the American League had approved setting aside $10,000 from World Series receipts for five years to create a fund for that purpose. For several years they had been aiding former Boston catcher Lou Criger, who had lost a leg to tuberculosis in 1915.

In the spring of 1926 a new players' organization was formed that Connie Mack heartily endorsed. The Association of Professional Ball Players of America had only one purpose: to help in the care of indigent or disabled former players in their old age. When the secretary, Russ Hall, met with the Athletics before a game in Chicago on June 8, Mack and almost every player joined.

Mr. and Mrs. Mack, their five-year-old daughter Betty, and their close friends Mr. and Mrs. George Jacoby were among the players and writers who left Philadelphia for spring training in a blizzard on Friday, February 19. Lefty Grove used the quiet time on the train to approach the writers and request that they drop the "s" from his name and spread the word, which Isaminger did in his first dispatch after they arrived on Sunday. It would take some months for the wire services and other papers to make the change and several years for baseball publications to comply.

They were greeted in Fort Myers by warm sunshine, a large welcoming crowd, and an elephant covered by a banner prematurely claiming "Champions 1926." The elephant was owned by Billy Clark, a Philadelphia ex-fighter turned showman who had the midway concession at the Lee County Fair, which would open on Tuesday. Among the welcomers were Joe Hauser and his wife, who had been there for a month so Joe could exercise his wired-up knee. The real estate boom was still much in evidence. New stores and theaters were going up downtown. Brand new bungalows lined the avenues leading to the golf course and fair grounds. There were still no hotels big enough for all of them; they were scattered among the Royal Palm, Bradford, and Grand Central.

The practice field, inside the race track surrounded by the fair grounds, had been greatly improved as promised. A new grandstand had been built. But the A's and the fair didn't coexist calmly. On Monday they found Clark's elephant grazing in the outfield when they tried some light batting practice. The pitchers shagging flies had to run around it. When the pachyderm was hit in the side by a line drive, it kept right on pulling up grass. Kid Gleason yelled, "Hey, Billy, get that French poodle of yours out of the way." Clark whistled and the obedient elephant tromped away.

Mack had planned two workouts a day. On Tuesday the fair opened. The wild west show went on at 2:30 just outside the infield, where Kid Gleason was hitting fungos and the pitchers were playing pepper. The players enjoyed the show, but they were frightening the horses and distracting the bronco busters. Mack agreed to hold one workout a day, 10:30–2:00, until the fair closed on Saturday night. There would be plenty of red necks and arms from the hot midday sun.

Mack called all the pitchers together and lectured them on the merits of running to build their endurance—not for pitching but for base running. Mack, who would rather see a pitcher strike out than get on base on a hot day, had been an early advocate of a designated hitter to keep pitchers off the bases. "Last year there were too many instances of [a pitcher] running from first to third who so weakened himself he was valueless on the rubber in the next half," he told them. "His knees would shake from the effort and he lost speed and control. There was a reason for this. The pitcher never did enough running. All he did in practice was to exercise his arm."

They could get their arms in shape their own way, but he wanted to see them jogging around the park and doing fifty-yard wind sprints. "And jog around the park the last thing you do," he ordered.

One Wednesday morning a motorcar pulled up to the third base line and stopped. A few people got out and helped a white-haired gentleman down from the running board. The man walked slowly over to Connie Mack. One of his companions introduced him as the inventor Thomas Edison. Mack said a few words, but his soft voice didn't register. "I can't hear a word you say," the seventy-nine-year-old Edison said. "I'm deaf as an adder."

Mack shouted into his ear, "Do you like baseball?"

"I'm a real crank," said Edison, still using the obsolete nineteenth-century term for a fan. He said he had first come to Fort Myers and set up a work-shop forty years ago when the place was "a hamlet of about forty houses, thirty-seven buildings being saloons."

Some photographers handed Mr. Edison a bat and urged him to stand at home plate and swing it. Batting left-handed, he swung and missed at a ball lobbed underhand by Kid Gleason as the cameras clicked and flashed and movie cameras whirred. Gleason lobbed another. Edison hit a swinging bunt but didn't run. He and Mack shook hands, and the wizard of Menlo Park returned to his car. Later he invited the entire team and their wives and children to his home.

The next day Connie Mack was stunned by the news of the death of Eddie

Plank, who had suffered a stroke three days earlier and died on February 14. He was fifty. The frosty, awkward atmosphere of their professional parting of the ways after the 1914 season was long forgotten.

A visibly shaken Mack told reporters:

> I feel like a father must feel when he has lost a son. Any words I can voice will not describe the shock that I have suffered. It was a blow to me when I learned that Eddie had suffered a stroke. But I had hoped that he might recover from that. He was a rugged man, young enough, I was confident, to pull through and regain his health.
>
> Plank came to me right from college. He was with me in the days when our American League team in Philadelphia was fighting for its existence. I had to call on him to work pretty hard in those days. He never failed me, never complained.
>
> Eddie Plank was one of the smartest left-hand pitchers it has been my pleasure to have on my club. He was short and light, as pitchers go. But he made up for the physical defects, if such they were, by his study of the game and his smartness when he was on the pitching peak.
>
> Plank was the master of the cross-fire delivery, and that was one of his big assets. He worked hour after hour to perfect control of that cross-fire, and it made him.
>
> The world has lost a fine, clean sportsman when Eddie Plank died. I am certain he did not have a real enemy in the world. He was the salt of the earth. My heart goes out in sympathy to those of his family who survive him.

To James Isaminger he added, "Plank was a clean liver and worked a good influence on the younger players. Another point that made him stand out was that he always gave the club his best services. He never sulked or eased up, but always was at high pressure throughout the game."

Plank's World Series ERA was 1.30, but he won only 2 of his 6 complete games.

Connie Mack went to Fort Myers with sound reason for optimism. There would be little experimenting, no dozens of hopefuls to sort through and send home. His high-priced rookies, Cochrane and Grove, had a year's experience behind them. Mack shrugged off Grove's inconsistent performance, chalking it up to the fans expecting too much from him, and predicted that Lefty would be "sensational . . . before we get through with him."

They did a lot with Grove before they got "through with him" that spring.

Connie Mack told him if he didn't get control he'd be just another pitcher. But he could be more than that, much more. Mack suggested he pick a spot to aim for when he warmed up. "Try to hit the catcher's belt buckle."

In a 1932 interview with John Drohan of the *Boston Traveller*, Grove was ambivalent about whether it helped.

Ira Thomas blamed his wildness on not throwing from the proper angle. His curve broke away from the plate, allowing hitters to ignore it and sit on the fastball, if they could catch up to it. Thomas noticed that Bing Miller, a right-handed batter who hated facing lefty pitchers, had no trouble hitting Grove in batting practice. Thomas asked him about it. "I can see Grove's stuff," Miller said. That convinced Thomas he was right. He shared his views with Mack and Kid Gleason. They set about correcting his delivery.

Cy Perkins decided that Grove's control problems came from working too fast. Cochrane later wrote that taking his eye off the plate as well as hurrying his pitches caused Grove's wildness. He was ready to pitch as soon as he got the ball from the catcher.

Fiddle with the ball a little between pitches, Perkins suggested. But Grove was no fiddler. He was as opposite to Eddie Plank as you could find. He didn't want infielders coming over to talk to him, slowing him down. And they weren't eager to do it. Whenever Mack wanted somebody to walk to the mound to cool him off, Dykes was the one he signaled. "What's the matter, Mosey?" was about all he'd dare say before getting out of there.

"Connie Mack would tell his other pitchers to go high and inside or low and outside when in doubt," Grove recalled years later. "'But not you, Robert,' he would say, 'because you'll pitch your own way anyway.'"

In the past Grove hadn't needed any time to study the catcher's signs; he relied almost entirely on his fastball. Cy Perkins persuaded him to begin working on a slow curve as a change-up. It was new to him, and sometimes it threw him off stride. And when he tried to throw a fast curve, it did nothing because he was throwing it as hard as his fastball and it couldn't break. But he kept working on it, throwing to Earle Mack for an hour every day. By opening day Grove had mastered the hook.

Somebody—Cochrane later said it was Kid Gleason—suggested Lefty count to ten between pitches. He tried it, so audibly and visibly that first bench jockeys, then spectators, picked up on it and counted along with him.

In a 1941 *Saturday Evening Post* article, Stanley Frank wrote that Miller Huggins was the first to notice it. Hug had the Yankee batters count to seven, then step out of the batter's box. If they did, it didn't bother Grove. He beat them four times that year, striking out 10 in one game and 12 in another, which he followed up with 3 innings of relief in the second game of a July 5 doubleheader.

That his counting was common knowledge is evidenced by James R. Harrison of the *New York Times* referring to it in his account of Grove's June 28 7–1 win, in which Grove struck out Babe Ruth twice and never went to a three-ball count all day: "This season [Grove] counts fifteen before each pitch, juggling the ball up and down in his glove as he counts."

If Harrison knew what he was looking at, he also contradicted the later myth that Grove never developed a real curve until he lost the zip on his fastball ten years later. On that June day in 1926, wrote Harrison, "His fastball came up hopping like a kangaroo, his curve had the blind staggers; it whirled and sagged and took unique angles and his control was so perfect that he threw no more than two bad balls to any batter."

Whatever it was that worked, Lefty Grove became "pleasingly wild," in Branch Rickey's terms. He never again led the league in walks; for the next seven years his strikeouts more than doubled his walks. Sure, he'd blow up now and then, throwing as many as nine straight balls. But coming in with the bases loaded and nobody out, he could also throw nine straight strikes, against the Yankees or anybody else.

Connie Mack had no holdouts; Cochrane had signed a three-year contract, starting with an 80 percent raise to $8,000 for 1926, $9,000 for '27, and $10,000 for '28. Simmons signed a new three-year pact, almost doubling his salary to $11,000 for 1926 ($2,000 more than the Yankees' sensational 1925 rookie, Earle Combs, would earn), and calling for $2,000 raises in '27 and '28. Sammy Gray's salary went from $4,000 to $7,500. Grove was in the second year of his original contract at $6,500. Just about everybody else received a satisfactory raise of from $500 to $1,500. Even Joe Hauser, despite his uncertain status, was kept at the same $6,500, as much as the Yankees were paying their first baseman, Lou Gehrig.

After two years Al Simmons was now an established star. Mack called Simmons, twenty-three, "one of the greatest players I've ever managed," and said of Cochrane, twenty-two, "He possesses every quality that makes a great catcher, yet Cochrane has many years ahead of him. He is only a boy."

On October 17 the Pirates had paid a six-figure price for Paul Waner. Mack had been interested in him—everybody knew about Waner's big year in San Francisco—and once said he had missed buying him "by a week." Hard to say what that means; he had the money and the willingness to spend it. Maybe he waited too long to raise his bid. Clearly the urgency to add a bat that had impelled him to go high for Paul Strand two years ago was no longer there.

Mack considered buying Joe Boley from Baltimore to replace Chick Galloway, who had posted a disappointing year. But he decided to stay with his infield. Max Bishop had gained fifteen pounds over the winter and looked stronger than ever. But Mack was concerned that Bishop lacked the stamina to play every day. He picked up the fading veteran Bill Wambsganss from the Red Sox for bench strength. (Wambsganss was only thirty-two, but he was portrayed at the time of the deal as "not quite as old as King Tut's Tomb.") A lot depended on Joe Hauser's ability to come back. In addition to his team's inexperience, Mack pinned their failure to win in '25 on the year-long loss of the slugging first baseman.

Anticipating the return of a healthy Hauser, Mack had sent letters to other clubs trying to sell Jim Poole and Red Holt. This one, written September 23 to Garry Herrmann in Cincinnati, is illustrative of the frankness of Mack's assessment of his players and an example of why his contemporaries never doubted his word or his honesty.

Dear Mr. Herrmann:

Our club has an over-supply of first basemen, now having four and feel that we have a couple of players who would help your club a great deal.

Let me say that Hauser, who has been out of the game all season due to a broken knee-cap, is now in shape to play and next season will be in as good condition as ever, so will be our regular first baseman.

Poole has helped our club wonderfully this year. He is not a Hauser but he certainly is a good ball player. He has not been in the best of health, nevertheless will say again that he has been of splendid service to our club.

About September 5th I secured Holt, first baseman of the Jersey City Club, paying five thousand dollars down and agreeing to pay a further sum of fifteen thousand dollars by May 1st, 1926.

Holt in his first sixteen games with our club has batted .368 and has accepted 183 out of 184 chances. He was out of the game for a long period due to an injured groin and I can see where he is favoring the injury, but there is no doubt to my mind but that he is an exceptionally good player and am satisfied that he would help any major league club that was in need of a first baseman. He can hit and field and while he would not be considered a fast man at this time, and perhaps never would be, he is by no means a slow runner.

There is no denying the fact that for my part I would now like to get my money back on this player, the principal reason being that I am going to have Hauser. If you are interested in this player would like to hear from you. It might pay you to have one of your scouts look this player over for the balance of the season.

> With kind regards I am,
> Sincerely yours,
> Connie Mack

Herrmann received the letter the next day and immediately replied that he was "very much interested." Herrmann wound up buying a now expendable Wally Pipp from the Yankees. Mack, out $5,000, returned Holt to Jersey City.

Kid Gleason took charge of getting Joe Hauser into condition.

"The Kid's first order to me was to practice walking backwards as a means of strengthening my injured knee," Hauser later told Sam Levy of the *Milwaukee Journal*. "Then Gleason started in running me in reverse. When I mastered this trick the Kid was happy."

Gleason declared Hauser ready. But he wasn't. His right leg was stiff, as the doctors had predicted. He couldn't bend it enough to take a full cut at the plate. Taking throws at first base, he couldn't pivot or stretch the way he had been taught by Harry Davis. He complained about the wire hurting. Exercises were one thing, but the stress of maneuvering to play his position day after day was something else.

"I think it is the mental hazard that worries Hauser as much as anything else," Mack said. "He seemed to be all right until the time came for playing games and then he began to complain that his knee was bothering him. Poole is a good first baseman but he needs a day or two rest to be at his best. We figured it would be Poole helping out Hauser this year, but it looks like Hauser will be helping out Poole if he can play a few games now and then and pinch hit."

That's what happened. He looked like the Unser Choe of 1924 when the season started, nimbly making the plays, leading the club in drawing bases on balls, and hitting a long home run off a rooftop against Walter Johnson. He would have some other moments of glory; pinch-hitting for Cochrane on July 13, he hit a game-winning home run. But the leg bothered him. He would play in only 65 games, pinch hit in another 22, and bat .192 with 8 home runs. It was a good thing nobody had bid on Jim Poole.

For the first time in years Mack felt confident with his pitching staff of Gray, Walberg, Harriss, Rommel, and Grove. Ira Thomas wasn't so sanguine about Harriss. Nobody had better curves or speed, but he threw from the hip. No great pitcher, said Thomas, throws from the hip.

There was only one rookie—a thirty-three-year-old rookie—and therein lay a tale of five years of draft evasion.

Joe Pate was a rotund left-handed knuckleball pitcher who had been pitching in the minor leagues in Texas and the Southwest since 1911, with a spell as a lieutenant in an artillery regiment during the Great War. He joined the Fort Worth Panthers in July 1918 and had been there ever since, becoming the second winningest pitcher in Texas League history while the Panthers won six straight pennants. After going 16-4 in 1919, Pate had won 20 or more every year, twice chalking up 30 victories.

So how come he had never made it to the big leagues? The answer: he didn't want to, and the Cats' manager, Jake Atz, didn't want him to go.

Jake Atz, a light-hitting infielder with the White Sox in 1908–1909, had managed Fort Worth since 1914 (and would for sixteen years). Like Jack Dunn with Grove in Baltimore, he was in no hurry to sell his star pitcher. He paid Pate enough to keep him happy, more than some big leaguers earned. There was a bonus from their annual Dixie Series appearance. Pate acquired some business interests in the city and didn't want to be far from them for six months out of the year.

But unlike Baltimore and the International League, which had opted out of the draft system along with the American Association, Pacific Coast, III, and Western leagues, the Texas League didn't. Even in 1919–1920, when there was no major league draft agreement, an unlimited number of players could still be selected from the Class B Texas League by A and AA clubs. (The league became Class A in 1921.)

Jake Atz had plenty of friends in baseball. He had no problem finding somebody who would do him a favor to protect his meal ticket from predators. Since a Class A club could lose only one player in the draft, a cooperative club owner might draft someone else from the roster first or purchase Pate before the draft with the understanding that the pitcher would be returned the following spring. If a major league club made the phantom deal, unless it was a conditional purchase, there would have to be a wink and a nod agreement with the other clubs to allow the player to slip through the required waivers in order to return him.

It was the same form of collusion that Connie Mack had employed in the old days in Milwaukee with players like Ginger Beaumont, and had joined in helping the Columbia club hold on to Goose Goslin in 1920. But now there was a new commissioner in charge, and he might have something to say about such doings.

So it came to pass that the Boston Red Sox bought Pate and three other Panthers in August 1920; they were to report in the spring. The following March it was reported that Pate "refused to report." That usually led to the player landing on the ineligible list: "If you won't play for us, you can't play for anybody else." But, the records show, all four players were peacefully "returned" to Fort Worth for the 1921 season.

After Pate won 30 and lost 9 in 1921, Connie Mack claimed him during the October draft window and sent a check to Fort Worth for $1,900 as part payment on the $4,000 draft price. Pate was among four Texas League players named on the draft list issued by the minor league office.

On November 1 AP reported that Paul LaGrave, business manager of the Fort Worth club, had returned Mack's check to John H. Farrell, secretary-treasurer of the National Association of Professional Baseball Leagues, because, said LaGrave, Pate had been sold to the Toledo club of the American Association before he was drafted by Philadelphia.

The *San Antonio Evening News*, well aware of the draft-dodging tactics, ran the story under the headline: WAS JOE PATE SOLD TO TOLEDO TO "COVER HIM" FOR FORT WORTH TEAM?

The paper had it right. Pate's official transaction record makes no mention of a Toledo purchase. It shows simply: "Drafted by Phil AL Oct 1921; returned to Ft Worth April 1922," making it read as though the Athletics drafted him, then returned him.

The *Spalding Guide*, printed during the winter, said that Mack's draft claim was "being investigated." It was. And it wasn't the only one being investigated by the commissioner. Fort Worth and Charlotte had made the mistake of dealing with clubs in leagues that had opted out of the draft system.

On February 8, Landis issued this decision on "Attempted Draft Evasion":

On September 13, 1921, Charlotte transferred to Joplin the contract of Player Lloyd Smith, and on September 15, 1921, Fort Worth transferred to Toledo the contract of Players Whittaker and Pate.

These transfers to clubs in leagues that had refused to accept the draft were made for the purpose of excluding these players from the operation of the draft.

In the face of clearly demonstrative proof that the deals were in fraud of clubs having the right of selection, Toledo, Joplin and Charlotte stood firmly for the good faith of the transactions. Toledo also failed to comply fully with requests for information, and the president (now retired) of Joplin and of Charlotte, in an attempt to obstruct and frustrate the investigation, adopted every possible expedient, including loss of memory, misstatement of facts, and presentation of fictitious correspondence.

The investigation entailed a cost of approximately $200 for traveling expenses, telegrams, etc., which will be reimbursed by these four clubs, each paying $50.

In addition there will be a fine of $500 each against Toledo and Fort Worth, and of $750 each against Joplin and Charlotte. Checks for the amounts mentioned will be forwarded to the Secretary Treasurer within ten days.

The assignments above mentioned are nullified. The draft of Player Smith by the Boston National League Club is allowed. Draft of Player Pate by the Philadelphia American League Club would be allowed had that club not voluntarily withdrawn its claim. The player will therefore remain with Fort Worth.

So Joe Pate got what he wanted. Connie Mack, being a good guy, heeded Pate's pleas to let him stay in Fort Worth. And Jake Atz learned his lesson: don't fool around with bush league colluders. Although there is nothing in the transaction records, the story was that two years later Ty Cobb "bought" Pate for Detroit, then returned him because he "wouldn't report." Later Cobb was reported as telling Pate the Tigers would have won the 1924 pennant if they'd had him.

Connie Mack didn't give up. He had seen Fred Marberry create a new role for a pitcher—a relief specialist who appeared in 55 games and never started—for the pennant-winning Senators in 1925. Sure, Mack would still call on Grove and Rommel and Walberg as firemen when he needed them, but they were primarily starters. He wanted a Marberry. He wanted Pate, a tireless, wily, confident veteran with more soup in his noodle than his arm.

So with scout Mike Drennan's endorsement, he once again drafted Pate, who passed for thirty-one but was really thirty-three.

This time there were no delayed announcements of phantom sales. According to Philadelphia writer Stoney McLinn, Mack asked Pate to meet him in New York in December, where he persuaded the reluctant southpaw that the A's would be likely pennant winners with his help. It took $7,500—more than Grove or Walberg or Quinn would be earning—to sign him. Pate, remembering how close he had come to being claimed by the last-place A's of 1921 but for Connie Mack's reprieve, and possibly envisioning himself in a World Series, went home and sold his radio and battery store.

Despite his roly-poly appearance, Pate could hit and field his position adequately, and he was handy with a fungo bat for infield practice. Pate quickly made a believer out of Kid Gleason. "I hate to talk about Pate," he told skeptical writers, "for fear I will jinx him, but he showed me something I had never seen before, and that is putting his knuckler wherever he wants to."

Control the raw-raw, as the knuckler was sometimes called in those days? That was a laugh. Even the premier knuckleball pitcher, Eddie Rommel, said he never knew where the butterfly was going to land. But Gleason assured them Pate could do it. Ira Thomas agreed he had never seen the like.

Unlike modern-day knuckleball pitchers, Pate (and Rommel) didn't rely on the raw-raw entirely. Sometimes they would go through a complete game without using it once. That made it all the more effective when they sprang it in a tight spot.

One thing that made Connie Mack sore was talk of his being too old to continue on the job and his imminent retirement. There had been more of it than he cared to read that winter. He was more tired of talking about it than he would ever be of managing a team. One day during spring practice two Philadelphia writers, Cullen Cain and James Isaminger, were sitting on the bench with him. They were discussing pennant races of the past and those to come.

Then, wrote Cain, "This most serene and emotionless man was moved outside himself to make a florid gesture. . . . He appeared to speak with difficulty. Suddenly the flame burned up within him and he rose to his feet and stretched out one long arm. His words were clear enough now and they came in a tone that thrilled Jimmy Isaminger and me when he declared, 'There is no such thing as age in baseball. I tell you that Eddie Collins [thirty-eight] is twenty-two today and Hornsby [twenty-nine] is twenty-four. Their game proves it. They say I am too old to lead a team to a pennant but I tell you that in the spirit I feel like forty this year.'"

And watching his spirited and talented young team responding to the whip of Kid Gleason's tongue, Mack did feel young. On March 17 United Press baseball writer Henry L. Farrell found a relaxed Mack sitting in a corner of the dugout, his legs crossed, holding a scorecard—his only form of exercise to get ready for the season. Kid Gleason was sitting a few feet away.

"What's your club going to do this year?" asked Farrell.

Mack smiled. "Ask the Kid."

Gleason grinned. "We're in," he said.

Sizing up the rest of the league, Mack declared that Walter Johnson's days as a dominant pitcher were over, although Washington was still the team to beat. A healthy Babe Ruth would revitalize the Yankees, but they had two rookies in their middle infield—second baseman Tony Lazzeri from Salt Lake City and shortstop Mark Koenig from St. Paul. Lazzeri had hit 60 home runs and driven in 222, but Mack had learned to be skeptical of big numbers racked up in Utah. Koenig, a solid hitter, was not known as an outstanding glove man.

But something was bothering Mack about his team. He didn't mind his boys playing a little golf when they had a day off; he enjoyed it himself. What bothered him was the chatter on the bench, around the batting cage, and in the clubhouse and the hotel lobbies; it was all about their golf games, their strokes, their sand-trap woes. They weren't talking baseball. They were talking about PGA champion Walter Hagen, not Walter Johnson. One day before a game against Baltimore they were bragging about how far they could drive a golf ball. Orioles pitcher George Earnshaw said he could hit one from home plate over the center-field wall. That drew skeptical guffaws. Somehow Earnshaw located a driver and ball and proceeded to back up his boast.

Connie Mack remembered the days when his boys would discuss nothing but the last game and the next, how to do things differently or better—on or off the field. Today it was more like they were ballplayers three hours a day and golf nuts the rest of the time.

When the Giants and Yankees had arrived in Jacksonville on the same train, there were forty sets of golf clubs among the baggage. Many of them belonged to the writers, but a good number were the players', prompting Ed Barrow to growl, "That's what's the trouble with baseball. That's why pitchers can't work more than once a week. That's why we have to have special shift hitters for batters who can't hit lefthanders. That's why the game is softening up."

Blame it all on Bobby Jones, the soft-spoken, widely respected amateur golfer from Atlanta whose victory over the pros in the 1923 U.S. Open at the age of twenty-one and continued successes since then had inspired an epidemic of sedentary businessmen becoming Sunday duffers. By the time Jones retired in 1930, there would be 5 million of them, twenty times the number when Jones was a teenager.

Whatever the reason, Mack's boys looked flat and spiritless as they neared the end of March. "Worst looking bunch I ever saw," he was reported muttering. "They look rotten." On Monday of their last week in Florida, before a game with the Giants, Mack held a meeting to put some pep in them. They had no complaints about the weather, he said. They should all be in top condition and raring to go. And he banned golf for the rest of their stay.

They perked up and won the first four games of the city series against the Phillies before losing the last two.

It was cold in Washington on April 13, when Walter Johnson warmed up to start his twentieth season and Eddie Rommel his seventh. Vice-president Charles Dawes threw the first wild pitch. The umpires sported new blue suits in place of the pea green outfits of 1925. They didn't count pitches in those days; the half-frozen fans saw the kind of contest that is gone forever—two star pitchers battling for 14 scoreless innings before the Senators put together 3 of their 9 hits to score in the fifteenth. Rommel walked 6 and fanned 1. Afterward he said he didn't throw a single knuckleball. Maybe the wind was not strong enough that day to make it work. Or maybe the cold air stiffened his fingers too much. Whatever the reason, the hitters anticipating it made its absence as effective as its use.

Johnson was not as fast as he had been a dozen years earlier, but he was still formidable, smoothly flipping his sidearm buggy whip, his back and leg muscles easing the strain on his arm. He struck out 9, walked 3, and was lightly touched for 6 hits.

Lefty Grove was still inconsistent when the season began. In the Patriots Day morning game in Boston he was sharp, tossing a 3–1 3-hitter. But the last time Grove and Johnson started against each other, on April 23 in Philadelphia, it was no pitchers' duel. Grove walked the first two men he faced. Sammy Hale booted a grounder to load the bases. A visibly miffed Grove gave up a single to deep short by Joe Harris. Mack had seen enough. He rushed in Pate. Three more runs scored. Given the lead, Johnson relaxed and coasted to a 9–5 win.

Cochrane was now catching Grove. This was the kind of performance that infuriated him so, he'd turn beet red and threaten to beat up Grove. "Don't put a finger on him," Mack warned him more than once. "If you do, you'll regret it."

Was Grove faster than Johnson in his prime? Nobody knows. Batters swore his fastball jumped when it got to the plate. It was an optical illusion. When they saw it leave his hand, it looked to them like it would come in waist high, but when they swung it was up around the letters. It looked that way from the bullpen too, as White Sox pitcher Ted Lyons remembered it: "I don't know how fast Grove was. But we could sit out in the bullpen and see that fastball of his rising about ten feet before it got to the batter. Johnson threw a very heavy fastball; it would sink."

Perhaps that "hop" was why a few years later backup catcher Ed Madjeski described Grove's fastball as "light as a feather" to catch. And perhaps it looked that way to a batter because of his delivery. "He took a big step," said Madjeski, "and let the ball go in front when his arm was already horizontal, three or four feet closer to the plate than a pitcher with a higher release point."

One day in Chicago, Deacon White, a contemporary of Mack's in the 1880s, watched Grove in action. Visiting with Mack after the game, he said, "Imagine a batter trying to hit that speed while standing just forty-five feet from the pitching box."

The old catcher replied, "Imagine a catcher trying to hold those pitches barehanded."

Not every situation that tried Lefty's patience resulted in a tantrum. On June 24 against Washington, in the first inning Cochrane's wild throw into left field in a rundown between third and home was followed by Dykes losing a pop fly in the sun for a double. Ossie Bluege then hit a home run and it was 4–0. There was no sign that Grove had petulantly grooved one; Mack left him in, and he blanked the Senators for the next 4 innings, issuing no walks, until Mack pinch-hit for him. The A's eventually lost it in 10 innings.

In the second game that afternoon, the A's were losing when big black clouds threatened to open up in the fifth inning. The A's stalled, hoping the rain would come down and wipe out the game. The rain held off until the bottom of the sixth. When it came down, it took more than a dozen men twenty minutes to wheel out the giant steel drum and unroll the new tarpaulin that covered the infield. By then the field was unplayable.

In New York the Babe was back in full flower. The rookie infielders, Mark Koenig and Tony Lazzeri, lived up to their billing. Koenig would lead the league with 52 errors, but it seemed as if every time Babe Ruth launched one, Koenig was trotting home ahead of him. Traveling north from spring training with the Dodgers, the Yankees had reeled off almost daily romps, and they kept on rolling. Joe Dugan was off to a sizzling start. Gehrig, Combs, and Meusel were all hitting. By May 1 the Yankees were 13-3, the A's 6-11, 7½ games back.

Connie Mack was conceding nothing except that his boys, aside from Lamar and Dykes, just weren't hitting. He knew they would have to make their move in the long home stand that awaited them. They launched it by sweeping a 3-game series against the Yankees and kept on winning—9 in a row, 13 of 18 at home, then 4 out of 5 from the defending champion Senators. On the morning of May 13 they had cut the lead to 2 games. Trouble was, the Yankees began a 16-game winning streak of their own and were 30-9 before Grove stopped them, 2–1, on May 28. The A's won the next two in New York. But after all that, they were again 5 games back.

Connie Mack may have regretted his praising of Simmons to the skies. Great performances spawn great expectations, and Al wasn't living up to them at the plate or in the outfield. He considered himself a star and acted like it. "Uppity" was a word Joe Hauser used to describe him sixty years later and with a "big head." He had been voted the team's most valuable player by the writers in 1925, an award that did not sit well with some of the others. Simmons was born and raised in a Polish neighborhood and had a thick accent. He never lost it all, but with some tutoring from newspaperman Bill Duncan, his locution gradually improved. His sharp tongue and brusque manner never softened. It would take him a few years to trade in the flashy, garish outfits he wore when he first reached the big leagues for more conservative duds.

Al was touchy about his bats, didn't want anybody going near them. If anyone picked one up and hefted it, everybody heard the roar to "Drop it." He received more fan mail than anybody else. His locker was by the entrance to the showers. "He'd sit there reading his mail, blocking traffic to the showers," Hauser recalled. Simmons and Jimmie Dykes got into more than one hot argument over it.

This may have been the root—and substance—of a comment made by

Frank H. Young in the *Washington Post* in February 1928: "In 1926 rumors of cliques on the Athletics were heard all over the circuit; in fact, from a reliable source came the report of a 'free-for-all' fight in the Mackmen clubhouse."

Clubhouse fights and feuds have been common since the nineteenth century on pennant-winning teams as well as also-rans. The A's lack of hitting on the field had more to do with their place in the standings than any possible hitting in the clubhouse.

Bench jockeys around the league kept up their "foot in the bucket" routine when Al was at the plate. Young reported that some of the Senators thought the riding was affecting Simmons. They observed him changing his stance. The drives were not coming off his bat as hard as they had last year.

Simmons seemed to be playing for himself first, the team second. On May 25 the A's split a doubleheader against Washington in which the two teams combined for 51 hits, none by Simmons. "Fifty-one hits today," he complained, "and I had 8 for the collar." In the outfield he seemed distracted, his mind elsewhere—"a general air of lassitude in his work," Isaminger called it. Fly balls dropped in front of him for hits that could have been caught. When he made spectacular running catches that brought the crowd to its feet cheering, it was often because he had been in a trance and gotten no jump on the ball or misjudged it, breaking back for a blooper, then charging in to take it off his shoe tops, or breaking in on a ball over his head, then racing back and making a leaping catch of what should have been a routine out.

Connie Mack said nothing to him; he didn't have to. Jimmie Dykes and Mickey Cochrane did it for him. One of Dykes's favorite stories, which he placed in 1930, when Simmons was playing left field, illustrates how they would get on a loafing teammate. On this day Simmons was slow going after a single to left, and a runner on second scored:

After the side was retired, I glared at Al and kept glaring.

"Well, say it," he snapped.

"If you're the left fielder, play like one!" I shot back. "You could of thrown that man out if you'd tried."

One word led to another. The air was hot with blasts and counterblasts. From the end of the bench came Mr. Mack's voice. "Shut up, you two."

I continued to pop off. Mr. Mack came toward me. "Will you shut your goddamn mouth, Dykes," he quietly ordered.

I nearly fell off the bench. It was as close to profanity as I'd ever heard him go. I was so stunned that I lost my voice.

As a peacemaking gesture I joined Al as the inning ended and we went on the field together. "We sure got the Old Man mad," said Al with a laugh.

"Did you hear that g.d.?" I chortled.

Another player told me later that, as we went on the field, Mr. Mack had chuckled. "Know what those two are saying? They're gloating over getting the Old Man mad."

Connie Mack had his own way of dealing with the problem. En route to losing their third in a row to Detroit in the first game of a doubleheader on July 20 at home, he told Al to stay on the bench and sent Bug Welch out to center field for the top of the ninth. No big deal, thought the fans and the press box experts. The city was sweltering under a record heat wave. It must have been over 100 degrees on the field. Give Al a time out.

But when Al was not in the lineup for the second game, that made it news. It was the first game he had missed in an A's uniform after 394 in a row. The line that went out over the wire services was that Simmons had been benched for "light hitting and indifferent fielding." He had gone 1 for 11 in the series and skidded to around .325. It's easy to say, "Humph, some slump, some off-year," but for Simmons it was. He would pick it up in the last two months to finish at .343, his lowest average for seven years.

Simmons was back in center field the next day, but the A's were shut out again, their fifth loss in a row. After cutting the Yankees' lead in half from 10 games to 5 in mid-July, they were now 8 games back again. By the end of July they trailed by 14. The winning spirit of last year that Mack had found missing in spring training was still missing. They had a deep bench. When Welch and French and Miller were all sidelined, he could choose from Foxx, Hale, and Cochrane to fill in. When Cochrane had a split hand, Perkins and Foxx did the catching. The eighteen-year-old Foxx played his first complete game on July 30, catching Eddie Rommel flawlessly in a 4–1 loss at Cleveland. He was 0 for 2 batting sixth.

The Yankees were not running away from anybody. Since they'd opened the season winning 13 out of 16, they were no ball of fire. But nobody else was either. The A's could win 10 of 11 in the first half of May, then lose 10 of 11 in the next two weeks.

"You can't tell anything about the A's," Mack said as they headed out for two weeks on the road July 26. "They could win every game on the trip."

They hewed to the same pattern: lose 3, win 3, lose 4, win 5; they were 11-10 on the trip and came home 11 games out and in third place.

The New York lead would swell to 14 games at times and shrink back to 5, but that's as close as they got. The A's won 13 of 22 against the Yankees for the year and outplayed them by 8 games in the last two months, but when it was over, they would still trail by 6 games, with Cleveland slipping into second place ahead of them.

The Indians were the surprise of the year. With the same lineup that had finished sixth last year, they were picked to do no better by the experts. The rumor was that club president Ernest Barnard had told them if they didn't do better in '26, salaries would be cut. If they improved, there would be bonuses. They improved by 18 games.

In the losing years of the past, it was always the pitching and defense that the Athletics lacked. No more. For a change they had good pitching—the best in the league. Far from the days when Mack had not a single southpaw on the roster, he now had six. When Rommel was ill with tonsillitis and Quinn with bronchitis and Slim Harriss was on the shelf with a torn muscle in his pitching arm—all in early June—Mack still had Grove and Walberg and Gray. And Pate to go 2 or 4 or 7 innings when needed.

Galloway and Bishop were plugging the holes in the infield.

This time it was the hitting that held them back. By the middle of June Lefty Grove had lost 4 games in which the A's had been shut out. It wasn't just Simmons. Cochrane too was having what would be his worst year at the plate, fifty points below his career average. Dykes and Lamar had cooled off; both were significantly down from last year.

Bill Lamar had arrived with a reputation for an active night life. Philadelphia's breed of full-throated warblers, who had ridden home-grown first baseman George Burns out of town six year ago, got on him. Though it's been said that their riding so upset Lamar he dropped many a fly ball in left field, in fact he committed no more errors than most other left fielders in the league. A year ago his bat had made up for any fielding lapses. This year it didn't.

By July several of the Athletics were batting around .300, but not much over it, and the rest were around .200. The latter included Joe Hauser, whom Mack had stubbornly left in the cleanup slot in the order. With Simmons slumping, the four and five spots were death valley for rallies. When Mack replaced Unser Choe with Jim Poole in mid-June, it wasn't enough. They had led the league in hitting last year; they would be seventh this year.

Mack was using everybody to try to manufacture scarce runs and consistent victories. Their run production was down almost 20 percent. For the season Mack would average about one pinch hitter per game. Pitchers would be taken out for pinch hitters even if they were going well. More than once he would use 18 players—4 or 5 pitchers and pinch hitters, 3 catchers—to try to win close games.

There were reports the ball had been debugged or deadened; hitting and run production were down significantly for everybody from the year before (despite the new sacrifice rule that gave a batter no time at bat if he hit a fly ball that advanced a base runner from any base).

Nobody told Babe Ruth. By June 8 he had hit 21 home runs. He would finish with 47.

Connie Mack thought he had found enough young stars to win a pennant. Now it looked as if he hadn't. He would have to start looking for more young sluggers; he wouldn't swap one veteran for another. So it came as something of a surprise when, on June 14, he traded Bing Miller to the Browns for thirty-five-year-old outfielder Baby Doll Jacobson. Even Isaminger was fooled, calling it a move to boost the attack.

It wasn't. Jacobson was the key—a mysterious key—to acquiring a pitcher Mack had been after for two years: Howard Ehmke.

The 6-foot-3, broad-shouldered Ehmke was a workhorse at thirty-two. Touted by Washington scouts twelve years ago as a second Walter Johnson, he had not impressed Clark Griffith, so he signed with the Federal League. Bought by Detroit in 1916, he had posted double-digit wins and losses for seven years before the Tigers traded him to Boston. The common rap was that Ehmke "couldn't get along with Cobb."

In 1920 Ehmke had been described by Detroit writer H. G. Salsinger as someone who "has a lot of stuff including temperament of a certain rare quality. It is not the average temperament but a peculiar temperament that does not give to some of the rough treatment that has been accorded him. With the proper handling of [Detroit pitching coach Jack] Coombs, the kind of handling that is the law in the Connie Mack school of baseball, Ehmke will develop into a good twirler, a consistently reliable twirler. Physically he seems to have unlimited ability."

By 1921 Coombs was gone and Cobb was the manager, and "rough treatment" was the norm. After two years Cobb traded him to Boston, where he had pitched over 300 innings for the tail-end Red Sox in 1923 and '24, winning a total of 39 games. He had given up the first home run hit in the new Yankee Stadium, to Babe Ruth on opening day in 1923. Ehmke and Eddie Rommel could commiserate with each other over the number of games that had slipped away from both of them during those years, thanks to leaky defenses behind them.

Yearning to play for a contender, Ehmke begged Boston general manager Bob Quinn to trade him in 1925. Quinn said no. Ehmke didn't let down, tying for the league lead with 22 complete games, and was saddled with 20 of Boston's 105 losses.

At least five clubs, including the Athletics, had been after him at the winter meetings in December. Ehmke came down from his home in upstate New York and implored Quinn to take one of the offers. Quinn said it couldn't be done. (Quinn later said he turned down a $150,000 offer. He certainly could have used the money; eighteen months later the league had to lend him $75,000 to keep the Red Sox going.) Ehmke went home condemned to dwell in the cellar again. There were dozens of Philadelphia pitchers of yesteryears who knew exactly how he felt.

Rube Walberg had picked up his third win without a loss in Cleveland on the afternoon of June 15, a 5-hit shutout over the Indians. The baggage and equipment had been trucked to the boat dock for their overnight ride across Lake Erie to Detroit. It was past eight o'clock, but Mr. Mack had not appeared yet. The word spread that Bob Quinn had come over from Detroit and was in Mack's room conferring on a deal. The midnight deadline for trades that did not require waivers was looming. Most of the A's hung around the Hollenden lobby, speculating on who was coming and who was going. They were also saying a reluctant goodbye to Bing Miller, who had played his last game for the A's that afternoon.

It was after nine when a smiling Connie Mack emerged from the elevator and announced that he had obtained Ehmke and utility outfielder Tom Jenkins from the Red Sox in exchange for Jacobson, Fred Heimach, and Slim Harriss. There was no cash involved. "He is one of the most gifted pitchers in baseball," Mack said of Ehmke, "and I expect him to win a lot of games." Besides, over the years Ehmke had beaten the A's twice as often as he had lost to them.

Mack did not believe he had given up anyone vital to the team's future—or so he thought at the time. Bing Miller had lost the regular right-field job to Walter French. Mack didn't really want to part with Miller, but he had to in order to get Jacobson, who was Bob Quinn's choice. It's difficult to say why Quinn didn't take Miller instead; Jacobson had one more season in him; Miller, four years younger, would have ten more.

Although Slim Harriss had done his best work in six years in 1925, he had shown little so far this year to consider him preferable to Ehmke. He would never put up another .500 year. Fred Heimach had become an expendable lefty reliever.

Stan Baumgartner had been released outright to Portland on June 12, his salary guaranteed by the A's for the rest of the season. Mack's six lefties were now down to four: Grove, Walberg, Pate, and a rookie, Charles Willis.

When the trade was announced, Slim Harriss was at a movie, so Fred Heimach hailed a taxi to go to the dock and retrieve their bags and equipment rolls. The Red Sox would be in Cleveland in the morning.

That afternoon in Detroit Ehmke had lost his tenth game against 3 wins when the Tigers pulled a 2-out 3-run rally in the ninth, begun with what was called a "freak triple" by Harry Heilmann, to win 7–6. When Ehmke received a telegram from Mack telling him of the deal, he and Jenkins had to go to the dock where the Red Sox' bags were waiting for the boat to Cleveland. They retrieved their bags and rolled-up sweatshirts and gloves and returned to the Tuller Hotel to await the arrival of the Athletics.

Boston writer Burt Whitman, saying "Ehmke had failed to come through for the Red Sox," also alluded to Ehmke's temperament, adding to his "good riddance" that the pitcher "was more suited for Mack's patient attitude with his players. . . . At any rate, the writers here and those connected intimately with the game are one in their belief that the Red Sox did a wise thing."

Ehmke's $10,000 salary matched Rommel's as the A's highest-paid pitchers. He delivered as Mack had hoped, winning 8 in a row in August and September, 12 all together against 4 losses in an A's uniform.

The Athletics never gave up. They went to Yankee Stadium for a Labor Day doubleheader trailing by 10 games but full of fight. Despite the prospect of rain, about sixty thousand spectators jammed the aisles all over the three-tiered structure. They got their money's worth of excitement.

Sometimes Connie Mack's use of Lefty Grove in relief seemed to go against everything in the percentage book used today. He ignored both the lefty-vs.-righty conventions and Grove's occasional flights of wildness. Certainly he did not hesitate to use him against the Yankees.

In the first game Eddie Rommel's knuckleball behaved perfectly for 6 innings while the A's took a 2–0 lead. In the seventh he walked lead-off batter Babe Ruth and threw three balls to Gehrig. At this point Mack sent in Grove. Maybe he thought Lefty's fastball would throw off the timing of the

Yankees after Rommel's fluttery stuff. Grove poured two strikes past Gehrig, then threw ball four. Then he walked the right-handed batting Lazzeri, loading the bases. He threw one ball to Dugan, and the nervous Mack sent in Ehmke. Ruth scored as Dugan grounded out. Then Ehmke threw a wild pitch that caromed off Perkins's knee into the A's dugout as Gehrig scored the tying run.

In the eighth Sammy Hale claimed he had been hit by a pitch thrown by Dutch Ruether. Home plate umpire Billy Evans said no. Hale argued. The entire A's bench got on Evans. Jimmie Dykes recalled, "Mr. Mack stood on the dugout steps and was yelling as loud as the rest."

According to James Harrison of the *New York Times*, "Evans tore off his mask, rushed over in a fury, bending down poking his face into Mack's."

"You'd better shut up," Evans warned Mack.

"But Mr. Mack kept right on hollering," Dykes said, "and Evans evidently decided discretion was the better part of valor because he politely ignored the insults the rest of the game."

Reminded of the incident later, Evans said, "What a day. Imagine me threatening to throw Mr. Mack out of a ball game. The very thought scares me."

Hale then tripled and the A's went on to win, 5–2.

Despite the use of seven pitchers in the game, it was played in just under two hours.

In the second game Rube Walberg took a 1–0 lead into the eighth, when five o'clock lightning struck for 2 runs. Herb Pennock came in and shut the A's down in the ninth, and the delirious Yankee fans showered the field with straw hats, scorecards, and shredded paper.

The Athletics went on to win 10 of their last 16 and pick up 4 games, but it was too little too late.

After years of pitiful pitching performances, it was the mound staff that had carried the Athletics this year.

Splitting his work between starting and relieving, Rube Walberg posted what would be the lowest earned run average of his fifteen-year career, good for 12 wins.

Lefty Grove's 13-13 record is deceptive. He had the lowest ERA of his career: 2.51, best in the league. He led the league in strikeouts and allowed 11.44 base runners per 9 innings, combining the fewest allowed hits—7.92—with 3.52 walks. He started 33 games and relieved in 12.

Quinn, Rommel, and Gray all pulled their weight, starting and relieving. Like Grove, they were given too few runs to ease their burden.

Joe Pate did everything that was asked of him. He paid his first dividend on April 15, relieving Baumgartner in the third and shutting out Washington on 2 hits the rest of the way in the 9–3 win. In one stretch he threw 19 scoreless innings. He relieved long and short in 45 games, earning 9 wins without a loss. (He talked Mack into two starts, was kayoed in both, but the A's went on to win them.) His fielding was perfect: 45 assists and 4 putouts in 113 innings.

In August, after Pate had preserved victories in four consecutive games, Billy Evans said of him, "Pate doesn't appear to have much stuff on the ball, but his fast one has a little hop that makes the batters pop up, his change of pace is clever, and his knuckleball practically unhittable when he gets it over. But best of all Pate has plenty of nerve. He is what is known in baseball as a 'money pitcher,' doing his best work when hardest pressed. The Athletics would have been lost without Pate this year. He is the 1926 model of Fred Marberry in the hero role."

Connie Mack had been going to church on Sunday mornings and playing baseball or managing teams on Sunday afternoons for most of his life and saw nothing sinful about it. Neither did the Roman Catholic Church. But the Puritans, the Methodists, and other faiths whom H. L. Mencken described as living in fear that someone, somewhere, might be enjoying themselves, considered it a desecration of the Sabbath. Youngsters growing up in Philadelphia in those days, when just picking up a deck of playing cards might bring a scolding from a maiden aunt, described Sundays as a day of deadly boredom.

Ever since Connie Mack had come to Philadelphia in 1901, he and the Shibes had tried to persuade the legislature to amend or repeal the 1794 Pennsylvania Blue Laws that banned all forms of commercialism or recreation on Sundays.

They had come the closest in 1913, when they had a friend in the governor's mansion: John K. Tener, a former pitcher who had given up Mack's first major league home run twenty-five years earlier. Tener promised to sign a bill introduced by Philadelphia representative James Wiltebank if it reached his desk. It never did. The legislature, denounced regularly for corruption by the big-city newspapers, drew no condemnation from the pulpits of the ministerial associations. Pennsylvania had more churches of every denomination than any other state by the 1930s. Philadelphia alone had seven hundred of them. The preachers got their Blue Laws maintained and did not disturb the lawmakers' wheeling and dealing, an understanding that kept everybody happy except baseball fans and kids who worked six days a week and wanted to play ball on their only day off.

In Wilkes-Barre borough officials prohibited boys from playing ball on Sundays. So on Saturday, May 3, 1915, one hundred "door boys" and "patchers" had walked out of the Maxwell Colliery of the Lehigh & Wilkes-Barre Coal Company to play baseball, idling twelve hundred men. The boys said they would shut down the colliery every Saturday if they couldn't play on Sundays.

Even in places where Sunday baseball was legal, it was seen as a step on the slippery slope to damnation. In 1913 the *Indianapolis News* wrung its hands: "Sunday baseball is being used as an argument for Sunday theaters. One must draw the line somewhere."

In reality the Pennsylvania law was not uniformly enforced. An amusement park in Philadelphia operated on Sundays with no complaints. Had the law been followed to the letter, it would have been a crime to operate or ride on public transportation or in your own automobile (except to go to church), provide telephone service, publish or buy a newspaper, or play golf.

Baseball was a part of the city's culture, with fierce rivalries among neighborhood, company, and church teams. In 1926 Henry Ford became the first American manufacturer to adopt a five-day, forty-hour work week. Philadelphia was a manufacturing city, still on a six-day week. Sunday was the only day workers could play or watch a game. When a group of ministers called on Mayor W. Freeland Kendrick to stop the local sandlot games, His Honor said, "Why keep them penned up in the slums? Let them go out to the ball field and drink in the pure air."

A clergyman in Ashland wrestled with this dilemma and reached a similar conclusion: "Sunday baseball is deplorably wrong in principle. But it must be admitted that this year the Sunday games have broken up the Sunday beer picnics. . . . Besides this, it must be recognized that young people can attend ball games on Sunday afternoon and still be able to attend church services in the evening with a clear mind, if not a clear conscience. But those who are out on drunken carousals are totally unfit for attendance at public worship. If it comes to a choice of the two evils, baseball is certainly the lesser."

The good reverend did not consider the ingenuity of baseball fans who might combine both vices by getting drunk at a ball game.

In hundreds of towns throughout Pennsylvania local teams played on Sundays, often charging admission. All six Pennsylvania teams in the New

York–Penn League and Reading in the International played on Sundays. George Brand, guardian of the press gate at Shibe Park, managed a team in Lancaster that played on Sundays and charged admission. On July 18 the A's had played a Sunday exhibition game in Pottsville, Jack Quinn's home town, and would play an industrial team in Springville the following Sunday on their way to Cleveland. Most of the time these games were left alone. Small-town preachers knew they would not be popular if they went about calling for the arrest of some of the town's leading citizens.

In the restless postwar years, the public had begun to rebel, throwing off old taboos on dressing, drinking, dancing, or spooning with an undisguised nose-thumbing, anything-goes attitude. By 1926 amateur and semipro teams in Philadelphia were openly taunting the Sabbath Savers. A man named Clement H. Congdon announced in the *Sunday Transcript* that he was going to play baseball on Sunday in Fairmount Park. If anyone wanted to arrest him, they were welcome to do so. He would pay the four dollar fine or spend six days in jail, as the law prescribed, and be out in time to show up for another game the following Sunday.

The "white ribboners," as the Save the Sabbath forces were called, goaded the police into breaking up some sandlot games and arresting the team captains. Local politicians, sensing where the public was going and eager to get out in front of the parade, offered to pay the fines of the arrested players. Rev. William Fitzgerald, rector of the Church of the Blessed Virgin Mary, stood up in one courtroom hearing and said he had searched the decalogue and found nothing banning innocent recreation on Sundays. He invited the teams to play on the church lawn, then said, "Why should a man be pronounced guilty before he is tried? I am here in the role of a character witness for Williamson. I am his pastor and friend." He then offered to pay the fine for the guilty man, a wounded war veteran.

The justice of the peace said, "It's already been paid."

Connie Mack had no fear of hearing himself condemned at a Sunday Mass.

Mack and the Shibes knew the public was on their side. John Shibe was active in the Democratic Party. Mack's close friend and neighbor, Judge Harry S. McDevitt, was a power in Republican circles. They had their contacts in Harrisburg. But not enough. Phillies owner William Baker wished them well but did nothing to help. He would not play a Sunday game until it was clearly established as legal and not against public sentiment.

Only Massachusetts and Pennsylvania remained without Sunday baseball. John Shibe estimated that the Athletics' handicap versus the rest of the league except the Red Sox came to $20,000 of lost income for every Sunday they had to be idle or travel to play in another city for the day.

In 1876 Philadelphia had been the host of a grand celebration of the nation's one hundredth birthday. Built with state, city, and private funds and a loan from Congress, the Fairmount Park site included more than two hundred buildings—state and foreign pavilions, exhibition halls, art galleries, and amusements. Ten million people visited the grounds between May and November.

In 1921 planning had begun for a sesquicentennial in 1926, bigger and better than the earlier exposition. The grandiose plans were soon pared radically when potential backers showed little enthusiasm. Turning 150 didn't turn people on the way turning 100 did.

Sales of shares for the exposition at ten dollars fell far short of the goals. The state legislature finally approved $750,000 with the "preachers' provision"—thou shalt not be open on Sundays. It might be educational, the Sabbath Savers said, but all those rides and sideshows on the Gladway clearly were not. The planners plowed on, and the fair, located in South Philly roughly between Tenth and Twenty-Third Streets, opened on May 31.

And then, as if heaven-sent—at least from the Catholic precincts thereof— it rained more than half the days the fair was open. When it didn't rain, a record heat wave sent temperatures to 100 and people to the seashore, out of the city over the newly opened Ben Franklin Bridge across the Delaware River. The bridge, expected to bring thousands of people to the exposition, was taking more of them away.

The expo was losing money and faced unpayable debts. The fair directors decided their only salvation lay in opening on Sundays. They persuaded Mayor Kendrick to go along with it, with a caveat: they could charge the regular fifty cents admission, but all the exhibits, rides, and amusements must be free. They didn't want it to look like they were promoting fun for profit on Sundays. The show operators squawked and were promised a cut of the admissions, a promise that had to be pulled under pressure from the pulpits. Food vendors were allowed to sell their wares.

The Methodist Men's Committee of 100 went to work, seeking an injunction from Judge Thomas Finletter in equity court to stop this desecration. The fair had been open on three Sundays in July before the judge handed down his decision. John Shibe and Athletics attorney Charles G. Gartling were in the courtroom on July 22 when Judge Finletter went on at great length to make it clear he had no doubt the Sesquicentennial Exposition was guilty as sin as a commercial enterprise and he would declare its Sunday opening illegal if he could.

But the only words from the bench that interested John Shibe were, "I have no authority to grant an injunction to stop the Sunday opening. . . . As a judge in equity court I am a Chancellor with no power to enforce a criminal act."

Methodist chairman Thomas D. Taylor grimly foresaw "a wide open Sabbath." He vowed to appeal to the Supreme Court.

John Shibe said, "Other amusements are permitted to run or at most pay a small fine. Baseball should not be discriminated against."

The A's were about to depart on a western trip. "When they come back," said Shibe, "if the Exposition is still open on Sundays we will hold a Sunday game."

The exposition remained open on Sundays. The A's had three possible dates: August 22 and 29 and September 5. The only team available on the twenty-ninth was the Red Sox, but the two teams would have already played their 22 games for the year. The A's and Yankees were scheduled to face each other for five days before September 5 and a doubleheader on Labor Day. Moving a game to Sunday left no chance to make it up if it rained. That left August 22, with the White Sox arriving from Boston to start a series on Monday. If it rained, they had the next three days to make it up. They decided to switch the Wednesday game to Sunday.

The Athletics notified Mayor Kendrick that Shibe Park would be open for a game with Chicago on Sunday, August 22. The mayor replied that he would order the police to keep the park closed. The A's filed for an injunction in Common Pleas Court to prevent police interference, claiming "the police had no authority to stop it unless there was evidence of disorder, and not before such evidence occurred."

A hearing was set for Thursday, August 19. Meanwhile, the team circulated petitions in the neighborhood and collected about two thousand signatures from people saying they would have no objections to a Sunday game. Some of them showed up in court to testify that the crowd and the cheering would not disturb them.

The Philadelphia Sabbath Association presented its own petition with seventy-two signatures.

At the hearing before Judge Frank Smith, police Inspector William J.

McFadden said the crowd noise from inside Shibe Park could be heard three or four blocks away, but in sixteen years he had never seen any disorder in or near the ballpark.

Connie Mack testified:

A Sunday baseball crowd is a little bit different from a weekday gathering. Perhaps they have in mind they are attending a game on Sunday. Perhaps, I might say, the people dress a little bit differently, and they also seem to have in mind that it is Sunday and do not reprove the players. For over forty years as player and manager, I have taken part in the game of baseball, not only on weekdays but on Sundays also. While all games are orderly as a general thing, excepting unimportant disputes occasionally, there is something about a Sunday game that is just a little bit different.

I have observed Sunday games in every city where the major leagues play Sunday baseball, and I have yet to see a disturbance on Sunday. In my own mind I feel Sunday baseball is undoubtedly a good thing for the people of the cities where it is played.

Questioned by city solicitor Joseph P. Gaffney, Mack admitted that admission would be charged. He stated that the players received their salaries whether they played on the Sabbath or not but added that all the players were anxious to play on Sundays at home.

On Saturday morning Judge Smith granted the Athletics their injunction, adding a caution that any breach of the peace would invalidate it and allow the police to stop the game.

The short notice and rain, which washed out the Saturday game against Detroit and continued into Sunday, held the crowd down to about twelve thousand. There were few exciting moments to raise much racket. The A's gave Lefty Grove a 3–0 lead; the White Sox scored in the seventh and eighth, one on a solo home run, and Grove sailed through the 3–2 win in one hour and forty-five minutes. The sharp-eared Rev. Forney of the Sabbath Association rode around the neighborhood during the game and found the occasional evidence that somebody was having a good time on a Sunday "disgusting."

(If you're looking for a sign of divine requital: in his next start Grove was bowling over the Browns when a line drive tore the nail off the second finger of his left hand. He had to leave the game and didn't win another game that year.)

Five minutes after the game ended, Shibe Park was empty, and within a few minutes more the neighborhood was deserted. Connie Mack was all smiles: the A's had won, nobody misbehaved, nobody called the cops. On Monday the city's newspapers supported the A's, while the ministerial association, declaring it the worst calamity ever inflicted on the city, denounced baseball, Connie Mack, and everybody associated with the disgraceful act. Mayor Kendrick wasted no time in raising the flag of religion and charging the Athletics with violating the Blue Laws. In the meantime, said John Shibe, the Athletics had no plans for any more Sunday games. Given the schedule, that was not a significant gesture.

Nobody was surprised when the Athletics were found guilty of violating the 1794 law in Dauphin County court. The club owners could have paid the four dollar fine like anybody else, maybe played a few Sunday games next year to chip away at the opposition and achieve de facto acceptance at a cost of four dollars each time. They chose instead to take the path that future social activists would take, trying to get the courts to legislate. They appealed to the state Supreme Court. If the legislature wouldn't repeal the 1794 law or grant sporting events an exception, perhaps the court might overturn it or at least bend and twist it enough to inoculate baseball with innocence.

It was a mistake. The court took an activist turn but not in the direction hoped for by Connie Mack and the Shibes.

On June 27, 1927, the state Supreme Court handed down its decision, upholding the law by a 7–2 vote. So what, you might think. What was a four dollar fine compared to a Sunday gate? But the court also issued the chilling warning that the Athletics' next offense could cause the club's corporate franchise to be revoked.

The two dissenting justices agreed that the Athletics were guilty but maintained the court had no authority to go beyond the law itself and impose further punishment for future violations.

Justice John N. Kephart's opinion reflected the public's attitude toward baseball and the law. He condemned what he called the majority's corporate "death penalty," which, he wrote, "should be used only in very serious crimes":

It is imperative that the cause for the infliction of the death penalty in whole or in part should be one which the law considers as of a very serious nature. . . . The law looks on [the playing of baseball on Sunday] as a very minor offense compared with crimes generally. . . . The game of baseball is a sport; when played on Sunday it is not an indictable offense as a felony or misdemeanor, but is made illegal only by . . . a civil police regulation. It is not wicked in itself; it has no element of criminality. . . . If the act prohibits playing baseball on Sunday, then the club could not play on Sunday without subjecting itself to the penalty of the act, four dollars for each offense. By these proceedings an additional punishment is, in effect, added by judicial construction.

Wrote Chief Justice Robert von Moschzisker, "The penalty and also the appropriate remedy are provided in distinct and unmistakable terms by the Act of 1794 itself. . . . If the penalty therein provided is not a sufficient deterrent, it is for the legislature to provide another."

Connie Mack was now 0 for 2 with the state Supreme Court, which had snatched away the heart of his 1902 team on opening day.

Any change in the Sunday laws would have to come from the legislature. As it turned out, that would take another six years. In the meantime the Athletics made occasional noises about building a bigger ballpark across the Delaware River in Camden, New Jersey, ten minutes from City Hall, and playing Sunday games there. But it was all bluff.

MR. SPEAKER AND
MR. COBB

Despite a 20 percent decline in attendance and an outlay of $127,250 for old and new player purchases, Connie Mack had another $200,000 in net cash inflow to spend. And when Connie Mack smelled pennant, he was willing to spend all they had made and more to bring it home. One prospect that got away was a twenty-five-year-old outfielder, Fred Schulte, who had batted .347 for Milwaukee.

The Browns had paid $60,000 and three players for Schulte in July 1926. Mack had enjoyed many beneficial deals with Brewers owner Otto Borchert, whom he admired as "a great business man [who] would make a success in any business as well as in baseball." In a letter dated December 6, 1926, Mack told his longtime friend and volunteer bird dog Otto Schomberg, "The St. Louis club was very fortunate to secure Schulte at the price they paid for him as I am sure there are a number of clubs that would have paid one hundred thousand dollars for him, our club being one that would have paid that figure." It seemed that Borchert had given Browns owner Phil Ball first crack at the outfielder in gratitude for Ball's having sent him a few pitchers when the Brewers were shorthanded. Despite losing out on Schulte, Connie Mack understood and appreciated Borchert's loyalty to a benefactor.

In that letter, the last he wrote to his old friend, Mack revealed his yen to travel, even after riding the rails from March to October.

> Note you will be leaving for California for the winter. Have had a great desire to go to California the past few years but on account of the large young family it is impossible for me to get away.
>
> Note that you will look over that young pitcher and first baseman and will be pleased to hear from you in regard to them.

I trust that you will spend a very pleasant winter and that Mrs. Schomberg and yourself will return in the very best of health. Wishing you a Merry Christmas and Happy New Year, I am,

Sincerely yours, Connie Mack

Otto Schomberg never returned. He died of a heart attack on the train on the way home on May 3, 1927.

Connie Mack had assembled a nucleus of outstanding young players with tremendous potential. But only one of them—Jack Quinn in 1921—had ever been on a big league pennant-winner. He wanted one or two veterans who knew how to win and could add the punch he needed to close the gap with the Yankees.

Then suddenly, as if someone had lit a Roman candle, a shower of stars fell out of the skies. Like a crazed lepidopterist, Connie Mack grabbed his butterfly net and set out to capture every one of them. With an assist from a disgruntled former pitcher and a pair of exiled Black Sox, he nearly succeeded.

In Chicago Eddie Collins and Charles Comiskey had not been a compatible couple during Eddie's two fifth-place finishes as the Sox manager. Injuries and eighteen years of action had made it evident that at thirty-nine, Collins was no longer an everyday second baseman. Comiskey, not interested in paying him $35,000 just to manage, released him. Connie Mack eagerly offered Collins $15,000 to return to Philadelphia. Eddie just as eagerly accepted it. After twelve years both men were happy to be reunited.

When George Sisler, thirty-three, was fired as the Browns' manager after a seventh-place finish, Mack momentarily had a vision of solving his first base problem, but the Browns retained Sisler as a player. Unwilling to give up on Joe Hauser but uncertain if Unser Choe would ever regain his earlier form, Mack went into the minor league market and paid $25,000 to Kansas City for twenty-nine-year-old first baseman Dudley Branom, a .353 hitter. As part of the deal, the A's sent Bill Wambsganss outright and Hauser on option to K.C.

Baltimore shortstop Joe Boley was now thirty. A consistent .300 hitter with some power—19 home runs in '26—he had been the Orioles shortstop for eight years. A native of the Pennsylvania coal country, he had grown up playing on lumpy fields where every hop was a bad hop. Jack Dunn, reluctant to sell him, had put a six-figure tag on him in the past. Now he decided to get what he could for the aging shortstop.

Chick Galloway was the same age as Boley, but Connie Mack had become disenchanted with him. His range had declined, his error totals hadn't, and he had become a .240 liability at the plate.

Once again Mack and Dunn did business. The terms were $50,000 cash and three players valued at $5,000 each. When Mack decided not to send the three players, he wrote another check for $15,000.

In January thirty-eight-year-old Zach Wheat, after eighteen years patrolling left field for Brooklyn, was handed his release following a miserable .290 season. Mack asked him what he wanted to play for the A's. The answer: a $5,000 bonus and a $12,500 contract. The Giants were also interested in him, but McGraw balked at paying the bonus. Mack didn't hesitate.

On November 3, after Tris Speaker and Ty Cobb had returned from a hunting trip to Wyoming, Cobb resigned as manager of the Tigers. On November 29 Speaker resigned as the Indians' manager. In both cases the facts were not necessarily the truth.

Speaker had done a decent job in his eight years leading the Indians, winning the World Series in 1920 and spurring the '26 team to a surprise second-place finish. But managing may have palled on him. The *Boston Herald* quoted him on August 30 complaining that the high salary earned by the average player led to a lack of desire to improve, resulting in "less intelligent baseball on his part and often a bit of laziness."

The Indians had drawn so poorly in recent years (although attendance had rebounded with the team's performance the previous year), the club had pleaded for a reduction in the taxes on League Park, which it didn't get. "Casual Comment" in the December 9 *The Sporting News* estimated Speaker's annual salary at $50,000 or more, including attendance bonuses. He was thirty-nine and had slumped so much in the first half of the season that the press was on him to bench himself. He picked it up in the second half and finished at .304. The Cleveland owners' explanation for Speaker's resignation was plausible: his waning abilities were no longer worth his hefty paycheck, and he resigned rather than taking a cut.

During the season Connie Mack had noticed something about Speaker, who still played the shallowest center field in the game. On July 29 Mack had brought up a rookie, Dave Barbee, from the Piedmont League and put him in the lineup batting fifth. In the first inning, with two men on, Barbee hit a fly ball to deep center. Speaker raced back for it, but it fell beyond his reach for a triple. It was, Mack noted, the first time in twenty years he had seen Speaker fail to make that kind of catch.

But Mack had also seen Speaker a week earlier put a bunt down the third base line and race to second while Jimmie Dykes stared at the ball willing it in vain to roll foul. That kind of heads-up—at any age—was what Mack was after. Now that Speaker was available, Mack wanted him.

Ty Cobb was the epitome of what no club owner looks for in a manager. He hated the man he worked for, Frank Navin. He had no tact, no patience with players who wouldn't or couldn't bat or slide or play the game his way, no matter how much he tried to teach them. Cobb put down his players in front of their teammates and showed them up on the field before the fans. He had no aptitude for handling men and getting the most out of them. The placid rookie Charlie Gehringer, the Mechanical Man who would say hello in the spring and goodbye in the fall and bat .320 in between for seventeen years, was an enigma to him. His attempts to give them batting tips, even when they were at bat and he was on the bases, were contrary to what he told Grantland Rice for a July 10, 1926, *Collier's* article: "At the plate I must be so prepared that I need do no thinking while at bat. It should all be instincts and fundamentals. If I had to think about my stance, etc. I would be easy pickings. Instinct and muscle memory have to carry you at that point."

No wonder his players resented his constant advice. Even if he knew what he was talking about, they didn't want to be doing any thinking at the plate either.

In trying to help them become better ballplayers, Cobb wasn't mean or malicious. His instincts were as generous as a gardener nurturing a plant. He simply ran off the rails in a hurry whenever his attempts failed to bring forth his desired results. He was the same way at home in Georgia, where he financed many local boys through medical school. Baltimore sportswriter John Steadman told of one such student sponsored by Cobb. When the student needed $200 for school debts, Cobb loaned him the money for ninety days. On the ninety-first day the student received a registered letter from Cobb blasting him in Cobb's trademark green ink for lacking the honor and integrity to repay the loan when due.

After a sixth-place finish in 1926, Cobb let it be known he had no confidence in the Tigers becoming a winning team for at least the next two years.

Frank Navin, who had had enough of Cobb as a manager and probably would have fired him anyhow, already had his replacement, George Moriarty, lined up.

Cobb's quitting was called "a surprise" in the press, but it shouldn't have been. After twenty-two years he had worn out his body and his welcome in Detroit. For the past two years attendance had sagged, and those who turned out had begun to boo him. He didn't need the money. As a player he had accomplished all he set out to do. He held a folio full of records. At forty he wanted to get out, he said, "while still one of the best. I'm tired." He was going to take his family on a tour of Europe.

On December 1 Connie Mack said, "I know nothing of the reasons, but I suppose [Cobb] thinks he has had enough of an active part in baseball."

Connie Mack knew more of the reasons than he let on, but he had no reason to think that Ty Cobb would ever play another day. Not yet.

It's impossible to pinpoint exactly when Mack first learned about the accusations of former Detroit pitcher Hubert "Dutch" Leonard against Cobb and Speaker. Despised by Cobb, who had had him waived out of the American League in 1925, and holding a grudge against his former teammate Tris Speaker for not claiming him for the Indians, the veteran left-hander decided to sell some memorabilia—letters written by Cobb and Joe Wood to Leonard that hinted at Speaker's and Cobb's conspiring with Joe Wood to fix a Detroit-Cleveland game in 1919 and betting on the game. Cobb's awkwardly worded letter dealt obliquely with "our business proposition" and rambled in similarly vague and ambiguous language.

What Leonard really had in mind was using the letters to extort money from the Detroit club. He went first to Chicago to see Ban Johnson, then to Detroit. By the middle of June, Johnson, Frank Navin, Cobb, Speaker, and possibly some other players and club officials knew about Leonard's intentions. Whatever Connie Mack knew about it had to come from hearsay or the minutes of AL board meetings. The story was circulating among clubhouses in both leagues. Cobb later told the *Atlanta Journal*, "So far as I know, Judge Landis first heard about this Leonard business from me. I told him about it . . . in July or August."

John McGraw had heard something but didn't take it seriously. When he read of Cobb's release in November, his first reaction was to try to sign him for the Giants. But as a precaution he inquired of the commissioner's office if there was any reason why he shouldn't deal with the player. Landis replied, "Lay off Cobb."

Afraid of Leonard's selling the letters to a newspaper and causing a scandal involving two of the game's biggest stars, Johnson and Navin agreed on the Tigers paying Leonard $20,000 in exchange for the letters. The cover story was that the payment represented compensation Leonard claimed he had lost during 1922, 1923, and part of 1924. In fact, he had refused to sign in 1922 and had been on the suspended list while playing for Fresno in an independent league. He was reinstated in 1924. The Tigers owed him nothing. Even if they did, why would the American League vote to reimburse the Detroit club the $20,000 in December?

Ban Johnson took possession of the letters. It was a surprisingly well-kept secret from the public. There were no newspaper accounts of a meeting of the league's board of directors at the Union League Club in Chicago on September 9. In addition to directors Phil Ball, Jake Ruppert, Bob Quinn, and Ernest Barnard, league attorney Henry Killilea and Frank Navin were present. After a lengthy discussion of the situation and what action should be taken, the board voted 4–0 that all the evidence in the matter be submitted to Commissioner Landis for his consideration, with "directors and president of the American League to be present when such players are given a hearing before the commissioner."

There is no record of any league meetings on the subject, nor do the minutes of subsequent league meetings contain any mention of it.

As far as Ban Johnson was concerned, the issue was closed. The board's action in referring the case to Landis was just to keep the commissioner informed. Johnson considered it a league matter. On behalf of the league he decided that Speaker and Cobb had, at best, exercised poor judgment and, at worst, violated a trust. He took it on himself to persuade Cobb and Speaker to resign as managers, even if they were innocent as they said they were, and that would be the end of the matter, sparing them any embarrassing publicity. Their clubs would release them, and of course they would never again play in the American League.

Bad idea.

The manner of their careers ending—being pushed instead of jumping, and by that no-good bum Dutch Leonard and his phony charges—ate at them. Meanwhile, Judge Landis did his own investigating. In September Cobb informed Landis that he intended to make Leonard's charges public and explain the letter he had written. His attorney, James O. Murfin, talked him out of it. Instead Cobb and Speaker asked Landis for a hearing in which to confront their accuser in the commissioner's office. Leonard refused to go to Chicago. They asked for a hearing anyhow. Landis scheduled it for December 20.

Five days before the hearing Landis attended the AL board meeting in

Chicago with his assistant, Leslie O'Connor, and league attorney Henry Killi-lea. After a lengthy discussion of the Leonard charges, the board amended its September 9 resolution referring the matter to the commissioner by deleting the requirement that the president and the directors be present at any hearing given the players.

Johnson reacted as if he'd sat on a spur. The walls of the austere Union League Club shook as he roared at Landis: "Has there been on your part in the last two years any thought or well-conceived plan to absolutely safeguard the game from corruption?" He talked about his report of a year ago on the widespread throwing of games in California prior to 1919. "You were plainly indifferent," he thundered. "There was a recurrence of that gambling episode on a larger scale this past season. I had in my personal employ this past year one of the best equipped detectives on the coast. . . ." He went on and on, reeling off the names of members of an eastern gambling ring—"Nick the Greek, the Levy Brothers, Zelzer, Chapman."

The others in the room sat in silence.

Despite the AL owners' promise to Landis two years ago to stifle their president's eruptions, Johnson's public statements critical of the commissioner had become less guarded, more embarrassing to the league's owners. It was a delicate situation for them. They seemed to be constantly apologizing and pledging their allegiance to Landis, who repeatedly threatened to resign if Johnson continued to attack him. Their leader was a sick man. The earlier patina covering his resentment and hatred of the commissioner—the position more than the man—had completely eroded.

For the past two years Frank Navin had been acting as the league's representative on the commissioner's advisory council, which was supposed to consist of the two league presidents. The council's existence was almost meaningless anyhow, as Landis never consulted the others. In the league meeting that followed the board meeting, the club owners looked for a way to show support for Johnson. On a 7–0 vote (by this time Charles Comiskey was voting no or abstaining from almost every motion affecting Johnson, even on approving a new constitution), they reinstated Johnson to the advisory council. They supposedly had Landis's okay to accept Johnson, but they weren't sure what the judge's reaction would be.

After a brief adjournment, Johnson told them he declined to serve on the council. Jake Ruppert then made an extraordinary speech. It was like trying to coax a child into playing with another child when neither one liked the other:

Two years ago a different score was between Landis and Mr. Johnson. At the time I was one of the men selected to call on [Landis]. Mr. [Alfred] Austrian [Charles Comiskey's attorney] took me to the Federal Building and I had a little talk with him. I realized Mr. Landis was big enough and broad enough to realize we are all of us in the same boat for the benefit of baseball. I have my personal likes and dislikes, but I do not permit my dislikes to interfere with my business. At one time I may have been in baseball for my health, but I am through with that. Now I am in baseball for the business end of it. I am very sorry to hear Mr. Johnson withdraw from the advisory council. Mr. Johnson and I have had our differences. I do not believe there was ever a greater difference in baseball than we had. But that is all in the past. Mr. Johnson was big enough to forget and so was I. We all feel he is fit to be our president. I think we should go to Commissioner Landis and find out why he does not want Mr. Johnson. If the commissioner can give us a good and sufficient reason why, that is another thing. I am asking this for the good of the American League. The papers are constantly carrying stories to the effect that we are being dictated to by the National League. I would like very much to ask Mr. Johnson to defer his action until we can call on Mr. Landis.

A committee of Ball, Barnard, and Ruppert was named to call on the commissioner, who had no objection to Ban Johnson's rejoining the advisory council.

Was it a vote of confidence? An attempt to placate and calm their turbulence-churning president? A public relations move? Or, as the press saw it, an expression of hostility toward Landis, which the league denounced as "an atrocious libel"?

Whatever; in the joint league meeting that followed, Landis's term was unanimously extended for seven years at a salary increase of $15,000 to $65,000, after which Johnson and Landis posed in a hearty handshake—at any rate the appearance of a hearty handshake. There was more ice in their smiles than there was in Lake Michigan.

Cobb, Speaker, Joe Wood, and Fred West, the man who had allegedly placed the bets on the game, testified in a closed meeting before Judge Landis on December 20. All the testimony exonerated the two stars. Both Cobb and Speaker denied betting on the game, and nobody said they did. Wood, who had not played in the game in question, admitted betting on Detroit.

For some weeks reporters had been nipping at the heels of the secret scandal. They had learned of the investigation of "a new and startling case of crookedness." The rumors had their boots on. Landis knew it was inevitable that the story would appear in print, complete with inaccuracies, unfounded innuendos, and hearsay. The next day, with the acquiescence of Cobb and Speaker, Landis lay bare the entire record, including the letters and the testimony. His statement included no conclusions. All the players involved were now out of baseball, so as far as he was concerned, that was the end of it.

Ban Johnson was shocked that Landis had made it all public. He was more than shocked. He was berserk. He accused Landis of publicity-seeking and sensationalism at the expense of the players' reputations. And he wasn't alone. Typical were two Detroit municipal judges, who joined Tigers' fans in calling Landis's actions "indefensible."

"He has unnecessarily gone out of his way to destroy two of the greatest idols of the day," said one.

The *New York Times* came to the commissioner's defense. Several newspapers and wire services were prepared to break the story, it said. "By announcing the facts the Commissioner is labeled a 'muckraker.' If the story had been released by a news association he could have been accused of suppressing the truth."

Players and fans from California to Cobb's neighbors in Augusta, Georgia, were universal in their support of the two players. Evangelist Billy Sunday came out in their defense. Congressmen from Georgia spoke out in Cobb's behalf. Sportswriters generally had no qualms about the honesty of the two stars. Westbrook Pegler was regarded as a demon at smelling out crooked fights, races, or people—"a veritable Savonarola at denouncing corruption," Paul Gallico called him. Pegler sympathized with Cobb for the doubt that had been put on his reputation, "which, in the light of subsequent developments, never should have been there at all." The Philadelphia writers immediately invited Speaker and Cobb to be guests of honor at their February 8, 1927, banquet.

Cobb brooded over the cloud that still hung over him. Etched in his mind were headlines like the misleading subhead on the front page of the *New York Times* on December 22: "Landis Accuses Two Famous Players of Agreement to Throw a Game in 1919."

Landis had made no such accusations, but people who scanned the headlines and didn't read the lengthy account that followed would carry the impression that he had. There had been no specific verdict of "Not guilty" from the judge. Ty Cobb couldn't live with that. At a big rally in his hometown on Christmas Eve he said, "Let me tell you, I intend to clear myself of these charges before I'm through. . . . What I want is a verdict from Commissioner Landis."

Cobb saw it as a challenge, and he took it on in the same all-out way he would look for new ways to intimidate an infielder or steal home or hit a left-hander who had stymied him or catch fish barehanded in Lake Tahoe. He had really been ready to retire from the game, but not this way. If the American League didn't vindicate him by reinstating him and letting him play, he was ready to take it to court and sue for damages, to "bust it," as he wrote Connie Mack twenty-eight years later, and take "my pound of flesh from American League or Major League baseball." He and Speaker went to Washington, where they found sympathetic supporters but nothing else. They went to Cleveland, where Speaker's friends offered to finance his efforts to clear his name. Then Cobb went on to Detroit, where a wealthy friend offered to pay for the highest-profile legal counsel available.

Acting together, lawyers for both players confronted Landis, demanding the players' reinstatement.

Meanwhile, like Hamlet's battalions of spies, tales of ancient crookedness assailed the commissioner's desk. One story by Swede Risberg and Chick Gandil of the banished Black Sox involved Ty Cobb only insofar as the White Sox allegedly had taken up a collection and bribed the Tigers to throw four games to Chicago in the 1917 pennant race. This time Landis held a publicized open hearing, his long, narrow office jammed with the press and public. The hearings were widely covered at the time and are amply described in numerous books and articles. On January 5 players from both teams began three days of testimony. It came out that a fund had been raised, but it was used to reward Detroit pitchers for beating the pennant-contending Red Sox three times in late September. Eddie Collins admitted, "In those days it was nothing out of the ordinary to give a player on another team some sort of a gift if he went out of the way to turn in a good performance against one of the team's leading rivals in the race."

In the end, nobody believed Risberg and Gandil.

Five days later Landis handed out a lengthy legal decision, exonerating all the targets of the accusations. He called the practice Collins described "reprehensible and censurable but not corrupt." That would soon be remedied.

Landis made four recommendations: a one-year suspension for rewarding a player on another team; a one-year suspension for betting on a game a player was not involved in; permanent suspension for betting on a game in which a player was involved; a statute of limitations to prevent the resurrection of any more old stuff. (Beginning in 1928 the rules against players, umpires, and anyone else connected with the game betting on games were posted in big, bold red letters in every clubhouse. They are still posted there.)

Ban Johnson sniffed, "This is just a retrial of charges made six years ago when all were absolved of wrongdoing."

Connie Mack said, "That's fine—they can say what they want about the Judge, but he knows how to handle a case."

The two comments, taken together, are an indication of the further weakening of Mack's once-firm support of Johnson. Like his fellow owners, Mack had watched the deterioration of Johnson's judgment and behavior since the appointment of Judge Landis with sadness and concern for his onetime fearless leader. The "loyal five" that had stood behind Johnson in past disputes had now withered to one—Phil Ball of St. Louis.

Being dragged into another hearing had added fuel to Ty Cobb's burning desire for vindication. But he and Speaker, probably restrained by their attorneys, bided their time.

The public dismissed the whole business as old news, an enthralling off-season diversion and nothing more. Not Ban Johnson. He raved on. There was more damaging evidence that Landis hadn't seen, he claimed. He said he never believed either one of them was crooked. Speaker had really been eased out for betting on horse races and allowing his players to do the same, and Cobb for being "too violent" in the handling of his men. (Cobb later admitted he might have ridden his players too hard, but nobody ever accused him of knocking them about.)

Another time Johnson said "the league" had dismissed the two managers for incompetence, as though it was still twenty-five years ago when Ban Johnson *was* the American League and had his nose and hand in everything that went on. Anyhow, he declared, no matter what the commissioner said or did, Cobb and Speaker would never be allowed to play in the American League again.

Landis had had enough. Was evidence withheld from him? Was the league incapable of leashing Johnson's tongue? He called a special meeting of the league for Monday, January 24, in Chicago. A "showdown" the press called it. The betting was on Landis to stay, Johnson to go.

Johnson blustered on. He called a board meeting for noon Sunday at the Union League Club and a league meeting that afternoon at the Blackstone

Hotel. (Johnson reportedly omitted Charles Comiskey from the invitation. But Comiskey showed up anyhow with Alfred Austrian.) Declaring he had done nothing wrong, Johnson looked forward to jousting with Landis and coming out on top. As for holding his tongue, "I have never talked except for the good of baseball and I'm not going to shut up now."

As Connie Mack and Tom Shibe left for Chicago, Mack was the ultimate diplomat. "We've always been friendly with Johnson, and we have a high regard for Commissioner Landis. In fact, we are on friendly terms with everybody."

When the board members—Jake Ruppert, Bob Quinn, Phil Ball, and Ernest Barnard—saw Johnson on Sunday, they were stunned by his condition. He could hardly stand, barely mumbled, had difficulty recognizing people. In place of the fearless warrior they had expected, they saw a man in a state of near-total collapse. The only business recorded was a recommendation to dispense $25,000 to each club from the surplus in the league treasury. Ruppert then hurried to Landis's home to report that Johnson was in no shape for a confrontation and request that the showdown meeting be postponed. Landis agreed.

When the league met that afternoon in Ruppert's suite, Landis was there. Johnson was not. He had left them a written statement conceding that Landis had in fact received all the evidence in the Leonard matter. His physician, Dr. Robert B. Drury, told the owners that Johnson's poor health required an extended rest away from his duties. He would go to Excelsior Springs, Missouri, to recuperate. But they didn't have the heart to fire him or ask for his resignation; they named Frank Navin acting president. Those who had seen Ban Johnson that morning believed he would never recover enough to continue in office. They underestimated him; by the start of the 1927 season he would be back on the job.

But they couldn't let Johnson's attacks on the commissioner go unaddressed. They voted unanimously to appoint Ruppert, Austrian, and Killilea to draw up a statement for the press, repudiating "any and all criticism in the public press emanating from Mr. Johnson reflecting in any way upon Judge Landis or his handling of the several investigations."

That unanimous vote was significant. Ban Johnson had lost the support not only of Connie Mack, but of Phil Ball, his staunch ally since Ball had bought the Browns as part of the Federal League settlement of 1915.

In the only routine business, the league approved a new contract with A. J. Reach to supply baseballs at a cost not to exceed fifteen dollars a dozen.

Speaker and Cobb had been hanging around the Blackstone to see what would happen. Ignoring Johnson's edict that neither would play in the American League again and anticipating the players' imminent reinstatement, Clark Griffith cornered Speaker and asked him to name his price. After a lengthy discussion, they parted with no commitment by either one.

Mack extracted from Speaker a promise not to sign with anyone before giving the A's a chance to make an offer. He was the first to extend to Cobb the belief that the players were innocent and indicated his desire to have him play for the A's. The next day Speaker and Cobb asked Landis to act quickly to settle their status. Then they went home. Their attorneys remained and, according to Cobb's later accounts, dictated the lengthy statement that Landis issued on Thursday, January 27, declaring their innocence.

"As they desire to rescind their withdrawal from baseball," the statement concluded, "the releases which the Detroit and Cleveland clubs granted at their request . . . are canceled and the players' names are restored to the reserve lists of those clubs."

Frank Navin immediately notified every AL club that it was free to negotiate with Cobb directly. If he came to terms with any of them, the Tigers would transfer his contract at no cost. He also informed Cobb that he was free to sign with anyone.

Ernest Barnard put it a different way in a telegram to each club:

For reasons which any baseball man can understand, the Cleveland club will not be able to use Tris Speaker who has been assigned to us by Commissioner Landis in connection with his decision that Speaker's retirement from the game was unnecessary.

Am asking every club in the American League which may be interested in securing Speaker's services to make us a cash proposition for his release and also state salary they are willing to pay him. Please mail your propositions to me special delivery.

It is our intention that Speaker will receive the consideration as well as the salary specified. The Cleveland club will refuse to profit at the expense of Speaker in this matter. We will assign him to the club of his choice after propositions have been considered by him.

Duck hunting in Georgetown, South Carolina, Ty Cobb told reporters he would play another year. "I fully intended to retire permanently. But since this thing has come up I have decided I will have to go back and have one more big year." He was in no hurry to sign with anybody.

On hearing the news, an elated Connie Mack reacted like a teenager turned loose in a mall with an unlimited credit card. "I certainly would like to have both Cobb and Speaker, also Babe Ruth and a few others."

It wasn't as if the Athletics were starved for outfielders. But Mack believed the stars still had a lot of good baseball in them and incidentally would make the A's a stronger gate attraction around the league.

Mack was not alone. The line quickly formed, like customers taking numbers in a busy bakery on a Sunday morning. The White Sox and Yankees were interested in Speaker but not Cobb. The Browns wanted Cobb, not Speaker. Jack Dunn offered Cobb $25,000 to come to Baltimore. Folks in Martinsburg, West Virginia, offered Cobb the entire franchise, including a new ballpark, if he would take it over. Two National League teams were interested in Cobb. But he and Speaker were not free agents; they would have to clear waivers before changing leagues, and that wasn't going to happen. Clark Griffith, in Tampa awaiting spring training, immediately wired Speaker. He took Barnard's wire to mean that Speaker would cost the $4,000 waiver price, if anything.

Mack realized his chief competition for Speaker was Clark Griffith, who had quickly secured a promise from Speaker to give him a chance to top any bid. As soon as Speaker arrived in Philadelphia on Friday for a sports banquet, he conferred with Mack and Eddie Collins at Shibe Park. They met again on Sunday before Speaker headed to New York. The Yankees had an outfield of Ruth, Combs, and Meusel. When Speaker could not get a commitment from Miller Huggins that he would play regularly, the Yankees dropped out of the picture. On Monday evening Griffith called Speaker from Tampa and agreed to Speaker's terms. The next day Mack called Speaker with an offer he knew was better than Griffith's and was so confident, Bill Dooly reported, he even had the cashier's check for the bonus ready to mail. But Speaker said he had given his word to Griffith and wouldn't break it. He signed for a basic salary of $30,000, the same as he had earned in Cleveland. There may have been a signing bonus involved; league contract cards didn't record bonuses.

Mack now turned his full attention to signing Cobb. He wrote to Cobb that he was coming to Augusta. His principal rival was Dan Howley, the new Browns manager who had been a coach for Ty in Detroit. Like a silent movie in which a pair of rival suitors show up on the porch of America's Sweetheart Mary Pickford, Dan Howley and Connie Mack went to Augusta at the same time to win Ty Cobb's hand. Mack arrived on Friday, February

4. Cobb met him at the station and took him to the hotel, where Mack made his pitch. Howley had arrived earlier. That evening Cobb invited them both to his home, where they enjoyed a pleasant, noncommittal evening with their coy host and his family. The next morning the three of them boarded a northbound train. Cobb was going to New York for the writers' dinner on Sunday, then to Philadelphia for a similar event Tuesday night. A large crowd saw them off at the station, where the three men posed for a photo that shows Mack and Cobb smiling broadly, Howley looking more as if he had sucked a lemon. "Dan's expression is interesting compared to yours," Cobb wrote Mack years later. "He doubted or knew I would not sign with him, your expression a smile and reflected confidence."

Cobb had made up his mind that he would not go to St. Louis for two reasons. He preferred to join a team that had a chance to win, and he didn't want to upstage his old friend in his first year as a manager. But he kept that to himself. The hopeful Howley went with him to New York and Philadelphia.

The first chance Mack had to be alone with Cobb in his drawing room on the train, he pulled out a blank contract. "Put down any amount you want, Ty," he said, "and sign it and it'll be done."

Cobb declined. He would prefer to wait until he was in Philadelphia in a few days. The story that he was finally persuaded to sign on the train doesn't fit the records. Mack probably put his offer on the table—a $10,000 signing bonus, $50,000 salary, a cut of exhibition game receipts (which would earn him an additional $5,350.83), and $15,000 if the A's won the pennant, according to club ledgers. But Cobb didn't grab a pen and sign. And Mack made no announcements when he arrived home.

In New York Cobb drew a standing ovation when his presence was acknowledged. Dan Howley told St. Louis papers he had offered Cobb $50,000. Wilbert Robinson said that Brooklyn would go high for him. But that was all just PR. Howley reportedly was resigned to Cobb's going to the A's.

Cobb arrived in Philadelphia on Tuesday and met with Mack at Shibe Park. That evening Cobb addressed the crowd of more than seven hundred in the Adelphi ballroom. Connie Mack was not present. After thanking the writers for inviting him weeks before he was officially reinstated to baseball, he said, "I am happy to announce I will be associated with the Athletics this season."

Bedlam broke out. The whistles and cheers went on for several minutes. When they died down, Cobb expressed regrets that he had not made the change a few years earlier, when his legs had more spring in them. Somebody yelled, "You still have enough left," touching off another outburst of applause.

Chief Bender, Eddie Collins, and Kid Gleason were the first to shake his hand.

The next day the contract was signed. The *New York Times* reported the total terms as $75,000, but had the wrong mix. The numbers didn't bother anybody except Ruppert, who now had to sign Babe Ruth for something more than the $52,000 of last year.

Two days later a jubilant Connie Mack left for Tampa to get in some golf before spring training opened in ten days. The New York betting commission shared his optimism, picking the A's and Giants as 2–1 favorites to meet in the World Series. The Yankees were 3–1.

Clark Griffith had an outfield of Sam Rice, Goose Goslin, and Tris Speaker, with Earl McNeely in reserve. Connie Mack had Al Simmons, Ty Cobb, Zach Wheat, Bill Lamar, and Walter French. With powerhouses like these, they sang, who's afraid of Ruth, Combs, and Meusel?

22 | STRUCK BY LIGHTNING

It is in the nature of baseball fans and players to hate an aggressive player in another uniform who regularly wreaks havoc on them and their pennant chances, then cheer for that player if he should wind up on "our team." If John McGraw had moved from the Giants to the Cubs, say around 1914, Chicago fans would have switched from throwing brickbats to bouquets at him. There was nothing personal about it. It was all about winning.

For twenty years those seven hundred Philadelphians who gave Ty Cobb a rousing welcome at the 1927 writers' dinner and the rest of the city's fans had hated Cobb and made him feel less welcome than in any other city in the league. There are many stories about his disagreeable—mean, loathsome—nature. Perception may be more lasting than reality, but it's not the same thing. Still, if there is a sand grain of truth in every story of what he would do to win, they would add up to a beach the length of Florida. On the field—any field—of competition, Ty Cobb seemed to be wired in such a way that he had no off switch.

Ed Danforth, longtime sports editor of the *Atlanta Journal*, related the story of an exhibition game against a college team in Georgia. People turned out to honor Ty as a neighbor. But when he slid into second and threw a handful of dirt into the eyes of the young second baseman, the infuriated crowd turned against him.

Philadelphia fans weren't interested in the demons of his nature. They respected him as a winning player. After years of running wild against them, he would now be using that fighting spirit to win for them. That's all that mattered. He was no longer "that Ty." He was "our Ty."

Fourteen-year-old Connie Jr. had read the stories about the terrible Ty Cobb. "I thought he was some sort of an ogre," he recalled. When he heard the A's had signed him, Connie expected him to be a grouch. On Junior's first 1927 trip with the team, he quickly learned otherwise.

"Cobb was friendly right from the start. He often asked my father to let me sit with him on the train or on the bus. He told me stories and taught me card tricks and we became pals."

Old-timers recalled how Cobb had knocked them out of the pennant twenty years ago with a ninth-inning home run off Rube Waddell and spiked their chances in 1909 when his slide into Home Run Baker in late August had drawn blood and a furious denunciation from Mack. In the heat of the moment Mack had vowed that "I would not have [Cobb] on my team if he played for nothing." Cobb had responded in kind, and the press furor that followed ended up giving the Tigers the psychological edge. They swept the series and moved past the A's into first place to stay. Baker had stayed in the game, but another slide by Cobb in September had put Jack Barry on the bench, and that hurt the A's even more. Mack and Cobb had probably forgotten it all by now. They certainly acted like it, swapping words of warm and sincere admiration for each other.

What of the players? They all had their Cobb stories. How would they react to his being a teammate? Eddie Collins was the only active player who had been there twenty years ago, when the Athletics always looked at Detroit in terms of Cobb and not as a team. Collins had been a wild mustang on the bases himself. He didn't believe Cobb was a "dirty" player then and had never changed his mind. Frank Baker and Jack Barry felt the same. In 1930 Collins said, "Ty Cobb has always been my ideal ball player, the best I saw or hope to see, and 50 percent of his offensive ability was the threat he was to the defending team, the anxiety he caused opposing pitchers and fielders who had always to wonder just what he would do next."

Cobb and Collins often hunted together in the winter.

Ballplayers acknowledged that the baselines belonged to the runner. If you got in the way you might be spiked. Washington third baseman Ossie Bluege said of Cobb, "He would fake a slide as if going directly for the baseman, and at the last minute throw his body in the opposite direction, away from the infielder and the base. He would overslide, then reach for a corner with his hand." Cobb's aim was always to elude a tag, not slide into it, providing the smallest possible target. They understood that.

Plenty of catchers carried scars inflicted by Cobb. Ira Thomas had one. Wally Schang, now with the Browns, said that Cobb never cut him. "He was too pretty a slider to hurt anybody who would put the ball on him right." If a catcher had the marks of Cobb's spikes on his legs, Schang said it was probably the catcher's fault for trying to tag Cobb by going up the third base line to meet him. Cy Perkins had made that mistake in his first year and had a two-inch scar on his right knee as a souvenir. "Cobb plowed into me," Perkins recalled, "and the next thing I knew I was stretched out on the ground, my mitt lying in one place, my mask in another, my chest protector twisted around my back and my pants all the way up to here. While I was looking for the mask so I could bang him with it, he leaned down and rasped out, 'How'd you like it, you dirty little punk? This is just a sample. The next time you try to stop me, I'm going to knock you into the stands.'"

The next day, Perkins said, Cobb told him, "You're going to be a great catcher. I like you, but that's not going to stop me from tearing your guts out if you get in my way. All I want from you is three inches on either side of the plate when I'm trying to score. Is that asking for too much?"

While the fans were howling for Cobb's scalp, the players understood that it was all part of Cobb's game of intimidation. Jimmie Dykes said, "When I broke in, I played second. Every time Cobb passed me on the field, he said the same thing: 'You stink.' He'd say it after every inning. He was trying to bull me."

But Jimmie never backed down or took it personally. Cobb had never done him any harm except to go all out to beat the A's. Dykes respected that and was happy to have him on his side now. He wasn't too proud to listen to Cobb's advice. One day he noticed Cobb and Simmons in a huddle and moved closer to listen in. "Cobb is showing him how to hit lefthanders. He's telling Al to get up on the plate against them. The next day we're facing a lefty and I get up on the plate and go three for four. After the game I'm sitting in front of my locker all smiles. Cobb comes by, looks at me, and says, 'Well, rockhead, you're finally learning, aren't you?'"

Max Bishop was thrilled to be on the same team with Cobb, who had been his hero growing up in Waynesboro, Pennsylvania. When the kids played toss with their baseball cards and the one whose card landed closest to the wall took them all, Max never risked his Ty Cobb card.

"Ty was my big hero," he told Bill Dooly. "I read everything I could lay my hands on about him. At night the other kids and me would sit around and tell each other all the stories we ever heard about Ty."

Max was right-handed, but he batted lefty because Cobb did. "All the kids wanted to play outfield like Ty, bat like Ty. They tore up their stockings and clothes trying to slide like Ty."

The one player who was most upset by the arrival of Cobb was Howard Ehmke. They despised each other. Ehmke had pitched for Detroit during

Cobb's first two years as manager. Cobb had no idea how to handle anyone of Ehmke's sensitive temperament. Howard couldn't take the manager's riding and talked back. Cobb traded him to Boston in 1923.

The first time Ehmke pitched against the Tigers, in Detroit on May 18, Cobb went hitless in the Red Sox' 6–2 win. At times he rode Ehmke from the first base coaches box. When Cobb batted in the seventh inning, Ehmke hit him with a pitch. The fans booed. On his way to first, Cobb yelled at Ehmke, "That was deliberate."

Ehmke admitted that it was.

After the game they tangled under the stands. The next day Cobb told the press:

> You know people cannot throw things at me and get away with it. Had he said it was an accident, I would have done nothing but take his word for it. As it was, there was nothing for me to do but slap his face.
>
> Before doing so I told him I didn't intend to muss him up and hurt him seriously. After knocking him down I merely slapped him with my open hand, until he promised he would not throw at me again. I think he will keep his promise for he knows I will lick him every time he throws at me.
>
> I make a personal issue of such assaults. I could not retain my self-respect unless I did.

According to Ehmke, that wasn't the end of Cobb's revenge. In 1952 he told Ed Pollock of the *Bulletin* the rest of the story. "[Another] time I pitched against the Tigers, Cobb hit one toward right which [first baseman] Phil Todt knocked down. I ran over to cover first, but stopped at least a yard, maybe two, from the bag when I saw Todt couldn't recover in time to make a throw. I had my back to Cobb, but I heard him hit the dirt, and luckily I lifted my right foot. Cobb's spikes hit the heel of my shoe. If I hadn't lifted it, he would have cut off my foot."

The bitterness between the pitcher and Cobb continued after Ehmke joined the A's in 1926, according to another Dykes story: "One afternoon on the bench I was screaming insults at Cobb. He knew I was doing the hollering. But there was a pitcher on the A's he didn't like. I forget his name. I hollered up something and Cobb charged into the dugout. I was ready for him. But he ignored me and punched the pitcher. He just wanted an excuse to slug him."

The pitcher was probably Howard Ehmke.

When Cobb and Ehmke came face to face in Fort Myers at spring training, they shook hands and went their separate ways. There were no known incidents of friction between them after that.

Once he arrived at Fort Myers, Cobb tried his best to fit in. He told Connie Mack he would curb his tendency to try to correct every flaw he saw in other players and teach everybody how to do things his way—unless asked. It wouldn't be easy, and he wouldn't always succeed. Washington third baseman Ossie Bluege recalled a close game in which Collins was on third in the ninth inning. Cobb hit a grounder to Bucky Harris at second. Harris threw home. Collins was caught in a pickle between third and home and was unable to elude a tag before Cobb could get to second, where he was tagged out. Cobb raced at Collins shouting, "How long have you been playing this game?"

Ballpark errand boy Jim Morrow hadn't known Cobb before, but he didn't like him when he found that Cobb fit into the tightfisted category, along with Walter French and Lefty Grove: "They'd sit in the right field corner bullpen and send me up for ice cream or a candy bar and never even give me the money to pay for it," he recalled. "They'd holler, 'Don't let Mr. Mack see you.' I never got a nickel from any of them. No tip. Nothing."

Once, Morrow said, "Cobb gave me a dollar and asked me to take a telegram to the Western Union office. I took it and it turned out to cost $1.20. When I went back and told him, he wouldn't give me the twenty cents."

Cobb had few friends among ballplayers and didn't care. He didn't know how to give or take good-natured ribbing or needling, and the A's had some pretty sharp needlers. Cobb kept his distance. He was not a beer-with-the-boys kind of man. He preferred wine—champagne mostly—and the company of business tycoons. On a day off or a rainy day, he might take in four or five movies, usually but not always alone. Writer Al Horwits said he often went with Cobb but would have enough after sitting through two flicks.

When Cobb offered players stock market advice, they usually tuned him out. But Max Bishop listened, bought some Coca-Cola stock, and years later was grateful that he did.

One player Cobb took to was Mickey Cochrane. They became close, lifelong friends, maybe because they had the same temperament on the field. Just as Cobb believed the base paths belonged to the runner, Cochrane was equally vehement that home plate belonged to him. He dared a runner to try to reach it. Admitting that Cobb was "a little crusty at times," Mickey told

F. C. Lane, "He gave me some fine advice in batting and was an inspiration to me in every way." During Cobb's two years with the A's, Mickey regularly drove him to the ballpark. Cobb kept after him to buy Coca-Cola stock, which Cochrane finally did thirty years later. In the 1950s he would offer to get Cochrane a Coca-Cola franchise. According to Cochrane's wife Mary, "Cobb never helped Mike financially, just with advice." Cochrane and catcher Ray Schalk would be the only two ballplayers at Cobb's funeral in 1961.

Connie Mack had signed Cobb hoping the veteran might be an example to his younger players. When Ty Cobb had a weakness, he devoted hours on and off the field to overcoming that weakness. Mack hoped that attitude would rub off on some of his less industrious youngsters. He also hoped that Cobb's brand of baseball would ignite some competitive fire in his boys. Cobb was an exemplar of Mack's belief, "If you get the other fellow worried, the battle is half won." When his boys saw the forty-year-old Cobb going all out on every play, hustling singles into doubles, and jarring pitchers into balks and wild throws, it might put some ginger in them. He had one particular boy in mind—Al Simmons.

Westbrook Pegler once wrote, "Connie Mack often judges ball players not so much by what they can do as by their love of doing it." Miller Huggins called it a "winning quality," which a few were born with, some acquired, and others never had. The last were of no use to a championship team.

Connie Mack hadn't seen it in Herb Pennock or Joe Bush or hundreds of others in the parade that had passed through Shibe Park over the years. He saw it now in Dykes and Collins and Cochrane and Grove and Rommel—and Ty Cobb. He wasn't sure yet about Al Simmons.

Maybe Mack knew that when Al was a youngster, he would borrow a friend's collection of cigarette baseball cards and sit in the alley behind his home for hours, studying them and memorizing the statistics. Maybe he knew that, of all those cardboard images, Ty Cobb was the kid's hero.

Mack sensed that Simmons would be a willing and eager disciple of his idol. He assigned the forty-year-old Cobb to room with the twenty-four-year-old Simmons on the road.

It paid off. Simmons was thrilled. He soaked up all the advice Cobb had to offer. "You swing at too many bad pitches," Cobb told him. "You need more patience at the plate."

On breaking a slump: "Choke up on the bat and try to slash the ball back at the pitcher's or first baseman's shins hard as you can."

On hitting left-handers who were giving him trouble: "Crowd the plate."

On base running: "When you're headed for the base, watch the infielder's eyes. The way he looks to take the throw tells you which side of the base to slide on."

Cobb favored long-sleeved uniforms. Simmons adopted the same style.

While Al Simmons never became a base-stealing threat, for the next five years he would tear up the league with his bat, averaging .375 and 133 RBIS, and become a great defensive outfielder, with no more than 4 errors a year. Twenty years later umpire Bill McGowan told Arch Ward of the *Chicago Tribune* that during those years Simmons played "with the same fire and determination that marked Cobb's style."

Like they did with Cobb, other clubs soon learned that it didn't pay to get Simmons fired up. New York catcher Bill Dickey recalled that before a series in New York in June 1929, "Somebody suggested we rough him up, so we tried it." In the five games Simmons went 13 for 21, with 4 home runs, 3 doubles, and a triple.

By 1930 Simmons would be carrying himself with the same swagger of superiority on the field as Cobb had displayed. Ty Cobb deserves some of the credit for what Al Simmons achieved, and Connie Mack an assist.

On Ty Cobb's first day in an A's uniform on March 7, 1927, a gang of fifty newspaper and movie photographers was there to greet him. When Thomas Edison showed up, Cobb joined in the festivities, offering to pitch to the eighty-year-old inventor. Mack led Edison to the left-hand batter's box, took a bat from Zach Wheat, and handed it to Edison. Wearing a straw hat and small catcher's mitt, Mack stood behind the plate. Cobb stood about halfway to the mound and lobbed the ball. Edison took a mighty swing and connected; the ball hit Cobb in the shoulder and knocked him to the ground. Amid cries of "Sign him" from the spectators, Cobb picked himself up and shook hands with the smiling Edison.

"Think you will be able to do that when you are eighty?" Edison said.

"I hope so," Mack shouted to the deaf Edison. "It will mean a lot of pennants to us in the next forty years."

Occasionally Edison's neighbor Henry Ford accompanied him. New York writer Bill Corum once observed Edison and Ford sitting with Mack on a bench along the first base line. Corum overheard some of the conversation. "One of the things I heard was Mr. Ford saying to Edison, 'I was just saying to Connie that baseball was the best run business in America.'"

The A's settled down to a productive and enjoyable spring training. There was plenty of enthusiasm. Eddie Collins said he felt like a young colt again.

Joe Boley and Max Bishop were Mack's kind of players. Both were quiet, unflashy, smart students of the game. Unlike the more placid Bishop, Boley showed that he enjoyed playing the game.

It would take the intuitive Boley a while to learn to read the hitters and the A's pitchers in order to position himself properly. Then other infielders began to play off him, and Mack realized he didn't have to wave his scorecard at his shortstop anymore. Boley responded to Mack's patience. When he messed up a play, Mack might say to him, "John [Boley's real name was John], it might have been better if you had done it this way."

Max Bishop was all business, almost mechanical, on the field. He did his job every day, win or lose, and collected his paychecks. At bat or on the bench he studied the pitcher, watched how and where the ball came out of his hand and where it went. He had developed the ability to read the pitches quickly and accurately. But the most important element of his offense was discipline at the plate. His attitude on every pitch was, "This is it," and he was ready to swing. But if it wasn't his pitch to hit, he didn't bite. And he had the quick bat he needed if it was his pitch.

Bishop needed resting; he would never play a full schedule. But as a lead-off man, between his hits and walks, he was on base almost half the time.

Dud Branom, a left-hander, was the A's best-fielding first baseman since Stuffy McInnis. The pitchers were all in good shape.

Ty Cobb and Zach Wheat took orders from Connie Mack and Kid Gleason like everybody else.

For all his aggressiveness, Ty Cobb was, in Billy Evans's words, "never a hard man on the umpire." Cobb went into the season determined to avoid controversy. He wasn't a manager anymore and didn't have to argue for his team. On May 23 he would tell Alan J. Gould of the AP, "I started out the year with an entirely different idea—simply to play the game, have the very best year I could, and work my head off for Connie Mack, one of the finest leaders this game has ever had. I made up my mind I wouldn't stir up any fuss or do anything that might arouse criticism."

Ty Cobb didn't go looking for trouble with umpires, but trouble found him. It began in a spring exhibition game. Frank Wilson, a thin-skinned umpire who had joined the National League after Ban Johnson let him go in 1922, had had a few run-ins with Cobb back then. Apparently Wilson was still looking to have the last word. During a game against the Braves, Wilson was behind the plate. Suddenly, for no apparent reason, he tore off his mask, turned, and ordered Cobb, who was standing there minding his own business, out of the game. Cobb had said nothing to warrant it, but he didn't argue. He returned to the bench and sat down instead of leaving the field altogether. Whereupon Wilson forfeited the game to the Braves. To placate the angry crowd, the two teams agreed to play another game without Cobb in the lineup. Based on Wilson's report, Landis fined Cobb $100.

Several days later, when the A's got on Wilson over the incident, the jumpy ump cleared the bench, something he had done in a similar spring game a year earlier.

Connie Mack eagerly accepted an invitation to make the presentation of a silver service from baseball men in both leagues to John McGraw, marking his twenty-five years in New York, at a dinner in St. Petersburg. It was a love fest. Mack had grown into the most beloved and respected man among his peers in baseball. When the jovial, rotund Brooklyn manager Wilbert Robinson spied the tall, lanky Mack, Uncle Robbie (who was only six months younger) greeted him, "Dear old Connie," embraced him and kissed him on the cheek.

Mack and McGraw sincerely admired each other as baseball men. No two managers had ever fought harder for victory than they had in their three World Series clashes. The emcee, Bozeman Bulger of the *New York World*, wrote, "Mr. Mack made the prettiest and one of the most feelingest speeches I have ever heard. He accorded McGraw the honor of being the greatest baseball manager of all time and pointed to the record in proof rather than it being an empty compliment. McGraw's grateful response was as flattering of Connie Mack."

America was enjoying one big party. Clarence W. Barron, editor of the *Wall Street Journal*, predicted forty years of great prosperity for the nation. Automobile sales topped 4 million a year. More than five hundred new models had been on display at the 1926 National Automobile Show. Nobody paid any attention to the rising unemployment and economic instability in Austria and Germany. The stock market was soaring like a hot air balloon, carrying about 20 million investors (out of a population of 119 million) to unlimited riches. Miller Huggins complained about his players, "When they pick up a newspaper now, they turn to the financial page first and the sports page later. Those things aren't good for a ball club which is trying to beat a club like the one Mr. Mack has."

Gertrude Ederle swam the English Channel. Gene Tunney defeated Jack

Dempsey for the second time to retain the heavyweight championship. Bobby Jones, twenty-five, won more golf tournaments and made his first hole-in-one.

But it was the year of the Bambino. Babe Ruth overshadowed them all. "The Ruth is mighty, and shall prevail," Heywood Broun had written. And so he did.

Despite a winter of scandals involving baseball's top stars and the fixing of games, *New York Times* columnist John Kieran foresaw no fall-off in attendance. Like the farmer who predicted that a severe rainstorm would stop because "it always has," he wrote that the fans will keep coming despite the scandals because "they always have."

He was right. Record crowds turned out on opening day at Yankee Stadium (helped by the double decking of the left-field stands), at Wrigley Field, and at Redland Field in Cincinnati. Capacity crowds also showed up at the Shibe Park and Polo Grounds openers.

Connie Mack was unusually vocal in his optimism for the coming season. On his sixty-fourth birthday in December he had predicted a pennant for his team. Many spring training observers now agreed with him. *Time* magazine saluted his resurgence by putting him on the cover of its April 11 issue.

Before leaving for Florida, Mack had said, "Unless some team starts going above its normal speed, we should be out in front at the end."

That "unless" is what happened. The Yankees caught lightning in a bottle. They sprinted to a 6-0 start with 3 wins and a tie in the opening series against the A's, were 21-8 by May 19, 44-17 by June 23, and led the A's by 14½ after the Fourth of July. They set league records with 975 runs scored, 110 wins, and a 19-game lead at the end. Ruth's 60 home runs were more than any entire AL team hit; he and Gehrig drove in a total of 339 runs.

Philadelphia fans hated the Yankees, not a rare condition—then or now—when the New Yorkers seemed to win with the regularity of Henry Ford turning out Model Ts. But they loved and admired Babe Ruth.

Jim Morrow recalled that Ruth sometimes drove his car down to Philadelphia from New York. "He would park his big twelve cylinder Packard convertible and on his way out after a game, he'd stop at a concession stand and get several dollars worth of change. When he went out all the kids were hanging around his car and he'd throw a handful of that change in the air and the kids would scatter and he'd get in his car and drive away."

Nineteen-year-old Mary Jenkinson worked for Western Electric near Shibe Park. Years later she described the Yankees arriving in town in the morning at North Philadelphia station and walking past her building to Shibe Park:

> Our office was on the first floor and everybody was excited waiting to see them pass. As the team went by we all called out the window at them, mostly at Babe Ruth, calling 'Hey Babe' and the Babe smiling and nodding and waving to all of us. They looked like businessmen, wearing suits and hats, and always conducted themselves as gentlemen. I was very impressed to see these important ballplayers walking from the train six blocks. Some of them were carrying suitcases and equipment bags. But not Ruth. The others knew he would be picking up some kids along the way. He was like the Pied Piper, always surrounded by children and carrying one of them on his shoulder or in his arms. One day he had one perched on his shoulder and another one in his arms at the same time.
>
> The girls cooed over the handsome Lou Gehrig, but it was the prospect of seeing Babe Ruth that had us all absolutely breathless.

The Babe drew thousands of early arrivals to ballparks to watch him in batting practice. No matter what the score was in the eighth inning, nobody left if there was a chance of Ruth batting in the ninth.

That powerful aura, that magnetism, never faded. Mary's fourteen-year-old brother Bill went with his uncle, Jim Dugan, to a doubleheader against the Yankees on May 22, 1930. Bill was disappointed when they found the grandstand sold out and had to pay twenty-five cents to sit on a rooftop on Twentieth Street overlooking right-center field, about 425 feet from home plate. The Yankees won both games, 10–1 and 20–13. There were 14 home runs, including 3 by Lou Gehrig in the second game. But only one of them stood out in young Bill's mind for the rest of his life.

In the third inning of the first game, Ruth teed off on a Howard Ehmke pitch. Bill recalled many years later:

> I thought it was coming right at me. In a split second it kept right on rising far over my head. I snapped my head up as it zipped past. It was a jaw-dropping experience. I was so disappointed at not being in the ballpark and all of a sudden Babe Ruth hit it so far over my head, I felt so much closer to the action. With that one swing he had pulled me right inside the ballpark. I was aware of the extraordinary power of

this man, not just physically to hit a ball of that magnitude, but also the power of his personality, whereby he could act in so decisive and definitive a manner to take this fourteen-year-old kid and yank him right into the ballpark and do it in such an emotional manner that years and years later the experience was still fresh and still powerful.

The ball had gone so far over the youngster's head, it cleared the alley behind his rooftop perch and the next row of houses too before crashing through a window of a house on the far side of Opal Street, having traveled well over five hundred feet.

Connie Mack tried everything he could think of to stymie Ruth. He would stand on the top step of the dugout, waving his outfield around for a minute or two until the players stood where he wanted them, then watch Ruth hit it over the fence. He used an infield shift, with three men to the right of second base, and Ruth plopped a bunt down the third base line to beat him.

For the first two weeks the A's stayed with the Yankees. After losing the opening series in New York, they took 5 of 6 from their nemesis of the past two years, the Senators, and went into New York for a single game on Sunday, May 1, tied for first. Before a throng of seventy thousand, Jack Quinn gave up 1 hit in the first and 1 in the sixth. But they happened to be home runs by Ruth and Gehrig, each preceded by a walk to Koenig. Ruth hit another homer off Walberg, and the A's bid farewell to first place for the season.

The wags called Collins, Wheat, and Cobb "Mack's Ancients," but they delivered for Connie Mack. As he had promised, Ty Cobb gave the A's everything he had. And he still had plenty. Sure, he was a few steps slower in the field and on the bases, but the fire still burned in the old furnace, and the mind still fired on all cylinders. On April 26 in Boston he was the whole show in a 9–8 win, stealing home, driving in 2 runs. In the ninth he raced in to make a circus catch and kept right on running to double off the potential tying run at first base. He was still capable of destabilizing an infield. When infielders played in to protect against a bunt, he would slap it past the third baseman. When he was on base, they all played closer to the bases, leaving bigger holes. Pitchers got jittery; his fake starts to steal home caused balks. And they weren't all fakes. He stole home twice in April. At forty he was still good for 22 stolen bases, in an era when the league leader stole only 27.

In May Cobb had a 21-game hitting streak; at the end of the month he was batting .381, Simmons .392. They both would stay close to that pace all season, Simmons battling Harry Heilmann for the batting title. In September umpire Bill McGowan gave him an assist in that battle: "One day I called Al out on a close play at second base and he threw dust at me. That meant an automatic suspension. After the game Connie Mack came to me in the dressing room and asked if it would be all right if Al apologized. I accepted the apology of course and did not report the incident to president Ban Johnson. This gave Simmons a chance to stay in the batting race, but Heilmann won it anyway."

On the last day, Simmons was 2 for 5; Heilmann was 7 for 9 and beat him, .398 to .392.

Connie Mack didn't defer to his veterans. He moved them with his scorecard as if they were rookies. The practice had begun during the dark years, when his teams had been evergreen and it seemed as though none of them knew how to play the game. Mack had devised a system in which he moved his infielders while holding the scorecard below the waist, and the outfielders while holding it chest high. Over the years he had proven so good at it, whenever players around the league were discussing outfielders, someone would say, "The best outfielder in the American League is Connie Mack," and nobody would disagree. (Mack also used the scorecard as a decoy while sending a signal by a movement of his hands, feet, legs, or head. Sometimes he would be doing all of that while a rookie on the bench was the real source of the sign.)

Zach Wheat was new to the league; Cobb had been around for twenty-two years. He knew all the hitters as well as anybody. But he didn't know the Athletics' pitchers the way Mack did and how the deliveries of a tiring pitcher would change a batter's tendencies.

Cobb and Mack enjoyed talking about it over the years with, of course, the customary variations and embellishments as time went by. Cobb said he went to Mack at the start of the season and told him to wave the scorecard and he would follow his directions. According to Mack, on opening day a man was up who Mack knew would hit Grove's pitch down the right-field line to Cobb's left. "I stood up in the dugout and waved him over with my scorecard. Even the pitcher turned in the box to look. Ty saluted like the good sport he was and trotted over to the new position. I felt relieved when the batter lined a drive so close he hardly had to move a step to grab it."

In 1956 Cobb told a small group of baseball people and fans this version in a room at the St. Francis Hotel in San Francisco. Syndicated columnist Henry McLemore was there, and this is how he reported it:

I [Cobb] took my place in right field and I had been in the American League for more than twenty years. Nobody is going to tell me anything. Then I see Mr. Mack waving to me to move over. He waves his scorecard and says, 'Move twenty feet to your right.' I yelled back to the second baseman and said, 'I ain't moving.' Mr. Mack keeps waving and I don't move a foot. Mr. Mack still keeps waving that scorecard. I finally say to myself, 'He's an old man so just go ahead and please him.' So I move twenty feet to the right. Then the hitter hits one right in my kisser. If I hadn't been just where Mr. Mack told me to be, it would have had to go for a double or a triple. I caught it without moving an inch. When I walked to the bench I told the old man he knew more about baseball than I did, and from then on I'd obey him like a slave.

This happened on more than one occasion . . . and I'm sure Mack was the only man in baseball who could be right on so many occasions.

Zach Wheat recalled a game on June 16 in which the White Sox had men on second and third and one out. He misremembered some of the players involved and the exact sequence of the play when he told it to *The Sporting News* fourteen years later. But it did happen. Willie Kamm was the batter. Wheat was playing him deep in left field. Al Simmons yelled to him, "The old man's waving to you." Wheat said:

I looked toward the bench. There was Mr. Mack beckoning to me and waving his scorecard. I moved in ten feet. He signaled me to come in further. I advanced three or four more steps. He kept wigwagging with his scorecard and soon I was standing not more than twenty feet behind Joe Boley and Sammy Hale. I was mad clear through. Old Connie is a fool, I said to myself. Then [Kamm] pickled one on the nose. It came to me like a shot. I squeezed it and tossed to [Bishop] at second base for a double play ending the rally.

When I came in the dugout, Mr. Mack said, "Zach, I knew what the pitcher was going to throw and figured that [Kamm] would hit exactly the shot he did. That's why I kept signaling you to come in. Always watch me and do as you're told and then you will never get in any trouble."

When Ty Cobb failed to set the proper example, he heard about it from Mack. They were in Cleveland for a Sunday doubleheader on July 24. A wild throw by Joe Boley with the bases loaded had let in 3 runs to break a 6–6 tie in the first game. In the second game they faced a left-hander, Jake Miller, a fair but inconsistent pitcher, not overpowering. Back on June 3 Miller had beaten the A's, 3–1, a game in which Cobb had 2 hits off him. This afternoon the rest of the A's collected 11 hits, but Miller had Cobb bamboozled every time at bat. After a fruitless fourth time up, Cobb came back to the bench muttering, "It's impossible to hit that guy."

Mack bristled but said nothing. Two walks by Walberg led to 4 runs in the eighth and they trailed 5–1. The A's scored 1 in the ninth and had runners on second and third with Cobb due up. As Cobb picked up a bat, Mack said, "Maybe I better send up a pinch hitter for you."

Cobb glared at him. As Mack related the story years later, "He could have eaten me alive, he was so mad. He went right up there and started swinging again."

Cobb hit a roller to shortstop that ended the game.

Nothing more was said about it until several days later, when Mack and Cobb happened to be alone in the clubhouse. Cobb brought it up. "Why did you say that to me about a pinch hitter?"

"Because you've been a great batsman," Mack said, "and you never should make a statement like that about it being impossible to hit that pitcher. What about my boys sitting on the bench? They're not batsmen like you and when they hear you say such a thing, they're bound to think to themselves, 'Well, if Cobb can't hit him, what's the use of us trying?'"

One writer listening to Mack tell the story asked him how Cobb took the remark.

"He never took anything like that with good grace," Mack chuckled. "Not Cobb."

Putting himself in the heads of his players was typical of Mack. One day Al Simmons was having a bad day at the plate. After another fruitless at-bat he came back to the bench grumbling, "How can a guy be expected to hit against that lousy background?"

Later Mack said to him, "By golly, Al, don't ever say a thing like that as long as you live. If you're going to react that way about the background, and you're a .350 hitter, what do you think the effect is going to be on the .275 and .250 hitters?"

They were lessons that, later as coaches and managers, Mack's boys never forgot.

Trouble found Ty Cobb again on Thursday, May 5, at Shibe Park. The

Red Sox were leading, 3–2, when he came up to bat in the eighth inning. Right-hander Tony Welzer pitched. Cobb lined it down the right-field foul line, over the fence, clearly to the left of the pole. When he saw the ball go over the fence, he started to jog around the bases. But the ball curved to the right, and the last time home plate umpire Red Ormsby saw it, it appeared to be to the right of the pole. He held up his hands and hollered, "Foul."

Al Simmons, on deck, leaped and wailed like a banshee, "It was fair," and was quickly thumbed out. After the game Ormsby claimed that Simmons had made motions to the fans that the ump was blind. Bill Dooly of the *Record* denied that Al had done any such thing, just yelled that the ball was fair.

Eddie Collins rushed out and pulled Al away and calmly discussed the matter with the umpire. Kid Gleason talked with first base umpire Brick Owens. They had no case under the rules. In mid-June 1920 a new rule defining a home run based on where it had passed over the fence had been rescinded after numerous complaints from umpires that it was too difficult to determine a ball's fair or foul status that way. They had gone back to the old rule, basing their calls on where they last saw the ball. Ormsby had been an umpire since 1923. He went by the only rule he knew, although most umpires now no longer watched the ball once it cleared the fence. Connie Mack later said Ormsby made "an obvious blunder, digging up that ancient section one of rule forty-eight as an alibi."

(The next year National League umpires asked that the home run rule be made uniform. Balls hit into the seats would be judged by where they passed the foul pole; those hit over the outer walls or the roof would be judged where last seen. But they couldn't make it uniform because most foul poles did not go high enough.)

The crowd in Shibe Park that day didn't know from the cockamamie rule. All they knew was what they saw, an obviously fair ball clearing the fence. The noise was deafening.

And what was Cobb doing? Standing beside Boston manager Bill Carrigan watching it all. Then, according to Dooly, "Ty stepped toward the plate to bat and made a remark to Ormsby. To everyone's surprise Ormsby pulled off his mask and ordered Cobb to the showers."

According to James Isaminger, there was a "near-riot"—whatever that means. "In a second the spectators were inflamed and bellowed and boiled their indignation at the umpire, who was quickly surrounded by a cluster of gesticulating Macks. One irate customer hurled a seat cushion down on the field and several other small missiles were thrown."

The *Boston Globe*'s account by "Special Dispatch" made no mention of pop bottles or a game-delaying riot. It said simply that the row between the players and the umpire lasted ten minutes, and after the game Ormsby was "struck by a cushion thrown from the upper pavilion as he walked into the dugout" escorted by the police. Hardly a deadly downpour of debris. The brief AP account that ran in other papers said only, "Ty was ejected from the game for disputing the decision too strenuously. Al Simmons also was ordered from the game for taking part in the debate."

Both Ormsby and Cobb said afterward that Cobb had not argued. In stepping into the box, he had accidentally brushed against the umpire's shoulder. That brought an automatic ejection. After the game, Cobb apologized to the umpire and said it was accidental. Ormsby said he believed him, but he couldn't retract the ejection. Ormsby was also quoted as saying, "I can't umpire for the Athletics."

By the time a "special" report in the *Chicago Tribune* got hold of the story, it had become a full-blown riot on the field amid a murderous barrage of soda bottles: "Eight thousand irate baseball fans swarmed onto the playing field at Shibe Park today, hurling pop bottles, cushions, and everything else they could pick up. . . . Police on duty at the park were unable to hold the crowds back, and a riot call was sent in. Reserves were able to clear the field after much difficulty, and when the game ended the fans again swarmed out to 'get' Ormsby who sought protection and was escorted from the park by police cutting a swath through the crowd with their clubs." The article implied that Cobb and Simmons had incited the fans to riot.

Isaminger responded that there were no pop bottles thrown. "One man threw a cushion down in the field to register his disgust, but did not aim it at Ormsby who was fifty feet away. The story was grossly overcolored in every detail."

But the A's hadn't seen any of those reports when they boarded a train that night to Buffalo, where they had an exhibition game on Friday. On the train Simmons griped about being ejected just for bawling, "It was fair." Cobb explained why he was tossed. He had entered the box with a smile, not a sneer. "I jumped out of the box and on the way back I accidentally brushed Ormsby's shoulder and he thought it was intentional and put me out. I never at any time uttered a word of protest over the decision, although Ormsby made the mistake of his life."

A few days later Cobb added, "We talked after the game and Ormsby was very much broken up because he had put me out. At the time he was confused by the noise of the crowd and the arguing following his decision."

They were all aggravated because the home run meant the difference in a 3–2 loss. But it was behind them now, and that was the end of it. Or so they thought.

In Buffalo Cobb sprang a charley horse sliding into second on the back end of a double steal and limped off the field. It looked like he'd be sidelined for the next series in Cleveland.

When they arrived in Cleveland on Saturday morning, Connie Mack was handed a telegram from Ban Johnson's secretary, Will Harridge, notifying him that Cobb and Simmons were suspended indefinitely. What they had done might justify an ejection, but an indefinite suspension? What did that mean?

Connie Mack was furious. He was convinced that Ormsby had filed an exaggerated, distorted version of the incident. The heart of his team was being cut out unjustly. It had been twenty years since he'd been so outraged by an umpire's conduct. And what remained from a quarter century of marching side by side with "Friend Ban" blew away with his fury. He immediately called the league office and gave Will Harridge an earful. He lambasted the work of Red Ormsby and the umpire's statement that he could not umpire for the Athletics. "Such a statement should not be permitted on a major league staff," he stormed. "It's outrageous." He asked Harridge to see that Ormsby was not assigned to any further Athletics games. (He was.)

When they saw the AP version of the *Tribune* story that went out all over the country with a Chicago dateline, Mack and Cobb boiled over. They believed that Ormsby's report had influenced Ban Johnson, who fueled the *Tribune* story. Cobb was trying to play his best baseball and avoid controversy, and here he was, the center of a storm. He had never had any quarrels with Red Ormsby and considered him a friend. Cobb's brother Paul had served in the same company of Marines with Ormsby in the war, and they had talked about it. He didn't deny the accidental physical contact, but he branded anyone "a liar" who claimed he had argued about the call.

When Connie Mack received a wire from Johnson asking for the club's report of the incident, Mack said, "How can I make a report when I haven't the slightest idea what charges were made by Ormsby?"

Johnson was in St. Louis, where he had read Ormsby's report. Before leaving for Chicago at noon Sunday, Johnson told reporters, "I am waiting word from Mr. Mack of the Athletics for anything the club may have to say on the side of the offenders. Thus far I have been advised of no reply on the part of the club. My report from umpire Ormsby states that Cobb shoved him around. Then, realizing his offense, Ty began apologizing, but only after the actions of Simmons and himself had incited the crowd to the extent that the umpire had to be escorted from the field."

The A's lost a raggedy 11–10 game in 11 innings on Saturday in Cleveland, and another, 4–2, on Sunday. Monday morning Mack went into a 6-foot-2½-inch rage when he called the American League office and Ban Johnson wouldn't take his call.

After he hung up, Mack sputtered, "It's the most outrageous thing I ever heard of in baseball and there must be a complete investigation. Mr. Johnson wouldn't talk to me personally and ordered me to submit a written report of my version of the row. What I can't fathom is the insistence of Johnson that I file a written report. I had wired him that the incident was overcolored in some newspaper stories. Nothing I could add in a further written report would help clarify the situation. That is what I wanted to explain to Mr. Johnson over the telephone."

His anger was aimed as much at what he considered Ormsby's misleading report as it was at Ban Johnson's brush-off. Mack then sent a telegram to Johnson demanding a hearing with the players and Ormsby in Detroit Tuesday morning and the release of Ormsby's report. "I want Ormsby to explain why he apologized to Ty for putting him out of the game and then made a report to Ban Johnson that has apparently inflamed him. I also want Ormsby to tell Ban Johnson that at no time was there an attack made on him and that he never was in danger of being harmed. If the league officials are playing the game square, they will grant my request for a hearing. I am going to fight this case to the finish."

The last time he had said that was in 1918, when he had taken baseball to court over the Scott Perry case. That time Ban Johnson had been his ally.

Mack's telegram was one of hundreds flooding the league office. Most of them came from Detroit, where civic leaders and the fans who had booed Ty Cobb last year had prepared an all-day lineup of festivities to welcome back their erstwhile hero on Tuesday. Every seat in Navin Field had been sold weeks ago. The luncheon and dinner and pregame ceremonies could go on regardless, but they wanted the suspension lifted in time to see Cobb in action on the field once again, even in an enemy uniform.

Ban Johnson rejected Mack's request for a hearing. He said he would decide the length of Cobb's and Simmons's suspensions on Tuesday morning.

Claiming that the report of the other umpire, Brick Owens, had not arrived until Tuesday, Johnson used that as his out pitch. Owens reported that he did not observe Cobb pushing or shoving Ormsby and did not know what had occurred until after the game. He made no mention of a "murderous" hail of pop bottles or hordes of rioters storming the field.

Johnson announced, "I do not see how I can keep Cobb out of the game any longer after considering Owens's report." Simmons was also reinstated. At the same time Johnson imposed fines of $200 on the players, payable by personal checks within forty-eight hours or there would be "further suspensions."

Connie Mack received the telegram of Johnson's decisions as he left the Hotel Tuller to attend the luncheon. On the way he stopped in a telegraph office and wrote out a long protest of the fines. A trivial incident had been blown up and no such fines were appropriate. When reporters asked for comments, he had plenty to say: "The suspension was unnecessary and should never have been made." He said the umpires had too much power. "Nine times out of ten that players are suspended, it is due to an umpire's bad decision. Very seldom a first-class umpire puts a man out. Before any player is suspended he should have a hearing before the president of the league and the umpire making the complaint. It is all right to put a player out of a game for one day, but not for several days."

There were those who considered Ban Johnson's actions the spitefulness of a man still reeling from the humiliation of the ascendancy of his bitterest enemy, the commissioner, and his own declining influence. Never a temperate man, he had apparently lost some balance of mind and step since Ty Cobb and Tris Speaker had been readmitted to *his* league over *his* ultimatum that they would never appear there again. And to see Connie Mack, his most loyal comrade in arms from the beginning, with whom he had gone to war against the National Commission and all of baseball in the Scott Perry affair, lead the rush to sign the disgraced Cobb and seek out Speaker as well? That put Mr. Mack up there with Judas and Brutus in the traitors' league.

All that bile went into a letter Ban Johnson wrote to Connie Mack blaming *him* for the May 5 disturbance. The letter went on at length, excoriating Cobb and Simmons for their "reprehensible" conduct inciting the spectators to wrath against the umpire, which "stamps the offender as entirely devoid of the highest principles of manhood." He cited "the throwing of great numbers of murderous pop bottles . . . the swarming of angry spectators on the field." Cobb was fined for his "lack of intelligence in 'bumping' the umpire at that crucial moment. . . . Much of this, unfortunately, must be attributed to the lack of fairness, intelligence, and true sportsmanship on the part of the Philadelphia management."

The letter then went into much irrelevant detail about Ormsby's wartime service in France as evidence of his integrity.

Since the letter went to Shibe Park while the A's were on the road, Mack didn't see it before it was printed in the papers. Asked to comment, he was probably seething when he said, "The letter as printed requires no answer from me. I am not going to launch any long-range rebuttal in the newspapers. We'll say that the incident is closed."

Connie Mack was fed up with Ban Johnson. As far as he was concerned, his old friend was no longer physically or mentally fit to conduct the business of the league.

On May 10 Connie Mack and Ty Cobb rode together in the parade to Navin Field, where the overflow crowd, a weekday Navin Field record 27,410, greeted Cobb as Charles Lindbergh would be welcomed in Paris eleven days later. The president of General Motors, of which Cobb was an original stockholder, presented him the keys to a new LaSalle. During the 4-game series Cobb rekindled some memories for Detroit fans. He beat out a bunt, worried a pitcher into a balk, doubled and stole third, and scored when the catcher's throw was wild. Twice he tripled but pulled limping into second base. Relieved of the burdens of managing, he visited with fans in the outfield and enjoyed beating the Tigers in 3 of the 4 games.

By May 28, although still only 4 games back of the Yankees, the pundits who had made them the preseason favorites were asking what was wrong with the A's. In St. Louis that day Sid C. Keener put that question to Mack and received a quick reply: "Weak pitching by a good staff and you have it all. It is the biggest mystery I have handled in my entire managerial career. . . . I thought I had a pitching staff that would be strong enough to get us off to a nice start. And I haven't changed my opinion either. But there's something wrong someplace."

Mack had left Florida convinced his pitching staff was the best conditioned he'd ever had. But cold weather gave Ehmke and Rommel aching arms. Of their first 15 starts, only 5 were complete. Mack used 32 pitchers in the other 10. Even the veteran Jack Quinn was having control problems. Kid Gleason put all the pitchers on batting practice duty. "Warming up in the bullpen doesn't help a pitcher's control," he said. "It only loosens up their arms. What they need is a plate and a batter to throw at and I think pitching BP every day they will get control. Anyhow, we're going to give it a whirl."

Mack was so desperate he even reached back eight years and persuaded thirty-two-year-old Jing Johnson to rejoin them. Johnson had been one of Mack's young prospects who went off to war in 1918 and returned to win 9 games in 1919, his last in the majors. Now he was coaching at Lehigh University.

Connie Mack still kept an eye out for youngsters. A young pitcher named Ike Powers had had a brief trial with Martinsburg in the Class D Blue Ridge League with no success in 1925. The club owner, one of Connie Mack's many friends in the minor leagues, persuaded Mack to take him on as a batting practice pitcher for $350 a month. Powers appeared in 11 games, started and lost the last game of the season, and ended up with a full share—$1,178.32—of the second-place World Series money and a $2,500 contract for 1928.

The Yankees came to Shibe Park for a 5-game series on May 30. In a holiday split doubleheader that drew more than forty thousand to each game, Grove gave up 15 hits in the morning game but hung on to win, 9–8. Babe Ruth won the afternoon game with an eleventh-inning home run off Walberg. The next day the new Murderers' Row mowed down the A's, 10–3 and 18–5. On June 1 Joe Dugan, taunted by fans with long memories and leather lungs chanting, "I want to go home," drove in the winning run in the ninth, leaving the Athletics in the dust, 7 games back.

In the fourth inning of the May 30 afternoon game there arose another incident that had Connie Mack sputtering at Ban Johnson. With Collins on second and Cobb on first and one out, Simmons hit a pop foul close to the A's dugout. Catcher Johnny Grabowski dashed over, made a brilliant catch, then dived head first over an iron railing onto the dugout floor. Collins and Cobb, with Grabowski out of sight, alertly tagged up. Collins scored and Cobb was about ten feet from home plate when Grabowski emerged from the dugout. But none of the Yankees was covering home and Cobb scored. The umpires ruled that both runs counted. Then Miller Huggins persuaded them that under Rule 72, the runners were entitled to only two bases. Collins's run counted. Cobb had to go back to third.

The fans were in an uproar, and so was Connie Mack. He sent Collins out to announce that he was playing the game under protest. Umpire Clarence Rowland came over to the A's dugout to discuss the decision with Mack, who argued that Rule 72 dealt solely with an overthrow into the dugout or the seats. "A caught foul ball is not the same as a wild throw," he told Rowland.

It took almost two weeks for Ban Johnson to deny Mack's protest. "The interpretation of the play is simple," his decision read. "The player by accident fell into the pit, gripping the ball as he fell. The ball was then temporarily out of play. [He didn't say the ball was dead, just *temporarily* out of play.] It must of necessity be placed in the same classification as a ball thrown in the players' dugout."

Fuming, Mack said he would abide by the decision. He had no choice. (Realizing the rule was vague, that winter the umpires decided to allow base runners to advance only one base if the catcher fell into a dugout after making a catch.)

It didn't take Connie Mack long to realize that Dud Branom, like Lefty Russell and Paul Strand and so many others, was just another high-priced quintessential minor league star who flopped in the big leagues. He was smart and alert. But he couldn't hit big league pitching for sour apples and had zero power. By June 1 Mack had sold Branom to Portland, where he regained the batting eye that would bring him a .315 lifetime average over fifteen seasons in the minors. Back on first went Jim Poole, who was even worse and was soon gone too.

An unhappy Jimmie Dykes had been riding the bench most of the time until Sammy Hale was injured on May 29 and Dykes took over at third base. On June 16 Hale was ready to return to action. It didn't matter that Dykes had hit .411 during those few weeks. Hale was a key man that Connie Mack intended to build his new champions around.

Stan Baumgartner reported what happened as Dykes told it to him.

That morning Mack saw Dykes come through the press gate and beckoned to him. "Jim," he said, "Hale is in pretty good shape now."

"I guess that means I take a rest on the bench," said Dykes.

"Well, I would like to have him in there," Mack said.

"All right, go ahead. Take me out," said Dykes. "I don't give a continental. I am only the dishrag around here."

"Calm yourself, Jim. I know you often get angry at me, but there is one good thing about you. You get mad as hell and then forget it. Some of the others sulk for weeks. Did you ever play first base?"

"Never saw a first baseman's glove in my life. What's the matter? Have Branom and Poole developed fallen arches?"

"You practice around the bag this morning," said Mack.

Dykes told Baumgartner, "I figured that Connie was just trying to make me feel good, so when the time came for infield practice, I was sore as the devil. The first ball Kid Gleason hit at me I stopped with my foot and flipped to second with my thumb.

"'Get serious, Dykes,' roared Gleason, as he hit another down the line. I didn't even bend over for it and the ball bounced between my legs.'"

Gleason disappeared for a few minutes and returned with a paddle and chased Dykes into right field, where he caught him and walloped him until Dykes promised to take the drill seriously. But when it was over, Dykes left the park determined to take the day off: "It was quarter of three before I returned to the park. The daily skull practice was in full swing when I reached the dressing room. Not a soul paid the slightest attention to me, even to say hello. When the session finally broke up and all the players had left the room Connie came over, tapped me on the shoulder and said, 'Jim, you are the first sacker today.' He kept right on walking and was out of the clubhouse before I could recover my bearings."

On the first play of the game, Dykes made a backhand stop of a grounder and tossed to Ehmke covering first for the putout. When he came back to the bench, he smiled at Mack and said, "That first base job is a cinch. You ought to make a first sacker pay to get in the park."

Dykes wound up playing eighty-two games at first that year. The most versatile player in the game, he would also play third, second, short, and the outfield—and take two turns on the mound—and still hit .324. Bill Dooly called him the league's MVP.

Connie Mack had to find a way to have both Cochrane and Foxx in the lineup. Foxx was a catcher first and a good one, then a third baseman. Sammy Hale and Dykes were ahead of him there. Why not see how the kid from Sudlersville handled himself at first base? In early June he occasionally played Foxx at first against left-hand pitching. The youngster was no natural first baseman, but he was a big league hitter. He hit his first home run on May 31 off Urban Shocker after replacing Cochrane behind the bat in an 18–5 rout by the Yankees. He hit his second eight days later. He demonstrated the confidence at bat that a successful pinch hitter needs, batting .350 in that role. When Dykes pulled a muscle during a game on September 10, Foxx replaced him and played first the rest of the year.

The pitching woes continued. By early July Eddie Rommel had won only twice. After getting nobody out in a July 4 start in Boston, Howard Ehmke was sent home "in no condition to pitch." The rest, including last year's invincible Joe Pate, were in and out like an inept burglar who keeps getting caught. In a June 25 doubleheader Pate curved over a third strike on Lou

Gehrig with the tying run on third to end the first game and pitched 2 hitless innings to close the second. Three weeks later, on July 12, he blew a lead relieving Rommel in the fifth in Chicago and was pulled after he inexplicably leaped in the air and deflected a throw from Cochrane trying to nip a steal of second. A week later he came in in the ninth at Detroit to try to stop a Tiger rally, walked 2, and gave up the hit that drove in the winning runs. With a 5.20 ERA, he was sent back to Fort Worth to live happily ever after.

Connie Mack may have known as much about baseball as anybody ever would. He certainly knew that pitchers were a breed apart. When William Brandt asked him how he explained all his pitchers getting cold at the same time, Mack said, "I can't explain it. How can anybody explain it? Quinn hurt his hand shagging flies in Cleveland. It threw him out of turn. He wanted to work in Chicago and not St. Louis. St. Louis is about the easiest place in the west for a pitcher to win. Jack didn't mind Detroit, but he shied away from St. Louis. Just one of those personal peculiarities, like Grove not liking to work in Washington." (Grove had started twice in three years in Washington, with a 1-1 record.)

From July 4 on, the pitching finally appeared to straighten out. Joe Boley, who had not been the shortstop Mack thought he had bought, woke up and began to fulfill Mack's expectations.

Despite the loss of Al Simmons, who missed six weeks with a groin injury, the Athletics almost kept pace with the Yankee juggernaut, going 53-28 in the second half. During that stretch, Rommel was 9-1. Walberg, considered by some hitters as fast as Grove with a better change-up, was 9-5. Grove won 6 of his last 7 decisions. Quinn was 9-4.

But it was too late.

Eddie Collins demonstrated the old adage that the legs go first, the batting eye last. He could give Max Bishop a rest now and then, but he was unable to cover the ground beyond his shadow. He was on base almost 150 times and stole only 6 bases. But at forty he could still hit .338, above his career average.

Connie Mack realized that Eddie didn't have it in the field anymore. Collins realized it too. So he wasn't surprised when Mack asked him to stop in the office one morning in July. Several years later Collins recalled the hesitant, faltering conversation that ensued.

"Er, I've been thinking," Mack began, then stopped, then started again. "You know that coach we have at third base?"

Collins nodded.

"I'm not satisfied with him. I need a very competent man there. I feel that you. . . ." He paused again.

Suddenly it dawned on Collins where Mr. Mack was going.

"Listen," he said, "this isn't going to hurt me. I mean it. Look, I'm so happy just being back here with you again, anywhere you want to put me is all right with me. If it's your judgment I can serve you better by coaching than playing, just say the word."

A relieved Mack could only nod vigorously.

Collins remained on the active roster, pinch-hitting and filling in for Bishop occasionally. Gradually he began to take on more responsibilities and became Mack's adjutant in the clubhouse. If a player had something on his mind, he would take it to Collins, knowing it would get to Mack's attention. Not a bench coach—neither he nor Gleason considered themselves as assistants to "the boss"—Collins was the third base coach, and in the dugout sat at the far right while Mack sat in the middle. It was the same role that Chief Bender had filled for Collins in Chicago. But it went further. Each morning Collins would meet with Mack in the office or his hotel room, discuss the previous game, and draw up the lineup for that afternoon, which Collins would post in the clubhouse and dugout. Their conversations covered every aspect of running a ball club on and off the field.

One of the topics that came up often was Mack's frustration with Lefty Grove.

Collins was experiencing Grove as a teammate for the first time. He didn't like what he saw. To him Grove was undisciplined, "a rude-tongued young man," a self-centered clubhouse disrupter who got on anybody he might blame for a loss while tossing chairs and knocking over furniture. It didn't enhance his opinion of the pitcher when Grove would playfully pick him up and lock him in a locker.

Connie Mack saw all that too and dealt with it in his own way. There are several variations on the stories of a disgruntled Lefty Grove being taken out of a game and saying either "Nuts to this ball club" or "To hell with you, Mr. Mack" and Mack getting up, walking over to him, looking him in the eye, and replying in the same manner to Grove, causing everybody, including Lefty, to burst out laughing.

Outfielder Roger Cramer once said, "The only time I saw Connie Mack upset was when Grove threw his jacket in Mack's lap. Mr. Mack just kicked it out of the way."

(Asked about ever seeing Connie Mack angry or upset, players invariably began their answers with "The only time. . . .")

Mack saw Lefty's explosive potential greatness as well as his temper. Grove could be literally unhittable. But Connie Mack knew there had to be some thinking on the mound for a pitcher to be great, and so far there had been none.

Having seen Firpo Marberry help the Senators win two pennants pitching primarily as what was then called a finisher and watching Wilcy Moore, with perfect control and no nerves, now succeeding in the same role with the Yankees, Mack envisioned Grove, with his overpowering speed and trouble-free arm, going in for two or three innings to protect a lead—in addition, of course, to taking his regular turn starting.

More than once, Mack said to Collins, "If I can only get Grove to finish games for us the way he starts them."

The idea turned ugly in a hurry.

On May 7, two days after taking a 3–2 complete game loss, Grove pitched the last 4⅔ innings of an 11-inning 11–10 loss and went on a rampage in the clubhouse.

It wasn't that Lefty minded the workload. From May 26 through May 30 he would start twice and relieve twice, but the A's won them all. He just didn't like the idea of trying to finish somebody else's assignment—"taking up somebody else's ball game" is the way relievers put it—and making one mistake at the wrong time and being stuck with a loss. He was mad at himself and the rest of the world after any loss, but these "finisher" losses really sent him into a rage. He wasn't alone; Bill Dooly claimed that this attitude was shared by most pitchers, even Firpo Marberry.

On June 15 Grove relieved Jack Quinn in the fifth inning of a 4–4 tie with the White Sox and struck out 5 of the first 9 he faced. But in the eighth inning his own error led to the tie-breaking run when Ted Lyons followed with a single that got by Ty Cobb for a triple. At the end of the inning Grove stormed into the dugout, flung his glove against the back wall, and snarled, "Never gonna finish another game." He got into his Pierce Arrow and disappeared for a few days, came back desteamed and beat the White Sox, 6–2.

One day, so the story goes, Mack asked Grove to warm up and go in in relief. Lefty refused. "I won't go in," he said. "Nuts to him. Let him save his own game."

"For shame," said Mack. "They relieve you often enough. Go in and relieve right now."

After that, whenever Mack asked him to warm up in the late innings, Grove didn't try to hide his reluctance, slouching out with what Collins called "a surly expression."

In the evenings on the road Mack would talk quietly with Mose, explaining how much it meant to the team if they knew they could count on him to go in and hold a lead late in a game. The welfare of the team was more important than any man's record. Some of the players were beginning to think he was putting his own numbers first.

Mack kept sending him out there—23 times along with 28 starts—and while Grove picked up 3 wins that way, he was charged with 5 of his 13 losses in relief.

Grove reached 20 wins for the first time. He reached his peak on September 3, handing the Yankees their only shutout of the year, a 1–0 4-hitter in which he walked only 1 and struck out 9. In the second and third innings he threw 19 pitches before a ball was called, striking out the side on 10 pitches in the second. But he was still a work in progress.

"What a wonderful pitcher Grove would be if his disposition were different," Mack told Gordon Mackay. "Grove has his days. Whenever you see him come out laughing, joshing, cutting up, that's the day to use him. He is a great pitcher then. When he is in one of his bad days, that's when things happen. He doesn't pitch the way he should. He'll get over that. He gets upset too easily now. He isn't able to stand an error or two. If an umpire misses a few on him, then he takes it too seriously. It is something experience will smooth over. Then he should be one whale of a pitcher, the best left-hander since Waddell."

On July 23 *Collyer's Eye* claimed that Ty Cobb was the cause of dissension wrecking the Athletics, the players had appealed to Mack to get rid of him, Mack had admitted he was causing trouble, and the veterans were just going through the motions. It concluded, "So don't be surprised if the A's hit the skids."

The team was 48-41 at the time. It was 43-22 the rest of the way. Some skids.

It was all nonsense, wrote Bill Dooly. "Anyone who is even remotely familiar with the club knows that these deductions have no basis in fact, that they are fabricated out of whole cloth. Cobb has been particularly careful about offering his advice this season for the sole reason that he knows the reputation that has been fastened upon him. It is the truth that Ty has never offered a word of criticism or expressed an opinion without being invited."

Other writers agreed. Ed Pollock said that Cobb had fulfilled everything he promised. Bill Brandt called him a sparkplug and an inspiration to the young players.

Stoney McLinn wrote in *Baseball Magazine* that the pitchers not performing up to expectations, and not the bunk about morale-scrambling cliques or Connie Mack's age, was the sole reason the A's were not winning.

Asked by Gordon Mackay if there was any jealousy of Cobb, Mack said, "Bosh. Ty has been one of our biggest helps. He has done wonders."

Cobb's presence inspired them to bring back the double squeeze for the first time since the glory days of 1914. On August 3, with Perkins and Dykes running from third and second, French bunted a two-strike pitch down the third base line and beat it out for a hit as both runners scored. Thirteen days later they did it again.

Cobb never slackened his pace, never let up. On July 18 in Detroit he got credit for a double when Heilmann failed to come up with a shoestring catch. It was Cobb's 4,000th hit, but it didn't get much notice. Three days later in Cleveland he took off on a delayed steal of second. Nobody covered the base and the throw went into center field. Cobb kept on going and scored ahead of the center fielder's throw to the plate. On August 10 he showed a glimpse of his old derring-do, but his old legs failed him. He hit a triple and was thrown out trying to turn it into a home run. Two days later he gave twelve thousand Boys Club members (admitted free) a look at the Cobb of old in a 7–1 win over Boston. He turned a deflected infield grounder into a double, stole second and went to third on a bad throw, and faked a steal of home that caused the pitcher to throw wild and allowed 2 runs to score. He and Wheat had 4 hits each. They went west and he batted over .500 in a 12-game streak. He played in exhibition games in Allentown and Pottsville, pitching the last 3 innings on September 7 in Allentown to raise money for the police pension fund. The only hit he gave up was a home run by an eighteen-year-old named William Klucharich, probably the biggest thrill of the youngster's life.

In a 5-game stretch in September Cobb was 17 for 25. He worked a double steal with Walter French and was on third with one out when Foxx hit a shot to third baseman Willie Kamm. As soon as Kamm threw to first, Cobb dashed for home, like the Tyrus of twenty years ago, and beat the throw.

But Cobb was tired. Once the A's clinched second place, he left the lineup in the fifth inning on September 21 at Shibe Park. He changed into street clothes, came back to shake hands with several players, waved to the fans behind the dugout, and left for a hunting trip in Wyoming after a stop in Chicago to see the Dempsey-Tunney rematch. Asked about playing another year, he said, "Well, I'm no young fellow anymore. I really don't know. The association with Mr. Mack this year has been the finest thing that ever happened to me in my baseball career. I never played under a man who treated me with as much kindness and consideration. I wouldn't like to say anything one way or the other and I guess this is hardly the time for me to be talking about next year, anyhow."

One example of the kindness referred to by Cobb occurred during the season when Cobb's son Herschel and his son's friend Jimmy Lanier, who had been Cobb's personal batboy in Detroit, came to Philadelphia for a visit. Cobb asked Herschel to take Jimmy up to the tower office to meet Connie Mack. Years later Lanier told his friend Millard Fisher, "We found Mr. Mack having a sandwich and glass of milk for lunch. He welcomed us, ordered sandwiches for us, and talked baseball with us until it was time for him to go down to the dugout just before the game."

Mack made it clear he wanted Ty back next year, "even if he just sits on the bench." So much for that team-wrecking troublemaker blarney.

Like Cobb, Zach Wheat later said he wished he had played for Connie Mack years earlier. Wheat batted .324, sharing left-field duty with Bill Lamar and pinch-hitting. (Imagine having a bench with Zach Wheat, Eddie Collins, and Jimmy Foxx to call on as pinch hitters. They batted .321 collectively in that role.)

Bill Lamar was unhappy, and it had nothing to do with Ty Cobb or money. He was only thirty, but four years in Philadelphia had aged him. A capable outfielder who consistently hit .300, he had joined Sammy Hale, Al Simmons, and Jimmie Dykes as prime targets of the raucous razzberry artists of Shibe Park. When Zach Wheat replaced Lamar in left field, the riders got on him just as much. Wheat was unaccustomed to it. Dykes shook it off; Hale and Lamar let it get to them. Writers cited errors made by several players that coincided with vocal projectiles fired from the stands. Despite his rabbit ears, Mack considered Hale the best third baseman in the league.

Bill Lamar went to Connie Mack in July and asked to be traded. Mack asked waivers on him. Washington claimed him, but Lamar chose to retire instead of reporting. Maybe the prospect of playing even eleven games a year in Shibe Park was too much for him.

Some of the human megaphones worked alone, some in tandems, shouting across the field from opposite sides of the infield. They were usually produce vendors (called A-rabs in Baltimore) who sold their wares from wagons in residential areas in the mornings, leaving them free to go to the games in the afternoon. They developed powerful lungs by announcing their presence as they walked the streets. Most of their taunts were intended to get under a player's skin with what passed for bleacher wit, giving other fans a laugh. The Kessler brothers, Bill and Eddie, known as Bull and Dutch, worked together, one on each side of the infield. Their voices boomed without shouting, enough to be heard a block away.

They rode the Philadelphia natives like Dykes the hardest.

"Who is this bum coming up?" one would yell.

"Pop-up Dykes," boomed the reply.

When Simmons was at the plate: "Who is this bum?"

"Simmons, the bucketfooted honkie."

One day Simmons came in from left field drenched in root beer, orangeade, crackerjack, and popcorn. "The youth of America—phooey," he said to Dykes.

Stan Baumgartner wrote, "Connie Mack never bent his ear till he was positive the fans had the player down; I've seen him keep Dykes in a game when I thought the stands would fall down from the boos they gave out. Mack even went so far as to put police in the stands to pick up fans who were particularly abusive in a profane way."

Philadelphia's reputation for having "the most snaggle-toothed wolves of any city," as Hugh Brown of the *Bulletin* quoted one locally produced player, continues to this day.

Harry Donnelly, who worked alone out of the left-field stands, was a different case. He used language that offended rather than amused. In 1926 umpire George Hildebrand had once ordered him escorted out of Shibe Park.

On August 10 Brick Owens, working behind the plate, had had enough of Donnelly's bellowing. In the seventh inning Owens stopped the game, walked out to the left-field pavilion, and ordered the police to put him out of the park. Afterward Owens said the language was so objectionable that he had to take action. "The American League has always striven to make baseball a game clean of rowdyism and one that ladies might attend without fear of hearing or seeing anything objectionable . . . and when a fan goes beyond the pale of common decency and shouts remarks that reek with filth and vileness, then it is time to interfere. Baseball can be enjoyed without that sort of rooting and it can get along without the type of man whose mouthings are full of oaths and indecencies. I'll have them run out of the park as fast as I can spot them."

On September 15 Connie Mack had the police evict Donnelly during a game against the White Sox. After the game, Mack went to the Twenty-Second Street station house and swore out a warrant against Donnelly for disturbing the peace. "This man's rooting has damaged the morale of my team," Mack told the magistrate. "He has been razzing us all year with a voice that carries like a three-mile loudspeaker. Because of him I have had to dispose of Bill Lamar, a competent outfielder. He has assailed other players until they are of little use to the club at home. Sammy Hale, for instance, is a nervous wreck. I want Donnelly under a bond that will restrain him from any more of this abuse."

At a hearing the next day Donnelly pleaded innocence of any "downstairs motive. I'm a regular rooter for the Athletics and I've only been doing this so the team will win. Many times the players have given me baseballs."

To which Mack snapped, "They gave you baseballs in hopes you would keep your mouth shut."

The twenty-eight-year-old Irishman's photo made the front page of the *Record*, along with his plea for free speech. He said he never rode the players and never used profanity; besides, they were a bunch of temperamental crybabies who couldn't put up with a little panning, which, by the way, he didn't do anyhow.

He was ordered to post a $500 bond to stifle himself at the ballpark.

Looking back over the season, Connie Mack called it disappointing. Not because the A's didn't win. The hitting had come through, but the pitching wasn't up to last year's. Still, he conceded, even if the pitching had been top-notch all year, they would have finished second, just not by 19 games. When you win 12 of 14 on a western trip in August and can knock only 2 games off an 18-game lead, what more can you do? With it all, they finished with a 91-63 record, matching the Yankees' pennant-winning total of last year.

In late June some American League club owners had requested a league meeting ostensibly to amend the constitution. But the buzz—accurate for a change—was that any such amending would deal only with finding a way to remove Ban Johnson from office without breaking his contract, which ran through 1935. Johnson called the meeting for July 8 at the Hotel Belmont in New York. On the train from Chicago he said he had no intention of resigning. Anything more that he had to say would be said at the meeting.

Johnson didn't attend the meeting, remaining in his seventh-floor room a few doors away from the meeting room. Nor did Connie Mack, who was in

St. Louis with the team. Tom Shibe represented the Athletics. All afternoon a committee led by Ruppert shuttled between the meeting and Johnson's room, trying to find a formula agreeable to everybody that would remove Johnson from office and resolve the league's contractual obligation to him. Worn down, Ban Johnson signed a note of resignation effective November 1 "or earlier should I so decide" and refused any further compensation.

Johnson had been sick for the last six years, had lost a lot of weight and some bravado, but not his pride. And proud he should have been of his accomplishments. But he could not separate his person from his creation. He had stayed at least two years too long. Had he resigned after completing twenty-five years, he would have gone amid a chorus of "Hail and farewells." Now he went quietly, unheralded in his exit. He considered that he had been betrayed by ingrates, but he had betrayed himself with his increasingly erratic, antagonistic behavior.

Johnson held his last league board meeting at his office in room 1510 of the Fisher Building in Chicago on October 17 to turn over all his papers and records. He had less than four years to live.

In 1928 Marietta College asked the American League for $50,000 for the building fund of the Ban Johnson Memorial Gym. The league turned the college down.

There is no record that Ban Johnson and Connie Mack ever met again. Johnson died on March 28, 1931, the same day his successor, Ernest S. Barnard, also died.

Late in the season, everywhere the Athletics went the writers renewed the speculation about Connie Mack's retiring. The presence of Eddie Collins, a logical successor, fertilized the guesswork. Mack no longer let it bother him. He measured age by a man's spirit, not the calendar, and his spirit was as youthful as ever. He told Bill Dooly:

They wrote, "Poor old Connie Mack. He's getting too old. Why, he'll be sixty-five next December."

There was a time when twaddle like that would have made me angry. No more. This thing of writing daily baseball comment is hard, and I know the boys have to call on their imagination a lot to keep the fans supplied with something to talk about. They have a tough job and I realize it. But, as to the truth of their stories, why, they're all bosh.

Why should I step down? What reason is there for me to quit? My advice is just as good now as it was twenty years ago, maybe better. Perhaps I've learned a little more about baseball than I knew then.

If the team loses games or goes on a bad streak I seem to get the blame. But I can't hit for the boys or run or field for them. I get players that I think can do those things for me. If they fall down going for a grounder or trip going around the bases, I can't go out and pick them up. And if they fall down in all ways it isn't my fault. It means I have to go out and get somebody else to do the job I thought they could do.

But the idea that I am getting too old to manage anymore is absurd and ridiculous. Why I know loads of businessmen in their seventies who are handling their affairs with just as great wisdom and sagacity as they showed when they were years younger. Many of them in fact are doing a lot better.

As for people who are calling me through now, they are probably the sort of folks who enjoy the rattle of their tongues.

On Mack's sixty-fifth birthday in December the usually terse, acerbic John Shibe confirmed Mack's self-assessment. He told Bill Brandt:

It seems to me that the older Connie gets, the better he looks. I was looking at him along the table at a dinner the other night, in his dinner coat, there with these other men, all leaders in their professions, prominent citizens, you know, and I said to myself that the word to describe Connie is "distinguished."

A lot of the men there I did not know, and I thought to myself if I did not know Connie I would have taken him for a judge or a distinguished lawyer or surgeon. I guess I had often thought about it, but it took that dinner and the viewpoint it gave me to put it into words.

Additions to a man's age mean different things to different men, but to Connie Mack you can put me on record as saying that every year makes him look better, younger and more keenly alive. It's a great thing to see, I can tell you.

A close four-way race, won by Pittsburgh, boosted NL attendance to over 5 million for the first time. The Cubs, in the race until mid-September, became the first NL team to draw a million at home. The lack of a race sliced the AL gate by three hundred thousand. Despite the presence of Cobb, the early evaporation of the Athletics' pennant hopes cut their attendance by over one hundred thousand. The second straight decline in receipts coincided with a payroll that topped $279,000—about matching the Yankees' as the highest in the league, despite a home attendance barely half that of New York. Still, Connie Mack had another $73,000 profit to spend.

The Yankees couldn't be that good two years in a row. He was still determined to pass them, whatever the cost.

23 | THE GOOD FIGHT

On February 1, 1928, the Washington Senators released Tris Speaker. Clark Griffith had gone high for him in an effort to regain the Senators' winning form of 1925. There were stories of resentment among some of the players over the wide gap between Speaker's $30,000 salary and theirs. But they may have been as exaggerated as the tales of dissension among the A's over Cobb.

Connie Mack had released one of his ancients, Zach Wheat, but he was still interested in Speaker. Four days after Griffith released Speaker, Mack interrupted his golfing vacation in Mount Plymouth, Florida, to telephone Speaker, who accepted a $15,000 offer to play for the Athletics.

Writers filled their wintertime column-inch quotas with speculation that Connie Mack had been seized by senility. In their opinion he clearly didn't know what he was doing. Dissension among the lesser-paid players was sure to erupt over the signing of Speaker, although it was generally conceded that the same prediction in the case of Cobb a year ago hadn't panned out. This was different. The temperamental Al Simmons would be sore over making way for Speaker in center field, and when he was sore, he would jake. Besides, the A's hadn't won in '27 with Cobb and Wheat. What made Mack think he could win in '28 with a year-older Speaker?

Like Cobb, the forty-year-old Speaker had slowed. In his prime nobody had gotten a quicker jump on a fly ball or played a ground ball better. He still had a good arm, could still tell at the crack of the bat where a ball would land. He just couldn't get to it as quickly. No outfielder played hitters better, except Connie Mack, who wouldn't hesitate to stand on the top step of the dugout waving his veteran newcomer over a few steps.

Passing up the player draft, Mack shelled out $16,000 ($6,000 of it the cancellation of a debt) on scout Mike Drennan's recommendation for twenty-three-year-old outfielder George "Mule" Haas, who had led Atlanta with a .323 batting average. In addition to Haas's on-field abilities, he also brought a loud, vibrant voice to the squad of bench jockeys Mack was assembling.

Like a glutton trying to make up for childhood starvation, Connie Mack was haunted by his years in the wilderness with skimpy reserves. He was loading up with reinforcements, stocking a deep bench against the inevitable sprains and bruises and charley horses and weary old legs that came with a six-month season. He sent Chick Galloway and $30,000 to Milwaukee for powerless spray-hitting left-handed pitcher-outfielder Ossie Orwoll, twenty-seven. Orwoll, known as the blonde ghost in his native northwest, had a 17-6 record and .370 batting average to recommend him. But behind that lofty average was a rap that he couldn't hit southpaws and had been used only against right-handers. From Waterbury came a young shortstop, Joe Hassler.

AP sports editor Alan J. Gould estimated that the Athletics' and Yankees' payrolls, which had been above $250,000 each in 1927, would approach a combined $600,000, an amount probably exceeding the total of the other six American League clubs. Having swept the Pirates in the World Series, the Yankees' stars were in for hefty raises (Lou Gehrig went from $8,000 to $25,000) that would push their total closer to $300,000 than Philadelphia's $255,000 payroll. (The A's were more generous than the Yankees in other money matters. They set no limits on what players spent in hotel dining rooms on the road. According to Yankee pitching ace Waite Hoyt, the Yankees had no limits until one day when two rookies shared a fifteen dollar breakfast at the Brunswick Hotel in Boston. After that the traveling secretary doled out four dollars meal money every morning on the road.)

Connie Mack had reluctantly parted with Bing Miller in 1926 as part of the three-way deal that brought him Howard Ehmke. When the Browns were willing to take the disappointing Sammy Gray in exchange for Miller, Mack leaped at the chance. He predicted that Gray would have one big year for the Browns, then go downhill as he had done with the A's. (Gray was 20-12 in 1928, then was 48-70 the next five years.)

Even if Ty Cobb decided to play another year, Mack knew that neither he nor Speaker would be a full-time outfielder. Now he had French, Miller, and Haas behind them.

When Connie Mack sent Lefty Grove a contract for $8,000 and Grove asked for $12,000, Mack decided to entice Grove into accepting the finisher's role in addition to starting by offering him a $6,000 deal loaded with incentives for wins and relief appearances. Not interested, said Lefty. He signed for

$9,000 and a $1,000 signing bonus. (Grove would relieve only eight times, without a loss. It was this, not Grove's superlative starting pitching, that was behind Mack's later reported comment that "we could have won [in 1928] but we couldn't count on Lefty.")

Mack decided to forgo the fireball for a butterfly. Eddie Rommel was thirty-one, not old for a pitcher, especially a knuckleball tosser. But a sore arm had limited his work to under 150 innings, barely half his totals of four or five years ago. Considering his diminished production, Mack asked him to take a pay cut, from $10,000 to $6,000, with the same incentives he had offered Grove: if he won 12 games, he'd get $500 for each additional game he started and won, and $200 additional for each game he finished that resulted in a win for the team. Rommel wasn't happy about it, but he did it, and earned an additional $2,000.

Mack also brought back Joe Bush, released by the Giants after stints with six teams since he had left the Athletics after the 1917 season. Bush signed a similar contract to Rommel's but won only 2 games and collected no bonus.

Connie Mack kept after Ty Cobb to play again in 1928. Cobb kept saying no. Most experts speculated that Cobb, the first active millionaire player, had had enough of the grind of the long season. Mack's phone calls and letters persisted until Cobb agreed on March 1 to sign for $35,000.

In June Cobb would give Bill Duncan of the *Washington Post* some insight into how he had wrestled with the decision: "Every winter one voice says to me, 'You are a slave to your records. It is time for you to quit the game and stay home with your wife and family.' But another voice says, 'Keep going, Ty. You hit .357 last year. You're still a good ballplayer. Once you quit you are through forever, and forever is a long, long time.'"

He described three reasons he had decided to "unretire" and return for the 1928 season: "The first is that I do love to play baseball. I love the game today just as much as I did before I entered the major leagues. Another reason is my strong sentimental attachment for a great manager and a great gentleman, Connie Mack. . . . I had intended to retire this year but when Mr. Mack told me he wanted me to help him in the 1928 pennant fight, that was all I needed to make me reverse my decision." Cobb's third reason for coming back was that he considered it injurious to stop a physical life suddenly for a stagnant one.

Ty Cobb's admiration for Connie Mack was genuine. Watching him managing men on a daily basis, Cobb recognized in Mack what he himself had lacked as a manager. Once Mack sent up a rookie to pinch-hit after the pitcher had walked a man to load the bases. The pinch hitter swung at the first pitch and grounded out to end the rally. When he came back to the dugout, Mack just shook his head and said quietly, "You should have taken a pitch." Ty Cobb would have flayed the kid in front of everybody.

During the 1928 season Grantland Rice asked Cobb what he thought of Mack as a man and manager. Cobb replied:

About the greatest I have ever known. He is smart and square. He understands baseball and men. He knows how to build up youngsters without breaking them. I'll give you an example. In a certain league game one of the younger players made a wild throw that cost the game. Connie asked him afterwards what his idea was. The youngster explained what he was trying to do. He showed at least that he was trying to think. Connie didn't interrupt, and after the player had finished, all he said was, "Well, it might have worked, but the best plays don't always go."

Look at the ballplayers he has built up from unknowns. He can suffer through a ball game and he can be as happy through a ball game as any man I ever saw, but he doesn't show it either way. The ballplayer who won't work his head off for Connie Mack isn't much good. And most of them do.

Cobb never liked spring training. He didn't think he needed it; his winter hunting trips kept him in good condition. At first he told Mack he would report March 8. Then he decided to stay home and work out with the Giants until the A's reached Augusta March 16. That was okay with Mack.

"Baseball is always an uncertain game," Mack told the AP on March 21. "One never can tell what may happen over the season. When you think you are right you are frequently wrong. I know I have a good ball club that will show our power. Last year we were slow in our start. This year I'm hopeful that we will get away much better. Our pitchers are in good shape now and will be better. Cobb was a great help to our ball club last season. He will be just as useful this year, and with Speaker in the outfield we will be very strong in that department. The return of Joe Hauser in fine condition has strengthened us."

After a big year in Kansas City, Unser Choe appeared fully recovered from his knee injury of 1925. He had hit .353 and led the team in doubles, triples, and home runs.

The A's had the top two strikeout kings of the league in Grove and Walberg, the best catcher and infield, and an all-star, albeit aged, outfield in Cobb, Speaker, and Simmons. There wasn't expected to be much playing time in the early going for Haas, Miller, and French. But Simmons showed up at Fort Myers crippled by rheumatism. He could hardly walk. Mack said it looked like he would be out until July and maybe all year. That gave Miller and Haas some unexpected playing time. (French was the most affected by the presence of Cobb and Speaker. Playing regularly, he had hit over .300 the past two years. This year he would pinch-hit more often than he wore a glove. "It was a very disappointing year for me," he wrote fifty years later. "Sitting on the bench just wasn't my cup of tea.")

Simmons made his first appearance as a pinch hitter on May 22 and tripled. He didn't start a game until May 28.

The infield of Hauser, Bishop, Boley, and Hale kept Jimmie Dykes doing a lot of sitting and fretting too.

Bishop changed his bat to a heavier Travis Jackson model and decided to go after fat pitches that he had previously let go by, hoping to draw a walk. As a result he would hit a career-high .316 and draw his fewest walks in eight years.

To change his luck, Mack removed the white elephant from the uniform shirts after thirteen years and replaced it with a large script "A."

All they needed was a good start for a change.

They didn't get it.

It looked like the same old story when the Yankees drove out Grove after three innings of the opener, winning 8–3, as they had done a year ago, before a freezing turnout of twenty-five thousand. Another thorn in Connie Mack's side was the pitcher who beat them—Herb Pennock, the boy he'd given up on a dozen years ago. The script looked familiar: the Athletics lost their first 4 games while the Yankees were winning 4.

And then, suddenly, they shed their annual spring slows, winning 13 of the next 14.

They went to New York for the Yankees' home opener in the expanded Yankee Stadium, where the three-tiered left-field stands now extended beyond the foul pole. The New York writers joked about Mack's veterans. During the lengthy pregame pennant-raising and handing out of the world championship diamond rings, wrote Pegler, "The A's grew older by the minute."

The fifty-five thousand New Yorkers on hand laughed when Speaker was unable to reach a fly ball that fell near him for a double, but they didn't laugh when Speaker drove in the visitors' first run, or when Ty Cobb led off the ninth with a triple over Combs's head and Speaker drove him in with the run that won it, 2–1, behind Grove's 5-hitter.

Joe Hauser began like the Unser Choe of 1924. He hit 2 home runs in the second game of the season, 2 more on April 24, and 5 in May. Mack confidently kept him in the cleanup spot in the lineup.

Speaker drove in at least one run in 14 straight games. Cobb was still hitting, giving it everything he had. He played four doubleheaders in late May, occasionally relieved by French in the late innings. But he had lost a few more steps. Singles that got by him for doubles last year were now good for three bases before he could catch up with them.

The Yankees came to Philadelphia for 6 games beginning with a doubleheader on Thursday, May 24. They led the A's by 3½ games. More than forty-two thousand fans stood, sat, hung from the rafters, or filled the aisles—while another fifteen thousand pushed against the closed gates. They got their money's worth; the home team almost pulled out the first game in the ninth, then won the second. But that would be the only home victory of the series. When the Yankees shelled Lefty Grove in the series finale, 11–4, and led by 8 games, Richards Vidmer of the *Times* declared the season virtually over: "There may never be another crucial series. Not in the American League. Not this year. After the Yankees finished with the faltering Philadelphians in this one, the antiquated Athletics are about willing to admit they belong in the second division, which includes seven teams in this circuit. If they're not, they ought to be."

Connie Mack and his men were not admitting anything. On June 1 they were a respectable 25-14, a .641 pace good enough to win most years. But the Yankees had a 7½ game lead. Their 34-8 record and .810 percentage were way ahead of their record-setting 1927 pace. A week later the gap was 10 games. "Only 103 more games until the World Series," chirped Vidmer.

Connie Mack pressed on. He believed it when he said you never knew what might happen over a season. In late May the Baltimore Orioles, after their glory years of seven straight pennants, were in last place in the International League. When Jack Dunn said he was ready to sell his star pitcher, George Earnshaw, on June 1, Connie Mack was ready to buy.

Earnshaw was huge for the times: 6-foot-4, 220 pounds. They called him Moose. He had reported for spring training overweight and had not gotten into shape yet. In the last three years at Baltimore he had racked up a 68-

43 record. So far in 1928 he was 3-5 with a 6.15 ERA. That didn't discourage Mack. On a spring stop in Baltimore, he had seen Earnshaw set down the first ten of his A's in order, striking out the side in the third after Grove had done the same to the Orioles in the second. He had watched him at Baltimore and tagged him as a smart pitcher who could win in the big leagues.

Earnshaw cost $80,000, plus pitchers Jing Johnson outright and Bill Shores on option. It was a conditional sale: $30,000 was due on July 1. If Mack kept Earnshaw beyond that date, he owed another $25,000 a year later and again on July 1, 1930.

In February 1930 Ed Pollock was sitting with Connie Mack on the train from Philadelphia to Florida when Mack mentioned what he had paid for some players, something he had never talked about.

"When he did I almost fell off the chair of the Pullman luncheon table where we were sitting," Pollock wrote. "Mack invited me to lunch with him. We were passing through Baltimore. I remarked, 'This has always been a good baseball town, hasn't it, Mr. Mack?'

"'No, it never was,' he disagreed.

"'I thought Jack Dunn made a lot of money here, 'I said.

"'He did,' Mack exclaimed, 'but he made his money selling players to major league clubs. We gave him a lot—$100,600 for Grove, $80,000 for Earnshaw, $65,000 for Boley, and Bishop was a great bargain at $20,000.'

"Timidly I asked him if it would be all right to quote him on costs. 'I don't see why not,' he consented."

Six years earlier Mack had advised Earnshaw to stay in school and signed his Swarthmore teammate Curly Ogden instead. Now, the story went, when Earnshaw reported in Chicago, he said to Mack, "I've often wondered if you remembered that time I came to see you for a tryout?"

"I remember," said Mack, "but I've been trying to forget."

But a month after reporting, Earnshaw told Bill Dooly he had never thought of playing pro ball while he was in college and repeatedly turned down Jack Dunn's entreaties. George came from a wealthy family, related to the Clothiers of Strawbridge and Clothier's department store. After he graduated in 1924, he worked in Newark and pitched semipro ball. The following spring he told Dunn he'd sign for a big league salary—$900 a month—just to get rid of him. Dunn surprised him by agreeing to his terms.

After joining the Athletics, Earnshaw still was in no hurry to get into shape. He failed to last in his first five starts. Throughout June the Athletics spun their wheels. And they couldn't beat the Yankees to save their necks.

After New York drove Grove to cover on June 27, a dispirited Connie Mack complained about his pitchers. He believed he had the best pitching staff in the league—on paper. But on the field they still trailed New York by 11 games. He told Dooly:

It just seems that when Grove can't beat the Yankees, nobody can. It doesn't seem to do any good how I work them. I give them plenty of rest. I tell them what to do, but I can't do it for them. And that's what a lot of them seem to need, somebody else to pitch for them. I've done almost everything I can think of to get them straightened out.

I'd like to know how to get them working in some kind of rotation. Quinn has pitched well for us, but really needs five days of rest between games. Grove and Walberg can pitch every fourth day but are better with four days off. Ehmke—I'm lucky to get a game out of him once in seven days. The only thing left now for me is to try to get Earnshaw into shape.

The next day Walberg lasted 2 innings against the Yankees. Earnshaw pitched 7 innings, gave up 7 hits, walked 6 but struck out 10. Ford Frick reported that Mack mentioned his pitching quandary to Miller Huggins and said of Earnshaw, "I don't know whether he will do or not. You know I paid a lot of money for him and by sending him back now I could save a lot of that purchase price. I've a mind to do it."

Huggins said, "Connie, hold on to him. He may not show it now, but he's got a lot of stuff. Don't let him get away."

With Kid Gleason on his case, Earnshaw finally got into shape. On July 5 he shut out the Red Sox, 5–0.

The Athletics' pitching staff may have been the league's best; it was definitely the league's toughest for a catcher to handle.

Earnshaw was as mean on the mound as Grove and almost as fast. When either one showed signs of letting up a little and Cochrane walked out to the mound to inquire if they needed a little help, they would "get so sore at me, they'd try to knock me down with their fastballs."

They were wild, not in the sense of walking a lot of men—the A's issued the fewest free passes in the league. They had so much stuff on the ball, the breaks were sharp and wide. Curves might break four or five feet to either side of the plate or hit the dirt in front of the plate, the hardest pitch for any catcher to handle. Earnshaw could throw his curve with the same velocity as his fastball. He occasionally threw a one-fingertip knuckle-curve and a spitter he called his "August sweater-ball."

Wildness also meant not always putting the ball where Cochrane called for it.

"Walberg has a beautiful curve," Cochrane told F. C. Lane in the August *Baseball Magazine*. "But sometimes when he is putting a lot on it and is a little wild in the bargain, he'll give anxious moments. When I caught him recently in Washington, he made what I call about five wild pitches in that game. I managed to knock them all down, but it kept me hustling."

As for Eddie Rommel and his knuckler, "Sometimes it hit me in the chest, sometimes in the shins. It was impossible to know."

Cochrane dealt with it by always looking for a wild pitch, "so when it comes, I'm not surprised."

Those kinds of wildness don't show up in the box scores, but they show up in a catcher's aching body.

Cochrane called all the pitches; Mack never did. But sometimes on the bench Mack might make a suggestion like, "Don't you think so-and-so hits curve balls best? Let's not throw him any curves."

In addition to Cochrane's handling of the pitching staff, his baseball sense, and leadership on the field, no catcher could outrun him. Despite an off-year at the plate, the eight writers selected to name the Most Valuable Player gave Cochrane the honor and the $1,000 check that went with it.

On July 1 a throng of more than sixty thousand New Yorkers whooped it up while their Yankees took two from the A's, 12–6 and 8–4. The lead was now 13½ games. "The pennant race is all over but the shouting," wrote James Harrison in the *Times*, "and there isn't any shouting to be done."

For the second year in a row, New York seemed as invincible as Mack's own unbeatables of 1913–1914.

Even the Philadelphia papers were conceding the race. An unsigned editorial in the *Record* declared the Yankees a shoo-in "short of a railroad wreck or an earthquake. The other magnates must settle down to plenty of red ink on the books except for such gala occasions as [when] Babe Ruth and his brothers visit the rival playgrounds. It certainly cannot go along for another season if Barnard expects to have any league whatever."

A rash of injuries hit the A's, testing Mack's reserves. Joe Boley pulled a muscle and was out for ten days. A charley horse sidelined Cochrane for his first injury-related rest in four years. Jimmy Foxx replaced him despite a sore wrist and finger. By now Tris Speaker's creaking knees had put him on the bench. He made his last start on July 16. Two days later Cobb was hit in the chest by a pitch and Haas replaced him. Cobb started a few more games, then pinch-hit the rest of the year. His last hit, a double off Bump Hadley, came on September 3 in Washington.

Mack was concerned about what he considered his players' obsession with the Yankees and their constant scoreboard watching. Before opening a 5-game series on July 19 against the surprising third-place Browns, which would conclude the home stand, he called a meeting. The Yankees were a distant 12½ games in front. The Browns were only 5 games back of the Athletics. Two years ago about this time the A's had been chasing the Yankees in vain when the Indians had overtaken them and claimed second place.

"Don't pay attention to the team in front, but watch the team in back of you," Mack warned his men. "The Browns are ready to force you into third place if you are caught napping."

According to the *Inquirer* column "The Old Scout," Mack used another psychological ploy in the meeting: "Men, we are out of the pennant race this year. Let's forget it. But there is one thing you must not lose sight of. I am going to make many changes in the lineup next season and there is not one man who is sure of his job. Think it over."

"The Old Scout" said players left the meeting knowing they were playing for next year's jobs and contracts. If Mack made those comments, it may have been another means of getting them to quit thinking about the Yankees and tend to the day's business on the field. That was clearly his primary concern.

With the outfield of Simmons, Haas, and Miller starting for the first time, the Athletics swept the St. Louis series. Walberg, Rommel, Earnshaw, Grove, and Quinn pitched complete games, giving up a total of 8 runs. A week later they swept 4 games in St. Louis to end the threat from behind them. They won 7 in a row, lost 1, then won another 10 straight.

Jimmy Foxx was playing third, with Sammy Hale out with a sore arm that hampered him most of the year. Occasionally playing first base, sometimes catching, Foxx had quickly become a Shibe Park favorite, hitting safely in each of the first 25 games he played and coming through with some big pinch hits off the bench. He was batting over .400.

At twenty, Foxx was already considered the strongest man in baseball. In 1929 *Time* would quote him: "When I was 12, I could cut corn all day, help in the wheat fields, swing 200-pound bags of phosphate off a platform into a wagon. We had games on the farm to test strength and grip. A fellow had to plant both feet in half a barrel of wheat and then pick up two bushels of wheat or corn and balance them on his shoulders. Another trick was to lift a 200-pound keg of nails without letting the keg touch your body. I could do that easily."

In the clubhouse he could grip a standing man's ankles and lift him straight up off the floor.

On July 21 Foxx hit the first home run to clear the left-field roof at Shibe Park. Press box observers said it crossed Somerset Street, which ran parallel to the left-field wall; sailed over the houses; and dropped into a parking lot behind them. But John Rooney, one of the neighborhood boys who chased foul balls and home runs, was in the lot and later swore that the ball had hit high up on a building beyond the parking lot before landing in the lot. The kids patrolling the streets around Shibe Park soon learned to identify the unique crack when Foxx's bat sent the ball out of the park.

Flashy middle infielders claimed that the only qualifications a third baseman needed were a strong chest for balls to bounce off and a strong arm. Foxx had both of those, but he was stiff, unable to get down quickly for a hard-hit grass-cutter.

Jimmie Dykes remained a man with no fixed address. He would play every infield position during the last two months of the season.

After a strong start Joe Hauser was struggling. In June he went almost a month without hitting a homer. Of all the Athletics, Ehmke and Joe Hauser probably disliked Ty Cobb the most. In later years, through a Dutch Masters haze, Unser Choe often told of how he was outhitting Cobb in the early going (after 24 games he was batting .329, Cobb .340) and Cobb was jealous and began pestering him with unwanted advice about moving up in the box until he got Hauser thinking too much at the plate and his hitting fell off. As Joe told it, one day Detroit outfielder Harry Heilmann was on first base and said to Joe, "You don't look the same at the plate. Has Cobb been giving you hitting advice?"

"Ja ja," said Joe.

Maybe that's why he went into his home run drought in June. Maybe that's why his hitting fell off in July. Maybe that's why he and Cobb almost came to blows in the clubhouse and afterwards, in the shower, Earle Mack said to him, "Why didn't you belt that guy?" And Joe said, "That would have cost me my job. You know how he stands with the old man."

Maybe. Those were Unser Choe's stories. But he hit 5 more homers in July and finished with 16, good enough for fourth in the league, in only 300 at-bats. For the first ten days of July he was hitting at a .400 clip, culminating in 4 hits in the first game of two on July 11. Then suddenly the hits disappeared. In the next two weeks, except for one 3-for-4 day, he was 5 for 37. It must have ruined Joe's dinner when Mack sent Cobb in to pinch-hit for him on July 23 in a 5–0 loss at Washington.

When the Athletics arrived in Chicago to start their western trip on July 25, they were 11 games back of the Yankees. That afternoon Mack decided that with the addition of Earnshaw, he could spare Orwoll from the pitching staff. He didn't need him in the outfield, so he put him at first base and Foxx at third. Orwoll had been an outfielder in Milwaukee when he wasn't pitching; Mack wanted his bat in the lineup and took a chance that he could do the job. Joe Hauser was benched. The day's twin bill was a blend of the old and the young. Cobb started in right field. They walloped the White Sox in the first game, 16–0, behind Howard Ehmke, and pulled out the second, 8–7, with 4 runs in the ninth. Speaker and Collins drove in the tying and winning runs as pinch hitters.

Meanwhile the Yankees were losing two in Detroit. Two games were cut off the lead in one afternoon.

"I think our whole club sensed their opportunity that day," Mack said a few weeks later.

Miller Huggins was experiencing miseries that Connie Mack was all too familiar with—slumping hitters, injuries, and wobbly pitching. Tony Lazzeri was out with a torn tendon in his right shoulder. Wilcy Moore had a lame wing and was unable to repeat his 1927 career year. Huggins had given thirty-nine-year-old Stan Coveleski a chance but gave up on him in August. He obtained former Athletics left-hander Fred Heimach from St. Paul and Tom Zachary on waivers from Washington.

But Babe Ruth in his syndicated column blamed the Yankees' woes squarely on a hitting slump. "When a contending team slumps, nine times out of ten it isn't the pitching, it's the hitting that has fallen off. Pitching, be it good or bad, is more likely to be steady. We've had bad pitching from time to time all season. But hitting is the most inconsistent thing in the world. One day a club smacks the cover off the ball and the next day they can't hit the broad side of a barn with a scatter gun."

Visiting with his old friend, Browns manager Dan Howley, in St. Louis in August, Ty Cobb agreed that veterans could wilt under pressure the same as youngsters. "When veterans get into a slump, they tighten up and start worrying."

"When a team like the Athletics starts to pick up, it's the hitting punch that comes alive," Ruth had written.

That's what happened. Sparked by the bats of Foxx, Cochrane, Haas, and a gimpy but game Al Simmons—who was leading the league at .386 on August 10—and the steady play of the reshaped infield, the Athletics went on to win 10 in a row, and 12 of 13 while the Yankees were 5-9. The lead melted to 3½ games.

New York began to take notice. On August 3 the *New York Graphic* sent its Yankee beat writer, Jim Kahn, to Detroit to cover the A's

After Lefty Grove struck out 11 in a 5-1 win in Detroit on August 5, Mack visited with Tigers manager George Moriarty. They had known each other for twenty years. Moriarty had been a player and, for ten years, an umpire before succeeding Ty Cobb at Detroit. Moriarty, who was also a poet, wrote for North American Newspaper Alliance. He described his conversation with Mack:

> I expressed the opinion that the team had taken a sudden bound toward greatness. With a characteristic twinkle, he replied, "I have tried to believe that for years, and I hope I am not kidding myself now. To have Haas, Foxx, and Orwoll come through at one time is a great stroke of fortune. Usually a manager is tickled to have one player blossom out in an emergency. Haas, however, impressed me last spring when he played so brilliantly in the Philadelphia city series. Orwoll, as a first baseman, frankly surprised me, as I figured he would make an excellent outfielder."
>
> [Orwoll had been a little at sea the first few days, trying to get at everything hit between first and second, but quickly adjusted.]
>
> "Foxx has fine possibilities as an infielder. Our club started uphill at a rapid clip with these three players in the lineup."
>
> Asked what he thought of his chances, he said, "We have a chance, if our boys will just play the game. That's all I am asking of them now. Tightening up till it becomes a state of mental pressing is the real danger a ball club faces in a crisis."

A buoyant, bright-eyed Connie Mack and the Athletics came home on August 9, talking—but not predicting—pennant. Jimmy Foxx's inexperience showed at third base one day in Cleveland when, Mack said, he was given 2 errors but "missed at least four balls that he should have come up with. I was thinking of taking him out, but he came right back in the game with a couple of marvelous plays and has been going great ever since."

Sitting on the bench beside Mack that day in Cleveland, a restless Jimmie Dykes asked, "Is Foxx really a better third baseman than I am?"

"No, Jimmie," said Mack, "but he hits so much better."

Mack never gave a thought to moving Foxx to first because he was more than satisfied with Ossie Orwoll's performance there, telling Bill Dooly he was "a wonder. His fielding has opened my eyes. He makes plays that look impossible. Orwoll isn't just a ball player, he's a HELLUVA player."

(Bill Dooly, who admitted to paraphrasing quotes—which all writers did but few admitted—wouldn't have dared to put that last one into Mr. Mack's mouth unless it had come out of it.)

But Orwoll's weakness against left-handed pitching showed up in the west. So did a tendency for Mule Haas's work in the field to be affected by a slump at the plate.

Mack was reluctant to keep Cobb and Speaker on the bench, but he wasn't about to break up a winning combination. Still, Speaker found other ways to contribute. He was coaching at third against Washington on August 11. The A's trailed, 2–1, in the ninth. With 2 out and 2 men on, Haas hit a short fly down the left-field line. Bluege went out for it. Sam Rice came in for it. Speaker yelled, "Watch out." Bluege pulled up and the ball fell between them. The tying run scored. Cochrane followed with a single, driving in the winning run. Lefty Grove picked up the win with 2 innings in relief of Earnshaw.

Two days later Grove won his ninth in a row, beating Detroit 7–1. That night the A's were guests of the Aldine Theater for a baseball movie, a silent film with sound effects called *Warming Up*, with Richard Dix. The cast included a few former players, including Pinch Thomas and Truck Hannah, whom the older Athletics recognized.

The Athletics kept pace 3 or 4 games behind the defending champions. Walberg and Grove were winning. Eddie Rommel seemed to be working every other day, complaining but never jaking. Rommel still didn't want to be the primary reliever. He didn't like it. And he wasn't shy about letting it be known.

"I'm no relief pitcher," he'd tell one and all in the clubhouse. "I don't pitch that kind of ball. I hate it. It's a pain in the neck, taking up somebody else's ball game. I'm not going to do any more of it."

All season the players heard it; the press heard it; Eddie Collins heard it but didn't bother reporting it to Connie Mack, who had heard it all before.

Nobody took it seriously. They all knew if the game was on the line, Eddie would be busting to go in and try to win it. In his heart Eddie knew it too.

During the A's August climb, from the fourteenth through the twentieth, Rommel worked 3 no-decision relief stints in six days. On August 22 he spouted off in the clubhouse. "I don't give a damn what happens out there today. I don't care two hoops in hades if 16 pitchers get their blocks knocked off and we lose a 15-run lead. I'm not going into that box today. I wouldn't go in for the ex-czar of Russia. I wouldn't care if Rasputin himself came and asked me. That's final. I'm no relief pitcher. It's a lousy dirty job."

A few hours later it wasn't the ex-czar but Connie Mack who asked him. In the bottom of the eighth Mack pinch-hit for George Earnshaw during a 3-run rally that cut the Indians' lead to 5–4. He had a hunch his boys would win it in the ninth. "Ed," he said, "do you think you can go an inning?"

"Gimme the ball," Ed grumbled and headed for the bullpen.

The Athletics tied it in the ninth. Rommel pitched 9 shutout innings until Mule Haas won it with a home run in the seventeenth.

Three days after pitching 9 innings, Ed Rommel volunteered to start on Saturday and go as long as he could and turned in 5 innings before Earnshaw finished it. Three days later, after Grove beat the White Sox 1–0, Rommel relieved in the second game and pitched 5 shutout innings before the A's won, 4–3, in 11. The next day he turned in 5 hitless innings in relief of Walberg as they beat Ted Lyons again, 6–2. The knuckleballer was warming up in the ninth the following day when Ehmke lost a 2–1 lead and the game.

They were still a relatively young team, more experienced than they had been in 1925, when they had been in the race until August then caved in under the pressure. They had also faltered down the stretch the following year. So when Mack saw a possible crack-up coming, he acted quickly to shore up his boys.

They trailed by 3 games on Saturday, August 25. The White Sox were in town for a doubleheader while the Tigers were playing two in New York. Howard Ehmke started the first game against Ted Lyons before a standing-room crowd of thirty-seven thousand. Ehmke had been erratic all year, rarely surviving the seventh inning. He and Mack had an understanding: whenever the pitcher felt himself weakening during a game, he was to tell the manager.

After 7 innings the A's led, 3–0. Ehmke had breezed along with no need to bear down at any time. Mack asked him how he felt. "Good," said Howard. So Mack left him in. As they took the field for the top of the eighth, the players saw that Detroit was beating the Yankees. They saw a chance to gain a game on the leaders. The first three batters scratched out singles, loading the bases. Bill Hunnefield hit a made-to-order double play tap back to Ehmke. The crowd roared. Ehmke picked it up and threw it over Cochrane's head. The crowd groaned. Instead of 2 outs, 2 runs scored. Mack hastily, reluctantly, waved Lefty Grove into the box. It was just the kind of situation Grove hated. The first batter he faced, Alex Metzler, drove a liner up the middle. Joe Boley dove for it and stopped it, then threw to Cochrane to trap Johnny Mostil between third and home. Grove struck out Bill Barrett, then walked Kamm to load the bases again. Bibb Falk doubled in 2 runs and Chicago led, 4–3. In the ninth they roughed up Grove and Carroll Yerkes for 5 more runs.

Connie Mack watched his boys slouch off the field to the clubhouse. They were clearly back on their heels. He could see from their expressions that the spirit had been drained out of them. They needed bucking up. He felt shaky himself, and he had been through this kind of dismaying shock who knows how many times. So he went into the clubhouse, something he rarely did between games, and spoke to them along these lines: "Forget that game. It's over. It was a tough one to lose but we've lost it and it's too late to do anything about it now. Don't let it rattle us. We have to take the slaps with the pats. Now go out there and bump them off."

To Mack's delight, his boys bounced back, pounding Red Faber and Ed Walsh Jr. 13–4. After the game Mack went into the clubhouse again to compliment them on their gameness and fight.

By the time they played their last home game of the season on September 1, the Athletics trailed by 2. If they were going to win it, they would have to do it on the road during the last four weeks. The Yankees would finish with two weeks on the road.

It had been almost twenty years since the sixty-five-year-old Mack had known the excitement of a September pennant race. When he had won four pennants between 1910 and 1914, they weren't close races. Three years ago they had been in the chase until a 12-game losing streak, begun in late August, knocked them out.

After losing 2 of 3 in Washington, the Athletics faced 5 games in three days in Boston starting Thursday, September 6. Looking ahead to the following 4-game series in New York, the A's were confident that if they could split those 4 and leave New York still 2 games back, they would win it in the west, where they had fared better than the Yankees.

In an exhibition game in New Haven on Wednesday, Jimmy Foxx played first base and hit 2 home runs. Mack decided that his strongest infield for the stretch run would have Foxx on first and Dykes at third.

When Connie Mack made his first appearance in the dugout at Fenway Park, the Red Sox fans stood and cheered. Like most of the baseball fans in the country, they were pulling for the Athletics to overtake the Yankees. It had nothing to do with any Sox-Yankees rivalry; that was still far in the future. The Red Sox were the perennial doormats of the league.

It was partly a tribute to Connie Mack, as the entire nation was rooting for the old man to succeed after fourteen years of struggling to come back. This was no surprise to the Philadelphia writers who knew him best. As Bill Dooly wrote:

> Probably there has never been a man in baseball so universally respected as the leader of the Athletics.
>
> His rivals and associates, players, club owners, umpires, the whole kit and crew, all speak in glowing terms of Connie. But there is one simple, heartfelt tribute they pay him that we like best. The sentiment is merely, "Connie is a wonder."
>
> In explanation, that word "wonder" is frequently used by the diamond profession. When a ballplayer wants to use the highest superlative to express his feelings, that's the word he chooses. So it has an especial meaning among the fraternity that it has not elsewhere.

The support for the A's was also based on the nation's fans being fed up with New York's domination of the World Series. Part or all of the past eight Series had been played in New York or Brooklyn, and the Giants were hot on the heels of the Cardinals to make the next one another all–New York show. It was a sign of the honesty of the game that throughout the Athletics' month-long road trip, everybody on the field and in the stands—except in New York—was rooting for Connie Mack, but still the home team played all out to win each game against the A's.

In Philadelphia the resentment against the Yankees wasn't just because of their winning. Philadelphians wouldn't have minded so much if it had been, say, Chicago or Cleveland dominating the league. But "Noo Yawk," ninety miles away, where the writers still looked down their noses at "Slowtown" and everything west of the Hudson was nowhere—that was worth hating.

Rain washed out the first Boston doubleheader on Thursday. That meant they could play only four of the games in the next two days. Mack was disappointed to lose another chance at the Red Sox; the A's would be 17-4 against them for the year. (Both teams had an open date September 13, but no effort was made to make up the rained-out game.)

In the first game on Friday, Lefty Grove struck out 11 and gave up 4 hits, beating Red Ruffing, 1–0, for his fourteenth straight win and twenty-second of the year. The Yankees were in Washington for two. Everybody was watching the scoreboard, which reported Washington defeating the Yankees in the first game. In their second game, the A's scored 3 in the top of the first. Earnshaw then walked the first 3 batters he faced and Mack quickly yanked him. He sent in Orwoll, but went to Rommel in the third to finish the game. Rommel pitched 7 shutout innings in the 7–3 win.

The Yankees lost the second game in Washington.

Their 13½-game lead of July 1 was down to zero.

Connie Mack's friend, Dr. James Penniman, possessed thousands of rare old documents and books in his home and had donated more than one hundred thousand volumes to various university libraries. But the most prized possession of this world-traveling scholar was the scorecard Connie Mack used in that first game in Boston.

That evening Mack wrote on it, "To my good friend, Dr. James Penniman," then signed and dated it above each team's data for the game. In the middle he wrote

Athletics tied the Yankees on this date with
87-47
87-47

(Mack held on to the scorecard until he returned to Philadelphia and delivered it. Finding nobody home, he slipped it through Dr. Penniman's door.)

The next day Babe Ruth's seventh-inning home run broke a 3–3 tie at Yankee Stadium, but the Athletics topped it with another doubleheader sweep in Boston to move into first place. In the first game Ossie Orwoll pitched 3 scoreless innings and contributed a single to the tenth-inning scoring that gave the Athletics a 7–6 win. George Earnshaw went the distance to win the second game, 7–4.

The Associated Press announced the news to the nation:

After fourteen years of effort, half of it in the nethermost depths of the American League, the silver pate of the grand old man was bobbing along tonight in front of all the rest. . . .

The dean of all the masterminds drew up alongside Miller Huggins in the shadows of last evening. For a day they marched upon even terms, but this afternoon the ancient Connie succeeded in pulling away—just half a stride, it is true, but nevertheless away.

The Red Sox put their best foot forward in a vain effort to stay the rush of the Mackmen, but the ringing cheers of 25,000 Bostonese told Connie the home folks were glad the Sox had failed. The veteran manager was the objective of an ovation as he led his men away after the second game to make ready for a double charge upon the citadel of the Yankees on the Harlem tomorrow.

"The story of the Mackmen's game fight and the fall of the New York idols is amazing," wrote Frank H. Young in the *Washington Post*, "and, even if they fail in reaching their pennant objective, the Athletics will bask in their share of the printed sunshine of the season's doings and in the minds of fans throughout the country for years to come."

The Athletics raced from Fenway Park in taxis to the station to catch the train that would arrive in New York before midnight so they'd get a good night's sleep in the beds of the Alamac Hotel instead of the Pullman cars. Connie Mack and his merry Mackmen weren't interested in just basking in printed sunshine. They went into New York for a 4-game showdown like lions scenting red meat. Even though they were 5-13 against the Yankees for the year, they were a different team—with Foxx and Miller and Haas and Dykes in the lineup—from the one that had taken most of those losses. And the Yankees were not playing anything like their early-season form.

New York fans were just as hungry for a real late-season battle after the Bronx Bombers' ho-hum romp through the field in 1927 and most of the '28 season. On Thursday thousands stood in the rain outside the club's office on Forty-Second Street and nearly rioted when the reserved seats for Sunday's doubleheader were all sold before they could get inside. A week earlier Connie Mack had tried to get some reserved seats for friends, but Ed Barrow had told him there were none left. The demand was so great that the club added seven thousand standing-room tickets and sold them all. Special trains formed a long line from Philadelphia to New York on Sunday morning. The *Inquirer* sent two writers to cover the story. On Monday morning Philadelphia papers gave the games front page, upper-right play as the top story of the day.

The final count was 81,622 paid plus 3,643 who went through the pass gate. Another 50,000 remained outside the stadium. "Mob is the word," wrote John McCullough in the *Inquirer*. "It pushed. It shoved. It tramped on toes just as its toes were tramped on." With people sitting and standing on every available horizontal surface, concessionaire Harry Stevens said the crowd cost him record sales because his vendors could not move through the occupied steps.

(The league's decision to help finance the building of Yankee Stadium was paying off, as visiting clubs were taking home shares of bigger crowds than they had ever seen. On July 4, 1927, Washington had shared in the receipts from an attendance of 72,644.)

Frank Graham of the *New York Sun*, highly regarded by other writers for his factual reporting, wrote that before the game some of the A's had opened a window in the clubhouse to watch the turmoil on the street as the mob tried to get into the ballpark.

Soon they became involved with the fans in an exchange of insults. This caused an even greater jam. Finally Capt. Houk of the police, in charge of moving the traffic, went into the clubhouse. Houk, a tall, handsome officer, and courteous, could be stern and unyielding. Looking about him and not seeing Mack, he asked, "Who's in charge here?"

A player asked, "Who wants to know?"

"I do. I want to ask him to close those windows before you snarl traffic worse than it is now."

With that the players directed at him the fire they had directed at the fans. Among the colorfully embellished suggestions were that he drop dead, get lost and jump in the river. He listened to them calmly for a moment, then the door opened and Connie Mack walked in. The spectacle of his players baiting the officer seemed to captivate him, for he stood there a minute in silence.

"Mr. Mack," the captain said, "I am sorry I have to say this, but here it is. Tell your men to close those windows immediately or I'll arrest them, and there may be some delay in starting the ball game."

Connie was startled. "Why, er, why yes, captain." Turning to the players he said, "Put those windows down immediately." The players obeyed him. He apologized to the captain for their behavior and the captain thanked him and left the room. Connie Mack still seemed a trifle dazed.

If there were tight nerves among the Yankees, they weren't in Babe Ruth. As the Athletics came out of the tunnel through the New York dugout to get to the field, Ruth was sitting on the bench. "You're never getting into the World Series," he joshed them. "Forget about spending that money. By tonight you're nothing."

But shortstop Leo Durocher was worried. Years later he told Jimmy Cannon of the *New York Post*, "I needed that World Series money to bail me out of my hotel. I hated the A's; they were taking my money."

It was a warm day. Mack doffed his suit coat and managed in vest and shirtsleeves. The bench jockeying was raw and robust. Wally French led the A's chorus, which was as formidable as the Mormon Tabernacle Choir—Miller, Haas, Dykes, Simmons, Cochrane, and Rommel all singing zingers.

Frank Graham quoted somebody in the press box commenting, "Connie is like a refined old gentleman with a house full of brats, a pain in the neck to the neighbors. Sometimes he must get a secret kick out of their antics."

Leo Durocher and coach Art Fletcher were the biggest mouths on the Yankees' bench. Durocher and Tony Lazzeri were the visitors' main targets. Four umpires were assigned to work the series instead of the usual three.

The Yankees won both games, 5–0 and 7–3. In the first, the Athletics made 9 hits off George Pipgras but none at the right time. Their best chance came in the eighth, when Jimmy Foxx struck out with the bases loaded. In the second game, onetime Athletic Fred Heimach and Rube Walberg started. Walberg had a reputation for pitching his best when he was behind. Given a lead, he seemed to ease up. But today he was rolling along with a 3–1 lead, showing his best speed and stuff of the year. Then, in the seventh, an unusual umpire's action may have sparked a fleeting memory in Connie Mack's mind of the day in 1909 when a rank call by Silk O'Loughlin had, he believed, cost him a pennant.

With a run in and men on second and third and 2 out, Miller Huggins sent Mike Gazella up to pinch-hit for Benny Bengough. The count went to 2 and 2. Walberg delivered. Brick Owens, behind the plate, called strike three. Or did he? Cochrane started for the dugout. Walberg strode off the mound. Owens called Cochrane back. The umpire spread his hands as for a safe sign and said it was ball three. Perhaps in a split second of indecision Owens had said "strike" but did not indicate it with any hand signal. Players, managers, and writers were confused. Nobody could remember an umpire reversing his own strike call, if indeed he had. Walberg went back to the box and threw ball four to load the bases. Then he walked pinch hitter Pat Collins, forcing in the tying run. Mack rushed Eddie Rommel in to put out the fire. But Rommel lit his own bonfire in the eighth. Koenig singled.

Gehrig doubled. Ruth was walked. Bob Meusel hit a grand slam. After the last out Connie Mack left the dugout and went directly to the hotel. He spoke to no reporters.

In the Yankees' clubhouse, Babe Ruth gave Meusel a big bear hug and said, "We broke their hearts today."

The *Times* reported that when the last club employee departed at nine thirty that night, there were still five cars unclaimed in the parking lot. "Where do you suppose the owners are?" asked the attendant.

"Better look in the East River," said the ballpark worker. "Maybe they came from Philadelphia."

That evening in the hotel lobby a bitterly disappointed Mack said, "The Yanks didn't look right. They didn't look like the same team that we faced earlier in the season. But somehow or other, I don't know why it is, our boys just can't seem to play their regular game against them. The second game was sad. We had that one until Walberg lost his control. All Rube had to do was get the ball over the plate to lick them."

Unlike the O'Loughlin incident, for which he never forgave the umpire, Mack bore no ill will toward Owens for what appeared to be an indecisive decision.

Ten years later Yankee pitcher George Pipgras was an American League umpire. One day he ran into Mack in a hotel. "You beat me out of a pennant," Mack said.

"Well, Mr. Mack, I needed the money," Pipgras said.

Monday was a day off. Mack took time out to conclude the purchase of a left-handed pitcher, Stewart Bolen, from Jack Dunn for $100,000 down, with the option of returning Bolen to the Orioles if he didn't make the team in spring training. (Mack returned him.) It was the last deal between the two old friends. On October 22 Dunn, fifty-six, suffered a fatal heart attack while on horseback watching bird dog field trials.

With the Yankees leading by 1½ games, Ed Barrow expected maybe forty thousand, a good weekday crowd, on Tuesday. More than fifty thousand paid their way in, confident of seeing the Yankees pull further away from the A's. After all, Henry Johnson and Lefty Grove were the pitchers. Johnson was a sure winner against Philadelphia, and the Yankees often got the best of Grove.

But the A's broke out on top and led 3–1 after seven. Grove had walked only 2 men and given up 4 hits. Combs led off the eighth, ran the count to 3 and 2, and walked. Koenig hit a hard grounder that Dykes stopped, but it bounced away. He picked it up. Instead of eating it, he threw it past Foxx at first. Combs made it to third. Some observers in the press box thought Dykes had had a sure double play if he'd fielded it cleanly, but he was given only one error. With Gehrig up, Grove uncorked a wild pitch. Combs scored; Koenig went to second. Gehrig then ducked away from another erratic pitch, but it hit his bat and blooped into left field. Simmons raced in to pick it up. Koenig dashed home and slid in ahead of the throw. Gehrig went to second. A walk, an error on a ground ball, and an accidental blooper, and the score was tied with nobody out, a man on second, and Babe Ruth at the plate.

Lefty Grove may have been the only person in America who hated Babe Ruth. Nothing personal, of course. He just had to turn up the heat every time he faced the slugger. Ruth, under orders, bunted to move Gehrig to third. The ball rolled just foul. On a 1 and 1 count, Grove grooved a fastball. Ruth drove it into the bleachers as clouds of straw hats sailed out of the stands.

The temperature around Grove's neck must have been thirty degrees hotter than anywhere else in Yankee Stadium. He fired three fastballs past Bob Meusel. After another walk, he closed out the inning.

Connie Mack used three pinch hitters in the ninth—Cobb, Collins, and French. They all popped up. It was Ty Cobb's last time at bat.

The Yankees now led by 2½ games.

Taking into account that all hearsay is filtered through the relaying narrator in the middle, this is the way Detroit pitcher Elden Auker later related the story of what happened after the game, as Mickey Cochrane loved to tell it when he was managing the Tigers six years later:

> In the clubhouse Grove's tearing up chairs and lockers. In walks Connie Mack. The clubhouse fell dead quiet. Mr. Mack walked up to Grove and said, "Mr. Groves, I'd like to talk to you."
>
> "What do you want?" Grove snapped.
>
> "I would like to talk to you about that pitch you made to Mr. Ruth." Grove glared at him and said, "Oh, horseshit."
>
> Mr. Mack straightened up and said, "Yes, and horseshit to you, Mr. Groves."
>
> Grove busted out laughing. The other players did too. Even Connie Mack chuckled.

When the game ended and both teams headed for the dugout steps to the tunnel that led to both clubhouses, the verbal warfare turned physical.

Lazzeri was looking for Howard Ehmke. There had been ill will between them last year when, Lazzeri later claimed, Ty Cobb had tipped him off that Ehmke intended to throw at him in a game at Yankee Stadium. Ehmke had forgotten the incident. Lazzeri hadn't.

As they reached the steps, Lazzeri said, "Hey, what are you riding me for?"

Ehmke, who was not a bench jockey, said, "I haven't even been thinking about you, much less riding you."

Lazzeri pushed against him and continued ranting.

"Say, if you're looking for trouble," Ehmke said, "I'm not the guy to run away." He threw down his glove and sweater and started after Lazzeri. Just then Cochrane tackled Lazzeri and brought him down. Babe Ruth picked up Lazzeri and dragged him into the clubhouse.

Later the perplexed Ehmke could only guess that "maybe they planned to get me into a fight and see if they could jam me up so I couldn't work against them, although it didn't look like I was going to be used. I have not been going very well lately."

Ehmke hadn't won in a month, but after four doubleheaders in a week, Mack had little choice. He gave the ball to Howard to start the last game of the series.

A big Wednesday crowd of thirty-five thousand turned out hoping to see the Yankees put away their challengers for good. Ehmke was hit often but not hard. The Athletics took a 3–2 lead against Waite Hoyt into the last of the eighth, and Ehmke said he felt strong enough to continue. Combs led off with a single to deep short. Koenig singled to left, but Simmons's throw to third cut down Combs. Koenig took second. Ehmke struck out Gehrig on a 3-2 curve. Mack ordered Ruth walked. The Yankees were taunting Ehmke fiercely. Ehmke threw an inside fastball that grazed Bob Meusel's arm. Meusel headed for the mound, but umpire Bill Dinneen intervened.

"[Bob] didn't mean anything," Ehmke said later. "I know Bob; we were in the submarine service together. It was just part of the riding the two teams were giving each other."

The bases were loaded and Tony Lazzeri stepped into the batter's box.

"I was out to strike him out," Ehmke said, "and I guess I was a little too anxious."

Trying to put too much spin on a curve, he twisted his knee and down he went. Mack frantically called on Ossie Orwoll.

"I hated to walk off the field," Ehmke said. "I would have had [Lazzeri] breaking his back going after my curves. It's tough to be forced out of a ball game that you've just about won with only four men to retire. But it is tougher to have to walk off the field with a bum knee when a bird like Lazzeri is wagging a bat and you've nearly come to blows with him the day before."

With Cochrane hollering at him to bear down and Connie Mack squirming on the bench, Orwoll walked Lazzeri, forcing in the tying run. He went 3 and 2 to Gazella before the pinch hitter flied out to Haas.

In the ninth the walking man, Max Bishop, stole the five o'clock lightning from the big sluggers, hitting a home run to break the tie. Rube Walberg gave Connie Mack fits by walking lead-off batter Pat Collins to start the bottom of the ninth. But he retired the next three and the lead was cut to 1½ games.

(A combined twelve future Hall of Famers had seen action in the series, with five more—Herb Pennock, Bill Dickey, Tris Speaker, Mack, and Miller Huggins—in the dugouts.)

For all their disappointing showing against the Yankees, the Athletics went west a half game better off than they had counted on. "We're in," was their attitude.

Ehmke wound up in Graduate Hospital in Philadelphia, out for the rest of the year. In the third inning Joe Boley had jammed a finger and bruised a bone on his throwing hand stopping a low throw from Ehmke at second base. Though he finished the game, he was also sidelined. Unlike the days when his star shortstop, Jack Barry, had suffered September injuries that derailed pennant drives, Mack had a Jimmie Dykes to plug in this time, with Hale playing third.

After two days off, Quinn shut out the Indians while the Yankees were losing in St. Louis, and the A's trailed by a half game. That's as close as they got.

On September 17 in Cleveland, Ty Cobb announced his retirement. "I want to know my children [three boys and a girl] better than I do," he said. "I leave Connie Mack and my present team with sincere regret. I have thoroughly enjoyed the two seasons as a private in the ranks under one of the greatest and fairest managers baseball has had."

Twenty-seven years later Mack received a photograph of Cobb taken in his rookie year. It was inscribed, "To Mr. Connie Mack with regrets that at the time that this was taken I could have been with you."

September 19 was a day off in Detroit. In his morning meeting Connie Mack continued to exhort his boys to forget about watching the Yankees and concentrate on the team they were playing. Then, speaking "contentiously," according to Isaminger, he told the writers, "The Athletics must conquer themselves before they can conquer the Yankees. That has been our great drawback. If the team would only forget the Yankees and play the game they are capable of, they would be out in front by a big margin. It is not too late yet even if the season is nearing the end and I feel that the team will play. We are not quitting yet."

"A brave front," Dooly called it. "[Mack is maintaining] a public show of confidence, but he is sad and dejected."

The next day Jack Quinn beat Detroit, 6–1 on a very cold day braved by fewer than eight hundred fans. The New York lead was 1 game with 9 games remaining for the A's, 10 for New York.

Then every time the Athletics won, the Yankees won too.

On the twenty-first the failure of Grove and Rommel to handle bunts led to big innings for the Tigers and a 9–4 loss. Three days later in St. Louis 4 errors undermined Jack Quinn's efforts.

The Yankees' lead was back to 2 games.

The season ended with the Athletics in Chicago for 4 games and the Yankees in Detroit for 5. The day before the final series, the A's played an exhibition game against the Studebaker plant team in South Bend, Indiana. Only Foxx, resting a pulled back muscle, and Simmons, with his aching ankles, sat it out as the entire work force of ten thousand turned out.

On Thursday Grove struck out 9, including 3 on 9 pitches in the seventh, and hit a home run for his twenty-fourth win. But Mack's prayers for an assist from the Tigers went unanswered. The Yankees, with Ruth hitting numbers 51 and 52, won twice.

That evening the writers were waiting for Connie Mack when Mack entered the hotel lobby on his way to meet some of his many Chicago friends and relatives. They expected him to be downhearted, but he smiled at them. "I hear New York won the second game," he said. "It doesn't look so good, does it? No, it looks kind of bad for us. But they still have to win another. I hope we can force them to win that one. That's what we must do now."

And they did. On Friday a 6-inning relief job from Rube Walberg completed a 7–5 win. But the Yankees won again and clinched their third straight pennant.

Connie Mack took the news with his customary quiet dignity. "We have no excuses to offer," he said. "I figured though that the Tigers would make a far better showing against the Yanks than they did."

Isaminger summed up three reasons the Athletics finished second:

1. The failure to win more than 6 of 22 against the Yankees
2. A September slump of Foxx and Simmons
3. Ehmke was of no use down the stretch.

The first reason really tells the story. Henry Johnson, 9-8 against the rest of the league, beat the A's five times against one loss. On the other side, Lefty Grove was 1-6 against the Yankees, 23-2 against everybody else. Isaminger's other reasons are hardly fair. Foxx and Simmons had carried much of the offense in the six-week charge to the top. Simmons was tortured with aching ankles and could hardly walk after every game. And with or without Ehmke, there was no shortage of strong, healthy pitchers. Grove led the league in strikeouts for the fourth year in a row and cut his walks in half from his rookie season. Twice he struck out the side on 9 pitches, an unmatched feat.

If Connie Mack had been waiting for Mose to achieve greatness, his wait was over.

The ageless Jack Quinn continued his mastery of the spitter, issuing the fewest walks per 9 innings in the league and matching Grove with 4 shutouts among his 18 wins. Eddie Rommel was the Athletics' answer to Wilcy Moore and Fred Marberry.

Given some playing time when Orwoll had a charley horse in late August, Joe Hauser was 2 for 15. When Orwoll's hitting fell off, Mack switched him back to the pitching staff in early September and put Jimmie Dykes, then Foxx, on first. Unser Choe was just a reserve now. On September 22 at Detroit, Sammy Hale made 2 errors at third base. Mack took him out, moved Foxx from first to third, and sent in Hauser. "That was the only time Ty Cobb said something nice to me," Joe recalled. "I had been hitting line drives all over the field in batting practice. When I went up to bat for the first time that day, he said to me, 'Let's see you hit 'em like you did in practice, Joe.'" Hauser drove in 2 runs with a sacrifice fly and a single and the next day had 3 hits, including a double and home run. But in the next 4 games he was 2 for 16 and finished at .260. His days with the A's were over.

Despite his disappointment over falling short of catching the Yankees, Connie Mack thanked four of his lesser-paid players for "a good season" with year-end bonuses: $500 for Max Bishop, $1,000 for John Quinn, $1,500 for Jimmy Foxx, and $2,000 for Eddie Rommel. When the books were closed for the year, showing a profit of $164,000, the stockholders were rewarded with another $50,000 dividend.

For the Athletics the next three seasons had actually begun in the middle of July. Walberg and Earnshaw looked ready for stardom. The outfield of Simmons, Haas, and Miller was set for years. The twenty-year-old Foxx had earned a permanent place in the lineup.

After fourteen years of Connie Mack's juggling act, all the pieces had finally fallen into place. Sadly, at that same time their biggest fan, Emory Titman, suffered a fatal heart attack at the age of thirty-nine and wouldn't be there to see the glory years. Titman was employed as a dispatcher for a taxi company after having spent his inherited fortune on chorus girls and traveling with the A's. A friend and unofficial mascot to the players of Mack's earlier champions, Titman had been welcome on the bench and on the practice field during years of spring training trips. He received a prominent sendoff in the *Record*'s sports section on July 10, 1928: "His heart was as big as his bulk. He was as open-handed and generous as he was large, as careless of his wealth and possessions as he was immense in girth. When his wealth was gone, he went to work uncomplaining, all but forgotten. The writer [unnamed] was proud to call Emory Titman his friend."

BACK ON TOP

The day after the 1928 season ended in Chicago, Connie Mack arrived home in time to watch his friend, light-heavyweight champion Tommy Loughran, win a 10-round decision over heavyweight Jack Gross at Baker Bowl on October 1.

After baseball Connie Mack's first love was boxing. It seems incongruous that Mr. Mack, this kind, gentle leader who avoided conflict whenever possible, had been an avid fan of what French fight manager Leon See called "a barbaric, unnatural way to settle an argument or entertain a crowd" since the bare-knuckle days of the nineteenth century, when prize fights were outlawed in many states and were staged—an apt word for the many that were rigged—in smelly, smoky lofts and saloons and honky-tonks and barns.

Tommy Loughran, a south Philly native, was Mack's favorite fighter. One of his most prized possessions was a pair of miniature boxing gloves given him by Loughran. Mack encouraged Connie Jr. to take up boxing and induced Loughran to give Junior a few lessons.

"I went to the Loughran fights with Dad," Junior said, "and it was rough on me. Dad was so enthusiastic, he would be swinging his fists and elbows along with the action in the ring. I went home with sore ribs."

On Friday, September 14, 1923, it had been cool enough for an overcoat but probably not too cold to play the Browns at Shibe Park. Nevertheless, Mack had postponed the game, setting up a Saturday doubleheader. This allowed him to take an earlier train to New York to see the Jack Dempsey–Luis Firpo heavyweight championship fight at the Polo Grounds that night. Bing Miller may have gone with him. It was a fistic hurricane. The first round opened with Firpo knocking Dempsey to the canvas. Dempsey then floored Firpo seven times. Firpo then walloped Dempsey clear out of the ring onto the ringside typewriters. Dempsey was boosted back through the ropes just in time to avoid being counted out. In the second round Dempsey dropped Firpo three times before the South American giant would stay down for the count.

Connie Mack became so excited, said Miller, "he said he didn't think he'd go to another boxing match." He recovered and went to a lot more.

Mack remained a fight fan all his life. On fall Saturdays he would sometimes go to a college football game or listen to one on the radio, but he never missed a radio broadcast of a championship fight. Years later his daughter Ruth could still picture him shadow boxing while a fight was on, occasionally swinging a one-two punch in the air at an invisible opponent. In his nineties, he would watch the bouts on the small television screens of the early 1950s two or three nights a week.

"If you asked him who he thought was leading, he'd tell you," Junior said, "and he would be right 90 percent of the time."

Connie Mack went to New York for the first two World Series games in October 1928, but he was too worn out to go to St. Louis, where the Yankees completed a sweep of the Cardinals. He stayed in New York and watched the games at Madison Square Garden on the big electric scoreboard.

The September battle with the Yankees that had gone down to the wire had exhausted him. In a way the job had been easier during the years when the Athletics were losing 100 games. There wasn't much to be tense about. Not that a close race to the finish was anything new to Mack. He had been there before—in baseball, Connie Mack had been *everywhere* before. But the last had been nineteen years ago. He had been a young man of forty-six when he had battled the Tigers down the stretch. Since then either his champions had breezed home or his also-rans had been out of the picture long before Labor Day.

Connie Mack had accepted that in the long run the breaks evened out and slumps were inevitable. He has often been described as a stoic, sitting immobile in the middle of the dugout imperturbably, with unchanging expression, taking everything that happened with equanimity.

It may have looked that way, but it wasn't so.

Grantland Rice had him pegged: "When a game is in progress, there is no manager who feels greater emotional tension. He keeps it repressed but that makes it all the harder on his system. Looked upon as a great conservative, he is actually one of the greatest gamblers and takes many daring chances."

Eddie Collins observed it up close. "Now and again," he told Pegler, "when a tense situation develops, you will see Connie's hands tighten on the score-card. He will sit up tight and straight and rigid with anxiety. But when the next play is done, whether it goes our way or the other way, it is past and his grip on the scorecard loosens and his body sags. He knows how to relax, whether naturally or by cultivated habit."

Mack, who normally shot around 90, was the same way on the golf course, Collins said. "When he dubs one, it's finished. He doesn't get upset. I never saw any man who could stand the strain and tension as he can at the age of sixty-six. He rides the railroads all summer long and runs the ball club in all kinds of weather from the terrible cold of the spring to the awful heat of St. Louis in July and August, but he leads a regular life and moreover he has a mind that doesn't waste energy on nonessentials."

Connie Mack was that way at home too. Ruth was a basketball star at Mt. St. Joseph's in Chestnut Hill, where her older sister Mary had been the team captain. Connie Jr. played football and basketball and pitched for German-town Academy. Their father seldom went to any of their games or talked to them about their athletic activities. He neither encouraged nor discouraged Junior to be a ballplayer.

"He had his emotions so under control," Junior recalled. "I don't remem-ber him being pleased or displeased at anything I did."

Occasionally Mack's stoic facade cracked in the presence of his family. After graduating, Mary had entered the Mt. St. Joseph's convent adjacent to the school. "When we were at the convent saying goodbye to her," Ruth recalled, "Dad had tears in his eyes. It was unusual for him to show that much emotion in front of us."

From their campus Ruth and Rita caught glimpses of Mary carrying big laundry baskets in the building where the nuns did the wash. When their father went with them on visiting days and they sat in a circle around Mary, Mack's blue eyes were moist.

(Mary wasn't cut out for convent life. She left and went back a few times before leaving for good. According to family friend Ted Gorsuch, "The mother superior told me they had to get rid of her. She wanted to smoke and wear silk stockings and had a mind of her own. They called the Macks and said, 'You better come and get your daughter. Her trunk is in the hall.'" That was in 1932. On December 31 she married Francis X. O'Reilly.)

When the cold weather hit Philadelphia in 1928, Connie Mack was too run down to fight off the flu. Right after Christmas he fled to Mount Plymouth,

Florida. But the flu hung on for weeks, draining his energy. When his friend of over thirty years, Henry J. Killilea, died after a heart attack in Milwaukee on January 23, 1929, Mack was too sick to go to the funeral. Killilea, an attorney and principal owner of the Milwaukee Brewers, had hired Mack to manage the team in 1896 after Mack had been fired in Pittsburgh. Killilea had been instrumental in the founding of the American League. His daughter, Florence, a twenty-four-year-old graduate of the University of Wisconsin, inherited the Brewers with the intention of running the club.

Mack wired his regrets that he could not be there. "The death of Henry Killilea means the loss of one of my dearest friends for the last thirty years and baseball loses one of the greatest figures in our national game. When closing his last deal with me for players, it was his great desire to give Milwaukee a pennant for 1929."

That last deal with Henry Killilea landed Mr. Mack in hot water with Judge Landis. Back in the old days he and Killilea had more than once engaged in the common practice of arranging phantom deals with higher clubs to protect players from the draft. Despite the new commissioner's increased vigilance, the practice had continued throughout baseball.

On August 31, 1928, the A's agreed to purchase a big left-hander, Ernie Wingard, from Milwaukee for $5,000 down and another $17,500 on June 1, 1929, with this "if": If we don't like him by April 15, we can cancel the agreement. Wingard, who earlier had been with the Browns for four years, had won 23 games while batting .350. Mack also recalled pitcher Bill Shores from Wichita Falls and outfielder Bevo LeBourveau from Milwaukee. Shores had been 8-3 in the Texas League, and Mack planned to keep him for '29. LeBourveau, thirty-four, had been up with the Phillies a few times. According to Casey Stengel, who had him at Toledo, Bevo was "a nervous Frenchman," a career .349 hitter for whom "fly balls were an adventure."

On December 15—the draft window having opened and closed—the A's optioned Wingard back to Milwaukee along with Bevo LeBourveau and sent Joe Hauser outright to the Brewers in place of the second payment of $17,500.

The shenanigans were described in a notice sent out from the commissioner's office on March 13, 1929, headed "Illegal Transfers and Player Returns":

September 14, 1928 Milwaukee filed agreement transferring player Ernest Wingard to the Philadelphia American League club outright. No right of return was stipulated. An initial payment of $1,000 was made by Philadelphia check to Milwaukee in September. This check was not cashed by the club but was deposited on December 28 to the personal credit of President Killilea who on December 31 refunded the same amount by his personal check to the order of Connie Mack of the Philadelphia club. Meanwhile, under date of December 15, Philadelphia sought to transfer Wingard to Milwaukee, but approval of this transfer was withheld by the commissioner and an investigation instituted, which has brought out the foregoing facts. Philadelphia and not Milwaukee reserved Wingard, although its "payment" had not been cashed.

There was no mention of LeBourveau, who would spend the year with Milwaukee before being recalled on August 26.

(Landis had also caught Killilea in the same kind of deal with Phil Ball, who was a part-owner of the Brewers, involving pitcher Claude Jonnard, as well as Clark Griffith for acting for the Birmingham club in buying two players from the Southern Association and another from Peoria and being reimbursed by Birmingham.)

Landis fined each club $500 and made Wingard and Jonnard free agents.

Whoever was keeping the books for the A's made no effort to gloss over the commissioner's finding, noting that "Landis decided we had not made a bona fide deal."

The decision left the status of Joe Hauser up in the air. Mack assumed that Landis's decision had voided his sending Unser Choe to the Brewers as part payment for Wingard. He wired Joe to report to Fort Myers. Florence Killilea asked Mack to leave Hauser with the Brewers. Mack agreed. Landis wired Hauser that his case was still under investigation. Apparently (the wording of official records of the time is vague) Landis ordered that Hauser could be optioned to Milwaukee, not released outright to the Brewers.

Unser Choe's homecoming wasn't pleasant. He struggled, hitting .238 with only 3 home runs by June. The Brewers sent him back to Mack, who asked waivers on him with the intention of sending him outright to Portland. Cleveland claimed him and used him primarily as a pinch hitter. Then the major leagues gave up on him, and he was sold to Baltimore, where Joe Hauser began the most spectacular stage of his career, hitting 63 home runs in 1930. He was finally swinging freely. But no major league club would take a chance on him. Three years later he hit 69 homers with Minneapolis. In 1935, while running the bases in Kansas City, his left knee cracked, just as his right knee had in 1925, and down he went. But he continued to play until 1942 and managed in the minors until 1959.

Still too weak to enjoy the facilities of "America's new golf capitol," as the Mount Plymouth Hotel billed itself, Mack dealt with a holdout. The three-year contract of his star MVP catcher had expired. Mack had offered him a $2,000 raise to $12,000. Egged on by some of his teammates and a few friends on the Yankees, Mickey Cochrane asked for $13,000. In his letter to Mack, Cochrane cited newspaper stories alleging the big salaries the A's had paid Ty Cobb and Tris Speaker.

High among Connie Mack's pet peeves—even more so than being quoted as saying things he had never said—was writers guessing players' salaries and purchase prices. That irritation was running higher than his fever when he picked up a pen and a sheet of hotel stationery on February 7 and replied to Cochrane. The letter is transcribed exactly as written.

Dear Mickey,

Yours received and pleased to hear from you. Also feel that I should reply.

Ever since our club was organized our rule was not to have any player come to our camp who had not signed. This rule was broken twice by the same player very much against wishes but allowed for the player. A great deal has been said about Cobb and Speaker and the salary they received from our club, players are not the only ones who should have there heads examined some of those newspaper boys need to be ex-rayed from there toes to there heads. Don't want you to think for a minute that this means an argument with you on the salary question. Our club has offered you the full limit that we can go, and no club outside of the Yankees can afford to pay more and all the two hundred or more players cannot play with the Yankee. Am not telling you what you should do, am simply telling you what our club can do for you and after you have thought it over am sure you will realize that 12000 is some salary. I believe Schang received this sum the last year he was in N.Y. also may have received the same salary last season. N.Y. got rid of him and St Louis wants too. You know our club wants you, but if you cannot see your way clear to sign its alright with our club, so whatever your decision may be its alright with us and no hard feeling on our part.

Yours very truly,
/s/ Connie Mack

Cochrane settled for $12,000, putting him equal to Grove.

In the A's ledgers, Bob Schroeder wrote, "The first week in January [Max Bishop] dropped into office and stated he felt he should receive contract for 25,000.00 due to the Cobb contracts the past two season." These are the only known instances of a player citing Cobb's salary in negotiations. Bishop held out until March before signing for $10,000. Al Simmons remained the highest paid at $15,000.

Several pitchers would benefit from bonus clauses for wins and relief appearances. Earnshaw's paid him $4,500 extra and Walberg's, $1,000 over his $8,000 salary.

Once again the A's payroll was second only to the Yankees. The 1951 congressional subcommittee chaired by Rep. Emanuel Celler studying baseball's monopoly power listed the 1929 New York payroll as $365,741; Philadelphia, $250,231; Washington, $231,618. The Athletics' 1928 attendance had been four hundred thousand less than New York's; Washington's was seven hundred thousand less.

As the start of spring training drew near, Connie Mack still did not feel up to par. He had always maintained that his health would be the only reason he would give up managing. Now for the first time he sensed—dreaded—that possibility. "I doubted that I would be able to go through another season as manager," he admitted a few months later, "and I came closer to quitting then than ever before."

But there was a pennant to be won, not the "just one more and then I'll retire" goal the writers speculated about year after year. And nothing could keep Connie Mack from that pursuit. For a change, the optimism that prevailed throughout the nation was also felt in the offices of the Philadelphia Athletics. On March 4 in a cold, hard rain, Herbert Hoover was sworn in as the new president. In his address he said, "We in America are nearer to the final triumph over poverty than ever before in the history of any land. The poorhouse is vanishing."

Connie Mack's optimism proved a little better grounded than the president's.

Beneath the veneer of Wall Street prosperity, unemployment had been rising for more than a year. Still, a record 4.6 million automobiles had been sold, many on the installment plan. That total would not be matched for another twenty years. Only 2.3 percent of American families—industrial tycoons, bankers, entertainers—had annual incomes of over $10,000. The wealthy partied on. Harpo Marx said of them, "There were grave responsibilities to face . . . plants to be watered, poodles to be walked."

Meanwhile, 60 percent of American families earned below the $2,000 annual minimum considered adequate for basic necessities.

His reserves and bench weakened by the departure of Cobb and Speaker, Connie Mack bought veteran outfielder Homer Summa from Cleveland to join Walter French and Ossie Orwoll as backup outfielders. (Fed up with his lack of playing time, French had retired from baseball. Mack arranged a job for him with Sears, Roebuck in Chicago. After a week, French decided that riding the bench beat riding the bus to work and "unretired.") Eddie Collins remained on the active list but would make only nine hitless pinch-hitting appearances. Mack talked about looking for a first baseman, keeping Jimmy Foxx at third. But he had Sammy Hale, and if Hale had a lame arm, there was Jimmie Dykes—unless Dykes was filling in for Boley or Bishop. So in the middle of March Connie Mack told the twenty-one-year-old Foxx, "You're my first baseman."

Playing first on a regular basis, Foxx proved to be an agile target for infielders' throws. High, low, wherever—he would catch them all. He was awkward at first and would never be a graceful first baseman, but he was a good one. Connie Mack and Eddie Collins made it a special project to give him daily booster shots of confidence. Gradually he learned how to field bunts and had a strong enough arm to throw out runners going from second to third.

For a change, Mack believed he had all the pitching he needed. Bill Shores was the only rookie to earn a regular spot.

Mack had no interest in starting a farm system, but he bought the Martinsburg club of the Blue Ridge League—rescued it really, as a favor to a longtime friend in the town, Lewis Thompson—as it was about to fold. Mack chose as the manager a veteran minor league manager, Dan O'Leary, whose teaching ability he respected. The club lasted only one more season.

In Fort Myers the A's looked indolent, indifferent. They didn't seem to share their boss's optimism. They had been deflated when they lost out the past September, and they still looked like they hadn't gotten over it. They won some spring games but didn't look sharp doing it. For all its charms as a training site—good warm weather, top-notch facilities, supreme hospitality—Fort Myers's location in the southwest part of the state was a drawback. It was at least a four-hour bus ride to the nearest other spring training base, a lot of limb-stiffening lost time riding over primitive roads. That didn't help.

After the season Mack told Alan J. Gould, "Everybody was pessimistic about our chances of beating the Yankees and I kept quiet. I thought we had the winning combination at last. I chose to encourage the pessimism about our chances. I didn't want premature enthusiasm."

Maybe so, but in early April he thought his boys needed a jolt to wake them up. He went directly home, leaving Collins and Gleason in charge of the northbound barnstormers, and told the press he was disgusted and disappointed by what he had seen in spring training. Mack called his team "sloppy. They didn't hustle." He knew the players would read it; he hoped they would react.

He had used that strategy before as a wake-up call. In the past nobody outside of Philadelphia had paid any attention to it. This time it was different. The entire nation of baseball fans noticed, and they reacted. Mack received hundreds of letters from fans everywhere, telling him to let up; he was being too critical of the team; it was better than he thought.

The plan worked. The players read his remarks or were filled in by the writers accompanying them. When the team started north, Eddie Collins told them, "Let's show the old man he's wrong about us."

They opened in Washington. The Senators came in with a tailwind. They had rolled over everybody in the spring so impressively that the nation's leading baseball predictor, Hugh Fullerton, tabbed them the front-runners. Washington had beaten the A's twice out of the gate last year and played them tougher than anybody except the Yankees all year.

It was Mack's custom to give his boys a pep talk before the opener. This time there was none. Al Simmons had been hurt in an exhibition game. Joe Boley was nursing a sore arm. Mack was leery of their chances of winning that day. He decided to start a rookie, Carroll Yerkes, figuring it wouldn't hurt morale as much if they lost with him instead of with Grove or Earnshaw. At least that's the way the experts figured it.

Or was Connie Mack playing a different game? No manager knew his men better than the cagey Mack. By now his boys knew and respected the depth of his insight into their heads. Was he counting on their determination being so strong to "show the old man" that it didn't matter if he started a rookie? Then he'd have his big guns ready for the next game.

Mack had to wait a day when rain postponed the opener in the capital, but then he got his answer in a hurry. The Athletics scored in each of the first 5 innings—Foxx had 3 hits, including a double and home run—and they ran up a 13–4 lead. Mack didn't stay with Yerkes long. He was wild, and Mack pulled him in the second. Enter Eddie Rommel, who shut out the home team the rest of the way.

The next day Mack had his first team meeting. He told them, "If you play like you did yesterday, you can win." They exploded for 6 runs in the fifth, and Rube Walberg cruised to an 8–2 win.

They went to New York and Jack Quinn lost 2–1, both runs scoring on fly balls lost in the sun and shadows of Yankee Stadium by Mule Haas in center field. Was the New York dominance of 1928 still haunting them? Delayed a day by a downpour, a frustrated bunch of Mackmen jumped on their old nemesis Henry Johnson, scoring 4 runs in the first on the way to a 7–4 win for Lefty Grove in a rain-shortened 5-inning game.

On that rainy day in New York AP writer Brian Bell reminded Mack of the deluge of critical mail he had received after his remarks about his team before the season. Bell suggested that the Athletics were sentimental favorites all over the nation.

"Fans generally like to see a champion taken down," Mack said.

Bell pressed him. "Perhaps the interest in the A's among outlying fans might hinge on their affection for the manager."

Mack deflected that notion: "I will be glad when we have some warmer weather. The concrete floors in the dugouts make my feet cold."

After winning 6 of 9 games against Washington and New York, the A's went to Boston and scored 24 runs on May 1. Grove started and left after 5 innings, then came back the next day and pitched a complete-game 5–1 win. Foxx and Simmons, who had missed 5 games, already had 4 home runs each.

The Athletics went west and moved into first place on May 14. On that day the Yankees were in Cleveland watching the rain come down. Gordon Cobbledick of the *Plain Dealer* asked Miller Huggins if he thought the Yankees would overtake Philadelphia.

"No," said Huggins. "The Yanks are getting old and are glutted with success. They read the financial pages with more interest than the sports pages."

The Athletics came home and took 4 straight from Washington. By May 26 they had beaten Washington 12 out of 13 games and led the Senators by 14½. A 17-1 run opened a 7½-game lead over New York by June 3. They no longer quaked at the sight of Yankee pinstripes. They went into New York with the same lead on Friday, June 21, for the kind of make-or-break 5-game series that had broken them a year ago. Before a paid crowd of 66,145 and another 4,000 freebies, Lefty Grove was overpowering in the first game, walking nobody and fanning 6 in an 11–1 romp. In the second game Babe Ruth hit 3-run home runs in the seventh and eighth off Earnshaw and Shores for an 8–3 Yankee win, the kind of fireworks that would have demoralized the A's of '27 and '28. Not this time.

Before another full house on Saturday, Rube Walberg held Gehrig and Ruth to 1 hit between them and had the Yankees shut out, 7–0, aided by home runs by Foxx and Cochrane until New York scored 3 in the ninth. The crowd got more than its money's worth in the second game. They saw Quinn and Pipgras go 14 innings, Babe Ruth drive in Combs from third in the eighth by dropping a bunt down the third base line that caught a dumbfounded Jimmie Dykes shifted over toward shortstop, Pipgras shut out the visitors after Simmons's 3-run homer in the first, the Athletics set a record of no men left on base in the entire game, and Quinn scatter 18 hits before the last one drove in a run for the Yankees' 4–3 win.

On Monday Howard Ehmke pitched 7 innings in a 7–4 win. Foxx, Haas, and Simmons homered to make it clear that the powerhouse of the American League had moved from New York to Philadelphia.

On July 4 the A's were 53-17, a .757 percentage (still the American League record for that date), leading by 9½ games. Grove was 13-2, Walberg 11-3, Earnshaw 10-3. As a team, they were batting .313. Foxx led the league at .412; Cochrane was hitting .363, Simmons .360, Miller .355, Haas .332. Miller had put up a 22-game hitting streak.

They weren't the only ones hitting. As of mid-July more than a hundred major leaguers were batting over .300. (National League president John Heydler apparently didn't think there was such a thing as too much offense. Prior to the season he had resurrected the idea of the designated hitter. With John McGraw leading the way, the National approved it. The American League said no.)

The *New York Telegram* sports department crusaded against the lively ball. Someone at the *Telegram* got hold of a 1919 ball and a new one and cut them open. They found a layer of rubber in the new ball that was not in the old one.

At first the president of Spalding's, which made the NL balls under the Reach label, denied any change in the ball since the introduction of cork in 1909. Responding to the *Telegram's* findings, he said, "Let me assure you that the life of the ball has not been changed since 1920."

The phenomenal rise in home runs since Babe Ruth had changed the game picked up a tailwind in 1929—a 30 percent increase over 1928—causing the usual cries of alarm from baseball's reactionaries. When screens were put up in front of the right-field stands in Sportsman's Park to curb the home run barrage, *The Sporting News* applauded: "By and by more owners of major grounds will begin to cage the home run. Then there will no longer be special home run departments in the sports sections."

Time magazine devoted a few pages to the phenomenon, putting Jimmy Foxx on its July 29 cover as the face of the new game.

The *St. Louis Post-Dispatch* surveyed the managers on their views of the home run splurge. The majority said it was ruinous to the game and pitching had to be improved. Ten of them blamed a pepped-up ball. Connie Mack was not one of them. He was the oldest in the business, but he was the youngest, most forward-looking of them all. Only Mack, Cubs manager Joe McCarthy, Miller Huggins, and Braves owner (and manager for a year) Judge Emil Fuchs thought the home run craze helped the game.

"The fans like it," said Mack, "and that's good for the game."

Mack adjusted to the explosive big-inning era. He wasn't stuck in the time when a 2-run lead and Bender in the box meant a sure win. On July 31 at home against Detroit, the Athletics scored 9 runs in the fifth inning to take a 10–1 lead. Some of his boys made noises like, "This one's in the bag." Alan J. Gould quoted Mack as telling them, "I won't feel easy until we have about twice as big a lead. You can't tell nowadays when the other club may break out with nine runs or more. You boys keep hustling in there and get all you can."

That day the 10–1 lead held up.

Mack was comfortable but not complacent. So he was queasy when in the morning game on July 4, Mickey Cochrane fell to the ground to avoid a high inside pitch and the end of his bat banged into his ribs as he fell. He stayed in the game—hit 3 doubles and a home run—and between games was taped up and played the afternoon game. Then they went to Chicago where X-rays revealed a broken rib and Cochrane went home. Bishop and Boley were on the injured list. Haas became ill. They lost 3 of 4 to the White Sox. Their lead melted by 2 games, to 7½.

Mack had discontinued his daily morning meetings, but when they reached St. Louis, where they played three doubleheaders in four days, he called one. His biggest concern was the effect of the loss of Cochrane. He reminded them how well they had played all season. Now they had run into some bad luck from injuries, but they had good subs, especially in the veteran catcher Cy Perkins, who had been 5 for 13 in Chicago.

"We are not broken reeds," he said. "We have subs for every man out who would be regulars on many other teams. So get it out of your heads that we are crippled. All you have to do is hustle a little harder, put forth some stronger licks, and we will win with these reserves in the lineup."

Later he told Isaminger, "I hammered that point in strong and I noticed the players left the room in high spirits."

They won 4 of the 6 in St. Louis and went to Cleveland, where they found a beaming, taped-up Cochrane and Mule Haas ready to play again and won 8 of their next 10.

"I knew then that I had a championship team," Mack said.

By August 2 they were 74-26 with an 11½ game lead. They lost as many as 4 in a row only once, in the west in mid-August, with Simmons and Miller sidelined. That slide ended when Simmons came back with 3 hits in a 5–2 win in Chicago.

German World War I flying ace Baron Manfred von Richthofen believed that "the aggressive spirit is everything." He would have applauded the 1929 Athletics.

"We played to win," said Al Simmons. "Connie Mack wanted us to be a fighting team. He held a bridle on us if anyone got too tough."

Mack's bridle consisted of an insistence that no abusive language be aimed at an umpire. Otherwise he tolerated language he would never use himself. If he thought a comment to a player was in order, it would be calm but pointed—sometimes barbed; sometimes, according to Collins, with "some damning and helling," but never what they'd call a "bawling out." When Mack had had enough of Haas's bellowing one day, he snapped, "You've said all there is to say, George. You now hold the championship for today." If a pitcher showed his agitation over being taken out of a game—as pitchers did in those days—Mack might say, "Well, you'd better take your glove and go on in the clubhouse."

The origins of some stories—where or when they happened for the first time or if they ever happened at all or who first narrated them—are often impossible to pin down. But given that caveat and allowing for misremembered details, if they are good stories—that is, if they are accurate illustrators of the people involved, if they could have happened—they are worth retelling. One such involves Max Bishop trying to stretch a hit into a triple and being thrown out by a mile. Mack told him quietly, "Next time you hit a triple, please stop at second base."

Connie Mack didn't drive them. He didn't have to. He had assembled a team of drivers. Fierce and scrappy as Cochrane was, he was far from alone. Dykes drove them. Eddie Collins and Kid Gleason drove them. Besides, that wasn't Mack's style. No firebrand he. No charge-'em-up orator or flint-sparking lasher. When he felt he had to deliver a message, he did it more like a parish priest than a fire-eating preacher. His strength lay in knowing and understanding the men he led, knowing them even better than they knew themselves.

Mack's pitchers had some idiosyncrasies. Grove didn't want any infielder except Foxx to throw the ball to him on the mound. Earnshaw refused to warm up at the start of an inning with anyone but the catcher in the game. If the catcher had been on base and Earnshaw had to wait for him, he would wait or throw to Foxx at first.

It was a harmonious team. Everybody got along. If they had any differences, they settled them among themselves. Rube Walberg later likened the club to a family. "They just enjoyed being together," he said. "We never had to come out in the mornings but everybody would be there at ten or 10:30."

Earnshaw might call Walberg "Meathead" and throw around a bunch of big words and Latin phrases, but it was just for laughs. Nobody took it seriously. Bishop, Boley, and Foxx were the quiet ones. Unlike Simmons, who was hot-tempered, nobody ever saw Jimmy Foxx angry. He always had a smile on his face, taking everything in through his pale blue eyes, which were mirror images of the old man's. He was popular with fans and players in every city. No bench jockey, he was more likely to exchange friendly banter with the opposition. White Sox pitcher Ted Lyons, another easy-going guy, once asked him, "Jimmy, how many pounds of air do you put in your arms?" "Thirty-five," Foxx said.

"[Foxx] never said anything to the umpire," recalled pitcher-turned-umpire George Pipgras, "never looked back to show you up. He'd say, 'You can miss the first two, just don't miss the third one.'"

Bing Miller was even-tempered. Al Ruggieri, John Shibe's all-around handyman, was about fourteen when he was working one day under the left-field grandstand. "The players parked their cars near Shibe's speedboats," he recalled. "I was washing Miller's Pontiac. I was wearing rubber boots and when I got into the car to back it up, my foot slipped off the brake and the car backed into the prow of a boat. I banged up his car, but Miller never said a word about it. If that had been Al Simmons's car, he would have killed me."

Earnshaw, Haas, Cochrane, and French were always up to some deviltry—hotfoot, shoes nailed to the floor, sweatshirts tied in knots, itching powder in jockstraps, smelly cheese smeared inside a hat.

Everybody knew Eddie Collins considered paper littering the dugout steps was bad luck. During a game they'd crumple a piece of paper and throw it while Eddie wasn't looking. When he picked it up, he'd warn them, "Go ahead. Keep it up and we'll lose."

Harold C. Burr recalled in *The Sporting News* that the younger players would get into wrestling matches with Kid Gleason, who was almost as old as Mr. Mack. "Not even big Al Simmons could keep him pinned to the floor for long," wrote Burr. "The Kid always whipped one of those little souvenir bats from his hip pocket and belabored Simmons with it, as if it had been a billie."

Collins always had a fancy name for Gleason. "How are things today, Algernon?" he'd greet him. Another day it might be "Abernathy."

They were competitive with each other. Prior to an old-timers' day, when the current team would play the 1914 team, Lefty Grove teased Eddie Collins, "I'll strike you out."

"You won't strike me out," Collins said. "I'll get a piece of it." Collins fouled off a few and didn't strike out.

They got on anyone who wasn't doing his job. At the same time they were willing to help each other. Bing Miller was as much a hitting coach as an outfielder. An exceptional curveball hitter and a scientific hit-and-run expert, he used his wrists to put the ball anywhere. Some players went to him for batting tips.

Dykes would get on any player who didn't hustle or made a mental mistake. Connie Mack recognized Dykes's value in that role. "Lookit," he told *Daily News* sports editor Ted Von Ziekursch, "he's worth his weight in gold because he keeps the boys going. He's what I'd call a great team player. Why, he has them all on their toes and playing to win no matter how far behind we may be. I'll say he's a great ball player. You know," he said, poking a long, gnarled-knuckled finger in the air, "I mean that. I'm not just talking to praise a ball player."

Dykes was also the one to cut through tension with a wisecrack. Connie Mack appreciated that role:

> You know, the boys get all tightened up and disagreeable on any team sometimes. It's a strain, especially when you're out front, and the team right back of you keeps on winning as regularly as you do. Some of the boys get to thinking mean things about each other, or saying them. First thing you know there's bad blood or ill feeling, and it doesn't make for good teamwork. That's where Jimmie Dykes helps a lot. He's the kind of a fellow that's just naturally a swell fellow. He'll say something that makes the fellow who is sore see how foolish he is. Or he'll make everybody laugh, not like a clown, but just like a regular fellow, and that ends it.

Dykes and Bing Miller swapped insults all day long but were the closest buddies in baseball. Arthur Daley of the *New York Times* wrote of a day when Dykes was riding one of the Athletics' favorite targets, Washington pitcher Firpo Marberry. The next time Dykes was at bat Marberry threw at him. Dykes swung and flung the bat toward the mound. The umpires had to separate them. After the game Marberry was waiting for Dykes.

Before they could tangle, Miller brushed Dykes aside. "Okay," Miller said to Marberry, "if you want to fight, let's go." They stood looking at each other, then Miller said, "There's no action here, Fat Boy. Let's go."

Cochrane took up flying, until Connie Mack found out that he had gone up in a glider and put a stop to that foolishness.

On the long train rides they worked crossword puzzles, read magazines and mysteries and westerns, played cards and the match game, sang, talked baseball, and argued about anything and everything. Kid Gleason played solitaire. There was usually a low-stakes crap game—known as African golf, galloping dominoes, or Alabama marbles—in the washroom.

Not everybody in the league appreciated Mack's boys. Bucky Harris, possibly smarting under the Senators' disappointing dive into the second division, told John Kieran the A's were "a stiff-necked bunch of guys, and if they win the pennant they will be even more impossible."

The players read it, and the next time the Washington club came to Shibe Park, the mortar fire from both dugouts was louder than ever.

In the National League the Cubs had an 8-game lead over the Pirates in mid-August. But neither Connie Mack nor Joe McCarthy was doing any predicting. In the previous two years the Cubs had been in front with two months to go and had finished fourth and third. It didn't take a long memory for Mack to recall that just a year ago the Yankees had led by 12 or 13 games in August only to see it all evaporate. But John Shibe went ahead and ordered the construction of an additional seven hundred temporary box seats for the World Series.

Connie Mack's biggest concern at this point was that his boys would ease up, begin celebrating too soon, and lose their edge if not the pennant. There were reports of some of his stars' hats getting tight, and they were asking for a fee to be interviewed by the press. Mack chose to do something about it when they stopped off in Toledo for an exhibition game on August 9. At a luncheon at the Willys-Overland automobile plant before the game, he was asked to speak. Ed Pollock was there and wrote about it:

He introduced each member of the club, then said something like this: "Because I don't go into the dressing room, I don't have a chance to talk to my boys very often, and if you don't mind I'm going to talk to them now, just as if we were in the clubhouse."

He really tore into them, told them he knew some of them had been partying, that he wasn't going to do anything about it, but would if it continued, said it wasn't fair to the players who were trying so hard, and advised them to give up good times until after the season was over and they had won the pennant and world series. Everyone gave him a great hand when he sat down. The players applauded as much as the auto execs. The toastmaster had no sooner taken over than Connie was on his feet again, asking if he could have another minute. He had forgotten to make any remarks about the home town ball club and he wanted to square himself with the home town men who were there. The club wasn't doing so well, but Connie Mack assured them it wasn't the manager's fault. The manager, he said, was a very good baseball man and given sufficient time would bring the club around where it would be in contention for the pennant.

The toastmaster then introduced the [home team] manager to say a few words of thanks to Connie. "I'm sure what you have said about our manager is true, Mr. Mack. Let's hear from the manager of the Toledo club, Mr. Casey Stengel."

The Athletics rolled through August, adding to their lead until all doubts disappeared. Just before they returned home for an extended September stay, Connie Mack called another meeting in a hotel ballroom. He had a core of thirty-something veterans—and one who was past forty-five—but most of them, along with the younger players, had never been on a big league championship team. Mack thought some fatherly advice was in order. Westbrook Pegler, with confirmation from Kid Gleason, reported his comments: "Well, you are great fellows with the public now and beginning to meet strangers who want to take you out to drinking parties, and women who suddenly think you're a hero. They weren't hunting you up last year, and I think you all know the reason why they are chasing you now. It's because you are up. You are the champions. I don't need to tell you what this kind of friends can do to you, either, because you know as much about that as I do. Just remember how fleeting fame and celebrity can be."

Kid Gleason told Pegler, "He is no glory-be-to-God man, you understand, but when he takes it into his mind to talk to a ball club about things like that, he is the greatest preacher I ever heard in my life. I am no young squirt myself and I knew Connie before most of these ballplayers were born, but he even made my hair stand on end, what few hairs I have."

Fans all over the country were happily rooting the Athletics home. In Atlanta the *Constitution* sportswriter Ed Danforth received a constant flow of poetic tributes to "the old man," of which the best, said Danforth, was this:

> Wave the flags for Connie Mack
> For he has come back
> After stumbling along all those years
> Amid the bleachers' grinding jeers
> At last old Connie's out on top
> This time the A's will not flop

Mack picked up veteran first baseman George Burns, a local boy who had been ridden out of town by the Philadelphia hecklers in 1919 after two years with the A's, to give Jimmy Foxx some days off. He gave neophyte infielder Newell "Bud" Morse a line in the record books by using him in 8 games to rest Max Bishop and gave good-field-no-hit shortstop Jimmy Cronin some playing time. They were all in the lineup at 4:24 on the Shibe Park clock on Saturday, September 14, when George Earnshaw threw the last pitch in a 5–0 win over Chicago to clinch the pennant.

For the next three weeks Mack gave his regulars more time off, with one admonition: "No golf."

Rudell Miller was a veteran minor league third baseman who had played on a semipro team against the A's in Battle Creek, Michigan, in July. Connie Mack had signed him and sent him to Martinsburg, then brought him up in September. On September 19 his name was on the lineup card. After infield practice Miller was sitting on a trunk in the dressing room. Connie Mack walked over to him and patted him on the shoulder. "Relax," Mack said, "this is just another ball game."

"The memory of Connie Mack's doing that to calm an obscure rookie's nerves stayed with me," Miller said sixty years later.

"Al Simmons had broken Mack's no-golf rule and Mack found out about it," Miller recalled. "So Mack made him show up and play that day—the only regular in the game with us reserves."

Rudy Miller played in 2 games for the Athletics, then was sold to Montreal. He carried with him one other unforgettable memory of Connie Mack: "He wrote me a letter the following January from Mount Plymouth, Florida: 'Dear Mr. Miller: You have by this time no doubt received a contract from Montreal, and if you have not you will very soon. Hope you have a good season[,] many of them. With very best wishes.' He didn't have to do that. I appreciated it."

Two other rookies made their debuts in late September and stayed around a while.

One Sunday afternoon in June of 1928 Cy Perkins and Jimmie Dykes had gone to the Jersey shore, where they took in a semipro game. Somebody recognized them and asked Perkins to umpire the game. Perkins was impressed with one of the pitchers, a husky 6-foot-2 right-hander named Roger Cramer, and invited him to come to Shibe Park for a tryout. There Connie Mack watched him throw to Perkins, then take some swings. He wasn't impressed with his pitching, but he liked the way Cramer swung the bat.

"Don't let that boy out of the park without signing," Mack told Perkins.

Cramer finished the season pitching batting practice for the A's and signed for $2,000 for 1929. In the spring Mack told him, "I'm sending you to Martinsburg for [manager] Dan O'Leary to make an outfielder out of you."

O'Leary's third baseman was hurt, so that's where Cramer played in addition to pitching a few games. When the third baseman returned, Cramer moved to the outfield. He had a big, fast stride and covered a lot of ground, which earned him the nickname "Flit" among the players. But he had a lot to learn out there. Connie Mack was right about his hitting potential. He could drag a bunt or reach the walls, and he set a league record, batting .404 in 104 games.

Recalled in September, Cramer pinch-hit for Ed Rommel on the eighteenth and played one game in left field four days later without a hit.

Eric McNair had the most noteworthy debut among the recruits. "The first look I had at him," said Mack, "I thought he would make good. There was an indescribable something about his swing and gait on the field that impressed me. I knew he was always on his toes and hustling." Bought from Memphis, which had farmed him out to Knoxville, where he had hit .391, for $30,000, the twenty-year-old shortstop from Mississippi had 3 hits and scored the winning run in the tenth inning to beat Detroit, 2–1, on September 20. In 4 games he batted .500.

The season ended on Sunday, October 6, in New York. Before the game, eight of the A's received their first endorsement deals, from Majestic Radios.

That night the Majestic Theater of the Air presented a one-hour drama with a World Series background written by Ring Lardner. The players didn't hear it. They were on the train to Philadelphia, where they changed to a sleeper headed for Chicago.

Bill Brandt once asked Connie Mack to describe a perfect baseball team. After going over the specifics for each position Mack added, "Then, when you get that team, you'll win the pennant if the breaks are with you."

The 1929 Athletics didn't need the breaks. They made their own. They had Eddie Collins coaching at third base and reading pitchers and telling batters what was coming. Al Simmons didn't want to know. Jimmy Foxx did. Even if Collins missed a few, those who wanted the tips maintained their confidence in him. They read the shortstops who were taking the catchers' signs and relaying them to the other infielders.

The Athletics won 104 games and finished 18 ahead of the Yankees. They were the first team to have five players score 100 or more runs. Al Simmons's 212 hits went for a league-best 373 total bases. He led in RBIs and missed the batting title by .004. Had the league not dropped its MVP balloting that year (the writers would resume it in 1931), he would have won it.

Max Bishop led the league in walks, twice collecting 8 in a doubleheader. He would wind up with the highest on-base percentage for lead-off men in the twentieth century—.423. The peripatetic Jimmie Dykes played second and third and short and hit .327.

Ring Lardner had been turned off by baseball after the 1919 World Series, but his interest was revived by the colorful characters corralled by Connie Mack. He was particularly intrigued by Jimmy Foxx's power and speed.

Foxx displayed the same kind of power that put him alongside Babe Ruth in the memories of those who saw him. His wallops over the Shibe Park left-field roof would be later described to the next generation of Philadelphia fans with the same expressions of awe and wonder as Babe Ruth's launchings over the Twentieth Street rooftops.

The A's outfield was filled with good, accurate arms. They knew how to hit a cutoff man and rarely made a mistake. Later Connie Mack recalled seeing Simmons throw to the wrong base only once.

The peerless Mickey Cochrane caught 135 games and batted .331. After the season, Connie Mack thanked him with a check for $3,000.

With Rommel, Walberg, and Quinn for relief work, Mack had little need to call on Lefty Grove, who finished 4 victories but had no decisions in relief in his 20-6 record. Earnshaw had stayed in shape from the start of spring training and emerged as a dominant pitcher, winning 24 games.

On a trip to New York in August, Connie Mack had chatted with Miller Huggins, who conceded the Yankees were out of the race. "But I already am building for next season," Huggins said, "when we'll be right back in there giving you the battle of your lives."

Within a few weeks Huggins was battling for his own life. He lost that fight on September 25, defeated at fifty by pyemia with complications of infections and pneumonia. About a week later Eddie Collins was contacted by someone in the Yankees' office. Jake Ruppert wanted to see him. Collins had turned down three offers to manage other clubs since rejoining the Athletics, preferring to stay with Connie Mack, earning $15,000 a year as a coach.

Collins had never told Mack about those offers, rejecting them without a second thought. But this was the Yankees, considered by people in the business as the best job in baseball. Collins went to Mack and told him that Ruppert wanted to see him.

Collins later wrote in a June 23, 1934, *Saturday Evening Post* article that after asking Tom Shibe to join them, Mr. Mack said, "Be sure of what you want to do, Eddie. You know we'd be the last ones to stand in the path of your advancement. But Mr. Shibe and I feel you should know something before you go to New York. If you stay here it is our plan to have you succeed me as manager."

Collins went to Ruppert's apartment in New York and said, "Colonel, I would feel more comfortable if you did not go further with your offer. I'd rather not know what I'm refusing. I talked with Connie Mack and Mr. Shibe and they have plans for me."

"[Collins] knows for sure that he had the big chance—and passed it up" to stay with Connie Mack, commented New York columnist Ford Frick. "That's real friendship when a man does that."

Why did Connie Mack say what he said to Collins? Perhaps he had meant it when, during his illness the previous winter, he had said he hoped to manage until he was seventy—only three years away. When he wrote the article five years later, Collins had just left to become general manager of the Red Sox. Perhaps he realized by then that he would be an old man himself before Connie Mack ever quit.

The Cubs maintained their lead and finished 10½ games in front of the Pirates for their first pennant in eleven years and the first for Joe McCarthy.

When he had signed to manage the Cubs in 1926, some friends in German-town had arranged a dinner for him. Connie Mack was one of the speakers. He predicted a long big league career for McCarthy.

When McCarthy got up to speak, he said he was happy to see Mr. Mack and hoped to have the pleasure of meeting him in a World Series soon. The Cubs had finished last in 1925.

"Everybody laughed," McCarthy recalled. "They thought that was funny."

As a teenager Joe had waited with other kids outside Columbia Park for a glimpse of the manager of the new Philadelphia Athletics. He had never played in the major leagues. He knew that when he was managing at Lou-isville, Mack had recommended him to Cubs president William Veeck for the big league job. Connie Mack was his idol, the man he hoped to emulate as a manager. (Forty years later Red Sox scout Broadway Charlie Wagner was visiting McCarthy at his home in Buffalo. Wagner noticed that there were no baseball photos in the living room. As they walked upstairs to the den, at the top of the stairs Wagner saw one large photo of Connie Mack. McCarthy noticed Wagner looking at it and said, "That fellow gave me my chance to manage in the big leagues.")

Connie Mack had not seen the Cubs, who trained in California. He sent Ira Thomas to Wrigley Field primarily to scout their pitchers. At the end of the season he asked White Sox pitchers Ted Lyons, Red Faber, and Tommy Thomas to come to his office and tell him what they knew about the Cubs' hitters that they had faced in the city series. Lyons had been a 20-game win-ner twice with the second-division Sox, who had finished seventh. When Lyons arrived, Mack reminded him that the Athletics had tried to sign him nine years earlier and Lyons had turned them down. He'd been toiling in the second division in Chicago ever since.

"If you'd signed with my ball club, you'd be on a pennant winner," Mack said.

"Mr. Mack, I could have been down in Podunk somewhere too," said Lyons," 'cause you've got Earnshaw, Grove, and Walberg and I'd have a hard time breaking in there."

"We could have found a place for you," Mack said.

Joe McCarthy had not seen the Athletics all year. He asked Joe Tinker to scout them in their last series in New York. Later some Cubs complained that Tinker had come back with all the wrong dope.

That was Connie Mack's intention.

25 | WORLD CHAMPIONS

For the next twenty years, whenever Connie Mack was called upon to speak at a luncheon or banquet, his favorite subject was how Howard Ehmke came to pitch the 1929 World Series opener. Mack was a showman, understated—unlike (say) a Jimmy Durante—but a showman nevertheless.

Just as there are eight different towns in the West claiming the burial ground of Billy the Kid, there are as many versions of the Howard Ehmke story. That's partly because the participants told it in different ways at different times. Sometimes the fateful conversation Mack described took place outside the clubhouse before a team meeting or in Mack's office or while Mack and Ehmke rode downtown together. Sometimes it happened in mid-August, other times in mid-September.

Here's the way Mack often told it:

"Just before the team went west for the last time that year," Mack would say, "I called Howard into my office and said, 'Howard, the time has come for us to part.'

"He looked at me. 'Mr. Mack,' he said, 'I have always wanted to pitch in a World Series.'"

Then Mack, raising his right fist in the air, lifting his thin, high-pitched voice about as loud as he ever did, would portray Ehmke's declaring, "I've got one good game left in me and I'd like to give it to you in October."

"That was what I wanted to hear," Mack would say. "'All right, Howard,' I told him. 'When we go west I want you to stay here. When the Cubs come in to play the Phillies, you watch them. Learn all you can about their hitters. Say nothing to anybody. You are my opening pitcher for the World Series.'"

Immediately after that historic World Series opener of October 8, Howard Ehmke said, "I knew a month ago that I would start and my boss knew it too. Barring injury or illness there never has been any doubt about it."

These accounts have some problems squaring with the facts.

For example, the Athletics' last western trip began on August 8, two months before the World Series began. There was no way that Connie Mack would make such a commitment to Howard Ehmke a month, a week, or even an hour before the Series opener.

Let's begin with Ehmke the pitcher. At Detroit and Boston in the ten years before coming to the A's, Ehmke was typed as peculiar, temperamental, hard to handle, undependable. At thirty-five he was a smart pitcher with good control and an assortment of slow curves that made his occasional fastball that much more effective. But his innings pitched had fallen sharply each year with the A's. Most of the time his arm felt dead. He needed two or three weeks' rest between starts. By mid-June of the '29 season he had appeared in only five games.

Connie Mack had studied him and concluded that Ehmke had to believe that he was "ready," his arm had to feel "right" to him, or he couldn't get anybody out. When he felt ready, he could be almost unbeatable. To his teammates, Ehmke was one of those pitchers who could win if he was "in the mood."

So Mack learned to ask him if he felt "right" before handing him the warmup ball. And he made it clear that he expected a straight answer. On June 23 in New York Ehmke pitched into the eighth inning before Earnshaw came in and finished the 7–4 win. Seventeen days later in St. Louis he pitched a 2-hitter against the Browns, winning 4–1. On July 26 he gave up 4 hits and no walks in beating Chicago 3–1.

Then on August 7 at Shibe Park the Yankees clobbered him for 8 runs, a second-inning grand slam by Babe Ruth driving him off the mound. Mack was furious. According to Eddie Collins, after the game Mack said to Ehmke, "That's the last game you will ever start for us until you come and tell me you are ready to pitch. You were not ready today. You knew it, and you should have told me so when I sent you out to warm up."

The Athletics were starting on their last western trip the next night. "Don't bother packing," he told Ehmke. "We don't need you."

According to Connie Mack's 1938 *Saturday Evening Post* account, that was the day the basis of his later after-dinner oratory occurred. The Athletics had a 10½-game lead at the time, but Connie Mack was not about to start planning his World Series pitching rotation on August 8, especially with the National League race between the Cubs and Pirates still far from settled. An exhibition game between the A's and Pirates in Pittsburgh was being advertised as a preview of the World Series.

"Weeks before the end of the season I arrived late for a clubhouse meeting," the *Post* article quoted Mack. "I hesitated at the door, caught Ehmke's eye and beckoned him to follow me. Outside the locker room door I said, 'Howard, it looks as though I'm going to have to let you go. I'm sorry to do this so late in the season, Howard, but I don't think you can be any help to us.'"

Mack went on to say he was testing Ehmke, looking for a show of spirit. When Ehmke said he had always wanted to be in a World Series and this was as close as he had ever gotten, Mack asked him, "Do you think you could win a game in the series?" That's when the right arm came up and the declaration was made that "I've got one good game left in me and I'd like to give it to you in October."

Mack said he told Ehmke to stay home and scout the Cubs and he would pitch a game—not necessarily the opener, but "a game"—in the Series.

This was the ghostwritten story that appeared nine years later. Perhaps it was written to back up what had become Mack's standard dramatic rendition or because he had recited it that way so often he now believed it.

The Athletics' first stop of the western trip was Toledo. When the writers asked why Ehmke was not with them, Mack said, "Ehmke was left at home because of the reaction of certain men to his many failures." In the *Post* version he said it was "because the fellows all thought he wouldn't be much help to us" and claimed it was a subterfuge to put the writers off the trail. Some writers at the time guessed that Ehmke was left home because he was out of condition.

Back in Philadelphia, Ehmke laughed at the idea that Mack was angry over his showing against New York. "In fact he told me he was gratified at the showing I had made in my three previous games. My arm isn't any too strong and I need a few days' rest."

How do we reconcile this version with the one piece of handwritten evidence we have—the following letter written by Mack (exactly as he wrote it) at the Detroit-Leland Hotel on August 11, three days after the supposed meeting outside the locker room.

Dear Howard:

Have been giving you some thought since leaving Philadelphia and find myself still very much at a loss in regards to your pitching. You probably know as well as myself that all the clubs you have pitched for are under the same impression and this is you can pitch if you wanted to, and the players are of the same opinion. The impression among our players are that you could pitch if you worked one game a week and would then put your stuff on the ball otherwise they figure you are of no help to them. I have come to the conclusion that you figure too much on your soft stuff and in my opinion you cannot get away with it without first showing plenty of speed and both Cochrane and Perkins say you have the speed when you let it go. My letting you remain at home was due to your poor game against New York having had at least fifteen days rest. also had in mind that the players felt the same as I did that you could have done better and for the good of all decided to let you remain at home. Am going to be frank in saying that you have me guessing regarding your pitching. dislike to think that you are thinking wholey about saving your arm and giving no thought to the club. You have been pitching a good many years and the past few years you have not worked in many games so cannot see any club taking you on next season.

Have given you my straight opinion, don't say that its right as I am not a mind reader but want you to get the view of others + myself so you will not view your case from wholy your own view.

Can you help us by working one game a week? Are you sure you can? Must not be any half way about it it's yes or no. If after giving the matter plenty of thought and your decision is that you can do as outlined and help the club by working one game a week join club at Cleveland. In case you feel that its better for the club and yourself to remain at home do so and its OK with me.

> With kind regards,
> Sincerely yours, Connie Mack

Not a word about the World Series or scouting the Cubs. This letter was no crafty deception to mislead the press but a private letter, not meant for publication. If Mack had told Ehmke to stay home and scout the Cubs, who would be in Philadelphia August 22–24, why was he asking him to join them in Cleveland August 14–17 if the pitcher felt he could "help the club?"

Howard Ehmke did not join the team in Cleveland or anywhere else on the trip. He stayed home and worked out on his own.

Every ballplayer yearns to be in a World Series at least once. Ehmke had been in the big leagues for fourteen years. He knew this would probably be his last chance. He also knew that Connie Mack had used few pitchers in his past Series victories—just two in 1910 and three in 1911 and 1913. With the likes of Grove, Earnshaw, Walberg, and Quinn ahead of him, Ehmke's chances seemed slim.

Determined to do everything he could to be ready if given the opportunity, Ehmke went to see Dr. Charles J. Van Ronk, a noted osteopath, for some easing of his shoulder pain. He worked on refining his delivery by sliding farther to the right as he threw. It seemed to him that to the batter, the ball would be coming out of the pitcher's shirt as well as the outfield background. He also decided to heed Mack's advice and mix more fastballs with his curves and change-ups.

Ehmke apparently scouted the Cubs August 22–24, but not because Connie Mack asked him to or had assured him that he would pitch. (Whether he scouted the Pirates too he never said.) He told more than one writer that he went to Baker Bowl each day Chicago was there, sat by himself, kept score, and watched "how every one of the Cubs batted, how they stood in the box, the kind of balls they hit, and the kind they looked weak against. I watched how the Phillies pitched to them, figured how I would pitch to each man. I got all of them except Grimm." (If he had made up the story, Ehmke probably would have missed the detail about Charlie Grimm not playing. Grimm was out at the time with a broken hand.)

When the Athletics returned home on August 29, most of the players assumed that Ehmke was through for the year. Ehmke asked Connie Mack what his status was. Mack said, "When you tell me you are ready to pitch, I will use you."

On September 2 against the Yankees, Ehmke relieved Walberg in the sixth and allowed two base runners the rest of the way, picking up the 6–5 win when the Athletics scored 2 in the ninth. More than seventy thousand turned out for the morning-afternoon sweep of the dethroned champions. On September 13 Ehmke said he was ready, and pitched 8 innings beating the White Sox, 5–2.

That makes the next day the most likely time that Connie Mack had his first conversation with Ehmke about starting a World Series game. It's the date that Ehmke used on an NBC radio program two months after Mack's death (although he also quoted Mack as telling him then to stay home and scout the Cubs, who had been in Philadelphia three weeks earlier). He recalled that Mack told him, "I will take all the responsibility if you pitch and the game is lost." But there were still no promises.

During the last three weeks of August the Cubs got so hot and the Pirates so cold that Pittsburgh's winning 4 out of 5 over the Cubs at the end of the month still left them 11½ games out. Connie Mack then began planning his World Series strategy.

The Cubs had a predominantly right-handed batting order—Rogers Hornsby, Riggs Stephenson, Hack Wilson—all but Charlie Grimm. They were good curve as well as fastball hitters, but they hit like lefties, primarily to right field. The experts at the time said they hit southpaws with ease and gusto, but incomplete stats show only a slightly higher batting average against lefties, whom they faced only about 20 percent of the time. Mack didn't think the National League had anybody with the power of Grove and Walberg, but he decided those two would be more effective in relief than starting. That way the Cubs hitters might see them only once in a game, following a knuckleballer or spitter expert or slow curver like Rommel or Quinn or Ehmke, with no chance to hone their timing in three or four at-bats against the fastballers. And for right-handed power pitching, he had George Earnshaw.

As for Ehmke, his excellent control, off-speed curves, and sidearm delivery coming out of the Wrigley Field crowd to the left of the center-field scoreboard would certainly make him difficult to hit. Tony Lazzeri claimed that Ehmke was the only pitcher who could hide a pitch perfectly beyond detection.

But would Howard Ehmke declare himself "ready" on October 8? Mack would make no decision until he learned the state of the pitcher's mind and arm at game time.

That's the way he explained it to James Isaminger a year later:

I wanted [Ehmke] to pitch in the World Series if his arm was right. We agreed that he would notify me on the morning of the game if he felt right and then I would decide if I would use him. That's why I didn't name my pitcher before the game. A pitcher with such a cranky arm knows alone when he is right. I wanted to hear it from him. Earnshaw would have been my choice for the opener if Ehmke had not been right. I counted on him big to start and relieve. I intended to start Quinn and use Rommel and Shores only in relief. I intended not to start left-handed pitchers unless the series went long and I had to. Had it gone to Game 6 Grove would have started in Chicago. But I would use them in relief. In a short series I thought it best to play out the right-handed pitcher string first and stick to the righthanders as long as they delivered. Game 6 would be Grove, Game 7 Walberg.

That's why Connie Mack truly did not know who would pitch the opener until that day arrived. That's why he was not being coy or evasive when, on September 25 in Boston, he told Bill Brandt, "You can name my pitcher for the first World Series game as well as I can. The pitcher himself won't know until I hand him the warmup ball on October 8. I am not even going to talk about it between now and then."

The Athletics' seven Pullman cars and club car arrived in Chicago about two thirty on the afternoon of Monday, October 7. The Cubs had worked out between eleven and one, leaving Wrigley Field available for the visitors. The A's didn't go near it. They strolled around downtown or took in a movie or lobby-sat at the Edgewater Beach Hotel. Mule Haas was the only man who had played in Wrigley Field, but Mack didn't want them worrying about shadows and angles. He wanted them to relax. Some reporters ventured that Mack didn't want his sluggers taking batting practice in an empty stadium with temporary bleachers that had been erected above the left-field wall to bring the capacity to fifty-one thousand, then having to hit against a live, shirt-sleeved crowd and a busy scoreboard during the game. Eddie Collins pointed out that the last time the Athletics had played the Cubs, in 1910, they hadn't practiced at the old West Side Grounds then and had still won two out of three.

There was a miniature golf course behind the hotel. That evening Ehmke and his roommate, Jimmy Foxx, played until it was dark, then went to bed about nine o'clock. Foxx had not yet heard that his wife, Helen, was giving birth to their first child, a son, at that hour. Ehmke recalled Foxx telling him, "I have an idea the old gentleman will pitch you tomorrow."

"Get in bed and go to sleep and forget about it," Ehmke told him.

"If you do," Foxx said, "I'll hit one for you anyway."

Jimmy Foxx related the same conversation to Herb Haft of the *Washington Post* in 1950.

At eleven the next morning the team meeting began in Connie Mack's suite. It lasted about thirty minutes. Mack went over the Cubs lineup and explained how they would be playing the Cubs' right-handed batters around to the right, infield and outfield, to varying degrees, because that's the way they hit (a shift that paid off, as Bishop and Boley would cut off several hits). Jack Quinn and George Burns were the only players who had been in a World Series. "It's natural for you to be a bit nervous at the start," Mack said, "but after the first inning the nervousness will be gone."

That was it. The players left—all but Ehmke.

"Connie and I were standing over by a window," Eddie Collins told Joe Williams two months later, "with our backs turned, discussing some further details about the game. I didn't even realize that Ehmke was still in the room. But evidently Connie did. At any rate, he suddenly turned, looked at Ehmke, and said, 'Is there anything you want to say to me, Howard?' Ehmke stood in the middle of the room with his hat in his hand.

"'I just wanted to ask if you plan to use me in the Series.'

"'You know what I told you. When you are ready to pitch I will use you.'

"'Well, I'm ready to pitch, and I'm ready right now.'

"All right, Howard. You pitch the game today.'"

Collins was stunned but said nothing. This was the same Connie Mack he had watched play to Rube Waddell's eccentricities and Chief Bender's ego and Eddie Plank's foibles to get their best out of them. Nobody knew Howard Ehmke—or any ballplayer—better than Mack. If Ehmke said he was ready, Mack knew that nothing would faze him and he would pitch the game of his life.

But it wasn't game time yet.

Connie Mack stayed at the hotel for lunch with Collins and Gleason and a guest. Thirty years ago Mack had had a pitcher, Pete Husting, in Milwaukee. A lawyer, Husting had quit the team over a salary dispute. Husting was back pitching for Mack in 1902, winning 14 games for Mack's first pennant winner. Now living in a Chicago suburb, Husting contacted Mack for help in obtaining tickets to the first game. Mack not only did so, but he also invited Husting to lunch that day. Husting brought his eleven-year-old nephew, Tom Erickson, with him. Years later Erickson recalled, "I was embarrassed when I knocked over a glass of milk which luckily spilled into a dish of radishes and not on Connie Mack."

(When Husting died in 1948, the family returned from the funeral to find their home filled with flowers from Connie Mack.)

The Athletics went out to warm up around twelve thirty. Grove, Earnshaw, and Ehmke stayed in the clubhouse. Ehmke ate a chicken sandwich he had brought for lunch.

"Grove couldn't stand it and he went out," Ehmke told Bill Brandt a year later. "Then Earnshaw left. I finally went out. They were shooting Grove and Earnshaw with cameras. Nobody bothered me on the bench."

Al Horwits of the *Ledger* had picked up on the rumor of Ehmke's starting. His paper had headlined Earnshaw to start but hedged with a discussion of Ehmke's shrewdness and extreme sidearm delivery.

"[Al] sat down beside me," Ehmke said. "'Don't worry, Howard,' he said, 'it's just an ordinary game.' I laughed. 'Why, I've got nothing to worry about,' I said. 'If I haven't got my stuff I won't be in there. If I have let the Cubs worry.'"

Earnshaw and Grove were tossing casually in front of the dugout. Cy Perkins and Bing Miller were playing catch. Westbrook Pegler asked Perkins if he knew who was going to start. "I hope Ehmke pitches," Perkins said, "The people don't know what a good pitcher he is when he's good, and I think he is very good just now. He is a finished product."

Just about then Connie Mack appeared. The esteem—approaching awe—that the nation felt for him was captured by John Carmichael ten years later in the *Chicago Daily News*: "We never shall forget the day he paused in his box at Wrigley Field for the first game of the 1929 World Series. . . . As he strode, spare and serene, to greet friends, the athletes on the field were forgotten, and 40,000 fans turned and twisted to look at baseball royalty."

The pioneering syndicator Christy Walsh had signed Mack, Al Simmons, and Mickey Cochrane, along with Babe Ruth and John McGraw, to turn out ghostwritten commentaries on each day's game. Mack's popularity produced the biggest gross sales Walsh would ever see from a World Series—$43,252. Newspapers paid a record $9,662.50 for Mack's words (ghosted by James Isaminger) alone.

Two radio networks broadcast the games, Graham McNamee on NBC and Ted Husing on CBS. Using short-wave transmitters, the broadcasts were heard on 101 domestic stations and throughout the world. Connie Mack's rooters all over the country sought out scarce radios to hear the games. Huge display boards recreating the action went up in cities and towns from the outside of the newspaper office in Worcester, Massachusetts, to the plaza in front of the Palace of Fine Arts in Mexico City.

About one fifteen Ehmke headed for the bullpen and began to throw.

"Al Simmons was sitting next to me," Mack recalled. "He suddenly jumped to his feet and said, 'Is he going to work?'

"'Yes, any objections?'

"'Nope. If you think he can win it's good enough for me.'"

Mickey Cochrane later said he asked the same question and received a similar reply. (In his syndicated column he said, "I expected Ehmke to pitch the second game and was stunned when Connie Mack told me to go over the batters with him. We had a plan for each Cub batter and he executed it perfectly.")

In the Cubs dugout coach Jimmy Burke frantically reminded his hitters of Joe Tinker's scouting report on Ehmke, that he would throw nothing but slop—to put it politely.

But Mack wanted still more assurance. He waited until Ehmke returned to the dugout and said, "I have my stuff" before writing his name on the lineup card.

The start of the game was delayed about fifteen minutes, the result of a plea by William Wrigley to Judge Landis to give hundreds of ticket holders a chance to get through the jammed turnstiles. Ehmke's shoulder began to stiffen.

"Only my control carried me through those first two innings," he recalled. "But by the third inning I had all my stuff back."

It showed. After striking out Kiki Cuyler and Riggs Stephenson in the second, Ehmke faced his first tight spot in the third. Two hits put Cubs on second and third with one out. Ehmke fed Rogers Hornsby slow curves low and outside. Hornsby went fishing, swinging over and early three times. Hack Wilson then fanned on a high fastball, more from surprise than the modest speed of the ball. In the fifth and sixth Ehmke struck out five in a row, including Hornsby and Wilson again. They were all swinging, lunging, off-timed strikeouts.

From the first pitch the bench jockeys began. The Cubs later claimed that the Athletics started it, and they probably did. The Cubs rode Ehmke fiercely all afternoon. It didn't take long for both sides to get loud and personal.

Meanwhile Cubs pitcher Charlie Root was just as stingy with the hits. In the top of the seventh, Hack Wilson made a brilliant diving, skidding catch of a Simmons line drive a foot off the grass. The cheers had hardly died down when Jimmy Foxx drove a high fastball into the center-field bleachers for the first run of the game.

In the last of the seventh the Cubs again had men on second and third with one out. Joe McCarthy went to his bench. Cliff Heathcote lifted a fly ball to Simmons, whose quick throw held the runner at third. Pinch hitter Gabby Hartnett then went down swinging on a fastball.

The A's scored 2 in the ninth on a couple of hits and 2 errors by Cubs shortstop Woody English.

Hack Wilson led off the bottom of the ninth with a line drive into Ehmke's breadbasket. The pitcher threw to first as he went down in a heap. The trainer ran out; the infield gathered around the mound. Connie Mack sent Lefty Grove to warm up. But Ehmke was up in a few minutes ready to continue. Nobody was going to knock him out of this game. Cuyler hit a grounder to Dykes, who threw it into the Athletics' dugout. Stephenson singled to center, scoring Cuyler from second to make it 3–1. Grimm singled to right. With the tying runs on base and 1 out, Connie Mack was this close to calling on Grove. McCarthy sent up Clarence Blair to bat for the catcher Mike Gonzalez. Ehmke had seen Blair subbing for Grimm in August. Blair forced Grimm, Stephenson going to third. McCarthy then called on Chick Tolson, who had been recalled from Los Angeles to fill in for Grimm after the Cubs had left Philadelphia in August. Ehmke had never seen him.

This is how Ehmke described what happened next to Bill Brandt ten months later:

He had me worried. With the score 3–1, it took only one solid drive between the outfielders to tie the score. I tried to make Tolson hit a bad fastball. He wouldn't swing. I threw him five fast ones. The count stood 3 and 2. I called Cochrane out from behind the plate.

"Now Mike," I said, "when you go back there remind them of my control. Get him thinking, see? Tell him this next one is sure to be over the plate. I want him swinging, see? Then when the ball gets about halfway there, you yell, 'Hit it.'"

Well, Mike yelled and Tolson swung. But that yell kind of disturbed his timing. He swung too fast. He swung ahead of the ball and missed it.

On the 1956 radio program Ehmke said he had a 2 and 2 count on Tolson and threw a perfect strike that Bill Klem called a ball. Then he called Cochrane out to the mound and said

"You go back and we'll let this fellow stand in the batter's box just as long as we can and the longer he stands the worse he's going to get and more nervous. Then you get down and give me a sign and we'll still make him wait and I'll stand in the pitcher's box like holding a runner on first base and I'm going to shake my head 'No' and pitch. The pitch is going to be a fastball." Well, when a batter is up there hitting he usually guesses what you're going to throw and if he guesses what you're going to throw it's a little bit tough for the pitcher. But this was the story. I was to shake my head no and pitch immediately so as not to give him a chance for a second guess, and when the ball was on the way to the plate Cochrane was to yell out as loud as he could, 'Hit it.' Well, everything worked along nicely and I pitched and he yelled and Tolson struck at the ball and missed it.

In his syndicated account right after the game, Cochrane's only reference to the ninth inning was Ehmke's meeting him halfway to the mound and saying, "I'll strike this guy out and make him like it."

That was strikeout number 13, breaking Ed Walsh's World Series record of 12 set in 1906. Ehmke's record reigned for twenty-four years.

Home plate umpire Bill Klem said, "Ehmke had something on every ball he pitched and no three in succession were alike. It was a wonderful exhibition of smart pitching."

"Ehmke's sidearm and crossfire delivery coupled with almost perfect control of a change of pace made Cub hitters look small," wrote Frank Graham of the *New York Sun*.

Before the game, Ehmke had sent a request to Klem to hand any ball he was going to throw out of the game to the Athletics' batboy. After the game he selected the seven best as souvenirs for his seven brothers.

The eminent scholar and rabid Red Sox fan Stephen Jay Gould once called the choice of Howard Ehmke to start the 1929 World Series opener "the most famous successful hunch of postseason baseball history."

It was not a hunch as far as Ty Cobb was concerned. "If they are called hunches when they are based on the greatest background of detailed knowledge I have ever had contact with, all right," he told the AP.

"Masterminding with a vengeance," Heywood Broun called it.

John McGraw said it was "smart baseball."

Had the choice of Howard Ehmke to start the first game really been a well-kept secret? How big a surprise was it?

In the weeks leading up to the Series, most of the experts had concentrated on Grove or Earnshaw as the likely starters. The Cubs had lost to left-handers Larry French, Bill Walker, and Carl Hubbell in the last two weeks of the season. Ralph McGill of the *Atlanta Constitution* was one of the few who discerned Mack's thinking, "grooming Jack Quinn and Howard Ehmke to do some Series work."

Lee Allen in *The American League Story* wrote, "It was the best kept secret in the game, and perhaps the most daring bit of strategy in major league history. Eddie Collins was told about the plan, but the other players were kept in ignorance."

Allen based that on the 1938 *Saturday Evening Post* story, in which Mack said, "I took nobody but Eddie Collins into my confidence."

But just two months after the Series, Joe Williams quoted Collins that when Mack told Ehmke on the morning of the game that he would pitch, "I almost swooned on the spot, so great was my astonishment at the audacity of the aged leader of the A's."

Sometimes in later years Joe McCarthy would say it was a big surprise to him, but at the time he talked differently. In 1945 Red Smith revealed a story the late Ring Lardner had told him in the Phillies press box in 1930: "I was talking to McCarthy before the series and he told me, 'We're not afraid of Grove and Earnshaw. We can hit speed. But there's one pitcher on that club who is. . . . Here McCarthy used an indelicate expression to describe the stuff Ehmke threw. 'That pitcher,' Joe told me, 'is Howard Ehmke. And he's the so-and-so we're going to see in this series.'"

Connie Jr. was sixteen at the time. "I usually knew just about everything Dad was going to do on the field," he recalled, "but he never told me about planning to start Ehmke."

Bob Paul, sports editor of the *Philadelphia Daily News*, claimed that Bevo LeBourveau tipped him off on the train going to Chicago. Certainly Connie Mack did not take Bevo into his confidence. It may well be that Ehmke himself, although given no guarantee by Mack, could not resist dropping hints that he was going to start the opener, no ifs or maybes about it.

Paul said that when he told broadcaster Ted Husing an hour before the game, Husing refused to believe it until he saw it for himself.

Some books have Connie Mack telling Bill Brandt the night before the opener that Ehmke would start and Brandt hinting at it in his overnight *New York Times* dispatch. Brandt did hint at it, but it wasn't because Connie Mack told him. Brandt wrote:

The Mack camp radiates mystery in all directions. The first-line pitchers, Grove, Walberg, Earnshaw, and Quinn all expect to be called upon to pitch the opener, while the innermost wise whispers around the lobby hint that Howard Ehmke, of all persons, will toe the slab when umpire Bill Klem says, "Play ball."

One veteran Athletics fan, who has followed the team in all its vicissitudes for thirty years, whispered the following, "Connie told me last week that Ehmke could pitch any game he wanted to. 'I consider Ehmke the greatest pitching artist I ever saw,' were Connie's exact words. 'I figure him for one game in the world's series. I don't know which one, but whatever day he says to me, "I'm ready," that's the day Ehmke will go to the mound.'"

(The "veteran Athletics fan" may well have been Dr. James Penniman, who was well known to Brandt [a former Philadelphia writer], had indeed followed the team since its first season in 1901, and was a close friend of Connie Mack's.)

Brandt's story continued, "Your correspondent ran down Ehmke. 'How do you feel?' 'Fine,' was the reply. 'Don't be surprised if I'm in there tomorrow. All depends on how the arm feels in the morning.'"

This is another clue that Connie Mack had made no assurances to Ehmke about starting the opener back in August or September.

If Connie Mack had told anybody on the eve of the opener, he would not have been so evasive with Billy Evans. The veteran umpire, now general manager of the Cleveland Indians and frequent newspaper columnist, was a longtime friend and admirer of Mack's. He was covering the Series for a syndicate. Like most of the experts, he was sure that Grove would start the next day. When he said as much to Mack that evening, Mack said, "I'm not so sure of that. I have a half-dozen pitchers able to make trouble for the Cubs."

As he was about to depart, Evans later wrote in the *Rotarian*, he again mentioned Grove's starting to Mack. "I can still see the twinkle in his eye as he repeated, 'I'm not so sure of that. I may surprise you.'"

Back at his typewriter, Evans led off with his certainty that Grove would start. He looked at it, tore it up, and wrote that Grove was "Mack's logical choice," then hedged by adding that Mack might surprise with Jack Quinn or Eddie Rommel.

"I couldn't believe my eyes as I watched Ehmke warm up," wrote Evans. "Surely Mack was kidding. He wouldn't dare tempt fate by using a lame-arm pitcher with a half-dozen able-bodied stars sitting on the bench."

A little over three years later Connie Mack asked Ehmke, then a full-time tarpaulin salesman, to come up to his office in the tower at Shibe Park on

December 23. It was Mack's seventieth birthday. Mr. Mack handed him a signed photograph inscribed: "To Howard Ehmke, who I consider the greatest pitching artist of his day. Your pitching in the first World Series game of 1929, when you broke all World Series records by striking out 13 Cubs, gave me the thrill that will always be remembered by me."

"Every word comes from my heart," Mack told him. "It's a remembrance of an event that somehow will always belong to you and me."

Ehmke kept the photograph wrapped in tissue paper and stored away and never showed it to anyone until Connie Mack died in 1956.

Howard Ehmke's opening-game victory remains among the best-known World Series legends in the baseball world. Three generations later knowledgeable baseball fans could tell you who won that first game of the 1929 World Series but not who won the opener in any other long-ago year. In 1952 it would be recognized as "pulling a Connie Mack" when Chuck Dressen of the Dodgers announced he would start rookie right-hander Joe Landrum, who had won 1 game during the season, in Game 3 of the Series against the Yankees. (At the last minute Dressen switched to the veteran Preacher Roe.)

In 2006 a Minneapolis writer suggested Twins manager Ron Gardenhire use Mack's strategy and spring a surprise starter against the Yankees in the first game of the playoffs.

There were no surprises the next day. It was a cold, dreary day all around for Chicago fans. George Earnshaw, considered by some writers to be Mack's best bet against the Cubs, started against Pat Malone. In the third Jimmy Foxx launched his second homer in two days, a 3-run job into the temporary seats extending beyond the outer wall. In the fourth the A's scored 3 more and drove out Malone. When Earnshaw walked the bases loaded in the bottom of the third, Mack sent Bill Shores to warm up. But Earnshaw survived until the Cubs scored 3 in the fifth on 5 singles, and it was Lefty Grove time. Joe McCarthy sent Gabby Hartnett up to pinch-hit, representing the tying run. Grove struck him out. Al Simmons iced the 9–3 win with a 2-run home run in the eighth. By that time Grove's chronically sore fingertips were oozing blood, but Mack inexplicably left him in to the finish. Or perhaps he didn't feel secure enough with a 6-run lead to use Shores for 2 innings. Grove scattered 3 hits and struck out 6 in 4⅓ innings. Earnshaw had fanned 7. (Earnshaw earned the win despite pitching fewer than 5 innings. The standard was 4 innings for starting pitchers at the time.)

The trains were waiting to take them to Philadelphia.

A tale told by some Negro League old-timers and repeated in several books claimed that there was "talk" around Philadelphia that Connie Mack was short of players before the Series and wanted to sign some local black players—"Biz Mackey and Santop and all them"—to fill out his team. But, so went the story, Mack felt that other owners might not like it, or, in some versions, "they" wouldn't let him. This is pure bunk. Connie Mack never had any such idea. The Athletics were not short of players; their entire roster was healthy except for Joe Boley, who played despite a lame arm. Mack had a bench full of able-bodied reserves but used his regular lineup in every game.

The Athletics were a beaming bunch talking sweep when their train arrived at 2:10 on Thursday and was greeted by about five thousand fans. The Cubs had arrived a few hours earlier, feeling as though they hadn't gotten the breaks and their luck would turn. They went to the Ben Franklin Hotel, where they occupied an entire floor with their own private dining room and chef, private elevator, and gym. They even had radios in their rooms. When Connie Mack arrived home, he found a full house at 604 W. Cliveden. He had invited his cousin, Mary Dempsey, and her children (she had ten) to come down from Worcester and stay at the Mack home and go to the games. She brought two daughters and one son with her. Connie Jr. was an end on the Germantown football team. They had a game against Haverford on Friday. Junior would be able to stay for 5 innings before someone drove him to his own game. When he arrived, Haverford was leading 6–0 in the first quarter. Junior's pass receptions helped his team win 7–6.

It had been a long time since the club's front office had been busy in October.

Hoping to curb scalping and give a large number of fans a chance to see the games, the Athletics refused all requests for blocks of tickets. The players were entitled to buy ten sets. Boley, Rommel, and Cochrane were the first to pick them up. The public was invited to mail in requests for no more than two sets of tickets for three games, but those postmarked prior to September 16 would be discarded.

Dr. James Penniman was the first person to be assured of receiving World Series tickets. Having sent in a check before applications were being accepted, he received a note from Connie Mack: "Am returning you the check which you can destroy. Have approved of your receiving two (2) seats and the club will notify you later how you will receive and pay for same."

Tickets, marked "Greater Shibe Park" and signed "C. McGillicuddy, manager," were $5.50 grandstand, $6.60 box seats. The lucky applicants would be sent white notification slips that could be exchanged for the tickets. The scalpers were one step ahead of John Shibe. They immediately opened offices to buy and sell the notification slips, offering as much as $25 for a slip that had cost the lucky holder a two-cent stamp. At least five thousand tickets were said to have come into scalpers' hands. But John Shibe had made it clear that tickets bought from scalpers would not be honored, and they weren't. The government required scalpers to stamp tickets with their resale prices so the proper tax could be collected on their sale, and that was the tell-tale mark spotted by George Brand and his gate attendants. There were also reports of phony tickets being printed and sold for up to $75 each. More than one hundred ticket holders a day were refused admission, causing some chaos at the gates. Those empty seats at game time were quickly filled by standing-room ticket holders.

The line for the one dollar bleacher seats had begun to form around ten o'clock on Wednesday night.

Although the Athletics said they expected about forty thousand attendance, without the scalpers' tickets, the official announced attendance would be only 29,921 for each game.

Stewart Boggs was in charge of the Shibe Park second-tier press box, which had been expanded to the sides and back to accommodate four hundred, eight times its usual capacity for writers, radio men, and telegraphers. Stoney McLinn, chairman of the local writers' chapter, had to deal with more than twelve hundred applications, some from Japan, Germany, Cuba, and Canada. The local writers' association put together its own souvenir program, including a full-page profile of each player and past World Series records. Former Mackmen Jack Barry, Frank Baker, and Joe Bush were at the first game but were not admitted to the press box.

Concessions manager Bob Schroeder and head usher John P. Collins were busy hiring vendors and 231 additional ushers. The usual staff of ushers was 25 men and 15 women. The usherettes wore ankle-length dress uniforms and cloches in the latest style.

John Shibe hung no bunting around the ballpark. He engaged the comedy act of Al Schacht and Nick Altrock to entertain the crowd before each game. Gramophone records blaring through the right-field amplifiers had replaced the bands that used to play before the games.

Hopes of the homeowners on Twentieth Street for big paydays from rooftop bleachers were temporarily threatened when building inspectors pronounced the rooftops unsafe for spectators. The homeowners went to court, where a three-judge panel sided with them.

If the writers were surprised when Howard Ehmke started the first game, they were completely thrown when Mack came back with George Earnshaw after one day's rest. With Rommel, Walberg, Quinn, and Shores well rested—none had thrown a pitch so far—the consensus had been Quinn, with Shores representing "Mack's penchant for surprises."

It wasn't the first time Mack had gone with a big, strong pitcher on a day's rest. He had won two games with Bender that way in 1911 and two with Jack Coombs in 1910—all complete games.

Earnshaw, despite being the winner on Wednesday, had gone through a lapse of control in one inning and been driven out by a barrage of singles in the fifth. To Connie Mack that meant he had pitched just half a game, equivalent to a long relief job. He had thrown 112 pitches. But only the press box occupants counted such things.

It looked like a good move as Earnshaw held the Cubs scoreless for 5 innings, despite a lead-off triple by Hack Wilson in the second, which might have been scored as an error on Mack's scorecard-waving or Earnshaw's misplaced pitch. Mack had waved Bing Miller to right-center. Wilson's hit went to straightaway center and could have been caught if Miller hadn't moved.

The Athletics had never seen a pitcher's delivery like that of Cubs starter Guy Bush, whose follow-through ended with him kneeling on the mound "like a dervish on a prayer rug," said one writer. He completely handcuffed Simmons and Foxx. But the rest kept Bush in constant trouble. In the second the ever-alert Jimmie Dykes pulled what John McGraw called "one of the smartest plays ever seen in a world's championship series," although it never showed up in the box score. In the second inning Dykes was on third and Boley on second with 2 out and Earnshaw at bat. When Bush began a full windup, Dykes dashed for home and slid in safely. But the pitch was called strike 3, nullifying the steal.

The left-on-base column was adding up until Bing Miller drove in a fifth-inning run.

In the sixth the Cubs turned a lead-off walk to the pitcher, an error on a slow grounder toward third that Dykes failed to pick up (costing the A's a double play), and singles by Hornsby and Cuyler into 3 runs. That was it. Both sides threatened, but neither scored again. Earnshaw struck out 10. The A's left 10 runners on base.

"A tough game to lose, but the Cubs deserved to win," Connie Mack told reporters after the game. "Earnshaw pitched a good game, but so did Guy Bush. We had many opportunities, but we failed to make the most of them. Tomorrow is another day."

AP writer Edward J. Neil reported a less gracious reaction from Earnshaw in the runway to the clubhouse. "How do I feel about it? How would anyone feel about it?" The rest, Neil wrote, "passed on into the unreportable."

In the Cubs' quarters, Neil found a high-spirited bunch and an interesting story. The story was not attributed to any one source but was talked about by several players. Connie Mack, it seems, had figured that someone would be scouting the Athletics in late September. Maybe he had spotted Joe Tinker in the stands. Mack ordered his hitters to swing at pitches they normally let go by and deliberately miss those they liked in the games Tinker saw. Foxx, for example, let the high fastballs go by and swung at low ones. The result was a report from Tinker full of misinformation. Foxx had hit 2 home runs in the first 2 games. On the train from Chicago, McCarthy was bemoaning the situation to an American League pitcher who set him straight on the real tendencies of Connie Mack's sluggers. In today's game, Foxx had seen nothing but low pitches. He struck out once and hit three ground balls.

The National League team had won its first Series game since 1926. The tide of confidence had swung to the visitors, even though they were still down 2–1. Joe McCarthy was ready to come back with his ace, Charlie Root, who had pitched well against Ehmke on Tuesday.

Mack still had Quinn, Walberg, Grove, and Shores to choose from, and nobody was making any predictions. Only Mack knew it would not be Grove. He was not feeling well and was handicapped by sore fingers on his left hand. Because of the way he gripped the ball, Mack revealed later, the skin on the tips of the first two fingers was rubbed raw after 9 innings. He had pitched with that problem all season. By now the skin was worn away. He could work a few innings at top speed, but working 9 innings was out of the question.

That fit in with Mack's strategy of going with right-handers as far as he could and letting the Cubs see only late-inning glimpses of Grove and Walberg for maximum effect.

Asked late in life if he ever tired of watching baseball games, Branch Rickey said, "Never. The next game may be the best I ever saw."

Connie Mack had been in baseball for forty-six years before he saw the most unforgettable game of his career. He was not alone. Looking back over a lengthy career that began in 1909, writer Fred Lieb called it his biggest baseball thrill. Veteran Chicago writer and broadcaster Hal Totten said the same thing, calling it "a day never to be forgotten."

The date was Saturday, October 12, 1929.

During batting practice all the Athletics were on the field except Walberg and Quinn, leading the Cubs to speculate that either one of them would be pitching. They wondered if Quinn was still throwing a spitter. Rogers Hornsby, whose outspoken attitude would never change, said, "What's the difference who pitches or what he throws? It's up to you. Either you do or you don't."

It was Jack Quinn's turn to start. Quinn had been pitching for twenty years. He was really forty-six, though at the time nobody knew that for sure. ("Will Mack start Clark Griffith next?" quipped a few writers.) Unlike Ehmke, he had carried a full load of starting and relieving all season, working 161 innings. He was another mix-'em-up artist, the kind fastball maulers hate to face.

The Cubs began the game in the same strikeout style of the first three games, Hornsby and Cuyler each fanning for the seventh time. They made the first noise of the day in the fourth, when Cuyler singled and Grimm homered over the right-field wall.

The sun, which in the summer aimed at right field, was going down directly behind home plate by mid-October. It was also positioned higher at game time than during the regular season since the Series games started at one thirty, two hours earlier than usual. In the last of the fifth Hack Wilson came in for a high fly ball hit by Dykes, lost it in the sun despite his sunglasses, and dropped it. Two batters later he made an outstanding running catch on Boley's drive near the scoreboard that saved a run.

The Cubs opened the sixth with four straight singles that drove out Quinn. Mack called on Walberg. Grimm bunted. Walberg cut in front of Dykes, picked it up, and threw it into right field. Two runs scored. Grimm went to third, where he scored on Zack Taylor's fly to center. Walberg then struck out Root and MacMillan. The Cubs led 7–0.

When Walberg came into the dugout, Mack said to him, "Rube, I'm going to put somebody else in to pitch the next inning because I don't want the Cubs to see too much of you. But you are going to get another chance in a more advantageous spot later on."

Meanwhile, Charlie Root kept cruising along, having given up 3 scattered hits.

From the first pitch, the Cubs, led by jockeying specialist Hal Carlson, had been riding the A's loudly, profanely, continuously. As their lead grew, the blistering verbal attack intensified. The Athletics took it in uncharacteristic silence.

Rommel replaced Walberg in the seventh. With one out Hornsby tripled. Wilson walked. Cuyler singled to make it 8–0. A snappy double play started by Dykes prevented further damage.

Connie Mack mentally wrote off the game. "I'll let the regulars bat this inning," he thought, "then pull them and give the youngsters a chance to experience some World Series play." He got Bill Shores up in the bullpen to pitch the eighth.

Scouting teams is like scouting an enemy at war. For all the intelligence gathering, it still takes the foot soldiers to execute. Results are the product of physical forces, not plans. Facing lead-off batter Al Simmons in the seventh, Charlie Root made a mistake and put a pitch up where Simmons liked them. Al hit it onto the left-field roof. The same thought flitted through thousands of minds, including a few in the A's dugout: "Well, at least we won't be shut out." The Cubs infield gathered at the mound and asked Root if he was tired. "No," he said. Foxx singled, and another summit meeting took place. Miller hit a short fly to straightaway center field. Wilson rushed in and lost the ball in the sun's glare. It fell for a single. Root later called that the turning point. Dykes singled in Foxx. 8–2.

Boley started for the plate and Mack called him back. "That pitcher is losing his stuff," he said. "Hit the first good one he gives you." Boley singled to right, scoring Miller. 8–3. George Burns pinch-hit for Rommel and popped to short for the first out. Bishop bounced a single up the middle, scoring Dykes. 8–4.

Irish poet Thomas Moore wrote that hope is the grand exciter of industry, and hope was in the Philadelphia air, exciting the Athletics to extraordinary industry and their enthusiasts to yelling from their hearts, their lungs, their size 11 boots. Only the five hundred Cub fans who had made the journey from Chicago slumped silently in their seats.

Joe McCarthy summoned veteran left-hander Art Nehf from the bullpen. Nehf stood on the mound and shielded his eyes from the sun beaming directly into them. Mule Haas dug in at the plate and lifted a long fly ball to dead center. Hack Wilson followed its upward arc against the grandstand background, then it disappeared from his sight as the sun bounced off his sunglasses. He raced back to where it might land and saw it just as it was about to hit the ground. He stuck out his bare hand to grab it, but it bounced away from him. Haas circled the bases and scored behind Boley and Bishop. 8–7.

There was pandemonium wherever an Athletics' fan's heart beat. "Not once had the volume of roaring screaming thundering sound fallen the fraction of a note from its pitch or volume," wrote one local scribe with acres of space to fill. "It pounded in the ears like the scream of gales and the thunder of surf. It fed upon the excitement of the moment and excitement fed upon it. Sheer, stark insanity swept the field and clutched all in its gibbering, perspiring embrace."

There is a widely repeated story, probably begun by Jimmie Dykes, that as Haas rounded third, Dykes jumped up and yelled, "He's gonna make it," and exuberantly thumped the man standing next to him on the back, sending Connie Mack head-first into the bats arrayed in front of the dugout. Over the years Mack himself kept the story alive in interviews, being quoted as saying that he never saw Haas score. "I went sprawling into the bat pile. By the time I got myself untangled, Haas had scored." Sometimes in the telling, Dykes apologizes while helping him up, and Mack assures him at a time like that, anything goes.

A few years later, however, Alan J. Gould wrote, "Mack laughed at reports that he got so excited he fell off the bench during the 10-run inning. 'Why, I never so much as moved, much less lost my balance,' he told me. 'I guess I was the only one who didn't manifest excitement. I was too busy figuring plays to let my enthusiasm run away with me.'"

Some major newspapers had sent several men to cover every aspect of the games, looking everywhere for oddments to fill sidebars. The *Public Ledger* covered every detail from hotel occupancy rates to the names of three young men who drove three thousand miles from British Columbia and joined the line outside the bleacher gate at two o'clock in the morning Friday. The *Inquirer* assigned Stan Baumgartner to keep his eyes on Connie Mack. Jim Gantz and Ed Pollock did the same for the *Ledger*. Every scowl or smile by Mr. Mack was noted.

There were hundreds of eyes in the press box taking in everything that happened on the field and in the stands. While the rally was in progress, Pollock wrote, "Connie's employees were even slapping him on the back. They never took such liberties with him before."

If the long, lean, sixty-six-year-old manager had sailed through the air and landed among the bats, it's reasonable to assume that a dozen of his players would have leaped out to help him and somebody would have noticed.

After Haas's home run, wrote Pollock, "The A's dugout was seething with joyous and romping players. The retiring McGillicuddy found himself being jazzed around and embraced by a demonstrative employee. A dozen pairs of hands reached into the bat pile, so neatly arranged in front of the dugout, and sent the lumber skyrocketing in disorder."

The Athletics had been celebrating rallies that way forever.

Nobody mistook Connie Mack for one of the bats skyrocketing in disorder. No mention of Mr. Mack's landing among the bats was found in any of the next day's papers.

The Athletics still trailed by one run. The bases were empty and there was 1 out. Nehf walked Cochrane. McCarthy replaced him with Sheriff Blake. Simmons hit a grounder that bounced over the third baseman's head. Foxx singled to score Cochrane. 8–8.

When that score was shown on the scoreboard at Franklin Field, where thirty thousand were watching a Penn–Virginia Poly football game, all action on the field stopped. The spectators went berserk. Players on both sides stood and watched to see what would happen next.

Thousands more stood cheering in disbelief outside City Hall and newspaper offices, watching metal figures moving around the bases.

Lefty Grove and George Earnshaw began to throw in the bullpen. Bill Shores sat down.

McCarthy sent Pat Malone to the rescue. Malone's first pitch hit Bing Miller to load the bases. Jimmie Dykes sent a long fly ball toward the left-field wall. Riggs Stephenson raced back and leaped. The ball cleared his glove. Coaching at third, Eddie Collins waved Simmons and Foxx home while he ran in circles and slid in the dirt like he was scoring himself. 10–8.

Twenty years later Connie Mack said he remained calm outwardly, concentrating on planning his next moves. But he must have shown some emotion. Ed Rommel later said it was "the happiest I ever saw Mr. Mack. He was really beside himself with joy."

When Joe Boley and George Burns struck out to end the inning, the crowd sat back exhausted, all capacity for celebration depleted. Nobody tried to revive the collapsed Cubs fans. The scoreboard boy was frantic. The highest number on his slates was 9. He whipped out a brush, dipped it in the whitewash, and drew a 10 on a blank slate.

After Boley threw out Grimm to start the eighth, Lefty Grove struck out the next two Cubs.

When Hal Carlson went to the mound for the Cubs in the last of the eighth, Cochrane and Miller let him have it, accusing the Cubs of choking with unprintable embellishments.

In the ninth Grove struck out McMillan and English before Hornsby's fly ball to Miller ended it.

Reporters who rushed down to the field reported that Mack waved two clenched fists in the air but was unable to get words past the lump in his throat. It was a rare instance of his emotions breaking through his natural reserve. In a 1948 *Life* article by Bob Considine, Mack was quoted, "You know, there was talk that I danced with joy during that big inning. It is not true. I just sat there and when we won the game I walked off with hardly a word to the boys. It doesn't help any to appear to be too pleased before such an important series is won. Such an attitude might lead to overconfidence and that's fatal."

That's not how the observers on the scene reported it. Stan Baumgartner wrote that Mack bounded up the stairs to the clubhouse shouting, "The greatest thrill I have had in my years of managing." The first person he ran into was Bob Paul, sports editor of the *Daily News*, not one of Mack's favorite writers. Mack grabbed Paul's coat lapels with quivering hands, shook him with joy, and pounded his fists into Paul's chest as hundreds stood watching. "Wasn't that marvelous?" he chanted "Did you ever see such hitting? They can never say my boys are quitters now," he raved on. "No team in the world can stop them now."

The report said that Tom Shibe took hold of Mack and escorted him to his waiting car. But Mack made a rare postgame appearance in the clubhouse, which was closed to the press. He choked out a few words of pride in his boys, then hurried out. "I shall never forget it," Mack later told Gould. "Never have I seen a team rise so irresistibly, so magnificently. They said we got the breaks. Well, perhaps we did. Don't forget my players were forcing them. They refused to let an 8-run lead by the opposition discourage them."

Fred Lieb had a hunch that Mack might have gone up to his tower office. "As I started up the stairs, I was surprised to meet Rud Rennie of the *New York Herald-Tribune* coming down. 'I think you better not go up there, Fred,' Rennie advised. 'The old gentleman is pretty well fatigued. He just murmured to me, "I guess that seventh inning was a little too much for me." I think he may have had a slight stroke, either in that seventh inning or after the game. He's in no shape for talking.' I took Rud's advice and turned back."

In the Cubs' clubhouse nobody could recall seeing a run of breaks such as the A's had enjoyed. Joe McCarthy managed a weak smile. Nothing could eradicate Gabby Hartnett's perpetual good nature. The rest of the faces were sad.

McCarthy didn't blame Wilson. "The poor kid simply lost the ball in the sun, and he didn't put the sun there." The balls he missed were the toughest for an outfielder to get a bead on under any conditions, hit straight at him, instead of to the side where he could get a better read on them. He was wearing sunglasses but they did no good. It wasn't the background of the stands that bothered him; he had lost sight of the balls after they cleared the roof.

Charlie Root glared in silence at reporters and made no reply to their questions. But Hack Wilson faced them. "Couldn't see the balls," he said. "I dropped Dykes's fly in the fifth and put Root in a hole because I was late locating it. Miller's fly in the seventh was short and when I got a line on it I was too far back. Haas's hit later in the seventh never was in my vision until it was almost to the ground."

The press box denizens facing early deadlines had had little time to tear up their preliminary pre-seventh-inning leads and start over. It took a while to find the words to sum up the unbelievable. The AP's Gould, with less time than the morning papers to get his dispatch on the wire, came up with, "The bubbling World Series hopes of the Chicago Cubs were scattered all over Shibe Park today by a combination of lightning, cyclone, and tidal wave in the wildest inning of baseball championship history."

John Drebinger of the *Times* had more time to reflect: "Somebody dropped a toy hammer on a stick of dynamite today and touched off an explosion that shook to its heels a continent that Christopher Columbus had discovered 437 years ago to the day."

Ed Burns, the *Chicago Tribune*'s sardonic beat writer, put Hack Wilson at the top of the list of all-time World Series goats. "It remained for our beloved Cubs to furnish the greatest debacle, the most terrific flop in the history of the World Series. . . . Losing the balls in the sun usually is condoned, but Hack had his warning that his sun glasses were not adequate [when he dropped Dykes's fly in the fifth]."

With a day off on Sunday, Mack's cousin Dennis McGillicuddy, a businessman from Boston, hosted a dinner at the Bellevue-Stratford for a party of seventy-five, including the Macks, Ty Cobb, and writers from Boston and Philadelphia papers.

Nobody was doing any guessing about starting pitchers for the fifth game.

Connie Mack has been portrayed as a manager who would not tolerate rough jockeying, profanity, or personal insults from his players on the bench. Maybe so. But the language from both sides had been unrestrained and loud enough to be heard well back in the grandstand. Halfway through the Series Cochrane had said, "[The Cubs] should be in the Kentucky Derby instead of the World Series. They're the best jockeys I ever heard." Whether Mack's boys went beyond his line of toleration is not provable, but it apparently went beyond Judge Landis's, and Landis was an accomplished cusser himself.

On Monday morning Landis met with the two managers in his hotel room and warned them to clean up the language or it would cost offending players their Series shares. And if he couldn't tell who was doing the yelling, he would hold the managers responsible. That's what prompted Cochrane, when he went behind the plate to start the fifth game, to yell at the Cubs something about "serving tea and cookies today." When Landis went into the clubhouse after the game to congratulate the Athletics, he let Cochrane know that he had heard the "tea and cookies" comment.

After the Saturday game President Hoover decided he had to see the last game to be played at Shibe Park that year. He had been at Griffith Stadium to see the Athletics win their season opener. Tom Shibe provided his box for the president, two members of the cabinet, and their wives. Philadelphia mayor Harry Mackey joined them. Washington political reporters sat on cushions on the steps around the box, straining to catch every comment exchanged between the mayor and the president.

The police who lined up awaiting Hoover's entrance enjoyed a close-up view of the Altrock-Schacht comedy routines. When the presidential party entered through the left-field gate and walked across the field, the crowd cheered Hoover heartily. One report said that a superstition about leaving the dugout before a game kept Connie Mack from going over to greet the president. Another report said that Mack had earlier astonished onlookers by walking across the field to the Cubs' dugout during batting practice, a first according to old-timers. William Wrigley, Judge Landis, and Tom Shibe greeted the president, while Mrs. Mack handed Mrs. Hoover a bouquet of roses from her adjoining box.

Twenty-seven-year-old Pat Malone, the Cubs' 22-game winner, was fully rested. Mack decided to play out the right-handed string. But how? Ehmke was out; he needed two weeks' rest. Mack passed up Shores, possibly because the youngster had been arrested and fined twenty-five dollars for speeding outside Camden, New Jersey, Sunday night and 'hadn't gotten much sleep. He considered bringing Earnshaw back again on two days' rest.

Mack still hadn't made up his mind when he arrived at Shibe Park on Monday. The first man he saw was Howard Ehmke.

"Who is your pitcher today?" Ehmke asked.

"I haven't decided," said Mack.

"Well, I feel all right again and while I don't want to change your plans, I am willing to go in."

Mack knew that Ehmke could never go 9 innings and might not even get out of the first. But—and this was more of a hunch than the opener had been—he knew that when Howard Ehmke said he was ready to pitch, it was worth it to hand him the ball. Sentiment may have trumped judgment. They both knew that two weeks was his usual rest requirement, not six days. Mack decided to warm up both Ehmke and Walberg and go with Ehmke until the first sign of trouble.

Ehmke got through 3 innings, giving up a hit in each, fanning nobody. With 2 out in the fourth Cuyler doubled. Stephenson walked. Grimm singled. Taylor singled. The Cubs led 2–0. Mack waved in Walberg, who struck out Malone.

Meanwhile, the Athletics' bats were back in mothballs. Malone was cruising along, giving up a hit in the second and one in the fifth. Walberg kept pace, retiring the first ten he faced, three on three pitches in the seventh. When Grimm struck out in the ninth, it was Walberg's sixth, bringing the Cubs' record total to 50.

Cochrane drew a walk to start the seventh, and the fans took that as the curtain-raiser for a repeat of Saturday's dramatics and began to whoop it up. But Simmons popped up and Foxx hit into a double play.

In the eighth McCarthy had Bush and Blake warming up. Anticipating the use of a pinch hitter, Mack got Rommel up. But nothing happened. Three up and three down. Malone was confident and in complete control. He had been throwing a first-pitch high fastball for a strike to almost every batter. "I had more stuff on the ball in the eighth inning than I did in the first seven," he said after the game.

The Pennsylvania Railroad was preparing the Pullman cars for the trip back to Chicago. In the press box writers were asking telegraphers to wire for hotel reservations. Mack pointed a finger at Walter French and beckoned him, said a few words to him, and sent him up to bat for Walberg to start the ninth. From the press box Jim Gantz watched the manager, not the game. "Connie Mack leaned forward, rubbed his knee with his left hand, put his left hand to his face."

French struck out, came back to the bench, and said, "That fellow has everything." Mack shifted his scorecard to his left hand and marked a K. His focus shifted from the action on the field to thoughts of starting Lefty Grove in Game 6 on Wednesday.

Bishop slapped the first pitch over third base for a single. Mack fingered his scorecard. The crowd barely had time to start getting excited before Haas hit a first-pitch waist-high inside fastball over the right-field wall. Just like that, the score was tied. The frenzy that erupted matched Saturday's uproar. Mayor Mackey leaped out of the presidential box and raced to hug Haas after he crossed the plate. Hoover felt like doing the same but maintained the appearance of dignified neutrality. Malone and Taylor conferred heatedly halfway between the mound and home plate; writers speculated erroneously that the pitcher was complaining about the pitch call by the catcher. "I didn't mean to get it down his alley," Malone said later. "It simply strayed away from me."

"A smile [on Mack's face] was all that we could see," wrote Gantz.

Mack got Grove up to get ready to pitch the tenth. As Simmons picked up a bat, Mack was seen fidgeting again. Simmons doubled off the scoreboard. Mack sat still, coolly fingering that scorecard. McCarthy ordered Foxx walked. Bing Miller took four fastballs for a 2-2 count, then guessed curve. He changed his stance and moved closer to the plate, then guessed Malone might be reading his mind and throw another fastball, knowing that Miller was the best curve ball hitter in the American League. It was a fastball, Miller said later, and he lined it over Hornsby's head and it rolled unattended to the scoreboard, and the game and the Series were over.

Joe McCarthy flung his cap on the dugout floor in disgust, then dashed over to congratulate Mack.

The ecstatic crowd had been requested to stay off the field until after the president had left the grounds. They were content to do their joyful jumping where they stood, while the Athletics danced without restraint in front of the dugout.

Ed Pollock described the scene:

Bedlam broke loose. Eye-witnesses of that scene will never forget it. Grown-up athletes, dignified men of affairs, and just plain fans yelled, danced, jumped, and embraced their neighbors, strangers in some instances, in their delirium of joy.

The thrill-crazed Athletics half-carried Simmons and Miller to the dugout. Mayor Mackey rushed from the side of the President, fought his way through the dancing, jostling, hilarious players, and patted Miller on the back.

There in the dugout, the only man seated on the bench was Connie Mack. The ever-present scorecard was gript in both hands. A broad, happy smile multiplied the wrinkles on his Lincolnesque face. He was looking off into space—the veil of the years was lifting. . . . There he sat—the only one who wasn't letting off the steam of emotion.

Suddenly the form of a ballplayer came hurtling through the air. The manager . . . was almost knocked to the bottom of the dugout but he was caught in the strong arms of the athlete and embraced.

His hat was tossed off. He reached for it, arose and bent his long body under the low top of the dugout exit. He was gone.

Jim Gantz identified the player who lunged at Mack to give him a too-rough hug around the neck as Bevo LeBourveau. Another player retrieved Mack's brown felt hat and handed it to Mack, who then ducked out through the exit toward the clubhouse.

Graham McNamee had hurried down to the dugout for postgame interviews. Connie Mack had promised to be on the program but forgot and was in the clubhouse when McNamee arrived. The players interviewed mostly said hello to the folks back home and other platitudes that winners have been expressing in such interviews ever since. Asked what they would do with their winners' shares, most said they would put them in the bank. Al Simmons said he would pay off the mortgage on the house he had bought for his mother. Only Mickey Cochrane mentioned the stock market. He was feeling lucky, having carried a good-luck 20-franc coin brought back from Monte Carlo by Bill Eagelson, a friend of many of the players who had won a lot of money at the casinos. Cochrane had stuck it in his back pocket in every game except the one they had lost when he had "left it in my other uniform."

Connie Mack told Isaminger a year later, "I lost myself completely, hugging each player and jigging around the floor in joy. For a man of my years I must have made a pretty spectacle, but I couldn't help it. I felt as I did when I hit the first homer in East Brookfield when I was in my teens."

Hundreds of fans waited outside the clubhouse exit for the players to emerge. Miller, Haas, Walberg, and Simmons drew the biggest cheers. When Connie Mack came out, reporters asked for comments. With tear-filled eyes,

Mack said, "I am too happy to talk. It's a great ball club and I was sure they would come through."

Stan Baumgartner was there. "When he emerged," wrote Baumgartner, "he was out of breath. He dragged his way through the mob pounding him on the shoulders and made his way toward the catwalk to his office," which was jammed with reporters, employees, friends, and relatives. "Amid a torrent of questions and congratulations, he held up his hand. 'Just a minute, boys. Wait until I rest a minute.'"

The office became silent while the exhausted Mack lay down on the long couch in his office and closed his eyes. A full three minutes went by before he sat up, rubbed his eyes, and began to answer questions. Somebody asked him, "Was that your brother who hugged you in the runway?"

Mack said, "Gee, I don't know. It may have been my ice man."

He praised his boys for their team effort and predicted many future World Series triumphs for Joe McCarthy.

Mack called his boys "the gamest team in baseball. When Haas hit that home run I was stunned. It came too fast. Before I could 'get back,' Simmons came through and they had passed Foxx. Miller was up and my senses were just returning to normal when Bing connected. It was all over and I had to rush for the office. It was all too wonderful. I guess I overdid it."

No World Series before or after has ever packed as much excitement into 5 games. For Connie Mack this World Series surpassed everything in his baseball life. He was the first manager to win four world championships. Even into his nineties, in talks and interviews, he would give his listeners a play-by-play account of the Ehmke opener, the 10-run inning, and the ninth-inning rally of the final game.

At 6:20 a beaming Connie Mack walked into the press headquarters at the Bellevue-Stratford Hotel. The chatter of the typewriters stopped. Mack was surrounded by men and messenger boys offering congratulations. "You'll be back again next year," somebody said.

"I'd certainly be happy to meet you all here again next year," said Mack.

The next day Mack and his cousin headed for Atlantic City for a few days' rest. He was back for the city's celebration banquet at the Penn AC. Ira Thomas was set to lead two teams, headed by Foxx and Simmons, on lucrative barnstorming tours. Hometown celebrations awaited several players. But Connie Mack asked them to stay in town for this occasion. More than sixteen hundred fans filled the hall and the balconies. Many more listened to the proceedings on a local radio station. Players and coaches received engraved gold wristwatches. Walberg and Perkins received Temple radios. Connie Mack was given a clock. A showing of movie highlights of the Series drew explosive cheering.

Among the players who spoke, Bevo LeBourveau was the most eloquent in expressing their love and admiration for Connie Mack. The journeyman outfielder had been sent to Milwaukee after a trial with the A's in 1928. At the time Mack promised to recall him. "I had a good year out there in 1928," Bevo said, "but I wasn't recalled. I thought Mr. Mack had forgotten, but when I saw him in Toledo last August, he apologized. Mr. Mack doesn't have to apologize to ballplayers, but he apologized to me and told me he would take me back again. [Mack had then recalled Bevo when he sent Ossie Orwoll to Milwaukee.] I am here tonight because Mr. Mack keeps his word and doesn't forget."

When Connie Mack was introduced to speak, it was like a political convention saluting its presidential nominee. The hollers and whistles went on for five minutes.

When the din died down, Mack said he couldn't find words to express his emotions, then found enough to talk for almost thirty minutes. He thanked the Shibes for the complete freedom they gave him in all player transactions; retraced the building of the club over the past five years; recapped the momentous events of the Series; then said:

Let me tell you the boys fought hard all season. They deserve credit and I am glad to extend it to them. I cannot forget that during the spring I left our training camp and came back to Philadelphia and gave out an interview in which I stated that I did not think we had more than a fighting chance to win and that if we did win it would be because we were the better fighters rather than the better team.

I made that statement deliberately with the idea of keeping my men from being overconfident. It worked. They fought every inch of the way as if to show me, as I had thought they would do, that they were fighters.

When he finished, the cheering went on even longer than when he had been introduced.

A week later a dinner in Germantown honored both Mack and Joe McCarthy. That was followed by another at Cedarbrook Country Club, where Mack was a member. Then an exhausted Mr. Mack spent a few days in bed.

Connie Mack's return to the top brought a flood of congratulatory mail and telegrams from friends and strangers. He answered them all. One came from the widow of Sam Wise, a teammate at Washington and Buffalo forty years earlier. Mack replied, "Your dear husband and myself [were] on the same team together at Buffalo. What a great player Sam was. He could field and throw. I have never forgotten him as so many things came up while we were together at Buffalo that always kept him in my mind. I did meet Deacon White our third baseman in Chicago last summer. He must be well in his eighties [he was eighty-one], looked very old. Well do I remember going to the market Saturday night for our Sunday dinner. Well pleased to hear about your son and his family. Am just as much interested in the game as when I started out to play."

There were plenty of Irish Catholic players and managers in the major leagues. But among baseball-loving priests and nuns, none commanded the following that Connie Mack enjoyed. If massed prayers could guarantee wins, the Athletics would have been undefeated every year.

No one was more assiduous or devoted in her prayers for Mr. Mack and his men than Sr. Florence Cloonan. Born in Oswego, New York, when Connie Mack was five years old, Sr. Florence entered the Sisters of Charity novitiate in 1886, the same year that Mack made his big league debut with Washington. Her work took her to Kansas, Montana, and Colorado, but her baseball-loving heart belonged to Mr. Mack. She filled a scrapbook with clippings about the A's, the Macks, and the entry of Mary Mack into the convent.

The first known letter she wrote to Connie Mack was on the day after the final game of the 1929 World Series. In it she confided that she had been praying for the team's success, wished Mary well as a novitiate, and enclosed some clippings about them from the newspaper in Billings, where she worked at St. Vincent's Hospital.

Connie Mack, as always, responded, thanking Sr. Florence for her kindness and her prayers, "as well as the prayers of those throughout the country, who had been praying for us for a long time, at last were merited their reward. After all, I cannot account for our club's having won the last two games unless it were prayers."

This exchange began a fourteen-year correspondence between Mr. Mack and Sr. Florence, her letters sometimes accompanying gifts of "My Safe Guard" medals; prayer beads; packages of Lucky Strike cigarettes for the players; a gold cigarette case engraved "50th anniversary" sent at the time of a dinner held to mark Mack's fiftieth year in baseball in 1933; a photo of

Sr. Florence and her cousin, Fr. Edwards; and an unspecified gift that would be presented to a parish priest in Philadelphia. Sr. Florence also wrote to individual players.

The archives of the Sisters of Charity in Leavenworth, Kansas, contain only letters received by Sr. Florence from Mack and one from Babe Ruth. In them Mack chats about the team's fortunes and his health and comments about the state of baseball in general. He sends best wishes from Mrs. Mack and Earle and thanks for her kindnesses and her prayers.

Connie Mack and Sr. Florence never met, though she and Earle met in Billings, Montana, when Earle brought his barnstorming team there in the fall of 1930. Earle gave her a ball signed by a dozen major leaguers.

Connie Mack's last letter to her was written on November 3, 1943.

Sr. Florence died twenty-four days later. The Mother Superior advised him of her passing at the age of seventy-five.

On January 7, 1944, Mack sent this handwritten reply to the Mother Superior:

Dear Mother M. Francesca

Regret to hear of the death of Sister Florence may her soul rest in peace.

Seems only the other day that I had a nice letter from her. My son Earle had the pleasure of meeting her. I never did thou would have liked too and was in hopes that I could some day.

Am going to miss hearing from her but will not forget in praying or having masses said for her. Thank you dear Mother for informing me. With kind remembrance. Sincerely yours,

/s/Connie Mack

The pickup in attendance in the last half of 1928 and all of 1929 added to the economic impact that Shibe Park had on the neighborhood. The benefits were widespread and varied. Many of them fell to the young boys fortunate enough to live within a few blocks of the ballpark.

The increased use of the automobile was a boon. There was a garage and service station beneath the grandstand. The area beneath the left-field corner was filled with John Shibe's racing speedboats and an elaborate machine shop run by a full-time mechanic, Ike Steckler, and Shibe's racing driver, Armand DuPugh. Shibe spent a fortune maintaining and racing the boats all over the country but never won a Gold Cup event. The rest of the garage barely had room for players' and club executives' cars.

On a big day street parking was at a premium for a radius of three blocks around Shibe Park. The lucky kids who lived on Twentieth or Twenty-First staked out the spaces in front of their stoops. When a car approached and slowed, they would wave the driver to the curb, then ask, "Watch your car for you?" Nobody watched the cars during the game—they were too busy chasing foul balls and home runs to sell or use to get into a game free—but when it was over, they'd be right there, assuring the driver that nobody had touched the car and looking for a nickel or dime tip.

Before and after a game newsboys hawked papers for two cents outside the park. One-fourth of it was the newsboy's profit. An army of kids clamored for jobs sweeping the stands. On a slow day, when the Red Sox or White Sox or another tail-ender was in town, the demand for sweepers was small. But after a holiday doubleheader or a Yankee game, supervisor Bill Thompson would hire fifty sweepers. Each one was responsible for two and a half sections and was paid $1.50 to pick up the paper cups, crackerjack boxes, newspapers, and—the bane of all sweepers—peanut shells by the trillions. The brooms wouldn't pull the shells out from under the seats, which had to be lifted to get to them. The sweepers pushed it all into large garbage bags and dropped them under the bleachers to be picked up by trucks.

During the Depression Mack would help families who had no income by seeing that more boys and cleaning ladies were hired than he probably needed.

There were batboys, home and visitors' clubhouse kids, vendors, scoreboard operators, hustlers trying to pick up a nickel here, a dime there.

Many players rented rooms or apartments or took meals at homes within a few blocks of the ballpark. From his bedroom Al Simmons could look out at the outfield he patrolled. One lucky kid, Jerry Rooney, who lived three houses away, had the chore of waking Al, a slow riser, in time for breakfast and noontime practice. Lefty Grove had an eight-block walk home to 2938 Lehigh. They patronized the neighborhood clothing stores, dry cleaners, restaurants, and taverns. A Greek restaurant sold what they called "Texas hot wieners," hot dogs "as big around as Jimmy Foxx's forearm, with fried onions and a little chili sauce on them, two for fifteen cents," recalled Al Ruggieri, who fetched them for the players—"with a nickel Coke"—in the clubhouse before batting practice. "The Greek's was a little place, no more than fifteen feet wide, at Twenty-Second and Lehigh. There was a sign—'White trade solicited only'—right on the wall. In 1934 they passed an anti-discrimination law and the sign came down. But they still didn't serve blacks."

When the right-field gate opened after a game, you could hardly get into Quinnie's bar across the street.

Ruggieri, called "Little Man" by everybody around the ballpark because he was not much over five feet tall, was the most energetic and enterprising kid of them all. One of ten children who lived a half-block away, he began working for John Shibe when he was about eight. Before school, he swept out the machine shop where the boats were kept, then returned to run errands. He was quick and polite—"I called everybody Mister"—and when Ike Steckler needed something, Little Man went and got it and was back in a few minutes. He worked in the machine shop during the winter and when the team was on the road. Every Sunday morning was payday. Al would bring the Sunday papers to John Shibe's office and wait to be paid. "He might sit there an hour reading the paper. I'd sit and wait. He gave me ten dollars a week. During the Depression I was making more than my father. Mr. Shibe would say, 'Little Man, take this right home to your mother.'"

During the summer Ruggieri was in the clubhouse at noon with a bunch of other kids when the players began to show up. There was no food in the clubhouse. The kids took the orders and ran for the Greek's hot dogs, tuna fish, or ham and egg sandwiches and Cokes, never coffee.

Players bought their own kangaroo leather shoes. The kids wiped them down, took the pitchers' shoes to the shoemaker to get an extra piece of leather sewed to the toes. They went to Parissi's butcher shop to get bones to rub the bats. They all hustled; the quicker you returned, the better your chance of picking up an extra nickel or dime. A quarter tip was a big deal. Al Simmons was the worst tipper; you couldn't squeeze more than a nickel out of him. Jimmy Foxx was the best, good for fifty cents—a fortune—to shine and clear out the little holes in his French Shriner black and white wingtip shoes.

Nobody smoked ready-made cigarettes. A few Southerners had their own supply of what they called North Carolina twist, dried, twisted leaves they flaked and rolled in Bull Durham papers. Most of the players chewed Apple tobacco; many of them smoked cigars—Optimos were the most popular. Lefty Grove and Jimmie Dykes smoked the biggest and blackest.

Little Man's mother and father were involved too. "When rookies came in for a tryout, they used the rookie clubhouse," he recalled. "We rented them towels, a dime apiece. My mother washed them. She washed and ironed Jimmy Foxx's silk shirts, twenty-five cents each." At least twice each home stand she would cook up a big pot of spaghetti and meatballs and Al would take it to the clubhouse, where Eddie Rommel would give him three dollars. "A lot of guys would grab a plate and jump in and have some, but he paid for it."

For years Little Man's father had a stand in front of the house where he sold frozen Italian water ice in four flavors. "When night games came in and it was hot," Al said, "he made a fortune. After the war there were days he made a hundred dollars."

Concessions sales were a significant source of income to most clubs, netting am estimated $30,000 a year, enough to pay the salaries of a few stars or ten rookies. A doubleheader or a Yankee game provided work for about a hundred vendors and people to work the outfield concession stand. The lowest job was renting the thin leather cushions stuffed with horsehair. This went to the youngest kids; they received eight cents a cushion and had to collect them all after the game. The cushions became handy missiles to protest unfavorable decisions on the field.

Eddie Collins Jr. recalled, "One day the A's lost a close game because of an ump's decision. I was sitting with my mother near the A's dugout and people were sailing those cushions out of the stands and one hit my mother in the back of the neck and knocked her unconscious."

Scorecards were still handed out free with pencils for sale.

Some hustlers developed unique styles and rhythms for calling out their wares. They could make a lyric out of "Peanuts, crackerjacks, cigars, cigarettes, and all kinds of chewing candy," although the only candy sold was Goldenberg's Peanut Chew Bar. The hot dog vendor picked up his three dozen Voight's franks from hot dog "chef" Leon Gumpert and lugged the metal bin with hot water inside to keep them warm and a supply of mustard on the side. The buns came from the Freihofer bakery that blanketed the neighborhood with its fresh-bread aroma. Sandwiches of Burke's lunch roll—a baloney-like deli meat known in Philadelphia as lunch roll—were also offered.

The ice cream vendors had to move the quickest. On a hot day they faced the threat of their merchandise melting before they could sell it.

The only drinks sold were sarsaparilla and Barley's orange drink, made from a concentrate—no Cokes, no beer before or after Prohibition. A pregame chore for Bob Schroeder's concessions crew was mixing each gallon of concentrate into five gallons of orange drinks. The vendors put cups into a twelve-hole tray, filled them with ice, pulled a lever to add the juice, paid forty cents, and sold them for a nickel each. Spectators in the front row near the dugouts sometimes complained about spilled orange drink dripping on them from the upper deck. The "sass" was sold in bottles. The older vendors had their choice of product. (There was a league rule against selling soft drinks in bottles, but some teams, including the Senators and Athletics, ignored it.)

Shots Monaghan ran the visitors' clubhouse, Steve Pfleuger ran the A's clubhouse. Howard Crompton, known by all as "Yitz," worked the home clubhouse and was John Shibe's chauffeur. The locker room had a concrete floor, with wooden slats on the shower floor. The walls were lined with lockers, a stool in front of each. Pfleuger had a desk just inside the door, from where he gave orders. "The air in the clubhouse after a hot day's game was pretty raunchy and thick," Ruggieri said. The kids had to gather up the heavy sweatshirts worn beneath the flannel uniforms, hang them on steel racks, and take them to the gas-fired hot air oven behind two steel doors to be dried. Not washed, just dried. When they were dry, they still smelled.

Batboys collected broken and discarded bats and saved them for the head groundskeeper, Bill McCalley, who would split the salvageable ones in half down to the handle for use as fungo bats.

On hot days one of the kids would mix a bucket of what they called "Florida water"—ice, water, and spirits of ammonia and drop a sponge in it and take it to the dugout. The players would come in off the field and douse themselves with it, while Connie Mack sat in his dark suit, starched collar, tie, and straw hat, seemingly immune to the heat and the humidity. If he removed his jacket, you knew it was a scorcher of a day.

A few boys worked the scoreboard, an inferno on a hot day. They walked a narrow catwalk to hang the steel plates with numbers on them after each half inning. A telephone line to the press box provided them with the scores of other American League games to post. Shibe Park had the only scoreboard in the major leagues that displayed both teams' batting orders. (This was one reason given by John Shibe for the Athletics' not following the Yankees' lead in putting numbers on their players' uniforms in 1929.) The names were painted in whitewash on black four-foot-long metal sheets and hung on hooks. When a player left the game, his name was wiped off with a wet sponge and his replacement's name painted in its place. The scoreboard, visible from every seat, was supplemented by lineup and substitution announcements through newly installed public address amplifiers.

And when it started raining every working hand was expected to turn out on the field to drag the heavy canvas to cover the infield.

Connie Mack's brother Eugene directed traffic around the ticket windows until the game started. A local barber, Charlie Wanamaker, wore a badge and retrieved foul balls caught in the stands, saying, "Brother, that ball belongs to the club, not you."

There were black attendants in the ladies' rooms.

All told, from George Brand, who guarded the pass gate for more than thirty years and never saw a game, to the newsboys hawking papers, more than two hundred people depended on a game at Shibe Park for much-needed dimes and dollars.

For them a rained-out game was a disaster. But for others it was a blessing. When a game was postponed, a banner to that effect was put up on the wall near the main entrance. Families in the neighborhood knew what that meant. Even before it went up, a line began to form in anticipation at the Twenty-First Street gate, where the concession supplies were delivered. The pre-sliced hot dog buns and the lunch roll wouldn't keep. The hot dogs would. The buns came in bags of sixty. The lunch roll came in a fifteen-inch-long roll about four inches in diameter. Everybody in line was handed a bag of buns and a hunk of lunch roll. Kids would run home with it and return to the line.

"It was like animals going to a watering hole," Ruggieri said.

During the Depression the Athletics would send all concession stand leftovers to St. Joseph's Home for Boys at Sixteenth and Allegheny.

The families living in the row houses on Twentieth Street opposite Shibe Park reaped the biggest reward from their second-floor and rooftop views of the action over the right-field fence. The front bedrooms had four windows, which could be removed and stored for the summer. Portable bleachers were set up in one-foot gradations; the heads of those in the top row were near the ceiling. Outside the windows they sat two deep on the roof overhanging the porch. The rooftop was accessible by opening a skylight, usually in the bathroom, and climbing a ladder. This made the bathroom off limits to the occupants during the games. Assorted canvas and wooden chairs were placed on the roof. There was a constant controversy with city inspectors over how many people could safely occupy a roof at one time. Between the bedroom and the roof, twenty fans a day at fifty cents each over a ten-day home stand brought in a hundred dollars, a bonanza to a working man earning under $2,000 a year. Enterprising youngsters in the family made lemonade and bought hot dogs from street vendors for a nickel and resold them on the roof for a dime.

The World Series brought the biggest crush of customers, including newsreel cameramen, who paid twenty dollars a day for rooftop perches. Business was so good in 1929 that the families built bleachers on the roofs. During the Depression attendance fell; the price of the outlaw seats was cut to twenty-five cents. In 1935 the Athletics raised the right-field fence thirty feet, and the rooftop bleachers were out of business.

27 | A'S WIN; WORLD LOSES

Connie Mack's timing was terrible. The last time he had been on top, the Federal League and the Great War had knocked him off. Now he had regained baseball's center-stage spotlight just as the electric bill came due and the curtain was about to fall on the good times in America.

On Thursday, October 24, 1929, Wall Street borrowed an aviation term to describe the stock market's actions: air pockets. About eleven in the morning a tsunami of selling hit the market, driven by thousands of small customers who had no money to meet margin calls and were forced to sell. At one o'clock Thomas W. Lamont of J. P. Morgan & Co. said businesses were sound and many stocks had been driven down too far. That sparked an updraft. At the end of the day a system geared to handle a day's trading of up to 7 million shares had 13 million to clear, which took until five o'clock Friday morning.

Treasury officials blamed speculation and assured everybody there was no basic business weakness. The market was calm on Friday and Saturday. But on Monday the selling resumed with a vengeance. The Dow Jones Industrial Index sank 13 percent. Some stocks had fallen by one-third to one-half. Brokers who were still in business said the market was cheap; it was time to buy. Bankers sounded more optimistic than baseball managers in March. Democrats blamed Republicans.

On Black Tuesday, October 29, the Dow collapsed another 12 percent. More than 16 million shares traded. The next day John D. Rockefeller tried to lift it all by himself, then Wall Street closed for two days to catch up.

The Dow had made a high of 381.17 on September 3. By November 13 it hit bottom—temporarily—down almost 50 percent. The market rebounded in 1930. But as Al Jolson said in *The Jazz Singer*, "You ain't seen nothing yet." It began to slide again and wouldn't reach bottom until the summer of 1932. It's easy to believe the stories that some players were receiving margin calls during the next two World Series.

The first selling wave took out the small investors. Men and women of all circumstances who had given up bridge to play the market on 10 or 20 percent margin vowed to return to the bridge tables. Eventually many professional investors were wiped out, and some of the rich and famous would become just famous.

Connie Jr. recalled driving his dad to a banquet after the 1929 World Series. They were driving through Fairmount Park when Mack said he had achieved two cherished ambitions: winning another world championship and having a worth of $1 million—not for himself but for his large family.

Foresight is always in short supply. When it does surface, since it is ipso facto ahead of its time, it is often ignored, unappreciated, even unwelcome.

As Larry Budner, the grandson of Mack's close friend Hyman Pearlstone, remembered it, Connie Mack told Pearlstone during the 1929 season that his investments were worth $1 million. Pearlstone, the Texas banker who had traveled with the A's on at least one trip a season for more than twenty years, suggested it might be prudent to take some profits. Mack thought the market would go higher. Family lore is that Katherine Mack's brother, Frank Holahan, had a daughter, Helen, who married a stockbroker named Sheehan. Mack felt the time had come to sell out and Sheehan talked him out of it. Either way, he didn't get out. Most of the million was gone.

Al Horwits said that Mack told him a few years later, "I used to buy shares by the thousands. Now I buy them by the hundreds."

Between his stock market losses and speedboat racing expenses, John Shibe faced bankruptcy. He sold two of his racing boats but returned to the gold cup racing circuit later with a new, twenty-nine-foot craft, the *Miss Philadelphia*. He also kept two cabin speedboats, the *Ethyl Ruth I* and *II*, under the left-field stands. Connie Mack bailed him out and was nearly broke himself. But his family never noticed any change in their lives. The children still went to private schools. The help at home remained. The hospitality at 604 W. Cliveden never diminished.

The Athletics were generous in dividing their World Series winnings, resulting in each share being worth $5,620.57. In addition to twenty-five full shares to players—including Jimmy Cronin (25 games) and George Burns (20)—an equal cut went to Kid Gleason, Earle Mack, and Doc Ebling. A full share was divided between Bevo LeBourveau, who received a quarter, and Ossie Orwoll, who received three-quarters. Connie Mack donated his share to be divided among his scouts, traveling secretary, groundskeeper, and other park employees, and to bring Orwoll up to a full share.

For Jimmy Cronin, it was the biggest payday in his now-ended major league career. He used $325 of it to go home to Oakland in style, flying by day and riding trains at night.

Dartmouth pitcher William Breckenridge had received a $5,000 bonus to sign and was with the team all season. He appeared in 3 games, pitched 10 undistinguished innings, and received a full World Series share. His father was a lawyer in the Oklahoma oil fields and wanted his son to begin a legal career, so he quit baseball and used the money to go to law school.

Connie Mack concluded sadly, "He must not have loved the game enough."

Mickey Cochrane was quoted as saying he would use his entire check to pay off the margin on his stocks and own them outright. If so, he must have had very little invested to begin with. Whether he paid it off or simply invested more, he wound up losing it all. (Whatever else he may have lost was just paper profits, not his own money. Stories of his losing larger amounts out of pocket are not true. "We didn't have that much money to our names to begin with," said his wife Mary. It has been written that Cochrane lost $80,000 when the banks closed. When asked about it fifty years later, his daughter Joan said, "Nonsense. They didn't have that kind of money.") He made some of it back playing to packed houses as a headliner at theaters in Boston, Philadelphia, Newark, and Jersey City in an act with singer/dancer/comedian Arthur Brown and pianist Hildegard Selim. The act consisted of patter, songs, saxophone solos, and a little inside dope on the World Series. Mule Haas joined the act in Philadelphia.

From avid Athletics fans in the Pennsylvania coal country every A's player and club official also received a beautiful shining black baseball carved and polished from a piece of anthracite coal with the recipient's name etched into it.

Small banks were closing at the rate of five hundred a year; by the end of 1932 more than four thousand would fail. At one point Connie Mack asked Lefty Grove where he had his money deposited. "In the local bank in Lonaconing," Grove said.

"I would advise you to take your money out of that bank," Mack said, "and give it to me and let me place it somewhere. I'm a little uneasy about this currency situation."

According to Judge Getty, "Grove totally trusted Mr. Mack and moved it" to a Philadelphia bank.

The Lonaconing bank failed. The Philadelphia bank never closed.

"Grove was the only Lonaconing depositor who didn't lose his money," said Judge Getty.

Connie Mack also helped Grove earn some extra money. Ford Motor Company introduced shatterproof glass in its windshields. It contacted Connie Mack to inquire if it could use Lefty Grove to demonstrate the superiority of its new windows.

Mack said, "Robert, you can earn a little money here. All you have to do is throw a baseball at the windshield of a new Ford."

The demonstration took place in downtown Philadelphia. They measured off sixty feet, six inches from the car and handed Grove a baseball.

"I often wonder that I didn't kill somebody in the crowd," Grove told Judge Getty, "cause the first one went over the roof of the car. I got the next one into the windshield and glass didn't shatter, so they were happy."

He also endorsed Grainger pipe tobacco, posing in a hunting outfit with an English setter and a shotgun. They gave him the outfit, the gun, a lifetime supply of pipe tobacco, and $750. He didn't want the dog.

On October 16 Detroit asked waivers on four-time batting champion Harry Heilmann. Mack was tempted. He liked those veteran hitters; he knew that at thirty-five, Heilmann had not lost his batting eye. Mack told North American Newspaper Alliance writer Raymond Hill that most players quit the big leagues five years too soon. But he decided not to claim Heilmann, who was bought by the Reds and batted .333 for them.

By year end Mack released George Burns and sent Walter French, Jimmy Cronin, and Carroll Yerkes to Portland as part payment for pitcher Roy Mahaffey, twenty-seven, who had worked 370 innings with a 21-25 record. Yerkes never won another major league game. In 1937 French became baseball coach at West Point for six years until he went on active duty in World War II.

Although attendance at Shibe Park was up 150,000 in 1929, it was lower than it had been in 1925, when the A's had finished second in a close race. But with most of the big player purchases paid for, the club showed a $350,000 profit and paid another $50,000 dividend. The Phillies didn't offer much competition; they hadn't finished in the first division since 1917. Their annual season's highlight would be beating the Athletics in the spring city series. Detroit's population had doubled in the past decade; it was now the biggest one-club city in either league. The sixth-place Tigers had outdrawn the pennant-winning Athletics. The 5-game World Series had added little income.

John Shibe continued to expand and improve the facility. He had installed a public address system to replace the megaphone, allowing Babe O'Rourke to sit in the dugout and make his high-pitched, clearly enunciated announcements instead of rolling his 5-foot-6, 200-pound body onto the field. Shibe added more seats in the upper left-field stands, raising the capacity to thirty-four thousand. He considered adding seats in right field but decided not to shrink the playing field. Nor did he expand the box seats at the expense of the one dollar seats behind them. Shibe Park had the smallest proportion of box seats in the major leagues. It was also the only park where the fifty-cent bleachers were covered in the lower deck of the left-field stands. There were attended restrooms in all sections. Visiting writers called it the best equipped and cleanest park in either league. Only one sign appeared on the outfield walls:

Be A Good Sportsman
DON'T THROW Cushions or Paper

Connie Mack told his cousin Arthur Dempsey and others that it was more profitable for a club to finish second than first. "When you win a championship," he would say, "it's not like a boxing manager who has one champion. Every one of your twenty-five players thinks he was responsible for your winning and they all want raises. They don't think, 'We are champions,' but 'I am a champion.'"

Those who heard him make that statement understood that he was telling them the facts about the business side of baseball. Every winning manager and club owner experienced it. Nobody at the time took it to mean that Connie Mack or Clark Griffith or Charles Comiskey or anyone else in the game would *rather* finish second than win. Anyone who knew Connie Mack or worked or played for him knew how ridiculous that was.

Not all the world champions received raises for 1930, but the club's payroll rose to $275,000. Earnshaw went from a performance-based formula to a straight $12,000, as did Walberg, matching Grove. Foxx went from $7,500 to $10,000. Cochrane drew a $4,000 raise to $16,000. Dykes, who was second to batting champion Lew Fonseca in an unofficial MVP polling of one writer from each city, earned a $2,000 raise to $12,000. Mule Haas and Bill Shores also drew $2,000 raises. Rommel, Grove, and Bishop were unchanged.

Mack's biggest headache was Al Simmons. Simmons thought he was the best ballplayer who ever lived. Connie Mack didn't agree, but he did consider

Simmons the best outfielder he ever had. Simmons had hit .365 with 34 home runs and a league-leading 157 RBIs. He had been the highest-paid on the team at $15,000. He wanted $25,000. About a dozen of the Athletics headed for Hot Springs in February, Simmons among them. They hiked from the Imperial Bathhouse downtown over the Hot Springs Mountains, about seven miles. For diversion they visited the training camp of heavyweight fighter Primo Carnera and played golf. When it was time to go to Fort Myers, Simmons stayed in Hot Springs and worked out with the Minneapolis club.

On the first day of practice Connie Mack, wearing a new brown suit, told his team, "You're not a great team unless you can repeat as champions." He expressed his confidence that they would win again "if they hustle."

With an experienced lineup on the field, Mack felt comfortable going with youth on the bench. His utility infielders were Eric McNair, twenty-one, and Dib Williams, twenty. Williams, a native of Greenbrier, Arkansas, had been taught by his father, a semipro manager. His cheek bulging with a chaw of tobacco, he had worked in the Oklahoma oil fields and had only one year in pro ball, playing second base for Little Rock. Mack paid $15,000 for him. The only oldster was forty-one-year-old Wally Schang, who had started out with Mack seventeen years ago. Nicknamed "Tarzan" by the Yankees, Schang had been supplanted as baseball's strongest man by Jimmy Foxx. Mickey Cochrane played with such intensity, it was inevitable that he would get banged up enough to need some time off. Mack wanted two backup catchers, preferably veterans. He sent Sammy Hale to the Browns for Schang and $2,500. Schang and Perkins would provide dependable late-inning relief for Mickey.

Roger Cramer had hit .404 at Martinsburg. One day in an exhibition game Cramer took a third strike. Mack told him, "Boy, when you swing, you're dangerous. Hit anything you can reach." The advice helped Cramer amass 2,705 hits and strike out only 345 times in 2,239 games in his twenty-year career. With Cramer and minor league veteran Spencer Harris as his outfield reserves, Mack sold Homer Summa to Portland for $5,000.

"I must have confidence in every player," Mack said. "When I look down the bench and I have to bypass a ballplayer—if I don't think he can do the job—I might as well get rid of him. You're going to find yourself in a position where you'll have to use him."

Spencer Harris failed to meet that standard and soon went back to the American Association.

Mack considered his bench stronger than last year's and his pitching staff the best in the league. Dib Williams could play second or short, Eric McNair both those positions and third. He could use a pinch hitter for Boley or Bishop early in a game without weakening his defense. And Jimmie Dykes could stay at third base all year.

While Eddie Collins and Kid Gleason worked with the young infielders, Mack concentrated on the new pitchers, Al Mahon and Glenn Liebhardt, whose father had pitched for Cleveland twenty years earlier.

In June Mack would begin a practice he continued the rest of his managing days. He invited a local high school pitcher to pitch batting practice at Shibe Park, unsigned and unpaid, as a form of audition. The first was eighteen-year-old Lew Krausse. Given a chance to pitch in an exhibition game in Columbus, Krausse was impressive enough to be signed for $2,000 for 1931. (He won 5 games for the A's; his son, Lew Jr., would have a longer big league career thirty years later.)

Mack did not ban golf during spring training. Players clad in stylish knickers, knee-length argyle socks, sweaters, and caps frequented the local country club, as did Mack, similarly attired, who won matches with league president Barnard and Tom Shibe. But the social ramble was more subdued than in the past. There was less rebellion and rambunctious partying in the entire country. Skirts and spirits were lower, bobbed hair was fading out.

There was no Sunday baseball in Fort Myers, so the Athletics made weekend trips to St. Pete and Miami. On March 13 the unthinkable happened: it rained all day in St. Pete. The A's had gone there to play the Braves. Mack was kept busy attending a lunch, at which he spoke at the Princess Martha Hotel, and the annual Gangplank Villa baseball dinner that evening.

Baseball and radio and the movie newsreels had begun keeping company more regularly, opening new vistas of publicity for the game and material for the networks, whose broadcasts consisted mostly of academic or political talks and concerts by studio orchestras, vocalists, and jazz bands. In Chicago, station WGN broadcast a series, *Big Leaguers and Bushers*, about two rookies, Rube Appleberry and Tommy Malloy, that Connie Mack enjoyed listening to when the A's were in town. The rookies, he said, reminded him of Rube Waddell and other characters he had managed in the past. In addition to spring training roundups, network programs were enticing managers to appear for interviews. Connie Mack's national popularity made him a prime target for announcers. He always obliged. On March 24 he made his debut on a thirty-six station nationwide regularly scheduled program, the *General Motors Hour*, emceed by Graham McNamee from New York. Following

DeWolff Hopper's recitation of "Casey at the Bat," McNamee did a remote interview with Mack, who talked about his spring training routine.

The novelty of radio at the time was reflected in Mack's receiving telegrams after the program from all over the country, including one from the Portland club, which was training in San Jose: "Entire Portland team clustered around clubhouse in San Jose heard you as distinctly as if you were in the same room."

"My, what an experience," said Connie Mack.

A Movietone news crew arrived and spent a day photographing players while Mack talked into a recording device. He introduced Ehmke, Rommel, and Shores while the cameras ground away at them throwing to Cochrane, and he talked about Jimmy Foxx, who slid at home plate for the cameras. The film would be shown in Philadelphia theaters before opening day.

A thirty-year-old Fort Myers housewife, Mildred Johnson, made candy bars in her kitchen. Her two young children peddled them in parks and door to door. During spring training in 1930 she created one from nuts coated with caramel and covered with chocolate. As a promotional gimmick, she put a question mark on the wrapper and invited her customers to suggest a name. The most popular person in town was the manager of the world champion Athletics; the winning entry was "Connie Smack."

Mrs. Johnson and her husband, Fred, a printer at the *Ft. Myers Press*, had met Mr. Mack at Terry Park. When she approached him about naming the candy bar after him, Mack readily consented. There was no contract; Mr. Mack asked for no royalties. Tom Shibe predicted it would be a big seller in every ballpark.

The ten-cent candy bar, featuring a drawing on the wrapper of a pitcher having just thrown the ball, sold well in Fort Myers. Mrs. Johnson heard of only one complaint. Mrs. Mack bought one in Dick Richards's drugstore. When she bit into it, the caramel stuck to her upper dentures and she had a devil of a time removing it.

The Johnsons lacked the capital or resources for mass production and distribution. The editor of the *Press* wrote to several candy manufacturers on their behalf. The Eatmor Chocolate Co. of Pittsburgh (run by four Hershey brothers who were unrelated to Hershey's Chocolate), replied, "We came mighty near ditching this letter, but on second thought we will appreciate if you will send us a sample of this item and give us more information about it, and we can then write you whether or not we would be interested."

They showed no further interest.

Norris Candy Co. of Atlanta agreed to supply the bars and made up two cartons of them (at sixty-five cents a carton) to send samples to dealers. But the "Connie Smack" never achieved sufficient distribution to rival Baby Ruth, and Mrs. Johnson gave up her candy-making business a few years later.

The Macks and Shibes and players' wives skipped the barnstorming trip north and left Fort Myers on March 28. Considering him a good luck charm, the superstitious Mack invited his spring training clubhouse boy since 1929, Solly Meyers, to spend the summer working in the A's clubhouse in Shibe Park. On April 9 Mack took time out to throw out the first ball in the dedication of a new field at Temple University.

Al Simmons had still not signed. Mack reportedly offered him $20,000. Simmons said no. He wanted $25,000. When the Athletics headed north and Mack went home, Simmons went directly from Hot Springs to his rented room on Twenty-First Street. He played in one game in the city series, still unsigned. On the morning of the April 15 opener against New York, Connie Mack asked him to come up to the office. As Simmons later told the story, Mack said, "Al, it seems we are in need of your services. I suggest you play today."

Al said, "I'll play if I get my money."

"You'll get exactly what you asked for," Mack said. "Now I suggest you get out there and play."

Simmons signed for $25,000. He got out there and played, hitting a 2-run home run over the right-field wall in his first time at bat. A full house clapped their hands in joy and an effort to warm them on the cold, gray day. Among the New York writers in the press box, Hugh Bradley, a syndicated columnist for the *New York Post*, recalled, it became "a little less certain that the Yankees are 154 games from the World Series." In the third inning Babe Ruth hit an equal wallop but had to settle for a double when it hit the newly installed loudspeaker horn and bounced back on the field. (He would lose another home run the same way in his last game of the year at Shibe Park.) Lefty Grove fanned 9 in his 6–2 win.

Four days later Simmons hit 2 more and Rube Walberg shut out Washington, 7–0.

The A's lost their first game on April 21, to Washington. Earnshaw walked 3 to force in 2 runs in the fourth. Ehmke and Mahaffey pitched in relief. Down 6–3 in the ninth, Simmons and Foxx led off with hits and the fans anticipated the usual late-inning heroics, but a double play ended this one in a fizzle.

The next day the magic was back at New York's opener. The Yankees batted Grove out of the box in the third and led 6–5. Mack sent in nineteen-year-old Glenn Liebhardt, who gave up 1 hit in 3⅔ innings. But when the twenty-year-old left-hander Al Mahon walked to the mound to start the eighth, the crowd of sixty-six thousand so unnerved him that he threw four erratic pitches to Ben Chapman and Mack sent Rube Walberg to the rescue. Bing Miller hit a ninth-inning home run to give the A's the lead, 7–6. In the last of the ninth, Mule Haas saved it by racing back and crashing into the center-field wall to haul in a Ruthian drive with Earle Combs on second and 1 out. Combs tagged up. Bob Shawkey, coaching at third, waved Combs around third. Haas picked himself up and threw to Bishop, who relayed to Cochrane in time to tag the sliding Combs at home.

On May 16 Washington hit Walberg hard, took two from the A's, and moved into first place. The Senators were confident. Frank H. Young of the *Post* said Connie Mack was making the same mistake he had made in 1925—using starters in relief—and would "manage himself out of the race" if he continued.

Mack ignored Young's advice. Earnshaw felt better pitching with one day's rest than four. Grove was a low-maintenance pitcher. Doc Ebling said Lefty never needed much attention, just an alcohol rub now and then and he was as good as ever. Ebling would be surprised when Grove developed a sore arm in 1934.

Howard Ehmke couldn't get anybody out. His arm was dead beyond resurrection. Mack released him on May 30 but paid him his full salary for the season. Mahaffey and Shores were better starting than relieving. Quinn and Rommel could be effective but couldn't do it all. And Mack was not going to count on the rookies when the game was on the line. He had seen enough carnage on May 11, when Mahaffey, Mahon, and Liebhardt had been battered by Cleveland in a 25–7 shellacking, and six days later when Washington roughed up Mahaffey for 9 runs in a 16–5 romp.

Mack knew how powerful a weapon Grove or Earnshaw could be in the late innings to close out a win.

"If I could only get Grove to finish a ball game for us between starts," Mack lamented to Eddie Collins.

Sitting beside Grove in hotel lobbies in the evenings on the road, braving the clouds of cigar smoke, Mack patiently pointed out how much the team needed him to keep a game close in the late innings, how the team's record was more important than any individual's, how it would give a boost to the rest of the boys to see him come in in a tight spot and shut down a rally.

After his first look at the Senators, Mack had said they were the team to beat. In June they would trade Goslin for Heinie Manush and Alvin Crowder, maintaining their outfield power while adding a veteran pitcher. "But you can't count out the Yankees with all that power."

All that power was on display at Shibe Park and Yankee Stadium during three days in May. On the twenty-first, Babe Ruth hit 3 home runs for the first time in a regular season game, but the A's took two, 15–7 and 4–1. The next day Ruth hit 3 more in a doubleheader and Gehrig hit 3 in the second game. A record total of 10 home runs was hit in the second game, won by New York 20–13 after the Yankees had won the first, 10–1.

Two days later at New York Ruth hit 2 more as the Yankees swept another pair, 10–6 and 11–1.

Connie Mack missed the fireworks, out for about two weeks having some wisdom teeth extracted. (In 1933 he would have all his teeth pulled in the Philadelphia office of his friend, Dr. Walter Grier, in an agonizing session. The impression material for the dentures set before the dentist could remove it. He had to break it to get it out. Mack couldn't eat for several days while the dentures were being made in Milford.)

The bombs bursting in air prompted Ring Lardner to equate baseball to "stud poker with the spades wild, or chess with all the pieces moving like queens." He concluded that it was "very unfair to the pitcher; that it discourages the use of brains; that it renders one of the greatest features, base running, almost null and void; and that sooner or later the fans are going to be so sick of seeing victories won by pop fly balls that when a doubleheader is scheduled between the Athletics and Yankees they will spend the afternoon at the public library."

Managers complained that umpires weren't calling corner pitches strikes, forcing pitchers to groove pitches.

The Senators led by 3 games when they came to Shibe Park for a holiday split doubleheader on May 30. They had won 7 of their first 9 games against the Athletics. Grove started the morning game and was losing 6–3 when Spencer Harris pinch-hit for him in the ninth and scored on Simmons's 3-run game-tying home run. Mack called on Jack Quinn. In the thirteenth Simmons doubled, rounded third on Foxx's infield single, and dove back to the bag. As he did, he twisted his right knee. When McNair singled Simmons hobbled home with the winning run.

The length of the game left little time for the park to be emptied and the afternoon crowd to get to their seats. In the clubhouse Simmons stared at his right knee, swollen to twice normal size. "How did you do that?" asked Mack. Simmons didn't know. They sent for the club physician, Dr. Carnett, who was at the game.

"You've broken a blood vessel," the doctor said. He put a cold compress on it and told Mack, "He can't play, but he can sit on the bench and maybe pinch hit if you need him. But he won't be able to run. We'll take him to the hospital later."

Earnshaw started the afternoon game and had nothing. Washington led, 7–4, when Cramer pinch-hit for Earnshaw in the fourth and singled. Bishop doubled. Haas singled. Williams walked. With a run in and the bases loaded, Spencer Harris was due up. Mack aimed a bony finger at Simmons. "Go up and walk around the bases if you can," he said.

Simmons got hold of a pitch from Garland Braxton and sent it into the left-field stands for a grand slam that made it 9–7. Eddie Rommel was hit for 4 runs in the last 5 innings, but the A's kept slugging and finished on top, 15–11.

Al Simmons later called it his greatest day in baseball.

Rube Walberg turned in a rare complete game the next day, winning 7–3.

On June 1 in Washington Grove relieved Mahaffey with men on first and third and 1 out in the ninth and the A's leading, 9–6, and struck out two pinch hitters. The win lifted the A's back into first place. Then they went west, with Simmons resting in Graduate Hospital. Dykes had bruised his hand in a failed squeeze play attempt. Joe Boley had a sore arm and had not been hitting, giving Eric McNair and Dib Williams plenty of playing time. Cochrane was out with a sore ankle that had bothered him all spring. Without their two offensive sparkplugs, Simmons and Cochrane, both hitting above .380, they were not the same team. The pitching was wobbly. They fell out of the lead on June 13, when the Indians routed Walberg and Rommel, 15–2, to sweep a 3-game series.

Walberg in particular rarely survived 4 innings when he started. Somewhere about this time, Connie Mack realized the problem. Either through his own observation or tipped off by Doc Ebling or Rube's roommate, Mack learned that Walberg was a nervous wreck the night before he was to pitch. He paced the floor, chain-smoking for hours, pitching games in his head. In the clubhouse the next day he gulped down aspirins. That would explain why he was often more effective in relief roles, when he had no advance notice that he was going to pitch.

They went into New York for three games beginning July 8 in a virtual tie with the Senators. In the morning meeting Mack made a point of aiming most of his remarks about pitching to the Yankees in Roy Mahaffey's direction. He had Mahaffey take batting practice. Fifteen minutes before game time he handed a new ball to Walberg and told him he was pitching. Rube shut out the Yankees on 3 hits.

Perhaps it was seeing Simmons save him from his first loss of the season on May 30; or the stout work of the old man, Jack Quinn, who still started occasionally and never balked at relieving; or the team's inability to pull away from the rest as the weeks went by in June; or Connie Mack's persuasiveness. Whatever it was, one evening Lefty Grove told Mack, "I'll work for you any way you want me to, if I never get credit for a game."

He no longer complained about working out of turn or being called on to relieve between starts. Well, hardly ever. The day after he pitched a complete game, Mack might ask him, "Robert, can you give me an inning today?" And Grove would say, "Yeah." It reached the point where in a close game, without being asked, Mose would get up and walk to the bullpen and start throwing. For the year Grove would relieve 18 times in addition to his 32 starts.

By July 10 Cleveland had faded out of the picture, but not Washington, which held a slim lead over the A's. Connie Mack was disappointed that his team hadn't run away from the pack.

The A's went west in second place. First stop was St. Louis. To Connie Mack it was time to wake up the boys. "I'm disappointed in you," he said. Then, as Jimmie Dykes recalled it, Mack laced into each player. "It's up to you," he concluded. "You can win this pennant if you want to, if you don't keep on playing like the walking dead. That's all I have to say."

It was enough. They won 7 in a row and regained first place. When they reached Chicago July 21, Mack told Arch Ward, "Washington is hard to beat. I was a little worried about my boys until we started this trip. Pitching was unsteady and hitting not as it should be. But they are starting to click now."

Playing with all the moxie they had shown in 1929, they finished the trip 12-4 and came home July 28 with a 6-game lead over Washington, 10 over New York. The next day their reputation for late-inning fireworks was renewed. Rube Walberg pitched 8 strong innings against New York, but the A's trailed 5–3 until Jimmy Foxx hit a 2-run homer in the last of the ninth. Earnshaw then pitched 4 innings in relief and Cochrane drove in the winning run in the twelfth. For the year the A's would be 13-4 in games decided in the seventh, 7-7 in the eighth, and 13-5 in the ninth or later. Al Simmons hit 10 of his 36 home runs from the seventh inning on.

Connie Mack was confident enough to give his youngsters plenty of playing time. McNair and Williams were playing second, third, and short when Boley's arm hurt or Bishop needed a rest. Cramer was filling in for injured outfielders. For the first time in his career Jimmie Dykes played one position—third base—all season, except for one memorable experience in left field. It happened on July 9 in New York, and rookie third baseman Mike "Pinky" Higgins was part of it.

Higgins had played football and baseball at the University of Texas. A flock of scouts were after him when he graduated in June. Mike Drennan of the A's was one of them. He wasn't getting anywhere. Higgins went home to Dallas, where his father was a policeman. Connie Mack asked Hyman Pearlstone to help.

Pearlstone invited Pinky and his parents to his office and persuaded them that Connie Mack was the man to play for. As he later recalled, "The contract called for $3,000 [bonus], but there was one hitch. Pinky was a minor and had to have his parents' approval. That cost us another $2,500."

Higgins reported to the A's, and a few days later he was sent up to pinch-hit in a 7–3 loss. "I was so scared I could hardly find the plate," he told Arthur Daley twenty-nine years later.

It was an unforgettable experience for a green college kid. "What a bunch," he recalled. "They were good and they knew it. They were tough and they never let you forget it. On a road trip I'd never get to swing in batting practice. At home I'd have to get to the ballpark early to take my cuts. If I asked for advice I could get it, but no one volunteered. I learned how to play third base by watching the best—Dykes, Bluege, Kamm. They were artists."

On the day of the escapade involving Dykes playing left field, the Yankees led 9–3 after 5 innings. Al Simmons, who had homered in the third, complained that his ankles hurt. He wanted out of the lineup. Mack sent Jimmie Dykes out to left field and put Higgins in at third.

Higgins remembered the game not just for his first big league hit, but for what he saw when a fly ball was hit to Dykes:

Jimmie judges it accurately and waits, but Mule Haas can't resist pulling a gag. "Come in on it, Jim," he shouts. "More, more."

Dykes knows he's wrong but he has so much respect for the Mule that he keeps running until he's overrun the ball. It falls back of him for a double. Dykes is furious and Haas nigh dies a-laughing.

Pretty soon another batter hits one to Dykes and Haas gives him the business all over again. "Come in on it, Jim," shouts Haas.

"Nuts to you," says Dykes, and makes the catch.

Those regulars were a crazy bunch. They played hard on and off the field. But they had fun and would do anything for a laugh.

Playing every day at third base, Jimmie Dykes was within range of the hecklers. Jimmie was the pride of Bryn Mawr, doing an outstanding job at the plate and in the field. But that didn't make him immune from the traditional royal razzing reserved for hometown players in Philadelphia. George Burns had endured it. In the future Del Ennis of the Phillies would hear it.

Connie Mack shook his head over it. "Lookit," he told Von Ziekursch one day, "there's something I can't figure, and I've thought about it a lot. It's that bunch of fans in Philadelphia who sit back of third base and razz Jimmie Dykes. You know, I can't figure these fellows at all."

They were just as rough on Al Simmons, no matter what he did. The one closest to him would holler, "You look bad today. Out all night, eh? Had a few too many?"

One would yell, "Think Simmons will ever get a hit?" Another would answer, "He may never get another one."

St. Louis first baseman Jack Burns recalled a time when Simmons hit a single and one of the leatherlungs yelled, "That's right, Simmons, always hitting singles, and you're getting $30,000 a year."

Simmons said to Burns, "Nothing I do is right."

They picked on visitors with equal enthusiasm. During the winter Detroit infielder Billy Rogell had been caught on a smuggler's boat that was shelled by a rum chaser. He was cleared in court, but the next season he heard "Bootlegger Rogell" from the hecklers.

Right fielder Lew Fonseca of the Indians and later the White Sox was a favorite target of one heckler on the right-field side.

"He climbed on me the minute I appeared on the field," Fonseca told Chicago writer Francis J. Powers. "He never pronounced my name correctly nor twice in the same way. 'Hey Fonsicky, why don't you go to work? Why don't you get a job? You can't play ball. . . . You oughta stayed in vaudeville. . . . You're just a ham. If you don't get some hits you'll be back singing before long. . . . You spend more money on beer than you do on your family. . . .'"

One day Fonseca, after going hitless for the fifth time, was greeted with "Now, Fosecker, will you give up?"

They rode Fonseca's teammate, left fielder Bibb Falk, just as hard and with precise knowledge of where he had been the night before.

The umpires got it too: "Brick Owens broke a leg jumping out a window at a Camden speakeasy."

"Every park has its grandstand jockeys," Fonseca said, "but those Philly hucksters were the worst of them all."

Out west in July the A's lost Mule Haas to a sprained ankle and Joe Boley to a bruised wrist hit by a pitch. Flit Cramer, Eric McNair, and Dib Williams filled in with no letdown, though Cramer's weakness on picking up ground balls in center field became apparent.

They finished July winning two games in Washington and led by 8. Grove won the first and preserved Earnshaw's win in the second. During the second game Flit Cramer was given a take sign. Instead he swung and popped it up. On the train back to Philadelphia, Connie Mack called him over.

"Sit down here, son."

Cramer sat down. "Doggone it," said Mack, "you missed the sign today."

"I know," said Cramer.

"You're going to Portland tomorrow," said Mack.

"I'm not going," said Cramer

"Oh yes, you're going. You're going out there to learn how to field and learn the signs."

Cramer was on the train the next morning. Mack gave the Portland club $10,000 to send Homer Summa back to him.

On August 2 in the second game of a doubleheader against Boston, the A's trailed 5–0 in the seventh. With McNair and Williams in the lineup, Mack used his graybeard platoon of pinch hitters, Wally Schang and Eddie Collins. Collins batted for Quinn and singled and scored a run before Al Simmons hit a game-tying home run. After falling behind again, the A's came back in the eighth, and Grove drove in the winning run in the ninth with a double to sweep the day's activity.

It was the last of Eddie Collins's 3,311 career hits.

Connie Mack had made the transition from the old game of speed and skill to the modern power game. "The A's do not play a bunting game," he said, "unless it is essential we get one run late in the game. It is no longer considered good ball to try for one run in mid-game. Before the game ends you may find you need six to win. Ballplayers of today have gotten so far from bunting, some regulars are not equal to it. Late in the game when one run may decide, then you bunt if you have a hitter who knows how to do it."

They had some power all through the lineup, headed by Foxx and Simmons. Even the walking man, Max Bishop, hit 10 home runs. Only Boley and Haas were not longball threats. On June 18, facing Wes Ferrell in the fifth inning at Shibe Park, Simmons, Foxx, and Miller hit back-to-back-to-back home runs. Al Simmons was all worked up about the possibility of the A's being the first team to hit four in a row. Joe Boley was up next. He bunted and beat it out for a hit. When the inning ended, Simmons yelled at him, "You chucklehead. Why didn't you go for that fourth home run?"

Boley smiled and said, "Smart baseball. Did you see where the third baseman was playing? They weren't looking for a bunt."

In recent years the Athletics had usually been last or next to last in the league in stolen bases. They didn't even have a sliding pit in spring training anymore. But once in a while the "old man" turned back to the "old game." On July 25 against Cleveland they pulled the rare feat of two triple steals in the same game—Simmons, Miller, and Williams in the first inning; Cochrane, Simmons, and Foxx in the fourth. Bishop, Miller, and Simmons also hit home runs in the 14–1 rout. It was as if Connie Mack wanted to show the world they could do it all.

In August Mickey Cochrane, anticipating another World Series check, celebrated the birth of his first child, a daughter, by fulfilling a longtime wish—buying a Packard convertible.

But Connie Mack was still keeping a wary eye on the Senators in his rearview mirror. Mack knew that one bad week could start a slump that could cost a pennant, especially if the second-place team got hot at the same time. An 8-game lead could vanish in a hurry.

On August 24 Mule Haas was out with a sore shoulder. Homer Summa's error led to the first Washington run in a 7–3 loss that cut the A's lead to 7½ games. The next day the Senators whittled another game off the lead. Mack wanted another outfielder, preferably a right-handed batter, one who was swinging a hot bat.

Twenty-seven-year-old Jim Moore had started the year with the White Sox, then was sold outright to Dallas. There he got off to a slow start, batting .138 on May 30. From then on his average had risen every week until by August 20 he was hitting .363. Mack and Dallas business manager Bob Tarleton had agreed on a price of $10,000 and a player for Moore for delivery after the season. Now Mack decided he wanted Moore immediately.

On Monday, August 25, Mack wired Tarleton, "Will be pleased to take Moore. Have him report Brunswick Hotel Boston at once." Mack told writers he would have a new outfielder by Thursday.

The Dallas club was in Beaumont. Tarleton relayed the message to Moore, who took a train to Dallas to pack his belongings on Tuesday. The next day he apparently missed the eastbound train. The telegram had said "report at once," and Moore was eager to do so. He decided to fly. There weren't many choices in those days. Based on Air Transport Association archives, the best guess is that on Thursday he took a Southwest Air Fast Express twelve-passenger Ford Tri-Motor from Dallas to Kansas City and changed airlines for a flight to Columbus, Ohio, a thirteen-hour trip that cost $74.50. A fourteen-hour train ride to New York (fare $17.50) and a Colonial Air Transport flight from Newark to Boston ($17.43) brought him to Boston Friday night. Connie Mack was in the lobby of the Brunswick on Saturday morning after breakfast when he first set eyes on Jim Moore. "And was he mad," Moore recalled. "He didn't like the idea of 10,000 bucks in cash taking any chances like that."

Stoney McLinn wrote that Mack talked to Moore like a Dutch uncle: "Had I known you would do something as foolish, I would have left you with the Dallas club. It's too darn risky for a ballplayer to ride in airships for twelve hours." Yet, wrote McLinn, "there was the suspicion of a twinkle in Connie Mack's eyes as he laid down the law to Moore."

By September 1 the lead was down to 5½ games. Mack gave his boys a pep talk before the start of a 4-game series at home against Boston. "Don't worry about what Washington is doing. Go out and play your own game every day."

They responded, Lefty Grove most of all. Sailing along with an 11–4 lead in the first game, he had to leave in the seventh, when a line drive hit a finger on his left hand. Quinn finished it for him. Jim Moore made his A's debut, driving in 4 runs with a home run and double. For a day at least Mule Haas wasn't missed. The next day Grove relieved Mahaffey in the seventh inning of a 4–4 game and pitched 9 innings. Both teams scored a run in the tenth. After the Red Sox scored 2 in the fourteenth, Cochrane doubled and Simmons tied it again with a home run. In the fifteenth Simmons drove in his sixth run of the day to win it, 8–7.

Earnshaw needed no help winning the third game, 5–1. On September 6 Grove picked up his third win in four days, pitching 3 innings in a 1–1 game broken up by Cochrane's tenth-inning home run. Grove's record was now 25-5.

The lead was back to 7½ games. There would be no slump.

Moore continued to swing a hot bat, hitting .380 in 15 games. His 2-run home run against Detroit September 9 provided the 3–1 margin for Lefty Grove's twenty-sixth win.

The season-long feud between the A's and Firpo Marberry came to a head on September 7 in Washington. The home fans were all over Al Simmons, who had taken umbrage at Marberry's throwing at him earlier in the year. Dykes and the rest of the A's were letting Marberry have it. After the third out in the top of the seventh Marberry made a beeline from the mound toward the A's dugout. Two teammates grabbed him. When the Athletics came off the field after the seventh, a pop bottle aimed at Simmons narrowly missed. A police cordon guarded the visitors' dugout for the rest of the game, which the Senators won with 2 in the ninth, 7–6, to cut the lead to 6½ games.

The Athletics headed west, arriving in Detroit in time to huddle around a radio to listen to an old-timers game in Boston between a team of Red Sox old-timers and an all-star team that included Connie Mack's old $100,000 infield of McInnis, Collins, Barry, and Baker. They clinched the pennant in Chicago on September 18 in their accustomed style—falling behind and rallying two times, capped by a 5-run seventh. It was Connie Mack's eighth pennant.

The Cardinals led the Cubs and Robins by 2½ games. The A's were rooting for the Cubs because Wrigley Field would provide a bigger payoff than the smaller St. Louis or Brooklyn parks. But the Cardinals held the lead to the end.

When the champions arrived at North Philadelphia station at 6:00 p.m. on September 22, Connie Mack went directly home while a dozen players were whisked to City Hall for an official greeting from Mayor Mackey.

The Yankees had scored 1,062 runs in the year of heavy hitting. Gehrig had driven in a record 174 of them. If you didn't hit over .350, you wouldn't make the top five, which was led by Al Simmons at .381. Simmons had a monster year: 165 RBIs in 138 games, 36 home runs, and only 34 strikeouts.

The Athletics finished 8 games ahead of Washington and 16 in front of New York. Together, Grove and Earnshaw worked in 99 games, won 50 of the 102 victories, and pitched almost half the team's total innings.

There was truth in the possibly made-up story of a young reporter asking Connie Mack the secret of his success. "A good memory," Mack said. "All I have to do is remember the names of Grove and Earnshaw. I tell one he is pitching today and the other he is pitching tomorrow. So they win, and I am a great manager."

Lefty Grove had matured into a pitcher who realized how to use the talent he was born with for the greatest benefit. He took his time, thinking, not trying to strike out every batter. He knew the hitters, threw off-speed pitches, paced himself, bore down when he had to, and still struck out 209. He brought his walks down to 60 in 291 innings. Connie Mack gave him a $3,000 year-end bonus.

"It is a big help to me," Grove told Bill Duncan of the *Public Ledger*, "and gives me lots of confidence to know that I have my fast one to use in the pinch, but until the pinch comes I am content to have the outfielders and infielders retire the batsmen."

Max Bishop for the second year in a row drew more walks than his hit total for an on-base percentage of .426. (SABR statistical analyst Tom Hanrahan concluded that Bishop had baseball's best batting eye ever.) In Cochrane, Simmons, and Foxx, the A's had their own Murderers' Row. And they had the premier field general in the game.

"[Mack's] success," wrote Arch Ward of the *Tribune*, "has been remarkable because, as his contemporaries point out, he has made his men come around to his way of doing things. He has had his prima donnas and his duffers. But he ultimately turns them into the perfect machine. That requires patience, understanding, and restraint. He is a curious combination of the manly elements."

In the midst of the late-1930s Yankees' domination of all baseball, Red Sox manager Joe Cronin would rate the 1930 Athletics a better team than the 1938 Yankees.

28 | 1930 WORLD SERIES

St. Louis was the smallest two-team city in the major leagues. In the early 1920s the Browns were the toast of the town, narrowly losing the 1922 pennant to the Yankees. That year Sam Breadon, an émigré automobile dealer from New York, bought control of the Cardinals. The club had no money to compete with the deep pockets of the Cubs, White Sox, Giants, and Yankees in the open market. Breadon backed the idea of his general manager, Branch Rickey, to sign young players by the dozens and grow their own stars through a network of minor league clubs they would buy or control through working agreements. They were not alone in this when they made their first connection with Houston in 1919, but they built more aggressively than anyone else. By 1940 the Cardinals' farm system would grow to thirty-one teams controlling more than six hundred players.

The system had produced its first St. Louis pennant winner in 1926 and its first world champions after a seven-game World Series against the Yankees. They won the pennant again in 1928 but were swept by the Yankees in the Series.

With a homegrown nucleus of Jim Bottomley, Chick Hafey, Taylor Douthit, George Watkins, Charley Gelbert, and Bill Hallahan and astute trades that brought them Frank Frisch, Burleigh Grimes, and Jimmy Wilson, they were young, smart, and speedy.

Ira Thomas spent two weeks following the Cardinals. Connie Mack sent Mickey Cochrane home from St. Louis to watch the Cardinals at Baker Bowl September 19–23. The Athletics returned home in time for Mack to see the last game of that series. He was impressed by the Cards' speed and skill and said "Bosh" to the idea that they would be worn out from their grueling, hard-fought pennant race.

When the Cardinals worked out at Shibe Park, their main topic of discussion was how small it looked. And it was, compared to Yankee Stadium, where some of them had played before crowds exceeding sixty thousand in 1926 and '28. Observers noticed they hit very few long balls. But they were no lightweights with the bat, having outhit the A's by 20 points and scored 1,004 runs. Everybody in the lineup batted over .300, topped by rookie George Watkins's .373. They had some pop, although four of them hitting 10 or more home runs was modest in this popcorn-hitting season. A balanced pitching staff was headed by veteran spitball artist Burleigh Grimes and Jess Haines, with youngsters Flint Rhem and lefty Bill Hallahan. Connie Mack was not taking them lightly.

Center fielder Taylor Douthit checked out the outfield with his sunglasses and declared he saw nothing any worse than the conditions at Sportsman's Park. It was also ten days earlier in the year than it had been when Hack Wilson had had his problems a year ago, and that made a difference in the sun's early-afternoon position.

An attack of lumbago kept Frank Frisch in bed, but he would play, his back encased in tape and plaster. Shortstop Charley Gelbert would also have a sore leg taped every day. Nor would an ankle injury sideline first-string catcher Jimmy Wilson, although his condition was doubtful enough for Cardinals manager Gabby Street to obtain Connie Mack's permission to add an ineligible catcher, Earl Smith, to the active roster. For the A's Jimmie Dykes was slowed by a bruise below his right thigh that Doc Ebling taped up before every game.

With last year's experience behind them, the Athletics' office staff had no problems handling preparations. Bob Schroeder hired almost a hundred clerks to handle the flood of ticket applications—thirty-three thousand more than they could fill for the strips of tickets to three games. Speculating would be a bum business this year. Federal agents arrested eighteen speculators in the area. So many buyers had been denied entrance last year, prices on the street dropped below face value by game time. Official paid attendance would be identical for each home game: 32,295.

The stock market had turned around, at least temporarily, but the economic news continued gloomy. Christy Walsh's syndication sales nosedived to under $5,000, some of which again went to Connie Mack. Bob Paul ghosted for Lefty Grove, an endeavor that Paul would regret. "He's too tough to work with," Paul said. "You don't get anything out of him."

Millions of fans would hear all the action from Graham McNamee and Ford Frick on NBC, Ted Husing on CBS. Betting was light, the Athletics generally posted as 10–7 favorites.

While Nick Altrock and Al Schacht entertained the early arrivals with their pregame comedy routines, Babe Ruth—in person, not his ghostwriter—sat on the A's bench. When rookie Jim Moore entered, Ruth said, "Hiya kid. How do you feel about being in the big games?"

"A little nervous," Moore said.

"The same as I do," said Ruth, "every time I get to bat, and I've been in seven or eight World Series."

President Hoover attended the first game with five members of the cabinet. Unlike last year, Connie Mack crossed the field as martial music blared from the loudspeaker to greet the president. "I'm glad to see you here," Mack said, "because we always win with you.

Another visitor on the field greeting old friends was star of stage and screen Joe E. Brown, among the most fanatic of theatrical baseball fans. A naive *Inquirer* sidebar supplier turned in this interesting note: "Brown used to play with the Boston Red Sox. 'My biggest moment in the game,' he said, 'was when I batted for Harry Hooper.'"

That could only have happened, if at all, during a spring training game somewhere if Brown had been allowed to work out with the team and given a chance to bat.

On the eve of the opener Connie Mack insisted he still didn't know who would start for him, and he took plenty of ribbing from the writers. Some press box wags, when asked who they thought would open the Series for Mack, listed every pitcher on the staff, separated only by an "or" between the names.

John Kieran of the *Times* wrote: "Mr. McGillicuddy may warm up Grove before the game and then shoot Rube Waddell to the mound. Or Rip Van Winkle."

Maybe, Mack admitted, it was just a superstition with him to wait until the day of the game to name his pitcher. At least he had won last year doing that. But there would be no surprises this time. The Cardinals would see plenty of Grove and Earnshaw, just as the American League had all year.

As bench jockeys, the Cardinals were right up there with the Cubs. On the mound Burleigh Grimes was as ornery as Lefty Grove but a lot more talkative. Dick Bartell, who had played with him in Pittsburgh, called Grimes "the meanest, toughest, hardest-boiled pitcher I ever knew. . . . With that two-day stubble of beard, he snapped and snarled and glared at you. He was liable to knock you down on any pitch, whatever the count."

The jabs began before the Series with Grimes calling the Athletics "a bunch of bushers," and they never stopped. Grimes and Cochrane had never met. Bob Paul said he introduced them before the opener and they talked for about ten minutes. It probably didn't take that long for them to realize they didn't like each other, maybe because they were so much alike on the field—iron nerves and full of fight. Grimes made a big deal of Cochrane's protruding ears. "Some of his remarks got under my hide," Cochrane said later. Burleigh signaled his disdain for Foxx by the choke sign. He mimicked Al Simmons's habit of flicking bits of dust from his uniform. Other Redbirds joined in. Cochrane and Miller and Rommel and Haas and Dykes were in full throat too.

Grimes didn't stop at mouthing off at players. He later said he thought his first two pitches of the first game to lead off batter Max Bishop were strikes, but umpire George Moriarty called them balls. "I walked toward the plate and asked him what was the matter with them? Moriarty said, 'Don't you know who's batting? That's Max Bishop.' I said, 'Well, George, I thought I was pitching to the plate, not a name.'"

Grimes and Grove started the opener on a cold, windy Wednesday afternoon, October 1. In the first inning Connie Mack pulled a surprise. The A's almost never stole a base, especially early in a game. But after Cochrane walked with 2 out and a 2-strike count on Simmons, Mack sent Cochrane. Gus Mancuso threw him out. In the second inning Foxx's double off the wall was played into a triple by right-fielder Ray Blades. Bing Miller drove him in with a sacrifice fly.

Grove struck out 3 of the first 6 he faced, but in the third Mancuso and Gelbert singled and Grove fell down trying to field a bunt by Grimes. Three on, nobody out. But all they could muster was a pair of sacrifice flies for 2 runs. That was it for the day.

The A's pecked away. In the fourth Simmons homered. In the sixth Bishop walked and Dykes doubled him home. In the seventh Haas tripled and Mack played small ball again; Boley put down a perfect suicide squeeze. In the eighth Cochrane, who had exchanged words with Grimes every time up, hit the first pitch over the right-field wall and yammered at Grimes as he rounded the bases. The Athletics had scored 5 runs on 5 hits—2 home runs, 2 triples, and a double.

The A's clubhouse was open to the press after the game. Amid the joyful noise, Ira Thomas said Grove didn't look right to him—he gave up 9 hits. Thomas was surprised he had lasted 9 innings.

Grove refused to talk about his pitching. "If you're going to write anything about the game," he said, "give it to Boley. That play he made in the seventh just about decided the game."

The play he referred to came with Grimes on first, 1 out, and the score 3–2. Douthit hit a hot shot between short and third. Boley dove for it, knocked it down, picked it up, and threw to second in time to get Grimes. It was followed by another single before Bishop leaped high to snare a line drive hit by Frisch.

There must have been some long-stifled echoes in the visitors' clubhouse. The Cardinals sounded just like the Cubs of a year ago: "They got all the breaks. The breaks beat us."

The next day the weather was warmer but the action was not. Earnshaw fanned 8 and allowed only 7 base runners, one a bases-empty home run by Watkins for the only Cardinals' run. The A's scored 6 runs on 7 hits—another home run by Cochrane and doubles by Foxx, Simmons, and Dykes. Flint Rhem—either the victim or the perpetrator of a celebrated twenty-four-hour "kidnapping with bootleg whiskey forced down my throat" incident in September—should have stayed kidnapped. The A's scored 2 with 2 out in the first. Cochrane hit a home run. Simmons singled. Foxx doubled. In the third, again with 2 out, the A's scored 2 more. Frisch fumbled a grounder by Cochrane. Simmons doubled. Miller singled. In the fourth Boley singled, Bishop walked, and Dykes doubled them home and Rhem was gone.

A threat by the Cardinals in the eighth was stopped by what most writers called "a genuine bad break." But John McGraw saw it differently, describing the kind of play that caused many writers to single out Jimmie Dykes as the key player in the Athletics' World Series triumphs in both 1929 and 1930. McGraw's comments are worth quoting at length for his opinion of Dykes and the insight they offer into how John McGraw watched a game.

That brief mention [of a bad break] refers to one of the very best plays of the series which was more the result of alertness and quick thinking than luck. This brilliant play was made by Jimmy Dykes, a fighting ballplayer of the old-fashioned type. Jimmy may be somewhat slower than other stars in the league, but he is certainly not handicapped that way in the brain. He is a competitive player of the highest type—not merely a piece of muscular machinery.

Already [the Cardinals] had been robbed by several fielding plays that seemed impossible. . . . This particular inning started off with Sparky Adams driving a clean single into right. The Cardinals, still full of fight, jumped at the chance. Frankie Frisch, batting left-handed, picked one off on the outside, and with a vicious whack sent the ball toward third base. It looked like a sure single.

Jimmy Dykes evidently had been on the lookout for a ball hit down his way though the general thought was that Frisch would pull into right field. At the crack of the bat Adams was on his toes ready to tear around on the hit.

Dykes, taking one step backward, leaped high in the air, reached for the ball, and it hit him squarely in the outstretched glove. As the ball stuck the St. Louis rooters groaned.

Ordinarily, the making of that catch and getting one man would seem sufficient, but Jimmy Dykes, being a real ballplayer, thought out another possibility as he jumped. Anyway, Dykes' feet came to the ground in the right position for him to make a throw. Without hesitation he whipped the ball to Foxx at first base—a perfect peg—and Adams was caught off the bag for a double play. That was a really great play—correctly thought out and perfectly executed. Had Dykes failed to make the catch the Cardinals would have had two on and none out. It was indeed a bad break for the St. Louis outfit, but I give the credit to Jimmy Dykes and not to luck.

Calling Dykes a "money player" like Chief Bender, Connie Mack agreed with McGraw's assessment. "Jimmie plays a brand of baseball that is not particularly flashy during the regular season. That's why he has never been given the real credit which he deserves. When you put him into an important series, however, you have a new and different Dykes."

That was the game. A few of the Cards reached third, but no kayo punch followed. When Mancuso struck out to end the game, Cochrane ran to give the ball to Earnshaw, who jumped over the foul stripe and kept on jumping with joy into the clubhouse.

"I'm ready to pitch Saturday if Connie will let me," he said. "I feel best when I've had only one day's rest."

On the trains to St. Louis both managers had the same comment about the breaks: they had a way of evening up.

Connie Mack had good reason for not announcing his pitching plans ahead of time. He intended to start Rube Walberg, and he didn't want Rube pitching two or three games in his head beforehand. With a 2–0 lead, Connie Mack felt comfortable handing the ball to Walberg, who had suffered fits of wildness all year, although George Earnshaw would be well rested, having not thrown a pitch for forty-six hours. Not that Mack was overconfident. "The Cardinals will give us a terrific fight and will hit better on their own home grounds," he said. He expected Jimmy Wilson, sore ankle and all, would be doing the catching, which would steady the pitchers.

Added field boxes in front of the dugouts in Sportsman's Park forced Connie Mack to wave his scorecard in full view of the fans from a bench in front of the box seats. Everybody could see which players were doing the hollering and gesturing. Rube Walberg threw strikes—he walked only 1—but the Cardinals' Taylor Douthit homered bunched hits in the fourth. In the fifth Wilson executed a hit and run perfectly, hitting behind Blades, who had singled. Gelbert singled in a run. When Walberg walked Hallahan, Rube took a walk and Shores replaced him. Shores and Quinn, who is the oldest player—forty-seven years, three months, three days—ever to appear in a World Series, were also hittable, but Bill Hallahan, the National League strikeout leader, was not, at least not for extra bases. Six of the A's 7 hits were singles, 3 of them by Bishop, and they left 11 on base in the 5–0 loss. The only real threat came in the first inning, when they loaded the bases with 2 outs. But Miller struck out on a sharp curve.

Mack sent Jim Moore up to pinch-hit for Haas in the ninth inning. "I was trembling noticeably," Moore said. "But when I took my stance I thought, 'This is just another game.'" He singled. Bishop walked. But Dykes took a curve for strike three to end the game.

Almost forty thousand fans paid to sit and stand in a packed Sportsman's Park on Sunday. The breaks evened up. Lefty Grove was faster and sharper than he had been in the opener. Gabby Street started thirty-seven-year-old Jesse Haines, seemingly over the hill since shutting out the Yankees four years ago to the day. In the first inning the A's scored only 1 run despite 3 hits and a wild pitch. From then on Haines, relying on sweeping curves, pinpoint control, and pitching smarts, baffled every batter. "Our boys showed poor judgment sometimes in hitting bad balls," Mack said. Al Simmons beat out an infield roller for the A's only other hit.

In the bottom of the third Charley Gelbert hit a double down the right-field line. Bing Miller raced over for it, but it caromed off the boxes at an angle, eluding Miller long enough for Gelbert to make it to third. Connie Mack later called that the deciding break of the game. "If Miller had succeeded in holding Gelbert's triple to two bases," he said, "the game would have been different. Grove would have pitched all fastballs to Haines. But now he had to throw curves to induce a grounder that we could get Gelbert at home. The curve he threw did not break right."

With the infield in, Haines singled up the middle to score Gelbert.

But the breaks weren't finished. In the fourth with 2 out, Hafey doubled. Blades hit a grounder to Dykes, who looked at Hafey, hesitated, then made an awkward throw to first that was low. It bounced off Foxx's glove and rolled away. By the time Foxx picked it up, Hafey had scored. Wilson singled. Gelbert's bouncer glanced off Grove's glove and Blades scored to make it 3–1.

That was all the scoring for the day.

Twenty-four-year-old second-year shortstop Gelbert's two key hits were accompanied by equally key defensive plays. He dashed in for a slow roller to end the first inning, went deep in the hole in the third to start a double play, and dashed in to field a ball that bounced high over Haines's head in the eighth to nip Simmons at first after Dykes had walked.

After the game Dykes called his action in the fourth that had led to 2 runs the dumbest play of his life. Taking all the blame that he expected would come his way, he offered no alibis. "When the ball reached my glove," he said, "I saw Hafey coming toward the bag and immediately realized that I had an easy play at third. I was set to wait for Chick and tag him out. He appeared to be ready for it, too. Then all of a sudden something flashed through my mind that I should throw to first base. You know, you don't have all day to come to a decision, so I threw to first. And to add trouble to the rotten play, I threw the ball away. There is no one to blame but myself."

Connie Mack didn't see it that way. He blamed Jimmy Foxx for taking his time going after the ball. The next morning Mack summoned Foxx to his room. Stan Baumgartner quoted Mack's lecture: "Jimmie Dykes's error was excusable. Errors are all in the ball game, but you did not play the game with your head up. Had you been awake you could have picked up Dykes' wild throw and nailed Hafey at home by thirty feet. My boy, those are the lapses that hurt. Wake up. Keep alive."

Both managers considered the fifth game the pivotal one. Street came back with Grimes, Mack with Earnshaw. And they were both sharp, matching zeroes for 7 innings. Earnshaw gave up a single in the first and a two-out single that Haas fell asleep on, allowing Wilson to reach second, in the seventh. That caused Mack to order Gelbert walked to pitch to Grimes, only the second time he had ever called for an intentional pass in a World Series game.

Grimes was equally stingy, giving up 2 hits in 7 innings. He was thoroughly enjoying himself, dusting off Al Simmons more than once, yakking between pitches at the A's and their rooters seated behind them.

In the third inning Jimmie Dykes handed the Cardinals a break. After Gelbert walked and Grimes bunted him to second, Douthit hit a grounder to Dykes, who saw Gelbert hung up between second and third and chased him back toward second and never threw to Bishop. Gelbert reached the bag safely. Now there were men on first and second and 1 out. Up in the press box the name of Heinie Zimmerman was recalled. The Giants third baseman had chased Eddie Collins across home plate in the final game of the 1917 World Series. The writers began fitting Dykes with goat horns. Dykes said later he could feel them sprouting. Earnshaw remained calm. Adams popped up and Frisch grounded out to Foxx, and no harm was done.

(Syndicated humorist Will Rogers was listening to Ted Husing's broadcast of the game. He commented, "Only man I can't forgive, that's the radio announcer for Columbia, who kept comparing Dykes's bone-head play chasing Gelbert to one 'pulled years ago by Hans Wagner.' Hans Wagner in all his life never pulled one. It was Heinie Zimmerman.")

The A's threatened in the eighth. With 1 out Haas beat out a bunt and stole second. Boley's sharp grounder hit Grimes's glove and bounced away. Grimes picked it up and threw to third too late. With Grove up in the bullpen, Mack sent Jim Moore in to hit for Earnshaw. At this point it seemed likely that 1 run would be enough to win. This time Moore wasn't nervous and patiently drew a walk to load the bases. Max Bishop stepped into the batter's box. Grimes had struck him out twice, not an easy thing to do to Camera Eye. Grimes calmly induced Bishop to hit a ground ball to Bottomley at first, who threw to the plate to get Haas. Dykes hit a spitter at Gelbert, who threw to second to force Bishop, and the crowd went crazy.

Second-guessers questioned Mack's pinch-hitting for Earnshaw the way the big Moose was mowing them down, but at this time in the life of the planet, Earnshaw and Grove were interchangeable. The game went into the ninth still scoreless.

In the top of the ninth the Athletics' heroics of 1929 returned with the same hero in the leading role. Cochrane led off with a walk on a 3 and 2 spitter that was barely inside. Simmons popped up. Later Connie Mack credited third base coach Eddie Collins with a timely assist for calling Grimes's next pitch.

"Grimes was a master at masking his face with his hands and delivering his spitters with the identical delivery he used when he was faking and throwing something else," Mack said. "He had a great pitching brain, a good fastball, and a fine curve, but his spitter was his Sunday pitch."

Foxx was the batter. Grimes went through the motions to throw a spitter. Collins read curve and flashed it to Foxx. Grimes later confirmed it was a high curve—only the second he had thrown in the whole Series—a perfect pitch right where he wanted it, the same pitch he had used to strike out Foxx in the seventh. "I didn't think he could hit that one, so I gave it to him again." It was a pitch, Jimmy Wilson agreed, "we didn't think he could hit."

Foxx timed it perfectly, "and he knocked the concrete loose in the center field bleachers," Grimes said. "He hit it so hard I couldn't feel sorry for myself."

(After the game Foxx confirmed it was a curve, but he said nothing about Collins tipping him.)

"There should be a law against the thing Jimmy Foxx did," wrote Louis La Coss in the *St. Louis Globe-Democrat*.

The A's flung bats wildly in the air while most of the audience sat in deep silence, watching Connie Mack up on his feet with as much enthusiasm as his boys. Nobody on the bench gave a thought to the Cardinals touching Grove, not even when Frisch had singled with 2 out in the eighth or when Blades walked with 1 out in the ninth. Yesterday's hero, Charley Gelbert, looked at a fastball for strike three to end it.

Back in Philadelphia club secretary Bob Schroeder had a problem. For some unexplained reason, tickets had been printed for four home games, but they had been sold for only three. Perhaps the club had thought that it would be easier to distribute tickets for a seventh game if needed than to refund the money. Schroeder mulled his options. He could choose at random from the thirty-three thousand original applicants who had been turned down, put the tickets on sale outside the ballpark during the sixth game so only new buyers could get them, or sell them as the fans left the sixth game. He decided to do nothing until Commissioner Landis arrived from St. Louis.

Jimmie Dykes expected the hecklers to get on him for his boner in St. Louis, but the cheers that greeted him drowned out the razzes. For all his hecklers, Dykes had more friends than anybody in baseball.

The headlines said Grove was "almost certain" to start the sixth game. Instead it was Earnshaw, with one day's rest. The Moose cruised along with a shutout until the ninth, but it wasn't easy. A bruised heel, suffered during batting practice when a foul ball had banged his instep, bothered him. His two previous starts had taken something out of him. Fortunately the

A's gave him an early lead, finding Bill Hallahan no puzzle this time. Making the most of 7 hits—home runs by Dykes and Simmons and 5 doubles—they scored in 5 of the first 6 innings and led 7–0. Max Bishop was a silent offensive threat, walking twice, hit by a pitch, and scoring 2 runs.

"Lucky for me," Earnshaw said after the game. "My arm got heavier with every pitch. I was getting tired and was virtually exhausted in the ninth." The Cardinals went down fighting, scoring a run in the ninth on 2 hits and 2 walks around a double play. Grove was in the bullpen the entire game, ready to go in whenever called upon.

"When Wilson finally flied to Miller for the last out," said Earnshaw, "I felt like stretching right out on the grass and going to sleep."

Shredded paper and ticker tape rained down on the streets around City Hall.

There was none of the drama of last year's final ninth-inning comeback. The game and the Series had been all but over for the last hour. In the A's clubhouse the celebration was more like a day's work well done than exhilaration.

Connie Mack wasn't the least bit tired. He was, as Rud Rennie wrote, "as calm as a cup of cold consomme." Or was he just speechless with joy? The players were in the clubhouse shouting the time-honored clichés of the victors into Graham McNamee's microphone when Mack entered. He patted players on the back while McNamee waved for him to say a few words. Before he reached the microphone, he stopped and said to his boys, "You did what I asked you to do. You are a really great ball team."

In his office Mack sat and calmly brushed his long fingers through his grayish sandy hair, smiled, and said, "Well, there's not much to be said." He gave all the credit to his boys, who could now be called "a great team."

Earnshaw, whom Babe Ruth called a "horse" for work, and Grove had pitched 44 of the 52 innings, allowing 7 runs between them. Earnshaw pitched 22 consecutive scoreless innings and came close to winning 3 games. But he never resented being taken out for a pinch hitter in the seventh inning of the 0–0 fifth game. "Connie knew what he was doing," he said. When Bing Miller caught the last ball hit and raced to the clubhouse, he tossed that final ball to Big George.

As a team the A's had batted .197, second lowest ever for a Series winner (the Cardinals hit .200). Jimmie Dykes blamed it on the background of the St. Louis fans in the center-field bleachers, which were never filled when they played the Browns in Sportsman's Park.

The total player pool was smaller than last year, a total of $136,027.69 for the winners, which was divided into twenty-seven full shares, coming to $5,038.07 each, more than the average income for those filing tax returns in the state of Pennsylvania that year.

In addition, Jim Moore received a quarter share of $1,259.51; Higgins, $3,778.55; Perkins, Summa, and Cramer each a half-share. Each player received a fourteen-carat gold tie bar with a full cut round quarter-carat diamond. Once again Connie Mack's share went $1,000 each to Ira Thomas and Mike Drennan, with the rest distributed among clubhouse and park employees.

Foxx, Simmons, Dykes, Cochrane, Grove, and Earnshaw were all heroes. But, wrote Gordon Mackay in the *Record*, "The real victor was Connie Mack. It was his brain, his labor, his wig-wagging out there with that scorecard, dog-eared and distrest, that brought home the bacon. So go ahead and give the cheers to the boys in the trenches, but remember that the lad who always led the charge was the skinny General McGillicuddy himself."

Grantland Rice commented that Mack's brain was keener than it was twenty-five years earlier, when he had made his first World Series appearance.

Connie Mack demurred. A year later, asked about his success, he said, "There isn't any secret formula, and I don't see where I've been any better manager than a dozen others I know. Where a team wins championships it's because the men who make up that team work and fight together. It's cooperation, coordination, the interests of the individual, and the success of the whole group, and my men have given me that."

But what had brought his men to the point where they had the self-confidence and determination and fighting spirit to give him that?

Will Rogers supplied the answer: "Connie Mack at 99 years of age will be able to sit in bed and show fifteen other managers how to handle a ball team in a crisis."

29 | BASEBALL'S GREATEST TEAM?

Connie Mack didn't linger long in the afterglow of his fifth world championship. The next morning he was in the office dealing with the letters and telegrams of congratulations, then back on a train with Tom Shibe to Cleveland
for the minor league meetings. The higher minors wanted players to have
a four-year exemption from the draft and a $10,000 draft price. The draft
price was raised, but the four-year exemption wouldn't happen until 1945.

Many of the A's split up into three barnstorming units and rode the trains
in all directions. Others couldn't wait to go hunting. Kid Gleason was honored at a big dinner at the Penn AC at which Ira Thomas and Tom Shibe
spoke. The entire A's office staff—Bob Schroeder, Peter Flood, John Martin,
James Thompson—was there.

Back home on November 8 Mack attended the Notre Dame–Penn football
game with Al Simmons and Babe Ruth.

On December 4 Phillies owner William F. Baker died. Mack and Baker
had had little to do with each other, but Mack said the appropriate words:
"We in Philadelphia and major league baseball are going to miss him very
much. He was devotedly interested in the welfare of baseball, and I admired
him greatly." The Phillies had finished fifth in 1929 but returned to their usual
basement abode in 1930.

Mack came out in support of liberal Democrat John M. Hemphill for
governor, having gotten no help from Governor Gifford Pinchot in his quest
for Sunday baseball. He called Pinchot "vindictive and distrustful." Pinchot
was reelected and would continue to oppose Sunday ball.

There was little news on the player front. Connie Mack planned no major
changes. He released Wally Schang and Jack Quinn. Schang played one more
year, his nineteenth, with Detroit. Quinn signed with Brooklyn and hung

on for another three years. Before going off to the winter meetings, Mack became a Rotarian, joining the Philadelphia Rotary Club. On the road he would attend meetings whenever they coincided with his schedule.

The major leagues were still trying to bring some consistency and professionalism to the official scorers' position. In the early days, the chore had been assigned to some minor office employee. Gradually the writers covering the team were appointed by the club presidents, sometimes on a rotating basis. In 1917 the Athletics had used eight writers, paying each $200. After that they picked one and paid him $300 for the season. Beginning this year, the appointment power was given to the league presidents.

They were also tinkering with the scoring rules. Connie Mack agreed with American League president Ernest S. Barnard that the sacrifice fly rule, which had enabled Bill Terry to bat .401 for the Giants in 1930, was absurd. "It gets entirely away from the meaning of the word sacrifice. A bunt is a true sacrifice." Perhaps remembering the day Mule Haas had robbed Babe Ruth of a home run, which was scored as a sacrifice fly because it had allowed Earle Combs to go from second to third before being thrown out at home, Mack said, "A man who hits a sacrifice fly is trying to hit the ball out of the park. Even if the fly ball advances a man from second to third it doesn't count as a time at bat. Only a bunt is a sacrifice."

The sacrifice fly was abolished for 1931, then would be reinstated for a year—only for a runner scoring—in 1939, then disappear again until gaining immortality in 1954, when Connie Mack was no longer in a position to fight it.

Major league attendance had been up for 1930, but Philadelphia had been hit hard by the Depression and the Shibe Park gate was down 15 percent. In recent years new accounting rules on depreciating building improvements and players' contracts had reduced reported profits; even after taking that $112,000 debit, the bottom line showed a $162,000 profit. The Athletics declared a $100,050 dividend, half of which went to Mr. Mack.

The economy had been sliding throughout 1930. The amusement industry was hit hard. On January 1, 1931, five shows closed on Broadway. At curtain time at one theater there were four people in the audience. In 1929 movie theaters had sold 100 million tickets a week. Now the movie houses were starting to close; by 1933 nearly one-third of them would be dark.

Unemployment was still widespread, but the Athletics were the champs and they expected to be paid as such. For the first time since the Federal League war of 1914, Mack was signing players to three-year contracts:

$100,000 for Simmons, $56,000 for Cochrane, $50,000 for Foxx. Simmons was earning more than any Yankee except Ruth and more than most managers, including Mack. Grove signed for $20,000 (an $8,000 raise), Earnshaw for $15,000. Only Walberg, whose workload had dropped and whose earned run average had gone up a run, took a cut.

On the way to Fort Myers Mack stopped at Mount Plymouth for ten days of golf. While there, he went over to St. Pete for the dedication of the Yankees' practice field as Miller Huggins Field.

Mack's main concern was the possibility of injuries to key players. Jimmie Dykes made the point for him by missing most of spring training with a stubborn charley horse. Bill Shores had a sore arm. "Luck plays no part in a season except for injuries," Mack told Grantland Rice. "The breaks even up. But whether all your stars stay in good shape is the big factor. You can have strong reserves but they can't replace your stars." He told John Kieran that Higgins, McNair, and Williams could all play second, third, or short. To which Eddie Collins added, "They can play anything including the piano."

Mack realized that Mike Higgins would benefit more by playing full time and optioned him to his hometown, Dallas, but the Dallas club sent him back. So Mack sent him to San Antonio. To back up Foxx, he picked up first baseman Phil Todt, and for Cochrane, veteran catcher John Heving, both on waivers from Boston.

Simmons and Earnshaw trained at Hot Springs with the Minneapolis club. Simmons wouldn't sign until opening day, so he couldn't have joined the team in Fort Myers if he wanted to. Which he didn't; the Florida sand was not kind to Al's rheumatic ankles.

Thomas Edison, a regular at past Terry Park practices, was absent. At eighty-three, he was too feeble to leave his Fort Myers home. Mack would visit him and tell him about the players and how they were doing.

The pitching was thin after Grove and Earnshaw. Walberg was healthy and strong but wild all spring. The rest of the load would be carried by Hank McDonald (up from Portland), Bill Shores, and Roy Mahaffey, with occasional help from Eddie Rommel, who was near the end of the line. Mack wanted another veteran pitcher. It took him until the end of June to find one.

The experts asked, "Can Connie Mack win again with a three-man pitching staff?"

Connie Mack thought he could. To his critics he said, "Subtract the top three pitchers off any other club and you won't have much, either." Billy Evans called Mack's top three the equal of any five.

The Athletics were now the object of a different kind of joke: at a league meeting the other club owners told John Shibe they would provide the pension fund if Mack would retire Grove, Earnshaw, Simmons, and Cochrane.

Mack was confident that he had the best team in the field. Confident but wary. "A third pennant is hard to get," he said. "To win a third a team has to be 15 percent stronger than when it won its second. Players are not stirred up by the excitement any more. Keeping them up and hustling will be my job."

The annual debate over changes in the ball drew this explanation from league president Barnard: "Some years ago there was a change in the stitches. The cover is wet when stitched on. When it dries it tightens. The old stitches stood out so much there were complaints. The ridge was sharp and when it hit something hard the stitches broke. So they put in a finer thread and rolled the seams flat. This year they are using larger thread and the seams stand out a little more."

Barnard also revealed that the cover of the NL ball would be 2/100 of an inch thicker than that of the AL ball.

Would the higher seams aid the pitchers? Barnard didn't think so. The batters would still be swinging for the fences, he said. Connie Mack agreed. "I prefer the old-style method of attack, but the fans want slugging. The new ball will be of no physical aid to the pitcher. I cannot see that it will restore the mound duels and bring back the fine art of base running. Not this year at least."

Whatever the reason, run production, home runs, and slugging averages in 1931 would fall sharply in the National League, only slightly in the American.

For the first time the American League required all teams to put numbers on uniforms. The Athletics wore them on road uniforms only. Unlike other teams, they did not go according to the batting order but by position, using the same system as for keeping score, with one exception: there was no number 1. The catcher, Cochrane, wore 2, Foxx 3, and so forth. The pitchers began with Grove number 10, Earnshaw 11, Walberg 12. There was only one request: the superstitious Bill Shores asked for 13, the same berth number he preferred on the Pullmans. The coaches wore the highest numbers: Gleason 30, Collins 31, Earle Mack 32.

Mack was in Greensboro, North Carolina, with the second team when he learned that both Ban Johnson and Ernest Barnard had died on March 27. Mack was asked about rumors he might be named president of the league. "You can say for me that I am not a candidate for the office," he told

Isaminger. "The only position in baseball I want is the one I hold today. I cannot make my denial too strong."

Connie Mack would have been bored being president of anything instead of managing the Athletics. He lived to be in the dugout, teaching, developing young players, building champions, directing the strategy during a game. He would rather manage a last-place team, losing 100 games a year, watching even just one young player improve day by day, than sit in an office, no matter how high the office.

League secretary Will Harridge was elected to succeed Barnard.

Washington had the slickest infield in the league, the best pitching, and Sam Rice and Heinie Manush in the outfield. The Senators had outhit the A's last year but lacked power. They figured to be first or second this year.

Both teams were virtually unchanged from a year ago when they opened the season on April 14 in Washington before a DC opener record crowd of thirty-two thousand. With their good luck fan, President Hoover, on hand, the A's renewed their reputation as the comeback kids. Mack surprised everybody by handing the ball to Rube Walberg. In the first Haas doubled into the crowd in left-center field. Simmons was loudly booed and responded with an RBI single. For the next 7 innings lefty Lloyd Brown mowed down the A's in order and had a 2–1 lead until the ninth, when Haas again doubled, driving in Bishop to tie it. Enter Marberry and Grove. Both teams scored in the tenth. The A's scored 2 in the eleventh, and Grove finished it by striking out Manush and Joe Cronin. They lost the next 3 to Washington, and lost Jimmy Foxx, who pulled a muscle in his left leg rounding second and would be out for two weeks.

The opener in New York drew the second-largest crowd ever—80,403. Max Bishop, still the magic base-reacher, scored twice in the A's 3–2 win. Joe McCarthy, the new Yankees manager, displayed his own methods in the sixth inning, when, after Ruth walked, he ordered Gehrig to bunt him to second. But Mack's boys lost the next 2, including a humiliating 12–1 pasting in which the Yankees, aided by 6 walks, scored 8 runs in the second. Mack pulled Boley, Bishop, Simmons, and Cochrane and let the subs finish the game.

It was cold and windy for the Shibe Park opener against Washington. The Wingate American Legion Post band played the newly legislated official national anthem, and Eddie Collins raised the 1930 world championship flag. The players received their choice of a gold watch or ring. Grove cruised to a 5–1 win. When Mack called off the next day's game because of the cold wind, Senators manager Walter Johnson pressed Mack to play two the next day. Mack said no. His pitchers weren't pitching and his hitters weren't hitting. They'd make it up in July.

The next day Max Bishop led off with a single, and Simmons's home run made it 2–0. Mack went with Hank McDonald, who shut out Washington for 6 innings, then got nobody out in the seventh. In came Grove, his fourth appearance in the six games between the two teams. This time he was pounded for 6 hits amid the fickle crowd's jeers and boos. Washington led 7–2. But the A's pulled it out with 8 runs in the seventh and eighth. Simmons hit 2 triples, the second a most satisfying blow off Marberry to cap a 5-run eighth for the 10–7 win.

After five days of idleness, the A's looked listless at home against the Yankees, doing nothing with their old nemesis Henry Johnson, while Walberg and McDonald pitched poorly.

They were 5-6, in sixth place.

Connie Mack called a meeting. It wasn't too soon to get them fired up and hustling.

Seven years later in a *Saturday Evening Post* article written with Al Horwits, an accomplished embroiderer, Mack was quoted:

Big money, series checks, and fees from testimonials did their work after two World Series wins. We floundered badly to start the 1931 season. I was on edge while we were wallowing around or as nearly on edge as I have allowed myself to become. I wanted to be the first manager to capture three straight world championships. I knew we could win, but the chance was being tossed away. We were defaulting. I finally decided the time for drastic action had come. I told Eddie Collins to call a special clubhouse meeting.

"Eddie, I'm going to call a spade a spade," I informed him.

When the players assembled, sober faced and wondering, I singled out four of my stars. I told them they were leading too soft a life. They were putting more enthusiasm into taking bows for past performances than for hitting and fielding. Their heads were too big for their hats. I charged them with letting the rest of the team down.

One of those he mentioned by name was Mickey Cochrane, although he had no complaint about his efforts. He figured it would give the others a jolt, so he said, "It seems like a shame, even Mike is losing his spirit out there."

Five days later they started a 17-game winning streak. At first Walberg and Earnshaw carried the load. Grove had been out for two weeks with a heavy cold and didn't start again until May 12, when he beat Chicago to move the Athletics into first place. The new Grove was now itchy to go in and put out a fire whenever it looked like a game was slipping away. After pitching a complete game at Cleveland on May 16, he went in and got the last 2 outs the next day and relieved Walberg in the eighth a day later. Simmons had a 21-game hitting streak.

During the streak Earnshaw and Walberg won 5 each. Grove won 4 and finished 3. When it ended, the A's led Washington by 5, the Yankees by 5½.

"Those three pitchers are in there almost every day," said the Washington players. "They can't last. They're bound to crack."

They didn't crack.

The A's kept winning—Earnshaw won 12 straight before losing on June 25. But they couldn't relax. In June the Senators won 15 of 16 and cut the lead to 2½.

Walberg and Grove were ornery, stubborn pitchers who wouldn't give in to anybody, especially Babe Ruth.

"Rube was stubborn," recalled Flit Cramer. "He and Cochrane dressed near me. One day in New York I was down to play center field. I asked Rube how he was going to pitch to Ruth and he said, 'To his strength.' I asked Mike where he thought I should play Ruth and he said, "About the third row of the bleachers." In the fifth Ruth hit a long high home run into the bleachers. I came in and Mike says, 'You weren't playing him right.' I said, 'I know. I couldn't get into the stands.'"

Backup catcher Ed Madjeski never forgot a day at Shibe Park in 1933. "First two times up, Ruth hit home runs off Lefty Grove. Grove came in after the second one just fuming. 'That guy won't get another hit off me today,' he growled. That took guts to say that. And Ruth didn't. Struck out twice. Grove hung in there and won 9–5."

On June 30 Connie Mack found the veteran pitcher he sought, claiming Waite Hoyt off Detroit's waiver list for $7,500. To make room on the roster Mack moved Eddie Collins to the inactive list. Collins had played his first game for Mack in 1906 and his last in 1930.

After nine high-flying years with the Yankees, Waite Hoyt had been traded to Detroit in 1930. Hoyt found life with the seventh-place Tigers less than exciting. He was only thirty-one, but he was overweight and his lack of enthusiasm was evident. His record was 3-8 when the Tigers asked waivers on him. Nobody else claimed him. Mack took him and his $7,500 salary. Kid Gleason set to work getting him into shape by hitting him ground balls during batting practice.

"I wish he could learn to love the game again," Mack sighed.

Apparently being back on top rekindled the romance. Hoyt won his first four starts for the A's and 10 against 5 losses.

The Washington Senators came to Shibe Park for a doubleheader on Monday, July 13, trailing by 6 games. It may have been hard times for a lot of people, but this was still a hot pennant race and a Senators-Athletics battle in the 1930s was the equivalent of the Red Sox-Yankees rivalry of two generations later. The two club owners were the closest of friends, visiting each other every time their teams met, talking about the welfare of the league, attendance woes, how to help each other. But there was no love lost among the players. Forty thousand jammed into Shibe Park, sitting and standing on every available surface. Grove and Marberry started the first game, and the feud exploded in the fifth inning, when Firpo sent Al Simmons sprawling out of the way of a head-hunting fastball. After three more dusters Simmons ran for the mound instead of strolling to first. Marberry threw down his glove and assumed a John L. Sullivan stance as players ran out from dugouts, but plate umpire Bill McGowan broke it up. Only verbal brickbats were thrown until Marberry struck out Foxx and walked to the dugout as cushions rained down on him.

It was Grove's worst outing of the year. After Marberry left for a pinch hitter in the eighth, the Senators led, 7–5. The A's piled on his relief for 7 runs in the last of the eighth to salvage Grove's eighteenth win, 12–7. The game exemplified the difference between the two teams; 9 of the A's 11 hits were extra base hits, 5 of them home runs.

The Senators won the second game but gained nothing on the day.

From July 15 to September 1 the A's won 22 home games without a loss; the lead was 15½ games, and the race was over. There were no more crucial series. No more record crowds. Hard as it may be to believe, Philadelphia fans *did* get jaundiced by greatness.

"The team was so good," Mack's daughter Ruth recalled, "I couldn't even give a pass away to the milkman. He'd just say, 'Oh, they'll win.'"

But Connie Mack saw signs he didn't like. His boys were coasting, enjoying the social ramble too much. Everywhere they went, idolizers were eager to wine and dine them. None of it got by Mack. Once Simmons and Foxx skipped a train hop from an exhibition game to St. Louis and drove with some friends. "The Old Man didn't know a thing," Simmons recalled. "Everything went fine until the team was getting off in the St. Louis station. Then Connie pointed up to the luggage rack and spoke to the road secretary, 'You better take Fawksey's hat,' he said, 'he may want it.'"

Of one player Mack said later, "I had noticed a falling off in his play; his timing was bad and his eye was letting him down when it came to judging a hard-driven ground ball or a fast-breaking curve."

They arrived in Cleveland on August 15, leading by 11½. That evening Mack was standing in front of the hotel when that player arrived in a taxi. "Good night, Mr. Mack," he said and walked into the lobby.

"I was supposed to think he was on his way to his room and bed," Mack recalled. "I said good night to him and walked around the hotel to the rear entrance. Just as I got to the back door, out came the player and made a beeline for a taxi. I didn't say anything to him. I didn't have to. He saw me and went back in the hotel and up to bed."

The next day at a civic club's luncheon for the team, Mack warned his boys that it was still possible to fall into a losing streak and fumble away the pennant because they wouldn't stay in condition.

"I had planned to say all of that at our skull-practice meeting the next day, but I had a hunch that telling them there in front of outsiders would make a bigger impression."

The A's went 28-14 the rest of the way.

The lack of a pennant race in the last two months and loss of jobs in the area cut attendance by another hundred thousand from the previous year. Between the dwindling attendance and the frequent use of Moore, Cramer, Williams, and McNair, the rumors began that Connie Mack was getting ready to sell off his stars again.

Asked in Cleveland on August 16 if he intended to dismantle the team, he said, "No. I made that mistake with the 1914 outfit. One mistake like that is enough. . . . Now that we're on the top we're going to stay here until we're passed. I'm not going to tear down; the others must build up."

A few weeks later Pegler asked him, "Are you planning to break up this ball club as you broke up that other one?" Mack, tired of the subject, replied, "Do you know where I can pick up some men to make it a little stronger next year?"

In giving his young players some experience while resting his regulars, Mack was merely looking ahead. Joe Boley was getting old and had no arm left. Bing Miller was slowing down. Dykes's hitting had fallen off. McNair, Williams, and Cramer were the future.

On the road Connie Mack would often walk through the pass gate and climb to the last row of the lower stands to sit for a while watching batting or infield practice before going down to the dugout. Occasionally his wife and one of his daughters might accompany him on a trip to New York or around the western circuit. One day in August Westbrook Pegler waited for Mack at Yankee Stadium's press gate. Although Pegler had a reputation for writing with acid, not ink, he revered Connie Mack. As he watched Mack go up the ramp to the stands, he saw a small boy run in front of Mack and bump into him. It was Mr. Mack, he observed, who said, "I beg your pardon" to the boy. Fans who recognized the tall, thin manager came up to him, congratulating him and wishing him well. Mack made them feel that he was sincerely happy to see them.

Pegler sat down beside Mack. They talked about players' salaries. Mack said his highest-paid players were saving their money.

"I like them that way," Pegler quoted him. "A player who is saving his money isn't going in for a lot of gol-damn foolishness."

Mack said he didn't object to frivolous conduct in one man, "but I won't keep that kind of man on my club because he won't go out alone."

Three weeks later Pegler visited Mack again at Shibe Park and talked about the old days. Mack didn't yearn for the good old days because he knew they weren't that good. "People weren't all fine, moral and honest in grandpa's day." he told Pegler. "The world improves. Business methods are better. Education is much better. Each generation is a little bit smarter than the one before and the kids today behave better and show more sense than they did when I was young."

When Pegler began a question with, "Back in your day," the sixty-eight-year-old Mack interrupted him. "Back in my day? What was my day? My club has won two pennants in a row and we've just about won another. Isn't this my day? Isn't it possible that next year will be my day too?"

Mack felt sorry for men like Bishop and Boley and Hoyt who had reached the point where they saw baseball as a job. To him it was playing at a job, even after almost fifty years. He looked forward to the next spring training, the next season, the next game, the next play with as much enthusiasm as ever.

"If baseball weren't fun for me," he told Pegler, "do you think I would be trouping in cold spring weather and terrible summer heat year after year to make money?"

Mack had eased up on using Earnshaw and Grove in relief. But Al Simmons, a coach for Mack in the 1940s, enjoyed telling young players how Mose would sometimes get up from the bench and go out and take the ball from the pitcher on his own without Mack saying a word to him.

A typical performance occurred on Sunday, August 9, at Yankee Stadium. The Yankees had taken the first two games of the series but were still 13 games back in third place. Roy Mahaffey shut down the Yankee sluggers while Simmons's 2 home runs gave the A's a 5–0 lead. In the bottom of the seventh 2 errors and a walk loaded the bases. Mack sent Walberg in to face pinch hitter Earle Combs. Walberg fired a 3-2 fastball past the outmatched Combs. Then Sammy Byrd hit a fly ball that was headed for grand slam land, but Simmons reached over the low wall and turned it into a run-scoring out. Joe Sewell hit a 2-strike pitch for a single, and it was 5–2 with Ruth coming up.

Grove, squirming on the bench, grabbed his glove and headed for the mound. He took his eight warmup tosses, then fired 2 strikes past Ruth. But the third one Ruth grounded to right for a single, making it 5–3. The frustrated Mose didn't make the same mistake against Gehrig, who never saw the called third strike. Grove finished the game fanning 3. He pitched three complete games in the next ten days.

"Grove is a team player now," Mack told Westbrook Pegler. "He used to get sore and try to throw them by batters. Now he's as smart as almost any pitcher you'll see and plays for the team all the time. He's come out of himself, developed."

The Grove volcano was dormant but not dead. Billy Sullivan Jr., a catcher out of Notre Dame, recalled an incident at Shibe Park. "I was a rookie playing third base that day and Grove was going for his thirtieth win and I hit a home run in the first inning. He was so mad he followed me around the bases calling me, 'You college bastard.' I wanted to say, 'Yes, Mr. Grove.'"

On August 19 Lefty won his sixteenth in a row at Chicago, 4–2, tying a record set by Walter Johnson and Joe Wood in 1912. He struck out only 5 and walked nobody. Flit Cramer and Jim Moore were in the outfield. Al Simmons had hurt his ankle in Cleveland on August 15. When it became infected and he knew he'd be out at least a week, he had gone home to Milwaukee. Haas was out with a broken wrist. Grove's record was now 25-2.

The 16 straight wins might have been 24. But after 8 wins he had relieved against the White Sox and worked the seventh through the twelfth, when Lew Fonseca homered to win it. He hadn't lost a start since a 2–1 loss at Washington on April 18.

That night some of the players were invited by a police lieutenant to drop in at the detective bureau, where they took part in a mock lineup. Cochrane, Earnshaw, Cramer, and Earle Mack were put in the lineup before an audience of two hundred, charged with the crime of beating the White Sox that afternoon.

"Why did you commit such a crime?" Lt. Healy asked.

"Because the White Sox were defenseless," said Earnshaw.

Four days later in St. Louis Grove went after number 17 in the first game of a doubleheader. In addition to Simmons and Haas, Dykes and Boley were crippled. McNair and Williams played.

Dick Coffman took the ball for the fifth-place Browns. The twenty-four-year-old right-hander had been on the brink of being sent to the minors earlier, with a 2-9 record, but had won 3 games in the past two weeks, including a 1-hitter against Chicago. He had something to prove.

Grove pitched his usual game—7 hits, 6 strikeouts, no walks.

With 2 out in the third inning Fred Schulte singled. Oscar Melillo hit a line drive to left. Had Jim Moore stood still it would have hit him in the chest. But he took a few steps in, then began to backpedal—too late. The ball landed behind him. Melillo pulled into second while Schulte scored.

In later interviews Jim Moore said, "Connie Mack patted me on the shoulder when I returned to the bench and said, 'Don't feel bad. I've seen Speaker misjudge some, and he was a little better than you are, you know.'"

That was the only run Grove allowed. It was also the only run of the game.

Coffman gave up 3 singles in the A's only shutout of the season and lasted another ten years in the big leagues.

When the game ended, Mack suggested that Moore remain on the bench between games.

Al Simmons was in Milwaukee watching a softball game when somebody told him the Athletics had lost the first game, 1–0. "Holy smoke," said Al, "that's Grove's game. His streak is stopped."

Simmons could imagine the scene in the clubhouse. Flit Cramer witnessed it.

"My locker was next to Grove's. No words were said. He stood a half minute in front of his locker, then grabbed the top of his shirt with both hands and pulled. Buttons flew everywhere. The chairs were broken, lockers kicked, benches turned over. The next day it was all over."

Twenty minutes later they began banging out 17 hits for Waite Hoyt and won, 10–0.

One paper reported that Mack lost his usual cool when an irate fan yelled at him as he approached the clubhouse after the second game, "Hey, Mack, what do you keep that guy Moore around for anyhow?"

"I'll tell you," Mack snapped. "I keep Moore around because he is such a neat dresser. He inspires the rest of the boys to dress well, too."

That evening in the Kingsway Hotel lobby Connie Mack tried to smooth over Grove's fretful mood. According to Eddie Collins, Mack told his players, "What a game that Coffman pitched today." Then he analyzed Coffman's pitching inning by inning. "But for that bit of hard luck in the third we might have been playing out there 'til midnight, because both Grove and Coffman were pitching beautifully. Nevertheless the best pitching of the day had come out of Coffman's arm."

Grove was not angry at Moore but at Simmons for not being there. "It burned me up worse than a fever to lose," is the way he put it. "There are some pitchers who can laugh and take it as a joke, but not me. I would get angry at myself for losing." Angry at himself, but he couldn't take it out physically on himself, so the chairs, lockers, shirts, and furniture took the beating.

"Grove never said anything to me," Moore recalled. "In fact, he didn't speak to me for a long time, not even after I broke up a game with a [double] to [help] beat the White Sox for him a few weeks later."

On Connie Mack's orders, Mickey Cochrane flew home that afternoon for a much-needed rest. He was burned out. He had been unable to sleep for at least a week. His sinuses were killing him. His eyes were constantly red from the dust kicked up around home plate every day. For seven years he had given everything he had on every pitch, every inning, every game. Every catcher felt the physical and mental toll of squatting more than a hundred times during a game, being bruised by foul tips and collisions at the plate, blocking pitches in the dirt, and calling pitches while coaxing and cajoling and catering to a variety of characters on the mound. He had caught at least 120 games a year. Batting second or third in the lineup ahead of Simmons and Foxx—and hitting around .350—he had a lot more base running to do than any catcher batting eighth, scoring 601 runs in seven years. Cy Perkins figured Cochrane did a third more work during a season than any other catcher. Mike drove himself harder than anybody else, left it all on the field, and never took it home with him, said his wife. It had taken a toll on his nerves and body.

Mack also gave George Earnshaw a week off.

The pennant was clinched on September 15, when St. Louis beat Washington an hour after Ed Rommel had defeated Cleveland, 14–3, with a makeshift lineup including Lou Finney (recalled from York), Jim Moore, Phil Todt, third-string catcher Joe Palmisano, Eric McNair, and Dib Williams. Connie Mack heard the news when a reporter called him just as he arrived home.

"I am rather pleased," he said, "but it did not come with that thrill as it would have had we had a hard fight right down to the wire."

They won with pitching and power, topping the Yankees by 13½ games despite New York's scoring a record 1,067 runs as Ruth and Gehrig hit 46 home runs each and Gehrig drove in a record 184 runs. And despite Jimmy Foxx having the worst year he would have in an A's uniform, slipping to .291 and 30 home runs. Simmons repeated as the batting champion at .390. Cochrane hit .349. Billy Evans called Simmons and Foxx the best one-two punch in baseball and Cochrane the greatest catcher he ever saw. Usually overlooked is the prowess of lead-off man Max Bishop, whose 146 hits and 112 walks led to 115 runs. (Over three years Bishop averaged 1.77 hits plus walks per game; only 10 players have done better over the same time span.)

They did not win it with speed, stealing only 27 bases.

Grove, Earnshaw, and Walberg worked almost two-thirds of the team's total innings pitched—nearly 300 innings each. Grove and Earnshaw topped the league in strikeouts—the seventh and last year in a row Grove would lead in strikeouts. His 2.06 ERA was the league's lowest for the third straight year and would be the lowest of his career. The A's led the league with 12 shutouts and 97 complete games by a pitcher—27 of 30 starts for Grove—a huge jump over the previous two years. Grove's 31-4 record gave him pitching's triple crown. He didn't do it with soft touches. He was 6-1 against Washington, 2-1 against New York. A Baseball Writers Association poll of one writer from each city in the league voted him the MVP.

Lefty never wanted to come out of a game he started, and when he didn't want to, Connie Mack didn't argue. It was Earle Mack's job to come out to the mound, a job he didn't relish when Grove was out there. The players liked Earle, but they had little respect for him; they called him "Junior." And, in truth, he didn't show them much to earn their respect. One day Grove had given up a few hits in an inning and out came Earle. Foxx, Boley, and

Bishop strolled to the mound. Earle said, "Mose, Daddy says he's going to have to warm up somebody if they get any more hits."

Grove said, "Junior, you go tell Daddy what Mose starts, Mose finishes."

The A's won two of the three starts he didn't finish. The only loss was the last game of the season, when Mack used Grove, Earnshaw, and Walberg for 3 innings each.

Grove won 79 and lost 15 over three years. Rarely has a pitcher been so dominant. Connie Mack was asked if Grove was the greatest lefty ever. "On the record yes," he said, "but regardless of records, it would be Waddell. If Rube had taken care of himself, the books would back me up when I say he was the greatest pitcher."

Contrary to stories that Grove had no curve until he was older and had lost something off his fastball, Shirley Povich wrote of him in 1931, "No other twirler in the league has his fastball; no other pitcher has his curve. The Cubs of '29 or the Cards of '30 had never encountered the speed or the curve of a Grove."

Perhaps the most amazing facet of Grove's dominance was Mickey Cochrane's testimony that Grove's fastball did nothing; it came in straight as a string. In 1934 F. C. Lane in *Baseball Magazine* quoted Cochrane: "Unlike Walter Johnson, whose fastball had a hop to it, Grove's fastball had no hop on it and no break—it was straight. If it had had any movement to it, nobody would have ever hit it."

Cochrane added the enigmatic statement that "a lefthander's speed looks faster than a righthander's."

George Earnshaw, 21-7, cut his walks almost in half after leading the league in that department for two years. One factor in the success of Grove and Earnshaw was their signaling to the outfielders what they were going to throw. It was especially helpful, said Cramer, when they were going to throw a change-up. "I'd know then that the hitter might get around pretty good on the ball, which they couldn't do with their fastballs."

Rube Walberg rang up more walks than strikeouts but had his only 20-win year; Roy Mahaffey earned credit for 15 wins despite an ERA higher than the league average.

Were the Big Three overworked? Of the two "broadbacks," as Cochrane called Walberg and Earnshaw, Walberg, now thirty-five, would work over 200 innings each of the next two years and over 100, primarily in relief, for four more years after that. Earnshaw, thirty-one, would average 185 innings for the next five years. Grove, thirty-one, would still be working 191 innings and leading the league in ERA for the ninth time at thirty-nine.

"Lefty's arm is like a rawhide whip," Doc Ebling said. "It's the kind of an arm that won't stay sore. He has the smoothest pitching technique I've ever seen. Almost perfect and just about effortless."

As long as he kept his legs in shape—and Grove did—the arm would last.

Were the 1931 Athletics a better team than the 1927 Yankees? The '27 Yankees had won only 3 more games, too narrow a difference to be conclusive. Man-to-man comparisons come close to evening out, although the Athletics had a higher-quality pitching staff.

Were the 1929–1931 Athletics better than the 1926–1928 Yankees? In their three pennant-winning years, the A's finished a cumulative 47½ games ahead of New York; the Yankees' 1926–1928 record was 27½ games ahead of the A's for those years. The Athletics won their pennants by average margins of 13 games to 8 by New York.

(Over the decade 1924–1933 the Yankees' won-lost record would be 3½ games better than the Athletics.)

It has been written: "You can torture numbers and they'll confess to anything." The Yankees' and Athletics' numbers are close enough to provide fodder for the endless inconclusive debates that baseball fans thrive on.

Ted Lyons pitched against both teams from 1924 through 1942. In 1939 he told Ed Pollock, "The best hitting club I ever pitched against was the old A's of 1929-31. Bishop, leading off, was enough to drive any pitcher crazy. He got five strikes every time he came up. He made you pitch and if you made one too good—bang—he'd hit. Haas, Cochrane, Simmons—what a hitter in those days—Foxx, Miller—you couldn't let up anywhere along there. Then Dykes and Boley, bad men in a clutch. Any one of them could break up a ball game. That was baseball's greatest hitting team."

The Athletics were 8–5 favorites in most betting circles. The St. Louis Cardinals were given a slight edge defensively in the infield. The outfield was a toss-up. Grove and Earnshaw had no equals on the St. Louis staff. And of course, there was no better catcher anywhere than Cochrane. A healthy Cochrane, that is. But Mickey headed the injured list. His arm was strong as ever, but his eyes and sinuses bothered him. Both his thighs had to be taped up before every game. Their soreness made it impossible for him to dig in and gain any leverage at the plate. He would manage only 4 singles in the 7 games. "At no time was he himself," Isaminger wrote.

Bob Paul ghosted Cochrane's syndicated commentary. Cochrane refused to let him write anything about the condition of his legs.

"He played the entire series on sheer nerve. His whole general physical condition was below par," Mack confirmed after the Series. "He was on the verge of collapse in every game, battled to stay in there—insisted on it—and went along on nerve alone."

Joe Boley had bruised his shin in practice before the A's left for St. Louis. Earnshaw and Bing Miller had heavy colds. Mule Haas's broken wrist had healed but remained weak and would hamper his ability to swing the bat.

For St. Louis, third baseman Sparky Adams had a sprained ankle and Jesse Haines, who had beaten Grove 3–1 last year, was definitely out with a sore shoulder.

On arrival in St. Louis on September 30 the A's went directly to the Kingsway Hotel without visiting Sportsman's Park. They were familiar enough with the field, which they considered the worst in the league. Used by both the Browns and the Cardinals, it was never free for maintenance or repairs. "When you start digging for a toehold," said Cochrane, "you scratch up rocks."

Meanwhile, the Cardinals held a three-hour workout. The superstitious Gabby Street refused to have a team photo taken. His announced opening game starter, right-handed rookie 18-game-winner Paul Derringer, also refused to pose for photographers.

Connie Mack said he hadn't the faintest idea who would pitch for him. "It might even be Lew Krausse." But nobody was fooled. Last year it had been all Grove and Earnshaw. Nobody believed Mack would depart from that winning combination.

Gabby Street had three top pitchers: Derringer, Burleigh Grimes, and lefty Bill Hallahan. His pitching plans were no secret.

The day before the opener Mack called a meeting at the hotel. Thirty years later, at a reunion of the two teams in St. Louis, Bob Broeg of the *Post-Dispatch* reported Phil Todt remembering it this way: "He told us, 'Gentlemen, I don't worry about their big hitters—Frisch, Bottomley, Hafey—but they've got a young man named Martin who bothers me. He's the kind of aggressive, unpredictable kid who could be the hero or the goat.'"

Mack was not alone in his opinion of John Leonard Roosevelt "Pepper" Martin. Gayle Talbot of the AP wrote, "Some smart baseball men expect Martin, if he plays [he had a wrenched knee], to prove the individual hero of the approaching series. He has never encountered either Lefty Grove or George Earnshaw, and is blissfully confident he can murder anything they toss at him. He might do it, but until he does, the great majority of the fans will look to Simmons for the main fireworks."

Bill Corum reported that Martin had seen Grove in spring training and had told Gabby Street, "I can hit that guy," then lined out 2 hits off him in an exhibition game.

Pepper Martin was no kid—he was twenty-seven. St. Louis scout Charley Barrett had seen him playing second base at Ardmore in the Western League in 1925 and bought him for $2,500. It took him until mid-1930 to make his way up the Cardinals' chain gang to the majors. He had come out of Oklahoma—ridden the rails like a hobo to spring training, the story went, charged around the bases like a wild mustang, and played center field the same way. Babe Ruth was still the most popular ballplayer in the nation, but the Babe was an old story. Pepper Martin was new. He was colorful copy at a time when the rest of the world was drab. He wore rumpled clothes and a broad-brimmed slouch hat, chewed tobacco, and smoked big cigars, and his uniform was always dirty and grass-stained. He claimed to have played football for four colleges. He loved practical jokes and hillbilly music, raced midget autos, and slid into bases on his belly with equal enthusiasm. "He can get more joy out of little things than almost anybody I ever knew," said Frank Frisch. Playing horseshoes or baseball, he went all out on every play. He batted .300 in his first full season and stole a modest 16 bases, which was enough to tie him for third in the league behind Frisch's 28.

October 1 was a warm day, near 80 degrees. Mack had both Grove and Earnshaw throwing before the opening game. When Gabby Street handed his lineup card to umpire Bill Klem at home plate, it had George Watkins, a left-handed hitter, in right field batting second. When Street saw Grove's name on the A's card, he wanted to replace Watkins with righty swinger Wally Roettger. Klem said he wouldn't allow the change unless Connie Mack agreed to it. Mack said he wanted to win right or not at all and allowed the switch.

Roettger singled and scored the first run in the first inning when the Cardinals collected 4 hits, the last an RBI double by Pepper Martin. Grove had gotten ahead of every hitter 0-2, then tried to put them away with curves that kept missing their targets. "I know it was bad pitching," Grove said after the game, "but it just seemed I could not put that next pitch where I wanted it. Connie talked to me during our time at bat in the second inning. I took more time after that and felt they wouldn't score any more and they didn't"

The crowd of 38,529 had plenty to cheer about but little to show for it. Grove gave up 12 hits altogether—3 by Martin—fanned 7, and walked none.

Paul Derringer had the A's lunging off-balance with an effective change-up and struck out 4 in the first 2 innings. They caught up with him in the third. With 2 out and men on first and second, Haas doubled, Cochrane and Simmons walked, Foxx singled, and the A's led 4–2. In the seventh Simmons hit a 2-run home run.

As they had last year, temporary box seats pushed the benches onto the field. The fans could see Connie Mack slapping a player on the back after a good play. Mack was described as "especially demonstrative" after Simmons's homer.

In the St. Louis sixth, with Hafey on second and Martin on first, Hafey stole third. Dykes thought he had him, and while he held the ball arguing with umpire Bill McGowan, Martin stole second. Charge that one to Dykes, not the catcher or pitcher. Grove bore down and left them stranded. He pitched the last 4 innings with a blister rubbed raw and bloody on the index finger of his pitching hand, a recurring problem that had caused him considerable pain for the past three years.

For the first time Connie Mack dictated a postgame statement to a stenographer to be typewritten and given out to the press, which was barred from the clubhouse. "They worried me by their failure to hit in recent games, but today they proved they can come out of a slump." Mack said their fielding saved the game several times, especially Al Simmons's leaping catch of a drive by Wilson against the fence. He thought Derringer had pitched too strenuously in the first two innings and that took its toll.

The next day Wild Bill Hallahan walked 7 but the A's managed only 3 hits, and as he had done a year ago, Hallahan shut them out, stranding 10 runners. The A's biggest threat came in the fifth, when Miller singled for their first hit after Foxx had walked. Dykes sacrificed them to second and third. Williams was walked to load the bases. Earnshaw then hit into a double play.

Earnshaw was just as good as Hallahan against everybody but Pepper Martin. In the second inning Martin singled to left. Simmons slipped picking it up, and Martin kept right on going to second. With Jimmy Wilson up, on the third pitch Martin touched his nose, the sign he was going on the next pitch. Wilson missed a bunt, and Martin dove headfirst into third under Cochrane's high throw. He then scored on Wilson's fly. Paul Gallico of the *New York Daily News* timed him in 3.9 seconds from a standing start at third to home. In the seventh Martin singled again, stole second, went to third on an infield out, and came barreling into Cochrane as Gelbert put down a perfect squeeze bunt. The score was Martin 2, Athletics 0. When the inning ended, Martin headed out to center field amid the roaring crowd and calmly took a blue tobacco tin from his hip pocket and replenished his bulging cheek.

The A's almost pulled it out in the ninth, and Jimmy Wilson narrowly escaped the goat's horns. Foxx and Dykes were on second and first with 2 out. Mack sent Jim Moore up to hit for Earnshaw. On a 1-2 count, Moore hit a foul tip that Wilson couldn't hold. On the next pitch Foxx and Dykes were running. Moore swung and missed for strike 3. The pitch was low and hit the dirt in front of Wilson, who saw Foxx running and threw to Jake Flowers at third. Flowers instinctively swiped a tag at Foxx, who was in safely. Meanwhile, Moore, thinking he had struck out, headed for the dugout. The Cardinals were heading off the field as the spectators rushed onto it. The game was over.

Or was it?

Coaching at third, Eddie Collins had seen the ball hit the ground in front of the catcher. He yelled at Foxx and Dykes to stay put and hollered at Moore to run to first while he raced toward plate umpire Dick Nallin to argue that under the rules, Wilson had to tag Moore or throw to first to complete the play. When Flowers saw the commotion, he threw the ball back to Wilson. By now Bottomley was long gone from first base and there was nobody to throw to, and Moore made it to first. The entire Cardinals bench surrounded Collins and Nallin, who ruled that Collins was right. Everybody was safe. (The three official scorers debated for twenty minutes before giving Wilson an error.)

"I would bet Wilson aged a couple years during those moments," Collins said later.

Afterward Wilson admitted that he had made "a dumb play." He'd had his eye on Foxx heading for third and instinctively threw to third without thinking.

The police cleared the celebrating fans off the field. When order was restored, the bases were loaded with the tying run on second and Max Bishop was up.

Bishop hit a high foul ball down the right-field line. Bottomley raced back for it and dove over the bench filled with the A's bullpen crew, carrying them in a heap into the temporary box seats behind them. Umpire Dolly Stark pried the tangle of players apart and saw that Bottomley still held the ball. His right hand went up and the game was over.

Pepper Martin must have reminded Eddie Collins of himself and Ty Cobb in their younger days. "Nothing else in the world won for the Cardinals today but Pepper's speed and daring on the bases," Collins wrote. "More power to him. Incidentally, it is too bad from the spectator's viewpoint that there are not more of his type in the game right now. He is my idea of a ballplayer's ballplayer."

With a day for travel and no Sunday baseball in Philadelphia, the teams had two days to consider their positions. They both had reasons to be confident. Although Grove had beaten them, the Cardinals had hit him lustily and held no fear of him. The Athletics were going home after breaking even on the road.

Demand for tickets in Philadelphia was overwhelming despite the sour economy. Baseball was one necessity its consumers couldn't do without. The A's received 150,000 ticket applications. On Wednesday they sent out 15,000 special delivery letters to the lucky applicants, inviting them to come to Shibe Park to buy two tickets for each home game at $5.50 each. Ticket sales would be reported at 32,295 for each game. On Tuesday night, September

29, George Calhoun, a semipro player wearing his uniform, had arrived at the bleacher gate at ten o'clock to be the first in line when the gate opened the following Monday morning. His teammates brought him an overcoat and supplied him with food.

President Hoover had plenty of world crises on his desk. The Japanese were bombing Manchuria. Meetings were going on to bail out the failing banks and deal with the flood of delinquent mortgages. But the erstwhile sandlot shortstop and lifelong fan was not about to miss a World Series game in Philadelphia. He had seen the Athletics win each of the previous four Series games he had attended.

The president and Mrs. Hoover emerged from the third base dugout and entered Tom Shibe's box as Grove and Grimes were warming up. Hoover waved his hat and smiled as a slight patter of applause greeted him. It was quickly interrupted by a boo, then a chorus of boos, then a thundering of boos. Did the booing reflect unhappiness over the failed economic policies of the president or the high unemployment rate?

The answer came when a loud voice boomed out, "Beer! We want beer!" The chant was taken up, and soon Shibe Park rocked like the student cheering section at a football game. The president sat implacably; Mrs. Hoover studied her scorecard intently. When the presidential party left after the game, the same chorus was reprised like an operatic theme.

That's the way the story has been told and retold. Did it really happen?

In its October 19 issue, *Time* magazine said, "Last week the nation's press was embroiled in a controversy as to whether or not President Hoover had been booed by rooters at the Philadelphia World Series baseball game. Sports editors Paul Gallico of the *New York Daily News* and Joe Williams of the *World Telegram* reported booing. The Associated Press heard none. [The *New York Times* heard none and said the crowd was cordial. Sid Mercer, writing for Universal Service, made no mention of it.] Consensus was that on the entry and exit of President Hoover respectful folk in the grandstand near him cheered, folk in the bleachers, farther away, jeered."

Hardly "a barrage of angry boos that seemed to shake the ancient stands of Shibe Park," as Joe Williams described it. (If they had booed Hoover, it would not have been surprising. At the time he was the most criticized president since Lincoln, blamed for all the nation's problems except the severe drought in the Southwest.) As always, the truth depended on what paper you read and how the writer voted.

There were also mixed accounts of when Hoover left the game. The

Times said he smiled frequently at the applause of the throng and "obviously enjoyed every moment of the game," rising with the crowd for the home seventh-inning stretch, and remaining until the last out. Others have him leaving after the seventh inning, having received two telegrams, one telling of the death of Senator Dwight Morrow, a close friend and ally of the president. The *Times* reported that the news had been received during the game by the NBC announcer and the listening audience was told, but it was withheld from Hoover until he was on the train back to Washington.

Hoover's press secretary, Theodore G. Joslin, in his book, *Hoover Off the Record*, told of a group of White House correspondents seated behind the president who kept pestering Joslin to ask the president about matters of state, which Joslin refused to do. "It is his first opportunity to have any relaxation in weeks," Joslin told the reporters, "and he is going to get the benefit of it." When the press got word of Senator Morrow's death, Joslin again refused to let anyone tell Hoover during the game.

Joslin wrote nothing about any outbursts from the crowd upsetting Hoover. There was no mention of such an incident at Hoover's press conference the next day.

As for the game, the Shibe Park crowd had little to cheer about. Spit won out over speed. Grove was hittable. Burleigh Grimes, determined to avenge his two Series losses a year ago, was not, at least for 7 innings, in which only Foxx and Bishop reached base on walks. Unlike last year, Grimes was all business, no gabbing and gesturing at his opponents.

After a lead-off walk to Foxx in the eighth, Bing Miller broke up the no-hitter with a single. But Grimes set down the next three in order.

The Cardinals led 5–0 in the ninth; Mule Haas hit a line drive that smacked Grimes in the hand. The ball was deflected to Gelbert, who threw him out. The infield gathered around Grimes, who stood flexing his stinging hand for a few minutes while Syl Johnson warmed up. Grimes took a few practice tosses and stayed in. After Cochrane walked on a 3-2 pitch, Al Simmons made it 5–2 with his second homer—and second hit—of the Series. They were the first runs for the Athletics in 19 innings. Grimes then struck out Foxx, his 1930 nemesis, to nail down his first World Series win since 1920.

To celebrate, Gabby Street took his wife to New York to see the Ziegfeld Follies.

The next day Street turned to his number 4 starter, veteran right-hander Syl Johnson. His primary reliever, Jim Lindsey, was throwing in the bullpen from the first pitch, a fact that Eddie Collins needled Johnson about from the coaching box.

Anticipating a low-scoring game, Mack departed from his regular-season strategy and played for 1 run from the start. After Bishop's lead-off single, he ordered Haas to bunt. Simmons's double drove in Bishop. There was no more scoring until the sixth. With 2 out, Foxx hit the first pitch over the left-field roof. Miller doubled, Dykes singled, and it was 3–0 and Lindsey replaced Johnson.

Meanwhile, George Earnshaw, with a full three days' rest, was in complete command all the way. He walked 1 and fanned 8. The pesky Pepper Martin had the only 2 hits for St. Louis, a single in the fifth and a double in the eighth. When he slid headfirst stealing second in the fifth, he came up looking like a chimney sweep.

Everybody in baseball knew then and knows today that bases are stolen on pitchers more than catchers. A pitcher's time to home plate can vary from 1.2 to 1.8 seconds, a vital difference. The first time Pepper Martin saw Earnshaw lean way back before he threw, Martin knew anybody could run on him. Grove never paid any attention to base runners.

There was nothing wrong with Mickey Cochrane's arm. Nor was the stock market on his mind. Pepper Martin ran wild on the pitchers. Even without his sore eyes and legs and swollen hand, Cochrane had no chance.

"When pitchers let a runner get halfway to second base," said Connie Mack, "the catcher cannot throw him out with a shotgun."

But there was something bothering Mickey—his mail. Stan Baumgartner reported that Cochrane was receiving anonymous letters blaming him for the A's losing two of the first three games. Before the fifth game, wrote Baumgartner, a photographer passed Cochrane on the way to the bench. Cochrane was mumbling to himself, "The dickens with them all."

"What's the matter?" asked the cameraman.

"Oh, another poor sport wrote me a letter and he didn't have the nerve to sign it."

"Where is it?"

"I tore it up."

"What did he say?"

"What do they all say—you know. They think I ought to hit every ball over the right field wall and I ought to run down to second base and tag Martin out myself. They accuse me of everything after I have given my best to the club for seven years. They forget all I have done. They make accusations that are not only silly but insulting, and if I knew who they were I would stand them up against the wall and wallop them."

Bob Paul later confirmed that Cochrane was averaging about five hundred letters and telegrams a day by the fifth game. "He was taken over the coals as few ballplayers in the game's history ever have. He was called everything from a quitter to a cheat who had sold out his teammates."

Paul suggested Cochrane keep the letters and use them for a magazine article on the fickleness of the fans.

"No," said Cochrane, "that wouldn't be fair to the fans who wrote them. After all, these people are fans. Rabid fans who want the A's to win just as much as I do. They've written these letters and telegrams while peeved over our defeats. They'll forget all about their letters if we win."

Having used Earnshaw the day before, Mack needed a third starter. He considered Roy Mahaffey, Rube Walberg, and Waite Hoyt. He picked the veteran Hoyt, who had been in six World Series with the Yankees and had beaten the Cardinals twice in 1928. Some of the players had noticed on the train to St. Louis that Hoyt had been drinking. This is the story that Bob Paul never wrote but related years later:

The night before the game he was to pitch [Hoyt] went to a restaurant in Fairmont Park run by a Frenchman who was serving liquor despite prohibition. I was there and I saw Hoyt staggering by. I went up to him and said, "Waite, I see the condition you're in but I am not going to say anything. If you want to be like this it's your decision, that's up to you."

"Well," he says, "I just came from Broad and Locust where the gamblers all were, and I took a lot of bets that I was going to pitch, not that I would win, but just that I would pitch. They were betting that I would never pitch in the series. But I am."

The next day it was hot as blazes. He was warming up. I went up to him and told him I had never said a word about the night before. "Oh," he says, "I'll be all right. The more I warm up the more I'm getting that stuff out of my system. By the time the game starts I'll be okay. I'll take control of Pepper Martin."

Gabby Street moved Martin from sixth into the cleanup spot in the batting order, and Martin responded with 3 hits, including a home run, and 4 runs batted in. The Cardinals scored in the first, when Martin's fly ball brought home High from third. In the sixth Frisch doubled and Martin hit a home run into the left-field stands. In the eighth with Rube Walberg pitching, he singled and drove in Watkins to make it 5–1. He was then caught stealing for the first time.

The A's hit Lefty Hallahan but never in the pinch. He scattered 9 hits and walked only 1, and 8 of them were stranded in the 5–1 loss.

In the sixth inning Mack replaced Bishop and Haas, neither of whom had been hitting, with McNair and Cramer.

Pepper Martin now led the Series, 3 games to 2. He was 12 for 16 with 2 sacrifice flies and 4 stolen bases.

In the press box three hundred writers had run out of adjectives to append to him.

"He has the bit in his teeth and can't be stopped," Frisch said of Martin. "Now he's doing a big thing you can imagine the fun he's having."

"Isn't he the darndest feller you ever saw?" said Mack after the game. "How are we going to stop him? They outplayed us and deserved to win. Hallahan pitched a fine game. His control was much better than it was last year."

"We never thought [Martin] could keep it up this long," Cochrane said, "so why try to figure he's through now? We have thrown everything at him so far except the bat bag and he has plastered it."

On the train to St. Louis, Connie Mack called Martin "a real ballplayer" whose performance reminded him of another player twenty-five years earlier whom most people had long forgotten. "That fellow [George] Rohe of the White Sox in 1906 was just as sensational a World Series performer. [Rohe, a fill-in third baseman, had 2 doubles, a triple, and 4 RBIs in the Hitless Wonders' 6-game upset of the Cubs.] But he wasn't anything like as good a man as Martin. I was at that Series. Rohe was a second-rater, just a substitute. I think they let him go about the middle of the next season. But Martin is going to be a star for a good many more years, judging by what he has shown us."

Judge Landis was heading west on the Cardinals' special. The AP reported that he encountered Martin in a Pullman aisle and said, "Young man, I envy you. I would love nothing better than to trade places with you."

"It's all right with me, Judge," said Martin. "I'll trade my $4,500 a year for your $50,000 any day."

The AP added, "Pepper didn't know the commissioner's salary was $65,000."

Crowds gathered at stations along the way to get a glimpse of the new hero. When the Cardinals arrived at Union Station in St. Louis, he was the center of attention. He acted the part of the hero, but as he and his wife got into a taxi he said, "Ain't all that the bunk. If I strike out tomorrow with a couple of men on they will give me the razzberry. But it is nice to hear it once in a while—makes you feel good."

The threat of rain in St. Louis was not welcomed by Mack. "We're ready," he said. "It won't help us to get any extra days off and it might help St. Louis." The Athletics had fielded flawlessly, going a record 5 games without an error. But they weren't hitting. Only Foxx, at .421, had as many as 6 hits so far.

Dib Williams had struck out 8 times. "There's a little something wrong with his swing," said Mack, who was his own hitting and pitching coach. "He'll get over it, but of course he may not get over it in time to help us in this series."

There was some second-guessing that Joe Boley would have been better at short than Dib Williams, but John McGraw didn't think so. McGraw lauded the rookie's steady, at times spectacular, play. He called a third-game play by Williams "a corker" when Frisch hit a high bouncer over Grove's head and Williams raced in, scooped it up on the first hop, and threw a shot to Foxx that nipped Frisch diving into the bag.

Frank Frisch dismissed Lefty Grove as a factor. "We hit him so hard Mack has to start Earnshaw in the sixth game and if he wins, start him again."

The press tended to agree, writing off Grove.

Connie Mack disagreed. On the train he decided to hold individual pep talks. He took a seat at one end of a car, and as a player passed, he asked him to sit down for a few minutes. "I told each one of them how well Grove and Earnshaw were primed for the final contests, and how good it looked for us with them ready," Mack told Al Horwits in the 1938 *Saturday Evening Post* article. "The last meeting was with Grove. I told him I wasn't worried, that all the boys knew he could win for them. Lefty liked that. He often has been described as sullen and crusty. But I found him human enough to enjoy appreciation as well as the next."

According to Phil Todt, before Game 6 Connie Mack decided to throw Martin nothing but fastballs down the middle. And that's what Lefty Grove did. Martin didn't strike out, but he didn't get a hit or steal a base or do anything for the crowd of 39,401 who gave him a thunderous reception when he first ran out to center field and again when he came up to bat the first time. John Drebinger of the *Times* described this conversation between Martin and Cochrane as the crowd cheered:

"Well, kid, you're sitting on top of the world now and you deserve it."

"Why man, I'm as dizzy right now as you are and don't know yet what it's all about. I'm just up here swinging, hoping I'll connect."

Lefty Grove was in his 31-game-winning form. He allowed 1 run on 5 hits, walked 1, struck out 7. With home plate in the shadows in the ninth, even Cochrane had trouble seeing his fastball. When Roettger swung and missed and the ball got away, Roettger reached first. "I never saw that ball," Mickey said.

Paul Derringer matched Grove for 4 innings, then blew up in the fifth. An error by third baseman Flowers, 2 hits, and 4 walks netted 4 runs and finished the Cardinal rookie for the day. At that point some fans reportedly left to buy tickets for Game 7. The A's added 4 more in the seventh off Jim Lindsey, helped by Chick Hafey dropping a fly ball, and more fans left to buy tickets for the next day.

Mack was gratified to see some hitting, especially by Williams, who had a single and double. But he lauded two key plays by Bishop that he said changed the game. In the first Bishop had turned a tricky hopper into a difficult double play to end a threat. In the third, with Gelbert on first and 1 out, Derringer bunted to the right of the mound. Grove went after it as Bishop charged in. Grove fell and tripped Bishop, who became entangled with Grove on the ground. But Bishop managed to get off a swift throw to Foxx to nip Derringer at first.

Asked how he would have felt if the Cardinals had won, Mack said, "I sleep as well on Pullmans as I do at home, and if we had lost today that's where I would be sleeping tonight and soundly."

An unexplainably low turnout of 20,805—about the lowest for a World Series in twenty years—was on hand on a midsummer-like Saturday for Game 7. Nothing, not a sore hand nor probably a broken hand, could keep Burleigh Grimes from pitching this game. Gabby Street had Bill Hallahan ready to go in at the slightest trouble. Connie Mack had managed his pitchers so that George Earnshaw was ready again with three days' rest. In 17 innings the Moose had given up 2 runs and 8 hits.

Connie Mack's often-stated warning that the big guns will get their hits but you better bear down on the weaker guys or they will hurt you proved prophetic. Andy High, the third third baseman used by Street, and right fielder George Watkins, who had 2 hits so far, did all the damage. In the first inning, High and Watkins singled. Frisch sacrificed them along. High scored on a wild pitch and Watkins went to third. Martin walked and stole second. Ernie Orsatti struck out on a pitch that bounced. Cochrane threw to first but the ball stuck in Foxx's glove, and by the time he dug it out and threw to Cochrane, Watkins had scored.

In the third High singled again and Watkins hit a home run. Those 4 hits were all Earnshaw gave up. But they were enough.

Burleigh Grimes held the first five A's in the lineup to a lone single and kept the 4–0 lead until the ninth. Walks to Simmons and Dykes and Williams's single loaded the bases with 2 outs. Rube Walberg, who had pitched the eighth for the A's, was due up. Connie Mack waved a finger at Flit Cramer. "Hit for Walberg," he said.

"I was stunned," Cramer recalled. "I'd been sitting on the bench yelling at the Cardinals. Grimes was throwing spitballs that seemed to break a foot. I fouled off several, then singled to drive in two runs. It was my biggest thrill in baseball."

The score was 4–2 and Max Bishop was up. Gabby Street waved in Bill Hallahan. Bishop hit a high fly ball that was fated to be caught by Pepper Martin for the last out.

Surrounded by writers and fans, Connie Mack sent Eddie Collins to the Cardinals' clubhouse to congratulate Gabby Street.

"Martin just got hot," seemed to sum it all up for the Athletics.

Connie Mack, who had hoped to become the first manager to win three championships in a row, took it calmly. A few weeks later Mack told a group of students at Temple University, "The Cardinals were the better team. Last year Grimes spent too much time jeering and lost two games. This year he attended to business and won two games."

Losing never affected Connie Mack's sleep or appetite. Not even when he blamed himself, as he did for the loss of the seventh game. Horwits quoted him:

I didn't feel it necessary to call a clubhouse meeting after those individual meetings on the train. It's practically revolutionary of course to skip a meeting before a World Series game. But I thought we were up and would stay up. The Cards looked like a beaten outfit when they took the field. But two quick breaks put them in the lead and we never caught them. In the first Dib Williams and Al Simmons got snarled and let a pop fall between them for two runs. Expecting George Watkins to bunt, Earnshaw put everything he had on a fastball down the middle. He hit a home run. Breaks, yes. But breaks that might have been prevented by a clubhouse meeting to consider all possibilities. In the box score of the seventh game after losing pitcher–Earnshaw there ought to be a line, losing manager–Connie Mack.

Maybe. Neither team hit for much—another way of saying both pitching staffs were superb. Grove and Earnshaw had held Martin hitless and scoreless in the last two games. But the wild mustang of the Osage was the reason it went to seven games. Years later Joe Williams wrote of Mack, "I once heard him say conversationally of a ballplayer, 'He sure gave me one hell of a time.' It may have been Pepper Martin, but I am not certain."

If it wasn't, it certainly could have been.

The pain of losing was soothed somewhat by checks for $3,023.09. (Jimmie Dykes said he lost his when the bank closed the day after he deposited it.) Connie Mack added $600 to his share to see that his scouts, his new public relations man, Jim Peterson, and park employees received something. The seven-game series enabled the Athletics to show a profit of $110,000 instead of a loss and declare the eighth dividend in eleven years, this one the biggest—$150,000.

Mickey Cochrane was bitterly disappointed in himself. Connie Mack tried to console him. "It's done," he said. "We did our best and that's all we could do. Forget it. Have a good time on your trip."

Right after the World Series several of the A's left for a trip to Japan arranged by Fred Lieb and promoter Herb Hunter. The first leg of the trip was a TWA flight from St. Louis to Glendale. Then in San Francisco they would be joined by some of their wives, Lou Gehrig, and a half-dozen other players and board the *Tatsuta Maru* to Tokyo.

During the first leg of the trip reporter Frank Roche of the *Los Angeles Times* asked the players if Connie Mack planned to retire and name Eddie Collins to replace him. None of them wanted to be quoted, but Fred Lieb said, "It is not improbable."

It was improbable. On the train back to Philadelphia, wrote Cy Peterman of the *Bulletin*, Mack was observed "writing, erasing and rewriting on an old scorecard, planning the new lineup for 1932."

A small, subdued crowd greeted Connie Mack on his arrival at North Philadelphia station Monday evening. "The Cards played better than we did," Mack told them, "and that's why we lost. Our boys didn't click as they have in the past, but it's silly to say that they've slipped permanently. They all played hard and I have nothing but praise for them. It's over now and I'll start thinking about next year."

On October 29 Mack made the sorrowful trip to Chicago for the funeral of Charles Comiskey. They had never been close friends but had been allies of Ban Johnson's in the Western Association in the 1890s and during the founding of the American League. In February Pirates owner Barney Dreyfuss would be gone too. Of the principal participants in the founding of the American League and the 1903 peace agreement between the leagues, only Clark Griffith and Connie Mack remained.

Many baseball students and old-timers like to think of the 1920s and 1930s as the golden age of baseball, but at the time some writers deplored the trend of other sports drawing youngsters away from baseball, resulting in a decline in the quality of players.

Connie Mack never so deplored. He believed a diversity of sporting interests made for a better society. "We can't be a one-sport nation," he said in an interview in a Catholic magazine, *The Queen's Work*, in 1931. "If baseball were our only sports interest we'd be in a frightful rut. I encourage the men on my club to play golf. It's healthy for them and gives them a new physical and mental relaxation."

In some interviews after he retired, Ty Cobb was quoted as knocking the caliber of the players then in the game. But in others he acknowledged that there was greater pressure on the players than when he had started twenty-four years earlier, and clubs now had more depth and fewer mediocre players.

Mack agreed. In a 1934 interview with Louis Atchison of the *Washington Post* he laughed at the suggestion that modern players didn't stack up with the old-timers:

Certainly the game has changed, but the change has been for better, not worse. The players today are just as good as any I saw in the old days. I don't see how we can improve on our outfielders. I know we had Cobb and Speaker and others, but we have Ruth and Simmons and others who are every bit as good. I get as big a thrill watching present day outfielders pick balls off outfield walls as I did out of seeing others.

I can't truthfully say the old players were better. Just let these pitchers do what they want to with that ball, and you'll see batters choking up from four inches to a foot. Now everybody has a toehold and swings from the heels simply because pitchers haven't got control over the ball the way they used to have. If the ball gets scratched or a little dirt on it they throw in a new one. Let them do what they want with it, and the pitchers will hold their own.

Mack also saw an improvement in the character of players at the major league level. "Years ago, if a man could play we signed him without knowing anything else about him. Today we want to know about the boy's home life. . . . I'll stack ten average young men of today up against ten of the same age twenty years ago, and the modern youngster will be so much cleaner cut, no further question can be raised."

In October Indians general manager Billy Evans had turned back efforts of an airplane manufacturer to sell the Cleveland club flying machines to carry the Indians on their road trips. There was talk of clubs flying on long jumps. John Kieran envisioned a Boston–San Francisco World Series, with a travel day by air.

While Connie Mack was not ready for travel by air, in many ways he was far more visionary than his younger colleagues. In an April 27, 1932, interview about the game's future he said, "Baseball is an imperishable part of our national life. It has thrived and will continue to thrive sympathetically with the expansion of our cities." Asked if the present popularity represented a peak of popular interest, he said, "No. Twenty years ago they said the same thing. We had wooden stands and average crowds of 5,000. Double deck stadiums were unthought of. A crowd like that at Yankee Stadium a week ago when we played to 80,000 was beyond the wildest dream. Why not look ahead as well as back? Perhaps to the time when there will be baseball fields on the top of immense skyscrapers with perhaps a weatherproof dome to remove the rain hazard?"

At sixty-nine Connie Mack was still looking to the future.

31 | MR. MACK

At the conclusion of the first third of the twentieth century, Connie Mack was the most admired and respected man in America. The unschooled son of Irish immigrants was beloved by all who knew him professionally and socially and by millions more who did not know him but were inspired by his optimism, his pluck and perseverance, his refusal to quit the quest for success, his innate fairness and sportsmanship, and his generosity. They seemed to sense his old-world graciousness and warmth without knowing that he would tip his hat to a lady working behind a concession stand as he walked through Shibe Park or greet any stranger who approached him in a hotel lobby as if he (or she) were a lifelong friend.

An unnamed reporter once described the lengths to which Mack would go to make an admirer feel welcome. One afternoon in Fort Myers two men came across the field toward him. Mack turned to Earle and asked, "Who is that man?"

"That's Mr. Brown from Philadelphia," said Earle.

"Hello, there, Mr. Brown," shouted Connie before the gentleman could say one word. Mr. Brown smiled and said to his companion, "Pay me." To Mack he said, "I just bet my friend that you would remember my name."

No politician, no general, no leader of industry, no athlete commanded so deep and heartfelt a following for so many years. Connie Mack was the only manager called "Mister" by everybody connected to baseball.

In a booklet put out by the Philadelphia Sporting Writers Association to honor the 1929 pennant winners, Mayor Harry Mackey wrote, "Mr. Mack exemplifies the very best that is in a citizen. Quiet, unassuming, determined, industrious and persevering, he has ever commanded the admiration and respect of those to whose attention his great work has been called. It is a privilege to have known Connie Mack and we honor ourselves as we sing his praises today."

When the Athletics were in the World Series, Mack's national legions of followers sought out scarce radios to listen to the action. In 1929 most of the population of eighty-seven in Swenson, Texas, crowded into the depot agent's house and huddled around one of the two radios in town to root for Connie Mack and the Athletics.

The 1931 World Series was broadcast by fifty-eight NBC stations and eighty-two CBS links. One of them could be picked up in the far north of Glenburn, North Dakota, near the Canadian border, where Elmer Oiseth had come from Norway in 1901 and settled. His son Ed said:

> He became interested in baseball from town teams. He was an Athletics fan because he had no use for McGraw but had great respect for Connie Mack, even at so great a distance, and those two were the dominant figures in the game. With his poker winnings and farming income he went to see the A's play in Chicago and Detroit and Philadelphia. When the 1931 Series began he went to school and took me out of the fifth grade to listen to it on the radio. "You should close the school," he told the teacher, "so all the kids can listen to Connie Mack and the Athletics in the World Series." The teacher didn't agree, but he took me out of school anyhow.

Eugene M. Rhodes was a prolific author of popular historical stories and novels of the southwest. Born in 1869, he lived all his life in the west. When he died in 1934, his obituary said "that his keenest interest was in baseball, and that he would rather be a second Connie Mack than a second Alexandre Dumas."

The only other man who may have surpassed Connie Mack's standing with the public at that time was himself an ardent admirer of Mr. Mack—folksy humorist, gentle fun-poker at everything and everybody, America's favorite movie star, Will Rogers.

Edward W. Bok was a Dutch immigrant who became editor of the *Ladies' Home Journal*. He wrote several books on the pursuit of success that Connie Mack had read. In 1921 Bok endowed an annual award of a gold medal and $10,000 to the person considered by a committee as having done the most for the city of Philadelphia during the past year. Leaders in music, medicine, the arts, and academia had been honored since then. Following the Athletics' 1929 World Series victory, some of the baseball writers and friends of

Connie Mack thought he deserved the honor, not just for that year's World Series triumph, but for all he had done to bring seven American League pennants to the city.

With little expectation of success, they put his nomination before the Bok awards committee. Eugenia Goldsmith, sister-in-law of George Graham, the former sports editor of the *North American*, now vice-president for public relations of Willys-Overland, wrote two letters to the committee on Mack's behalf.

Invited to Bok's home for dinner one evening in late December, Connie Mack was informed that he would be receiving the award. Bok did not live to see it. He went to Lake Wales, Florida, on January 5, 1930, and died four days later. Mack was in Mount Plymouth, Florida, when he received the official notice.

In a February letter to the *New York Times*, Bok's son Curtis explained why his father had chosen Connie Mack:

The present high standard of sportsmanship and of personal living among the players is very directly traceable to Connie Mack's efforts, so that today when thousands and thousands of boys regard these players as heroes and seek to emulate them, they have as exemplars a class of men who live cleanly and play the game according to best ideals of sportsmanship. Quite apart from this, Mr. Mack takes a direct and personal interest in the boy movement throughout the country, and seeks by his own personal effort and example to give boys a sense of the importance of decent living and clean athletics.

It is also safe to say that during the dark periods of baseball when there has been scandal and corruption . . . the name of Connie Mack has acted as a backlog on which has rested the ultimate confidence of the American public in the integrity of professional sport. He is a man of the highest integrity and modesty, and is beloved, as a person, by every one who is attached to the game.

"I feel good about receiving this honor," Mack told reporters, "the more because the committee deemed a man of baseball worthy of it. It is the last thing I expected. I confess it makes my heart pulse to think I should have received such an honor."

Mack was certainly the first and probably the only recipient who regularly rode to work on the streetcar, insulated in the cold, wet spring, with newspapers wrapped around his body under his shirt by an insistent wife. This recognition of the importance of baseball in the conservative city's culture boosted the game's standing as much as it did Mr. Mack's personal prestige. The fact that it was a New York team that Connie Mack's boys had toppled as pennant-winners may have helped.

In view of Bok's recent death, the February 13 dinner was a small, private affair at the Bellevue Stratford Hotel for the committee and a few prominent citizens. Mack, accompanied by Connie Jr., returned to the city with no publicity. The award was presented by Bok's son William, an assistant district attorney. Since the occasion was not public, no members of the press were present. No record of Connie Mack's acceptance speech could be found. Seventy-five years later a quote attributed to Mack was sent to his grandson, Dennis McGillicuddy: "Humanity is the keystone that holds nations and men together. When that collapses the whole structure crumbles. This is as true of baseball teams as any other pursuit in life."

It could have come from the Bok dinner.

The honor was widely applauded, not just by Philadelphia writers, but in New York as well.

James Isaminger wrote, "Mack, who came here in 1901, has passed every test and there is not one black mark against him. He has been Lincolnian in his stature, and while this may seem a preposterous assertion to the average man from a distance, he doesn't know the leader of the Athletics and what a really great man he is."

Ed Pollock reminded his readers that in addition to his public achievements, Mack kept an unpublicized payroll of old-timers he supported that ran "up to six figures."

Commented the *New York Herald-Tribune*, "Connie Mack has given the Bok prize publicity it never had before." Most people outside of Philadelphia had never heard of it.

John Kieran had earlier written in the *New York Times*, "It is probable . . . that there never was in any sport a more honest, engaging, straightforward, capable and courtly figure than kindly old Connie Mack."

Joe Williams seconded that in the *New York Telegram*: "There probably never has been a finer character in baseball."

Recognition of the attributes that made Connie Mack successful were not confined to the sports pages. Dr. Albert C. Barnes was a student, lecturer, and collector of art. His foundation in Merion, outside Philadelphia, houses one of the world's largest private art collections.

In 1936 Barnes gave a lecture at his old high school, Central High, in Philadelphia. According to his biographer, Henry Hart, this student of the masterpieces of the art world declared that the greatest artist Philadelphia had ever produced was Connie Mack.

"Let me reconcile this apparently wild assertion," Hart quotes Barnes, "with the facts of the case. Connie Mack would not accept a recruit who would not rather play baseball than do anything else in the world. He gets teamwork out of men who are concerned primarily with their own excellence. When Connie Mack is successful, his team has the attributes which all aestheticians agree are the indispensable requisites of great art—unity, variety, individuality, and the production of aesthetic pleasure in others. . . . Connie Mack has given honest aesthetic pleasure to more people than anybody I know of in a lifetime spent in Philadelphia."

The Bok award was followed in May by the presentation of a silver loving cup to Mack for "his interest in Philadelphia boyhood" at the Boy Council meeting in which a young boy was chosen "most worthy boy" for giving up his dream of becoming a world-class organist to work to help support his family. Mickey Cochrane handed the boy a season pass to Shibe Park.

Mack's 1929 world championship had put him on the cover of lesson 13 of *Practical Selling*, a fifty-two-week correspondence course on improving selling skills, with this call to closing a sale leading off the booklet: "When Cornelius McGillicuddy—or Connie Mack, as he is familiarly known to a million adoring baseball fans—is away from the Philadelphia Athletics, his prime consideration is in the results of their efforts. It takes runs to win games. Let the fans read the flowery details of how the game was played—Mack is interested in results."

At this point in his life, Connie Mack personified the Greek definition of happiness: "The exercise of vital powers along lines of excellence in a life affording them scope."

What was it about Connie Mack that caused two generations of Philadelphia baseball writers, some of whom had almost daily contact with him for seven months a year from March to October, to commit to newsprint that they "loved" the man?

What would move Fred Lieb to write in his memoirs, "I really loved the old fellow with his stiff white collars of the 1900s"?

Why would the Philadelphia writers call their annual golf tournament trophy the Connie Mack Trophy, Ty Cobb name his favorite bird dog Connie

Mack, a dog trainer enter a hound named Connie Mack in the 1935 three-mile hound trials at a high society riding club (he won), an upstate New York horse breeder name a prize pacer Connie Mack in 1915, a steamboat owner in North Carolina name his boat for him, or a seed company develop a Connie Mack rose?

What was it that would cause a man in his seventies named Joe Elstner, who lived in San Benito, Texas, on the Mexican border, to get out of his sickbed against his doctor's advice and drive four hundred miles to the Athletics' spring training camp in Lake Charles, Louisiana, to shake Connie Mack's hand?

"If I die," Elstner said, "I'll be doing something I've wanted all my life."

What was it that led the elderly Joseph Chandler of Corydon, Kentucky, who could have met presidents and kings because his son was the governor and then a U.S. senator, to act as awestruck as a young fan of a teen idol on meeting Connie Mack? In 1947 baseball commissioner A. B. "Happy" Chandler said:

> My father before me was a great admirer of Connie Mack. I had an unusual experience about ten years ago. I took my father to New York to the World Series and he wanted to meet Mr. Mack.
>
> I took him down to where Mr. Mack was seated and I said, "Dad, this is Mr. Connie Mack."
>
> Dad just stood and looked at him and shook his head as if he'd never expected that moment to come in his life. He came from a little town down in Kentucky, only about 700–800. He was speechless for the first time in his life. When he was able he uttered just two words. He stood there and shook his head and said, "Cornelius McGillicuddy."

What was it that motivated people by the hundreds to drive in cars or horse-drawn wagons a few hundred miles to a whistle-stop railroad station in hopes of getting a glimpse of Mr. Mack on the train carrying the Athletics home from spring training? He was an early riser. When the train stopped at a station, even in the predawn hours, they were often rewarded by Mr. Mack's appearing on the rear platform of the observation car, in suit and tie and high collar, and visiting with them. If the stop was long enough, he might get off to stretch his legs.

What was it that inspired the long-distance adulation of Mr. Mack that led young mothers and fathers to name their sons for him? There were dozens, hundreds—who knows how many—boys named for Connie Mack, beginning at least as early as 1913. Many became priests. Typical was an incident recalled by Mack's grandson Connie McCambridge. "One day in Chicago a priest came into the Cooper-Carlton Hotel and came over to Connie Mack and said, 'My name is Cornelius McGillicuddy. I was named for you.' Dad [the McCambridge boys called him Dad] was tickled to death to hear that."

What is remarkable about these namesakes is their diversity of geography and background and the commonality of the motivation behind their parents' actions.

Here are some of their stories.

In 1913 in the tiny town of Fort Duchesne in the middle of the vast empty Uintah and Ouray Indian Reservation one hundred miles east of Salt Lake City lived Elmer and Mary Harris Denver. Elmer played ball on local Uintah tribal teams. Both were avid sports fans. Somehow—possibly from a Salt Lake City newspaper—they kept up with major league baseball. Mary became a Philadelphia Athletics and Connie Mack fan—the two entities were inseparable. On October 14, three days after the Athletics defeated McGraw's Giants for Mack's third world championship in four years, Mary gave birth to her second child. Because of her admiration for Mr. Mack, she named her son Connie Mack Denver.

Connie Mack Denver (he always proudly identified himself by his full name) played on local town teams and ran in the 1931 *Los Angeles Times* marathon as a '32 Olympics candidate. He attended BYU and USC and became a Uintah leader. In 1942 he named his son Connie Mack Denver Jr. His grandson, Connie Mack Denver III, lives in Ontario, California.

Connie Mack Gravitte was born July 12, 1933, in the small textile mill town of Ca-Vel, North Carolina. His mother, Lucy Hamlett Gravitte, was an avid baseball fan (her sister was married to Claude Wilborn, a minor league outfielder who played in 5 games for the Braves in 1940). Lucy Gravitte listened to the World Series on the radio and any other games she could find on the dial. Since the Athletics had been in three World Series in recent years she had read and heard enough about Mr. Mack to inspire her to name her second-born son for him.

"As a child Connie was very proud of his name," said his older brother Willie. "He would tell everybody he was Connie Mack number two. He looked up Mack's records and whatever he could learn about him and his life."

Captain Connie Mack Gravitte was killed in a C-130 crash in Vietnam on June 17, 1966.

Connie Mack Luce was born in San Augustine in the east Texas pine country in 1941.

In 1956 he wrote to Mack's daughter Ruth, "My daddy was a great fan of his, so my mother tells me. You see, my daddy died two months before I was born. As she knew my dad would be pleased, she named me Connie Mack Luce."

Connie Mack Butler, born in Greensboro, North Carolina, in 1933, was one of the few namesakes to meet Connie Mack.

"My father was an amateur baseball player and he and my mother named me after the grand old man. My father was a fan of Mr. Mack. I met him when I was about seven years old in the visitors dugout at the Memorial Stadium in Greensboro."

Butler played for Rollins College, which lost to Missouri in the championship game of the 1954 College World Series.

Connie Mack Horned was born May 7, 1930, near Black Oak, Arkansas.

"My grandfather was the patriarch of the family and he named his grandsons. He was born in Marmaduke in 1868 and became an early admirer of Mr. Mack and followed his life through the newspapers. He named me for him. I was teased about the name but grew to like it, or at least live with it. One day I was driving in southern Illinois and I stopped at a farm to ask directions and it turned out the farmer was named Connie Mack too."

Connie Mack Krivanek was born August 14, 1936, in Samaritan Hospital, Oklahoma City. His father was a local sandlot pitcher, but it was a delivery room nurse who, discussing a choice of name with the young mother, suggested naming him for Connie Mack. In 1948 Krivanek wrote to Mr. Mack and received a reply and a ball signed by the Athletics.

Connie Mack McIlvoy was born September 11, 1936, in Lawton, Oklahoma. He was *not* named for Mr. Mack but has gone through life being asked if he was.

"My father's name was Orville. My mother had a friend who lived on a farm who admired the boxer Max Baer and named her son Connie Max.

'That sounds good to me,' Ma said. But she made it Connie Mack, after my father, who was known to everybody as 'Mac.'"

In 1948 the two young Connie Macks, Krivanek and McIlvoy, both short-stops, met when they played against each other in a YMCA midget baseball league in Oklahoma City.

McIlvoy played left field for Oklahoma State when the Cowboys won the 1959 College World Series. He was named to the all-tournament team.

Connie Mack Berry was born April 15, 1935, in Greenville, South Carolina.

"My dad idolized Connie Mack so much he named me for him."

Berry played baseball, football, and basketball at North Carolina State and several years in the NFL.

Connie Mack Stubbs was born September 20, 1929, in Shawnee, Oklahoma. The Athletics had just won the pennant after fifteen years of struggling.

"My father, Grady, was a big Philadelphia Athletics fan and he was celebrating their being back on top when I came along so that's how I came to be called Connie Mack."

Connie Mack McCoy was born August 12, 1939, in Lyons, Kansas.

"My father, Carol 'Ted' McCoy, was not a baseball fan. He grew up on a farm in northern Oklahoma and didn't care if he never saw a ball game. But he knew enough about Connie Mack to admire him as a gentleman of high standards, a great American hero. He named me after Mr. Mack and told me he wanted me to be like him. I was never a ballplayer, but the name has gotten me a lot of attention."

Connie Mack Seymore may be the only boy named for Mr. Mack by a Yankee fan. Born August 31, 1934, in Merkel, Texas, he was the third of eight children of Joseph and Dolly Seymore. Nobody knows how a cotton farmer in the middle of Texas, born in 1906, became a Yankee fan. Maybe the fourteen-year-old Joseph was swept up in the Babe Ruth mania when the Yankees acquired Ruth and began to win in 1920.

"We don't know why," said his son Riley, "but he was, and so we all were too. Even so, Dad admired Connie Mack at the same time."

Joe played ball when he was not working in the fields. The farm, ten miles out of town, had no electricity until 1952. So he rigged up a wind charger on the garage roof that generated enough power to run a little radio.

"When the World Series was on," Riley continued, "everybody got out of pulling cotton while Dad lay down on the floor with his ear pressed up against the radio trying to hear what was going on so he could tell us."

Connie Mack Seymore was sixty-seven when Riley took him to New York to see Yankee Stadium for the first time.

Connie Sparks became a "nicknamesake" of Connie Mack, thanks to an elementary school principal.

Born in 1919 in Panhandle, Texas, near Amarillo, Sparks was christened John Sparks Jr. Everybody called him Junior. He hated the name.

"There was another boy in his class at Panhandle Elementary named John Jr.," recalled his sister, Nancy Garner. "The teacher called the other boy John and my brother Junior. He didn't like that one bit."

John took an early interest in baseball. Connie Mack's Athletics became his favorite team. The school principal, J. L. Naylor, was also a baseball fan. He took Junior to area high school games, where they would discuss the big league pennant races. In the 1930 World Series Mr. Naylor rooted for the St. Louis Cardinals. John, of course, was pulling for the Athletics. They made a bet on the Series. Nobody remembers what the stakes were, but Junior won.

Junior was so fervent in his admiration for Connie Mack and his team that one day Mr. Naylor said to him, "I'm going to call you Connie."

Junior beamed. He liked the idea of carrying his hero's name. He told everybody he knew in Panhandle that his name was now Connie. He told his family, "From now on you all call me Connie. I never want to hear John or Junior again."

Junior went to Texas Christian University in Fort Worth as Connie Sparks. He played fullback on the 1938 TCU national championship team as Connie Sparks, scoring the first touchdown in the Orange Bowl.

When he was inducted into the TCU Hall of Fame for baseball and football, it was as Connie Sparks. Nobody in the school's athletic department knew him by any other name.

Connie spent thirty years in the Air Force, during which he flew a B-29 dropping bombs over Japan. Three days after the atom bomb was dropped on Hiroshima, he dropped leaflets over the city urging surrender. During his career Connie commanded the physical education department and coached the baseball team at the Air Force Academy.

If anyone called out "John" to him, he didn't respond. He didn't think they were talking to him. He was Connie Sparks.

Bill Veeck's son Mike wasn't a namesake but he identified with them.

"My dad had one hero in his life—Connie Mack. He had tremendous respect for Mr. Mack, who never put him down or criticized him. I was his first-born. He named me Mike but he called me 'McGillicuddy' 'til the day he died."

Dr. James Penniman was an authority on George Washington, having written several books on the first president. He once compared Connie Mack's handwriting to that of George Washington and told Harry Robert in *Baseball Magazine* in 1929:

> When one studies the formations made by his pen, it is very easy to understand why Connie Mack has been so successful in his work. Every movement of the pen shows strength of character. . . . Connie's writing has many strokes similar to those penned by Washington. People think of our first president as a warrior and statesman. In reality, he was a scholar, a true man of letters.
>
> So it is with Mr. Mack. Although he did not attend school after he was twelve years old, he has become a scholar in his own line. Baseball calls for as much study as other lines of endeavor, and sometimes it calls for more. You have to know Connie Mack intimately, really to appreciate him.

That was not necessarily so.

People in some of the most remote areas of the nation who never set eyes on him seemed to appreciate the essence of Connie Mack without ever knowing that he answered every letter he received, no matter how young the writer; never forgot his small-town New England roots; never turned down a chance to do a favor or an act of kindness, creating a range of enduring friendships that adorned his life like pendants on a Christmas tree. They never knew how many cash-filled envelopes he handed to poor families for coal or food or rent.

They didn't know that whenever a son or nephew or young friend of a friend of a player went on a trip with the team to New York, Mack would hand him fifteen dollars, saying, "Here's some spending money for you."

If a high school coach wrote asking for some used baseballs, the coach would receive a handwritten note that they were on the way. When students at the North American College in Rome told a visitor they could use some baseball equipment, the visitor suggested they write to Connie Mack. They did. Soon seven dozen baseballs and twenty-one bats arrived. A few months later a priest came to Connie Mack's home with a Papal blessing from Pope Pius XI for him and his family.

As far as Connie Mack was concerned, none of this was anybody's business. No public relations operation churned out press releases. No media vacuum cleaners sucked up every morsel and tidbit of everybody's life and dumped it all on the populace. The things Connie Mack did naturally, without fanfare, were known only to the recipients and their friends and neighbors.

These are the kinds of things he did.

When an obscure nineteenth-century ballplayer named Ray Cardiner died, Mack wrote to the player's daughter:

Dear Jeaneth:

Your father was a credit to baseball and I know his daughter will be a great credit to her father. Wish you both all the good things this world can possibly give.

In 1929 and 1930 Mickey Cochrane's brother Archie was a student at Staunton Military Academy in Virginia. Each spring Mack brought the A's to the school for a game for the students.

When the Athletics were in Boston, Connie Mack always welcomed visits from old friends and teammates from East Brookfield and invited them to lunch with him before the game. One of those old town team players, Walter Carroll, lived in Portland, Maine. Whenever he visited with Mack in Boston, he brought along his young nephew, Tom Murphy. "When you're old enough," Mack told Tom, "you can be a batboy for the Athletics."

When the A's left Boston in July 1931, fifteen-year-old Tom went with them for the rest of the summer.

"I lived with Mr. [Rudy] Ohl in Philadelphia, and roomed with Kid Gleason on the road," Tom recalled. "Gleason watched over me. On the train I would flip a coin with him for the lower berth. The team was a very friendly group. They would invite me to go to the movies with them."

Among Murphy's memories were the many priests who called on Connie Mack at every stop around the league.

That fall the Athletics played an exhibition game in Portland. "I told Mr.

Mack the thirty-seven boys in my class expected me to get them into the game free because of my association with the team. He told me they could all help carry in the equipment through the gate. Years later I learned that Mr. Mack told the promoter to take thirty-seven student admissions out of his guarantee."

Any time a class from Brookfield High School came to Fenway Park on a field trip, Mack would invite them into the dugout after the game and to the hotel that evening or the next day to meet some of the players. Brookfield coach Marty Leach recalled a day in 1928 when the class was introduced to Cobb, Speaker, and Grove. He carried away two lasting impressions of Ty Cobb: "A diamond ring the size of a rock on his pinky, and his discretion in disposing of a cigar wrapper while seated in the hotel lobby."

On the team's first visit to Boston in 1930 Connie Mack and Earle went after a game to Spencer, where his first wife and Earle had been born, for a Knights of Columbus dinner in his honor that could have sold five times the capacity of 160. The rosewood bat, trophy of East Brookfield's 1883 championship, when Mack was their catcher, was borrowed from the fire hall and hung over the dining room. Hundreds of old friends and well-wishers kept him busy all evening. They stayed the night at the Massasoit Hotel, and the next morning Mack spoke to a large group of schoolchildren assembled on the steps of the Town Hall. "He showed an unusual capacity for understanding the minds of youth," noted the *Spencer Leader*, "in the manner in which he spoke to them: simple, offhand, direct sentences." He told them of his start in East Brookfield, answered questions, and advised them of the importance of self-discipline and the benefits of physical exercise and athletics as well as the importance of their school studies.

"At the conclusion three rousing cheers were given with great enthusiasm."

On April 9, 1926, Max Bishop and Walter French were missing from the lineup. They had gone to see a dentist in Milford, Delaware, about one hundred miles south of Philadelphia. Why Milford?

Like most towns with at least nine men and boys on the Delmarva Peninsula, Milford had been a hotbed of baseball since just after the Civil War. In 1914 the local team, backed by the L. D. Caulk Company (manufacturers of dentures and other dental supplies), and their rivals from Dover ended their season series tied 5–5. The Grier brothers, who owned the company, were dentists. Determined to win the playoff against Dover, Dr. Walter Grier took a train to Philadelphia looking for a non-roster pitcher and catcher. The sponsor of the Dover team was on the same train with the same mission. The only thing that's clear is that Dr. Grier called on Connie Mack, who told him, "I can't help you."

Both teams wound up hiring either minor leaguers or semipros. But as so often happened, Mack had made another lifelong friend. According to family lore, Walter Grier read one day in 1925 that Mickey Cochrane was out of the lineup with an abscessed tooth. He called Mack and offered to treat Cochrane at no cost. Mack said the problem had been taken care of. Well, said Dr. Grier, any time your players need dental work, send them down to us and we'll take care of them.

By this time the Griers were running the Caulk business and were no longer practicing dentistry. One of their lab men, Dr. Clyde Nelson, took care of the patients. The players would take the evening train to Milford, stay overnight at Walter Grier's home, have the work done in the morning, and be back in time for the game that afternoon. Walter's son Garrett remembered the gregarious Jimmie Dykes as the family's favorite visitor. He always brought candy for Mrs. Grier.

When the players offered to pay, Dr. Nelson pointed to a bank on the windowsill of his office marked "Milford Emergency Hospital," a new facility the town was trying to build. "Contributions welcome," he said. When Connie Mack heard about it, he brought the entire team to Milford on June 28, 1926, and would again in 1930, to play exhibition games to raise money. A plaque still hangs in the emergency room of Milford Memorial Hospital: "Donated by Connie Mack and his Athletic Baseball Club June 28, 1926."

Over the years the Macks were frequent guests for several days at the Grier home in Milford. The Griers often sat in Mack's box seats on the home plate side of the A's third base dugout. Walter Grier accompanied the team on a road trip. Garrett, a prep school shortstop, spent a few weeks each summer working out with the team in the late 1920s. It was a young boy's dream come true.

Garrett recalled, "I stayed at Mrs. Truitt's boarding house on Lehigh, where a lot of the players ate their meals. We were on the field at 8:30 every morning." He remembers Tris Speaker took a liking to him; Ty Cobb didn't. And Connie Mack gave him a few lessons in playing shortstop: "Two things I want you to keep in mind. I don't want you to throw that ball underhand. Throw it overhand. It'll be more accurate and save time. When a ball is hit and it's not hit to you, don't stand out there and do nothing. Cover a base or back up things. Don't be caught out in the middle doing nothing. Be somewhere."

One day with the Yankees in town coach Art Fletcher gave Garrett permission to field grounders at second base during New York's batting practice. "I wanted to catch a ball Ruth hit, and I did, and Gehrig and Lazzeri too. It was a thrill."

When the Athletics went to Milford to play an intrasquad game to benefit the hospital in September 1930, Mack let Garrett, then a student at Lehigh, play shortstop for the first-string A's squad. On one play he charged a slow grounder and threw hard to second for a force. After the play Jimmie Dykes said to him, "Don't kill that guy at second base. We're going to need him in the World Series."

Lee Thompson and his identical twin brother Ralph were born in the tiny town of Nowata, Oklahoma, in 1901, the year Connie Mack founded the Philadelphia Athletics. Over the next twelve years the Athletics won four pennants and became Lee's favorite team. In 1913 he organized a team of twelve-year-olds and called them the Nowata Athletics. On December 27 Lee wrote a letter to Connie Mack telling him about the team and expressing his admiration for the A's leader. He enclosed a photo of himself and his brother.

To his surprise he received an immediate reply, a handwritten note on the club's letterhead dated January 2. Mack thanked him for the picture, which, he wrote, would be placed in the office.

"Hope you had a very pleasant Christmas also a Happy New Year," the letter concluded, "and best wishes to brothers and yourself."

With the letter came an autographed baseball.

Lee's son, retired federal judge Ralph Thompson, later said, "It was the biggest news in Nowata. The baseball was put on display in the storefront window of one of the main street businesses, sitting on blue velvet for all to see."

As usually happened with Mr. Mack, once a correspondence began, it didn't end. It didn't matter how high or low the correspondent's station in life. Write to Connie Mack, he'd write you back, wishing you well, thanking you for thinking of him, inviting you to come and see him, sometimes sharing his views on his team's performance. By 1925 Lee Thompson was a senior at the University of Oklahoma. That summer he planned to travel in the east. Lee, whose father had recently died, wrote to Mr. Mack asking if they might meet. The Athletics were in St. Louis, tied with Washington for first place on the morning of July 20, when Connie Mack sat in his room and wrote:

More than pleased to hear from you and while sorry to hear of your losing your father am pleased to hear that you were able to remain at school also that your brother could continue at school also. You did not mention Philadelphia as one of the five city you will visit in the course of the next two month. If I was in Phila would have been able to send you a pocket schedule—just this moment looked in my grip and am enclosing schedule I found in same, so you can see when our club plays—try and make Phila if you can. You could stop off on way to N.Y. from Washington. If you come through in day time jump off at North Philadelphia only five minute walk from station to ball park will be pleased to see you. Many thanks for your kind letter.

Mack added a P.S.: "When I write again will tell you about the team & its chances."

They finally met in Chicago.

In 1942 Lee Thompson was in the army, stationed at Fort Devens, Massachusetts. When the Athletics were in Boston, Connie Mack invited Lee, his wife, and their three children to lunch at the hotel before a game. Judge Thompson recalled sixty-five years later:

I was eight years old. We sat around a large round table in the hotel's dining room. I sat next to Connie Mack. I remember being amazed at his fingers—knotted and bent. . . . The experience made such an impression on me that I even remember what I had for lunch—a peanut butter and jelly sandwich, garnished with parsley which I considered the last word in elegance. The true elegance, of course, was Connie Mack himself: Friendly, kind, courtly—a true gentleman. Imagine him taking the time and interest, first, twenty-eight years earlier, in a letter to a boy in Nowata, Oklahoma and then, twenty-eight years later, continuing the unlikely relationship in such a thoughtful manner.

That afternoon the family sat behind the A's dugout at Fenway Park. When first baseman Dick Siebert broke a bat, Connie Mack had the batboy give it to the young Thompson boys.

"Believe me, that bat was the talk of our pals at Edgemore Park in Oklahoma City when we returned home," said Judge Thompson.

Connie Mack was retired and past ninety when he sent a piece of silver as a wedding present to Lee Thompson's son—forty years after the twelve-year-old fan in Nowata, Oklahoma, had first written to him.

Red Smith had been a columnist for the *Philadelphia Record* for about five years in 1941 when he tried to answer the question, "What was it about Connie Mack that touched the lives of so many people who knew him and who didn't know him?"

> These people aren't hero-worshipping children. They aren't simple-minded. They aren't looking for anything. . . . They are just normal, decent, ordinary folk who go along working at their jobs and rearing their children and counting their change and paying the installment man and quietly, honestly worshipping their idols.
>
> It is hard for Philadelphians to appreciate the place their first citizen holds in the hearts of people who never have met him.
>
> Not that he is a prophet without honor in his own country. But Philadelphians have known him since they were children. He was their neighbor when his lean Irish features, imprisoned between a hard, high collar were only becoming known to sports page readers across the land. . . .
>
> It isn't that way at all in places where his visits are rare enough to be exciting events. There, public demonstrations of affection, and his response to them, have a quality that bring a lump to the throat.
>
> There is something curiously and importantly American about the hold this man has on the imagination and respect and esteem of the crowds that gather wherever he goes. . . .
>
> The honors that are his cannot be won by threats or bribery or cajolery. The fealty that is paid him cannot be commanded. The tribute he receives cannot be levied.
>
> His is an eminence that can be awarded only by free men acting of their own free will. And he has not won it because he has enjoyed unparalleled success in his own field, because he is the shrewdest and most successful of baseball managers.
>
> Buttonhole manufacturers are successful, too, sometimes, and make more money than Connie ever will, and die unmourned.
>
> No, he is what he is and where he is because he stands for everything the American people consider desirable and admirable—tolerance and

sportsmanship and kindly justice and patience and the gentility that stems from within.

Lots of words up above there, huh? Fancy words, some of 'em. All they mean is that Connie Mack is one of the most terrific things that ever happened to the human race.

1926 season, 402, 414; 1928 season, 482, 502, 504; 1929 season, 525, 548, 555; 1930 season, 578, 583, 586, 590, 595, 597; 1931 season, 603, 604, 612, 619, 622, 624, 626, 627; batting eye of, 368, 586, 595, 614; and Cobb, 445, 447; on Grove, 377; Mack and, 320–21, 450, 518; nicknames of, 368, 377
black ballplayers, 543
Blackburne, Lena, 91–92
Black Sox scandal (1919), 253, 394, 436; Ban Johnson and, 248, 249, 355; fan reaction to, 251–52, 271; game fixing in, 246, 248–51; initial rumors about, 203, 204; lifetime suspensions for, 261; Mack and, 249, 250. *See also* betting and gambling
Blades, Ray, 590, 594, 596
Blair, Clarence, 538
Blake, Sheriff, 550, 554
Bloom, Harry, 317
Bloom, Sol, 354
Blue, Lu, 301
Bluege, Ossie, 341, 410, 444, 447, 491
Bodie, Ping, 83–84, 111, 130, 167, 319
Boger, John A., 148–49
Boggs, Stewart, 544
Bok, Edward W., 632–34
Bolen, Stewart, 499
Boley, Joe, 346; 1927 season, 457, 467; 1928 season, 486, 502; 1929 season, 514, 548, 550; 1930 season, 578, 582, 583, 590–91; 1931 season, 607–8, 610, 615; Mack purchase of, 402, 428–29, 484; qualities as player, 450, 519
Boone, James, 202
Borchert, Otto, 280, 304, 427; and Simmons, 315, 316, 317, 318
Boston Braves, 69; and Perry dispute, 139–41, 149–58, 169
Boston Globe, 31, 51, 73, 283, 459

Boston Herald, 73, 124, 127
Boston Post, 35
Boston Red Sox, 37, 42, 119, 193, 494, 496
Bottomley, Jim, 587, 595, 619
boxing, 264; Mack as fan of, 122, 506–7; at Shibe Park, 118, 382
Boykin, Annie and James, 93–94
Bradley, Vernon S., 56
Bradley Hugh, 575
Brand, George, 252, 421, 544, 565
Brandt, William E. (Bill), 44, 299–300, 467, 470, 525, 538, 540–41
Branom, Dudley, 428, 450, 465
Braxton, Garland, 578
Brazill, Frank, 270, 271, 272
Breadon, Sam, 395, 587
Breckenridge, William, 569
Bresnahan, Roger, 375
Bressler, Rube, 19, 27, 30, 62, 69, 71, 107
Broeg, Bob, 616
Brooklyn Eagle, xi–xii, 136, 223
Brooks, Leonard, 288
Broun, Heywood, 33, 59, 452, 539
Brower, Frank, 233
Brown, Arthur, 569
Brown, Hugh, 473
Brown, Joe E., 589
Brown, Lloyd, 603
Brown, Warren, 183
Bruggy, Frank, 299, 310, 328, 334
Budner, Larry, 568
Bulger, Bozeman, 451
Burke, Jimmy, 537
Burke, John and Ellen, 93
Burkett, Jesse, 115
Burns, Dennis, 330, 350
Burns, Ed, 552
Burns, George, 568; and hecklers, 237, 414, 523; Mack and, 130–31, 570; seasons and games, 143, 167, 191, 194, 225, 371, 523, 548, 550

Evans, Billy, 301, 394, 419, 630; on Athletics team, 601, 612; on Baker, 62; on Cobb, 450; and Hornsby, 316; and Mack, 27, 199–200, 276, 302, 418, 541
Evers, Johnny, 23, 79, 173
Ewing, Buck, 352
Excelsior, 160
Ezzell, Homer, 309

Faber, Red, 28, 527
Falk, Bibb, 493, 581
Falkenberg, Fred "Cy," 114–15
Farrell, Henry L., 408
Farrell, James T., 267
Farrell, John H., 152, 405
Federal League, 33; ending of war with, 56–57; impact of war with, 1–2, 41, 43, 103; lawsuit by, 2–6; Supreme Court ruling on, 259
Felsch, Happy, 51, 267
Fenway Park, 244, 330
Ferrell, Wes, 583
Fife, Shannon, 96
Finletter, Thomas, 422–23
Finneran, Joe, 146
Finney, Lou, 612
Firpo, Luis, 506–7
Fisher, Harry, 349
Fitz Gerald, J. V., 205, 209, 231, 236
Fitzgerald, William, 421
Flaherty, Pat, 48, 107
Fletcher, Art, 498, 645
Flood, Peter, 599
Flowers, Jake, 618, 619, 626
flu epidemic (1918–19), 185
Fohl, Lee, 188, 189
Foley, Joe, 203, 204
Fonseca, Lew, 571, 581–82, 609
football, 264, 306–7, 366, 368, 392; Mack attendance at games, 11, 599; at Shibe Park, 342, 392

Ford, Henry, 104, 361, 420, 449, 452
Fort Myers FL, 361, 365, 397, 573; as site for spring training, 361–63, 370, 513–14. *See also* spring training (1925–31)
Fort Worth Cats, 259–60
Fort Worth Panthers, 404, 405–6
Foster, Rube, 218
Fournier, Jack, 51, 52
Foxx, Jimmy, 376, 519, 563; 1925 season, 376; 1926 season, 413; 1928 season, 486–87, 488, 490–91, 493–94, 498, 503, 504; 1929 season, 513, 515, 516, 534, 537, 542, 545, 548, 550, 554; 1930 season, 575, 579, 583, 590, 591, 594, 596; 1931 season, 603, 606, 612, 617, 622, 625; as athlete, 366; as catcher, 466; contracts and salary, 571, 601; and Dykes, 491; as first baseman, 513; hitting style and ability, 525; joins Athletics, 361; Mack and, 338–39, 367, 369, 490, 513, 594; in minor leagues, 338, 376; speed of, 367–68; strength of, 487–88, 572; as third baseman, 466, 487, 490–91
Frank, Charlie, 67, 200, 201, 294–95; and Perry dispute, 138, 139, 140, 141, 150, 171
Frank, Stanley, 400–401
Franklin, Nelly, 100
Frazee, Harry, 129, 134, 185, 186, 187, 208, 281; and Babe Ruth, 217; and Ban Johnson, 163, 165, 207, 211
free agency, 4
Freeman, Buck, 201
French, Larry, 539
French, Walter, 447, 519, 643; as bench jockey, 377, 498; as football player, 306–7, 366, 388; Mack and, 306–7, 377, 570; seasons and games, 388, 416, 482, 513, 554–55
Frick, Ford C., 100, 331, 485, 526, 588

Griffin, Ivy, 200, 202, 225, 237, 272, 280
Griffith, Clark, 11, 80, 218, 224, 226,
243, 257, 318, 329, 330; and Ban Johnson, 162, 163–64, 165, 215, 356; and
baseball rules, 219, 395, 396; becoming Senators owner, 208–9; financial
strains of, 135, 169; generosity of, 176;
and Landis, 290–91; Mack friendship with, 99, 208, 341; steps down
as Senators manager, 268; trades
with, 281–82, 510; trading deadline
advocated by, 213, 221; and Tris
Speaker, 439, 440, 478; and World
War I, 107, 146; and Zachary, 160–61
Griffith Stadium, 330, 386, 553
Grimes, Burleigh, 587, 588, 589–90,
594–96, 621, 626–27
Grimm, Charlie, 78, 532, 533, 547, 554
Groh, Heinie, 272–73, 283, 324
Grove, Lefty (Robert Moses Groves),
361, 562, 563, 576, 612–13; 1925 season, 373, 374, 375, 387, 388; 1926 season, 409–10, 414, 417–18, 424; 1927
season, 464, 470; 1928 season, 482,
483, 490, 491, 492, 493, 495, 499–
500, 502, 503, 504; 1929 season, 515,
525–26, 542, 550, 551; 1930 season,
575, 576, 577, 582, 584, 585, 590–91,
593–94, 596, 597; 1931 season, 603,
604, 605, 606, 609, 610, 612, 617, 621,
625–26, 628; as American League
MVP, 612; and Babe Ruth, 500, 605,
609; and baserunners, 622; brushback pitches by, 376–77; Cochrane
and, 378, 400, 410, 613; and Collins,
468, 520; contracts and salary, 401,
479–80, 571, 601; curveball of, 400,
613; Dykes and, 381, 400; fastball of,
344, 388, 410, 613; generosity of, 381;
Mack on behavior of, 381, 468; Mack
discussions with, 381, 400, 569–70,

576, 625; Mack on greatness of, 399,
469, 470, 609, 613; Mack scouting
and purchase of, 337, 344–48, 484;
maturation as pitcher, 585–86; in
minor leagues, 279, 337, 344–45,
346, 366; name and nicknames, 377,
397; Perkins as catcher for, 378, 400;
pitching control of, 344, 366, 400,
401; relief pitching by, 417, 469–70,
476, 480, 525, 576, 579, 609; and
sportswriters, 379–81; superstitions
and idiosyncrasies, 400–401, 467,
519; temper of, 298, 377, 378–79, 381,
469, 609, 610–11; tightfisted with
money, 381, 447
Grover, Roy, 84, 85, 108, 191
Gumpert, Leon, 564

Haas, Bruno, 32
Haas, George "Mule," 307, 519, 569, 571,
600; 1928 season, 482, 487, 491; 1929
season, 515, 516, 518, 534, 548–49,
555; 1930 season, 576, 578, 582, 583,
590, 594, 595; 1931 season, 603, 609,
615, 617, 621, 624; Mack and, 478–79,
490
Hafey, Chick, 587, 594, 617, 626
Haft, Herb, 534
Hagen, Walter, 19, 408
Haines, Jesse, 588, 593–94, 615
Hale, Sammy, 306, 572; 1924 season,
332, 336; 1925 season, 373, 375, 388;
1926 season, 409, 418; 1927 season,
465, 466; 1928 season, 487, 504; 1929
season, 513; Mack purchase of, 304–
5; and Shibe Park hecklers, 472, 474
Haley, Ray, 73–74, 82
Hall, Russ, 397
Hallahan, Bill, 587, 588, 593, 597, 618,
626, 627
Hannah, Truck, 491

Huggins, Miller (*cont.*)
489, 498, 515, 517; death of, 526; on
Earnshaw, 485; on Grove, 400–401;
Mack trading with, 130, 281; and
Simmons, 338
Hughes, Charles Evans, 71
Hulvey, Hank, 320
Hunnefield, Bill, 493
Hunter, Herb, 628
Husing, Ted, 536, 540, 588, 595
Husting, Pete, 23, 535
Huston, Cap, 17, 55, 80, 208, 221; and
Ban Johnson, 198, 211, 215; criticisms
of Mack by, 209–10

Indianapolis News, 420
industrial leagues, 144, 145, 238, 274
inflation, 104, 134, 215
intentional walk, 218–19
International League, 148, 275, 279, 321;
and draft system, 404; Mack scouting of, 201, 344–45
Investor's Business Daily, 75–76
Irwin, Arthur, 64
Isaminger, James, 8, 63, 127, 166, 189,
192, 196, 350, 458, 459, 615; on
Athletics salaries, 235, 284–85; on
gambling in baseball, 246; on Grove,
397; on home runs and high scores,
277; on Johnson-Landis feud, 355; on
Mack, 59, 176, 194, 407–8, 634; Mack
interviewed by, 126, 128, 337, 399,
556; on pennant race of 1928, 502,
503–4; on Perry, 141; on Simmons,
324, 385, 412; as sportswriter, 133, 176

Jackson, Joe, 33, 52, 250
Jacksonville FL, 107, 129, 137. *See also*
spring training (1915–18)
Jacobson, Baby Doll, 415, 416
Jacobson, Charles, 150

Jacoby, Jean and George, 96, 397
James, Bill, 17, 193
Jamieson, Charlie, 117, 187, 189
Janvrin, Hal, 72, 73
Japan, 628
Jenkins, Tom, 416, 417
Jenkinson, Mary, 452–53
Jennings, Hugh, 31, 130, 327, 365, 393
Johns, Pete, 84
Johnson, Ban, 33, 60, 107, 289, 343, 395–
96, 433–34, 438; and Baker dispute,
22; and baseball season schedule,
117, 135, 148, 161–64, 186; and Black
Sox scandal, 248, 249, 355; clipped
authority of, 222; and Cobb-Speaker
allegations, 432, 433, 435, 437–38;
death of, 475, 602; dictatorial methods of, 165; and Federal League war,
1; and gambling in baseball, 244,
248, 249, 353; and Harding death,
311; and Landis, 260–61, 352–54, 395,
433, 434, 437–38; and Lasker plan,
254, 256, 257; loss of owners' support
for, 164, 207, 211–15, 220–22, 257–58,
355–57, 396, 438, 474–75; and Mack,
155, 199, 355, 357, 462–63; Mack's
growing disenchantment with, 255,
355–56, 437, 438, 461, 462, 463, 464–
65; and Mays, 193, 198–99, 242; and
McGraw, 354; and National Commission, 214, 223, 254; and National
League, 257, 354; and Perry controversy, 140, 150–51, 152, 155, 169, 170;
Players Fraternity opposed by, 102;
and resin bag issue, 395, 396; reversal of scorer decisions by, 71, 237;
suspension of Cobb by, 460–62; on
wartime draft exemptions, 147–48,
173; and Yankee Stadium, 242–43
Johnson, George F., 226, 227–28
Johnson, Henry, 504, 515

owner and team architect (*cont.*)
285–86, 526; breakup of 1914 team,
43, 62–63, 132, 252–53, 607; as
diplomat, 215, 438; effort to cut
payroll, 41, 43–44, 65, 175; and Federal League war, 2, 3, 8, 57; Griffith
friendship with, 99, 208, 341; and
John Shibe, 9, 286–87, 476; and
Landis, 258, 292–93, 437, 438; lawsuit
filed by, 156, 157, 158, 200; obtaining
Cobb, 440–42; obtaining Cochrane,
348–50; obtaining Dykes, 79–80;
obtaining Foxx, 338–39; obtaining
Grove, 337, 344–45; obtaining Lajoie,
9–10; obtaining Simmons, 318; obtaining Speaker, 430, 439, 440; and
Pate draft controversy, 404–7; and
Perry dispute, 141–42, 149, 151–52,
153, 156, 157, 158, 171, 199–200; personal finances of, 58–59, 65, 132,
168–69, 303, 365, 568; and player
contracts, 41, 61, 65, 135–36, 187,
358–59, 511–12; on player salaries,
41–42, 103, 175–76, 216, 284, 511,
608; reticence on giving public information, 34, 63, 123–24, 304; and
Rickey, 207, 229; on roster limits, 11,
175; sale of players, 8, 33, 36–37, 58,
113–14, 123–24, 124–25; and spring
training locations, 206–7, 288, 306,
361–63, 370; on Stallings, 155; and
veteran-rookie mix, 19, 63, 76–77,
143, 278–81, 308, 428
—relationship with players: Baker, 13–
14, 26–27, 55–56, 62; Baumgartner,
266–67, 334; Bishop, 320–21, 450,
518; Bressler, 30; Burns, 130–31, 570;
Cobb, 306, 376, 431, 444, 455, 456–57,
471, 472, 480–81, 635–36; Cochrane,
359–61, 376, 383, 500, 521, 628; Collins, 507–8, 529; Cramer, 468, 524,
572; Davis, 132; Dooly, 475–76, 491,
494, 503; Dugan, 206, 232, 238, 280–
81, 282; Dykes, 79–80, 200, 225, 232,
269–70, 294, 340, 384, 387, 418, 520,
579, 592; Earnshaw, 485, 585; Ehmke,
415–16, 417; Evans, 27, 199–200,
276, 302, 418, 541; Foxx, 338–39, 367,
369, 490, 513, 594; French, 306–7,
377, 570; Galloway, 200, 402, 429;
Grove, 337, 344–45, 381, 399, 400,
468, 469, 470, 569–70, 576, 609,
613, 625; Haas, 478–79, 490; Hauser,
137–38, 280, 336, 428; McInnis, 38,
128–29; Miller, 382–83, 507; Myers,
71, 178–79; Naylor, 180, 190; Orwoll,
479, 489, 490, 491; Perkins, 191–92,
206, 383, 524; Rommel, 291–93, 297,
298, 303, 550; Roth, 188–89; Shannon, 238–39; Simmons, 267–68,
317, 325, 328–29, 385, 401, 413, 457,
571–72, 599; Strand, 320; Strunk, 67,
109–11, 176; Thrasher, 107; Witt, 188,
206; Zachary, 159, 160, 161
—welfare of baseball: on baseball integrity, 119–20, 247, 251; on baseball
schedule, 135, 186; on Chapman
beaning, 240–42; on designated hitter, 398; on fan rowdyism and heck-
ling, 473–74, 581; on gambling and
Black Sox scandal, 204, 244–45, 247,
249–50, 251–52; on home run craze,
517; on Major League expansion,
630; on resin bag, 395; on sacrifice
fly, 218, 600; on Sunday baseball, 59,
421, 424; on spitball, 66, 135, 219; on
use of scuffed baseballs, 327
Mack, Connie, Jr. (son), 96; birth of,
88; on father, 92, 507, 508; as football and basketball player, 508, 543;
traveling with Athletics by, 131, 335,
443–44, 540

CPSIA information can be obtained
at www.ICGtesting.com
Printed in the USA
LVHW04*1832160718
583944LV00005B/74/P